A MANAGERIAL ODYSSEY

Problems in Business and its Environment

A MANAGERIAL ODYSSEY

Problems in Business and its Environment

by
ARTHUR ELKINS
Chairman and Associate Professor
Department of Management
University of Massachusetts, Amherst

and

DENNIS W. CALLAGHAN
Teaching Associate
School of Business Administration
University of Massachusetts, Amherst

ADDISON-WESLEY PUBLISHING COMPANY
Reading, Massachusetts • Menlo Park, California
London • Amsterdam • Don Mills, Ontario • Sydney

ISBN 0-201-01578-1
ABCDEFGHIJ-AL-798765

To Barbara and Sara and Michael and Steven

PREFACE

The area of Business and Its Environment—or Business and Society—is presently in the take-off stage relative to other business-school courses and curricula. While much of the subject matter is fad-prone and many of the issues transitory, the field is, nonetheless, certainly relevant as corporations and managers increasingly face problems previously unmet. Indeed, at times the whole concept of private enterprise become subject to question in fits of social and political unrest.

As a new area, however, the materials are far from standard. A few descriptive texts and some casebooks are available, and Business and Environment cases have been added to traditional policy and strategy books. From our point of view, however, the existing materials have several limitations which reduce their effectiveness.

First, much of the writing is overly dogmatic. A steady diet of topics such as corporate ethics, social responsibility and the like do not make a satisfactory experience for either student or teacher. Articles and books on these subjects rarely operationalize the concepts, give little training on the solving of real problems and, in our experience, plainly bore students after about two weeks of exposure.

Second, existing materials in text or case form seem to lack a managerial orientation. Many are merely descriptive and some are set in adversary rather than managerial modes.

Third, too much of the existing literature focuses on the top of the managerial pyramid in large firms. Very little concern is shown for the operating manager, small businessman, or entrepreneur—and those are the levels where most students will be for some years to come. Also, as the evidence increasingly shows, those are the levels where the problems hit hardest and the solutions must come the quickest. Indeed, the problems from the field and the pressures from the organization merge at the operating manager's level and create the value and role conflicts that should form the substance of a Business and its Environment course.

We aim to overcome some of those drawbacks. Our first objective is to get to "bread and butter" or "nuts and bolts" issues. While the first major part of the book covers social responsibility, business ethics, and theories of managerial behavior, the rest of the book deals with operational problems.

Secondly, we aim toward a managerial problem-solving approach. Each of the areas covered is current and the material is geared to providing a sound educational experience as well as background and various views in preparation for the cases. While we have disregarded some topics typically covered in a Business and Society course, those we have selected lend themselves to forcing decision situations upon students.

Finally, the cases and incidents, where possible, are geared to the lower-level manager, small businessman, or entrepreneur. Students will be sensitized to the conflicts and pressures involved in positions they will occupy after graduation and for a good part of their managerial careers.

The format of the book consists of three major parts. In the first, we expose the student to the various philosophies of the corporation—prescriptions of corporate behavior—and then weigh those against theory and evidence of actual corporate and managerial behavior.

The second section consists of eight socio-politico-economic problem areas affecting managerial decisions. Each section consists of an introduction and background readings followed by a case or two. Students should be encouraged to pursue further readings in each of the areas. We have included brief bibliographies for that purpose.

The final section focuses on social accounting and the problems faced in quantifying nonmarket decision-making.

The materials in this book have been course-tested and we have found that the action orientation lends much to student involvement and interest. Sometimes, the dilemmas facing students may simply demonstrate the difficulties confronting modern managers in responding to contemporary corporate existence. That is, there is no easy solution.

Acknowledgments

We wish to thank the many authors and publishers who allowed us to reprint the readings in this book. Also our thanks to the companies who furnished us data for the cases. Tim. L. Bornstein, Thomas McAuley, Joseph Thomas, Robert Comerford, Leslie Ball, and Nicholas Speranzo researched and contributed cases and assisted us in case development. Judy Duncan and Judy Rose did more than we can acknowledge in typing the manuscript, and in trying to decipher our scribbled notes.

Finally we owe the greatest debt to several hundred students who were patient and helpful while we attempted to construct a meaningful and useful educational experience for them. We hope that we have, in some small way, contributed to their effectiveness as they start on their own managerial Odyssies.

Amherst, Massachusetts   A.E.
January, 1975   D.W.C.

CONTENTS

FOUNDATIONS
AND A FRAME
OF REFERENCE

The *Odyssey,* as you recall, was the title of Homer's epic travelogue of Odysseus' perilous journey back to Ithaca after the conquest of Troy. In his travels Odysseus faced a series of complex, difficult, and relatively unknown challenges before returning safely home.

We have chosen the title *Odyssey* for this book because the area of Business and Its Environment is about the complex and difficult problems being newly thrust upon the manager. Business and its Environment, or Business and Society, is the study of the relationship of the firm and managers to social problems and issues. These issues, albeit old in the context of human history, are relatively new in the context of managerial decision frameworks. It is only within the last ten or so years (10 years, incidentally, was the length of Odysseus' journey) that managers have been constrained to give social problems more than minimal consideration (and business-school curricula usually reflected that minimum consideration). Questions of race and ethnicity, pollution and environment, peace and war, conservation, politics, government relations, international relations, and the like are now important factors in management decision-making. These topics are the stuff of Business and its Environment—a Managerial Odyssey.

Nor are the newly challenging problems necessarily isolated in their contexts. Older, traditional business decisions are taking on new dimensions. For example, a plant location decision traditionally involved consideration of transportation costs, low labor costs, access to markets, fuel and energy availability, and similar other factors—in a few words, the typical business parameters. Now, for that same decision, a manager must consider environmental spoilage, affirmative-action hiring in terms of minorities, dealings with local agencies (planning boards, zoning boards, citizens' action groups), the impact of the plant on local schools, sewerage systems, roads and community facilities, and a host of other "social" factors, along with the more traditional economic and business considerations.

1

THE MODERN MANAGER: TARGET FOR CRITICS

The manager faces today new challenges of several sorts. In the most extreme forms, these challenges are directed at his very existence as a decision-maker or at the form of business organization currently sustaining him. That is, critics in this furthest mode would like to replace the corporate or private form of business operation with some other forms, be they government owned or controlled enterprises, cooperatives, or some other supposedly more responsive type of organizational control mechanisms. Despite the sometimes vociferous nature of these critics, however, their numbers are small and their position is not taken very seriously.

But other critics are taken seriously. These include the generalists who condemn the roles and behaviors of modern managers, as well as the particularists singling out for correction specific attributes of the corporation or business. In many cases, no mutual exclusivity separates these critics—a Ralph Nader, for example, brackets both categories.

The general critic questions the profit motive—that is, whether business should pursue profit as its primary objective or whether managers should deemphasize profit and guide the corporation toward objectives encompassing social welfare. The term *social responsibility* is generally applied to corporate behavior prescribed under this critique.

Critics of specific acts of business and managers focus on such problems as pollution, minority or female hiring, occupational safety and health, defense contracting, and the like.

Whatever the content, today's critics put the businessman or the manager in a new role. The traditional cost-and-profit calculus is now altered to include value formulations and responses that may consume organization resources for no apparent benefit to the firm or at least none to the traditional recipients of business efficiency, the shareholders. Indeed, demands promulgated by the various interest groups now surfacing about the business firm may put the manager into a severe value-conflict situation. Such demands may be inconsistent within and between groups, may require drastic and sometimes impossible reallocations of the firm's resources, and may challenge a manager's personal mores or creeds, perhaps even forcing the manager to reexamine his adherence to some of the established norms of the American enterprise system.

A STRATEGY FOR STUDYING BUSINESS AND ITS ENVIRONMENT

Our objectives in this book are to acquaint you with the challenges presently facing managers, and to make you aware of the managerial roles (and role conflicts) in responding to them. We hope to move beyond the level of abstract generalizing to that of operational problems. Many managers operate at levels and positions in direct contact with the firm's publics. It does them little good to vaguely pontificate about social problems or social responsibilities, it does them more good to be aware that they might meet a real, perhaps explosive, problem and be prepared to tackle it in a decisive manner.

The general format for each section of the book, and hence for each problem area to be covered, is an introduction, a series of readings and a case or two. The readings are designed to provide background for the case. We have tried to be scrupulously fair in presenting background readings, exposing you to as many sides of an issue as possible. The issues are complex and each has many sides. Social problems involve values, and various interest groups may have conflicting values. The manager who is meeting social issues must try to understand the values, views, and tactics of all the participant interest groups. The manager may not come to agree with all or any of them; nor may his decision reflect any values but his own. Nevertheless, in this age of activism the alert manager should, at the very least, try to understand the basis for the activism.

THE PLAN OF THE BOOK

Generally the book follows a concept, problem, measurement scheme. Major parts deal with concepts and theories, specific operational problems, and social measurement or accounting in that order.

Concepts and theories

The first major part is divided into two sections. Section A deals with prescriptions of business behavior—that is, what scholars, practitioners, and laymen think corporations and businesses *should* be, whom business *should* serve, and what groups *should* reap benefits from the firm. The discussion in this part is normative, and obviously the articles reflect the value systems of the respective writers.

Juxtaposed against the prescriptions of corporate and managerial standards presented in Section A are the theoretical descriptions of corporate and managerial behavior presented in Section B. The student is alerted to comparing the prescribed or normative patterns of Section A with the patterns scholars describe in positive terms in Section B.

Although the theme of the book centers about operational problems and operational managerial responses, we include this general overview to give the student a framework of value systems that might condition behavior in specific situations. For example, the behavior of a firm which is guided by a profit-maximization creed might be quite different in a pollution controversy from the behavior of a firm that professes a "social responsibility" philosophy.

Operational problems

The second major part of the book moves us into several specific operational problem situations. Obviously, more problems exist than we have room to include, but we think the issues we have included are representative of those which the operating manager or the staff person on the firing line might face. First, in section

A, we cover the business firm as it relates to changing lifestyles. In recent years we have seen profound changes in outlook toward some of the traditional institutions and practices of our society. Religion, the family, government, sexual conduct, and education are being increasingly confronted by new values and new practices. A cornerstone traditional value, commonly called the work ethic, also shows signs of crumbling, and this challenge has profound implications for business decision-making.

Closely related to changing lifestyles and their effect on the corporation are the relatively new problems for the firm in the area of equal opportunity. As women and minority group members demand places in the social and economic hierarchies of society, the business firm must face the complex problem of applying equal-opportunity legislation and affirmative-action guidelines, as well as emerging social standards in hiring, promotion, pay, and assignment decisions. At the same time, managers must be careful to avoid discriminating against white males (reverse discrimination).

Section C involves the business firm and pollution. Environmental protection is probably the most basic topic in the whole panorama of business–society issues. It certainly has received the most attention in the media. But the pollution problem is also one where the local manager is apt to be in the spotlight. The chairman of the board rarely is the person under fire to clean up; usually the division manager, who may be five or six levels down in the hierarchy, bears the brunt of local crusades against pollution. The local manager represents the corporation to the local community and he must respond to the petitions of local officials.

Closely related to environmental issues are those involving the energy crisis (Section D). Although this is a relatively recent problem, no one issue has come onto the scene with more resounding force. At least three business positions in the energy area are relevant to business and its environment students. The first involves those firms engaged in the supply of energy. In this case, decisions ranging from power plant siting, nuclear energy, and new or untapped sources of energy, to those involving the rationing of oil, gasoline, and electricity among customers, are all relevant. The second involves businesses that are trying to sustain the necessary energy supply to keep operating. In this case, managers must apply efforts to switch fuels or conserve in other ways, and sometimes these efforts cycle right back to the pollution issue. The final position concerns those firms that manufacture energy-consuming devices and the effects that society's new energy consciousness has on them.

Two sections on American business abroad are included. In the first, we focus on apartheid in South Africa. The objective here is not so much to study apartheid, but primarily to focus on another country's problem and the effects of American business presence. Apartheid is a significant problem for illustration, but similar problems in Latin America, other parts of Africa, or the Middle East and their relations to American business can be similarly instructive. A second objective in the section on apartheid is to study its effect on the operations and relationships of the American firm back in the United States. How does the firm respond to local protest groups, American blacks, and others who see a connection between the corporation's presence in South Africa and its operations in the United States? For example, how does a corporation respond to boycotts called against it as a U.S. parent to protest actions of a South African subsidiary?

Another international section covers the American manager working overseas —an assignment that will be held by increasing numbers of today's students in the future. We have entitled this section the "Ugly American" (even though, you may recall, the Ugly American was the *hero* of the book of that title). The objective in this section is to prepare the student for the cultural expectations and the appropriate stance of the American manager working in another country. The manager overseas faces a completely different social and political milieu than he would face in the United States, and progressive companies are conditioning managers toward appropriate profiles. But the instances of American firms and managers imposing American standards on other nationals, or attempting to manipulate political and social processes in host countries, demonstrate that social acculturation is a two-way street. The problem, then, is the proper balance of countercultural influences to make for successful and productive relationships.

Section G of Part II deals with Business and Government. Governmental relationships are complex; and the subject, which includes topics such as antitrust laws and various other types of regulation, consumes whole courses, let alone sections of a single book. But in an age when government is becoming more involved in business affairs and when the protests in other areas—pollution, affirmative action, energy policy, and the like—manifest themselves in government action, the relationships of managers and governmental agencies become even more crucial. Nor should the businessman confine himself to thinking in terms of the federal government; relationships with state and local officials, particularly for the small businessman or the manager of the local plant, are equally as important in such areas as licensing, regulation, zoning, and certification.

Finally, we include material on Business and Activism. While this topic cuts across the lines of the substantive issues previously covered, it is important that businessmen be familiar not only with the problems raised by activists, but with the strategies and tactics they employ as well.

Measurement

The third major part of the book focuses on measurement. Social accounting is a new and emerging tool designed for measuring the degree of business actions in socially important areas. At the present stage of development, social accounting is imprecise and not widely adopted. But we believe that exposure to social accounting is necessary if one is even to start the application of efficiency and effectiveness criteria to the firm's ancillary activities.

One last word about our intent in this book. In recent years, the process of education in business administration has come to stress less the inculcation of specific bits of information and more the grounding in broader concepts and tools —in short, a managerial approach. In line with such a focus, we hope the student will find that our topic and case selection will aid in developing a process of critical thinking, an appreciation of the issues and types of problems that might arise beyond those of a traditionally business nature, and an ability to act in complex situations where no formulas are available for quick and ready answers. We trust that students will look on the problem situations and other material presented as *conditioners of critical thinking* in some rather complex areas, rather than as a *catalogue* of specific situations they are being trained to handle mechanically.

A word about cases

Some of the same caveats expressed in the last paragraph apply to the cases. These are not designed as preparation for a specific incident one may meet in his or her business career. Cases are, quite simply, vehicles to force the practice of systematic analysis and decision-making. Also, cases rarely have *school* solutions. Solutions can and do differ among students (and even among professors); the student's task is to analyze the data, logically derive a decision solution, and then prepare for the implementation of that decision.

Cases can be handled in many ways. A student may take the role of a consultant or staff analyst, in which he will prepare a logical, written recommendation of policy or action. Typically, the sequence of attacking a case in that mode includes fact analysis, problem formulation, tentative solutions, selection of the course of action, and development of a plan for implementation. Another use of the case is role-playing, in which the parts illustrated in the case are assigned to various actors (students) and the roles played out. Several of our cases lend themselves well to role-playing techniques.

The cases in this book are designed to be used with the readings. Typically cases require the use of assumptions and they almost invariably require more information than is included. The readings should help in this respect, although unrealistic and unwarranted assumptions should always be avoided.

USE OF OTHER SOURCES

Bibliographies have been included after each section. The student is encouraged to read further in the field. Since the area of business and environment is so new —less than the 10 or so years practitioners have been facing the problems—there is little in the way of standard literature. Indeed the literatures of economics, sociology, and political science, as well as business, are relevant to the field. The eclecticism of the discipline not only adds to the challenge—it enhances the perspectives one may need to operate in the field. It also adds to the fun of the course.

PART I
CONCEPTS AND
THEORIES

A. *Conceptual and Ideological Prescriptions for Business Behavior*

Suppose you are a seller of produce, and a local social-action committee comes to your outlet to ask that you remove nonunion lettuce from the shelves. How would you respond? How would you sift through your mind the many factors entering such a decision? Could you respond that nonunion lettuce is more profitable? Could you answer that working conditions for farm workers are none of your concern? Could you say that your customers want and are entitled to the lowest price? Or could you offer the rejoinder that one self-appointed group has no right telling others what to do, or what to buy or restricting their options?

And then how would you react to a picket line thrown up in front of your outlet by such a committee?

This is one of an increasing complex of new problems faced by businessmen and managers. They aren't the problems easily solved by resort to the profit calculus, nor by simple formulas, but they must be responded to.

These problems and the managerial responses to them are the topics of this book. What questions—in a social context and with social (as well as profit) ramifications—does the businessman deal with? And how does he deal with them?

In this section, we introduce the field by presenting general normative models and doctrines of corporate behavior. That is, the authors pose the question: "What is the role of business in American society?" Also included are some selections pointing up the problems and vicissitudes of corporate social involvement.

THE TRADITIONAL MODEL OF THE FIRM

Models or theories are abstractions. They do not encompass every element of the real situation; they can't. Models must be general enough to reasonably describe a range of situations. Thus, much of the complexity of the real world is omitted in favor of simplification. While oversimplification opens the door to criticism that a model is useless, one finds that same criticism many times emanating from sources that seek to use the model for unintended purposes.

Such simplification is the case with the traditional model of the firm. Developed in economics, the imaginary simple firm is nothing more than a mechanism in a much larger body of theory. The traditional assumptions of rationality, profit maximization, and the single mind of the firm and the entrepreneur are very useful shortcut tools and reasonable enough generalizations (descriptions of reality) to allow the economist to generate reasonably accurate predictions of resource allocation and income distribution.

Nonetheless, the firm as described in economic theory also closely approximates the prescribed firm of traditional political and economic dogma. Under the free enterprise system, business firms are expected to seek profits. That is, all relationships should be treated in a revenue–cost–profit context. Resources are to be purchased (cost), goods produced for sale to customers (revenue), and residual resources (profit) distributed to owners. Business decisions are to have extremely simple parameters; the businessman simply arranges the lowest-cost resources in the most efficient configuration, sells to customers willing to pay the highest prices, and derives his maximum profit.

But the real world is different from that of the simple model; it is probably more complex than the world of dogma as well. The mythical businessman is much brighter than one in the real world, and the real world is a more difficult place in which to operate than is the mythical world. Many problems cannot be solved swiftly or easily through resort to profit calculus. Others involve *values,* in that the most profitable way may not be the "right" way according to the businessman's scale of ethical values. What introduces this complexity and what brings questions of values into managerial decision-making?

First, we must consider market structure. Few instances of pure or perfect competition exist, and there are few examples of totally powerless firms. Almost every firm has some sort of power, be it the local drug store with its several-city-block monopoly (or its professional association limiting market forces), the firm that operates as a small town's only employer, or the only steel company in the country. Hence, free choice, the important element in economic doctrine, may be seriously constrained. This constraint may be even more evident when one is considering the concentration of sellers or buyers on the larger national or international level —four automobile companies, three aluminum companies, or seven major oil companies, for examples. Under such circumstances of monopoly, monopsony, high concentration, or limited individual choice, the job applicant who suffers discrimination may not have the option of applying to another, nondiscriminating employer. The customer who doesn't like a corporate or business policy (or even a product) doesn't always have the alternative of buying from another seller.

Second, the assumptions in economic doctrine of free information and maximum individual knowledge are tenuous indeed. Not all information is available, and individuals are sometimes incapable of making even simple decisions. For example, the small investor rarely possesses information (or the expertise to interpret the information that he does have) compared to that available to the large investment houses or funds. On a more mundane level, try dividing 49¢ by 6.8 ounces in your head at a supermarket counter.

In essence, the imperfections in the market mean that firms are not automatically driven—by the invisible hand—to behave in such a way that social problems or power are minimized. Firms and entrepreneurs have discretion, and with discretion business behavior does not result in market conditions that represent the optimal social results described or prescribed by the models. Thus the social issues loom important.

Approached from another way, the firm engaging in competitive struggle has its prices driven down and its profits squeezed (to the point of opportunity costs in economic theory). The (purely) competitive firm would have little time, energy, or resources to devote to social issues. Without discretion and without profits, social issues would be irrelevant to the firm. In such a condition, it would also not be in the best interests of the firm to act antisocially in its own affairs; employees would be hired according to skills, information would be made understandable and easily accessible, products would be produced under the demands of a severe and controlling market.

THE SOCIAL RESPONSIBILITY DOCTRINE

Recognizing the complex nature of the real world, a number of scholars and business practitioners have proposed that business firms should become more socially responsible. That is, business firms should use the discretion and power they possess in a socially acceptable context.

The social responsibility doctrine holds that firms are surrounded by various constituent or interest groups, each having some call on the firm's resources or energies. Shareholders hold no special status in this doctrine, sharing importance with labor, government at all levels, customers, neighbors, suppliers, minority groups, other financial factors, etc. Management, acting as a hub of activity, is entrusted with equitably distributing its effort and its corporate rewards or resources fairly among each of these groups. Thus, the doctrine calls for the firm to simultaneously strive for lowest prices, good products, fair wages, clean attractive plant sites, voluntary pollution-control efforts, contributions to charity, training programs for the disadvantaged, and other social and economic actions, along with fair dividends for its shareholders.

But the social responsibility view, while seemingly attractive, has some serious operational and philosophical problems.

First, no rules for decision-making exist for the manager. With a profit-maximization philosophy, the manager at least had a single operational objective at which to aim. All other considerations become either constraints on his action or costs. But the socially responsible manager is reminded of multiple objectives or of fulfilling obligations to all constituent groups. About the only operational decision rule that exists is a sequencing of decisions—take care of one group first, then the other. But this might leave the manager with a whole host of equity problems.

Other, more serious problems of a philosophical nature exist, however. Several critics have pointed out that the businessman's role is economic. He can act privately in the role because he is expected to do so, but he is not empowered to (nor is he especially capable of) acting in social areas. These are the areas of decision usually reserved for elected representatives. This distinction becomes more important when one couples to social responsibility the question of power. The socially responsible manager can be socially responsible only because he has the power to gain excess resources through some exclusive market position. That is, his (powerful) position allows him to price goods in such a way as to secure pure profit—or a privately raised tax that supplies him the resources to be socially responsible and to distribute corporate rewards according to his own or to some perceived societal value system. Thus, the question becomes, "Who elected the businessman to tax and then distribute rewards according to his own values?"

The problem, then, is also to decide whose values are appropriate. The socially responsive manager's behavior in Birmingham, Alabama, for example, may not coincide with the socially responsive behavior of a manager in Boston, Massachusetts. Yet both may be responding to social values. Whose values are correct?

Social values are by no means universally accepted. Those who would criticize the businessman for using power to exploit a community resource for his own interest should be equally critical of the businessman who uses power to exploit a community resource for some other group's interest, even though in the latter case, the values behind the businessman's decision happen to coincide with those of the critic. The process of exploitation is still present, but the ox is being gored for a different purpose.

And finally, the social responsibility doctrine vests power with the businessman, yet provides no mechanism (other than a moral trust) which would prevent the businessman from turning and using that power in another way. In many ways, the doctrine resembles a call for a benevolent dictatorship, but gives no indication of what happens when the benevolent dictator leaves the scene. It also implicitly requires that all businessmen assume the same posture, but offers no mechanism for assuring so.

An example

Let us briefly trace out an incident to illustrate a socially responsible manager's practical problems. Suppose a management responded to a local group and instituted a training and placement program for hard-core unemployed. What pressures might arise among other interest groups?

Older employees might gripe "It took me three years to apprentice to this job and now they're getting it handed to them on a silver platter." Customers might be affected by higher prices, poor quality, or late deliveries. Shareholders might express concerns over higher costs and lower profits. Government might pressure the firm into moving faster. If a union were involved, it might complain over violations of established apprenticeship or training programs. Foremen may complain about becoming trainers.

In essence, the problem becomes much more complex than just providing jobs or doing a "socially responsible" thing. It also raises the question of values. Whose values is the manager responding to? What makes him socially responsible in this case? Aren't the complainers' values of equal importance?

Thus, neither model makes it easy for the manager. The economic doctrine suffers from being descriptive and prescriptive for a structural condition that doesn't exist; and the social responsibility model is vague and poses serious philosophical questions.

Yet the world goes on and the manager must move with it. Problems will arise that require decisions. No two managers may choose identical paths, and indeed the problems facing a manager may turn him into a political person rather than the Economic Man he has often been labeled.

THE READINGS

The four selections in this section present varying prescriptions for a general posture for the firm and its managers. The first article is an excerpt from a policy statement issued by the Committee for Economic Development. The CED is an organization of 200 businessmen and educators involved in research and study of political, social, and economic issues. Their statement on the *Social Responsibility of Business Corporations* was issued in 1971.

The CED statement strongly emphasizes "The Doctrine of Enlightened Self Interest." The corporation is viewed as "dependent on the goodwill of society" for its supply of essential resources. An element of fear is also present: " . . . if business does not accept a fair measure of responsibility for social improvement, the interests of the corporation may . . . be jeopardized. Insensitivity to changing demands of society . . . results in public pressures for governmental intervention . . ." On the other hand, the statement then goes on to stress the profit potential of fulfilling social needs by placing them in a market context, clearly a not too revolutionary idea.

The second selection by Milton Friedman, well-known University of Chicago economist, is essentially a restatement of classical economic and political doctrine. Viewing social responsibility as basically a subversive doctrine, Friedman is incisive in cutting through some of the political, economic, and philosophical weaknesses of the thesis.

The selection by Gilbert Burck (from *Fortune*) is much in line with the Friedman manner of thinking. Clearly sympathetic with the approach of the "strict constructionists," Burck is critical of the self-righteousness of social responsibility advocates as well as their thinking on the cost–benefit parameters of the concept.

On the other hand, the article from *Business Week* is cautiously laudatory of the results of social responsibility. While the *Business Week* article does not squarely face the philosophical issues, it is quite obvious that the writer and *Business Week* look kindly on the doctrine since the article is primarily a recapitulation of Business Week Awards for Corporate Citizenship.

The reader might find it interesting to compare assessments of social action by *Business Week* and *Fortune,* particularly as they relate to firms such as Levi Strauss and Co.

Excerpts From Social Responsibilities of Business Corporations

Committee for Economic Development*

This statement† deals with the social responsibilities of business enterprises in contemporary American society. It is intended to contribute to a clearer view of these developing responsibilities and to show how business can best respond to the changing requirements of society.

To focus sharply enough on such a complex and fluid situation, the Research and Policy Committee has defined its frame of reference in this way:

> • To address ourselves predominantly to the *social* rather than the *economic* aspects of business responsibilities, although we recognize that business serves society mainly through carrying out its basic func-

---

*Committee for Economic Development, *Social Responsibilities of Business Corporations,* Chapters 1 through 4 (New York: CED, 1971).

†Various CED members added "Memoranda of Comment, Reservation or Dissent" to this statement. Space limitations in this volume prevented the inclusion of these memoranda.

tions of producing goods and services and generating wealth that improves the nation's standard of living.[1]

• To concentrate on the large publicly-owned, professionally-managed corporations which account for most of the country's productive capacity and which generally bear the burden of leadership within the business community. Nonetheless, much of what we say about social responsibilities applies as well to smaller enterprises and to businessmen as individuals.

• To consider the structure of corporations as it affects social responsiveness and accountability, but not undertake a thorough analysis of organizational matters which would require a study in its own right.

• Similarly, to treat business–government relationships as these impinge on our central concern with social responsibilities, without attempting a detailed analysis of the business–government interface which would also necessitate a separate study.

• Finally, we have restricted our scope to the United States to make the subject manageable, although we recognize that there are international implications and interactions involved in the social responsibilities and performance of American business enterprises operating abroad.

Within this frame of reference, we have sought to set forth a fresh and enlightened point of view about the role of business as an important instrument for social progress in our pluralistic society. While this statement emphasizes some general policies and new approaches which seem to us necessary to achieving better balanced economic and social development, it does not make specific recommendations for action as the Committee normally does in its statements on national policy. Primarily, this is an educational document which aims to provide the background and perspective for the development of solid reasoning and sound policy on the part of business, government, and the public.

1. THE CHANGING SOCIAL CONTRACT WITH BUSINESS

Business functions by public consent, and its basic purpose is to serve constructively the needs of society—to the satisfaction of society.

Historically, business has discharged this obligation mainly by supplying the needs and wants of people for goods and services, by providing jobs and purchasing power, and by producing most of the wealth of the nation. This has been what American society required of business, and business on the whole has done its job remarkably well. Since 1890, the total real national product has risen at an average

---

[1] The economic performance of business has been treated in our earlier statement, *Economic Growth in the United States,* a Statement on National Policy by the Research and Policy Committee, Committee for Economic Development, updated and reissued by the Program Committee (New York: October 1969).

of more than three per cent a year compounded, almost doubling every 20 years. Even with a threefold growth in population and greatly increased taxes, real disposable income per person has more than tripled and work time has declined by a third over the past 80 years.

In generating such substantial economic growth, American business has provided increasing employment, rising wages and salaries, employee benefit plans, and expanding career opportunities for a labor force, many of whose members are still subject to intermittent unemployment, which has grown to 83 million people. More than 30 million stockholders—and some 100 million people who have life insurance policies, pensions, and mutual fund shares—have benefited over many years from dividends and appreciation of their investments in business. All other major institutions of society, including government, have been sustained in substantial measure by the wealth produced by a business system which provides a strong economic foundation for the entire society.

Most important, the rising standard of living of the average American family has enabled more and more citizens to develop their lives as they wish with less and less constraint imposed on them by economic need. Thus, most Americans have been able to afford better health, food, clothing, shelter, and education than the citizens of any other nation have ever achieved on such a large scale.

Business has carried out its basic economic responsibilities to society so well largely because of the dynamic workings of the private enterprise system. The profit-and-loss discipline continually spurs businessmen to improve goods and services, to reduce costs, and to attract more customers. By earning profit through serving people better than their competitors, successful business concerns have been able to contribute importantly—through taxes and donations—to the financial support of public and private organizations working to improve the quality of life. By operating efficiently, business concerns have been able to provide people with both the means and the leisure to enjoy a better life.

Moreover, the competitive marketplace has served as an effective means of bringing about an efficient allocation of a major part of the country's resources to ever-changing public requirements.

Notwithstanding these accomplishments, the expectations of American society have now begun to rise at a faster pace than the nation's economic and social performance. Concentrated attention is being focused on the ill-being of sectors of the population and on ways to bring them up to the general well-being of most of the citizenry. Fundamental changes are also taking place in attitudes, with greater emphasis being put on human values—on individual worth and the qualitative aspects of life and community affairs.

Society has also become acutely conscious of environmental problems such as air and water pollution produced by rapid economic development and population pressures. And the public has become increasingly concerned about the malfunctioning of important community services such as those provided by the post office, mass transportation, and some utility systems; about inadequacies in education and health care; and about mounting social problems such as poverty, crime, and drugs.

There is now a pervasive feeling in the country that the social order somehow has gotten out of balance, and that greater affluence amid a deteriorating environment and community life does not make much sense.

The discontinuity between what we have accomplished as producers and consumers and what we want in the way of a good society has engendered strong social pressures to close the gap—to improve the way the overall American system is working so that a better quality of life can be achieved for the entire citizenry within a well-functioning community. The goals include:

• Elimination of poverty and provision of good health care;

• Equal opportunity for each person to realize his or her full potential regardless of race, sex, or creed;

• Education and training for a full productive and rewarding participation in modern society;

• Ample jobs and career opportunities in all parts of society;

• Livable communities with decent housing, safe streets, a clean and pleasant environment, efficient transportation, good cultural and educational opportunities, and a prevailing mood of civility among people.

These goals for some years have been articulated, advocated, and worked for by leaders in American politics, business, labor, and education. Their efforts have produced considerable progress toward most of the goals, and have contributed to the development of a broad consensus in support of more intensive efforts to realize all of them more fully, especially since the productivity of the economic system now makes this feasible.

Today there are also newer forces at work—pressing for rapid and, in some instances, radical changes in the social order. These include a highly idealistic and restless generation of American youth; a cultural leadership class of writers, film makers, artists, and intellectuals which is exerting considerable influence through communications media, literature, theaters, and universities; and numerous citizens' groups which are crusading for conservation, consumerism, black power, and other objectives. Many of these movements tend to assault the status quo and "establishment" institutions, which are viewed as obstacles to social progress and as too rigidly orthodox.

More broadly, the sluggishness of social progress is engendering rising criticism of *all* major institutions—government, schools, organized labor, the military, the church, as well as business. In this context, the large business corporation is undergoing the most searching public scrutiny since the 1930's about its role in American society. There is widespread complaint that corporations have become cavalier about consumer interests, have been largely indifferent to social deterioration around them, and are dangerous polluters of the environment.

The interaction between protagonists of substantial reform of major institutions and a generally concerned citizenry is producing significant changes in public expectations of business. As evidence of this, studies by Opinion Research Corporation during 1970 show that:

> • Sixty per cent of the population 18 years and older still consider that a main responsibility of business is to satisfy consumer needs for more and better goods and services. Corporations get good marks for innovativeness in developing new products to improve the nation's living standards. But twice as many people think companies are not doing as much as they should to satisfy consumer needs at reasonable prices as those who believe business is doing a particularly good job for consumers. At the heart of this dissatisfaction is the complaint that consumers are not provided with sufficient product information to make wise choices, and sometimes are misled by deceptive packaging and marketing practices.

> • Most significant, 60 per cent of the electorate also consider that another main responsibility of business is to keep the environment clean and free of pollution. Public criticism has increased to the point where 49 per cent do not believe corporations are doing as much as they should to improve the environment, as against only 7 per cent who think they are doing a particularly good job. Most of the public are not convinced that companies are making any real progress toward solving their pollution problems, and about 80 per cent favor closing plants that violate pollution regulations.

> • Substantial percentages of the public also identify as main corporate responsibilities such functions as hiring and training blacks and other disadvantaged people (38 per cent); contributing money to support public education, health, and charities (36 per cent); and helping to clean up and rebuild the ghettos in big cities (29 per cent). Slightly more of the public is satisfied with corporate performance in philanthropic activities than those who believe companies should increase their contributions.

Over all, a clear majority of the public thinks corporations have not been sufficiently concerned about the problems facing our society. Two-thirds believe business now has a moral obligation to help other major institutions to achieve social progress, even at the expense of profitability.

The fact is that the public wants business to contribute a good deal more to achieving the goals of a good society. Its expectations of business have broadened into what may be described as three concentric circles of responsibilities.

The *inner circle* includes the clear-cut basic responsibilities for the efficient execution of the economic function—products, jobs, and economic growth.

The *intermediate circle* encompasses responsibility to exercise this economic function with a sensitive awareness of changing social values and priorities: for example, with respect to environmental conservation; hiring and relations with employees; and more rigorous expectations of customers for information, fair treatment, and protection from injury.

The *outer circle* outlines newly emerging and still amorphous responsibilities that business should assume to become more broadly involved in actively improving the social environment. Society is beginning to turn to corporations for help with major social problems such as poverty and urban blight. This is not so much because the public considers business singularly responsible for creating these problems but because it feels large corporations possess considerable resources and skills that could make a critical difference in solving these problems. Indeed, out of a mixture of public frustration and respect for the perceived efficiency of business organizations, there is a clear tendency to look to corporations to take up the slack resulting from inadequate performance of other institutions, notably government but also education and health care in some measure. At the same time, the weight of informed opinion seems to be that these tertiary areas are not the responsibility of business in the first instance but that of the public sector and/or other private institutions. Even so, there is growing support for a more self-conscious partnership between business, government, and other institutions in some of these areas, most of all in urban affairs.

These broadened expectations of business have been building up for some time. This is indicated by the trends in public opinion over a number of years, and by the resultant actions of government in responding to the public will through an increasing variety of measures to protect consumer interests, to clean up the environment, and to enhance equal opportunities for employment and career development in industry. The evidence strongly suggests that these are solid and durable trends, not momentary frustrations or fads, and that they are likely to increase rather than diminish in the future.

Public opinion trends, of course, are not the only criteria for formulating sound business or public policy. Yet public opinion is a basic consideration, and in democratic society it usually is determinative over the long run, as demonstrated throughout the history of American business.

Today it is clear that the terms of the contract between society and business are, in fact, changing in substantial and important ways. Business is being asked to assume broader responsibilities to society than ever before and to serve a wider range of human values. Business enterprises, in effect, are being asked to contribute more to the quality of American life than just supplying quantities of goods and services. Inasmuch as business exists to serve society, its future will depend on the quality of management's response to the changing expectations of the public.

2. THE EVOLVING CORPORATE INSTITUTION AND MANAGERIAL OUTLOOK

The American business corporation, like the society in which it has its being, is a dynamic and changing institution. The corporation has gone through several major transformations and demonstrated great adaptability to societal changes over the past century. Its remarkable growth as an institution provides evidence of this fact. To survive, expand, and prosper it has had to adapt and serve society well.

Corporations have developed beyond anything imagined by the early economists. In Adam Smith's day and in his mind, the typical business establishment was that of the small entrepreneur who produced a simple product or service in competition with a large number of similar entrepreneurs.

American industrial enterprises on the modern scale had their beginnings in the middle of the nineteenth century with the spread of the railroad network and the steam-powered factory system. By the end of the century, many companies that had begun as comparatively simple organizations devoted solely to manufacturing had expanded to become vertical complexes embracing also the sources of raw materials and the marketing of products.

Corporate growth and responsibilities

During the twentieth century, corporations have grown enormously in size and power as they have followed the economic logic of complete integration from raw materials through all phases of manufacturing to the sale of products to the ultimate consumer. Many have also diversified horizontally into related and sometimes distinctively different lines of business, directed from a central management point. And a great many American corporations have also expanded internationally to such an extent that they have become truly global enterprises. They find raw materials wherever these are least costly, process them wherever it is most economical, transport goods great distances, and sell in the most advantageous markets irrespective of national boundaries.

Whether its size is dictated by the need for capital, mass production and mass marketing, or other forces, the large corporation has assumed a crucial role in the modern economy. The 500 largest American industrial corporations now account for nearly two-thirds of all domestic industrial sales, and 120 of these have annual sales exceeding $1 billion.

There have also been some notable failures as the profit-and-loss discipline weeded out enterprises which had become so poorly managed that they went into bankruptcy and were reorganized, or had ceased to be socially viable as independent firms and were absorbed into more efficient enterprises.

Contrary to fears of an earlier era, the growth of large corporations has not restricted opportunities for small enterprises to start up and flourish. Over the past 15 years, the number of proprietorships in the United States, comprising individually-owned businesses and farms, has increased from about 8 to 9 million, while active corporations have increased from about three-quarters to one and one-half million.

Nonetheless, the large corporations are the dominant producers in the industries in which they operate, and their influence is pervasive throughout the business world and much of society. Large corporations' price and wage changes strongly influence the economic actions of other companies—inside and outside their own industries. The leadership or inaction of large companies and their representatives frequently sets the pattern for the social performance of most of the business community—in terms of contributions to educational and cultural organizations, participation in job training and equal employment programs, and improvement of the environment.

As corporations have grown, they also have developed sizable constituencies of people whose interests and welfare are inexorably linked with the company and whose support is vital to its success. The constituencies include:

Employees. Many major corporations have more than 100,000 employees, while some (G.M. and A.T.&T.) have about one million. Employees are usually dependent on the corporation for their livelihood, work satisfaction, and career development, and often for much of their social life. Conversely, many employees wield considerable power within business organizations through their individual skills and through their labor unions, and increasingly exert important influence in community affairs.

Stockholders. Many corporations have hundreds of thousands of stockholders who are dependent on the company in varying degrees for their income. The understanding and allegiance of these stockholders is very important because by buying in or selling out they affect the financial standing of the company in the market, its ability to raise capital and acquire other firms, and its general reputation.

Customers and Consumers. Most corporations also have millions of customers and ultimate consumers who look to the corporation for the products and services they want. Customers usually are not dependent on a single source and their allegiance must continually be courted. At the same time, the corporation can affect their purchasing habits through advertising and merchandising.

Suppliers. A major corporation has thousands of suppliers of all sizes who, in substantial measure, are dependent upon it as an important market. The purchasing company, in turn, looks to its suppliers not only for quality products and services at competitive prices but often as a source of technical innovation.

Community Neighbors. Large corporations have operations in numerous communities throughout most of the country. Many of these operations are on a large enough scale in nonmetropolitan communities that they have considerable effect on the hundreds of thousands of people who live in or near such corporate facilities as mines, oil fields, forests, manufacturing plants, and research laboratories. The very appearance and tone of a small- or medium-size community, as well as its economic well-being, is often greatly influenced by its dominant industry. This is also true of cities as large as Seattle or Rochester. In this symbiotic relationship, the goodwill of the community is a positive contribution to the morale and performance of the corporation and its employees as well as a factor in the corporate image nationally.

In fact, the constituencies of large corporations have become so sizable and diversified—encompassing millions of employees, stockholders, customers, and community neighbors in all sections of the country and in all classes of society—that they actually constitute a microcosm of the entire society.

Beyond its interrelationships with these constituencies, the corporation also continuously interacts with other important elements in our pluralistic society. There are the *competitors,* both the producers of the same type of product and others seeking to substitute new products, vigorously striving to take away customers. There are *labor unions,* sometimes competing with management for the allegiance, welfare, and wages of employees, sometimes cooperating in the pursuit of productivity and other common goals, and generally exercising strong political influence. There are a wide variety of *interest groups,* continually monitoring what the corporation does in conservation, employment, and other sensitive areas, and often agitating for specific changes in corporate behavior. There is *education,* which has brought new kinds of business talent into the corporation, fostering ideas and pressures for change. There is the *press* and other media, alert to the news value of David-and-Goliath confrontations and to its watchdog role of publicizing any shortcoming of corporate as well as governmental institutions. There is *government* at federal, state, and local levels in its various capacities as customer, scrutineer, regulator, and lawmaker, and, in all instances, tax collector.

In relations with their constituencies and with the larger society, American corporations operate today in an intricate matrix of obligations and responsibilities that far exceed in scope and complexity those of most other institutions and are analogous in many respects to government itself. *The great growth of corporations in size, market power, and impact on society has naturally brought with it a commensurate growth in responsibilities; in a democratic society, power sooner or later begets equivalent accountability.*

The growth of corporate responsibilities has been reflected in part by the growth of formal and informal constraints on the exercise of corporate power. A considerable body of law and government regulation has been developed to ensure that *all* corporations conduct business ethically, compete vigorously, treat employees fairly, advertise honestly, and so on. Corporations are also expected to behave in accordance with social customs, high moral standards, and humane values. Not all corporations have lived up to these standards, and increasingly the public reacts very strongly against those in positions of great power who are arrogant or insensitive to either their legal or social responsibilities.

The new managerial outlook

As corporations have grown in ways that are visible from the outside, they have also been developing internally in ways which are not so obvious but are of great importance in shaping their role in society. The internal developments can be described in terms of the professional managers who have risen to the top in publicly-owned corporations. These new managers have brought about significant and continuing changes in corporate philosophy, organization, operations, and performance.

One of the most important changes is that the corporation is regarded and operated as a *permanent institution* in society. Whereas the proprietor of an earlier era saw his company as an expression of himself during his own lifetime and perhaps that of his sons, the professional manager sees the corporation as an institution very much more enduring than himself, an institution in which he plays a significant but transient role. In ascending to authority in a going enterprise, his aim is to further the continuous institutional development of the corporation in a very long time frame. His obligation, therefore, is as much to plan for the future —for example, by investing substantially in long-range research or in planting trees which will be harvested in 60 to 80 years—as it is to improve the current operations of the company during what is usually a comparatively brief term of office. His obligation is also to improve the qualitative aspects of the institution through the development of its personnel, the excellence of its performance, and its growing stature and reputation.

As a permanent institution, the large corporation is developing long-term goals such as survival, growth, and increasing respect and acceptance by the public. Current profitability, once regarded as the dominant if not exclusive objective, is now often seen more as a vital means and powerful motivating force for achieving broader ends, rather than as an end in itself. Thus, modern managers are prepared to trade off short-run profits to achieve qualitative improvements in the institution which can be expected to contribute to the long-run profitable growth of the corporation.

The modern professional manager also regards himself, not as an owner disposing of personal property as he sees fit, but as a trustee balancing the interests of many diverse participants and constituents in the enterprise, whose interests sometimes conflict with those of others. The chief executive of a large corporation has the problem of reconciling the demands of employees for more wages and improved benefit plans, customers for lower prices and greater values, vendors for higher prices, government for more taxes, stockholders for higher dividends and greater capital appreciation—all within a framework that will be constructive and acceptable to society.

This interest-balancing involves much the same kind of political leadership and skill as is required in top government posts. The chief executive of a major corporation must exercise statesmanship in developing with the rest of the management group the objectives, strategies, and policies of the corporate enterprise. In implementing these, he must also obtain the "consent of the governed" or at least enough cooperation to make the policies work. And in the long run the principal constituencies will pass judgment on the quality of leadership he is providing to the corporate enterprise.

Thus, recent generations of professional managers have been opening up more and more channels of communication and participation for various corporate constituencies. Whereas the traditional management structure was almost exclusively concerned with raw materials, manufacturing, sales, and finance, the modern management group includes executives who give specialized attention to all the constituencies: employees, stockholders, suppliers, customers, communities, government, the press, and various interest groups.

Some new managers are concerning themselves with the role of the individual in large, highly-structured organizations. They are experimenting with new ways of restoring more of the sense of personality and craftsmanship that has been virtually extinguished in assembly-line operations. And, in some instances, encouraging progress is being made in enriching the jobs of blue-collar workers, fostering a spirit of teamwork, and bringing employees into fuller and more constructive participation in the corporate enterprise.

Increasing attention is also being given to broadening the composition and enhancing the effectiveness of boards of directors. In some instances, boards have been filled with cronies of the management who rubber-stamped its decisions. The trend today is toward more independent directors who take their fiduciary responsibilities seriously, bring expertise and insights from different fields to bear on management, and guide and audit the performance of the management group to optimize the development of the company as a whole.

These developments in the organizational aspects of the corporation are of major importance and deserve deeper analysis and greater attention than can be given them in this statement. There is obviously under way a quest for better ways of integrating the various interests of major constituencies into the governance structure and processes and of relating the entire enterprise to society. In a broad sense, therefore, these developments are designed to make the corporation more responsive to its constituencies and to the larger society—while maintaining the managerial decisiveness that is required for efficient operations in the business world. Thus, the modern manager sees the corporation as a social as well as an economic organization, functioning in the whole of society rather [than] just in the marketplace.

All these developments are being greatly influenced by education. It is most significant that today's corporate leaders are the first truly college-educated generation of business executives. A *Fortune* survey of the chief executives of the 500 largest industrial corporations in 1970 showed that some 44 per cent had postgraduate degrees, another 36 per cent had undergraduate degrees, 14 per cent had some college education, and only 4 per cent had not attended college. The college education of these executives was almost equally divided among science and engineering, humanities and social sciences, and business administration. And their graduate degrees are equally diversified, about a third in business administration, and another third in law.

The full impact of education is just beginning to be felt throughout the managerial structure. Universities have been sending more than 20,000 M.B.A.'s alone into corporations each year. And several hundred thousand management people already in corporations are receiving additional formal management training each year.

Modern professional managers have been exposed to concepts of business and its relations with society that were not available to previous generations. Today's managers are also more involved in the world outside their business establishments through contact with people in many other sectors of society and through participation in public causes. They have a far better perception than their predecessors could possibly have had about society's problems, how the company looks from the outside, and how it impacts on society.

With the benefits of education and exposure, the modern manager is able to see the life of the corporation in terms of both its social and its economic ecology. A company functioning in the midst of a dynamic society may be compared to a living organism striving to live and develop within its environment. Relationships are extremely complex. The world around is at once sustaining and threatening. Multiple causes and multiple effects are continually at work. To be insensitive, even to subtleties, could be disastrous. It becomes necessary for the corporation's own existence that it be highly responsive to the environment in which it lives.

3. ENLIGHTENED SELF-INTEREST: THE CORPORATION'S STAKE IN A GOOD SOCIETY

The changes under way in the corporate institution and managerial outlook are significant. They are tending to bring about a constructive response to growing public insistence that business take on more social responsibilities while continuing to improve the performance of its basic economic functions. *This process of adaptation of business structure and performance to the changing requirements of society can be facilitated greatly by the development of a clearer corporate rationale of the role business must play in the national community—a role as a responsible participant determined to resolve any conflict with humane values or the social environment.*

The development of this rationale needs to deal with such questions as:

- Why should corporations become substantially involved in the improvement of the social environment?

- How can they justify this to their stockholders?

- How can companies reconcile substantial expenditures for social purposes with profitability?

- What are the limitations on corporate social responsibilities?

Some executives and economists argue that the business of business is just business; that management has no right and no qualifications to undertake activities to improve society, or to tax its constituents for such purposes, since the general welfare of society is a governmental responsibility. There are many who believe business should become more involved with public problems but who are nonetheless concerned that the assumption of broad social responsibilities could erode the professional discipline of profitability and blur the accepted criterion of corporate performance. *The answer to these quite legitimate concerns lies in a clearer perspective of business as a basic institution in American society with a vital stake in the general welfare as well as in its own public acceptance.*

The doctrine of enlightened self-interest

In classical economic thought, the fundamental drive of business to maximize profits was automatically regulated by the competitive marketplace. As Adam Smith put it, each individual, left to pursue his own selfish interest (*laissez-faire*), would be guided ''as by an unseen hand'' to promote the public good.

The competitive marketplace remains the principal method of harmonizing business and public interests, because it has proved, over a very long time, to be an efficient way of allocating economic resources to society's needs. Yet governmental intervention has been required to promote and regulate the conditions of competition. Government also has intervened to guide economic activity toward major public objectives, as determined by the political process, when these cannot be achieved through the normal working of the marketplace.

The self-interest of the modern corporation and the way it is pursued have diverged a great deal from the classic *laissez-faire* model. There is broad recognition today that corporate self-interest in inexorably involved in the well-being of the society of which business is an integral part, and from which it draws the basic requirements needed for it to function at all—capital, labor, customers. There is increasing understanding that the corporation is dependent on the goodwill of society, which can sustain or impair its existence through public pressures on government. And it has become clear that the essential resources and goodwill of society are not naturally forthcoming to corporations whenever needed, but must be worked for and developed.

This body of understanding is the basis for the doctrine that it is in the ''enlightened self-interest'' of corporations to promote the public welfare in a positive way. The doctrine has gradually been developing in business and public policy over the past several decades to the point where it supports widespread corporate practices of a social nature, ranging from philanthropy to investments in attractive plants and other programs designed to improve the company's social environment.

In a 1935 amendment to the Internal Revenue Code, which for the first time permitted corporations to deduct up to 5 per cent of pretax income for charitable contributions, the doctrine was explicitly recognized by the state. Since then it has been substantially refined through corporate practice and sanctioned by the courts.

In various decisions, the courts have established the legality of corporate contributions for social purposes that serve the interests of the firm as broadly defined, even though they provide no direct benefits to it. In the 1953 landmark A. P. Smith case, the New Jersey Superior Court upheld the right under common law of a manufacturing company to contribute funds to Princeton University. *The court held that it was not just a right but a duty of corporations to support higher education in the interest of the long-range well-being of their stockholders because the company could not hope to operate effectively in a society which is not functioning well.*

The basic reasoning is simply that a corporate grant, say to a department of engineering which will help to provide trained personnel for the company, is no less appropriate than a payment to a supplier of raw materials for inputs provided to the firm. Neither of these involves an intrusion of management into an area beyond its legitimate concern, and neither is in any sense a giveaway of the stockholders' resources.

By the same logic, expenditures to help improve community educational, health, and cultural facilities can be justified by the corporation's interest in attracting the skilled people it needs who would not move into a substandard community. Similarly, a corporation whose operations must inevitably take place in urban areas may well be justified in investing in the rehabilitation of ghetto housing and contributing to the improvement of ghetto educational, recreational, and other facilities. In this case, of course, management must determine that these improvements are required to help make the company's environment safer and more acceptable to its employees and generally more conducive to effective business operations.

Indeed, the corporate interest broadly defined by management can support involvement in helping to solve virtually any social problem, because people who have a good environment, education, and opportunity make better employees, customers, and neighbors for business than those who are poor, ignorant, and oppressed. It is obviously in the interest of business to enlarge its markets and to improve its work force by helping disadvantaged people to develop and employ their economic potential. Likewise, it is in the interest of business to help reduce the mounting costs of welfare, crime, disease, and waste of human potential—a good part of which business pays for.[2]

---

[2]This is a moral proposition as well as a matter of self-interest. The corporation as a legal person has the same obligation as all citizens to participate in and contribute to the general welfare, and to treat human beings humanely. Many businessmen understand this and act from moral impulses—"we should do this because it's the right thing to do"—without explicitly calculating self-interest. They implicitly recognize that the corporation benefits from strengthening justice in the society. In civil rights, for instance, some businessmen acted on moral grounds in pioneering fair-employment practices long before this became legally required, in aiding black educational institutions, and in going well beyond the traditional scope of corporate activities to combat racial discrimination.

The doctrine of enlightened self-interest is also based on the proposition that if business does not accept a fair measure of responsibility for social improvement, the interests of the corporation may actually be jeopardized. Insensitivity to changing demands of society sooner or later results in public pressures for governmental intervention and regulation to require business to do what it was reluctant or unable to do voluntarily. Today, the public strongly wants the environment cleaned up and Congress is responding by enacting stringent antipollution measures which will require substantial technological and economic changes in many industries.

Public expectations are also expressed through direct citizen actions. In recent years, a number of companies have been challenged by racial, religious, and educational groups ready to divert purchases and investments away from firms not doing their part to eliminate barriers of discrimination in employment. Other companies have been confronted by petitions, by publicity generated by groups of indignant citizens, even by picket lines or more violent expressions of protest.

Experience with governmental and social constraints indicates that the corporations's self-interest is best served by a sensitivity to social concerns and a willingness, within competitive limits, to take needed action ahead of a confrontation. By acting on its own initiative, management preserves the flexibility needed to conduct the company's affairs in a constructive, efficient, and adaptive manner. And it avoids or minimizes the risk that governmental or social sanctions, produced out of a crisis atmosphere, may be more restrictive than necessary. Moreover, indiscriminate opposition to social change not only jeopardizes the interest of the single corporation, but also affects adversely the interest all corporations have in maintaining a climate conducive to the effective functioning of the entire business system.

Enlightened self-interest thus has both "carrot" and "stick" aspects. There is the positive appeal to the corporation's greater opportunities to grow and profit in a healthy, prosperous, and well-functioning society. And there is the negative threat of increasingly onerous compulsion and harassment if it does not do its part in helping create such a society.

Redefining stockholder interest

As a practical matter, the doctrine of "enlightened self-interest" applies to the stockholders of a corporation as well as to management and other participants in the enterprise. Yet some additional attention to this point is warranted because traditional economic theory holds that the stockholder's interest is served only by corporate investment policies which yield benefits that are fully recovered by the corporation, and therefore maximize the market value of its stock. Many corporate expenditures for social purposes—such as manpower training or urban renewal—produce benefits which cannot be fully recovered because the worker may move to another employer, or because environmental improvements also accrue to other businesses and to the public in general. Circumstances like these have tended to inhibit some corporations from expending funds for social improvements, especially when management doubts that such actions can be reconciled with what is presumed to be the "interest of the stockholder."

However, the widely diversified nature of business ownership today alters the interest of the stockholder as classically defined.[3] Nearly all investors now hold equities in more than one company. Moreover, a substantial and growing proportion of stockholder investment in business is not through individual portfolios of a few stocks, but through large investment media—such as pension trusts, mutual funds, and insurance companies—which invest regularly in hundreds of different companies in different industries. Stockholders' interests, therefore, tend to ride with corporations as a group and with investment policies which provide benefits to the corporate sector as a whole—in the form of improved environmental conditions, a better labor force, and stronger public approval of private business. That is, corporations as a group—and singly as well, under reasonable assumptions—will earn more on their invested capital, and stockholders will be better off if these broader investment policies are adopted.

Inasmuch as the business community as a whole clearly has a vital stake in a good, well-functioning society, it can be argued that the stockholder's interest in the long run is best served by corporate policies which contribute to the development of the kind of society in which business can grow and prosper. Indeed, this long-range stockholder interest would justify governmental regulation to bring about improved environmental operating conditions—in, for example, pollution abatement—if corporations singly or as a group cannot achieve such results on their own.

Social improvement and profitability

The positive perspective of enlightened self-interest provides the framework for reconciling social improvement with profitability. Changing public expectations and the urgent quest for a good society are beginning to generate new demands for the kind of goods and services that in many respects business is demonstrably well qualified to provide. Some of these markets will come into existence fairly naturally, some will have to be created by business initiative, and others will have to be fashioned primarily by government. Altogether, they will provide substantial opportunities for business to profit by serving society's new requirements.

There are a great many social areas—such as housing, education, manpower training, health, transportation, large-scale urban redevelopment, and new cities— in which public pressures for improvement are already strong enough to create profitable markets, or markets that can be made profitable by a combination of greater business initiative and more effective governmental incentives. As these new opportunities develop, corporations with the entrepreneurial zeal to anticipate

---

[3] Henry C. Wallich and John J. McGowan, "Stockholder Interest and the Corporation's Role in Social Policy," in *A New Rationale for Corporate Social Policy,* CED Supplementary Paper Number 31 (New York: December 1970).

what the public is going to want, instead of merely supplying what it has wanted in the past, are apt to improve their profitability by discharging their responsibilities to society. Environmental quality standards, for instance, are creating large new markets for designers and producers of pollution-abatement equipment and systems, and for manufacturing-process and technological changes that could eliminate industrial pollution at the source. Public pressures for social improvements, and the resultant market opportunities, will grow substantially over the next 30 years as the country has to provide for some 75 million more people and an even more highly urbanized population.

To respond to such opportunities, business must recognize that the pursuit of profit and the pursuit of social objectives can usually be made complementary. From the standpoint of business, profit can be earned by serving public needs for social improvements as well as for goods consumed privately. From the standpoint of society, public services can be improved by enlisting the efficiencies of business organizations through the opportunity for profit. Thus, market incentives can serve the common interest of business and society.

There are likely to be more areas of social improvement in which the prospects for profit do not meet prevailing corporate investment criteria. In such cases, corporations will need to reexamine the traditional concepts and measurements of profit in the newer context. This may well involve, among other things, a substantial diversion of resources away from private consumption into higher-priority social improvements.

Conversely, government will need to reexamine the comparative advantages of public- and private-sector capabilities for getting the great social tasks done as efficiently as possible. And government will not only have to develop an adequate pattern of incentives for business to do its part of the job in those social markets which otherwise would not be sufficiently attractive but also in some instances impose penalties on socially harmful activities.

Limitations on corporate social activities

Business establishments obviously cannot solve all the problems of society, with or without help from government. Corporations are necessarily limited by various internal constraints on what and how much they can do to improve society. One of the conditioning factors is corporate size and capability. A very large corporation with extensive resources and skills is able to do a good deal more than a small company which might have to stick exclusively to its traditional business to stay alive in a highly competitive market. Even the large corporation must give its main attention to its mainstream business to keep competitive and it will have to find the best balance between these basic requirements and newer social market activities. Some companies may well find this balance on the social side because their interests, technologies, and skills are inclined in that direction. Others will not be well suited to do much more than extend their main lines of business into social markets wherever this is possible.

Cost–benefit considerations are a very important factor. No company of any size can willingly incur costs which would jeopardize its competitive position and threaten its survival. While companies may well be able to absorb modest costs or undertake some social activities on a break-even basis, any substantial expenditure must be justified in terms of the benefits, tangible and intangible, that are expected to be produced. Since major corporations have especially long planning horizons, they may be able to incur costs and forego profits in the short run for social improvements that are expected to enhance profits or improve the corporate environment in the long run. But the corporation that sacrifices too much in the way of earnings in the short run will soon find itself with no long run to worry about.

Thus, management must concern itself with realizing a level of profitability which its stockholders and the financial market consider to be reasonable under the circumstances. This means that substantial investments in social improvement will have to contribute to earnings, and the extent of such earnings will be a major factor in determining the mix of a company's commercial and social activities.

This suggests that criteria need to be developed for the range of profitability that will attract an adequate flow of corporate investment into various social markets. To be effective, the opportunities for profit should be reasonably related to comparable opportunities in traditional lines of business. In some cases, the risks might well be lower than in commercial areas, because competition is less or the social market is partially subsidized or guaranteed by government, and therefore the profit level can be correspondingly lower.

It can be expected that corporate social activities via the philanthropic route will be circumscribed by public policy considerations. Congress has established a ceiling of 5 per cent of pretax income on deductible corporate contributions. This is not currently restrictive because the average level of such contributions is only about one-fifth the allowable maximum, but it is a clear delineation of the scope of such activities.

Corporate philanthropy is also constrained in many cases by management's reluctance in making grants to substitute its own judgment for the judgment of its various constituencies in society. Corporate philanthropy necessarily reflects the value system of management. The political process, in an imprecise but effective way, reflects the values of all constituencies. In such instances, management may prefer that the decisions be left to the political process in which all corporate constituents participate as well as management executives in their capacity as citizens. Exceedingly good managerial judgment will be required to achieve the right balance between the internal constraints on corporate leadership and external social needs and pressures.

Clearly an alternative to philanthropy for supporting a social activity that is not only of particular interest to management but also of wide public benefit would be a new government program financed by taxation. Corporate participation in financing such programs through the corporate income tax amounts, at the marginal rate, to 48 per cent of profits. The history of corporate philanthropy contains many cases in which a social need was first met by philanthropy and later assumed by government.

In helping to meet social needs, as for better education or equal housing opportunity, companies may take the philanthropic route or lend support to government programs, or both. In addition, some may enter the business of providing the services needed on a profit-making basis. Thus, corporate activities in the social area encompass the full range from philanthropy through tax-supported government programs to profit-making business.

4. WIDENING PARAMETERS OF SOCIAL PERFORMANCE

As corporations recognize that their enlightened self-interest necessitates more substantial efforts to help improve their social environment, they are increasingly exploring and experimenting in a new terrain. This reaching out into new social fields is in an embryonic stage, however. There is not sufficient accumulated experience to formulate the kind of strategy and methodology that is generally employed in the mainstream of corporate business.

Even so, there are patterns of corporate social involvement and performance that are beginning to emerge. These patterns, along with developments in business thinking and in social science research, can facilitate the formulation of needed guidelines and principles with respect to such questions as:

> • What is the appropriate scope of corporate social involvement from the standpoint of management—considering the limitation of company resources, cost-benefit ratios, and good judgment about balancing the primary needs of the business with efforts to help improve social conditions?

> • What is the appropriate scope from the standpoint of society—as judged by the comparative advantages in getting social problems dealt with by business corporations and by such other institutions as government, education, labor, private foundations, and volunteer groups?

> • How much of the task can corporations undertake on an essentially voluntary basis under prevailing market conditions, and how much will need to be facilitated by changes in the governmental rules that govern the economic system?

> • How can the social performance of business be evaluated?

Clarification of these issues would help society understand what business can reasonably be expected to accomplish, and how it can best be done. This could forestall exaggerated public expectations that corporations somehow can and should solve most of the country's social problems, and thus prevent a blacklash of resentment when business performance falls short of unrealistic expectations. Conversely, clarification would facilitate the process by which business could find its optimum social role in a rational fashion. This would minimize the dual danger of under-response and resulting public dissatisfaction, or of overresponse which could lead companies well beyond their competence, bring about destructive rivalry rather than healthy competition with other institutions, and stretch corporate capabilities so far as to sap performance in the mainstream business.

Spectrum of current corporate activities

The spectrum of aggregate business activities to improve society covers, in widely varying degrees, ten major fields. The following is a reasonably comprehensive list of the sorts of things being done by business in the aggregate; each company must select those activities which it can pursue most effectively.

Economic Growth and Efficiency

- Increasing productivity in the private sector of the economy
- Improving the innovativeness and performance of business management
- Enhancing competition
- Cooperating with the government in developing more effective measures to control inflation and achieve high levels of employment
- Supporting fiscal and monetary policies for steady economic growth
- Helping with the post-Vietnam conversion of the economy

Education

- Direct financial aid to schools, including scholarships, grants, and tuition refunds
- Support for increases in school budgets
- Donation of equipment and skilled personnel
- Assistance in curriculum development
- Aid in counseling and remedial education
- Establishment of new schools, running schools and school systems
- Assistance in the management and financing of colleges

Employment and Training

- Active recruitment of the disadvantaged
- Special functional training, remedial education, and counseling
- Provision of day-care centers for children of working mothers
- Improvement of work/career opportunities
- Retraining of workers affected by automation or other causes of joblessness

• Establishment of company programs to remove the hazards of old age and sickness

• Supporting where needed and appropriate the extension of government accident, unemployment, health and retirement systems

Civil Rights and Equal Opportunity

• Ensuring employment and advancement opportunities for minorities

• Facilitating equality of results by continued training and other special programs

• Supporting and aiding the improvement of black educational facilities, and special programs for blacks and other minorities in integrated institutions

• Encouraging adoption of open-housing ordinances

• Building plants and sales offices in the ghettos

• Providing financing and managerial assistance to minority enterprises, and participating with minorities in joint ventures

Urban Renewal and Development

• Leadership and financial support for city and regional planning and development

• Building or improving low-income housing

• Building shopping centers, new communities, new cities

• Improving transportation systems

Pollution Abatement

• Installation of modern equipment

• Engineering new facilities for minimum environmental effects

• Research and technological development

• Cooperating with municipalities in joint treatment facilities

• Cooperating with local, state, regional and federal agencies in developing improved systems of environmental management

• Developing more effective programs for recycling and reusing disposable materials

Conservation and Recreation

• Augmenting the supply of replenishable resources, such as trees, with more productive species

• Preserving animal life and the ecology of forests and comparable areas

• Providing recreational and aesthetic facilities for public use

• Restoring aesthetically depleted properties such as strip mines

• Improving the yield of scarce materials and recycling to conserve the supply

Culture and the Arts

• Direct financial support to art institutions and the performing arts
• Development of indirect support as a business expense through gifts in kind, sponsoring artistic talent, and advertising
• Participation on boards to give advice on legal, labor, and financial management problems
• Helping secure government financial support for local or state arts councils and the National Endowment for the Arts

Medical Care

• Helping plan community health activities
• Designing and operating low-cost medical-care programs
• Designing and running new hospitals, clinics, and extended-care facilities
• Improving the administration and effectiveness of medical care
• Developing better systems for medical education, nurses' training
• Developing and supporting a better national system of health care

Government

• Helping improve management performance at all levels of government
• Supporting adequate compensation and development programs for government executives and employees
• Working for the modernization of the nation's governmental structure
• Facilitating the reorganization of government to improve its responsiveness and performance
• Advocating and supporting reforms in the election system and the legislative process
• Designing programs to enhance the effectiveness of the civil services
• Promoting reforms in the public welfare system, law enforcement, and other major governmental operations

---

Corporate activities across this wide spectrum, notably in the areas of social progress, break down into two basic categories. First, there are purely voluntary activities where business takes the initiative and exercises leadership. Next are activities induced by government incentives, or required by law and regulations.

In this chapter, we examine those activities that are voluntary in nature—ranging from those which are generally considered as philanthropic to those which are essentially profit-making ventures in social markets.

Voluntary corporate activities

Altogether, corporate contributions to "charitable and educational institutions" total nearly $1 billion a year. This represents a doubling of such contributions in slightly less than a decade, generally paralleling the rise in business profits and hovering around 1 per cent of total pretax corporate income.

A survey of patterns of giving in 1968 by 401 major corporations indicated that about 40 per cent of their contributions went to education; a slightly smaller proportion to United Funds, hospitals, and organizations collecting for health and welfare; about 7 per cent to civic causes; about 5 per cent to cultural activities; and the remainder to miscellaneous groups. The emphasis has been shifting toward education, and in smaller but increasing amounts corporate grants are also flowing toward cultural and civic projects, such as symphonies, little theaters, libraries, and museums.

A number of corporations, especially larger ones, have taken steps in recent years to systematize and facilitate their philanthropic activities. Many have established contribution committees with secretariats specifically assigned to survey worthwhile projects, evaluate results of grants, and prepare annual contributions budgets. A large number, well over 1500, have established company foundations to devote continuous and more professional attention to the philanthropic area, and to stabilize the flow of donations—e.g., during the economic downturn of 1969–71—by separating foundation resources from year-to-year fluctuations in corporate earnings.

A survey of more than 1000 small, medium, and large corporations in 1967 showed that 92 per cent were making financial contributions to education, health, and welfare. The major corporations, which set the pace on most social fronts, actually lag behind smaller companies in philanthropy—averaging only about 0.66 per cent of their pretax income in 1968 as compared with 1 to 3 per cent for small concerns and the maximum allowable 5 per cent for several companies.

The greatest voluntary involvement of companies, of course, has always been in the *local community,* where business support for social improvement programs is so traditional that it is generally taken for granted. Of more than 1000 companies surveyed in 1967, eighty-three per cent reported that they made gifts of equipment and talent to community enterprises; 87 per cent said they encouraged employee participation in community service organizations, with most of them giving formal recognition of employees' public service; and 75 per cent also encouraged employee service on public boards and commissions.

Even in national problems such as racial discrimination, a company's concern usually is focused on the local community. This is true not only of smaller concerns, but also of major national corporations. As businessmen have come to realize the high costs and damaging effects of discrimination on nearly every aspect of society, many of them have directed the influence of their corporations not only to eliminating discrimination at the workplace but also to providing community leadership in solving this corrosive social problem.

Some companies have refused to build plants or offices in areas with restrictions on open housing until these were eliminated. As Robert D. Stuart, Jr., the president of Quaker Oats, put it:

> We expect to make a positive social contribution, as well as an economic contribution, wherever we go. Specifically in the area of race relations, we expect the communities we locate new facilities in to offer equal opportunities comparable to those we offer in our own employment.
>
> Thus, prior to our decision to locate a major food plant in Danville (Ill.) two and a half years ago—and of course Danville was interested in attracting new industry—we advised the city fathers that passage of an open-housing ordinance would impress us as an indication of the city's intent for social progress. The ordinance passed, and two days later we approved location of a new plant in Danville.[4]

Increasingly, voluntary corporate activities are also taking the form of *cooperative action.* Cooperation among firms has the advantages of pooling their talents, spreading the costs and risks of social improvement efforts, integrating these efforts and enhancing their effectiveness. These are a few examples:

> • Under the auspices of Plans for Progress, some 37 clusters of companies have been formed to distribute help among predominantly black colleges. Representatives of each cluster of seven or eight companies meet regularly at their "adopted" school and provide assistance in a multiplicity of ways: funds for specific projects, donation of equipment, consultation on technical problems, visiting lecturers, and summer positions for teachers.
>
> • Two New York City corporations have established a profit-making venture, Construction for Progress, which is building about $6 million worth of low-rent apartment units in ghetto areas as turn-key projects. So far, construction has cost about 15 per cent less than it would have under governmental sponsorship, has been completed in one-third the time, and the first building has been sold to the New York City Housing Authority at a reasonable profit.
>
> • On a larger scale, 30 leading companies in the Greater Hartford (Connecticut) region have established The Greater Hartford Corpora-

---

[4]As stated in an editorial, "Something Socially Constructive," *American Banker* (October 9, 1970), p. 4.

tion to plan and direct development of the 750 square-mile metropolitan area. As a profit-making operating organization, a development corporation is raising $30 million for the acquisition of land to produce a new community out of a North Hartford ghetto area as the first stage in a $3 billion regional development plan.[5]

• The life insurance industry has pooled its resources to provide some $2 billion in capital for long-term loans at low interest rates for redevelopment of ghetto areas.

Even so, the overall pattern of voluntary individual and cooperative corporate activities to improve the social environment is quite spotty and not really substantial, either in terms of the magnitude of the nation's problems or of the business resources that could be applied to them. *These voluntary efforts need to be expanded and intensified. Voluntarism is a power that has always contributed a great deal to the improvement and functioning of our pluralistic, democratic society. It should be utilized to the fullest extent possible by the business community in discharging its responsibilities to society. By exercising greater initiative and leadership, business can be more effective in shaping the future development of its social environment. In this way, business can guide change and enhance its operational scope and flexibility, rather than lapse into the constricting role of a rearguard defender of the status quo.*

Asserting the initiative

Business enterprises have demonstrated many of the qualities and capabilities that appear to be critically needed in the solution of many of the country's social problems. They often possess comparative advantages over other institutions in such respects as innovation; technological competence; organizational, training and managerial abilities; and certain performance characteristics and disciplines. These comparative advantages could be more fully employed in relevant social areas, such as those in which corporate resources and experience can make a particular contribution or those with which the company has some logical connection.

Business itself could promote greater involvement in various ways. Top management, for example, could provide stronger leadership within many corporations to develop the policies and climate that would stimulate employees, especially young managers, to apply their interests and skills to relevant social as well as conventional business matters. The additional duty could be more widely and explicitly recognized as a normal, rather than extracurricular, part of managerial

---

[5]Hartford business leaders took this initiative not only because the cost of community services was rising rapidly but also because the quality of services was declining to the point that business would be most seriously affected unless a new and effective community life-support system were created.

responsibilities, and as an essential ingredient for managers aiming to equip themselves for broader executive responsibility. Managers at all levels could be encouraged and given adequate incentives to seek out relevant social market opportunities for the corporation.

The corporation itself can be organized for the systematic exploration and development of social markets *as a risk-taking, profit-making entrepreneurial line operation.* This requires not just the addition of staff specialists but also the development of new programs which are built into the main structure of the organization and its operating procedures. The restructuring might start by organizing a corporate "public business" group under a top executive with adequate staff and funds. Such a group would research social market opportunities as vigorously as conventional markets, and would develop a strategic plan for capitalizing on these opportunities—the corporate resources that would be required, the priorities, the extent of company and of any intercompany involvement, the requirements if any for governmental incentives, and the results to be attained.

To mobilize the resources and skills required to deal with social matters that are too large and costly for any single company, major corporations might also exercise greater leadership in industry and trade associations, and in developing new consortium arrangements. So long as no restraint of trade is involved, these cooperative activities are permissible under the antitrust laws. If trade restraints may be involved, corporations should compete in social as well as any other markets unless in particular instances the public interest is clearly better served by specific governmental exemptions. In such cases, the government could permit the cooperative development under proper supervision of major new technological systems that are urgently required and cannot reasonably be produced by individual company efforts.

The possibilities of consortium arrangements should especially be explored on a more imaginative and vigorous basis. The consortium method enables corporations to form groups of companies which include all or most of the firms that would benefit from specific social improvements—such as improving educational, medical, and cultural facilities in their communities. In this way companies could recover the benefits completely or substantially enough to justify the group going ahead with a project which would not seem worthwhile to a single company or to only a few companies.

The consortium approach could also minimize competitive disadvantages, without reasonable antitrust constraints, of more substantial corporate expenditures or investments in larger-scale social improvements. In retrospect, corporations probably could and should have taken more initiative, individually and cooperatively, to abate industrial pollution prior to the onset of progressively more stringent governmental controls. Voluntary action on an equitable burden-sharing basis would have demonstrated business' willingness to accept and act on its social responsibilities to the fullest extent possible, would certainly have alleviated the problem, and would have defined more clearly the point at which regulation was not only necessary but desirable. *Indeed, if corporations cannot deal individually with major social responsibilities such as pollution because of competitive cost disadvantages, and if they are unable to cooperate in resolving such difficulties, then they logically and ethically should propose and support rational governmental regulation which will remove the short-run impediments from actions that are wise in the long run.*

All this is to suggest that there is more scope for corporate initiative across the spectrum of philanthropic, burden-sharing, and profit-making social activities than has yet been realized. Even so, it is also clear that voluntary business actions alone will not be nearly sufficient to cope with the full range of corporate social responsibilities and to make the necessary contribution to the solution of the country's socioeconomic problems. This will require government-business collaboration.

Evaluation of corporate performance

As the corporation adapts to the changing requirements of society and moves into uncharted social terrain, there is a clear need to develop better methods for determining corporate goals and evaluating performance.

At present, these goals are predominantly financial in nature. Performance is likewise measured in financial terms—earnings per share, return on investment, sales income. Yet as investors become more sophisticated, they are looking into other factors that are likely to influence the corporation's performance in the future —including its policies with respect to employment of minority groups, consumerism, and protection of the environment.

Security analysts, in particular, are probing deeply into management and are making judgments about the quality of the human organization and its capabilities for innovation and growth in changing environmental conditions. This is becoming an increasingly professional activity, and leading security analysts have much influence on the decisions of large investment groups to buy or sell a company's stock which, in turn, greatly affects its price in the market. Thus, the price-earnings ratio of a company's stock is made up of a *fact*—the measured and reported financial results—and a *judgment or opinion* about all the intangible and seldom reported factors that determine future performance. The importance of intangible corporate assets is also demonstrated by the substantial difference between a company's *book value* (which accounts only for the physical and financial assets) and its *market value* as established by the market price of its outstanding stock.

Until recently, these intangible assets could be appraised only by informed opinion and good judgment, because there were no known ways to quantify them. However, a group of social scientists at the University of Michigan is developing theories and methodologies which could provide the means for measuring the worth of the productive capability of a firm's human organization, and may even eventually allow the value of the goodwill of its customers, stockholders, and financiers to be more systematically taken into consideration.[6] They are also applying experimental systems of human-asset accounting in business.

These efforts could in time provide managers with additional means of determining how to use the full resources of the business in the most productive and socially adaptive manner. The Michigan group, for example, has found that some of the conventional methods of cutting costs, increasing productivity and improving current earnings actually tend to have the opposite long-term effect by impairing the functioning of the human organization. The ability to detect and measure such changes in the human organization could enable management not only to improve its long-run economic performance but also to discharge better a responsibility to the key employee constituency which frequently influences community and public attitudes toward the company.

Improved measurement methods might also facilitate the governance of the corporate institution with respect to such other constituencies as investors and customers. In balancing the interests of various claimants, management needs to know as much as possible about the effects of products and of pricing and marketing practices on consumer satisfaction; the impact of a high wage settlement on stockholders; or the employee reaction to increased executive compensation and dividends. Conversely, more objective and accurate information about the business could enable these and other constituent groups to play a more constructive role in helping optimize the results for *all* those who have a stake in the enterprise.

Most important, the development of improved social indicators and measurement techniques would aid management in finding the most appropriate corporate role in social improvement, determining the correct strategy, evaluating the results, and justifying its actions to its constituencies. At present, many businessmen and economists are hesitant about corporations moving into social activities because neither social requirements nor corporate capabilities, actions, and results can be quantified with the exactness of commercial activities. Correspondingly, corporate constituencies and the larger society lack adequate means for judging what the corporation is really accomplishing in efforts to improve its environment.

The mounting public demands for better social performance necessitate corporate goal setting and performance measurements—just as demands are being made for an improved process for formulating objectives and measuring performance in government.[7] There is little in the present accounting and reporting systems of corporations that enables anyone to determine whether corporations have well-formulated sets of goals for social performance, or to measure the extent of progress toward realization of these goals.

---

[6]Rensis Likert, "The Influence of Social Research on Corporate Responsibility," in *A New Rationale for Corporate Social Policy,* CED Supplementary Paper Number 31 (New York: December 1970).

[7]This subject is being covered in a forthcoming CED Statement on National Policy, *Improving Federal Program Performance.*

The first step is to formulate corporate goals, not just for the stockholder constituency in financial terms but also for all constituents in as definitive terms as possible, and for the relevant scope of corporate social activity. For example, it should be possible to establish reasonably tangible goals with respect to pollution abatement on the basis of air and water quality standards and criteria projected three to five years ahead. Similarly, goals with respect to employment and advancement of minorities can be projected without great difficulty.

The second step is to utilize the advanced methodologies which are beginning to emerge to develop means for measuring corporate performance in meeting its various goals. Some of this may not be as difficult as it seems. The biological oxygen demand (BOD) load of effluent on receiving waters is now being measured precisely, as are an increasing number of other pollutants, and these measurements can be related to goals previously determined.

The third step is to report to the corporate constituencies and the interested public the definitive measurements of performance toward established goals. These clear objective evaluations of actual corporate performance will be more credible to the public than general rhetoric about how well the company is living up to its social responsibilities; they will also be much more meaningful than expenditure data alone.

By operating in a goldfish bowl of reporting progress toward goals, a management veering too far in pursuit of one constituency to satisfy its interest at the expense of another is likely to be brought into check by those whose interests are slighted. In the *laissez-faire* system, it was the *unseen hand* that was counted on to lead the pursuit of selfish private interests into realization of the public good. In the alternative system suggested here, it is the *visible hand* that is expected to achieve the same result.

The Social Responsibility of Business is to Increase its Profits

Milton Friedman

When I hear businessmen speak eloquently about the "social responsibilities of business in a free-enterprise system," I am reminded of the wonderful line about the Frenchman who discovered at the age of 70 that he had been speaking prose all his life. The businessmen believe that they are defending free enterprise when they declaim that business is not concerned "merely" with profit but also with promoting desirable "social" ends; that business has a "social conscience" and takes seriously its responsibilities for providing employment, eliminating discrimination, avoiding pollution, and whatever else may be the catch-words of the contemporary crop of reformers. In fact they are—or would be if they or anyone else took them seriously—preaching pure and unadulterated socialism. Businessmen who talk this way are unwitting puppets of the intellectual forces that have been undermining the basis of a free society these past decades.

The discussions of the "social responsibilities of business" are notable for their analytical looseness and lack of rigor. What does it mean to say that "business" has responsibilities? Only people can have responsibilities. A corporation is an artificial person and in this sense may have artificial responsibilities, but "business" as a whole cannot be said to have responsibilities, even in this vague sense. The first step toward clarity in examining the doctrine of the social responsibility of business is to ask precisely what it implies for whom.

Presumably, the individuals who are to be responsible are businessmen, which means individual proprietors or corporate executives. Most of the discussion of social responsibility is directed at corporations, so in what follows I shall mostly neglect the individual proprietor and speak of corporate executives.

In a free-enterprise, private-property system, a corporate executive is an employee of the owners of the business. He has direct responsibility to his employers. That responsibility is to conduct the business in accordance with their desires, which generally will be to make as much money as possible while conforming to the basic rules of the society, both those embodied in law and those embodied in ethical custom. Of course, in some cases his employers may have a different objective. A group of persons might establish a corporation for an elee-

The New York Times Magazine, September 13, 1970, pp. 33, 122–126. © 1970 by The New York Times Company. Reprinted by permission.

mosynary purpose—for example, a hospital or a school. The manager of such a corporation will not have money profit as his objective but the rendering of certain services.

In either case, the key point is that, in his capacity as a corporate executive, the manager is the agent of the individuals who own the corporation or establish the eleemosynary institution, and his primary responsibility is to them.

Needless to say, this does not mean that it is easy to judge how well he is performing his task. But at least the criterion of performance is straightforward, and the persons among whom a voluntary contractual arrangement exists are clearly defined.

Of course, the corporate executive is also a person in his own right. As a person, he may have many other responsibilities that he recognizes or assumes voluntarily—to his family, his conscience, his feelings of charity, his church, his clubs, his city, his country. He may feel impelled by these responsibilities to devote part of his income to causes he regards as worthy, to refuse to work for particular corporations, even to leave his job, for example, to join his country's armed forces. If we wish, we may refer to some of these responsibilities as "social responsibilities." But in these respects he is acting as a principal, not an agent; he is spending his own money or time or energy, not the money of his employers or the time or energy he has contracted to devote to their purposes. If these are "social responsibilities," they are the social responsibilities of individuals, not of business.

What does it mean to say that the corporate executive has a "social responsibility" in his capacity as businessman? If this statement is not pure rhetoric, it must mean that he is to act in some way that is not in the interest of his employers. For example, that he is to refrain from increasing the price of the product in order to contribute to the social objective of preventing inflation, even though a price increase would be in the best interests of the corporation. Or that he is to make expenditures on reducing pollution beyond the amount that is in the best interests of the corporation or that is required by law in order to contribute to the social objective of improving the environment. Or that, at the expense of corporate profits, he is to hire "hard-core" unemployed instead of better-qualified available workmen to contribute to the social objective of reducing poverty.

In each of these cases, the corporate executive would be spending someone else's money for a general social interest. Insofar as his actions in accord with his "social responsibility" reduce returns to stockholders, he is spending their money. Insofar as his actions raise the price to customers, he is spending the customers' money. Insofar as his actions lower the wages of some employes, he is spending their money.

The stockholders or the customers or the employes could separately spend their own money on the particular action if they wished to do so. The executive is exercising a distinct "social responsibility," rather than serving as an agent of the stockholders or the customers or the employes, only if he spends the money in a different way than they would have spent it.

But if he does this, he is in effect imposing taxes, on the one hand, and deciding how the tax proceeds shall be spent, on the other.

This process raises political questions on two levels: principle and consequences. On the level of political principle, the imposition of taxes and the expenditure of tax proceeds are governmental functions. We have established elaborate constitutional, parliamentary, and judicial provisions to control these functions, to assure that taxes are imposed so far as possible in accordance with the preferences and desires of the public—after all, "taxation without representation" was one of the battle cries of the American Revolution. We have a system of checks and balances to separate the legislative function of imposing taxes and enacting expenditures from the executive function of collecting taxes and administering expenditure programs and from the judicial function of mediating disputes and interpreting the law.

Here the businessman—self-selected or appointed directly or indirectly by stockholders—is to be simultaneously legislator, executive, and jurist. He is to decide whom to tax by how much and for what purpose, and he is to spend the proceeds—all this guided only by general exhortations from on high to restrain inflation, improve the environment, fight poverty, and so on and on.

The whole justification for permitting the corporate executive to be selected by the stockholders is that the executive is an agent serving the interests of his principal. This justification disappears when the corporate executive imposes taxes and spends the proceeds for "social" purposes. He becomes in effect a public employe, a civil servant, even though he remains in name an employe of a private enterprise. On grounds of political principle, it is intolerable that such civil servants —insofar as their actions in the name of social responsibility are real and not just window-dressing—should be selected as they are now. If they are to be civil servants, then they must be selected through a political process. If they are to impose taxes and make expenditures to foster "social" objectives, then political machinery must be set up to guide the assessment of taxes and to determine through a political process the objectives to be served.

This is the basic reason why the doctrine of "social responsibility" involves the acceptance of the socialist view that political mechanisms, not market mechanisms, are the appropriate way to determine the allocation of scarce resources to alternative uses.

On the grounds of consequences, can the corporate executive in fact discharge his alleged "social responsibilities"? On the one hand, suppose he could get away with spending the stockholders' or customers' or employes' money. How is he to know how to spend it? He is told that he must contribute to fighting inflation. How is he to know what action of his will contribute to that end? He is presumably an expert in running his company—in producing a product or selling it or financing it. But nothing about his selection makes him an expert on inflation. Will his holding down the price of his product reduce inflationary pressure? Or, by leaving more spending power in the hands of his customers, simply divert it elsewhere? Or, by forcing him to produce less because of the lower price, will it simply contribute to shortages? Even if he could answer these questions, how much cost is he justified in imposing on his stockholders, customers, and employes for this social purpose? What is his appropriate share and what is the appropriate share of others?

And, whether he wants to or not, can he get away with spending his stockholders', customers', or employes' money? Will not the stockholders fire him? (Either the present ones or those who take over when his actions in the name of social responsibility have reduced the corporation's profits and the price of its stock.) His customers and his employes can desert him for other producers and employers less scrupulous in exercising their social responsibilities.

This facet of "social responsibility" doctrine is brought into sharp relief when the doctrine is used to justify wage restraint by trade unions. The conflict of interest is naked and clear when union officials are asked to subordinate the interest of their members to some more general social purpose. If the union officials try to enforce wage restraint, the consequence is likely to be wildcat strikes, rank-and-file revolts and the emergence of strong competitors for their jobs. We thus have the ironic phenomenon that union leaders—at least in the U.S.—have objected to Government interference with the market far more consistently and courageously than have business leaders.

The difficulty of exercising "social responsibility" illustrates, of course, the great virtue of private competitive enterprise—it forces people to be responsible for their own actions and makes it difficult for them to "exploit" other people for either selfish or unselfish purposes. They can do good—but only at their own expense.

Many a reader who has followed the argument this far may be tempted to remonstrate that it is all well and good to speak of government's having the responsibility to impose taxes and determine expenditures for such "social" purposes as controlling pollution or training the hard-core unemployed, but that the problems are too urgent to wait on the slow course of political processes, that the exercise of social responsibility by businessmen is a quicker and surer way to solve pressing current problems.

Aside from the question of fact—I share Adam Smith's skepticism about the benefits that can be expected from "those who affected to trade for the public good"—this argument must be rejected on grounds of principle. What it amounts to is an assertion that those who favor the taxes and expenditures in question have failed to persuade a majority of their fellow citizens to be of like mind and that they are seeking to attain by undemocratic procedures what they cannot attain by democratic procedures. In a free society, it is hard for "good" people to do "good," but that is a small price to pay for making it hard for "evil" people to do "evil," especially since one man's good is another's evil.

I have, for simplicity, concentrated on the special case of the corporate executive, except only for the brief digression on trade unions. But precisely the same argument applies to the newer phenomenon of calling upon stockholders to require corporations to exercise social responsibility (the recent G.M. crusade, for example). In most of these cases, what is in effect involved is some stockholders trying to get other stockholders (or customers or employes) to contribute against their will to "social" causes favored by the activists. Insofar as they succeed, they are again imposing taxes and spending the proceeds.

The situation of the individual proprietor is somewhat different. If he acts to reduce the returns of his enterprise in order to exercise his "social responsibility," he is spending his own money, not someone else's. If he wishes to spend his money on such purposes, that is his right, and I cannot see that there is any objection to his doing so. In the process, he, too, may impose costs on employes and customers. However, because he is far less likely than a large corporation or union to have monopolistic power, any such side effects will tend to be minor.

Of course, in practice the doctrine of social responsibility is frequently a cloak for actions that are justified on other grounds rather than a reason for those actions.

To illustrate, it may well be in the long-run interest of a corporation that is a major employer in a small community to devote resources to providing amenities to that community or to improving its government. That may make it easier to attract desirable employes, it may reduce the wage bill or lessen losses from pilferage and sabotage, or have other worthwhile effects. Or it may be that, given the laws about the deductibility of corporate charitable contributions, the stockholders can contribute more to charities they favor by having the corporation make the gift than by doing it themselves, since they can in that way contribute an amount that would otherwise have been paid as corporate taxes.

In each of these—and many similar—cases, there is a strong temptation to rationalize these actions as an exercise of "social responsibility." In the present climate of opinion, with its widespread aversion to "capitalism," "profits," the "soulless corporation" and so on, this is one way for a corporation to generate good will as a by-product of expenditures that are entirely justified in its own self-interest.

It would be inconsistent of me to call on corporate executives to refrain from this hypocritical window-dressing because it harms the foundations of a free society. That would be to call on them to exercise a "social responsibility"! If our institutions, and the attitudes of the public make it in their self-interest to cloak their actions in this way, I cannot summon much indignation to denounce them. At the same time, I can express admiration for those individual proprietors or owners of closely held corporations or stockholders of more broadly held corporations who disdain such tactics as approaching fraud.

Whether blameworthy or not, the use of the cloak of social responsibility, and the nonsense spoken in its name by influential and prestigious businessmen, does clearly harm the foundations of a free society. I have been impressed time and again by the schizophrenic character of many businessmen. They are capable of being extremely far-sighted and clear-headed in matters that are internal to their businesses. They are incredibly short-sighted and muddled-headed in matters that are outside their businesses but affect the possible survival of business in general. This short-sightedness is strikingly exemplified in the calls from many businessmen for wage and price guidelines or controls or incomes policies. There is nothing that could do more in a brief period to destroy a market system and replace it by a centrally controlled system than effective governmental control of prices and wages.

The short-sightedness is also exemplified in speeches by businessmen on social responsibility. This may gain them kudos in the short run. But it helps to strengthen the already too prevalent view that the pursuit of profits is wicked and immoral and must be curbed and controlled by external forces. Once this view is adopted, the external forces that curb the market will not be the social consciences, however highly developed, of the pontificating executives; it will be the iron fist of government bureaucrats. Here, as with price and wage controls, businessmen seem to me to reveal a suicidal impulse.

The political principle that underlies the market mechanism is unanimity. In an ideal free market resting on private property, no individual can coerce any other, all cooperation is voluntary, all parties to such cooperation benefit or they need not participate. There are no "social" values, no "social" responsibilities in any sense other than the shared values and responsibilities of individuals. Society is a collection of individuals and of the various groups they voluntarily form.

The political principle that underlies the political mechanism is conformity. The individual must serve a more general social interest—whether that be determined by a church or a dictator or a majority. The individual may have a vote and a say in what is to be done, but if he is overruled, he must conform. It is appropriate for some to require others to contribute to a general social purpose whether they wish to or not.

Unfortunately, unanimity is not always feasible. There are some respects in which conformity appears unavoidable, so I do not see how one can avoid the use of the political mechanism altogether.

But the doctrine of "social responsibility" taken seriously would extend the scope of the political mechanism to every human activity. It does not differ in philosophy from the most explicitly collectivist doctrine. It differs only by professing to believe that collectivist ends can be attained without collectivist means. That is why, in my book *Capitalism and Freedom,* I have called it a "fundamentally subversive doctrine" in a free society, and have said that in such a society, "there is one and only one social responsibility of business—to use its resources and engage in activities designed to increase its profits so long as it stays within the rules of the game, which is to say, engages in open and free competition without deception or fraud."

444 52 128 4 GILL JASWANT S   000.0   JAN 05 06:40 PM

SOC. SEC. NO.   STUDENT NAME   MON   DAY   TIME

(1) DO NOT FOLD OR MUTILATE THIS CARD OR REMOVE IT FROM
    THE PACKET. IT MUST BE PROCESSED ALONG WITH YOUR
    CLASS CARDS.

(2) ENTER THE REGISTRATION CENTER ON THE DATE AND TIME
    SPECIFIED ABOVE TO OBTAIN CLASS CARDS.

REGISTRATION APPOINTMENT
CARD

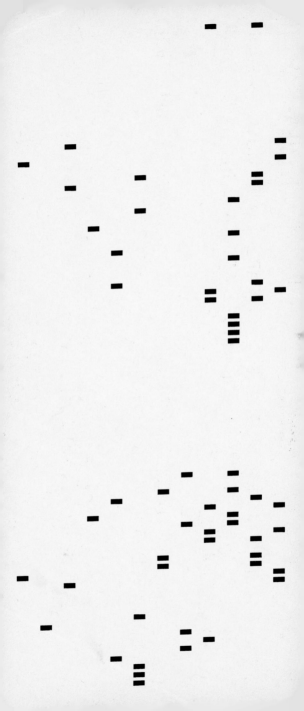

The Hazards of Corporate Responsibility

Gilbert Burck

Every Friday evening, Walter Fackler, professor of economics at the University of Chicago's Graduate School of Business, has been addressing a class of seventy-five high-ranking executives on the problems of public policy and corporate social responsibility. A more appropriate and exigent activity these days is hard to imagine. Fackler says he has never seen businessmen so confused and defensive. The doctrine that business has responsibilities "beyond business," which began to gather momentum a dozen or so years ago, is still picking up steam. Never before has the U.S. business establishment been confronted with such a bewildering variety of animadversion, such a Vanity Fair of conflicting demands and prescriptions. A detailed inventory of the "social" demands being made on business would fill several volumes; reconciling the numerous and conflicting prescriptions would baffle a synod of Solomons.

Perhaps because businessmen are so defensive, they themselves have not done much talking back to those who are making all the demands. When businessmen essay to discuss their role in society these days, they all too often sound like young ladies fifty years ago talking about sex. They cough and clear their throats and come up with moralistic platitudes. The back talk has come principally from economists—notably from some, like Milton Friedman and Henry Manne, who have generally been identified with the classical school. These "strict constructionists" argue that business serves society best when it minds its business well, and that it should take part in social activities only to the extent that these are necessary to its own well-being.

Fackler himself manages to sound like a strict constructionist much of the time. The great, the dominant, the indispensable *social* role of business, he tells his executive students, is a familiar one. In this most uncertain world, their prime job is to evaluate risks wisely, to allocate the nation's resources prudently, and to use them with optimum efficiency. Business fulfills its real social role by striving endlessly to take in more money than it pays out, or, as some of its critics would put the case, by lusting incessantly after the Almighty Dollar.

Reprinted from the June, 1973 issue of *Fortune* magazine by special permission. © 1973, Time, Inc.

Arrayed on the other side of the argument are the social-responsibility advocates—those who want an enlarged social role for industry. For all the immense variety of their prescriptions, these advocates agree on one general proposition: business ought to accept social responsibilities *that go beyond the requirements of the law.* In addition to mere compliance with the law, say the advocates, business should actively initiate measures to abate pollution, to expand minority rights, and in general to be an exemplary citizen, and should cheerfully accept all the costs associated with this good citizenship.

SUPPRESSING THE CONTROVERSY

Many of the most vocal social-responsibility advocates, including those affiliated with one or another band of Nader's raiders, tend to extreme forms of self-righteousness. Their proposals are often couched in rather general terms; they imply that the justice of their ideas is self-evident and that only a moral delinquent, or a businessman consumed by greed, could resist them. The notion that some schemes for implementing the proposals might actually be controversial, or that there might be serious questions of equity involved in asking corporate executives to tackle social problems with money belonging to other people (i.e., their stockholders)— these thoughts often seem to be suppressed in the advocates' minds.

But there is also a more sophisticated version of the social-responsibility proposition. According to this version, corporate executives who are strict constructionists at heart, and who harbor powerful lusts for Almighty Dollars, might nevertheless conclude that an activist social posture was good for their companies. They might decide, in other words, that social activism was good public relations. They might agree with Paul Samuelson, the Nobel laureate, who takes a simple view of the new demands on corporations. "A large corporation these days," he says, "not only may engage in social responsibility; it had damn well better try to do so."

A similarly pragmatic view of the matter has been propounded by Professor Neil Jacoby of the Graduate School of Management at the University of California, Los Angeles. Jacoby has been a dean of the school, a member of the Council of Economic Advisers under Eisenhower, a fellow of the Center for the Study of Democratic Institutions, and a member of the Pay Board. His forthcoming book, *Corporate Power and Social Responsibility,* describes corporate social involvement as a fact of life. "I don't really ask companies to do a single thing that isn't profitable," Jacoby remarked recently. "But political forces are just as real as market forces, and business must respond to them, which means it often must be content with optimizing and not maximizing immediate profits."

CORPORATIONS DO IT BETTER

Professor Henry Wallich of Yale has also advanced a rather sophisticated case for corporate social responsibility. Writing in FORTUNE last year (Books & Ideas,

March, 1972), Wallich made the point that corporations can perform some social activities better than can government; and in undertaking to do more than the law requires, they are shifting activities from the public to the private sector. When one corporation undertakes social obligations not borne by its competitors, it would, of course, be at a disadvantage. Therefore, Wallich proposes, companies in an industry should be allowed to work together toward social goals without fear of antitrust action.

Some serious economists regard the social-responsibility movement as a harbinger of major changes in the business environment. Professor George Steiner of the U.C.L.A. Graduate School of Management, for instance, believes the movement implies "a new area of voluntarism" that will change large corporations' basic operating style. Generally speaking, Steiner says, the old authoritarian way of running a company will give way to permissive and statesmanlike methods; the single-minded entrepreneur will be succeeded by the broad-gauge "renaissance" manager. Centralized decision-making will be accompanied, if not largely superseded, by decision-making in small groups. Financial accounting will be augmented by human-resources accounting, and the "social" costs of production will be increasingly internalized. Inevitably, government and business planning will complement each other. "We are," says Steiner prophetically, "in the process of redefining capitalism."

HOW SUPREME LIFE GOT THE BUSINESS

A few companies are beginning to act as if they believe Steiner. One is Standard Oil Co. (Indiana), which is spending about $40 million a year on pollution control —far more than it legally has to. It also boasts a long list of other social achievements, including efforts on behalf of Chicago's schools, and a determined program to hire and promote minority employees and to help minority suppliers and businessmen. Recently, for example, Standard arranged with Chicago's Supreme Life Insurance Co. of America, a company owned by blacks, to insure two plants of its Amoco chemical subsidiary in California. Standard's policy is to use not only qualified but "qualifiable" minority suppliers—i.e., it helps some to qualify.

The company's director of public affairs these days is Phillip Drotning, author of three books on the black movement in the U.S., and an advocate of a high level of corporate involvement. If Drotning has his way—and so far he has been backed by top management—the promotion of executives will depend not only on their cost and profit records but on their approach to social objectives. Managers will be supplied with the information they need to evaluate the social consequences of their decisions, and they will plan strategies that benefit both the company and society. "The heads of the company," says Drotning, "will exercise leadership among their peers in the broad business community and the public at large, to generate support for the far-reaching, long-range changes in social policy that must occur."

The goals of Chicago's CNA Financial Corp., an insurance-centered company with revenues of $1.6 billion, are pretty ambitious too. Last year the company spent close to $660,000 on dozens of selected social projects, compelled its insurance subsidiaries to demand that their clients take "corrective action" on a variety of pollution problems, and insisted on a 30 percent minority representation among the workers erecting its new headquarters building.

CNA's vice president in charge of social policy is a former social-agency administrator named David Christensen, who argues that companies typically go through several phases in the perception of their social responsibilities. First there is the "do-good" phase, in which the company builds libraries with its name on them—but goes right on dumping waste in the lake. Later comes a more systematic effort to coordinate public relations and corporate involvement in, say, urban affairs. Finally the company gets to the phase of genuine corporate responsibility, in which it is concerned less with public relations than with developing responsible ways to improve society. Conscience money is no longer needed, because the company doesn't have a bad conscience.

NOBODY TALKS ABOUT COST

Christensen says that CNA is just now entering the third phase. To guide it in this period he has helped the company develop an elaborate manual on corporate responsibility—a document that details just how CNA proposes to involve all its executives in social goals, and how they in turn should involve their charges. The whole opus has a somewhat evangelical tone, suggesting the marching orders for an all-out war on the devil. What it all will cost and who will finally pay for it are matters nobody seems to talk about. Presumably, however, CNA can afford it. That is to say, CNA, unlike many less opulent and more price-competitive companies, can absorb the costs—i.e., reduce the profits of its shareholders.

Given the natural inclination of managers to demand records and evaluations, it is not surprising that many businessmen who are interested in being socially responsible are also interested in what is known as the "social audit." Just as a conventional audit sums up a company's financial performance, a social audit would describe its social performance. Hundreds of articles, pamphlets, and books have already been written about the social audit, scores of workshops and seminars have been held to discuss it, and some sizable companies are experimenting with ways to implement the idea.

So far, it is fair to say, little has come of the effort. The problem, says Professor S. Prakash Sethi of the University of California at Berkeley, is that nobody has yet drawn up an objective definition of socially responsible behavior; hence nobody has succeeded in measuring it consistently. And who, in any case, would certify that the accounting was accurate? Professor Raymond Bauer of the Harvard Graduate School of Business Administration says, "We still need to learn how to get on the learning curve."

The social-audit concept has been scoffed at even by some of the most ardent advocates of corporate social responsibility. Milton Moskowitz, a financial columnist who edits a crusading biweekly sheet called *Business & Society,* derides the social-audit concept as "nonsense, redemption through mathematics, and useful to companies only as a laundry list." F. Thomas Juster, until recently a senior economist at the National Bureau of Economic Research, has been exploring social and economic measurement. "Given the state of the art," says Juster, "we're all kidding ourselves if we think we can measure [social] output. One reason is that real outputs are very long range . . . We can't measure that, not now . . . probably can't measure it in ten years."

One of the most insistent of all recent efforts to develop a social audit was presented in the Winter 1972–73 issue of the quarterly *Business and Society Review,* in an article by David Linowes, a partner in the accounting firm of Laventhol, Krekstein, Horwath, & Horwath. Linowes, who likes to be alluded to as the father of socioeconomic accounting, presents a model of a social audit. The model differentiates, logically, between mandatory and voluntary corporate outlays, and proposes to put dollar figures on the employee time, the facilities, the training, etc., that a company voluntarily invests in social areas. Linowes anticipates that FORTUNE's 500 list will someday include a corporate responsibility rating. In the same issue of the review, however, six friendly critics who were asked to comment on Linowes' suggestions raise a host of substantive and technical objections. As one puts it, Linowes tries "to shoehorn . . . into the framework of the orthodox income statement model" what are essentially nonfiscal data containing highly subjective determinations.

Meanwhile, the social-audit enthusiasts seem determined to find a way of making the thing work. A host of consultants who specialize in advising companies on the art and mystery of carrying out their responsibilities to society have got behind the idea of the social audit. "Anytime there is money to be made in some area requiring newly developed expertise," says Ralph Lewis, editor of the *Harvard Business Review,* "a new breed of consultants seems to arise." Several serious enterprises are also showing interest in the social-responsibility audit. Abt Associates, Inc., a contract research organization, publishes an annual report accompanied by its version of a social audit. Meanwhile, imaginative newspapermen are setting themselves up as experts, and social audits seem to be giving the public-relations profession a new lease on life.

THE GREAT SOCIAL INCREMENT

All this may sound highly laudable at best and harmless enough at worst. But in some circumstances it might be very harmful indeed. It could very well threaten the phenomenon known as rising productivity.

Perhaps because most people are so used to the phrase, they often forget what a stupendous phenomenon it describes. Last year American business produced more than $900 billion worth of goods and services, more than two-thirds of which were accounted for by corporations. Owing in large part to the corporations' striving to make money, national productivity rose by 4 percent. (Corporations earned some $88 billion before taxes, $41 billion of which was taxed away for government and other social needs.)

That 4 percent figure means that business turned out roughly $36 billion *more* of goods and services than it would have if it had maintained only the productivity level of the year before. This great social increment, fluctuating from year to year but expanding at an average of about 3 percent a year, is the very foundation of the nation's way of life; these gains afford the only basis on which a better society can be built. Rising productivity alone made possible the first eight-hour day more than eighty years ago, just as rising productivity has more recently brought higher real pay, shorter hours, and larger fringe benefits. And rising productivity alone will enable the U.S. to achieve without inordinate sacrifice the benefits that the advocates of social responsibility are now demanding.

This is so important a matter that it deserves to be viewed from another perspective. Suppose productivity ceased to rise, or that it even fell a little. Unless more people worked longer, the average living standard would then remain constant or decline. The costs associated with cleaner air, training for minorities, and other socially desirable programs would increase the total price of other things by precisely the amount of those costs. Every benefit would be offset by a sacrifice. If productivity did not rise, one man's gain would be another man's loss.

IT'S THE CONSUMER WHO PAYS

Productivity, however, rises only when a business manages to innovate successfully and when it manages to cut costs, either by using fewer resources to make a product or by turning out a better product with the same resources. As the man in charge of costs, the businessman is the agent of what might be called the "consumer at large." When the businessman wastes resources on a bad risk, it is this consumer who principally pays (although the stockholders are presumably losers too). When he reduces his costs or innovates successfully, it is the consumer who benefits.

And so, precisely because the businessman's drive for profitability is identical with his drive for lower costs, his profit is a pretty good measure of social welfare. Suppose two companies make similar products and sell them at about the same price. Company A nets $10 million, but Company B nets twice as much because it is run by a tough crew of hardheaded, no-nonsense, endlessly striving managers motivated by abundant bonuses—the kind of men corporate critics often like to describe as s.o.b.'s. To an individual consumer, the two companies might seem to offer little choice. But so far as society at large is concerned, Company B has done a much better job, because it has used $10 million less of our resources, i.e., raw material and manpower, in doing the same job. So obviously, the s.o.b.'s have been better for society than easygoing and irresolute managers would have been. As the Lord remarked of Faust, "He who strives endlessly, him we can redeem."

It is just possible, then, that the U.S. could use more endless strivers, redeemed or not. The advocates of corporate social responsibility, indeed, seem to have overlooked what may be the real case against U.S. business: it may be using too many resources for what it turns out. Suppose, at all events, that U.S. corporations had managed to turn out that 1972 volume for 2 percent less than they actually spent. The incremental profit would have amounted to $11 billion, enough to eliminate, over the years, practically all pollution. "If the responsibility buffs really want to promote national welfare," one strict constructionist observed recently, "they should be complaining that companies aren't making *enough* money."

And so it seems reasonable to ask what effect the businessman's increasing preoccupation with those other social "responsibilities" will have on his endless striving to elevate productivity. Thirty-one years ago the late Joseph Schumpeter predicted that, as corporations grew bigger, businessmen would cease to behave like aggressive entrepreneurs, and would degenerate into mere bureaucrats. Schumpeter's prediction hasn't come true, but some now worry that it may. They fear that the new emphasis on Good Works will sicken the businessman o'er with the pale cast of thought, vitiate his drive to innovate and cut costs, and gradually convert him and his fellows into the kind of bureaucrats that infest so many marble halls of government.

OUR SOCIALLY RESPONSIBLE MONOPOLISTS

These are the kinds of considerations that bother Milton Friedman when he contemplates the contentions in favor of social responsibility. Friedman likes to dramatize his position by making the superficially shocking statement that the businessman's *only* social responsibility is to increase profits. He is against the acceptance of social responsibilities, because it implicitly expresses the socialist view that political, and not market, considerations should govern the allocation of resources, and over the long run this means reduced efficiency. What's more, Friedman says, "no businessman has money to spend on social responsibility unless he has monopoly power. Any businessman engaged in social responsibility ought to be immediately slapped with an antitrust suit."

In the same vein, Professor Harold Demsetz of U.C.L.A. insists that the word "responsibility" is being misused: "The only responsibility of businessmen or anyone else is to obey the laws of the land, no more, no less." If our society wants business to set up day-care centers for employees' children, for example, then it should pass a law to that effect, so that the burden will be shared by all business enterprises.

The problem of sharing that burden is one that most social-responsibility advocates seem not to have thought through. One trouble with leaving good deeds up to individual executives is that not all of their companies are equally prosperous. Now that the Kaiser empire is in trouble, for example, Edgar Kaiser is taking a hard line on demands for "responsibility" in his companies. "Not to husband resources," Kaiser says with considerable feeling, "would be social irresponsibility of the highest order." Hard-pressed companies obviously cannot undertake the social programs supported by companies with strong market power, such as utilities (whose regulated rates are based on costs). And healthily profitable companies like Standard of Indiana and CNA obviously have a great advantage over companies that are constantly battling to stay in the black.

Even companies that have the resources to undertake socially responsible projects do not necessarily possess the skills to solve most complex social problems. "The job of the public and government," says F. Thomas Juster, "is to tell business what the appropriate social objectives are; they shouldn't want business messing around with its own set of social objectives." Professor Paul Heyne of Southern Methodist University, a strict constructionist, argues that the economic system is not a playground in which businessmen should be exercising their own preferences. "Any economic system," he explains, "ought to be a social mechanism for picking up the preferences of everyone, matching these against available resources, and obtaining from what we have a maximum of what we want. The market is a mechanism of almost incredible effectiveness in the accomplishment of this task. The market works effectively because those who have command over resources continually reallocate them in response to the signals provided by relative prices. The businessman who wants to behave in a socially responsible way must depend heavily, overwhelmingly, on this information."

JUST LIKE EMBEZZLEMENT

Probably no economist has given more thought to corporate social responsibility than Henry Manne, professor of law at the University of Rochester, who began writing about the subject a dozen years ago. He observed that most companies maintained enough reserves to meet unforeseen contingencies and to offset unintended mistakes, and so could *temporarily* spend some money on social activities that raise costs without raising revenues or income. So far as consumers and employees are concerned, Manne has observed somewhat caustically, this spending is indistinguishable in its effects from simple inefficiency or outright embezzlement.

Manne believes that the whole concept of corporate responsibility suits government officials and intellectuals—particularly intellectuals who deride and even hate the idea of a free market. It also goes down just fine with bloviating businessmen who don't mind casting themselves as members of the divine elect. Of course, businessmen often interpret "socially responsible" policies as long-term profit maximization, i.e., "in the long run we make more money by spending to be good citizens now." Manne doesn't object to this line of reasoning so long as the spending really does maximize profits in the long run—and helps the firms survive in a free market. He says, however, that voluntary corporate altruism has never made a significant dent in any but insignificant problems. Manne has developed his own economic model of corporate responsibility—the first of its kind—and reports that it can accommodate a little, but not much, corporate giving; he finds it impossible to justify a model of substantial corporate social action.

Above all, Manne avers, any such action will result in more government controls. It implies that business and government should work together to promote social progress. "Corporate social responsibility, a doctrine offered by many as a scheme to popularize and protect free enterprise," Manne concludes, "can succeed only if the free market is abandoned in favor of government controls. The game isn't worth the candle."

There seem to have been some cases in which "socially responsible" behavior has actually hampered business operations. California's Bank of America, upset and moved by radicals' demonstrations against it, went in some time ago for being socially responsible in a big way. It appointed an executive vice president, G. Robert Truex, Jr., as custodian of social policy, and he is now dabbling with a social audit. The bank also set aside no less than $200 million for low-interest loans that would help to provide housing for minority-group members and other under-privileged persons.

But the bank has found itself in a dilemma. The 2500 loan officers in its thousand California branches pride themselves on knowing the credit-worthiness of people in their areas. Now many of these officers have been asked to lend money to people who had no conventional credit standing at all—indeed, they were being asked to *persuade* people to borrow. How, in these circumstances, do you preserve the loan officers' morale and esprit? The Bank of America is wrestling with that problem.

Some proponents of increased corporate responsibility have given high marks to Levi Strauss & Co. of San Francisco, maker of the famous Levi's and other informal apparel. As its many admirers note, the company contributes 3 percent of its net after taxes to carefully chosen social programs, does a lot of hiring from among disadvantaged minority groups, helps finance minority suppliers, and has established day-care centers for employees' children. At the same time, the company has done well. It has expanded sales from $8 million in 1946 to more than $504 million last year, and net income from $700,000 to $25 million.

GETTING THEIR MONEY'S WORTH

But Levi Strauss is obviously getting a lot for that 3 percent. It does business in an intensely liberal city and has a market in which tastes are heavily influenced by young people. And so, whatever its top executives believe in their heart of hearts, their social-responsibility outlays would appear to be rather effective public relations. So far as an outsider can determine, these outlays cost no more than would conventional high-pressure public relations in a different kind of company.

Many of the costs associated with social responsibility, such as minority training and aid, are often marginal, out of proportion to all the time and talent that have gone into arguing about them. Behaving responsibly often means no more or less than acting humanely, treating employees and customers with consideration, avoiding ineptitudes and blunders, cultivating a sharp eye for the important little things, and knowing how to spend where the returns are high. In this sense, responsibility can accomplish a lot with relatively small cost.

But many other expenses of behaving in a socially acceptable way, such as the cost of meeting the escalating demands of the consumer advocates, will not come cheap, and might easily get out of hand. Heavy social involvements can also cost a company dear in terms of managerial talent. And so the impact of the corporate-responsibility movement on companies that must husband their resources, on the endlessly striving cost cutters, indeed on competition itself, is not yet clear. Americans can only hope that businessmen will retain enough of the old Adam Smith in them to keep productivity rising.

How Social Responsibility Became Institutionalized

Business Week

"Corporations are bored and disgusted with 'good works.' They don't want to be good guys because they are doing a nifty thing in Bedford-Stuyvesant." The speaker is Owen Kugel, director of the U.S. Chamber of Commerce's Urban Strategy Center, and he is probably in touch with more corporate urban affairs and community affairs directors than anyone else in the country. Their mood, he reports, is "gruesome, especially those who built careers on those little deals and projects."

If Kugel who lives with this every day, is perhaps overstating things a little, it is obvious that something has changed in the attitude of business toward social goals that were considered unimpeachable only a few years ago. In part, what Kugel sees as disenchantment is merely one reaction to the increasing institutionalization of social action. When BUSINESS WEEK inaugurated its awards for Business Citizenship four years ago, the environmental protection movement was just starting and enforcement of employment statutes was uneven. Since then, a flood of federal, state, and local laws has put much of industry's antipollution efforts beyond voluntary action. Everyone must meet an increasingly high standard.

Similarly, the Equal Employment Opportunity Commission (EEOC) has galvanized companies with a wave of lawsuits to force compliance with antidiscrimination laws. "At some point," says William H. Brown III, EEOC's chairman, the commission's court record "on substantive issues" will persuade companies to meet the legal requirements without going to court.

The emphasis on the law may be why much of the steam has gone out of the National Alliance of Businessmen, a nationwide voluntary effort to stimulate hiring of minority employees. The NAB has been plugging along at something under a quarter-million "hires" a year, which officials concede does not even keep up with the growth of the minority labor force. And the organization's operating budget has been cut 20%, forcing it to drop support of offices in 60 cities. Fewer than half of those have continued on local funding.

Aside from the leveling effect of law enforcement, an increasing sophistication has called worthy social-action efforts into question. What once seemed bold now seems routine—or worse. Says Carl Holman, president of the National Urban Coalition: "We no longer like the phony deals—a bank staking a black man to a clothing store in a dying neighborhood. They're willing to write off the loss. But why not get that man into a shopping center?"

A good many companies seem to have gotten the message and pulled back from some of the more public relations-oriented projects that were peripheral to their businesses. Instead, they have in essence internalized social action by concentrating on things they can do well in the context of normal operations. As with Western Electric, for example, more and more companies are formalizing programs that develop lists of minority suppliers that can bid on business competitively. Levi Strauss has such a program, and so does Honeywell and Indiana Standard, both of which are considered models for industry in that area. Sears, Roebuck & Co. has been testing a program for several years. In all cases, the effort includes a good deal of counseling and patient advice to the minority businessman on exactly how to cost out a product and how to bid.

Dozens of companies have actively searched for minority banks in which to deposit money. They not only add needed funds to banks struggling for deposits, but they do it within the normal parameters of business operation.

What seems to have happened, says the U.S. Chamber's Kugel, is that the experience of the past few years has meant that "sensitivity to social problems has become institutionalized, at least on the first two levels of management." Chief executives have accepted the need to take certain actions and have tried to make those actions a part of regular operations.

At Borden, Inc., for example, Chairman and President Augustine R. Marusi two years ago established a Minority Affairs Council, with representatives from nearly every staff and line department in the company. The ultimate function of the council, says Thomas K. Hammall, Borden's director of civic affairs, was to make sure that Borden's social policy was "multi-dimensional." Every area of operations that conceivably could contribute has been rung in, including management development in the form of a draft for an MBA program for minority employees and a women's testing and assessment center at Columbus (Ohio) headquarters.

In addition, Marusi gave orders a year and a half ago that henceforward Borden would add another input to its site planning: "In the future, all investment proposals for new or expanded installations must contain a report that addresses itself to minority socioeconomic issues, i.e., how communities within which a site is viable act with regard to equal employment opportunities (including construction trades) and open housing. A condition for joining a community or expanding Borden's operations within it will be that it qualifies in every sense." Marusi's rationale: "Communities that have major racial prejudices and/or problems do not represent good investments for the future."

A couple of sites, says Hammall, have passed the test, and a couple of others are now being scrutinized.

Borden's kind of deep involvement in the day-to-day administration of social aims is becoming increasingly common. And while Borden is still in the planning stage for much of its program, some corporations have carried the process so far beyond the law's basic requirements that they stand out for that reason alone. This is why Owens-Illinois, Inc., and Polaroid Corp. have won BUSINESS WEEK's Business Citizenship Awards for 1972.

This year, also, BUSINESS WEEK felt that it was time to take stock of how other companies that pioneered in their time and were similarly recognized have fared over the years. The following report on past award winners is by and large encouraging. Nearly all the people and the companies are still committed. In some respects, of course, they would do things differently if they had it to do all over again. But even mistakes are valuable if someone else can learn from them.

THREE SUCCESS STORIES

Several of the award winners have had a comparatively smooth time of it. Without claiming perfection, they say that they have either achieved the results they set out to attain or that success is virtually assured.

In part, this is because the goals—while far from modest—are not quite so ambitious as, say, to attempt to remake the rotting core of a whole city. More important is the quality of the commitment, to the project and its goals. "I'm convinced," says Walter A. Haas, Jr., chairman of Levi Strauss & Co., "that to be successful in social programs is not dependent on the amount of money you spend, but the attitude and concern of management."

Haas's own company, where managers are held accountable for social policy decisions just as they are for production goals, received one of the first BUSINESS WEEK awards for business citizenship nearly four years ago. The company still enjoys a golden reputation for enlightened social action. And it still routinely allocates 3% of its net profits to community projects, ranging from an intensive care unit for the East Tennessee Children's Hospital ($7,000), to a program to explore ways of getting government and foundation money for Alabama's dirt-poor Green County ($20,000). The company has plants in both places, and like most of Levi's social programs, both projects are run by "community relations teams." These are made up of local employees and have been set up at many of Levi's nearly 40 plants in the U.S.

The plants were fully integrated long before the Equal Employment Opportunity Commission got busy. Its 33% minority employment statistic is impressive. Nearly 14% of the company's managers and officials last year were women, double the proportion of the year before, and 10.1% were classified as minority employees.

Levi has also set up a minority purchasing program, now six months old, under which the company will buy $1.7 million worth of goods and services from minority suppliers over the next two years. A letter announcing plans for a $1-million computer center in San Jose, Calif., required general contractors to "obtain bids from competent minority businesses for each subcontract." Three such subcontractors have won $144,000 in contracts. Says Walter Haas, "We'll pay competitive rates, but not a premium. Businessmen must keep their business hat on."

Coca-Cola Co. has also made great strides in dealing with its minority workers. Nine months after receiving a BUSINESS WEEK award for its attempt to improve conditions among migrant workers in its Minute Maid orange groves, Coke signed the first-and so far the only—contract in Florida with Cezar Chavez' United Farm Workers.

The contract did away with the infamous crew chief system of hiring, raised wages, instituted fringe benefits, and gave the workers some say in setting piece-work rates. But there is general agreement that Coke's goals, announced long before the contract, have been substantially achieved.

For instance, Coke's plan to develop permanent employees has worked out pretty much as planned. Some 300 are on hourly wages year-round. And when 350 fruit pickers on piece-work rates are not picking, they are switched to maintenance duties in the groves at hourly wages.

Coke is also getting rid of the squalid labor camps. Most of the fulltime employees have been able to buy their own homes with Coke's help. And near Frostproof, Fla., which lacks suitable existing housing, the company has built 85 houses in a planned development. All but eight have been sold to farm workers at a small loss.

In all, the company has plowed some $3 million into its program. And it thinks it has come out ahead, not only in benefits to its work force, but in increased productivity.

Productivity is also the watchword at Fairchild Camera & Instrument Corp.'s pioneering seminconductor plant on the Navajo reservation at Shiprock, N.M. This is due largely to the efforts of plant manager Paul W. Driscoll, who received a BUSINESS WEEK award for exceptional leadership in 1971. Driscoll built Shiprock from a small—and troubled—facility in the mid 1960s, nursed it through the 1969–70 recession into a successful plant employing 1000.

Driscoll himself is pleased with the way things are going. "The people had the basics to perform the task we wanted done," he says, "and there was sensitivity in our top management."

If there is any disappointment, it is in the pace at which the Navajos have been able to move into management levels. Driscoll's goal was to push them ahead at Shiprock and then into Fairchild operations elsewhere.

Two years ago, Driscoll fully expected a Navajo to take over his job as plant manager someday, but that hasn't yet happened. Driscoll left Shiprock in May for greater responsibilities in Fairchild's international operations, probably in the Far East. His replacement is another white man, Mercer E. Curtis, Jr. "Paul," says Curtis, "is going to be tough to follow."

THE FERMENT IN ECOLOGY

Of all the areas of endeavor covered by the BUSINESS WEEK awards, achievements in improving the physical environment are most likely to look routine when reexamined even a year later. That is because the whole environmental movement is so volatile: Attitudes, legal doctrine, and technology are moving so rapidly that it is easy to forget how bold the first steps seemed.

Five years ago, at its big, new molybdenum mine at Henderson, Colo., American Metal Climax, Inc., launched what was then a unique ecological experiment. The goal was to reduce the environmental impact of the mine. This involved tunneling through a mountain and building a 13-mile railroad so that the mill and tailing pond could be built away from public view. The mine has become a motherlode of expertise that a dozen companies have tapped.

The Henderson site is still, of course, far from perfect. For one thing, no one has come up with the technology to get rid of the ugly tailing pond. And in ecologically disturbed areas, the fragile tundra vegetation has not returned to cover the scars as fast as had been expected. "As a pioneer in the area of relating environmental concerns and environmental information to land-use decision-making, you do not expect a project to represent the ultimate in environmental planning," says Roger Hansen, executive director of the Rocky Mountain Center on Environment. "The Henderson project paved the way for others."

Paving the way is nothing new to giant Weyerhaeuser Co., which won a BUSINESS WEEK award in 1971 for its sustained efforts to control pollution in the pulp and paper industry. Now, the big Tacoma (Wash.) company is pushing for better coordination with regulatory agencies. Says President George H. Weyerhaeuser: "In the matter of pollution control, the major block to investment has not been the stringency of regulation *per se,* but continuous changing of the rules, accentuated by conflict between regulatory agencies."

The problem, as Weyerhaeuser identified it, was that the company had wound up as broker among overlapping environmental jurisdictions. For example, in the endless negotiations over its Longview (Wash.) facility, the company dealt with four agencies.

Weyerhaeuser wanted out of the coordinating role. What evolved was a "team concept" for joint planning by the company and all the concerned agencies, probably the first in the country. The parties at least agree on the facts concerning plant operation and waste volumes, and on joint plans for satisfying requirements.

In the case of the Longview plant, Weyerhaeuser was unable to get what it wanted, a "one-stop" permit for construction and operation. But the team approach looks promising. "If it works out," says George Weyerhaeuser, "it may provide a breakthrough not just on a state level but nationally."

Dow Chemical Co., which won an award last year for an abatement program that managed to pay for itself, is successfully continuing its ambitious efforts. "Dirty processes are inefficient processes," says Chet Otis, director of Dow's ecology council. "We're keeping the pressure on our people to solve pollution problems in the process itself."

The approach still pays off—both environmentally and economically. In 1972, Dow completed 400 abatement projects at a capital cost of $17 million. But the expenditure is producing an annual saving of $4 million in recovered chemicals, higher product yields, and lower raw material costs.

But Otis admits that by 1974, Dow "may be scratching to break even" on pollution control. "As we get closer to zero discharge—100% pollution control—costs soar and it's harder to offset them," he says. Zero discharge is the controversial goal of the 1972 Federal Water Pollution Control Act, and by next year, five of Dow's 25 U.S. plants will have achieved it, which is probably the best water pollution control record in the nation. "But in some plants," says Otis, "we don't know how to."

Like Dow Chemical, Aaron Teller stresses the recycling of waste streams back into production processes. The former dean of engineering at New York's Cooper Union won a BUSINESS WEEK award in 1971 for advocating this environmental concept. Now, he says, "the real problem emerging is not pollution control but resource preservation."

But Teller has had only moderate success in translating his ideas into business. His engineering company, Teller Environmental Systems, has grown, of course. In three years, its staff expanded from three to 16, and its annual engineering fees and royalties increased from $50,000 to $1.5 million, which represents perhaps $15 million in actual systems installations in such manufacturing industries as fertilizer and secondary aluminum smelting.

Now, Teller finds himself at something of a crossroads. He needs help in developing marketing techniques, in financial and profit-center controls, and in some branches of engineering. So he has been searching for a merger partner and hints that he may finally have found one.

FRUSTRATION IN URBAN RENEWAL

Many companies, trying to be good corporate citizens of their troubled cities, have taken on the endless frustrations of restoring blighted neighborhoods.

Consider William Wendel, president of Carborundum Co. As boss of the only national company in Niagara Falls, N.Y., Wendel decided in 1964 to do something about rehabilitating the blowsy old city that adjoins the great waterfall. With enormous energy, Wendel organized agencies to accomplish an ambitious urban renewal program, stimulate housing, and lay the groundwork for metropolitan government on the Niagara Frontier.

The early housing goals—about 1000 new or rehabilitated units—were subsequently trimmed. But 400 units are either built or under construction. And the Wendel-led Society for the Promotion, Unification & Redevelopment of Niagara, has pushed through some projects in public administration.

But a number of big projects have faltered, most visibly the redevelopment of the city's rotting downtown. So far, Rainbow Center consists of the new 10-story Carborundum headquarters and the adjoining Carborundum ceramics museum. A convention hall and hotel will be finished next year, along with some open plazas. But 75 acres of the urban renewal area remain unspoken for.

Even worse, the effort to develop regional government was defeated last November, when the voters rejected a referendum to establish an elected county executive.

Wendel, who puts about 10 hours a month into his civic work, says that his involvement has been both "good and frustrating." He notes: "I'm still as heavily involved as ever."

Campbell Soup Co. has found its efforts in city-saving even more frustrating, since it must deal with Camden, N.J. Camden has the second-highest crime rate in the nation, and parts of it look like Dresden after the fire storm.

Campbell has put a lot of effort into Camden, and top management has been deeply involved, including President Harold A. Shaub. Says Osborne Boyd, executive director of the Greater Camden Movement: "Every morning, Shaub drives around town. Then he calls, wondering why this or that isn't being done. He gets into the nitty-gritty."

But despite years of commitment and a good many millions of dollars in special projects and aid for housing development, progress is painfully slow. Still, Campbell can show 464 homes rehabilitated in North Camden, as well as construction of 93 low-income townhouses, and 104 high-rise apartments. Last week, the Housing & Urban Development Department released additional money for more rehabilitation.

Campbell is by no means pessimistic, pointing to the $26 million of construction contracts awarded or completed last year. Says Shaub: "Sooner or later, that amount of money must begin to show."

Another award winner—Hallmark Cards, Inc.—is considerably happier, because its renewal scheme in Kansas City, Mo., is considerably further along. Joyce Hall, Hallmark's formidable chairman, set out to transform the drab neighborhood in which his headquarters are located, and he has substantially done it.

Crown Center, designed to complement the central business district, boasts, in addition to the Hallmark building, a 730-room hotel, five low office buildings, landscaped terraces, a central square complete with fountain, underground parking, and a two-story bank. Slated for completion this fall are a tri-level retail complex housing 160 shops and a $2-million audio-visual communications center. The final target project, apartment housing, has just been started, and the first occupancy is due in 1975. By the time the whole project is completed in 1984, it will consist of 50 buildings, including apartments and condominums for 8,000 residents and a daytime population of 50,000.

But the happiest of the city stories among the BUSINESS WEEK award winners is Rouse Co.'s Columbia, Md., a brand-new city set down in the countryside between Washington and Baltimore. Columbia, which received its award for the sensitivity and sophistication with which its environmental planning was done, is a roaring success.

Columbia has had its flurries of publicity about drugs among teenagers, racial conflict, and environmental fights. But much of its plan seems to be working: the general design of the villages, the "downtown" shopping mall, and the orderly growth. Columbia now has a fully integrated population of about 35,000 in 10,000 pleasant housing units. It offers more than 10,000 jobs, including 2,300 at General Electric's appliance plant and 800 at a Bendix research facility. All in all, the town is about one-third of the way toward its goal of 110,000 population in an eminently livable community.

If any part of the plan has not panned out, it is internal transportation. Despite bus lines, bikeways, and walk-ways, nothing appears to be able to separate the American suburbanite from his car.

The developers stand to make a handsome profit in four or five years. And, says Padraic Kennedy, manager of the Columbia Assn., which represents the residents: "Most people here feel that this is a terrific place and that Rouse has done a terrific job."

A FAIR SHAKE FOR MINORITIES

If there is any place that business confronts its reponsibilities toward minorities most directly, it is in the economic areas: jobs, job-training, and the development of minority business. And probably the best-known man in all three is the Rev. Leon Sullivan of Philadelphia, who won a BUSINESS WEEK award last year for his singular influence and effectiveness.

Sullivan is the founder of the Opportunities Industrialization Center, a self-help job-training organization that spread to 100 cities and now has a national board. But because of repeated federal fund cutbacks, OIC is not growing, and industry and community financial support remains low. Sullivan is pinning his hopes on an ambitious OIC assistance bill now in the Senate.

Aside from OIC, Sullivan is probably best known as a director of General Motors Corp., probably the only GM board member many people have ever heard of. Sullivan joined GM's board in 1970, and took on himself the responsibility for promoting greater minority participation in all phases of the company. His assessment: "I am encouraged." Black dealers increased from six to more than 20 since he joined the board, and 24 more are in a special training program. His goal: 100 dealers by 1975.

Sullivan is also pleased with the GM Institute, whose black enrollment has risen from fewer than 40 to 350 men and women out of 2,000 students. "My goal," he says, "is to have at least 20% within several years."

Sullivan is not so happy with the number of blacks in salaried jobs. There are now 5,000 at GM, but Sullivan would like to see double that number. As for black suppliers, "there were very few of any consequence when I started. Today there are 400, doing $18-million worth of business."

If Sullivan provides the overview on minority employment, two other award winners provide specific object lessons. Last year, International Business Machines Corp. was singled out for its pioneering cable plant in Brooklyn's Bedford-Stuyvesant district, home of probably the largest concentration of hard-core unemployed in the U.S. Despite a general impression that this kind of ghetto enterprise is a passing thing, the IBM plant is very stable.

The plant still has 400 employees, and the proportion of black or Puerto Rican supervisors is up to 80%. Absenteeism is still an acceptable 6%.

In the opinion of plant manager Hal Leiteau, the plant would have become competitive quicker if IBM had started with a higher opinion of the employees' trainability and gone to more complex products more quickly. "There's opportunity in coming into an area like this," he says. "Business should focus on it, not on the good works."

Ghetto job training doesn't sound like so much fun when you talk to the people at Western Electric Co. "I would have to say," states J. G. Blake, Western Electric's manager of community relations, "that if you were a cost-effect guy and wanted to look at the manpower programs of this country, it's not something you'd want to get into today."

Blake was responding to a question about Western Electric's Newark Shop, once a high-visibility training center for the unemployed and unemployable. "The shop still exists," says Blake. "It performed the function for which it was designed: to employ, teach, and put to work in the mainstream.

"But today we'd wonder if we couldn't do that job better—and we have. For example, we have consolidated operations in Newark in a new office complex, rather than upstate New York or southern New Jersey."

Even more important to Western Electric is the progress of the program for which it won an award in 1969: the use of the company's vast purchasing power to encourage the development of minority businesses as suppliers. The program, which had begun informally in the late 1960s, was formalized in 1971. Last year, the company numbered almost 500 minority suppliers on its vendors' list, double the number in 1971, and it did $13-million business with them, compared with $5-million the year before.

The development of minority business as a viable economic goal is also the task of the Colorado Economic Development Assn., one of last year's winners.

CEDA was founded to offer management and marketing advice—and to help get loans—for small minority-owned businesses, and it has had a string of successes since 1969.

Still, CEDA has made some changes. For one thing, it broke off its supportive services into 12 separate companies—accounting, loan packaging, venture capital, and so on. Employees own 49% of their companies and CEDA owns 51%. CEDA supplies office overhead at no charge.

The other change is an emphasis on helping bigger businesses. "We put a construction company into a business a year and a half ago," says (CEDA) founder Edward Lucero. "They did $1.7 million in the past year with $275,000 pretax profit. We could have put together three $500,000 companies, but they wouldn't have made a profit."

Polaroid: An Award for Developing Human Resources

When it comes to innovative, costly, continuing, and unconventional involvement in social action and community affairs, Polaroid Corp. of Cambridge, Mass., towers as high over most U.S. companies as its price-earnings ratio, which reared to a lofty 98 at midweek.

This should come as no surprise to anyone familiar with Dr. Edwin H. Land, the 63-year-old founder, president, and company research genius who likes to talk of his camera and film company as ". . . not just a place to make a product but a place in which people can join with other people to say, 'What's worth doing? How do you have a rich experience all day long?' " Adds Peter Wensberg, senior vice-president: "Land has always felt that your job and your company should be things you can take pride in. He has always encouraged employees here to do things on their own. People know this and they realize Polaroid has a tradition of being concerned with more than the balance sheet."

Just how thoroughly Land's philosophy has shoved Polaroid beyond social tokenism shows up in statistics.

• Some 12% of the company's nearly 10,000 U.S. employees are black, with 6.4% in salaried jobs. Another 3% are disadvantaged in other ways: physically or mentally handicapped, or with a poor grasp of English.

• More than 150 ex-convicts have been hired during the past several years, and only two have gone back to prison.

• A five-year-old Polaroid subsidiary in Boston's black ghetto of Roxbury continues to expand. There, 243 "unemployable" workers have learned enough skills to graduate to regular jobs at Polaroid and elsewhere.

• Polaroid is involved with 143 community projects in Greater Boston and New Bedford, Mass., ranging from camera loans to family planning services.

While the figures suggest the company's broad commitment, they do not adequately reflect such factors as courage. Land uses that word to describe Polaroid's decision in 1971 to stay in South Africa rather than pull out as demanded by anti-apartheid forces within the company and around the world. It would have been far less costly, both financially and in terms of public image, if the company had simply abandoned its tiny, $1.5-million yearly volume. But Land and such top executives as Thomas H. Wyman, now general manager, dropped everything at the height of the buildup for the new SX-70 camera and launched into marathon meetings with militant civil rights representatives.

Higher Wages. Land's decision to keep the company in South Africa was strongly influenced by a group of Polaroid employees he sent there to find out what the blacks wanted. The answer: stay and work for better wages and conditions. Some church groups and others continue to castigate Polaroid's presence, but Robert M. Palmer, director of community relations, points to the record: The company's distributor is paying his black employees twice as much as in 1970, though still far below white levels. Insofar as possible under apartheid rules, it has increased supervisory jobs for blacks. On balance, Polaroid has gotten considerable mileage out of its South African experiment.

In the U.S., Polaroid is deeply involved in the politically dangerous area of prison reform. Palmer is president of a statewide movement that last year helped rewrite archaic corrections laws and push them through the Massachusetts legislature. This year he has been struggling to implement such reforms as furloughs for prisoners. He has drafted at least two dozen Polaroid people for projects behind prison walls. One personnel man was dispatched to Norfolk Prison for 90 days, at the request of inmates who wanted help in listing grievances.

Since the riots and killing at Walpole Prison, reform is something of a dirty word. But Palmer is fighting to keep it alive: "I don't have to check with anybody around here on what I'm going to say."

Offbeat Rules. Palmer and other Polaroid officials, including Wyman, are trying to persuade other Massachusetts companies to hire former inmates. They cite low training costs, low absenteeism, and almost no turnover. They tell skeptical executives how Polaroid trains offenders while they are still in prison, and carefully follows through when they get out. "Massachusetts will release 1000 men this year," says Palmer. "If bigger companies would hire only a couple each, it would provide jobs for most parolees and go a long way toward solving one of the worst failures of our society." He points out that 98% of Polaroid's former inmates have stayed out of jail, compared with only 30% of total inmates released. In part, of course, that is because Polaroid is fairly careful in its screening.

A broad involvement in community affairs is a hallmark of Polaroid policy and the company's rule on contributions is typically offbeat. It starts with the premise that the company will respond to community needs on the community's terms. The company reviews priorities each year. Palmer adds that an employee committee sifts through the proposals—5000 last year—and decides how to disburse money without interference or suggestions from Land or top management.

The company's most conspicuous internal program is in education. Classes are conducted, often on company time, in everything from basic English to advanced chemistry. There is generous financial support to employees seeking doctoral degrees. An astounding 20% of Polaroid's employees are in the educational curriculum, which probably qualifies Polaroid, or "Land University," as the third biggest school in Cambridge, after Harvard and MIT.

Owens-Illinois: An Award for Improving the Environment

The idea of Ralph Nader praising a major corporation seems as likely as the *Washington Post* defending the Watergate conspirators. Yet Nader's 1971 study on water pollution cited Owens-Illinois as "one of the very few pulp and paper companies that has consistently made it a practice over the last 20 years to install the best pollution-control system available —or to pioneer in developing new ones—almost always in advance of state requirements."

The praise is as deserved as it is surprising. Toledo-based Owens-Illinois, which earned $69 million on sales of over $1.6 billion last year, has compiled an outstanding record of environmental performance—not only at its four paperboard mills, but in the production of glass bottles and other packaging materials, too. Its glass factories are among the cleanest in the nation, it leads the industry in glass recycling, and it is actively pressing for a national system of resource recovery centers to help solve the solid waste problem.

In many ways, O-I's record of environmental concern reflects the attitude of Raymon H. Mulford, who was O-I's chairman until his death last February. Mulford, whose father was a glassblower, encouraged his employees to participate in community affairs, and he himself spent nearly half his time in later years on social and environmental programs. Most of O-I's plants are in small towns, and Mulford insisted that they be an asset to the community—in part by controlling pollution.

In 1966, well before the environment movement started, Mulford formally set out the company's role in a "policy on pollution" memo. It read in part: "We attach the same importance to air and water pollution abatement that we attach to quality, safety, fire prevention, and operating efficiencies. In constructing new facilities, we will . . . provide the best pollution control equipment available to meet or exceed community criteria."

While Mulford formalized O-I's commitment in 1966, the company had already demonstrated its innovative approach as far back as 1954. In planning a new containerboard mill at Valdosta, Ga., O-I abandoned the traditional industry practice of situating mills on rivers and using those streams as sewers. Instead, William Webster, an O-I vice-president, selected a site seven miles from the nearest river, then built a series of settling and oxidation ponds between the plant and the river to provide primary and secondary treatment for the plant's effluent. The system has been widely copied since then and ranks as one of the major advances in environmental management. Today, the system reduces the mill's pollution by 95%.

"They thought Webster had rocks in his head," recalls Frederick Adams, vice-president of O-I's Forest Products Div. "But he saw the day coming when you couldn't dump waste, and he knew it would be cheaper to do it sooner rather than later."

Over the last 20 years, O-I has achieved a number of other key innovations in pollution control. At its mill in Tomahawk, Wis., it became the first company to install recovery boilers to capture spent cooking liquors, a major papermaking pollutant. It has recently developed two new methods to remove most of the sulfurous "rotten egg" odor from its mills. And it has stressed recovery of chemicals and recycling of water to offset abatement costs. Today, says Adams, O-I mills use one-half the water needed by competitors' mills and one-fifth the chemicals.

Adams believes that O-I will completely eliminate water pollution from its mills by 1985—the "zero discharge" goal of the 1972 Federal Water Pollution Control Act. Indeed, Adams is one of the few paper-industry executives who believes the goal is not only achievable but "absolutely necessary." Perhaps it is this positive attitude that has enabled O-I to achieve the best pollution-control record of any paper company, according to a 1973 study by the Council on Economic Priorities.

In its other products, too, O-I has pioneered. In 1968, one of its glass plants issued the first public appeal for consumers to recycle glass bottles. Last year, O-I's 18 glass plants paid 1¢ per lb. for 163 million lb. of used glass bottles—up from 32 million lb. in 1970. O-I is also conducting basic research aimed at reducing emissions from glass furnaces, and, in 1971, its borosilicate furnace in Chicago became the first in the industry to be equipped with electrostatic precipitators.

With pollution rapidly coming under control at O-I's 106 plants, the company now sees solid waste as its major environmental challenge, according to Kenneth Van Tine, director of environmental affairs. Glass containers often end up as litter, and Oregon and Vermont have already passed laws requiring a deposit on all beverage containers. But while such laws may reduce littler somewhat, Van Tine believes they will not dent the solid-waste problem. Instead, O-I favors a nationwide system of recycling centers to reclaim glass, metal, and paper fiber.

To this end, the company is actively participating in the National Center for Resource Recovery, a nonprofit industry–labor group that will use the latest technology to recycle 6000 tons of glass and metal per day. O-I president Edwin Dodd serves as vice-chairman of the Center's board. The first facility is scheduled to open in New Orleans next year, and O-I has signed a contract to buy 50 tons of reclaimed glass a day for five years. The company has also designed the glass recycling system for an advanced, government supported solid-waste recovery system in Franklin, Ohio.

SELECTED READINGS

Anshen, M., *Managing the Socially Responsible Corporation.* (New York: Free Press, 1974.)

Chamberlain, N., *The Limits of Corporate Responsibility.* (New York: Basic Books, 1973.)

The Corporation and Social Responsibility, Proceedings of a Symposium, University of Illinois, 1967.

Eells, R., *The Meaning of Modern Business.* (New York: Columbia University Press, 1960.)

Friedman, M., *Capitalism and Freedom.* (Chicago: University of Chicago Press, 1962.)

Heyne, P. T., *Private Keepers of the Public Interest.* (New York: McGraw-Hill, 1968.)

Jacoby, N. H., *Corporate Power and Social Responsibility.* (New York: Macmillan Publishing Co., Inc., 1973.)

Manne, H. G., and H. C. Wallich, *The Modern Corporation and Social Responsibility.* (Washington D.C.: American Enterprise Institute, 1972.)

Votaw, D., and S. P. Sethi, *The Corporate Dilemma: Traditional Values versus Contemporary Problems.* (Englewood Cliffs, N.J.: Prentice-Hall, Inc., 1973.)

Walton, C. C., *Ethos and the Executive.* (Englewood Cliffs, N.J.: Prentice-Hall, Inc., 1969.)

B. *Positive Theories of the Modern Manager and Corporate Behavior*

In contrast to normative prescriptions of business behavior—statements of what managers *ought* to do—this section will present positive or *descriptive* studies of actual managerial behavior and corporate roles. Included is a sampling of the many theories and empirical studies of how firms and managers behave and the motivations behind that behavior.

In this introduction, we shall briefly discuss some selected models of the firm and of managers. The readings will expand on the models and introduce some recent illustrations of *managerial indiscretions.*

As the student digests the models in this introduction, he should try to compare the managerial types described with those prescribed in Section 1(A). Are the managers as seen in actual roles (both theoretically and empirically) so vastly different from the types that social critics would like to see? Are there any descriptive models that will allow one to understand the ease (or difficulty) a firm or manager may experience in trying to respond to environmental or societal pressures? We shall have more to say on this at the close of this introduction.

Most positive or descriptive theories focus on a particular level for study; that is, some focus on the firm as an entity, others on managers, and still others on markets or industries. In models of the firm, the thesis is that the firm as an entity has a life of its own—the firm acts, the firm behaves, the firm has objectives, etc. Although the firm, in reality, is a conglomeration of managers (and workers and technicians), the connecting link between managerial behavior and motivations and those of the firm is not always clear. That is, does the behavior of a firm result from the sum total of managerial behavior or from something apart from the motivations of managers? Do curious cross-cancellations of opposing personal behavior govern the firm's position?

Max Weber, and indeed most classical organization theorists, describe the manager or the bureaucrat as leaving personal feelings outside the organization and adopting the corporate point of view when on the job. More recent work and observations of managerial lifestyles, of course, reveal the unreality of that description. We still have much to learn about how individual managers acculturate the corporation and vice versa.

THE THEORY OF THE FIRM IN TRADITIONAL ECONOMICS

In the introduction to the previous section, we briefly examined the traditional economic theory of the firm. Since the theory of the firm is a positive descriptive model and since it is possibly the most misunderstood and most maligned abstraction of all, we should like to expand upon it in this section. Quite simply stated, the firm *in economic theory* is a magnificently powerful computer; it functions as an entity—objectives and actions are those of the entrepreneur—and the (possibly dysfunctional) actions of individual members of a bureaucratic structure are not part of the analysis. The external environment (markets) creates the need for action, and the entrepreneur (or firm) chooses rationally, from all possible alternatives, the course of action that will maximize the profits of the firm. Rationality, in the theory, means that the decision-maker seeks out (and can identify) all available alternatives and is able to choose the one(s) which will maximize returns. The key assumptions in the theory of the firm are profit maximization, rationality, and the single-mindedness of the organization.

Most observers, however, agree that when we move into the real world, particularly in dealing with its oligopoly, monopoly, or otherwise imperfect market structures, and consider the real-life frailties and abilities of managers as well as the complexity of organizations, the key assumptions of the theory of the firm become questionable. The real-life oligopolist or monopolist is under no compulsion to maximize; as a matter of fact, the oligopolist may be under compulsion from several quarters to limit profits. Some firms are satisfied with "adequate profits," and most managers do not know how to maximize, or indeed cannot determine whether (or when) they have in fact maximized.

Why, then, do economists defend with so much apparent vigor a model so obviously divorced from reality? Economists will argue that they are not really interested in actual firm behavior or objectives *per se,* but only in what occurs in the market in terms of resource allocation. Theorists must simplify, in their abstractions from reality, and economists pick out the assumptions of profit maximization, rationality, and single-minded action not because they form a precisely accurate picture of firm behavior, but because they are good enough mechanisms to lead analysts to what they are really interested in: reasonably accurate predictions of market behavior and resource allocation.[1] In a very real sense, what is called the theory of the firm is in fact a theory of industries or markets, not firms.

Even though some recent work does focus on the firm, it must be recognized that the economist's analysis simply doesn't include the firm as its primary frame of reference. And even though the traditional model of the firm fails to provide a basis for a sound theory of markets in oligopoly situations (a topic we cannot cover here), nevertheless the criticism levied by other scholars—whose primary interest *is the firm*—is unwarranted.

MODIFIED ECONOMIC MODELS OF THE FIRM

A number of economists focusing on the firm *qua* firm have offered an interesting variety of positive models, particularly of oligopolistic firms, those with some degree of market interdependence, yet a considerable amount of discretion. While we shall not explore these frameworks in great detail, we should like to sample a few simply to point out the variety of objectives attributed to the firm.

William Baumol pictures sales maximization as the firm's goal. Subject to a minimum profit constraint (adequate profits?), the firm will seek to maximize total revenue. The basic premise here is that business prestige rides heavier on sales, and that businessmen—particularly oligopolists—are more prone to nonprice competition (advertising, model changes, etc.) than to price competition.[2]

In another theory, the primary objective is the entrepreneur's need to retain control of the firm. The entrepreneur allows the firm to grow and make a profit provided that growth does not cause the portion of assets owned personally by the entrepreneur to fall below a required minimum.[3] In a third approach, the firm is pictured as a homeostatic mechanism (homeostasis is a tendency to return to an original state); in this model, the firm seeks to maintain a desired balance-sheet structure; and variance from that structure will cause the firm to take action to *return* the structure to its original state.[4]

Other models have been developed, but the previous ones are included simply to illustrate the richness in revised positive approaches in terms of alternative objectives ascribed to the firm. These alternative objectives seem to correspond more closely to both observed behavior and the utterances of business executives than does the objective of profit maximization.

MODELS OF MANAGEMENT AND THE MANAGER

A number of scholars choose to center on the manager or management, rather than on the firm as an entity. While we might bring in the whole field of organizational behavior and its related disciplines, we shall restrict our outline to a few descriptions relating most closely to the role of managers in determining the objectives of the firm and in guiding the organization toward those objectives—in essence, to those models that modify the traditionally assumed objectives of business behavior, profit, and growth.

Thus, for example, Herbert Simon's "Administrative Man" seems to reflect the frailties of managers more than does the powerful economic man of classical (or indeed modified) economic theory.[5] Whereas the imaginary man of economic theory is rational, always knows how to act, and can survey all the alternatives before him in order to maximize or achieve his goal, administrative man has *bounded rationality.* Bounded rationality implies that there are internal and external limits to the exercise of rationality by the individual. These limits include "skills, habits, and reflexes which are no longer in the realm of the conscious, . . . his values and those conceptions of purpose which influence him in making decisions, (and) the extent of his knowledge of things relevant to his job." The limitations increase as one progresses up the organizational hierarchy and deals with grosser and more inclusive problems. Thus, as Simon points out, he is interested in the "behavior of human beings who *satisfice* because they have not the wits to *maximize.*"[6]

Administrative man, then, is the one who is familiar with such terms as share of market, adequate profits, and fair price. He is a nonmaximizer simply because he cannot maximize or figures maximizing is not worth the effort.

Following along the path of the Simon work is the *Behavioral Theory of the Firm* by Cyert and March.[7] While the whole theory is much too involved to cover in detail here, in brief it interrelates subtheories of organizational goals, organizational expectations, and organizational choice. The firm is depicted as a coalition of interest groups, and the goals of the total organization become defined and clarified in the process of side payments made in response to the various demands of the members of the coalition. Thus, the firm has a high potential for conflict; the model includes mechanisms the firm uses for resolving conflict.

Cyert and March's firm avoids uncertainty through the use of standard plans and procedures when possible and the *avoidance* of planning when uncertainty prevails. The organization will gradually shift goals on the basis of learned experience, will learn to attend to some standards of performance and ignore others, will "learn to pay attention to some parts of (its) comparative environment and ignore others," and will learn to adopt as standard, search patterns for problems which have been successful for solving those problems in the past.

In essence, the firm of Cyert and March is basically a safety-seeking, slowly adapting organization, which changes behavior only if some given arrangement is altered or if some familiar behavior pattern does not succeed.

Another interesting view of the firm and managers, by Monsen and Downs, hypothesizes that "owners desire steady dividend income and gradual stock appreciation, while managers act to maximize their own lifetime earnings." Coupling these motives with a bureaucratic structure, the authors believe, "management will deviate systematically from achieving ownership objectives." The theory then goes on to explain the strategies of managers at various levels of management—top, middle, and lower—in meeting their objectives. In sum, the model assigns the roles of maximizers to managers—only in terms of their own personal incomes—and satisficers to owners—since they are so remote from the firm that it is impossible for them to press for maximization.[8]

One last description of managers is that of John Kenneth Galbraith from his book *The New Industrial State.*[9] Galbraith's thesis is that the modern corporation, because of the imperatives of large-scale production, heavy capital commitments, and sophisticated technology, must plan far into the future. In order to assure success for the plans, the consumer must be managed so that his behavior will correspond to the needs of the corporation; and the state must be an active participant, moderating economic fluctuations and providing certainty to the economic environment. The key group in the corporation engaging in all this planning and managing, Galbraith calls the *technostructure*, the highly trained and closely knit group that guides the corporation and its environment to the primary end of survival of the firm or the technostructure—in essence, the preservation of management.

SOME THOUGHTS ON NORMATIVE DOCTRINES AND POSITIVE MODELS

Few of the descriptions examined in this introduction present the manager as a selfless server of humanity. The manager is pictured as either a profit-seeker, sales maximizer, self-aggrandizer, survival-seeker, a satisficer, or pain minimizer. Yet certain of these models might accommodate the inclusion of environmental pressures as costs or constraints resulting from power phenomena. And that may be the only link between normative social responsibility doctrine and the real motivations and behavior of management.

By relying on terms of reference such as "Thou shalt because I think it is right," social responsibility proponents have neglected to build into the system the fact that others with power to act may simply not care or agree that "It is right." Rhetoric aside, there is no solid theoretical or empirical evidence to show that managers engage in social responsibility because it is the "right" thing to do, because some social critic calls for "multiple objectives," or because some reformer says that "a social goal is as important as your private goal." Rather, it is more likely that managers and firms engage in socially responsible activity because it is the advantageous thing to do in terms of the firm's or the managers' welfare. The firm either has something to gain or acts to avoid losing something it already possesses. And if socially responsible activity is not advantageous in those self-interest terms, it simply is not, in most cases, undertaken.

In those terms, the behavior which advocates might label socially responsible is explainable in terms of costs or constraints on the doing of business, much as is Social Security, workmen's compensation, overtime, or fire insurance. With such an outlook, socially responsible actions would be perfectly compatible with the self-interest behavior and motivation described in many of the positive models.

THE READINGS

Our first selection in this section, by Professor Harold Johnson of Emory University, is an exploration of alternative theories of business goals, purposes, and motivations. Covering models from organization theory, game theory, and behavioral research, Professor Johnson offers an interesting and provocative paper on the complexity of modern business goal systems, while seeking to explain "socially responsible" practices in the contexts of positive models.

The second article, by Monsen, Saxberg, and Sutermeister, separates the motives of managers from those of the firm. The authors explain several sources of pressure on managers as well as the nature of these pressures in terms of specific motivational processes and goals. They conclude that "The modern manager desires to maximize his self-interest in terms of lifetime income—but the maximization of lifetime income implies far more than money alone to the manager in contemporary Western society. It often includes other goals and reflects various motivational pressures."

Finally, we include the *Business Week* article, "Stiffer Rules for Business Ethics." Enough has been written to fill volumes about insider trading, political dealing, tax evasion, and other unethical practices. Obviously not all businessmen are unethical or dishonest, but cases of outright indiscretion (or gray-area behavior) are not uncommon, either. This article gives some examples of managerial indiscretions, as well as some useful advice to the manager on his role as a businessman subject to the temptations of unethical practices. The student might compare the pressures explained in the Monsen, Saxberg, and Sutermeister article with those implied in this *Business Week* selection.

NOTES

1. The essence of this rationale can ve found in Milton Friedman, *Essays in Positive Economics.* (Chicago: University of Chicago Press, 1953); or Sherman Krupp, *Patterns in Organization Analysis.* (Philadelphia: Chilton Company, 1962); pp. 6–10.

2. W. J. Baumol, "On the Theory of Oligopoly," *Economica* New Series XXV (August, 1958), pp. 187–89. See also Baumol, *Business Behavior, Value, and Growth,* Rev. Ed. (New York: Harcourt, Brace & World, 1967); Chapter 6.

3. M. W. Reder, "A Reconsideration of the Marginal Productivity Theory," *The Journal of Political Economy,* LV (October, 1947); pp. 450–8.

4. K. E. Boulding, *A Reconstruction of Economics.* (New York: John Wiley and Sons, Inc., 1950).

5. H. A. Simon, *Administrative Behavior,* 2nd ed. (New York: Macmillan Co., 1957).

6. *Ibid.,* pp. 40–1 and XXIV.

7. R. M. Cyert and J. G. March, *A Behavioral Theory of the Firm.* (Englewood Cliffs, N.J.: Prentice-Hall, Inc., 1963).

8. J. Monsen and A. Downs, "A Theory of Large Managerial Firms," *Journal of Political Economy,* LXXII (June, 1965); pp. 221–236.

9. J. K. Galbraith, *The New Industrial State.* (Boston: Houghton Mifflin Company, 1967).

Alternative Views
of Big Business Goals
and Purposes

By Harold L. Johnson

It is ironic that today only individuals imbued with an ideology of a crude "free enterprise" or with Marxism believe that the goals of the large corporation can be summed up simply in profit maximization. Economists studying "big business" or oligopoly markets, the market habitat of most big businesses, have concluded that, in these circumstances, the profit-maximization assumption is either meaningless, too crude, or in error. Economists have found that, in industries where there is interdependence among firms or where there is freedom of action within the loose confines of the market, the profit-maximization assumption is a rather poor analytical device.

But if many students of big business no longer equate large firms and profit maximization in a one-to-one sort of way, what do they put in the place of this idea? What alternative models are there of the goals of the large firm? Where do more broad corporate goals take us in the United States? Down the road to socialism, toward a more responsible economy, or to a twentieth-century feudalism? The answers to these questions are the subject matter of this paper, with the last two questions, however, raised more than answered. The paper focuses on the understandings or conclusions concerning motivations or goals arising out of organization-theory, game-theory, and behavioral-science approaches to the large business enterprise. Thus, this paper primarily probes *what is* rather than *what should be* concerning business behavior. The question of whether the large corporation should or should not have the goal characteristics described here is left to other contributors to this volume—though finally it is left with the citizens of the United States. What these understandings of the firm indicate concerning ethics in business and socially responsible business behavior is discussed. Some of the implications of *what is* concerning corporate objectives are examined at the close of the piece.

Reprinted from "Alternative Views of Big Business Goals and Purposes," by Harold L. Johnson in volume no. 343 of THE ANNALS of The American Academy of Political and Social Science. © 1962, by The American Academy of Political and Social Science. All rights reserved. Harold Johnson is Professor of Economics in the School of Business Administration, Emory University.

AN ORGANIZATION-THEORY MODEL[1]

The view that profits are the only goal of big business faces difficulty in awareness that the corporation is a person only in legal theory. Lawyers, for their purposes, may conceive of the corporation as an artificial person, but, for the purposes of explanation and prediction of corporate behavior, this seems to be a faulty beginning. One analyst has noted the "error in anthropomorphism" in constructing a model of the corporation simply in the image of individual man. The organizational character of the enterprise seems to require a different definition. Organization theory views the enterprise as made up of many participants, such as suppliers, the many categories of employees, executives, dealers, and stockholders. A business organization consists of partly conflicting, partly complementary participants or interest groups. It does not possess a single mind, "conscience," or set of motivations as does an individual, for it is, in an organization-theory model, a coalition of many individuals and groups. The monetary and nonmonetary inducements necessary to ensure the participation of these individuals and groups make organization objectives a miscellany of goals. The "side payments" to coalition members in the form of democratic supervision of labor force or fairness to dealers and suppliers shape, and indeed are a part of, organizational goals. The web of contractual relationships between suppliers and national mail-order establishments indicates that fair and equitable arrangements are a part of the "price" for participation of manufacturers in the mail-order business.

Stockholders with profit goals, of course, may be important members of contemporary enterprise, but, in this model, top executives are more strategic participants. Executives bring their own goals to the organization and they act as "peak coordinators" of the firm, facilitating bargaining and negotiation between other participants. In this model, executives act as brokers, so to speak, between the various members of the organization. In traditional legal and economic theory, this rich and complex pattern of goals is homogenized into the purposes of stockholders through the terms of legal contract. This, however, seems to be an unsatisfactory solution, judging from ample evidence in American industry that such a transformation of objectives does not take place.

The objectives of big business, then, are conceived of here as varied rather than monolithic and as shaped by interactions of many participants in flexible coalition rather than being only profits to owners. To go on, the goals of organization arrived at in a coalition manner take a "satisficing" rather than maximizing form. This feature of organizational goals can be seen by first looking at the

---

[1] This model is that of Chester I. Barnard, Herbert A. Simon, Richard M. Cyert, and James G. March. See Barnard, *The Functions of the Executive* (Cambridge: Harvard University Press, 1938); March and Simon, *Organizations* (New York: John Wiley, 1958); and the forthcoming book of Cyert and March, *A Behavioral Theory of the Firm* (Englewood Cliffs: Prentice-Hall, 1963).

objectives of individuals. According to psychologists, individuals have target aspirations which they seek to achieve. These aspiration levels are influenced by past performance in relation to goals, past aspiration levels, and by comparison with others in similar circumstances and conditions. Aspiration levels, furthermore, tend to change only slowly in face of achievement above or below target. Individuals and groups playing the game of life tend to take as acceptable or "good enough" activities or relationships which meet or exceed their aspiration levels. In the language of operations research, in the real world, feasibility rather than optimality tests generally are used to gauge behavior.

Maximization of goals is left aside because of the "bounded rationality" conditions under which individuals operate and because of the "suboptimization" consequences of optimizing a single goal out of a goal set. To explain this bit of jargon, the individual follows a satisficing approach because he does not know enough concerning his possible strategies or the state of the world to optimize his goals. He is rational in a partial or bounded sort of way. If the goals of individuals are plural rather than single, optimization of one goal often results in losses with other objectives. Maximization of one goal means other important objectives cannot be met satisfactorily, the result being a "suboptimizing" with some goals and with overall satisfaction. The individual must, just as the housewife in the supermarket [does], balance his "expenditures" on objectives, getting something of all and thereby hopefully getting the greatest total satisfaction.

Organization theorists by and large have transplanted these insights concerning the individual to an organization context. They posit that the miscellany of goals arising out of the coalitions called big business exist in aspiration-level, satisficing terms rather than in maximization. The goals of people in business concerning profits, sales, employee relations, growth, social responsibility, and market shares are subject to tests of "good enough" or feasibility rather than maximization.

This view of corporate objectives helps explain why conflict between participants seeking different things from organizations is not greater than it usually is. With goals subject to feasibility rather than optimality checks, the organization has a greater range of action in which the goals of many participants are satisfied. Conflict is partially sidestepped by the fact that the enterprise at any one time attends only to those objectives in which it is falling short. Particular goals receive attention only when achievement falls below target levels. Only in rare instances with many large firms—in deep recession, for example—would the goals and interests of many participants fail to be met, opening to serious conflict. Much of the time, conflict remains latent as the focus is on different goals at different points in time. Not often are the goals of enterprise examined all at once.

It is useful to see that the organization-theory view of firm objectives cuts in two directions. It is probably disappointing to those who believe that, by definition, the large corporation is a money machine. But it also must disappoint those who come equipped with a naive view of business ethics. This model indicates that profits assuredly are one of the goals of business organization and that, under certain conditions, will be a vital goal. The door is hardly opened to the proposition that the large business enterprise is an eleemosynary institution dispensing gifts and charity to one and all. It seems clear that one of the goals of the firm relates to profits as a total amount or a percentage return on investment or sales. It is significant, though, that many company officials, instead of talking and acting in terms of optimum profits, operate in terms of target rates of profits. This bears some resemblance to the organization-theory model of how goals are established and pursued. In circumstances such as a general recession, new rivals in a market, or changing consumer tastes, profit objectives may be the most crucial of a goal set.

This view, on the other hand, offers a framework for discussing ethics in business. Some critics have argued that talk of ethics in commerce is inevitably at the level of glittering generality, pleasing to the ear but without real content. The organization-theory model is a way of analyzing ethical or responsible behavior. Some of the participants in enterprise are the custodians of ethical or socially responsible practice. Labor unions and individuals as employees have, as part of the nonmonetary requisites for joining an enterprise, items often classified as ethical business behavior. A full elaboration of such items would be too time-consuming to describe here. It is enough to note that the humanization of the work environment, safe working conditions, freedom from harsh and arbitrary supervision, and proper notice of change in methods and place of work are part of the nonmonetary inducements necessary to get employees in twentieth-century America. In the case of retail dealers linked with national manufacturers, the nonmonetary requirements for participation are seen in the developing system of law and contract between automobile dealers and the manufacturers. Commercial practices labeled as socially responsible can be viewed as part of the nonmonetary inducements necessary to secure participation of various people in the firm. Nonprofit behavior can be handled not as an odd mutation in a world of profit maximization but as an integral part of the goals of business organization.

To indicate that this model is more than a few interesting hunches, there have been a number of efforts to test its basic propositions. These tests have been made in the traditional language of economics and in the newer techniques of computer simulation.[2] While these studies are not conclusive, they indicate that the model can be subject to various validation procedures.

---

[2]See, for example, R. M. Cyert and J. G. March, "Organizational Factors in the Theory of Oligopoly," *Quarterly Journal of Economics,* February 1956; Melvin W. Reder, "A Reconsideration of the Marginal Productivity Theory," *Journal of Political Economy,* Vol. 55 (1947), pp. 450–458; and R. M. Cyert and J. G. March, "Models in a Behavioral Theory of the Firm," *Behavioral Science,* April 1959.

A GAME-THEORY VIEW

It may seem at first sight a fool's errand to use game theory as a basis for discussing ethics in big business. Talk of payoffs, strategies, and malevolent foes who are seeking to do each other in seems out of harmony with such a discussion. To be sure, the idea of profit maximization gets short shrift in a game-theory model, for in the dynamics of rivalry survival appears to be a basic objective. Profits, market share, responsible practice, and cash in the bank are relegated to the status of means in a grand strategy to stay alive.

But, in many games in theory, in actual experiment, and in the real world, the players—instead of being brutish, nasty antagonists—are individuals open to the possibilities of cooperation, fair play, mutual restraint, and live-and-let-live. Parenthetically, investigators in game theory are at work exploring under what circumstances conflict and cooperation arise, and in studying the basic structure of cooperative games. In cooperative games of both theory and fact, neither profit maximization nor the goal of "do the other fellow in" is an appropriate way of characterizing the motivation or objectives of individuals.

Of course, often in many games, players get together tacitly or overtly for mutual benefit, with this cooperation to the disadvantage of parties outside the game or to the community at large. This is a criticism of the bargaining between labor and management in major industries in America or of the tacit cooperation between rival business firms to avoid price-cutting. These comments remind us that sometimes the substitution of industry or group benefit for individual self-interest leaves objectives well short of the highest and best! The cooperation and mutual sharing between members of a gang of juvenile delinquents to carry out mayhem, robbery, and murder does not seem altogether to fit the description of proper ethical behavior!

Game theory, however, makes available insights in addition to the propositions that cooperation among players and a philosophy of mutual restraint may change economic rivalry from dog-eat-dog to a policy of live-and-let-live. These additional insights are derived from game experiments in bargaining carried out by a number of investigators.[3] These games reveal that many players bring to conflict and bargaining situations ideas of fairness and equity which influence their decisions. Contrary to the themes of maximum pursuit of self-interest, many individuals are reluctant to push their position to the utmost when they possess the power to do so. They are interested in results which are fair and equitable. Principles of split-the-difference and pursuit-of-justice have been found in games where the advantage would seem to lie in different kinds of policies. These developments in game theory point to an economic motivation and behavior more complex than the assumptions of narrow self-interest. But where do such motivations, purposes,

---

[3]See the article by Ward Edwards, "Behavioral Decision Theory," *Annual Review of Psychology,* Vol. 12 (1961), pp. 490–493, for a summary of these developments.

and objectives come from? One answer to this question lies in the propositions to which the discussion now turns.

A BEHAVIORAL VIEW

It is undoubtedly trite and obvious beyond excuse to describe human beings as social animals, but perhaps some may forget that this cliché extends also to big-business executives! According to behavioral scientists, businessmen, like the rest of society, grow up in social relationships which give them a reasonably well-organized set of attitudes, concepts, and values concerning physical and social reality. The development of a "self" or personality arises out of the interrelation-ships into which the individual is thrust, with family, peer groups, schools, churches, and mass media socializing him. Without such social relationships, the individual is a virtual beast rather than a human being. He is directed and influenced by social circumstances, but they help make him into a person. By a behavioral model, people in a real sense are like electronic computers, in that social and cultural circumstances "program" them so that they react in particular ways of doing and thinking about things. By this framework, the motivation of people, businessmen included, is shaped and formed by the social relations in which they exist.

The flow of communication in which individuals inevitably exist as children and as adults relates both to facts and to norms. We learn what *is* from what *is not,* and we also learn about what *ought to be* rather than what ought not to be. In the language of this model, individuals, by taking up a pattern of attitudes and values, internalize a normative frame at the level of conscience. Attitudes and norms give an ethical dimension to life, indicating a group consensus of what should or should not be done in particular situations.

This view of behavior should not be dismissed as relevant only to matters of social custom, dress, or eating habits, for big business as an organization and businessmen as individuals live in a social environment. There are many norms concerning business action. Many businessmen seek to "give people their money's worth," partially because competition forces them to but also because the customs and norms of America suggest that to be proper commercial practice. Businessmen strive with rivals, but norms and laws prevent them from bombing competitors, running them down with automobiles, or from getting customers with promises of free opium. Changing social norms concerning business are apparent in procedures to dampen the adverse effects on employees and communities of automation and plant shifts. The relative success of people-centered in contrast with process-centered supervision of employees and the preference for a boss who is a boss but who does not act like it, reflect particular social norms of business.

A behavioral view of business action and attitudes is related to game-theory and organization-theory approaches. The normative circumstances in which business takes place influence the size and character of the payoffs in the game and the number of strategies available to the players. Some people do not use dynamite to dispose of rivals because the sanctions or negative payoffs with this course of action are so severe. With businessmen who have norms at the level of conscience, such strategies are not even included in their statement of the game matrix. Because of the psychological constraints laid on them by particular norms, executives do not even conceive of many strategies. Some may choose alternatives other than violence not because of conscience but because of the heavy sanctions of public disapproval and the hangman's noose! Thus the whole structure and play of the business game in real life are influenced by the social environment in which it is played. Increasingly, businessmen have an explicit awareness of this elementary but crucial point. Pursuit of fairness and equity in the experimental games—and, in real life, bargaining between rivals—flows out of the social milieu in which the players have been programmed, to use once more the computer language. It is clear, also, that many of the nonmonetary inducements to secure customers, employees, dealers, and suppliers in the coalition of large business enterprise reflect social norms of America concerning business practice.

The behavioral model is sometimes addressed in terms of role theory. A role lays out for the individual—or for the organization, if it is possible to think of a role for big business in contemporary culture—expected goals and expected ways of achieving goals in the position or job which he occupies. In fact, it is in the specific prescriptions of a particular role that general social norms are focused and get their meaning. Social values and attitudes as vague as justice and equality are precise in the role requirements of ample notice to employees and communities before transfer to other cities, the "open door" policy of the executive suite, and the grievance procedures for disputes between automobile dealers and the manufacturers.

The behavioral basis of business is illustrated both in studies by scholars and by episodes reported in the public press. The recent furor over steel pricing, the Katy railroad controversy in 1957, and the debate over the closure of a textile mill in Nashua, New Hampshire in 1948 demonstrate the impact of the social environment upon business. In a more scholarly setting, a sociologist has traced out in the steel-distribution industry the varying norms and motivations of businessmen in established concerns and in the transient firms of the industry.[4] Rensis Likert and his colleagues at the University of Michigan have reported in many studies about the influence of American values upon management practice.[5]

But what does all this mean concerning corporate or business goals? What does this framework suggest about ethics in business? It reminds us that, in some degree, the objectives and motives of executives are social in origin. The goals and

---

[4]Louis Kriesberg, "Occupational Control Among Steel Distributors," *American Journal of Sociology,* Vol. 61 (November 1955), pp. 203–212.

[5]See, for example, Rensis Likert, *New Patterns of Management* (New York: McGraw-Hill Book Company, 1961).

purposes of big business do not well up either out of instincts of altruism or out of monetary self-interest. They are framed by the social circumstances of business. Ethics in business do not rest altogether in the imaginations of public-relations advisers. A behavioral framework indicates that the value-laden concepts of ethics and social responsibility can be translated into the analytical concepts of sociology and social psychology. Nonprofit goals thus involve relatively little magic or mystery, for they reflect changing norms or a changing role prescription for the big-business executive.

This model suggests, further, that the meaning of social responsibility is not given by businessmen alone. A community or social consensus helps indicate what the goals and purposes of big business must be. Some critics of a "corporate-conscience philosophy" have characterized it as a twentieth-century *laissez faire* in which executives alone specify the content of such a conscience. A behavioral view indicates that a social consensus is involved in describing the goals and purposes of modern business. Of course, managers are not speechless in the dialogue and debate about the make-up of business purposes and goals, but they are hedged about and directed by this social consensus. Some companies and managers have learned this the hard way. In a competitive-market model, the firm is constrained by market forces; in a behavioral view, it is also limited by a social definition of the business role.

We have here an analytical base for approaching the study of ethical business behavior, placing this vague notion under the scrutiny of analysis. The model hardly suggests, on the other hand, that, in contemporary America, profits, efficiency, and cost cutting are excluded from the purposes of big business. Indeed, in America, corporate executives and the enterprises which they coordinate are expected to pursue profit goals, efficiency, innovation, and cost minimization. These items are key elements in the pattern of American business. There are nonprofit aspects to the business role, but, in an enterprise system, strong emphasis remains on pursuit of profits, economy with scarce resources, and watching the dollar. A behavioral model does not indicate that the executive has been made over in the image of Santa Claus. But, to complicate life for those who desire simple answers, this framework indicates that the modern executive is not styled after Scrooge or the robber baron of yesteryear. Decisions of sales, cost, price, capital budgeting, and employee relations are made within a social milieu which affects considerably the style and manner in which such decisions are made. To recognize this is not to make big business into Santa Claus nor is it to forget the basic function of business in American society.

Another insight is available, emphasizing the complexity of probing at business behavior and motivation. Social norms and roles are elaborated both in the community-at-large and in the small groups in which individuals participate. Often these sources of norms prescribe similar kinds of values and behavior, but, on occasion, the norms of small groups conflict with those of society. This is most obvious in a contrast of the normative pressures of a juvenile gang or an organization of gangsters with those of society. It may be apparent also when the norms of labor unions or business trade associations are measured by social goals and norms. Norms shaping big business thus come from society and from the particular industry and market settings in which companies operate. Often the norms from these sources coincide, but they may conflict. The relatively insulated atmosphere of a group of oligopolists may develop norms and rules of the game more suited to the interests of the small group than to those of outside parties. Industry attitudes concerning price-cutting, advertising, and innovation may vary from general norms on these matters. Thus, a behavioral view emphasizes that not all normative or "ethical" behavior will be that outlined by the general interest.

SUMMARY

With the organization-theory, game-theory, and behavioral models of this paper, an emphasis is upon a mixed package of motivations, purposes, and goals. The goals and membership of the large corporation are varied. Bargaining and conflict in real and experimental games goes on, but often within a fence of moral restraint and fairness. The norms and roles of big business include a conglomeration of profits, efficiency, democratic human relations, freedom, and justice. Big business is not cast in the simple molds of profit maximization or of pursuit of public welfare.

An economist would be practically derelict in his duty without pointing to the problems of conflict and complementarity which this mixture of goals and motivation creates for us all. Executives, other participants in enterprise, and the total citizenry have the difficult task of choosing out of this mixture of business means and ends—when many of the choices have commingled in them gains and costs in terms of other purposes of big business. The task is made more serious with the awareness that, as these choices are made, there is simultaneous impact on the institutional fabric of the American economic order.

Judging from the choices made thus far, these institutional changes will not take us to a twentieth-century version of *laissez faire* or down the road to doctrinaire socialism. Americans have shown an awareness of the dangers of "suboptimization" in which marked success with one purpose or objective is purchased at the cost of nonfulfillment of other important goals. To hazard a guess on the future, Americans will continue to fashion, in their choices of what they want big business to be, a mixed, pragmatic version of contemporary capitalism.

The Modern Manager: What Makes Him RUN?

R. J. Monsen,
B. O. Saxberg, and
R. A. Sutermeister

The development of a cadre of professional managers for publicly owned corporations has brought into focus the divergence between the self-interests of the manager and the interests of the business firm and its owners. This article attempts to integrate organizational behavior theory with recent developments in the economic theory of the firm. The thesis is that the owner-manager of the traditional firm in economic theory has been transformed into the modern professional- and bureaucratic-oriented manager who works to achieve personal goals that may not be the same as the goals of the business.

THE MODERN MANAGER

The motivation of the entrepreneur, in traditional economic theory, has generally been assumed to be that of profit maximization. While other motives (such as the perpetuation of the family firm and the attainment of power and prestige) have been mentioned, traditional economic theory even today relies upon a model in which the firm aims at maximization of profits.[1] This monistic theory of motivation can be defended where one individual both owns and manages the firm; in this case, his self-interest is congruent with profit maximization. The development of the giant corporation, however, has produced the professional manager, described by one author as follows:

> The primary responsibility for business leadership in the large corporation has devolved upon a group of men who are professional managers. Their position is not achieved through ownership. They are salaried experts, trained by education and experience in the field of management. Though only salaried managers, they find themselves responsible for making the decisions which affect not merely the dividends their stockholders receive but also the price consumers

---

From *Business Horizons,* Fall, 1966. Reprinted by permission.

[1] For a more extensive treatment of the motivation of the classical entrepreneur, see R. J. Monsen, B. O. Saxberg, and R. A. Sutermeister, "La Motivation Sociologique de L'entrepreneur," *Economie Appliquée,* XVII (December, 1964).

pay, the wages their workers earn, and the level of output and employment in their own firms and in the economy as a whole.[2]

In the modern giant corporation, ownership is usually diffused among shareholders who are divorced from the management of their corporations; in fact, most managers no longer have large ownership in the corporations they manage. Therefore, changes in the private assets of the managers are not tied directly to changes in the assets of the corporation, and they need not identify with the profit-maximizing goals of the owners. Only if corporate profit or performance falls badly, particularly compared to the performance of the industry as a whole, will the scattered and generally anomalous owners vote management out of office.

What then are the manager goals? The basic desire of the professional manager is to maximize his self-interest or lifetime income in monetary and nonmonetary terms.[3] He may not even attempt to maximize the firm's profits, for such attempts might involve risks endangering his own interests—success in increasing profits may bring a bonus, but losses may mean loss of position and lifetime income.

Public opinion has imposed additional restraints upon pure profit-maximizing behavior. Since the turn of the century, the self-interest of owner-managers has not been accepted as the only legitimate objective of a business firm. Any organizational unit functioning as a social system, such as a firm, exists as a subsystem in society, which ultimately legitimizes the continued existence of its subsystems. Such legislative measures as the Interstate Commerce Act, the Sherman Antitrust Act, the Clayton Act, and the Wagner Act have established the framework within which society permits business to operate.

The transformation of the owner-manager of the traditional firm to the professional manager of the modern firm is reflected in various motivational pressures.

SOURCES OF PRESSURES

Personality

Some of the motivational pressures on the modern manager arise out of his own personality, influenced by family background, education, and the culture of his society. For example, an individual may have an authoritarian personality, reflected, as discussed later, in a pressure for power. Another individual may have a high level of need for achievement.

---

[2]Robert Aaron Gordon, *Business Leadership in the Large Corporation* (Washington: The Brookings Institution, 1945), p. 318.

[3]For a complete development of this thesis, see R. Joseph Monsen, Jr., and Anthony Downs, "A Theory of the Large Managerial Firms," *Journal of Political Economy*, LXXIII (June, 1965), pp. 221–36.

The achievement motive in personality

The works of Darwin and Marx lead one to believe that man is mainly adaptive to conditions in the environment. The research carried out by McClelland and his coauthors establishes an interesting case that man is creative in response to consciously or unconsciously internalized motives.[4] Their investigations have concentrated on the thesis that some people have a greater need for achievement than others. Achievement is not equated with success in financial or material terms, or any other tangible or intangible results; rather, achievement *per se* is the motive, the need, and the goal. The achievement drive in the personality results in needs for such things as money, power, status, and so forth. Economic development depends upon the presence in society of a sufficient number of high achievers; the modal personality of one society may show a higher level of need for achievement than might be found in another.

Though the empirical investigations have not clearly delineated distinctions between entrepreneurs and managers, the results appear to suggest that a preponderance of men in business-leadership positions show high achievement personalities. In this context we are attracted by the finding reported by McClelland that the entrepreneurial manager evidently is not a gambler or habitual risk-taker. Confronted with a choice of potentially high profits in a situation of chance uncertainty, or moderate profits but a strong possibility that he can affect the outcome (a calculable risk), he will choose the latter.

McClelland regards the need for achievement as the crucial component in the personality of the entrepreneur-manager. In a cultural environment where the values of the Protestant ethic form a core, a child internalizes a need for achievement in greater measure than where they are absent. Moreover, the need for achievement is greater in families where children are encouraged to develop early self-mastery and independence; it is also affected by the family's social status. Thus we find that high need for achievement is associated with a middle-class family background in which the father is either a member of a white-collar or professional occupational group, or in business. This also suggests a better-than-average family educational background where education is regarded as an important avenue in improving one's position in life.

---

[4]This work is reported mainly in David C. McClelland, John W. Atkinson, Russell A. Clark, and Edgar L. Lowell, *The Achievement Motive* (New York: Appleton-Century-Crofts, Inc., 1953); David C. McClelland, A. L. Baldwin, U. Bronfenbrenner, and F. L. Strodtbeck, *Talent and Society* (Princeton, N.J.: D. Van Nostrand Co., Inc., 1958); David C. McClelland, *The Achieving Society* (Princeton, N.J.: D. Van Nostrand Co., Inc., 1961). See also the critical evaluation of *The Achieving Society* in Fritz Redlich, "Economic Development, Entrepreneurship, and Psychologism: A Social Scientist's Critique of McClelland's Achieving Society," *Explorations in Entrepreneurial History* (2d series; Fall, 1963), pp. 10–35.

The societal culture, as well as the experiences of socialization during childhood, will govern the level of aspirations and establish attitudes toward success and failure. For example, a strong motivating force in the manager's life may be fear of failure *per se*. Our professional managers are interested in maximizing their lifetime incomes, yet, regardless of monetary rewards, they are likely to be high achievers by the nature of their personality makeup.

If we accept Maslow's need hierarchy as relevant, a man is characterized beyond the needs for security, safety, and love by still higher-level needs, those of esteem and self-actualization. Profits, material wealth, and other tangible aspects of success can serve as a feedback for the entrepreneurial manager, indicating that he is still innovating, still creating. After all, the values, choices, and behavior of other individuals indicate that they compete for a common set of resources. He is therefore conditioned by them to see economic reality in terms of the choices they make. Wood has expressed this as follows: "... profits, in a competitive enterprise economy, are an objective test of the social value of ideas and innovations—and the ultimate test of business performance."[5]

Environmental pressures

Small groups. The executive of the corporation, together with members of top management, establishes the values that will permeate the behavior of the firm as a social system with a culture of its own. The personal value hierarchy of the executive serves to routinize some of the demands of the position, which otherwise might involve him in conflict situations rampant with psychological pressure. It enables him to make social decisions with some confidence. Employees will accept the values of the management and the firm for which they work, just as the executives and the firm itself must function within the value system of society as a whole. But it should also be acknowledged that there are, within the business enterprise, a number of collectives or groups based on hierarchical level, occupation, or some other unifying base, and characterized by value systems of their own. The values within these social systems may conflict or even be mutually exclusive —they remain ideals or standards whereby judgments and evaluations are made. Each member will therefore choose a value hierarchy that will provide for him a set of personal operative values.

Throughout his lifetime the manager will belong to numerous membership groups, such as social or business clubs, the values of which he will not necessarily embrace. It is significant that as long as such an organizational group functions only as a membership group the executive personality shows little effect from this membership. Many groups, however, go beyond this function and are, in fact, reference groups; their values are internalized in the member, forcing a commit-

---

[5]Laurence I. Wood, "The Corporation and Society," Conference on Education for Business (Crotonville, N.Y.: Aug. 2, 1963), p. 5. (Speech by vice-president and general counsel of General Electric.)

ment from him. Even though a reference group may later be reduced to the status of a membership group only, it is unlikely that the member will totally eradicate the influence of its values. In addition, there are groups to which he aspires that also serve as reference groups. In each case, through anticipatory socialization, his behavior reflects an approach to and adoption of the values he has imputed to the group. Thus, within the context of the business organization, the executive is subject to considerable pressure as he constantly tries to decide with which group's values his behavior should conform.

The immediate social environment of the manager contains a number of other small groups that exert pressure on his motivation. The most important groups within the firm are those of other managers and employees. Outside the firm are groups of peers, that is, managers of other businesses who meet for lunch, at clubs, or in community organizations. Competitors also affect the entrepreneur's motivations. Thus, it can be said that "modern management—especially in the large corporation—operates in a group setting, with group decisions—and group attitudes, constraints, and aspirations—although individual roles may be sharply differentiated."[6]

The relationships between the small groups inside and outside the firm and the various motivations of the entrepreneur are numerous and complex. If the entrepreneur is facing difficult competition in his industry, he may be motivated primarily to protect his own security by increasing his competence, and quite secondarily to increase his power, build up his status, and earn prestige from competitors. A manager who is seeking satisfactory relationships and interactions with his fellow managers strives for recognition, status, and prestige through their approval of his actions. Therefore, the manager's peers have a major effect upon the direction of his motivation. A manager interested in gaining approval from his subordinates may be more concerned with his actions, interactions, and the prestige enjoyed with this group than with competence and power. Likewise, if he is interested in his employees as individuals, he may be motivated by a desire to help them develop their own abilities.

Large external groups. The executive of the firm is under further motivational pressure from a number of large societal groups that form the external environment for the firm in modern industrial society. The major ones—unions, government, competitors, church, and educational institutions—play varying roles of importance in a manager's life. As restraints or incentives they affect his motivation—to action or inaction.

In recent times, behavior toward *unions* by professional managers in corporations with broadly diffused ownership has been strikingly different from that characterized by the typical two-person zero-sum game imagined in classical economic

---

[6]C. Addison Hickman, "Managerial Motivations and the Theory of the Firm," *The American Economic Review,* XLV (May, 1955), p. 550.

theory.[7] The modern manager's motivation stems from the fact that promotion within many large companies depends upon having, among other qualifications, a good "record with labor." As he becomes viewed as more of a conciliator between opposing groups—stockholders, unions, government, and consumers—the manager who is the most amiable and conciliatory, and whose decisions are less often attacked, often makes the most rapid rise in the modern corporate hierarchy.

In the modern large-scale enterprise, we question whether the two-person zero-sum game in the classical firm, with the manager on one side and the union on the other, applies; it is often management's own gain to solve speedily any labor crisis, even if the solution might be adverse in the long run to the company. The explanation for this may be that the manager has more to gain in income, status, and career opportunities by being conciliatory toward labor and unions than he has by driving a hard bargain to increase profits for the stockholders and the company in which he may own no or very few shares.

The *government* affects the motivations of the entrepreneur largely through taxation and regulation. In the classical firm the entrepreneur is thought of as resisting all government intervention in his decision-making and, in particular, increased tax burdens upon the firm because they lessen his own personal profit and income. This strong classical ideology is still quite common among management men and members of various industry associations.

However, in the large firm with diffused ownership, the ideology held by management is usually more liberal, and allows for a governmental role that is still commonly rejected by owner-managers of small businesses. The attitude prevailing in modern professional management is frequently referred to as the "managerial ideology," in contrast to the classical ideology of business. In the managerial ideology, management may resent government regulations, particularly as they impinge on their own sphere of decision-making. However, they are largely resigned to the influence of government; in fact, their business often depends upon government as a major purchaser. In addition, they are usually consulted in governmental decision-making more than management in middle-size and small business. Therefore, they actually have fewer feelings of alienation. Moreover, government taxation policies have less impact upon professional management because their income stems mainly from fixed salary, stock options, and company expense accounts, which are less directly related to company profits than the income of the

---

[7]The main effect of the trade union upon the motivation of the traditional entrepreneur is essentially that of an opponent in a game in which the less the entrepreneur concedes to the union the greater the return to him will be, as in the typical case of the two-person zero sum game. Likewise, the position of the union is essentially that of an opponent whose aim is to increase his share of the company income as much as possible. Traditionally the entrepreneur, therefore, is expected to be motivated by both fear of the union as an adversary and by the desire to enhance his own position and firm profit as much as possible by opposing the union's demands. This can be described as the classical type of impact of the union upon the entrepreneur.

owner-entrepreneur. Professional managers, then, generally think of the government as a cooperating partner. It is not possible to make blanket statements about the impact of government upon managerial behavior. It is more feasible to consider managers as representatives of distinct, though frequently overlapping, interest groups, holding ideologies that reflect their socioeconomic position and background. This also explains why business groups frequently exhibit very different patterns and degrees of frustration and antagonism toward governmental policies.

Various industry and business associations reinforce particular ideologies of management. Generally, such associations are based more upon industry aims and economic interests. They tend to call pragmatically upon government for whatever may be to their advantage.

The *competition* of other businesses obviously has a strong effect upon the motivation of professional managers. In the modern firm where the mores and rules of playing the game may be different from those in the classical firm, the competitor's image of himself as a professional manager is also likely to affect his behavior. To some degree, all managers think of themselves as members of a professional fraternity with certain horizontal mobility. As long as a manager's image as "a good manager" remains intact, his opportunity to move out and up in other firms is good. Thus, the modern manager plays to an audience (if indeed the managers of competing firms can be thought of as an audience).

In large oligopolistic industries (with firms involved in price-fixing or combined in cartels), one firm often considers other firms less as competitors than as cooperators with whom the market is shared, and with whom policies are compared and standardized, as among members of a professional management fraternity. How oligopolistic or monopolistic an industry may be, or how competitive it may be, therefore, will affect management motivation and behavior.

The impact of *religious affiliation* upon the motivation of entrepreneurs is difficult to determine in contemporary society. Certainly in the industrial revolution in England, various Protestant sects, such as the Quakers, originally played an influential part. It has become increasingly difficult to say that the Protestants in modern America have shown a greater entrepreneurial spirit than any other group. It is often argued that churches, although memberships are soaring, are having less effect upon the behavior of their members than they had upon earlier, more inner-directed generations. There is some evidence that today's other-directed individual, in Riesman's terms, responds much more readily to peer groups or economic interest groups than to religious organizations.[8] If this is so, business behavior might more easily be explained in contemporary society by psychological and sociological variables than by the religious or philosophical differences that Weber originally found in an earlier and perhaps more inner-directed society of previous generations.

---

[8]For additional information on the "other-directed" man, see David Riesman, *The Lonely Crowd* (New Haven, Conn.: Yale University Press, 1950).

The prestige of our *educational institutions* has increased tremendously. To-day, more than ever before, schools and universities are the major institutions that transmit cultural values and norms in our society. At the primary levels particularly, they may affect the personality of the individual through cultural conditioning. In this process seldom can one escape the pervasive impact of our educational institutions on his way of thinking or acting.

At the college level, programs are increasingly oriented toward professionali-zation. The graduate school of business itself is rapidly attempting to make manage-ment a profession, and the modern professional manager is accredited by his M.B.A. In addition, education often affects his motivation by raising his level of aspiration and achievement needs.

Bureaucracy. Concern has been expressed by Riesman that the inner-directed man of the Protestant ethic is being replaced by an other-directed man in response to the demands of bureaucratically organized work and life conditions. Instead of having a man equipped with a gyroscope that sets the course, we have developed a radar-equipped man constantly tuning in for course and direction from those surrounding him—mass society *par preference.* Whyte acknowledges this devel-opment in his description of "the organization man," who is geared to become a member of any group that he judges will further him in the business organization, and who regards success in terms of teamwork and group membership rather than individual performance and achievement.[9] Dale sharpens the question:

> . . . shortcomings of the new managers seems to be distrust of innovation in procedures and practices. 'What are other companies doing?' is the question most commonly asked management associations. . . . The new manager thinks of himself as a problem solver rather than as an innovator, and as such he seeks a ready-made solution rather than striking out on his own in a search for something better than anyone has yet tried.[10]

In Whyte's terms, the Protestant ethic has been replaced by a social ethic where "belonging" occupies a preferred position. Fromm has commented on the prevalence of the market-oriented personality—a man is worth something only in terms of the package of salable goods he represents and the demand that exists for it. Finally, Presthus speaks of the pressures of bureaucratically run organizations whose employees are characterized by addiction to routine and mediocrity, with deference to superiors and willingness to conform to the organizational require-ments. The modal personality, developed in such a bureaucratic context and characterized by these qualities of conformity, is represented by the upward mo-biles who know how to use the bureaucratic apparatus to their advantage as they make their way in the organization. They are likely to become the business leaders

---

[9]References in this paragraph to William H. Whyte, Jr., *The Organization Man* (Garden City, N.Y.: Doubleday & Company, Inc., 1957).

[10]Ernest Dale, "Executives Who Can't Manage," *The Atlantic,* CCIX (July, 1962), p. 61.

of the future. They leave behind them the great mass of indifferent employees who never cared to identify with the objectives and goals of the organization in the first place or became frustrated in the process, and the ambivalent who are imaginative and creative nonconformists frustrated by the bureaucracy in achieving the success they deem they have merited.

In designing the elements of his bureaucratic theory, Weber took into account only the structural parts of the organization and the anticipated consequences from this theoretical scheme.[11] In reality, as complex organizations have approached the conditions of bureaucracy outlined by Weber, unanticipated consequences have appeared in the satisfying of personal objectives by the organizations' personnel, including managers.

Social responsibilities. The firm is usually assumed to have four broad areas of social responsibility: the stockholders, the employees, the customers, and the government. Many stockholders claim that they are "the forgotten men." Generally, they are not given a great deal of information about the running of the company, and management usually feels that it fulfills its responsibility by maintaining the traditional dividend and seeing that the price of the stock follows the market relatively closely, at least on the upside. Recent court cases, however, have held that management owes to the stockholder wise and prudent decisions and a separation between the interests of the company and management's own financial interests.

The employees of the firm represent another area of obligation. The long-run trend has been for firms to assume increasing responsibility for the employment, health, and retirement of its employees. Part of this obligation, of course, has been assumed by government. Such concerns as safety regulations on the job have been pursued by both government and unions. Generally, the larger the company the more security it offers its workers in the form of sickness and retirement benefits. Unions have attempted to provide workers with bargaining power and have thus enabled them to exact various fringe benefits.

In this century, government regulations and agencies such as the Pure Food and Drug Administration, as well as consumer cooperatives and consumer testing groups, have provided increasing protection for the consumer. Firms today, then, do have some checks upon them beyond the power of the consumer to withdraw patronage; in the last analysis, however, the customer's main protection is to deal with firms of established reputation. The market mechanism still ultimately rewards the firms that can produce most efficiently. There exists, therefore, a premise that firms need to maintain a satisfactory image with their customers.

The firm's responsibility to the government can be separated into three areas: payment of taxes and conformance with regulations, adherence to specifications on products sold to the government, and compliance with verbal inducements by

---

[11] Max Weber, *The Theory of Social and Economic Organizations* (New York: Oxford University Press, 1947).

the government in the interest of avoiding price increases and other forms of economic and social unrest. Growth in the direct and indirect power of the government has brought about a change in the government's relations with business. The reluctance of U.S. Steel to avert a price increase until President Kennedy resorted to threats, or the exposure of illegal price-fixing by General Electric, Westinghouse, and other electrical goods manufacturers, indicates that a business philosophy of social obligation has not yet been fully accepted.

The concept of social responsibility of business and of stockholders, consumers, labor, and government has, in the course of recent history, become increasingly emphasized. The business firm has little choice but to be aware of the social responsibility attributed to it by the public.

Thus the pressures on the manager stem from a number of sources. The accompanying figure is a representation of these pressures and the sources from which they derive.

NATURE OF PRESSURES

The sources of motivational pressures on the professional manager have been discussed. The manager responds to these pressures by striving for specific intermediate goals in order to attain his personal goal of maximizing his lifetime income in both monetary and nonmonetary terms.

Money

The need for money derives from strong sociological as well as financial motives. Money serves in our society as a general symbol of success and thus becomes an indication in the marketplace of power, status, prestige, and competence.

Power

Managers frequently are possessed by an urge for personal power—control of resources, and freedom to manipulate persons and events both inside and outside the firm. In our society the enhancement of personal power is suspect; yet, in recognition of the concrete existence of personal power as a managerial motive, the prevalence of authoritarian personalities in executive positions is widely accepted. Hagen, for example, speaks of the authoritarian personality as one in which " . . . satisfaction in yielding to the judgment and wishes of superiors and satisfaction in dominating inferiors are interwoven." He further states:

> An individual who thus perceives each contact with other persons as involving a danger of conflict and a threat of pain may conceive of dominating others rather than merely attacking them as a solution to the threat and an outlet for the rage which is within him. This need will express itself as a need to obtain performance from others by command, to influence or direct the behavior of others, to affect others so as to obtain desired performance from them.[12]

---

[12]Everett Hagen, *On the Theory of Social Change* (Homewood, Ill.: The Dorsey Press, 1962), pp. 73, 108.

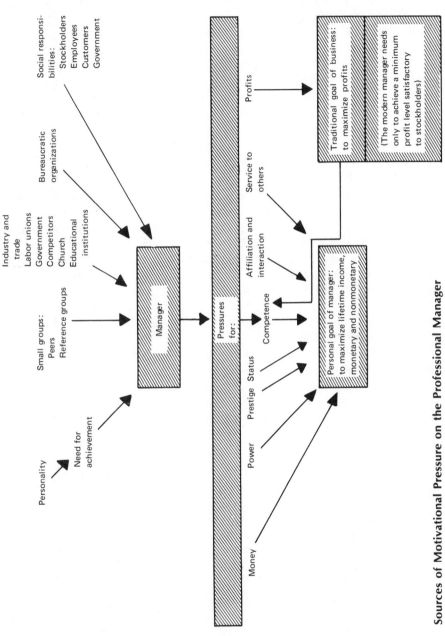

Sources of Motivational Pressure on the Professional Manager

There are, in practice, various ways in which power is reflected. The manager may be characterized by an authoritarian personality indifferent to the attitudes and needs of subordinate executives and employees; at the other extreme, he may be quite solicitous of and responsive to the ideas and feelings of his subordinates and go out of his way to gain acceptance of his authority. Tannenbaum and Schmidt view the various styles of leadership, ranging from autocratic to democratic, as points along a continuum; as one moves from the extreme autocratic to the extreme democratic style of leadership, unilateral decision-making through the use of authority by the manager decreases, and the area of freedom in decision-making by his subordinates increases.[13] The style of leadership chosen by a manager, then, partially reflects the motivations of his personality structure.

Status and prestige

Status refers to the position a person occupies in an organizational hierarchy or social system. Prestige, on the other hand, refers to his personal qualities in commanding the respect and admiration of others. Parsons points out several standards by which status can be measured: birth—membership in a particular family (which may include a company presidency), social class, race, or sex; personal qualities —age, strength, intelligence, and personality; achievements—results of personal efforts and the success that has thereby accrued to the company; possessions— especially such belongings as cars, houses, clothes, jewels, and art; and authority —the right to command action, frequently legitimized by being tied directly to a defined hierarchial position.[14]

The manager automatically achieves considerable status when he becomes his firm's top executive, and may move quickly to acquire the proper status symbols. These include money, usually considered an economic incentive only, titles, an elaborately decorated office, membership in elite clubs, and a home in the "right" neighborhood. These symbols are extremely important in the United States with its "success" culture and its high degree of spatial and social mobility.[15]

---

[13]Robert Tannenbaum and Warren H. Schmidt, "How to Choose a Leadership Pattern," *Harvard Business Review,* XXXVI (March-April, 1958), pp. 95–101.

[14]Based upon Talcott Parsons, *Essays in Sociological Theory Pure and Applied* (New York: Free Press of Glencoe, Inc., 1949), pp. 171–72. Parson's sixth standard of power, which he defines as status achieved by illegitimate means, has been omitted from this list.

[15]The reports about the increasing voluntary and involuntary professional mobility of corporation executives bear out the loss of the traditionally assumed close identification between the objectives of the company and those of its management. Managers today exhibit a marked change from a firm- or job-oriented view to a management profession-oriented view. See Seymour Freegood, "The Churning Market for Executives," *Fortune,* LXXII (September, 1965), pp. 152–54 ff.

Prestige is generally considered to be conferred by others and may involve fellow employees, colleagues in other businesses, stockholders, the public, and customers.[16]

Maslow's hierarchy of needs emphasizes esteem as one of the high-level needs, including self-esteem based on respect and esteem from others.[17] Thus, peer groups and other reference groups may often activate the latent desire of the entrepreneur for status, prestige, recognition, and importance.

Competence

There is little doubt that a strong motivating pressure on managers is the desire to do [their] work efficiently. At its simplest, this striving for competence can be attributed to fear of failure and a desire for security. At higher levels it is more likely to be a striving for excellence, a desire to be creative, or a desire to fulfill a need for self-actualization. As well as seeking intrinsic satisfaction, the manager may also cherish the recognition and prestige that will be conferred on him by competitors, fellow executives, and employees.

Many entrepreneurs are perhaps unconsciously motivated by a need to understand and manipulate their physical environment. In the broadest sense, they like to make things happen, to create events rather than merely await them passively.[18] For them the prosperity and growth of the firm become the outward manifestations of competence. Even if higher profits are not forthcoming, they may still be motivated by this strong desire for excellence—to do the job well for its own sake.

Affiliation and interaction

Although some entrepreneurs are probably satisfied with a pure power relationship over subordinates, others may desire to develop affective relationships and interactions with them. Some managers work hard to establish a personal bond with associates and subordinates to earn respect not only as competent managers but as individual human beings. Such a manager may, as Likert says, " . . . adapt his behavior to take into account the expectations, values, and interpersonal skills of those with whom he is interacting." He may choose to focus his attention on the personal worth of the subordinate and subscribe to Likert's principle of supportive relationships:

---

[16]Based upon William G. Scott, "Executive Incentives and Constraints in the Corporate Setting," *Human Relations in Management* (Homewood, Ill.: Richard D. Irwin, Inc., 1962), p. 361 ff.

[17]A. H. Maslow, "A Theory of Human Motivation," *Psychological Review,* L (July, 1943), pp. 370–96.

[18]See Robert W. White, "Motivation Reconsidered: The Concept of Competence," *Psychological Review,* LXVI (September, 1959), pp. 297–333. White treats the competence motive as one felt by most people, not just by entrepreneurs.

> The leadership and other processes of the organization must be such as to ensure a maximum probability that in all interactions and all relationships with the organization each member will, in the light of his background, values, and expectations, view the experience as supportive and one which builds and maintains his sense of personal worth and importance.[19]

Other managers may view successful personal interaction with others as a means of increasing the level of performance of the firm. Instead of emphasizing the formal organization as the instrument for achieving the firm's objectives, they stress the informal relations that cut across the formal organization structure " . . . when its own chain of command or decision or communication is tied into the informal network of groups within the organization, so that the network can be used to support the organization's goals."[20]

Service to others

Although it is not always readily recognized, there are managers who are motivated to subordinate self-interests and devote their efforts exclusively to serving the firm or the public, employees, and customers. Thus a manager's personal ambitions may change into a powerful desire to serve the business enterprise itself as an independent and living entity. Others may be concerned with the needs and development of subordinates:

> I believe it is practical and relevant to attempt a conceptual framework from which to derive practical applications in daily management and I believe that it is pertinent and sound for us, as managers, to concern ourselves with man's eternal struggle within himself to be free and yet to be ordered. I believe it is of special importance for us in management to attempt to rescue talented individuals from the lowered aspirations, the boredom, and the habits of mediocrity so often induced by life in an organization. I believe we should become painfully aware that we have established organizational settings in which order, harmony, and predictability have been given more emphasis than individual achievement and excellence. I believe that business management must continue to try to develop a process of life that strives for meaning and purpose, having as our goal the climate which permits every person to serve the values that have nurtured him, with the freedom of the mature and the responsible.[21]

---

[19]Rensis Likert, *New Patterns of Management* (New York: McGraw-Hill Book Co., Inc., 1961), p. 95. Quote in preceding paragraph, p. 103.

[20]Bernard Berelson and Gary A. Steiner, *Human Behavior* (New York: Harcourt, Brace and World, Inc., 1964), p. 370.

[21]James E. Richard, "A President's Experience with Democratic Management," in Paul R. Lawrence and others, *Organizational Behavior and Administration* (Homewood, Ill.: The Dorsey Press and Richard D. Irwin, Inc., 1961), p. 896.

Though behavior thus labeled as service to others can be altruistic, it is more likely to be related to the entrepreneur's personal motives to achieve prestige and rewarding personal relationships through interaction with the social environment.

Most entrepreneurs are probably motivated by a combination of psychological and sociological factors including desires for sufficient competence and power to ensure the perpetuation of the business and their own security, a position of status in the organization, in the industry, and in the community, and prestige or respect from all those with whom they associate.

This discussion of the interrelationships of economic self-interest theory and organizational behavior theory reveals the behavior of the modern professional manager to be necessarily at odds with the postulates of traditional economic theory. His interests are not identical to those of the owners of the firm. The modern manager desires to maximize his self-interest in terms of lifetime income—but the maximization of lifetime income implies far more than money alone to the manager in contemporary Western society. It often involves other goals and reflects various motivational pressures.

Many times these pressures are conflicting in nature and place the manager under considerable strain. The strain increases when there is a conflict between achieving his own personal objectives and working toward maximum profits for the firm. It is our contention that the manager will most frequently resolve the conflict by emphasizing his own personal goals.

Stiffer Rules for Business Ethics

Business Week

Bribing a purchasing agent to buy your product is illegal, and cheating on your tax return can send you to jail. But what about inadvertently leaking inside information about your company? Or how much pressure can you put on a government official? When is a subordinate merely being ambitiously aggressive, and when is he being flat-out dishonest?

The public wants stricter ethical standards from the men who run its government and its economy in this age of Watergate and of corporate responsibility. But what is ethical and what is not? Some acts are simply dishonest; some can be read either way. What looks ethical at first glance may not look that way in hindsight. What was acceptable yesterday may be out-of-bounds today.

There is a fine line between propriety and impropriety, and it is finer for the executive than for most because of the conflicting pressures that beset him. Society rewards him for performance, but penalizes him savagely if he is unethical in achieving that performance. The pressure to achieve is so intense that the temptation to cut a corner can be overwhelming; the reaction to a man caught cutting a corner, however, can be just as overwhelming.

"All the laws in the world won't prevent unethical conduct," says Richard L. Kattel, president of Citizens & Southern National Bank of Atlanta. "It's a matter of personal integrity." Adds Kenneth Andrews, a Harvard Business School professor who is also a director of Xerox Corp. and other companies: "If it's black and white, and a man has normal courage and security, he'll say no. It's in the gray areas that a businessman may more likely founder."

BALANCING ACT

The gray areas come up every day—where the law is not clear, where the ground rules are not hard, where the line between right and wrong is almost imperceptibly fine. How is the executive to deal with them? There are no final answers—only advice from other men who face the same problem.

First, there is the general advice—the self-searching "Watergate TV test," for instance, dreamed up by Arjay Miller, the former president of Ford Motor Co., who

---

Business Ethics: Guidelines for Eight Gray Areas

1. *The Incomplete Disclosure.* Provide more information rather than less, even if it goes beyond what the Securities & Exchange Commission and other agencies require. Put yourself in the investor's place and ask, "What do I want to know?" The SEC keeps requiring fuller disclosure, and failure to disclose can bring a suit.

2. *The corrupt boss.* Many middle managers have gotten into serious trouble—and a few have wound up in jail—by caving in to a boss who cared more about ends than means. Speak up as soon as you are faced with an ethical problem; you may set things straight. "If you can't, get out," says a Xerox director.

3. *The corrupt subordinate.* As a senior man, don't worry about rocking the boat, just get rid of him. A tolerant, "nice guy" attitude can put both of you in trouble. And his misdeeds can infect his co-workers.

4. *The inadvertent remark.* Think twice about what you tell anyone about your business—at lunch, in the locker room, over the bridge table. A chance remark might get you nailed for leaking company secrets. And

is now dean of Stanford University's business school. "Ask yourself," says Miller, "would I feel comfortable in reporting my action on TV?" If not, there is more searching in store.

If you get caught in a gray area, says Andrews of Harvard, talk it out. "Ventilate the problem," he says. "Get divergent views."

Sidney Davidson, dean of the University of Chicago School of Business, urges executives to avoid trouble by taking time to determine "the real purpose of the company." Every company exists to make money, says Davidson, but there are limits on how far it can go. Get the corporate purpose fixed in mind, he says, and make certain your fellow executives understand it.

A bit of common sense comes from Thomas J. Barlow, president of Anderson, Clayton & Co., a Houston-based food company. Says Barlow: "Anytime you see somebody making big talk about how much money can be made in a deal, scrutinize him carefully, because there is usually something in all that smoke that deserves scrutiny."

COMMON PITFALLS

A gray-area ethical conflict can pop up almost anywhere in your business, but some areas are particularly treacherous.

Reporting problems are probably the most common of all—not lying outright in reporting to the public, but stretching things just a bit. The director of accounting and auditing standards at a Big Eight accounting firm explains one common trap.

---

the law about passing "inside information" is vague. You could wind up in a courtroom.

5. *The "purified" idea.* You can usually find a lawyer or a CPA who will endorse a questionable idea or plan—especially if you phrase it just the right way. Just remember, the plan is still questionable and it can get you in trouble.

6. *The passive director.* Whether you are an inside or an outside director, don't just sit back silent and rubberstamp management. You can be sued, and the courts take a hard line nowadays on director liability. "Speak up or drop out," says one man who has served on 11 boards.

7. *The expense-account vacation.* Go easy on tax deductions for combination business–pleasure trips. Deduct for your wife only if she is actually involved in your business. This is a hot item with the IRS now.

8. *The stock-option trap.* Beware of "fast" option transactions—buying and selling your company's stock within the six-month trading rule period for insiders. More businessmen are getting tripped up on this one.

Often, he says, an executive will latch onto a rosy forecast from a middle manager —a sky-high sales forecast, for instance, or a very low cost estimate—and pass it on to the investment community as the company's "best estimate." Investors are misled, and the company may face trouble with the Securities & Exchange Commission or shareholders. "It's a common disease of overoptimism among executives," says the CPA.

Another reporting trap is simply leaving out a significant fact. Earlier this month the SEC charged Avis, Inc., with sending "false and misleading" reports to shareholders. The company failed to disclose that roughly 70% of its earnings for the first quarter of 1973 had arisen from sales of cars instead of from rentals and leases. In the first quarter of 1972, only about 25% of earnings had come from car sales. This, said the SEC, misled investors.

Where do you draw the line? Suppose the difference in earnings had been 40% against 35%, instead of 70% vs. 25%. Would the SEC have deemed this five-point spread a "material fact" that had to be disclosed? There is no hard answer. If you must err, it may be better to say too much.

CLOSING ONE EYE

Another pitfall is the failure to clamp down on the unethical conduct of a subordinate. It is easy enough for the manager to argue that the subordinate is, after all, meeting bottom-line profit requirements. "This is a variation of 'team pressure,'" says a Cincinnati machine-tool manufacturer. "But if you let one thing get past you this year, next year the guy will pull something twice as bad."

A tragic example of this pitfall is the case of Walter J. Rauscher, a former executive vice-president of American Airlines who was sentenced to jail this month. He had been involved in a supplier kickback scheme that was instigated by a subordinate. "He is a decent man," says an American Airlines official who has known Rauscher for years. "He was drawn into the trouble by a subordinate who was an s.o.b."

It is always difficult for the top men in a company to know how much pressure to put on the men beneath them. "The top manager has a duty not to push so hard that middle managers are pushed to unethical compromise," says Charles F. Luce, chairman of Consolidated Edison Co. in New York, the nation's largest electrical utility. Other chief executives agree, in principle. "I think the doing is harder than the saying," comments the machine-tool president. "The ethical question comes in," he adds, "when you push somebody hard and they do wrong—and you sit back and wash your hands of it."

The reverse of this—failing to oppose the domination of an unethical boss— has gotten many honest second-line executives into trouble, often because of a misguided sense of loyalty. "But failing to say 'no' to a corrupt boss can be the product of fear, as well," notes Mayo J. Thompson, a Texas corporation lawyer who became a member of the Federal Trade Commission in 1973. "I've seen too many cases in business," he adds, "where people caved in to a dominating and strong man."

CONSULTANTS' ROLE

An executive can get into trouble by "using" a management consultant, notes Albert McDonald, the managing director of McKinsey & Co., the management consultants.

"Often when the stakes are high—say a major acquisition—we're called in purely for an impartial opinion," explains McDonald. "But there are times when bad faith exists—when the top man knows he will benefit personally from the expansion. He wants us to help bolster his viewpoint."

The consultant soon realizes that the executive is seeking protection. "Ethics is surely involved," says McDonald, "when the project is marginal, and he still shows great enthusiasm for it."

A specialist in executive compensation insists that some managers use poor ethical judgment in pushing for "perks" that may be hard to justify.

This compensation specialist thinks that the executive treads a dangerous line in pushing too hard for such extras as company cars and free use of city apartments —especially when they are for personal, not business, use. That can raise problems with board members, shareholders and even with the Internal Revenue Service.

TWO-WAY DEAL

Businessmen are warned against testing doubtful schemes on their lawyers or CPAs. "The businessman does a double-think," says a New Jersey lawyer whose clients include several large companies. "He'll try to slip something by—inflating a crucial report, say—and if the lawyer or CPA lets it pass, he'll feel that somehow the idea has been purified."

Businessmen can expect to face a stiffer attitude from both lawyers and CPAs, since both professions have been shaken recently by well-publicized legal actions. The National Student Marketing Corp. case, which brought a string of indictments ending last year, involved false and misleading financial reports. The SEC complaint named, among others, one of Wall Street's most prestigious law firms, White & Case. On the accountants' side, the SEC last month censured Touche Ross & Co., a Big Eight firm, in connection with a San Diego securities fraud complaint against U.S. Financial, Inc., and others. This month Peat, Marwick, Mitchell & Co., another Big Eight member, was named a co-defendant in an SEC fraud complaint involving Republic National Life Insurance Co.

The mood of the accountants is summed by a prominent CPA in New York: "The ethical standard is on both sides. The auditor has a duty to investigate, but the businessman has a primary duty to report fairly."

Loose talk can cause trouble. White & Case partner Orison S. Marden, who was trial lawyer in the landmark Texas Gulf Sulphur case in the late 1960's, warns: "On the golf course or at the bridge table, a man may disclose information about his company and not realize that what he is saying is 'inside information' that might confront him later on in a courtroom."

You can land in hot water in dealing with your stock options in ways other than borrowing from the company at a bargain interest rate. Take the case, cited by a New York securities lawyer, of the executive who owns 3,000 shares of his company's stock and holds an option to buy 3,000 more. The option price is 10 and current market is 30. He sells 1,000 shares at 30 and buys 3,000 at 10. "The trouble is," says the lawyer, "he has an illegal profit—within the SEC's six-month insider trading rule."

NO EXCUSE

In today's climate, just sitting quiet and not asking questions can pose dangers for the executive. The 1968 BarChris decision held outside directors personally liable for the transgressions of a company. Lawyers now are quick to warn outside directors that ignoring what goes on within the company can mean trouble. Even if the director did not know, he still can be held liable because he should have.

Even the age-old game of padding the expense account draws fire from Justice Potter Stewart of the Supreme Court. "A lesser thing, like expense account chiseling, can undermine a man in time," he says. "It makes him prone to something more serious later on."

The Booby Traps in Everyday Lobbying

"In dealing with government," warns Supreme Court Justice Potter Stewart, "businessmen tend to be far too cynical. Too often they want a 'fixer'." That could not have been more apparent than during the Agnew and Watergate dramas this past year. Top corporations and corporate executives got into hot water for illegal contributions to Presidential campaigns, while corrupt politics at the local level led to the resignation of Spiro Agnew.

More than almost any other group in society, businessmen deal with government frequently and on every level, from Congress and the regulatory agencies in Washington to the hometown city council and zoning board. The ethical booby traps in all this are many—and sometimes scary.

You have every right, of course, to present your views—and present them forcefully—to elected and appointed officials. You can write, phone, or make a personal visit. But there is a line between what is reasonable and proper and what is not, and every businessman must learn how to draw that line.

Proper Examples

If you think you have a legitimate beef, do not be afraid to lean on your congressman. He is your representative in Washington and can often help. A St. Joseph (Mo.) company recently faced closing for lack of fuel. It appealed to Senator Thomas F. Eagleton for help—and got it. Eagleton's office bypassed the Federal Energy Office, called a major oil company directly, and got the fuel. And when some Delaware chemical companies thought they were getting less oil than they were entitled to, their state's senators jointly called an unofficial hearing to get all company information and then presented it to energy czar William Simon. Both approaches were direct, open, and entirely proper.

Representative Charles E. Bennett (D–Fla.) a longtime champion of setting stiff ethical standards for Congress, thinks you should go all out for legislation you support. Says Bennett: "Be vigorous. Pound the table for it even if the new law would make money for you. This is proper if you believe in it. What's wrong is to mislead as to your own personal interest."

Dealing with contract questions or with regulatory agencies is more ticklish. Seeking a congressman's direct help on a contract is out. Generally, he will do no more than request a "status report" or try to speed a dragging decision. But if you feel victimized—denied a contract even though you were low bidder, for example—your congressman might ask the General Accounting Office to look into it. That is standard procedure in Washington.

Do not hesitate to seek guidance in determining how to deal with a situation if you are inexperienced in the ways of Washington, your industry's trade association can give you some pointers. The local lobbyist can often be a goldmine of information—telling you whom to see, and whom not to see.

For the most part, a congressman will help a businessman from home without expecting direct favors in return. "But," says one veteran on Capitol Hill, "you'd be naive to think that a politician isn't more inclined to go out of his way for someone who helps him."

One way of helping him, of course, is with a personal campaign contribution—made in the normal way, and on the record. Offering one at the time you seek a favor, or even hinting of one in the future, is more than heavy-handed—it comes close to bribery.

Says Bennett: "Don't be confused by rationalizations such as 'others are doing it'—they're just garbage and make no difference."

Easy Does It

The facts of life in post-Watergate Washington are that a moderate personal campaign contribution—made at the next election—might well be in order. Only if private giving is banned by law will this change.

As to other gifts, the rule holds: "If you can eat it or drink it at one sitting, it's O.K." But birthday cigars, Christmas bottles, and such, have mostly faded from the picture. The topsy-turvy of political ethics is shown by the honorariums offered to congressmen when they make speeches —which are accepted by most. The range of fees is $300 to as high as $3,000.

Pretty much the same rules hold at the state and local government levels, with some important variations. One marked difference in working with state legislators is that you are almost forced by the surroundings to personalize your dealings. "The legislator has little staff or office space," notes Representative Thomas F. Railsbach (R–Ill.), who has had wide state and local government experience. "What you have to do is take your man to lunch and talk quietly. This is quite proper."

Railsbach and other professional politicians feel that there is no great difference in the basic attitudes at the state level. A smart businessman, says Railsbach, will be "low-key and noncoercive. Don't bluster because you are in your own state."

On state-level campaign contributions, one veteran political worker says: "Stay away from anything that smacks of a trade-off. Do it once, and you'll do it forever, and it will get more costly." Even if you are tempted to go along, the price of "going along" can dent the pocketbook.

Fight City Hall

On the local level, the businessman-government official relationship is even more personal—and often more treacherous—than at the state capital. The pressure to go along with the system can be intense, and staying above it can be hard. But Ambrose Lindhorst, a Cincinnati lawyer who spent 20 years in local politics, warns that condoning—"or suffering"—is the wrong way to deal with it. "Businessmen faced with kickbacks should get off their duffs and take action to clean things up at city hall," says Lindhorst. He argues that once you start making payoffs to policemen, building inspectors, and others, at "the curbstone level," you will be in for trouble. Once started, the practice never ends.

The thing to do in such a situation, says Lindhorst, is to try as strongly as you can to work with other businessmen to "flatten" graft. "If you 'go along,' you become responsible—you ask for it." he says.

Another problem is that dealings at the local government level can take you into contact with personal friends. You may have an old school chum or a country club crony who also happens to be the mayor, or a councilman, or a member of the zoning board. The question is how to proceed when your situation brings you in contact with the man. How close is too close? "There is nothing wrong with inviting your friend to lunch and presenting your problem," says Lindhorst, "as long as your position is legally sound and there is nothing clandestine about it."

No Year to Trifle With the IRS

The income tax form presents the businessman with one of the most agonizing ethical dilemmas he ever has to face. No matter how honest he sees himself, there is always the temptation to reach to the limit—and maybe a little beyond. And the way in which President Nixon has handled his taxes makes the dilemma all the more acute this year.

"The system of voluntary compliance is fragile at any time," says Sheldon S. Cohen, former Commissioner of Internal Revenue and now a Washington tax lawyer. "It won't crack, but it has been shaken."

The danger in 1974 is that even the businessman who normally files a perfectly straightforward return may try to stretch the rules this time—taking an overblown charitable deduction, perhaps, or listing some borderline travel and entertainment expenses. Yet, by all reports, the Nixon situation will make the IRS even tougher than usual this year. And even an innocent mistake on your return can mean an audit, and sometimes a penalty.

An audit can be time-consuming and infuriating. A penalty will cost you money, usually 6% of your total tax due, though IRS can also decide to audit your returns for the previous three years and penalties can pile up. The IRS seldom brings tax fraud charges in "gray-area" cases, but it can happen. At the least, that can mean some unfavorable newspaper publicity. Tax lawyers and advisers tick off three major areas where gray-area conflicts are likely to arise:

Donations

This is what tripped up Dr. Armand Hammer, chairman of Occidental Petroleum Corp., . . . He ran into well-publicized trouble with the IRS over deductions for donations of art works to charity. You can usually escape trouble if you have the work in question valued by two reputable appraisers. But other charitable deduction problems are getting more attention. Backdating a document proving a donation to charity is obviously one. Here the donor usually moves the date back across the Dec. 31 dateline, thus getting advantage of the deduction in the previous year. "Too many advisers and clients bend the truth to do this," notes Cohen. " 'Past intention' is used to justify it but it's flirting with fraud."

Travel and Entertainment

Here, the IRS seems to be paying most attention to the combination business–pleasure trip. "This is one of those gray cases where a little leeway is O.K., but there's been horrendous chiseling," says Michael Graetz, a former tax lawyer at the Treasury who is now teaching at the University of Virginia law school.

He cites the case of a businessman who takes his wife along on a business trip to the Caribbean. The question: Can the wife's costs be deducted?

"Say he pays $60 a night for a double room," says Graetz. "But the single rate is $40. He should deduct the $40, not the $60, and he knows it." There are federal appeals court cases, he explains, including *Disney* (1969). In that case, Roy Disney, Walt Disney's brother, convinced the court that his wife's expenses were deductible because she had assisted him in displaying a "family image" which was essential to his business.

"But a case like this," Graetz says, "is ammunition for the chiselers."

Shelters

Too many pitchmen have pushed too hard on tax shelters. IRS Commissioner Donald C. Alexander promised a crackdown last November, and some tax men believe it is now due.

Be especially careful about any shelter that offers an exceptionally big front-end deduction. An important Tax Court case, *Schultz* (1968), involving up-front deductions in a whiskey shelter, shows that reaching too far on these deductions can spell trouble. And the definition of "reaching too far" may be broadened. In a cattle-feeding deal, for example, writing off a huge feed bill at the start riles the IRS, and you might have to go to court to fight for the deduction.

Meanwhile, tax men are steering clients around other pitfalls. Here are some of current interest:

•*Fees for tax and investment advice are deductible. Fees for general legal work are not. Some businessmen have been hit by the IRS for writing off a personal lawyer's charge for both.*

•*Foreign bank accounts can cause trouble, warns Cohen. "Somebody says to a man at lunch, 'set up a Swiss account, everybody's doing it.'" Cohen explains. "He sets it up, and a year later is prosecuted for not reporting this on his 1040. The IRS has ways of picking up this sort of thing," he says.*

•*Interest paid on a loan to buy tax-exempt bonds is nondeductible. But income from tax-exempts is not shown on the 1040, so the interest deduction sometimes gets put on the form. Courts try hard, though, to protect the nondeduction rule. In a recent federal appellate court case, Mariorenzi (1974), the owner of some tax-exempts borrowed money from a bank. The court said that since he could have sold some of the bonds to raise money, part of the loan interest was not deductible.*

•*Lopsided real estate valuations can create problems for taxpayers. An investor will buy a building with land and place too much valuation on the building in relation to the land to pick up a bigger depreciation writeoff. But the IRS often unearths these cases.*

One of the most common traps is to follow the advice of a less than reputable tax man. Says David Kentoff, a tax lawyer with the Washington firm of Arnold & Porter: "You can't rid yourself of responsibility when you hire a tax man to do things you can't bring yourself to do."

When Not to Use 'Inside Information'

A businessman can make money from what he knows, and in years past many did—using inside information to make a killing in the market. But the rules about who is an insider and what constitutes inside information have been tightened in a series of cases, from Texas Gulf Sulphur to a Liggett & Myers case last year that helped define "public" information.

The hazard is that the new rules have not been drawn finely enough yet to follow without risking trouble.

You can get some idea of how "insider" is being defined these days by looking at the sort of people who have gotten into trouble.

Directors and top executives are clearly insiders. Department heads are too if they are privy to information not available to the general investing public. That holds true for lower-echelon people as well, such as the TGS geologist who talked about his company's Canadian mineral strike. And most experts believe that the definition of an insider will be extended still further. For example, you might get into trouble with the SEC by trading the stock of another company on the basis of information gained from it during merger negotiations. Other potential targets include longtime customers and suppliers of a company.

Be Close-Mouthed
The definition of what is inside information remains very fuzzy, and lawyers are telling clients to keep mum about company business outside the company. A good rule-of-thumb: Might a reasonable person make an investment decision based on the information that you provided?

You can be tagged a "tippee" and get in trouble simply by using material inside information gained from others. If you have a good reason to believe that what you have learned is no more than "street gossip," you are probably free to act as you choose. Otherwise, wait until the information has become public before acting—especially if you know that the original source of the information was himself an insider.

Even the definition of "public" is being broadened. The SEC insists that the public has not been adequately informed if the information in question has gone to just a few security analysts or is contained in a press release with limited distribution. For information to be public, it must be widely disseminated, and investors must have had adequate time to act upon it.

Do not expect early help from the SEC in the form of guidelines. Some have been promised, but the SEC will not say when.

SELECTED READINGS

Baumhart, R. C., *Ethics in Business.* (New York: Holt, Rinehart and Winston, Inc., 1968).

Berle, A. A., Jr., and G. C. Means, *The Modern Corporation and Private Property.* (New York: Macmillan, 1932); (Rev. Ed., New York: Harcourt, Brace and World, 1968).

Cyert, R. M., and J. G. March, *A Behavioral Theory of the Firm.* (Englewood Cliffs, N.J.: Prentice-Hall, 1963).

Galbraith, J. K., *The New Industrial State,* Rev. ed. (Boston: Houghton Mifflin, 1972).

McGuire, J. W., *Theories of Business Behavior.* (Englewood Cliffs, N.J.: Prentice-Hall, Inc., 1964).

Mintzberg, H., *The Nature of Managerial Work.* (New York: Harper and Row, 1973).

Monsen, R. J., Jr., and A. Downs, "A Theory of Large Managerial Firms," *Journal of Political Economy,* **73** (June, 1965); pp. 221–236.

Nader, R., and M. Green, *Corporate Power in America.* (New York: Grossman Publishers, 1973).

Reid, S. R., *Mergers, Managers, and the Economy.* (New York: McGraw-Hill, 1968).

Trebing, H. M., *The Corporation in the American Economy.* (Chicago: Quadrangle Books, 1970).

Case

SOCIETY LIFE INSURANCE COMPANY

Part I

In June of 1973, the Society Life Insurance Company was considering the matter of a corporate commitment, of both funds and human resources, to the fund-raising drive of the Essex Hospital Center, located in Salem, Massachusetts, which is also the location of Society's home office. This subject came up at a propitious time, since Society Life had already formally reviewed the topic of corporate citizenship or social responsibility.

COMPANY BACKGROUND

The Society Life Insurance Company is a mutual life insurance company; that is, its profits are returned to its policyholders through the declaration of dividends. Each policyholder, as a proportionate owner in the firm, has a vested interest in the firm's operations. Although the company has a favorable asset structure (over $300 million) and in-force policies representing over $1.3 billion of insurance, the Company is small by industry comparison, employing about 270 home-office personnel and ranking, in 1973, 200th in insurance volume among over 1,500 insurance companies. Exhibit A summarizes the Company's asset

---

This case was prepared by Nicholas Speranzo and Arthur Elkins as a basis for class discussion. While based on a true corporate situation, names, dates, places, and selected facts and figures have been changed.

© Copyright 1974 Nicholas Speranzo and Arthur Elkins.

and liability structure, and Exhibit B is a composite of its operating summary, both as of September 30, 1973.

Established in 1874, it has been only during the past decade and a half that the Company has enjoyed a rapid sales growth (an 8.2% in-force volume amount gain in 1972); its sales goal for the future is $2 billion of in-force insurance by 1980.

Such rapid sales growth has been achieved through an aggressive recruitment process for new salesmen in all of its forty-three agency offices in twenty-six states. Additionally, the Company offers a wide product line (Society deals in life, health, and mutual funds and is a recognized leader in noncancellable health coverages), competitive rates for its products, and a reputation as a small "blue-chip" firm. Because Society is small by industry comparison, the need to recruit and retain new agents is vital to its growth. (Currently, Society employs over 300 agents who sell exclusively for Society, and about 2,000 brokers who sell Society's as well as other insurers' products.)

An aggressive attitude has permeated the Company's outlook on corporate citizenship as well. Many of Society's executives serve as chairmen or committeemen on various fund-raising drives. Society has been an active supporter of the United Way campaign drives, and its executives have served as officers on Cerebral Palsy fund-raising drives, the Association of Business and Commerce, and various civic associations and campaign drives. Currently, the Company's President, Mr. Frank Seward, is the chairman of the Essex Hospital Center's fund-raising drive.

GENERAL FACTORS INFLUENCING THE COMPANY'S SOCIAL RESPONSIBILITY POSITION

Society Life, in an effort to determine how much of its resources should be expended toward fulfilling its social responsibilities, had recently spent $15,000 to participate in a research study involving several other insurance companies, as well as a variety of other firms. The results of the study, prepared by the Institute for Social Research located in Hartford, Connecticut, indicated:

a) Society Life spent, relative to the other firms surveyed, about the median percentage of its income and per capita employee time on activities falling under the category of corporate citizenship.

b) Based on other insurance companies of comparable size either participating in the study or about whom data was available, Society Life was in the top five percentiles for corporate giving and executive or employee time spent on "socially responsible" activities.

While the results of the study were interesting from a statistical perspective, Society's top management felt they were inconclusive, and that no concrete decision could be made, based on this study, as to the appropriateness of Society's pledge to the areas of social responsibility. Far more concrete, however, were several political and financial factors that loomed on the horizon:

1. Society Life, as one of several Massachusetts-based insurers, has been engaged in an intensive lobbying effort to change the state tax structure for home-based insurance companies. Essentially, in 1972, the State had increased the tax rate for domestic insurance companies, while leaving unchanged its tax structure for out-of-state insurers writing business in Massachusetts. Society and other insurance companies felt this resulted in an unfair competitive burden on domestic companies. In 1972, Society's state tax liability increased from its 1971 figure of $140,000 to $300,000.

2. The aggressive recruitment process Society had initiated for prospective salesmen continued to be a financial drain on current profits. New agents, whose income is subsidized by the Company for a period of 36 to 48 months, have a failure rate of 60%; often, in such cases, repayment of the subsidized portion of their income is impossible. In 1973 (see also Exhibit B), the dollar amount invested in the field sales staff increased $266,530, from $1,882,830 in 1972 to $2,149,360.

3. To continue its growth pace and achieve its 1980 goal of $2 billion of in-force insurance, Society Life has begun the laborious procedure of being licensed in all fifty states. (Currently, Society is licensed to write business in only twenty-six states.) It is hoped that this move, coupled with continued recruitment of quality salesmen, will bring further sales impetus as new sales territories, especially California, are explored.

4. The Company's entrance into the mutual-fund business, considered at the time to be a natural outgrowth of its insurance and financial interests, was ill-timed. Through its subsidiary, Society Equity Sales, the Company began its mutual-fund venture in 1968, and the disastrous results have kept mutual-fund sales low and profits in this area almost nonexistent.

5. While a recognized leader in health insurance, the Company, as of July 1, 1973, stopped writing hospital and major-medical coverages due to an unfavorable premium/claims loss ratio, an occurrence that has been industrywide and that has prompted similar action by many companies. The effect of this decision will eventually reduce the amount of the Company's claim payments as these policies lapse or terminate;

however, in the short run, adverse claims experience will still be present for this small but expensive line of business.

6. Society Life has also been subject to another industry trend—a significant increase in the number and amount of policy loans. This is due to policy provisions providing a stated interest rate on such loans of 5 or 6 percent, well below bank-loan rates. In 1973, there has been an outflow of over $4,000,000 to policy-owners for such loans, causing a continuous drain on the Company's cash position. (It might also be noted that with an interest rate of 5 or 6 percent there is little if any incentive to repay such loans.)

ESSEX HOSPITAL CENTER

The Essex Hospital Center is the largest of the two hospitals serving Salem, Massachusetts, and the surrounding communities. It is the only area hospital with maternity facilities and cobalt and X-ray treatment centers. In 1962, Essex Hospital merged with the now nonexistent Fairview Hospital to provide better and more economical service to the area communities, and to increase its patient capacity.

Presently, the Essex Hospital Center can accommodate over 300 patients on an in-patient basis. Room rates vary from $65 per day for wards to $190 per day for intensive care. While Essex Hospital has repeatedly offered to merge with the Clinic Hospital, also in Salem, on the basis of economy, better total service through a single cooperating staff and further expanded patient facilities and accommodations, Clinic has just as adamantly refused the offer.

CLINIC HOSPITAL

Clinic Hospital, the city's only other hospital, is small in comparison to the Essex Hospital Center. Clinic has facilities for 144 patients; it offers no maternity facilities or sophisticated cobalt and X-ray clinics. Clinic Hospital has maintained, throughout the merger controversy, that the total community can well afford two hospitals.

Clinic contends that a merger would result in a larger hospital bureaucracy with more "red tape" and, with no competition for hospital services, even higher hospital costs. Clinic's room rates are $65 per day for semiprivate rooms (it has no ward facilities) and $100 per day for intensive care. Clinic has also indicated that the only benefits to be gained from a merger would be a standardization of medical facilities and uniform doctor and nurse care quality, subjects which Clinic contends each hospital can just as well administer separately as together.

Both the Clinic Hospital and the Essex Hospital Center are engaged in fund-raising drives at the present time. Essex Hospital's fund-raising goal is $5 million over a three-year period; Clinic's fund-raising goal, though unannounced, is known to be more modest.

THE HOSPITAL FUND DECISION

In June of 1973, Mr. Seward met with the Board of Directors and the senior officers of the Company to decide on the Company's posture on the Essex Hospital Center's fund-raising drive. As Chairman of the drive, Mr. Seward noted: "Society Life has long recognized its responsibility, as a public citizen, to the community in which it resides. This commitment to the community can best be expressed in a corporate gift to Essex Hospital Center's fund-raising drive."

In addition, Seward cited the following three factors as important considerations for support of the Essex Hospital Center.

1. The insurance industry has a vested, albeit principally financial, interest in the health-care industry. Rising hospital costs have engendered ever-higher insurance premiums for health coverages. As noted earlier, Society, as well as many other insurance companies, abandoned the health-insurance field as a result of poor claims experience. Such adverse premium/claims ratios are, in great part, a reflection of both higher claims costs and the reluctance of state insurance commissioners in general to grant premium increases on such coverages when needed.

2. Inasmuch as the premiums for the Company's group employee health coverage (underwritten by Blue Cross/Blue Shield) are based on individual company experience, for which Society absorbs 55% of the cost as an employee benefit, the gift to the Essex Hospital Center would be an expedient one. It would, in the long run, both reduce the cost of such coverage and increase the quality of health care for its employees and the community in general.

3. An urban medical facility, as envisioned by the Essex Hospital Center, would enhance the area's attractiveness to other firms interested in new plant location sites. The further development of the area would result in lower taxes due to a larger and more diversified tax base, increased employment and a higher standard of living for the community.

Seward proposed that a "soft-sell" in-house solicitation be conducted. This, he felt, should best be spearheaded by an officer of the Company.

The Senior Vice President of the Investment Division, Mr. Berrigan, and the Vice President of Personnel, Mr. House, both expressed concern for this proposal in the following areas:

a) The subtlety of the in-house solicitation

Both Mr. Berrigan and Mr. House felt that, if improperly handled, an in-house fund-raising campaign might alienate some employees. This possibility was further enhanced by Mr. Seward's position as Chairman of the drive.

b) The Clinic fund-raising drive

Mr. House noted: "If we give to your drive, are we compelled to give to Clinic's drive? Any controversy about this gift could cause adverse publicity at a time when we need public support the most." Mr. House was referring directly to the proposed legislative change on the home-based tax-structure issue, an effort in which Society had asked for public support.

c) Financial considerations

Both Berrigan and House expressed concern over the size of the gift to either or both drives, especially in view of the Company's growth plans and its increasing expenditures to achieve these goals.

EXHIBIT A

Society Life Insurance Company
Balance Sheet
September 30, 1973
(All amounts rounded to nearest thousand)

Assets		*Liabilities*	
Cash	$ 2,707	Reserves	$254,238
Bonds	129,041	Accrued dividends and	
Stocks		proceeds	30,435
Preferred	1,481	Premiums in advance	2,045
Common	7,905	Unpaid claims	1,343
Mortgages and real		Premium taxes	220
estate	125,951	Securities valuation	
Policy loans	44,083	reserve	1,474
Accrued income	9,876	Dividend liability	6,026
Other assets	4,427	Reserve for prior years'	
		Federal income tax	450
		Other liabilities	7,092
		Total Liabilities	$303,323
		Surplus	22,148
		Total Liabilities and	
Total Assets	$325,471	Capital	$325,471

EXHIBIT B

Society Life Insurance Company
Summary of Operations
For the Year Ending
September 30, 1973
(Nearest Thousand)

Receipts

Cash premiums (adjusted for unpaid and in-advance premiums)	$29,366	
Reinsurance premiums paid	−663	
Earned premium income		$28,703
Gross investment income		13,888
Miscellaneous income		61
Total income		$42,652

Disbursements

Death benefits, surrenders, endowments, other paid benefits	$18,876	
Home office expenses	3,693	
Commissions	3,547	
Field expenses	2,149	
Insurance, real estate taxes and fees, depreciation	2,481	
		$30,746
Gain from Operations		$11,906
Less: Reserve liability	$ 5,963	
Dividends	4,310	
F.I.T.	1,052	
Surplus adjustment	491	
		$11,816
New Surplus		$ 90
Beginning surplus	$22,058	
New surplus	90	
Total Surplus	$22,148	

Part II

In June of 1973, Society Life allowed an in-house solicitation for the Essex Hospital Center's fund-raising drive. This solicitation was aimed at three levels: the officers of the company, the management staff, and the clerical staff. This solicitation was handled on a very low-key level, as follows:

1. Mr. Ames, a soft-spoken man who is also the Claims Director, was chosen to be chairman of the in-house solicitation. He held several short meetings with small groups of the Company's officers, at which he outlined the goals of the drive and the communities' needs. Each group was encouraged to contribute and given a brochure containing literature on the services the Essex Hospital Center provides, as well as a pledge form.

2. A general one-hour meeting of the management staff was held on a variety of subjects. At this meeting, Mr. Ames made a ten-minute presentation on the in-house drive, stressing that the contribution was purely a matter of personal choice. As he had done with the officers, he distributed brochures and pledges and stressed salary deduction as the preferable contribution route. Mr. Ames made no attempt to contact any employees beyond this initial presentation.

3. A general all-staff memorandum was distributed to the clerical and management staff, encouraging a contribution to the Essex Hospital Center's drive. The letter was signed by Mr. Ames and attached were pledge cards for any employees desiring to make a contribution.

Three weeks later, in early July of 1973, it was announced at a management meeting that the Company had donated $125,000 to the Essex Hospital Center's fund-raising drive. It was also announced that the Company's employees had contributed an additional $26,000 in pledges over a three-year period. It was also announced that Clinic Hospital would be allowed to solicit contributions for their fund drive at the Company's exits and entrances later that week.

PART II
PROBLEMS

A. *New Lifestyles and Corporate Response*

Hardly a single day passes that the news media does not have an article or two on the changing lifestyles of Americans and the effect of those changes upon employee attitudes toward work, assembly lines, or corporate life in general. More and more, we hear of young operative workers rebelling against the pace, monotony, and powerlessness involved in repetitive work, or of young executives opting out of the corporate "rat race."

Changing lifestyles encompass an entire spectrum of personal and group behaviors and attitudes, and form the fulcrum for significant changes in outlook toward work and the organization. The bases of changing lifestyles run deeper than the superficial facades of long hair and modish clothes.

In this introduction, we examine some of these bases, then some of the changes, and finally some of the impacts that changing lifestyles have brought to the workplace.* We briefly comment on some managerial response.

Specifically, what are the differences that separate today's generation from those of before? Most assuredly, today's younger people generally are better educated and more affluent than any preceding generation. As a result they have had exposure to fewer basic deprivations and fewer constraints on their thoughts. They have been exposed to more ideas and concepts and their aspirations for using their creative faculties are higher. Their education has given them higher expectations

---

*Obviously these changes have ramifications in the market as well as the workplace. While we shall not cover marketing here, we should note the irony in the fact that while many firms resist changing lifestyles in the workplace, they are more than accommodating to them in the marketplace.

and their affluence makes them much less tolerant of psychically unrewarding activity. Indeed the powerlessness to be creative and the inability to be one's own master, coupled with the sheer size, complexity, and power of organizations with which younger people come in contact, fuel many of the frustrations of younger aspiring men and women.

Allied to affluence and education is the fact that traditional patterns of authority in society are being challenged. If, on the outside, people are successful in using the courts, are challenging elected officials, are critically examining the dogmas of religion, are violating the taboos of society and, in the case of students, are confronting and receiving concessions from college administrators, then it is foolish to assume that such challenges would not penetrate the corporate structure.

Finally, the civil-rights movement engendered a greater stress on equality, not simply between racial groups, but for differing classes as well. So even people whose education or affluence are in the lower ranges are demanding their rights and expressing values similar to those of the highly trained and relatively affluent.

The lifestyle revolution manifests itself in myriad ways. The obvious, of course, are dress and styling. Your authors find so few students wearing anything but denim jeans today that when a student shows up in class "dressed up," we can be sure that some interviewer is on campus. But dress is superficial and masks the true changes, although changing dress standards have forced concessions in corporate offices, fancy restaurants, and formal gatherings.

More important are the changing values toward work, sex, religion, material possessions, housing, and other institutions, once governed by what we thought were inviolate, established norms. The press does an adequate job of covering attitudes toward sex, religion, marriage, and such social topics. We should like to center on the outlook toward work and the implications that outlook has for the firm.

The so-called work ethic was a key governing value in our society. Briefly, the work ethic stressed the value of work for its own sake, as well as the belief that hard work pays off in the end. In a romantic, Horatio Alger sense, Americans generally believed that the pot of gold lay at the end of the rainbow and that hard work would get you there.

The work-ethic view is now being challenged and tested severely. In a series of surveys of college students, conducted by Daniel Yankelovich, the drop in numbers believing that "hard work will pay off" was astounding. In 1968, 69 percent agreed with the idea that work pays off, while in 1971, the number dropped to 39%. Obviously events since then may change the data—many observers now see students "going straight" again—but the astonishing drop in just three years must be recognized as significant in demonstrating the fragility of a long-cherished value.

The real test of change in the work ethic, however, comes not from surveys, but in the workplace—what changes take place in the actual behavior and attitudes of people on their jobs? The evidence seems to be bearing out the thesis that outlooks toward jobs and work are changing markedly. Operative workers rebel at the dirty, boring tasks that their fathers and grandfathers grudgingly accepted and that generations of management consultants extolled as "efficient." Loyalty to one's employer may be an anachronism; loyalty to one's peer group becomes more important. Turnover rates in many plants and industries are increasing rapidly. Personal needs take precedence over organizational plans and schedules; for example, absenteeism is becoming epidemic for many firms, and employees feel no qualms in routinely taking days off.

All of this poses extremely difficult decision-making situations for management. Recruiting is becoming extremely difficult; one employer recently hired 20 young people through a special section of his state's employment service. The new employees were trained for routine jobs that required relatively little skill. Inside of four days, not one of these new employees still remained with the company. They simply rebelled at the routine work.

Work design is no longer a simple, readily accepted, engineering process. The most celebrated case, of course, involves the General Motors Corporation Vega plant at Lordstown, Ohio. Considered one of the most advanced plants in the world, the Lordstown installation used the latest in auto-building technology, including the use of robots and advanced and novel shipping techniques. Eventually, GM engineered the plant to produce one hundred cars an hour. But the workers, mostly young, rebelled at the pace demanded by the line. A twenty-two day strike idled some 10,000 employees. Speedup, job monotony, and the inability of workers to gain some voice in decisions affecting their assembly lines were all cited as factors. Discontent still exists at Lordstown and periodically strikes and protests erupt.

Even more significant than that one strike, however, is the fact that unions are raising the issue of "humanization of the workplace" in collective-bargaining negotiations. Traditionally and through the 1960's, unions emphasized wages, job security, seniority, unemployment benefits, overtime, and other such items. In essence, union demands reinforced the assumption of classical management theory that sufficient extrinsic rewards could buy someone to occupy almost any job at the workplace. That picture is changing as unions raise the job-design issue, the pace of the line, decision-making on the job, and other conditions formerly considered prerogatives of management.

The changes in lifestyle and the resultant modification of the work ethic are just as pronounced at the management level as they are at the operative level. Only a few years ago, the man in the gray flannel suit was the stereotype of a successful business executive; two or three hours of commuting on a dirty, hot, and crowded milk-run train were accepted as the standard pain of success. Today we hear of executives suffering the same boredom and role conflict that operatives do. We see them complaining of the meaninglessness of their work, their powerlessness in large, complex, bureaucratic organizations, their frustrations at competing in a "rat race," and their dissatisfaction at being beholden to dollars. In short, growing numbers of executives are finding corporate life intrinsically unrewarding in comparison to alternative careers. We see executives in larger numbers dropping out of the system, to take up lives of mysticism, rural farm living, handcrafting, or small business.

How do corporations respond to the new environment from which they draw their most important resource—employees and executives? Some do nothing, of course, on the assumption that enough people imbued with the work ethic will still be looking for jobs, or that new lifestyles are just a passing fancy. In many cases, they could be right, but they must be prepared to suffer the possible increased absenteeism and turnover accompanying their wait-and-see strategy. On the other hand, many organizations are engaging in job enlargement, job enrichment, team production, flexible hours and flexible-day scheduling, and similar techniques designed to reduce monotony and boredom and increase workers' participation in the planning for their own jobs. On the managerial level, some corporations are dropping dress codes and status differentials, and are enlarging the scope of work as well. Experiments with flexible arrivals and departures are also being conducted. Perhaps the best known undertaking is that of McDonald's new corporate headquarters—work areas are designed with no fixed walls and a waterbed room is available for personnel to relax and unwind.

We mention some of these techniques only briefly since this is not a book on organization design. But the changes in organizations are necessitated by changes in their environment; and the alert organizations and managements are the ones that can forecast these changes, understand them, and deal with them effectively.

THE READINGS

"Who Will Do The Dirty Work Tomorrow?" by Edward Faltermayer (from *Fortune*) is an interesting piece on the limits to filling the so-called menial tasks that have little possibility of being mechanized. Faltermayer describes some of the mechanisms that firms and organizations might have to use to induce people to take on the "dirty work." He also finds some surprising groups of people cleaning, hauling, washing dishes, and waiting on tables. Yet admittedly, the costs are high —turnover and absenteeism among the most serious ones.

Barbara Garson's "Luddites in Lordstown" is a no-holds-barred (albeit admittedly unscientific) investigation into workers' attitudes at that much publicized plant. Touring the plant, talking with workers, even spending some time at an auto-workers' commune, Ms. Garson poignantly captures the essence of worker aspirations in the face of assembly-line production methods.

Finally we include two articles (from *DUN'S*) that center on managers in this age of changing values. In the first article, "Management—Sitting on a Time Bomb?", George J. Berkwitt writes about managers who opt out of the corporate world and the reasons why they go. Most of the reasoning seems to center on a sense of frustration or powerlessness, or on the perceived lack of reciprocal loyalty exhibited by corporations to managers who "work their tails off." In the second article, "Top Management—and Turned-off Executives," Robert Levy reports on a survey of three hundred corporate presidents and chairmen. Some top managers seem sympathetic with the aspirations of frustrated middle managers, and call for carefully thought out programs for top management to communicate with and nurture aspiring young middle mangers. Others are less sympathetic. Some blame business schools for raising aspiration levels too high. Still others contend that only misfits leave industry while innovative managers stay on. What becomes clearest from these two articles is the existence of multiple perceptions of the problem and differing approaches to possible corporate response.

Who Will Do
the Dirty Work
Tomorrow?

Edmund Faltermayer

In the computer age, millions of men and women still earn wages by carrying food trays, pushing brooms, shoveling dirt, and performing countless other menial tasks in ways that haven't changed much in centuries. Traditionally, these jobs have been taken by people with no choice: high-school dropouts, immigrants with language difficulties, members of racial minorities, women, and young people (as well as unemployed family heads in desperate straits and disproportionate numbers of ex-convicts, alcoholics, the mentally retarded, and people with personality disorders). But various currents of change—including egalitarianism, rising expectations, and ever-more-generous government programs of support for nonworkers—are tending to make it harder to fill such jobs as time goes by. Some observers, indeed, foresee an eventual drying up of the pool of labor available to do menial work.

Yet many of these "jobs of last resort," as they have been called, involve essential tasks that it would be difficult to dispense with or to mechanize. Under the pressure of rising wages, the U.S. has traveled far down the road of reducing menial labor, which currently engages somewhere between 10 and 15 percent of the working population. But we are approaching the limits of how far we can go, or wish to go.

NO REPLACEMENT FOR ELBOW GREASE

On farms, for example, machines have replaced most manual toil. But a visit to California's Imperial Valley, one of the most efficient agricultural regions in the U.S., reveals that a surprising amount of "stoop" labor still survives. At construction sites, machines now do most of the heavy digging, but men with shovels still must work behind them. Much of the restaurant industry has shifted to self-service and throwaways, but growing numbers of Americans want to dine out in conventional fashion, with the food served on china plates.

In an effort to simplify cleaning, developers have modified the design of new office buildings, stores, and hotels, and industry now supplies improved chemicals and equipment. But Daniel Fraad Jr., chairman of Allied Maintenance Corp., which cleans offices, factories, and passenger terminals across the U.S., sees few remaining breakthroughs in productivity. Years ago, he says, his company abandoned a mechanical wall-washing device after it was found to be less efficient than a man with a sponge. Says Fraad, himself a former window washer: "In the final analysis, cleaning is elbow grease."

All this helps explain why the century-long process in which Americans have been moving out of low-status jobs is decelerating and may even be reversing. Productivity in the remaining menial occupations is growing more slowly than in most other fields, and shorter working hours often necessitate larger working staffs even where the amount of work remains the same. According to the Department of Labor, the percentage of Americans who were either "nonfarm laborers" or "service workers" was higher in 1972 than in 1960.

Declines in some menial jobs, most notably maids and housekeepers, have been more than offset by increases in other occupations. The 1970 census showed 1,250,000 "janitors" at work in the U.S., up from 750,000 a decade earlier. In the same period the ranks of unskilled hospital workers, i.e., "nursing aides, orderlies and attendants," rose by nearly 80 percent to 720,000, and the number of "garbage collectors" doubled. Between now and 1985, the Bureau of Labor Statistics has predicted, openings in many low-status jobs will increase faster than total employment.

DESPERATION IN DALLAS

But who, in this era when the Army feels compelled to abolish K.P., will want to wait on tables, empty bedpans or, for that matter, bury the dead? In some cities it's already hard to keep menial jobs filled. In the booming Dallas region, with its unemployment rate of only 2.1 percent, jobs for waitresses, private guards, trash collectors, and busboys were recently going begging.

One restaurant owner who is short of "bus help" revealed that his current roster consists of an illiterate black man in his fifties, a white girl who is somewhat retarded, a divorced white man in his sixties with personality problems, and an unattached white man in his forties "who goes out and gets drunk each day after he finishes his shift."

In slack labor markets such as Boston, where the unemployment rate has been running above the recent national figure of 4.7 percent, employers are experiencing troubles of a different sort. There seem to be enough people to fill most menial jobs, but they just don't stay around.

At the popular Sheraton-Boston Hotel, the turnover among chambermaids is about 150 percent a year. On pleasant weekends, when absenteeism runs high, the hotel hurriedly telephones local college students on a standby list. Down in the kitchens, turnover among dishwashers on the night shift exceeds a phenomenal 400 percent a year. Sometimes, the hotel has to ask the local U.S.O. to send over Navy men on shore leave who want to earn some extra money by helping out in the kitchens.

THE INCENTIVES *NOT* TO WORK

In Boston, as in many other cities outside the South, liberal welfare benefits make it possible for a great many people to stay out of the labor market if they don't like the work and wages available. Stricter administration of welfare, currently being attempted in a number of states, may remove some cheaters and induce some other recipients to work. Under a 1971 provision of federal law, welfare mothers with no preschool children are required to register for work. But it would be unrealistic to expect a tightening effective enough to make any large number of welfare recipients take menial jobs.

A number of factors besides increasingly generous welfare have been eroding the supply of people available for menial work. Perhaps the leading expert on this subject is economist Harold Wool of the National Planning Association. Wool points out that during the Sixties society's efforts to keep young people in school reduced the number of dropouts entering the labor force. At the same time, he says, the U.S. drew down much of its remaining "reserve" of rural labor migrating to cities.

Most important of all, minority groups, especially blacks, began pushing in earnest toward equality in employment. According to Wool's reckoning, black young men with at least one year of college (but not teen-agers or young women) have actually achieved occupational parity with their white counterparts. This remarkable social achievement has been too little noticed.

Today a great many young black people refuse to take jobs they consider demeaning. Wool observes that while a decade ago 20 percent of the black young women who had graduated from high school worked as domestics, only 3 percent were settling for that kind of work in 1970. "The service-type job," he says, "has become anathema to many blacks, even on a temporary basis." This helps explain why some service jobs are hard to fill even in cities where unemployment among young black people runs at dismayingly high rates.

It seems clear, then, that in years ahead the traditional supply of menial workers will not meet the demand. Some work will go undone. Many prosperous families whose counterparts even a decade ago would have employed household help now get along without any. Corners are clipped in services. Some restaurants, for example, have reduced the number of items on their menus, which among other things trims the customer's decision-making time and enables the waitress to move along faster.

THE $12,886-A-YEAR TRASHMEN

But a lot of menial work will have to be done, one way or another. Society will have to respond to the tightening of the labor supply by improving pay and working conditions. Right now there are many places where the federal minimum wage of $1.60 an hour cannot buy work. In northern cities, even members of the so-called "secondary labor force"—women and young people whose pay supplements a family's principal source of income—are usually not willing to work for $1.60. For those groups, $2 to $2.50 is the real market "minimum" needed to balance supply and demand.

It may be a portent of things to come that New York City now pays its unionized sanitation men $12,886 a year (plus an ultraliberal pension). Hardly anybody ever quits, and thousands of men are on a waiting list for future job openings. At Chrysler Corp., unskilled "material handlers," whose job includes pushing carts around the plant floor by hand, get $4.90 an hour, which draws plenty of young married men, both white and black.

At Boston's Massachusetts General Hospital, the minimum starting pay for "dietary service aides" and "building service aides" is $2.78, more than local hotels pay busboys and chambermaids. But even so, few native Bostonians, black or white, are entering such jobs these days. Most of the hospital's recent hires for entry-level jobs are immigrants from Jamaica and other Caribbean islands, or recent black arrivals from the rural South.

HIGH STANDARDS FOR SWABBING DOWN

Higher pay, if it's high enough, clearly helps improve the status of menial work. Another way to improve its status is to raise the quality and complexity of the work itself. Some of the credit for a fairly low turnover rate at Massachusetts General Hospital goes to a training program begun in 1968 for those "building service aides," who previously had gone by the relatively servile titles of "maid" and "houseman."

The one-month program, which involves eighty hours in a classroom and a loose-leaf manual resembling one used by higher-skilled workers at the hospital, is not mere industrial-relations gimmickry. "Janitorial work in a hospital is different than in an office building," says Ruth MacRobert, the hospital's personnel director. "Here they need to learn aseptic techniques, and the fact that they can't use slippery compounds that might cause a patient to trip and fall. If there's a spill, they can't leave broken glass lying around. It's a lot different than swabbing down a deserted office. Who cares if the John Hancock Building is wet and slippery after hours?"

A pleasanter work climate can also help make low-status work less lowly. Lack of amenity on the job is particularly noticeable in the clangorous kitchens where some of the country's 2,860,000 food service workers earn their living. Jan Lovell, president of the Dallas Restaurant Association, believes his industry is improving the work atmosphere but will have to do more in order to survive. In the most menial jobs, he says, "we used to have a tradition of taking the dregs of society off the street and working them twelve hours a day." This, he says, was bad for management as well as the worker.

"A few years ago it wasn't unusual for a restaurant to buy a $12,000 dishwashing machine and then hire two drunks or wetbacks at $75 a week who might forget to turn the water on. Today you pay one guy $150 a week who does the work of two. But maybe we also need to put in a radio and a rug on the floor. The restaurant business has been hot, dirty, and sweaty. Who needs it?"

TO REPLACE A "VANISHING BREED"

Still another strategy is to make menial jobs a stepping-stone to something better. Texas Instruments, for example, offers a prospect of advancement to anyone who signs on to push a broom. Six years ago, in an effort to get better-quality work (and save money too), T.I. terminated contracts with outside cleaning firms and created a staff of its own to clean its factories and offices in the Dallas area. As in so many menial occupations, the staff has a nucleus of mature people who never aimed much higher in life, a majority of them black men in their fifties and sixties who in one supervisor's words are "a vanishing breed."

To lure younger replacements, the company offers a starting wage of $2.43 an hour, exactly the same as in production, and allows anyone to seek a transfer after six months. And like other T.I. employees, the sweepers are entitled to an exceptional fringe benefit: 90 percent of the cost of part-time education.

In a way, though, "promotability" makes it even harder to maintain a staff. Over the course of a year about 40 percent of T.I.'s "cleaning service attendants" move on to other jobs within the company, in addition to the 36 percent who quit or retire. One recently arrived janitor who is already looking around is Willie Gibson, a soft-spoken, twenty-year-old high-school graduate. Willie has been talking to "the head man in the machine shop" about the possibilities of a transfer. "There ain't nothing wrong with cleaning," he says, "It's got to be done. But me, I feel I can do better."

Texas Instruments is forced to search ceaselessly for replacements, who these days include Mexican-Americans and a few whites as well as blacks. Recruiting methods have included the announcement of janitorial vacancies from the pulpit of a black church.

A MAGNET FOR ILLEGALS

Until the early 1920's, immigration provided an abundant supply of menial workers. And recent years have seen something of a resurgence. Legal immigration has grown to 400,000 a year and now accounts for a fifth of the country's population growth. While many of the newcomers are professionals from the Philippines and India, the ranks also include a great many unskilled men and women from Mexico, the West Indies, and South America.

In addition, it is estimated that between one million and two million illegal aliens are at large in the U.S., mostly employed in low-status jobs. And the number of illegal aliens, whatever it may be, is undoubtedly growing. "Suddenly, in the last few months, there have been more of the illegals," says an official of the Texas Employment Commission in Dallas. The hiring of illegal immigrants is against the law in Texas, and the federal Immigration and Naturalization Service periodically rounds some of them up and deports them. But the very low unemployment rate in Dallas, the official says, acts as a magnet pulling in the illegals, who work mainly in small enterprises that are not scrupulous about observing the law.

In northern cities, illegal immigration began to increase during the late 1960's. New York City alone may have as many as 250,000 illegals, including Chinese and Greeks as well as Haitians, Dominicans, and other Latin Americans. Such people can be an employer's dream. Often they have no welfare or unemployment compensation to fall back on, since applying for such assistance could reveal their existence to the authorities. In an era of liberal income-maintenance programs for the native population, says New York State Industrial Commissioner Louis Levine, such people "have a total incentive to work."

TOWARD SELF-SUFFICIENCY IN DIRTY WORK

To rely on increasing numbers of immigrants to perform menial jobs, however, is to put off true long-range solutions to the problem. Sooner or later, every mature nation intent upon keeping its cultural identity will have to figure out a way to get most of the work done with its own native-born.

The U.S. cannot, and should not, close the door to all immigration, but a crackdown on illegal immigrants seems overdue. In addition to penalties against employers who hire illegal immigrants, an effective crackdown might require some device such as identity cards for all citizens. While repugnant to many Americans, such controls have long been a fact of life in France.

The U.S. is in a better position than most countries to move toward a state of "self-sufficiency in dirty work." Americans are generally free of Europe's ingrained class consciousness, and under certain conditions are rather flexible about the jobs they will take. And in recent years, in fact, white Americans have been moving into low-status jobs as black Americans move out. Most of these native-born recruits to menial work are women or young people.

In view of all the attention given to the women's liberation movement in recent years, it may seem paradoxical that many women have been moving into the lower end of the occupational scale. But there is not really any paradox. The desire of *some* women to pursue careers in managerial and professional fields should certainly not preclude employment of a different kind of woman in a different kind of situation—the woman who is not a breadwinner and does not want a career, but who does want the freedom to divide her life between housekeeping and periods of work that entail no encumbering commitments between employer and employee.

A lot of these women are in jobs that are fairly pleasant, and whose "menialness" has more to do with society's prevailing view than the nature of the work itself. Some restaurant work falls into this category. That is the opinion, for example, of Peggy Easter, middle-aged white woman who waits on tables at Jan's Restaurant, a moderate-priced but clean and well-run establishment in a Dallas suburb. "Some people look down on this kind of work," she says. "But there's an art to this, and I like the hectic, fast pace because I have lots of nervous energy."

Like many waiters and waitresses, Mrs. Easter works only part time, coming in for three and a half hours each day during lunchtime. Her only child is married and her husband works full time as a diesel mechanic. With growing numbers of married women wanting to get out of the house, it is reasonable to expect that more Peggy Easters will turn up in the years ahead.

A BULGE FROM THE BABY BOOM

Young white people have moved into low-status jobs in even greater numbers than women. In 1960, according to census data, only 8 percent of the country's janitors were young whites under twenty-five. By 1970 that figure had jumped to 22 percent. Some of the movement of white young men *down* the occupational status scale (which partly accounts for that "parity" between blacks and whites who went to college) is a result of the postwar baby boom. Many of the young janitors, kitchen workers, and construction laborers are part-time workers from the ballooning population of high-school and college students. Others are full-time employees who, meeting heavy competition for jobs from their numerous contemporaries, have taken menial jobs until they can find something better. Another factor here is that many young whites live in the suburbs, where fast-food and other service jobs have grown more rapidly than in the cities.

Because the baby boom began waning in the late 1950's, the bulge in the number of employable young people will begin to recede during the middle and late 1970's. During the current decade as a whole, the sixteen to twenty-four age group will increase by 16 percent—somewhat less than the entire labor force, and far less than the phenomenal 48 percent growth during the Sixties.

To some extent, however, this demographic slowdown could be offset by a reduction in school hours, particularly in the high-school years. A growing number of educators and sociologists favor more part-time exposure of teenagers to the working world, where they can benefit by rubbing shoulders with adults. One principal at a high school in the Northeast confided not long ago that all the basic material in his three-year curriculum, including the courses necessary for entering college, could be given in half the time. Not many principals, perhaps, would go that far, but certainly high-school education is now a very inefficient process. Any reduction in classroom time, of course, would make more teen-agers available for work, and much of that would be work generally considered menial.

AGAINST THE GRAIN

In any event, it seems reasonable to expect that young people will be taking on more of those dirty jobs. According to a well-entrenched American tradition, almost unthinkable in much of Europe, it is healthy for sons and daughters of the middle class to wait on tables, scrub pots, and even clean toilets as part of their "rites of initiation" into the world of work. Late in the nineteenth century, the American author Edward Bellamy, in the Utopian novel *Looking Backward,* foresaw a day when all the onerous tasks of society would be performed by young people during a three-year period of obligatory service.

A formal period of "national youth service," a proposal that has been revived in recent years, runs against the American grain. But less extreme policies to encourage the employment of more young people would be a step in the right direction. Lots of young people might welcome earlier introduction to the world of work, especially high-school students, who these days seem increasingly inclined to work anyway.

"DIRTY WORK CAN BE FUN"

Charles Muer, who operates a chain of restaurants headquartered in Detroit, employs young part-time workers extensively and considers it entirely feasible that they could take over most of the kitchen work. "You might have to pay them more," he says, "but productivity would be high. Kids are strong and enthusiastic, and dirty work can be fun, especially if you enjoy your co-workers and the management is nice."

Others are skeptical. "You've got to screen young people," says a hospital administrator, "and you can't leave them off by themselves where they'll goof off." Some tasks cannot and should not be performed by the young, particularly those involving nighttime shifts or long commuting distances. And some parents, of course, would object to their children's taking jobs they consider demeaning. John R. Coleman, the president of Haverford College whose experiences last year as an incognito ditchdigger and trash collector are described in his book *Time Out,* advises many of his students to get a taste of menial work. The parents most likely to be upset by such an idea, Coleman says, are "people unsure of their own status."

There's another and perhaps more formidable impediment. Until now the large number of young people bumping from one job to another as they slowly settle into careers has provided much of the labor pool for temporary dead-end work. (See "A Better Way to Deal with Unemployment," FORTUNE, June, 1973.) But some of the desirable education reforms now being tested are designed to enable high-school graduates to jump right into jobs with career ladders. If "career education" or something like it becomes widespread, it may become necessary to get that menial work out of students *before* they graduate. That would entail new social arrangements of some kind.

In an ideal world, all menial work would be a passing thing, whether for adults seeking a temporary change from their normal routine or for young people who can count on better jobs later on. It won't turn out quite that way, of course. Some people, because of limited ability or sheer inclination, will mop floors or wait on tables throughout their working lives. If recent trends continue, however, their pay will rise and with it their self-esteem—and, of course, the costs of their labor, at a time when lots of other things are also getting costlier.

THE AIRLINE ROUTE

An indication of the direction things will move in can be seen in the way some airlines get their planes cleaned up between runs. The American Airlines system, for example, embodies nearly all of the features that society will probably have to incorporate into its low-status jobs. At New York's LaGuardia Airport a force of 185 "cabin service clerks" (an old designation rather than a recent euphemism) cleans floors, scrubs lavatories, and empties the ashtrays into which airline passengers grind their cigarettes. The men go about their work briskly, with no indication that they consider it demeaning. Two-thirds of them are white, the rest black and Puerto Rican. Their pay starts at $4.57 an hour, with a maximum of $5.15.

The job is not a dead end. Some recent hires are college graduates who, in the words of H. Lee Nichols, the staff's black manager, "get a foot in the door with an airline by taking a job like this." Most of these workers move on, replaced by a steady supply of new men attracted by the pay and the prospects for advancement. After all, Nichols says, "five years of cleaning ashtrays, if you have any drive, can get to you."

Luddites in Lordstown

Barbara Garson

Though labor unrest has long been commonplace in American society, more and more young workers now seem to be fed up with the whole ethos of the industrial system. Freer in spirit than their fathers, they often scorn the old work ethic and refuse to be treated like automatons, no matter how good the pay or how brief the hours. Their anguish and

boredom are likely to worsen in the next few years, perhaps infecting not only those on the assembly line but also white-collar workers who resent toiling at trivia. Nowhere has the new discontent been more forcibly expressed than by the young auto workers who recently shut down a GM plant at Lordstown, Ohio.

"Is it true," an auto worker asked wistfully, "that you get to do fifteen different jobs on a Cadillac?" "I heard," said another, "that with Volvos you follow one car all the way down the line."

Such are the yearnings of young auto workers at the Vega plant in Lordstown, Ohio. Their average age is twenty-four, and they work on the fastest auto assembly line in the world. Their jobs are so subdivided that few workers can feel they are making a car.

The assembly line carries 101 cars past each worker every hour. Most GM lines run under sixty. At 101 cars an hour, a worker has thirty-six seconds to perform his assigned snaps, knocks, twists, or squirts on each car. The line was running at this speed in October when a new management group, General Motors Assembly Division (GMAD or Gee-Mad), took over the plant. Within four months they fired 500 to 800 workers. Their jobs were divided among the remaining workers, adding a few more snaps, knocks, twists, or squirts to each man's task. The job had been boring and unbearable before. When it remained boring and became a bit more unbearable there was a 97 per cent vote to strike. More amazing —85 per cent went down to the union hall to vote.*

One could give a broad or narrow interpretation of what the Lordstown workers want. Broadly, they want to reorganize industry so that each worker plays a significant role in turning out a fine product, without enduring degrading supervision. Narrowly, they want more time in each thirty-six-second cycle to sneeze or to scratch.

John Grix, who handles public relations at Lordstown, and Andy O'Keefe for GMAD in Detroit both assured me that work at Lordstown is no different than at the older assembly plants. The line moves faster, they say, but then the parts are lighter and easier to install. I think this may be true. It is also true of the workers. These young people are not basically different from the older men. But they are

---

*The union membership voted to settle the twenty-two-day strike in late March, but the agreement appeared to be somewhat reluctant; less than half of the members showed up for the vote, and 30 per cent of those voted against the settlement. The union won a number of concessions, among them full back pay for anybody who had been disciplined in the past few months for failure to meet work standards. Meanwhile, however, UAW locals at three other GM plants around the country threatened to strike on grounds similar to those established at Lordstown. In early April GM recalled 130,000 Vegas of the 1972 model because of a possible fire hazard involving the fuel and exhaust systems.

faster and lighter. Because they are young they are economically freer to strike and temperamentally quicker to act. But their yearnings are not new. The Vega workers are echoing a rank-and-file demand that has been suppressed by both union and management for the past twenty years: *Humanize working conditions.*

Hanging around the parking lot between shifts, I learned immediately that to these young workers, "It's not the money."

"It pays good," said one, "but it's driving me crazy."

"I don't want more money," said another. "None of us do."

"I do," said his friend. "So I can quit quicker."

"It's the job," everyone said. But they found it hard to describe the job itself.

"My father worked in auto for thirty-five years," said a clean-cut lad, "and he never talked about the job. What's there to say? A car comes, I weld it. A car comes, I weld it. A car comes, I weld it. One hundred and one times an hour."

I asked a young wife, "What does your husband tell you about his work?"

"He doesn't say what he does. Only if something happened like, 'My hair caught on fire,' or, 'Something fell in my face.' "

"There's a lot of variety in the paint shop," said a dapper twenty-two-year-old up from West Virginia. "You clip on the color hose, bleed out the old color, and squirt. Clip, bleed, squirt, think; clip, bleed, squirt, yawn; clip, bleed, squirt, scratch your nose. Only now the Gee-Mads have taken away the time to scratch your nose."

A long-hair reminisced: "Before the Go-Mads, when I had a good job like door handles, I could get a couple of cars ahead and have a whole minute to relax."

I asked about diversions. "What do you do to keep from going crazy?"

"Well, certain jobs like the pit you can light up a cigarette without them seeing."

"I go to the wastepaper basket. I wait a certain number of cars, then find a piece of paper to throw away."

"I have fantasies. You know what I keep imagining? I see a car coming down. It's red. So I know it's gonna have a black seat, black dash, black interiors. But I keep thinking what if somebody up there sends down the wrong color interiors—like orange, and me putting in yellow cushions, bright yellow!"

"There's always water fights, paint fights, or laugh, talk, tell jokes. Anything so you don't feel like a machine."

But everyone had the same hope: "You're always waiting for the line to break down."

The Vega Plant hires about seven thousand assembly-line workers. They commute to Lordstown from Akron, Youngstown, Cleveland, even as far as Pittsburgh. Actually, there is no Lordstown—just a plant and some trailer camps set among farmhouses. When the workers leave, they disperse throughout southern Ohio. GM presumably hoped that this location would help minimize labor troubles.

I took the guided tour of the plant. It's new, it's clean, it's well lit without windows, and it's noisy. Hanging car bodies move past at the speed of a Coney

Island ride slowing down. Most men work alongside the line but some stand in a man-sized pit craning their necks to work on the undersides of the cars.

I stopped to shout at a worker drinking coffee, *"Is there any quiet place to take a break?"* He shouted back, *"Can't hear you, ma'am. Too noisy to chat on a break."* As a plant guard rushed over to separate us I spotted Duane.* from Fort Lewis, shooting radios into cars with an air gun. Duane had been in the Army while I was working at a GI coffeehouse. He slipped me a note with his address.

When I left the plant there were leafleteers at the gate distributing *Workers' Power*. Guards with binocular cameras closed in, snapping pictures; another guard checked everyone's ID. He copied down the names of leafleteers and workers who took papers. He took my name too.

DUANE'S MILITARY-INDUSTRIAL COMPLEX

That evening I visited Duane. He had rented a two-bedroom bungalow on the outskirts of a town that had no center. He had grown his hair a bit but, in fact, he looked neater and trimmer than when he'd been in the Army.

I told him about the incident at the gate. "Just like the Army," he said. He summarized life since his discharge: "Remember you guys gave me a giant banana split the day I ETSed [got out on schedule]? Well, it's been downhill since then. I came back to Cleveland; stayed with my dad, who was unemployed. Man, was that ever a downer. But I figured things would pick up if I got wheels, so I got a car. But it turned out the car wasn't human and that was a problem. So I figured, 'What I need is a girl.' But it turned out the girl *was* human and *that* was a problem. So I wound up working at GM to pay off the car and the girl." And he introduced me to his lovely pregnant wife, of whom he seemed much fonder than it sounds.

A couple of Duane's high-school friends, Stan and Eddie, wound up at Lordstown too. Stan at twenty-one was composed and placid, a married man with a child. Eddie at twenty-two was an excitable youth. Duane had invited them over to tell me what it's like working at the plant.

"I'll tell you what it's like," said Duane. "It's like the Army. They even use the same words like *direct order*. Supposedly you have a contract so there's some things they just can't make you do. Except, if the foreman gives you a direct order, you do it, or you're out."

"Out?" I asked.

"Yeah, fired—or else they give you a DLO."

"DLO?"

"Disciplinary layoff. Which means you're out without pay for however long they say. Like maybe it'll be a three-day DLO or a week DLO."

Eddie explained it further: "Like this foreman comes up to me and says, 'Pick up that piece of paper.' Only he says it a little nastier, with a few references to my

---

*Since many workers were afraid of losing their jobs, I have changed names, juggled positions on the line, and given facsimiles for identifying details.

race, creed, and length of hair. So I says, 'That's not my job.' He says, 'I'm giving you a direct order to pick up that piece of paper.' Finally he takes me up to the office. My committeeman comes over and tells me I could of lost my job because you can't refuse a direct order. You do it, and then you put in a grievance—ha!''

"Calling your committeeman," says Duane. "That's just like the Army too. If your CO [commanding officer] is harassing you, you can file a complaint with the IG [Inspector General]. Only thing is you gotta go up to your CO and say, 'Sir, request permission to see the Inspector General to tell him my commanding officer is a shit.' Same thing here. Before you can get your committeeman, you got to tell the foreman exactly what your grievance is in detail. So meantime he's working out ways to tell the story different."

Here Stan took out an actual DLO from his wallet. "Last week someone up the line put a stink bomb in a car. I do rear cushions, and the foreman says, 'You get in that car.' We said, 'If you can put your head in that car we'll do the job.' So the foreman says, 'I'm giving you a direct order.' So I hold my breath and do it. My job is every other car so I let the next one pass. He gets on me, and I say, 'It ain't my car. Please, I done your dirty work and the other one wasn't mine.' But he keeps at me, and I wind up with a week off. Now, I got a hot committeeman who really stuck up for me. So you know what? They sent *him* home too. Gave the committeeman a DLO!''

"See, just like the Army," Duane repeats. "No, it's worse 'cause you're welded to the line. You just about need a pass to piss.''

"That ain't no joke," says Eddie. "You raise your little hand if you want to go wee-wee. Then wait maybe half an hour till they find a relief man. And they write it down every time too. 'Cause you're supposed to do it on your own time, not theirs. Try it too often, and you'll get a week off.''

"I'd rather work in a gas station," said Stan wistfully. "That way you pump gas, then you patch a tire, then you go to the bathroom. You do what needs doing.''

"Why don't you work in a gas station?' I asked.

"You know what they pay in a gas station? I got a kid. Besides, I couldn't even get a job in a gas station. Before I got in here I was so hard up I wound up selling vacuum cleaners—$297 door to door. In a month I earned exactly $10 selling one vacuum cleaner to a laid-off steel worker for which I'll never forgive myself.''

"No worse than making cars," Eddie said. "Cars are your real trap, not vacuum cleaners. You need the car to keep the job and you need the job to keep the car. And don't think they don't know it. They give you just enough work to keep up the payments. They got it planned exactly, so you can't quit.''

"He's a little paranoid," Duane said.

"Look it," says that paranoid reasonably. "They give you fifty, fifty-five hours' work for a couple of weeks. So your typical boob buys a color TV. Then they cut you back to thirty hours. There's not a married man who doesn't have bills. And the company keeps it like that so there's no way out. You're stuck for life.''

I asked about future plans.

Eddie was getting out as soon as he saved enough money to travel. He thought he might work for three more months. He'd said three months when he started, and it was nine months already, but "things came up."

Duane figured he'd stay till after his wife had the baby. That way he could use the hospital plan. After that? "Maybe we'll go live on the land. I don't know. I wish someone would hand me a discharge."

Stan was a reasonable man—or a boob, as Eddie might have it. He knew he was going to stay. "If I'm gonna do some dumb job the rest of my life, I might as well do one that pays."

Though none of them could afford to quit, they were all eager for a strike. They'd manage somehow. For Stan it was a good investment in his future job. The others just liked the idea of giving GM a kick in the ass from the inside.

THE BLUE-COLLAR COMMUNE

Later in the week I stayed at an auto-workers' commune. Like so many other young people, they were trying to make a one-generational family—a homestead. Life centered, as of old, around the hearth, which was a water pipe bubbling through bourbon. The family Bibles were the Books of the Dead—both Tibetan and Egyptian. Throughout the evening, six to twelve people drifted through the old house waiting for Indian Nut (out working night shift at Lordstown) and his wife Jane (out baby-sitting).

Jane returned at midnight to prepare dinner for her husband. By 2:00 A.M. she complained: "They can keep them two, three, four hours over." Overtime is mandatory for auto workers, but it's not as popular at Lordstown as it is among older workers at other plants.

At two-thirty the Nut burst in, wild-haired, wild-eyed, and sweet-smiled. He had a mildly maniacal look because his glasses were speckled with welding spatter.

"New foreman, a real Gee-mad-man. Sent a guy home for farting in a car. And another one home for yodeling."

"Yodeling?" I asked.

"Yeah, you know." (And he yodeled.)

(It's common in auto plants for men to break the monotony with noise, like the banging of tin cans in jail. Someone will drop something, his partner will yell "Whaa," and then "Whaa" gets transmitted all along the line.)

"I bet there's no shop rule against farting," the Nut conjectured. "You know those porkers have been getting their 101 off the line again, and not that many of them need repairs. It's the hillbillies. Those cats have no stamina. The union calls them to a meeting, says, 'Now don't you sabotage, but don't you run. Don't do more than you can do.' And everybody cheers. But in a few days it's back to where it was. Hillbillies working so fast they ain't got time to scratch their balls. Meantime these porkers is making money even faster than they're making cars."

I ask who he means by the hillbillies. "Hillbillies is the general Ohio term for assholes, except if you happen to be a hillbilly. Then you say Polack. Fact is everybody is a hillbilly out here except me and two other guys. And they must work day shift 'cause I never see them.'

"Sabotage?" says the Nut. "Just a way of letting off steam. You can't keep up with the car so you scratch it on the way past. I once saw a hillbilly drop an ignition key down the gas tank. Last week I watched a guy light a glove and lock it in the trunk. We all waited to see how far down the line they'd discover it. . . . If you miss a car, they call that sabotage. They expect the sixty-second minute. Even a machine has to sneeze. Look how they call us in weekends, hold us extra, send us home early, give us layoffs. You'd think we were machines the way they turn us on and off."

I apologized for getting Indian Nut so steamed up and keeping him awake late. "No," sighed Jane. "It always takes a couple of hours to calm him down. We never get to bed before four."

Later that day, about 1:00 P.M., Indian Nut cooked breakfast for all of us (about ten). One nice thing about a working-class commune: bacon and eggs and potatoes for breakfast—no granola.

It took about an hour and a half to do the day's errands—mostly dope shopping and car repair. Then Indian Nut relaxed for an hour around the hearth.

As we talked some people listened to Firesign Theatre while others played Masterpiece or Monopoly. Everyone sucked at the pipe from time to time.

A college kid came by to borrow records. He was the editor of the defunct local underground paper called *Anonymity*. (It had lived up to its title before folding).

"I've been trying to get Indian Nut to quit working there," he said.

"Why?" I asked.

"Don't you know? GM makes M-16s."

"Yeah, well, you live with your folks," said one of the Monopolists.

"You can always work some kind of rip-off," replied the ex-editor.

Everyone joined the ensuing philosophical inquiry about where it was moral to work and whom it was moral to rip off.

"Shit," sighed Indian Nut. "It's four-thirty. Someone help Jane with the dishes." Taking a last toke, the Nut split for the plant.

As I proceeded with my unscientific survey, I found that I couldn't predict a man's militancy from his hair length, age, or general freakiness. But you could always guess a man's attitudes by his comments on the car. When someone said, "I wouldn't even buy a Vega, not a '71 or a '72," then he would usually say, "General Motors—all they care about is money. Not the worker, not the car, just the goddamn money."

A nineteen-year-old told me bitterly: "A black guy worked next to me putting sealer into the cracks. He used to get cut all the time on sharp edges of metal. One day his finger really got stuck and he was bleeding all over the car. So I stopped the line. [There's a button every so many feet.] Sure they rushed him to the hospital, but boy did they get down on me for stopping the line. That line runs no matter what the cost."

The mildest man I met was driving a Vega. He was a long-haired, or at least shaggy-haired, twenty-one-year-old. He thought the Vega was a "pretty little thing." When I asked about his job he said, "It's a very important job. After all, everybody's got to have a car." Yes, he had voted for the strike. "Myself, I'd rather work, but if they're gonna keep laying people off, might as well strike now and get it over with." Anyway, he figured the strike would give him time to practice: he was second guitarist in a band, and if his group could only "get it together," maybe he could quit GM. He had other hopes too. For instance: "The company lets you put in suggestions, and you get money if they use your suggestions." He was a cheerful, good-natured lad, and, as I say, he liked the Vega.

There's a good reason why attitudes toward the car correlate with attitudes toward the company. It's not just "hate them, hate their car." It's also hate your job and hate yourself when you think you're making a hunk of junk, or when you can't feel you've made anything at all. I was reminded of this by a worker's mother.

While her son and his friends talked shop—DLO's, strike, rock bands—I talked to her in the kitchen. Someone in the supermarket where she worked had said, those young kids are just lazy: "One thing, Tony is not lazy. He'll take your car apart and put it together any day. Ever since he's been in high school we haven't had to worry about car trouble. The slightest knock and he takes care of it. And he never will leave it half done. He even cleans up after himself.

"And I'm not lazy either. I love to cook. But supposing they gave me a job just cracking eggs with bowls moving past on a line. Pretty soon I'd get to a point where I'd wish the next egg was rotten just to spoil their whole cake."

At the Pink Elephant Bar I met a man who'd voted against the strike, one of the rare 3 per cent. He was an older man who'd worked in other auto plants. "I seen it before. The international [union] is just giving them enough rope to hang themselves. They don't ever take on speed-up or safety. And they don't ever help with any strike *they* didn't call.

"Meany and his silk shirts! Reuther's daughter hobnobbed with Miss Ford, but at least he didn't wear silk shirts . . . Woodcock?* Who cares what he wears.

"Like I was saying, they see a kicky young local so they go along. They authorize the strike. But it's just giving you enough rope to hang yourself.

"They see you got young inexperienced leadership—I'm not saying our leadership is young and inexperienced but what it is, is—young and inexperienced.

"So they let 'em go ahead. But they don't give 'em no help. They don't give 'em no funds. They don't even let the other locals come out with you. When it comes to humanizing working conditions you might as well be back before there was any unions."

---

*President, UAW.

"So the strike drags on, it's lost, or they 'settle' in Detroit. Everybody says, 'There, it didn't pay.' And the next time around the leadership gets unelected. See —they gave 'em enough rope to hang 'emselves."

Other GM plants are having labor troubles, but no coordinated union action has been authorized. It is difficult for an outsider to tell when the UAW International is giving wholehearted help. But with or without the international, workers will continue to agitate for better working conditions.

Local 1112 at Lordstown defined their demands as narrowly as possible. They asked GM to hire more men. They do not, they hasten to explain, want to limit the speed of the line. Gary Bryner, president of the local (an elder statesman at twenty-nine), said, "We recognize that it's management's prerogative to run the plant. But all we've got is our labor, so we want to see that our conditions of labor are okay."

Despite this humble goal, local 1112 is undertaking a fight that the international union has backed away from, even suppressed, in the past.

Every three years for the past fifteen, Walter Reuther bargained with auto manufacturers for higher wages and better benefits—off the job. And every three years for the past fifteen, auto workers rejected Reuther's contracts, demanding, in addition, better conditions—on the job.

In 1955 more than 70 per cent of GM workers went on strike when presented with a contract that failed to deal with speed-up or other local grievances. After the 1958 contract an even larger percentage wildcatted. In 1961 the post-contract strike closed all GM plants and many large Ford plants. Running from the rear to the front of the parade, Reuther declared the strike official. However, he failed to negotiate for the demands that caused the wildcat. In 1964 there was a rank-and-file campaign before negotiations began. Near all large plants, bumper stickers appeared on auto workers' cars, saying, *Humanize working conditions.**

The underlying assumption in an auto plant is that no worker wants to work. The plant is arranged so that employees can be controlled, checked, and supervised at every point. The efficiency of an assembly line is not only in its speed but in the fact that the workers are easily replaced. This allows the employer to cope with high turnover. But it's a vicious cycle. The job is so unpleasantly subdivided that men are constantly quitting and absenteeism is common. Even an accident is a welcome diversion. Because of the high turnover, management further simplifies the job, and more men quit. But the company has learned to cope with high turnover. So they don't have to worry if men quit or go crazy before they're forty.

The UAW is not a particularly undemocratic union. Still, it is as hard for the majority of its members to influence their international as it is for the majority of Americans to end the war in Vietnam. The desire to reduce alienation is hard to

---

*This information was given to me by Stan Weir, a former auto worker. His article "U.S.A.: The Labor Revolts" appears in *American Society Inc.* (Markham Publishing Co., Chicago, 1970).

express as a union demand, and it's hard to get union leaders to insist upon this demand. Harder still will be the actual struggle to take more control over production away from corporate management. It is a fight that questions the right to private ownership of the means of production.

Management—Sitting on a Time Bomb?

George J. Berkwitt

Grosvenor Ely, proprietor of Boatworks Inc., is hardly distinguishable from the hundreds of local "boat bums" who frequent the shores of Long Island Sound. Tanned from long hours outdoors, wearing sun-faded, stained slacks, a frayed dress shirt and ancient loafers, he looks born and bred to his job of servicing the yachts and other pleasure craft that tie up at the local basin in Rowayton, Connecticut.

Yet less than eighteen months ago, Ely was a full-time marketing manager for American Cyanamid Corp. He was earning a healthy annual income, getting lucrative fringe benefits, and was practically assured of a promotion. Why did he trade all that in for a twelve-hour day, seven-day week, doubtful income, no fringe benefits, and a fair chance of failure? In Ely's own words, "Most companies work your tail off, put you under tremendous pressure, but never really make you feel you are an important part of it all. Giving you stock in a company is just not enough. They are usually more concerned with bleeding you dry."

Grosvenor Ely is not just an isolated oddball "dropout" from the corporate scene. Hundreds of executives are leaving big business for other fields. They are starting up their own firms like Ely, becoming teachers and consultants, going into government and social work. "Frankly, I've never seen so many managers and graduates opting in other directions," says Albert W. Schrader, director of the Bureau of Industrial Relations at the University of Michigan's Graduate School of Business Administration. "They're opting for jobs in public service, their own businesses, or anywhere they can pursue their own interests and make more use of their talents and, in effect, get more fun out of working."

This growing exodus is evidence of a revolt in the executive suite that is unprecedented in kind and degree. To be sure, industry in the late sixties was inundated on all sides by complaints from middle-echelon executives ("The Revolt of the Middle Managers," DUN'S, September 1969), but those men were agitating for higher salaries, better fringe benefits, and all the other requisites of making it up the corporate ladder.

Today's revolt, in contrast, is against the corporate life. Increasingly, executives simply want out of the company. "For the first time," explains Harold M. Williams, dean of the Graduate School of Management at UCLA, "middle managers are not expressing their dissatisfaction with individual companies or their managements, but with the entire system of corporate life and style."

Evidence of the malaise that hangs like a black cloud over management is everywhere. Absenteeism, long considered a problem of the production line, is today known to be just as serious in the management ranks—and it is up 20% this year. Poor productivity, too, has hit the upper echelons. So bad has the productivity problem become at Bethlehem Steel, for one, that the company recently launched a full-scale productivity-improvement program involving middle and top management.

Even more damning, perhaps, are the reports that anxiety is rife among executives. A recent study by the Life Extension Institute of New York reveals that only one-sixth as many executives as in 1958 (the time of the last survey) are satisfied with the progress they are making on their jobs, and 17% fewer think their jobs are secure.

Still further evidence of serious trouble in the executive suite is the stepped-up agitation among middle managers to unionize. Executives have, of course, long complained that they lack the security of blue-collar workers. But now, according to a recent American Management Association survey, more of them than ever before want to do something about it. Fully half of the middle managers queried favor legislation for collective bargaining between top and middle management, and half also expect management to be unionized before 1980. Warns Willys D. De Voll, vice president of Union Camp Corp.: "When union sentiment seems to be mounting in this key group, you'd better find out fast about what is going on. Their strength as a unit is as powerful as that of the blue-collar group. If they all decide to take a walk or get sick, who would run the shop?"

A SELLOUT?

From DUN'S conversations with dozens of executives and former executives, what all this adds up to is the belief by a considerable number of managers that the corporation has let them down—or to put it even more strongly, that the business establishment that demanded so much loyalty from them has now betrayed them.

All during the profit-rich sixties, say the executives, corporations lured thousands of young men into their fold with promises of big salaries, lucrative fringe benefits, and unprecedented opportunity. Then the recession hit, and thousands of managers discovered that the one thing they did not have was job security. As Paul W. Kayser, a principal with the management consultant firm of Golightly & Co., International, puts it: "Middle managers are the first to be subjected to cost-cutting firings when the economy sours."

And indeed they were, as cutbacks slashed across industry in every area, from such conventional functions as engineering, research, and administration to more esoteric areas like long-range planning and operations research. It can be defined simply as "a breach of faith," believes Russell Marshall, once a manager of fabrication engineering with Collins Radio, now in consulting.

"Many of the progressive programs offered middle managers in the sixties," says Marshall, "were purportedly motivated on the basis of a generally good feeling toward managers. There were new kinds of perquisites, special payments for special skills, and more. Then when the crunch came a lot of redfaced executives had to bite the bullet and say, 'Gee, we really didn't mean that.' Top management," Marshall snaps, "ought to have admitted right at the outset that frills are tolerable when there is room on the bottom line and intolerable when there isn't. Instead, they told us they were ours for posterity. Those of us who thought so," he adds ruefully, "were pretty naive."

Paul Kayser agrees. In effect, he says, business found a convenient way to handle middle managers—and the middle managers have finally caught on. "Industry's practice of first falling in love with managers, and then blaming them when things get tough," he believes, "is what is beginning to bother more and more middle-level executives. They are beginning to wonder if there is any sense at all in working for large corporations, and that is why so many thoughtful executives are dropping out of the business scene entirely."

Edmund R. Hergenrather, a Los Angeles executive recruiter, tells a story that makes the point. Recently, Hergenrather reports, two topnotch executives came to him looking for jobs. One was John W. Lynch, the industrial-relations director of trouble-plagued Whittaker Corp. The other was Charles R. Chapman, who held the same position for the American Cement Corp.

When both these men's jobs had been eliminated, they were not fired but offered other jobs in their companies with less status and smaller income. Though both were corporate veterans—Lynch had been a labor expert at U.S. Steel before joining Whittaker, and Chapman had fifteen years of experience in management —they refused to consider another job in industry. In fact, reports Hergenrather, Lynch refused two highpaying offers from other companies.

Why? Certain executive functions like industrial relations still do not have strong positions in industry, explains Lynch. "You could be called in to solve a labor problem in a $40-million facility while the president of a division making four times as much as you was home asleep, and you were given all of the responsibility and accountability. But you got no authority. Remuneration is not always enough for all of the anguish and anxiety."

"There was just too little respect for the function of industrial relations," adds Chapman.

As Hergenrather interprets it, for high-caliber men like Lynch and Chapman, lack of security was "more psychological than material. They were insecure," he says, "because they lived with a false image of what they represented to the company. They thought they had meant more. When you see as many cases as I do of careers nipped in the bud by the decision of management," Hergenrather concludes, "you begin to wonder if the management ladder in the corporation is the way to travel. Many don't think so."

John Lynch and Charles Chapman are now in the executive recruiting business. Hergenrather hired both of them. "Industry," he says, "lost two good men."

A CONTINUAL EROSION

Indeed, although the executive dropouts gripe about job insecurity and low salaries, what really got them down was their dwindling influence in the corporation. There was a continual erosion in their decision-making power, they say, while their responsibilities kept increasing. As Stephen Cuthrell, who left his job as director of personnel at Boise Cascade's subsidiary Kidde Constructors, Inc., and is now in career planning, puts it, "I got tired of being constrained, and I wanted to be responsible and accountable for profit."

Another manager who felt constrained is Thomas Woods, who held a variety of positions in one of the country's largest rubber companies. Woods was, at one time or another, a systems specialist for the corporate controller, a production manager, an internal consultant and an assistant to the chairman of the board. Yet his frustrations became strong enough to move him out of industry into his present job as consultant at Rath & Strong, Inc.

Woods complains most about his former company's immovability. "No matter how good an idea I or my staff came up with," he says, "it was virtually impossible to implement it in such a way that you could observe any change in the motion of the corporation. I eventually chose something where originality would be more likely to produce change."

William H. Peters' last job in industry was as director of advertising for the Laboratories Division of Pfizer, Inc. He left to eventually became professor of business administration at the University of Wisconsin's Graduate School of Business. Says Peters: "It's tough to take when, no matter how high you are in the company and no matter what you do, you need to get approval from a whole hierarchy of people."

The dropouts also complain about top management's own insecurity. This, of course, is another fallout of the recession. For when those record-breaking profits of the sixties went down the drain, it was top management's job to cut the losses. The experience of slashing budgets, programs—and people—left them with a defensive stance they have yet to overcome. Even though the business climate is looking up, all indications are that companies in general are still playing it safe and making few commitments to new ideas or new expansion.

Not only that, corporate presidents seem to be playing their own game of musical chairs. According to a recent survey, the number of presidents who have been on their jobs less than a year is going up by 8% a year. Not only do frequent changes at the top hardly make for stability—or confidence—when a president is replaced; many of his subordinates can also find themselves out of work. For example, when John Phillips, president of R. J. Reynolds' RJR Foods subsidiary, resigned in June to go with American Home Products, some half-dozen of his staff managers, says an insider, were also let go. "It reinforces the notion," the insider notes, "that you ought to know what team you're on. If you are hired by a guy and he leaves, you may be out."

Perhaps the most intriguing area of protest among executives is their growing concern with corporate response to social issues. Of course, to the environmentalists, consumer advocates and other activists so vocal today, the business world has long been considered a major culprit. Now reports from many sources indicate that anti-corporate sentiment is also being expressed in the ranks—most particularly by the younger executives.

For instance, one former manager, who is now a civil servant, is highly critical of his former employer, an aircraft company. The company, he says, continually wasted government money on elaborate projects that could just as easily have been done simpler and at much less cost. And Thomas Woods claims that the rubber company he worked for "deliberately designed labels and promotions to keep the consumer from understanding the variations in quality of different models of the same product." "Managers," says UCLA's Dean Harold Williams, "are expressing concern that business is exclusively profit-motivated to the exclusion of concern for a lot of broader issues."

Adds one former Wall Streeter, who left and vows never to return: "A lot of us have gone from hard-core conservatism in love with the system to outright radicalism. We're against what the system does to people."

The new social-consciousness of executives is no doubt largely due to the influence of young college graduates who, having been exposed to the agitation of the campus, bring their views into the company. And it is also these young managerial types who seem to most quickly pinpoint what they consider the stultifying atmosphere of the corporation. As one former young executive who now runs his own business puts it: "I saw managers at the age of 55 doing the same thing they had been doing for eighteen years. That's depressing as hell for a guy like me."

As for the veterans the young man refers to, they are suffering, says Harold Williams, from "The Forty-Plus Syndrome." Many of the middle managers around forty, Dean Williams explains, sort of sense that they are running out of time. They begin to realize that the odds are pretty much against their moving further in the organization. Some rationalize that the company treats them pretty well financially, that they are pretty secure. But the better educated, more worldly manager, tells himself, "I don't want to turn off; there is more than this in me." Then he wonders, "What do I do now—go to another company, try something entrepreneurial, go into public service?"

"Many executives have come to me to ask for teaching jobs," Dean Williams says. But most, he adds, are not qualified.

WHERE THEY'RE GOING

College-level teaching is, in fact, one of the most appealing areas for the executive dropouts. So is consulting, where many disgruntled middle managers believe they can parlay their skills into more money, freedom and authority. Typical of the comments from those who have moved into consulting from industry: "You do what you want, and there is tremendous satisfaction in seeing a company turn around and know that you did it." "It gives you a chance to be creative. You can change things—change is the key word." "I came into it feeling it would be a springboard into another management job. I'm staying put."

For the dropouts starting their own businesses, William P. Palmer, a program manager at Fairchild Hiller Corp., left to open a car-painting franchise in Washington, D.C. And an American Can marketing manager left the company to open a fancy-food chain in plush Westchester County, New York. A recent Conference Board study showed that many executives have gone into fast-food, motel, retail and other franchise businesses.

A number of former executives are opting for social work. Several have gone into administration of community mental-health programs, a number into hospital administration, a few into programs for senior citizens, and some can be found running local YMCAs. This despite lower pay and smaller operating budgets than they enjoyed in industry. "No one should have illusions about social work," warns Mitchell Ginsberg, well-known for his recent tenure as head of New York City's trouble-ridden welfare program and now dean of Columbia University's School of Social Work. "It is essential that they know what they are getting into." Nevertheless, says Dean Ginsberg, many high-caliber people are attracted to the field. "They are willing to accept challenge over security."

For much the same challenge, the government is also attracting executives. Herbert G. Neal, a General Foods Corp. product manager, left to become Deputy Regional Director of the U.S. Department of Health, Education and Welfare. Michael Frankel, an engineering manager at TRW, Inc., who was enticed to Washington on a twelve-to-eighteen-month leave of absence to participate in the President's Commission on Personnel Interchange, has decided to apply for a permanent position with the Environmental Protection Agency, where he is acting special assistant in planning and management.

The inducements for such men are more tempting than ever. Since 1962, Congress has been steadily monitoring salaries of private industry to maintain equitable levels in government jobs. Furthermore, the jobs offered professionals by government are frequently in excess of anything offered by industry. Such programs as the Polaris and moon shots, the U.S. Civil Service Commission reports, are attracting high-caliber industry professionals out of science, technology, computers and management. "These men," says a Commission spokesman, "are attracted more to the mission than to compensation."

What seems most potentially damaging about the new revolt, then, is that the corporation is losing some of its best men—the ones who have the drive and ability to get out and find new areas of work. If the trend continues, it seems inevitable that, as the economy continues to pick up, industry will be facing a shortage of the innovative kind of managers needed in times of growth. Indeed, industry is already stepping up its search for middle-echelon executives. "The people who are left in the organization," says Albert Shrader, "are the belt-tighteners and cost-cutters. But are they researchers, developers? Can they contribute?"

If the present malaise continues, more self-generating managers will leave the corporation, Schrader believes. "It will be left with the self-seekers who will have more of an eye on their status than on their responsibilities. There will be fewer managers who can be assigned the job of running the organization. Inevitably," he concludes, "the situation will deteriorate in a dangerous loss of productivity and competitive edge."

Considering the U.S.' present difficulties in meeting foreign competition, it is an eventuality industry can ill afford.

Top Management—and Turned-off Executives

Robert Levy

"Except for those middle managers who are natural malcontents, the problem is basically a top-management failure in personnel relations."

That view, expressed by Chairman Russell Erickson of ITT Rayonier, sums up how industry's top executives generally feel about one of the biggest problems facing them right now: the widespread alienation of their middle-echelon executives. As reported by DUN'S last month ("Management—Sitting on a Time Bomb?"), many middle managers, distrustful of an Establishment that they believe treated them shabbily during the recession, have quit their jobs to go into other fields. Just as telling, talk of unionization is now rife in the executive suite, and diminishing productivity at the management level has become a matter of top-level concern.

Are the middle managers justified in feeling insecure and alienated? Given such attitudes, what can the men at the top do to halt the executive exodus?

Beyond that, how bad is the situation? And are there really unions in management's future?

To get the answers, DUN'S turned to the 300 corporate presidents and chairmen who make up its Presidents' Panel. As the men who set the policies and establish the goals toward which middle managers must work, it is perhaps surprising that a number of the panelists concede, like Russell Erickson, that the middle managers have a point. As President Peter G. Scotese of Springs Mills puts it, "Any corporation—barring those facing disaster financially—that went through its ranks with an ax instead of scalpel when the recession hit deserves the opinion held by those middle-management executives who feel they were harshly and unfairly treated."

Middle-management's reaction, adds President Richard J. Stockham Sr. of Stockham Valves, "is perfectly normal in the absence of aggressive and careful effort on the part of top management to listen to, hear, and communicate with middle managers."

To be sure, some top executives do not see it quite that way. In the view of blunt-talking Bruce Horst, president of Barber-Colman Co., for one, some middle managers have only themselves to blame. "During good times, almost anyone can succeed," says Horst. "They obtain results far below their true capability and get in the habit of working at a moderate speed. But the recession demanded much more, and in a number of cases people in middle management couldn't cut it."

For that matter, AMF Chairman Rodney C. Gott believes that middle managers have less to complain about currently than ever before. "In this day of constantly improving fringe benefits," Gott maintains, "the middle managers in most corporations have perquisites, privileges and compensation more generous then they ever had before. I am inclined to think that the situation does not exist where the corporation is vigorous, growing, and competitive in its compensation policies."

In a sense, of course, all these top executives are saying the same thing: that whether a company suffers from poor employee relations depends largely on how well it is run. As one panelist notes, many a company overextended itself during the high growth period of 1966–69, and consequently suffered management morale problems when the downturn hit and it had to cut back. "In well-managed companies that run a taut ship in good times and bad, and who take the long-run point of view," further contends Chairman Raymon H. Mulford of Owens-Illinois, "traumatic cost-control activities are not necessary, and the organization is therefore not disturbed."

THE FACTS OF LIFE

Yet even though they can understand what has turned executives off, most of the panelists also believe that many managers simply expect too much from the corporation. For one thing, says one chief executive, "Getting ahead and moving up the corporate pyramid is seen as the exclusive criterion of success. Yet inevitably, only a minority of executives can advance toward the top. So a great majority of managers are going to be dissatisfied and frustrated."

A further comment is offered by the president of a major paper company. "These young people," he says, "have received their first big disappointment in the business world, and they are understandably dissatisfied. But when it comes to corporate promises, it is a fact of life that they are conditioned upon the corporation's economic health."

Interestingly, some top executives see the real fomenter of managers' unrealistic expectations to be not business, but academe. They give low marks to business schools for encouraging in management students what one president calls "an exaggerated sense of their abilities and their prospects, which necessarily leads to frustration or failures." Adds President Joseph V. Quarles of Simmons Co.: "All young men are impatient—especially if they have the impression from business schools that industry will advance them to key positions immediately."

For top management, one of the big questions concerning middle-management alienation is whether it is a temporary problem or a long-lasting phenomenon that the corporation will have to learn to live with. Here, the panelists have mixed reactions. And most believe it depends on the quality of the managers themselves. In the opinion of Barber-Colman's Horst, "For good, aggressive managers, the alienation is transitory. For many of the others, they will probably carry a sour outlook on business for years to come."

Echoing this view is President James H. Hoffman of The Mansfield Tire & Rubber Co., who says, "The insecure and alienated will generally disappear from the scene."

But President George F. Dillon of Butler Manufacturing Co. disagrees. "I believe it is much more fundamental," says Dillon. "Credibility in the quality of business ethics has lessened; expectations of employees, young and old, is increasing. Human costs and rewards need to be more thoughtfully balanced against economic costs and rewards in the future."

On another point, though, the panelists are, not surprisingly, just about unanimous: management unionization. A recent American Management Association survey of middle managers shows that fully half of the respondents expect management to be unionized by 1980. The presidents do not think that Armageddon is nearly so close at hand. And they renounce the idea of management unions in terms ranging from "chaotic" to "disastrous."

Springs Mills' Peter Scotese reflects this viewpoint when he says, "I cannot believe that middle managers will unionize in any management climate that permits a high degree of participation and that rewards outstanding results."

President Herbert E. Markley of Timken Co. concedes that management unions are possible. But he brands them "bad for industry, since generally speaking unions are restrictive. A unionized middle management," Markley believes, "will make it most difficult to establish company loyalties, and inefficiency will grow."

Lest top management think that it cannot happen here, however, Richard Stockham Sr., reminds his peers, "A few years ago, few of us would have thought it possible to organize the teachers of the country into unions. I believe the answer lies within each organization and within the power of top management to provide an atmosphere that will eliminate the desire for such organizations."

"UNADULTERATED NONSENSE"

Over the long run, many management theorists are worried that defections from the executive ranks will result in the loss of creative, innovative people in industry. And this loss, they contend, will seriously affect U.S. industry's competitive stance in world markets.

While conceding that the disaffection is a serious problem for any company, the great majority of DUN's panelists doubt that its ramifications extend that far. R. G. Babcock, chief financial officer of Bird & Son, in fact, calls such a notion "absolute unadulterated nonsense. It is just a lot of academic theory perpetrated by the 'publish or perish' crowd sitting behind their ivy-covered walls," contends Babcock. "The creative, innovative managers generally have not gone anywhere. The competitive misfits who can't stand the pressure of bottomline performance have."

Agrees Timken's Herbert Markley: "I do not believe that the creative executive can be counted among the frustrated middle managers. Regardless of what detractors might say, business wants all the ideas it can get. People who are creative and innovative get a hearing, and get it promptly."

Yet the panelists continually emphasize top-management's responsibility for creating a proper working environment where managers can grow and flourish. To bolster personnel relations, says Russell Erickson of ITT Rayonier, industry must motivate middle managers with "incentives for outstanding performance, regular interviews, promotional opportunities, corporate recognition, reasonable job security and opportunities to participate in corporate planning, all the while providing managers with ample time for family and recreation."

Even R. G. Babcock, while castigating those managers who "spend too much time scheming for advancement rather than doing their own job to perfection," urges industry, "Let them know top management is aware of their existence, and definitely promote from within. 'They aren't ready,'" Babcock contends, "is a poor excuse for top management's unwillingness to gamble."

SELECTED READINGS

"The Blue-Collar Blues," *Newsweek,* May 17, 1971.

"Boredom on the Assembly Line," *Life,* September 1, 1972.

McGregor, D., *The Human Side of Enterprise.* (New York: McGraw-Hill, 1960).

Reich, C., *The Greening of America.* (New York: Random House, 1970).

Sheppard, H. L., and N. Herrick, *Where Have All the Robots Gone?.* (New York: The Free Press, 1972).

Terkel, S., *Working.* (New York: Pantheon, 1974).

Toffler, A., *Future Shock.* (New York: Random House, 1970).

Townsend, R., *Up the Organization.* (New York: Alfred A. Knopf, Inc., 1970).

Work in America, Report of a Special Task Force to the Secretary of Health, Education and Welfare. (Cambridge: M.I.T. Press, 1972).

Case

KINGSFORD MOTOR SALES, INC.

Kingsford Motor Sales, Inc., is a dealer for three lines of new cars—two domestic and one foreign—located in Kingsford, New Hampshire, a community about twelve miles above the Massachusetts border. Kingsford Motors is one of New England's highest-volume auto dealerships outside of the Boston area. Aggressive price cutting and a reputation for good service have attracted customers from an area radiating up to about 75 miles from the company's facility. On an average day, Kingsford sales personnel would move six to eight new cars and perhaps another six used vehicles. Sometimes sales reached 20 new cars a day. During the 1974 energy crisis, KMS was fortunate. While they did have over 120 large cars on hand, and these did not move well despite price cutting to below cost, they also had over 200 compact and foreign cars to sell; salesmen had little difficulty moving the smaller cars for full sticker prices.

Kingsford, the Community

The city of Kingsford is a community of some 68,000 people. It is primarily an industrial city, but its periphery and the surrounding towns are agricultural. Kingsford is an old community, founded in 1670 and incorporated as a city in 1864. The city's industrial plants are old and relatively inefficient, and have suffered the vicissitudes of business cycles, changing markets, import competition, and physical depreciation. Recently, two new plants were built on the outskirts of the city, the first new construction since the Second World War. Populationwise, the city has a mix typical of many New England industrial centers: old-line families descended from early settlers and factory owners, descendants from the immigrations of the late 1800's, and the "new" immigrants— unskilled blacks and Puerto Ricans—who have moved into some of the older homes in the city's core. Currently the community is experiencing the serious emigration of its younger citizens.

Kingsford's youth have not been isolated from the events and trends generally affecting youth throughout the country. Long hair and sloppy clothing are the vogue, along with the speech patterns common to the young. Some drugs have been reported in the high school. Students at the high school have demanded and won concessions such as the elimination of lunchroom attendance, restroom passes, and compulsory study hall. Kingsford High School hasn't had a senior prom for six years; and the student newspaper was recently the object of a state legislative investigation because of an article studded with four-letter words. The city's newspaper periodically runs editorials denouncing the new lifestyles and the general ''lack of discipline'' among Kingsford young people.

During the 1970 student unrest over the Vietnam war, events causing the most controversy were the smashing of windows at the local army recruiting office and the burning of the President in effigy on the city common. What made these events the talk of the city was the fact that the leader of the demonstrators was Jim Holson, son of Fred Holson, the President of the City Council, and Chairman of the Merrimack Republican Association.

Kingsford Motor Sales, the Organization and History

KMS was founded in 1929 by John Tilden to sell and service one prestige line of cars. Until 1950, John Tilden kept the agency relatively small, selling about one car a week and knowing all of his customers. Service was a byword with the agency, and the company was known as a place where ''you paid the price but were assured of being well taken care of.'' John Tilden was a conservative man and his dealership reflected that philosophy. Convertibles and station wagons were not stocked; of the ten or so cars kept on hand, all were sedans, and rarely was there a two-toned car on the lot. Tilden prided himself on the highest ethical conduct. In 1946, one local resident offered Tilden $400 extra to put his name higher on the waiting list for the first postwar automobiles. Tilden not only turned down the sum, but refused to sell the man a car at all.

John Tilden died in 1952 and his two sons, Jim and Steve, took over the business. In 1954, the Tilden brothers purchased 14 acres of land on the outskirts of town and built a new showroom and service center. They dropped the prestige car agency and took on one of the low-priced three. In 1959, they accepted the agency for a medium-priced, high-fashion line, and in 1965, added a foreign-car line as well. Soon after the new agency opened, the Tildens started advertising in the Boston papers and on TV stations around New Hampshire, Massachusetts, and Maine. Price cutting became standard (advertising stressed the low overhead of the New Hampshire location), and the agency used appeals with the newest style of vehicles and flashy accessories. In essence, the younger Tildens aimed at a mass selling dealership and keyed in on what they were convinced buyers were looking for—lowest price combined with high-style, high-performance automobiles. KMS salesmen felt no reluctance in pushing accessories, particularly those of a style appealing to the younger auto buyer. One of the city's sage older citizens, when passing the Tilden operation, was heard to comment, "If old John could see what those two kids did to his business, he'd turn over in his grave."

New Car Preparation

When a car was sold, the salesman would fill out the sales papers, arrange for financing and prepare a work order to service the car for delivery. KMS guaranteed 24-hour delivery of a new vehicle picked off the lot; and if the customer insisted, the car could be ready by the close of business on the day it was purchased.

Since cars were sold so rapidly, a special service area and crew were employed, separate from the repair service unit. The new-car preparation team consisted of two mechanics, an undercoating specialist, a body man, and a wash man. One of the mechanics, Sam Forbes, acted as foreman of the crew, but generally the salesmen went directly to whoever was working on "his car" to rush the work along. KMS had a 12-step standard new-car preparation procedure (called the "dirty dozen" by salesmen). These steps were:

1. Check lubrication and oil levels (sometimes cars were found to come from the plant unlubricated or with less oil than specified).
2. Winterize to 40 degrees below zero.
3. Check timing and ignition; adjust if necessary.
4. Align and balance wheels; check tire pressure.
5. Check and adjust brakes.
6. Check and adjust transmission.
7. Undercoat (if ordered by customer).
8. Install radio and other dealer-installed accessories.
9. Check and adjust door, hood, and trunk alignments.
10. Touch up scratches.
11. Test-ride.
12. Wash, clean, and vacuum.

The Wash Rack

Of all the jobs, the wash rack required the least skill, but was the dirtiest. After a car had gone through all the mechanical and body checks, it was delivered to the rack where it was washed and vacuumed, the stickers peeled off the windows, and the floor mats installed. This was the last station of the dirty dozen, and the one where salesmen waited impatiently to get the car for delivery. Sometimes a salesman directed his customer to the wash area to wait for the car. The wash-rack attendant was thus under pressure to get the car out. And if any scratch or imperfection, such as leaks, showed up, he was usually the first to hear about it in no kindly manner. Even though the wash-rack attendant had no role to play in the car's manufacture or preparation, he bore the brunt of a buyer's dissatisfaction. He was often asked such questions as "Can I trust that salesman?" or "Did he give me the best deal?" or "Is this car really gone over like they say it is?" Occasionally he was asked, "How do you disconnect the air-pollution device on this car?"

Tim Wallace

Tim Wallace was the fourth wash-rack attendant KMS employed in the last two years. He was 20 years old, having quit Kingsford High School at age 16 to work in a paper plant. He lasted at the paper plant four months, walking off the job complaining that the chemical smells made him nauseous. Tim then pumped gas on the 11:00 P.M. to 6:00 A.M. shift at the independent gas dealership on Main Street for about four months (one night, he just didn't show up). The next morning, he enlisted in the Army. After basic training, Tim was sent to infantry school and then to Vietnam for a year; he was wounded slightly and spent the final year of his service at Fort Dix, New Jersey, in a training company. Tim reached the rank of corporal before his discharge.

The Army and his war experience added little to Tim's skills for civilian life, but they did have an effect on his lifestyle. He grew a beard, wore long hair with a headband, and moved in with a radical commune in Desmond, Massachusetts. Tim experimented briefly with drugs, but stopped abruptly; he soon left the commune and returned with his girl friend, Lucille, to Kingsford, where they took up residence in an old farmhouse north of town. Tim had a motorcycle for transport. Some of the older residents had unkind things to say about Tim and Lucille, but generally they were not harassed.

When he applied for the wash-rack job at KMS, Steve Tilden at first was reluctant to even interview him. Tilden was hoping to get someone who was "straight," who could be relied on, and who would work hard, be punctual, and appreciate the fact that he had a job to do. After all, even though the wash-rack required little skill, it was still an important phase in new-car delivery, particularly for a high-volume dealer such as KMS. But when no one else applied for the job, Tilden hired Wallace.

Tim Wallace on the Job

For about four months, Wallace performed well; he showed up on time and his production rate, as well as the quality of his work, was quite satisfactory. One day, a customer complained about paper shavings in the back seat; the salesman brushed them out and said nothing, thinking the event a minor annoyance. But salesmen started receiving complaints about unwashed windows, cleaning compound left unwiped, water on the floors, etc. Steve Tilden talked to Wallace, who shrugged and said, "I'm doing my best. What do you have to do to please all those rich fat cats?"

Tilden also noted that Wallace started arriving five to ten minutes later and leaving five to ten minutes earlier each day. One day Tim called in sick (on sick days, a grease-and-oil man from the regular maintenance shop was called into service on the new-car wash rack). When asked the next day what was wrong, Tim just said, "Nothing much; just a 24-hour bug." Tilden could see no aftereffects of illness.

About a month later, Wallace called in sick again. At about 2:00 P.M. Sam Forbes, the foreman, called Wallace's house to find out how long he was going to be out. No one answered the phone. The next morning, Wallace replied to Tilden's questioning by saying that he was over at the drug store buying some aspirin. He seemed upset at having his whereabouts checked on.

Wallace called in sick again a week later. About 10:00 A.M., Forbes called Wallace's home and got no answer. At about the same time, a salesman told Tilden that he thought he saw Wallace and "some hippy girl" motorcycling down the interstate highway toward Boston.

Forbes burst into Tilden's office. "That damn Wallace is out again and I can't reach him. God, I know that they've got the same problems in the maintenance shop with the guys on the grease and wash racks, but the wash-rack on our end is too important. We've got to get those cars to customers. What the hell is this younger generation coming to?"

B. *Business and Equal Opportunity*

In the last quarter-century, most businesses at one time or another have faced the issue of discrimination. With the rapid development of the civil rights movement in the 1950's and the passage of the Civil Rights Act of 1964 (particularly Title VII covering employment), the elimination of explicit discriminatory practices and the reevaluation of procedures in recruitment and selection become important challenges for management. Certainly, personnel departments must now be increasingly professional and analytical in scrutinizing practices of recruitment, testing, screening, wage and salary administration, promotion, and evaluation.

The issues of employment discrimination and the growing aspirations of women and minority groups are, however, extremely complex ones. We introduce the topics by first discussing some basic data on the underutilization of women and minorities. Then we follow with a brief review of the laws, some indication of the problems in the enforcement of the laws, and finally some notes on managerial responses, problems, and opportunities resulting from the campaign against discrimination.

SOME DATA ON MINORITIES AND WOMEN

The civil rights struggle for blacks is the oldest of the contemporary campaigns and the earliest in terms of major impacts. While much of the publicity focused on sit-ins and boycotts instituted to secure such basic rights as desegregation in public facilities, restaurants, transit vehicles, and swimming pools, as well as on voting rights and school integration, considerable attention was also directed at employment practices and manpower utilization.

In 1960, blacks constituted about 9.5% of the civilian labor force, but the percentage of blacks in various categories of employment varied markedly from the percentage breakdown of the total labor force. For example, whereas 43.3% of the total labor force was employed in white-collar jobs, only about 16% of the black labor force was so employed (and of those, almost half were clerical workers as opposed to one-third clerical in the white-collar category for the total labor force). On the other hand, while only 12.2% of the labor force was employed in service work, fully 31% of the blacks were so employed.

By 1972, the picture had improved somewhat. Almost 30% of the blacks were now in white-collar jobs (although half were still in clerical work) as opposed to

47.8% white-collar in the total labor force. The percentage of blacks in service work declined to 27%, but this figure was still twice that for the general labor force. The largest change came in farm workers. While, in 1960, 12% of the black labor force was in farm work, by 1972 the figure dropped to 3%.

On the other hand, the data also show that black employment is still heavily concentrated in low-wage sectors and industries, and that blacks generally are more adversely affected by recessions than are whites. Black unemployment rates are consistently double those of whites and the median income of black families is about 58% of the median income of white families (up from 55% in 1960, but down from 60% in 1970).

A more recent civil rights movement involves the aspirations and rights of women and the placement of women in job categories where traditionally they were not found. In 1960, women comprised 30% of the civilian labor force; by 1972 that percentage had increased to 38%. But like blacks, the breakdown of women in specific job categories is heavily skewed toward relatively unprestigious work. Women are found primarily in clerical, operative, and service-worker roles. They are vastly underrepresented in craftsman, foreman, and management roles.

Similar problems of underrepresentation can be found with other minorities— Spanish-Americans, American Indians, and Asian-Americans. While one may doubt that proportional representation of blacks, women, Chicanos, or Indians in each of the specific occupational categories, according to their percentages in the population, will ever be attained (whether it is wise social policy to attempt to engineer such proportions is being hotly debated), nevertheless, a legacy of discrimination clearly shows in the data. Minority-group members and women often lack marketable skills and have historically been prevented from entry into many better-paying and prestigious positions.

THE LAW AND SOME CASES

Since 1964, the federal government and most of the states have enacted legislation aimed at preventing discrimination in employment. In the major federal law, the Civil Rights Act of 1964* (as amended in 1968 and 1972), Title VII covers employers with "fifteen or more employees for each working day in each of twenty or more calendar weeks in the current or preceding calendar year . . .," as well as labor unions and employment agencies. The Act prohibits discrimination on the basis of race, color, religion, sex, or national origin in hiring, firing, compensation, or any other condition of employment. The law also prohibits the segregation or classification of employees in any way that adversely affects an employee's status because of race, color, religion, sex, or national origin. Finally, the Act bars the publication of job openings or notices specifying race, sex, color, religion or national origin as job requirements.

---

*One year earlier, Congress passed the Equal Pay Act, eliminating pay differences based on sex or race.

Another discriminatory pattern, and one that should receive much more attention, is that involving age. The Age Discrimination in Employment Act of 1967 was passed to protect individuals between the ages of 40 and 65 from being discriminated against in employment and job conditions. The Act, enforced by the Secretary of Labor, also forbids employers to exclude individuals being hired from participating in pension plans if the age group of the new employee is already included.

Enforcement of Title VII rests with the Equal Employment Opportunity Commission. The EEOC, created by the 1964 Act, originally was empowered only to attempt rectification by conciliatory methods, with the complainant taking the case to court in the event EEOC intervention failed. With the 1972 amendment, however, the Commission was empowered to file suit in federal court to enforce compliance with its orders. The EEOC has been winning its cases, and its ability to go to the courts has allowed it to negotiate some substantial out-of-court settlements. American Telephone and Telegraph Company paid, in an out-of-court settlement, over $15 million in back pay to women and minority group employees who were discriminated against in terms of pay and job advancement. Recently, nine major steel producers agreed to a back-pay, interest, and future-pay settlement that could run as high as $80 million the first year.

In sex discrimination cases, women have won the right to all types of positions formerly reserved for men only, and men have sued for employment in jobs traditionally thought to be for women only—hosting on airline flights, for example. In the emerging area of age discrimination, Standard Oil Company of California agreed to pay $2 million in back pay to employees discharged because of age in the three years ending December 31, 1973. SOCAL agreed to also rehire 120 of the employees. The Labor Department has recently sued two railroads, the Baltimore and Ohio and the Chesapeake and Ohio, to restore $20 million in back pay and benefits to 300 employees allegedly discriminated against because of age.

Another stage in the government's campaign against discrimination is Affirmative Action. Under Executive Order 11246, promulgated by President Lyndon B. Johnson, all businesses and institutions holding federal contracts (or subcontracting for a federal contract) are required to develop numerical goals, plans, and timetables for implementation to increase the numbers of females and minority-group employees in all categories within their firms. The theory behind Affirmative Action is that special effort must be undertaken to compensate for past discriminatory patterns. Compliance with the Executive Order is guided by the agency awarding the contract or administering the area corresponding to the primary focus of the institution; the Department of Health, Education and Welfare, for example, monitors the affirmative action activities for universities.

Some concern has been expressed that, in the application of affirmative action, goals are turned into quotas and favoritism takes place for women and minority-group members over white males. Critics have charged that the federal contracting offices' application of affirmative action is substantially at odds with the Civil Rights

Act of 1964. In a recent case involving university admissions, a University of Washington Law School applicant, Marco DiFunis, sued the University for violating his civil rights when minority students with qualifications inferior to his were admitted and he was denied admission. A lower court ruled for the applicant and he was admitted to the law school. But DiFunis continued the case. When the case finally reached the U.S. Supreme Court, DiFunis was ready to graduate, so the Court ruled the issue moot. But there is little doubt that further cases of alleged reverse discrimination, some involving employment, will be brought before the Supreme Court.

MANAGERIAL RESPONSES, PROBLEMS AND OPPORTUNITIES

The new laws and court interpretations of them impose several obligations on management. First, traditional sources of recruitment may no longer be adequate. Management must expand its practices to include not only offering equal opportunity in the selection process, but also assuring that potential applicants have equal access to notices of job openings. Second, traditional selection devices such as tests, profiles, and employment reviews must be reevaluated for validity, reliability, cultural bias, and necessity. In a recent case, a company was found to be using tests and requiring high school diplomas when it could establish no specific basis for these requirements relative to the jobs at issue.

Companies must also reevaluate their concepts of sex requirements for jobs, and discard many of the prevailing myths about the performance of women and minority-group members. All of this, of course, increases the need for competent professionalization of personnel departments.

Lastly, some critics argue, companies and society should realize that having an essentially black or minority workforce with a white supervisory staff might entail costs in terms of lost productivity, job disruption, poor communication, and frustration. In essence, by actively promoting minority-group members to supervisory positions and managerial ranks, companies develop productive links with operative employees that they might not be able to develop with white-only supervision.

THE READINGS

The first two articles focus on the status of women and blacks in U.S. society. Shirley H. Rhine (in the *Conference Board Record*) traces changes in the status of blacks in recent years in terms of income, employment, entrepreneurship, education, and geographical location. The General Electric study analyzes the history of changes in the status of women, the present role of women in the labor force, and the issues raised by the Women's Rights movement. Finally, the study focuses on the implications of the movement for business.

The paper by W. H. Brown III, former Chairman of the Equal Employment Opportunity Commission, presents an explanation of Title VII, some of the areas in personnel matters where discrimination is highly possible, and some of the remedies sought by the EEOC and ordered by the courts. In his statement, Brown seeks to explain "numerical remedies," where the EEOC and the courts have mandated specific racial composition for new hiring or personnel assignments. Commenting on a decision involving a "specific racial ratio in faculty assignments," Brown concludes that "Careful reading of the Supreme Court decision makes it clear that where discrimination exists, it must be entirely eliminated and the remedy adopted must be appropriate to such elimination."

But the circumstances for applying "numerical remedies" are far from clear to lawyers and laymen alike. It is that problem and the associated ones involving affirmative action programs that Daniel Seligman examines in his *Fortune* article, "How 'Equal Opportunity' Turned Into Employment Quotas."

The Economic Status of Black Americans
Change has already lessened some of the historical differences

Shirley H. Rhine

Concern about the depressed condition of the majority of black Americans has undoubtedly broadened and deepened in recent years. It was fostered by a combination of events culminating in the civil disorders and race riots of the 1960's. Heightened pressure by blacks and other disadvantaged groups, as well as by many segments of the more affluent white population, certainly hastened the passage of the Civil Rights Act and the Economic Opportunity Act, in 1964.

The former prohibits discrimination in employment, education, public facilities, voting rights in Federal elections and primaries, and in programs receiving Federal assistance. The principal objective of the Economic Opportunity Act is the extirpation of poverty through a variety of programs for improving the education, training, work experience, and health of the disadvantaged so they may upgrade their earning ability.

Although less than a decade has elapsed since the passage of these basic legislative acts, they have apparently already had a significant impact. This article attempts to depict how much progress blacks have made in recent years, and how well off they are today compared with the white population.

From *The Conference Board Record,* August, 1972. Reprinted by special permission of The Conference Board.

The median income of black families[1] in 1970 was $6,279, or 61% of the $10,236 figure for white families.[2] While the gap remains substantial, it has shrunk markedly since 1965 when the average income of black families was only 54% that of the whites. However, black families are somewhat less well off vis-à-vis whites than is indicated by a comparison of median family income of the two groups, since black families are inclined to be larger. In March 1971 the average number of persons per black family was 4.26 compared with 3.52 per white family.

The narrowing of the discrepancy between incomes of blacks and whites since the mid-1960's undoubtedly reflects the influence of the Civil Rights Act. The relatively high rate of growth of the economy as a whole during the latter half of the 1960's probably also played a part in the reduction of the black-white income spread. Periods of rapid economic expansion, when demand for manpower is great, tend to be particularly favorable to the disadvantaged groups in the labor force. The competitive disadvantage of minority groups in finding employment and obtaining promotions tends to diminish in periods of rapidly growing manpower needs.

In recent decades the most dramatic annual rise in the ratio of incomes of blacks to whites occurred in 1966 when it rose to 58% from 54% in 1965. It is relevant to note that 1966 was the first full year in operation of the Equal [Employment] Opportunity Commission, which went into effect in July 1965. Moreover, from 1950 to 1965 there was no notable reduction in income differentials between whites and blacks.

From 1965 to 1970 the gap between average family income of blacks and whites narrowed proportionately more in the South than in the rest of the nation. Nonetheless, family income of blacks in the South in 1970 was still only 57% that of whites, markedly below the other three regions (Chart 1). The differential between incomes in the South and the rest of the country is considerably more pronounced for blacks than for whites.

Female heads of families are far more common among blacks than among whites. In 1971 some 29% of black families were headed by women as against only 9% of white families. This contributes significantly to the black-white family

---

[1]Statistical series from the Bureau of the Census and the Bureau of Labor Statistics do not always break out blacks separately. Some of the series apply to nonwhites, which include American Indians, Japanese, Chinese, Filipinos, Asian Indians, Koreans, Polynesians, Indonesians, Hawaiians. Aleuts, and Eskimos, in addition to blacks. (Persons with Spanish surnames, such as Puerto Ricans, are classified according to color, i.e., white or black.) Since blacks account for 90% of the nonwhite population, trends in the latter are virtually identical with trends in the former. For this reason, the designation "blacks" is used throughout.

[2]Here and below, "income of families" applies exclusively to families and does not include unrelated individuals.

Daniel Huff
How to lie with statistics

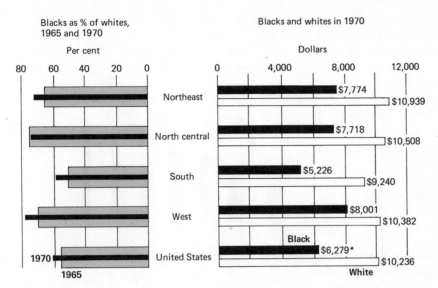

Blacks as % of whites, 1965 and 1970

Blacks and whites in 1970

Per cent

Dollars

* Since slightly more than half of the black families in 1970 lived in the South and only 8% lived in the West (region where incomes of black families were highest), the median income of black families for the United States as a whole is closer to that of blacks in the South than in the rest of the country.

CHART 1 Median family income

Source: Bureau of the Census

income gap since the median income of female-headed families is considerably lower than that of males—54% lower for black families in 1970 and 46% lower for white. Hence, among families headed by men, the median income of blacks in 1970 was 73% that of whites.

Blacks are far less likely than whites to have income from interest, dividends, rent, estates, trusts, or royalties. Only 11% of the black families had income from one or more of these sources in 1970, compared with 45% of white families. However, blacks are more likely to receive public assistance and welfare payments. Some 22% of the black families received income from these sources in 1970 as against only 4% of white families.

During the past two decades the number of black families with annual income of $10,000 or more has been increasing at a considerably faster rate than the number of white families in that income range, particularly between 1965 and 1970. During that five-year interval the number of black families in the $10,000-and-over bracket (in constant 1970 dollars) doubled, while the number of white families in that category increased by one-third. Even so, only 28% of the black families had incomes of $10,000 or over in 1970, compared with 52% for whites (Chart 2).

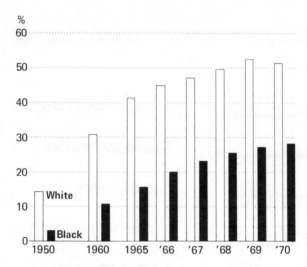

CHART 2. Percent of families with income of $10,000 or more
Source: Bureau of the Census

INCIDENCE OF POVERTY

In 1970 there were still 1.4 million black families and 3.7 million white families below the official low-income level[3] despite substantial progress during the past decade in reducing poverty. From 1959 to 1970 the proportion of families below the poverty threshold fell from 48% to 29% among blacks and from 15% to 8% among whites. Virtually all of this gain was achieved between 1959 and 1968, with no marked change in 1969 and 1970, the latest year for which data are available.

Unlike white families, black families below the low-income level are predominantly headed by women. In 1970 some 43% of the black families below the poverty line had a male head compared with 70% of the white families.

Among both blacks and whites, families with a female head are more prone to be below the poverty line than those with a male head. Among blacks, 54% of the families headed by women were below the poverty threshold in 1970 as against 18% of those headed by men. Among whites, the respective ratios were 25% and 6%. Moreover, the proportion of families in poverty headed by men has declined far more precipitously in the past decade than those headed by women (Chart 3).

---

[3]The concept of poverty, or low income, as used here was developed by the Social Security Administration in 1964 and revised by a Federal Interagency Committee in 1969. Poverty thresholds vary by family size, sex and age of the family head, number of children, and farm-nonfarm residence. They are updated annually to reflect changes in the Consumer Price Index. The poverty line for a nonfarm family of four was $2,973 in 1959, $3,743 in 1969 and $3,968 in 1970. In 1970 it ranged from $2,500 for a two-person family to $6,400 for a family of seven or more persons.

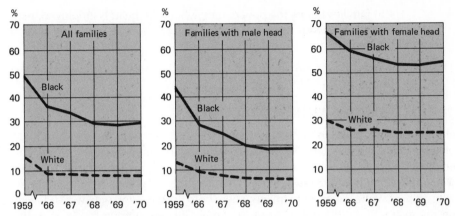

CHART 3. Percent of families below the low-income level
Source: Bureau of the Census

Explanations for the high incidence of poverty among families headed by women are quite obvious. First, a substantial portion of these women have young children. Consequently, many of them are unable to leave the home to take jobs or are able to work only a limited number of hours a week. As a result they tend to have no earnings or very small earnings, and often have to rely either wholly or partially on public assistance. Also, women on the average have smaller incomes than men. In addition, a woman head is less likely to have another adult in the family to contribute earnings, whereas a man may have a wife who can also work.

One reason why black families with a female head have proportionately larger numbers in poverty than their white counterparts is that black women tend to have lower-paying jobs and more dependents than white women. Secondly, it is more common for black women who are widowed to be less adequately provided for by life insurance and/or savings. Black women who are divorced or separated from their husbands are less likely to receive support payments from their erstwhile or estranged spouses, and when such support is received it is more likely to be smaller than for whites.

Some 45% of the black families and 21% of the white families below the poverty threshold received public assistance or welfare payments in 1969 (the latest year for which data are available). Among the reasons for the higher proportion of black families in poverty that receive public assistance are:

> • On the average, far wider presence of female heads among black families below the low-income level than among white. A substantially smaller proportion of women than men who head such families are employed. Among families in poverty, slightly less than 30% of the female heads were employed in 1970 compared with 58% of the male heads among blacks and 50% of the male heads among whites.

• In families below the poverty line where the head is employed, earnings of the heads in black families are, on the average, lower than in white ones.

• Whites are more likely to have assets, such as savings, which would disqualify them for public relief.

FAMILIES WITH TWO INCOMES

Husband–wife families in 1970 represented 89% of total white families[4] and 70% of total black families.[5] Wives in black families are more likely to be gainfully employed and to contribute a larger share to the family coffer. Among husband-wife families, 54% of the wives in black families were working in 1970 compared with 38% of white wives. For families where both husband and wife worked, wives on the average contributed 31% of the family income among blacks and 26% among whites.

Median income for families with both spouses working shows a considerably smaller gap between blacks and whites than for other types of families. In 1970 the median income of black husband-wife families where both worked was 79% of their white equivalents.

The income differential between black and white families in this category tends to be correlated with the age of the family head, i.e., the differential is smaller for families where the husband is young than where he is older. For example, in 1970 among families where both spouses worked and the husband was under 35 years old, the median income of black families was 89% that of white, compared with 66% for those families with a head aged 55–64.

In the North and West, among families with both spouses working, blacks seem to be well on their way toward achieving income parity with whites. (In the South, not only is the average income of white families below the rest of the country but the ratio of black to white is also lower.) Among families where both husband and wife worked, the median income of black families was 92% of whites. Also in the North and West, in 1970, the ratio of the median income of black families with both husband and wife working to their white counterparts graduated from 81%, where the head was between 55 and 64 years old, to 104%, with a head under 35 years old.

The achievement of parity with whites, or even slightly more, in the North and West for the latter group of black families can be attributed to the greater annual earnings of black wives compared with white. For families where the head was under 35 years old, the mean earnings of wives in black families was 130% that

---

[4]The other 11% are families with a female head (9%) and families, other than husband-wife families, with a male head (2%).

[5]The other 30% are families with a female head (27%) and families, other than husband-wife families, with a male head (3%).

Age	Men		Women	
	Black	White	Black	White
Total, 16 years & over	74.9	79.6	49.2	42.6
16 and 17 years	32.4	49.2	21.9	36.4
18 and 19 years	58.9	67.8	41.4	55.0
20 to 24 years	81.5	83.2	56.0	57.9
25 to 34 years	92.9	96.3	59.2	43.6
35 to 44 years	92.0	97.0	61.0	50.2
45 to 54 years	86.9	94.7	59.4	53.7
55 to 64 years	77.8	82.6	47.1	42.5
65 years and over	24.5	25.6	11.5	9.3

(1971 averages)

TABLE 1. Civilian labor force participation rates,* by age, sex, and race

*Percent civilian noninstitutional population in the labor force.
Source: Bureau of Labor Statistics

of white wives, while for husbands in black families it was 90% that of the white husbands. Higher earnings of black wives reflects more work time during the year. In 1970 in the North and West 52% of the wives in black families, where the husband was under 35 years, worked 50 to 52 weeks, compared with 36% of their white counterparts. Whether, among black families, working wives with husbands under 35 also worked more hours per week than their white counterparts cannot be determined since the relevant data are not available.

BLACKS IN THE LABOR FORCE

The percentage of the noninstitutional population 16 years and over that is in the labor force is, in the aggregate, virtually the same for blacks and whites—60.9% and 60.1%, respectively, in 1971. However, when viewed by age and sex, labor force participation rates between blacks and whites show marked differences.

Black men have lower participation rates than white men in all age groups, particularly among teen-agers. However, black women have a higher participation rate than white at all ages, except for the 16–19 group where it is substantially lower and the 20–24 category where it is only nominally lower (Table 1).

On the whole, black women of necessity carry a larger share of the family financial burden than white women. First, a far larger share of black families have female heads—29% in 1971, compared with only 9% of the white families. Second, since black husbands on the average earn less than their white counterparts and tend to have somewhat larger families to support, black wives are more strongly motivated to contribute to the family income.

Only 36% of the total black population was in the labor force in 1971 as against 41% of the white. It is quite evident that a significantly larger share of the black population is economically dependent, which is traced to the higher proportion of black children under 16 years old than white.

BLACK UNEMPLOYMENT

Unemployment rates historically have been considerably higher for blacks than for whites. This phenomenon stems from a variety of sources:

- Largely as a consequence of a relatively greater number of school dropouts among blacks in the labor force than among whites, blacks are more heavily concentrated in low-skill jobs whose holders are generally more vulnerable to both cyclical and secular unemployment.

- Since blacks on the average have fewer years of schooling, often of a lower quality than whites, they are frequently at a competitive disadvantage in the market for middle-range and upper-range jobs.

- Racial discrimination, while receding, has also been a deterrent in the hiring of blacks.

During the entire decade of the 1960's the jobless rate among blacks was at least twice as high as among whites, but in the past two years it was running about 80% higher. In 1971 the unemployment rate averaged 9.9% for blacks and 5.4% for whites.

In contrast to most previous periods of rising unemployment when blacks tended to suffer sharper increases than whites, the unemployment rate for blacks rose by 55% from 1969 to 1971 compared with 74% for the whites. The Bureau of Labor Statistics attributes the narrowing differential between the unemployment rate of blacks and whites to a combination of factors: (a) rising educational level of blacks has permitted them greater access to occupations that are less vulnerable to employment cutbacks during cyclical declines; (b) paucity of blacks in those industries which experienced the sharpest declines in employment such as defense and aerospace industries; (c) industries where relatively large numbers of blacks are employed, such as service industries and government, did not undergo severe reductions in employment; (d) relatively large enrollment of blacks in manpower programs; (e) decline in discriminatory practices among employers in laying off of black workers during a period of employment cutbacks.

MOVING UP THE LADDER

Upward mobility in the occupational scale during the 1960's was far more dramatic for blacks than for whites. From 1960 to 1971 the number of professional and technical workers among blacks rose 128% and the number of managers, proprietors and officials rose 92%, compared with 45% and 21%, respectively, for whites. Conversely, the number of blacks in those occupations which tend to be least remunerative—private household workers, farmers and farm workers, and nonfarm laborers—registered steeper declines in the past decade than the number of whites in these jobs (Chart 4).

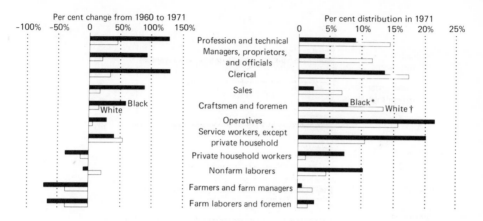

Per cent change from 1960 to 1971
-100% -50%   0   50% 100% 150%

Per cent distribution in 1971
0   5%   10%   15%   20%   25%

Profession and technical
Managers, proprietors, and officials
Clerical
Sales
Craftsmen and foremen
Operatives
Service workers, except private household
Private household workers
Nonfarm laborers
Farmers and farm managers
Farm laborers and foremen

Black
White

Black*
White †

*Percent of total black employment
†Percent of total white employment

CHART 4. Employment by occupation
Source: Bureau of Labor Statistics

The marked improvement in the occupation profile of blacks in the past decade has accrued from a variety of sources:

> • Heightened demand during the 1960's for professional and technical workers, particularly for teachers, engineers, and technicians. Opportunities for jobs are naturally more numerous in those occupations where demand is expanding and applicants become increasingly scarce.
> • Decline of racial bias in employment, undoubtedly partly attributable to the Civil Rights Act of 1964.
> • The level of educational attainment of blacks in the labor force has been rising at a faster rate than for whites.
> • The mushrooming of programs, sponsored both by government and private groups, for training the unskilled and upgrading those with low-level skills has enabled many blacks and other disadvantaged to obtain better jobs.

Despite the impressive growth in the number of blacks in the more coveted occupational groups and declines in the least desirable ones, their number is still disproportionately small in the former and large in the latter (Chart 4). Moreover, even within each occupational group, earnings for full-time male workers are consistently lower for blacks than whites. However, for women, earnings of blacks more closely approach those of whites for each of the occupational classifications, and for private household workers even exceed whites by 10% (Chart 5).

The black-white earnings differential has shrunk substantially more for women than for men in the past decade. Part of the explanation for this is that there was

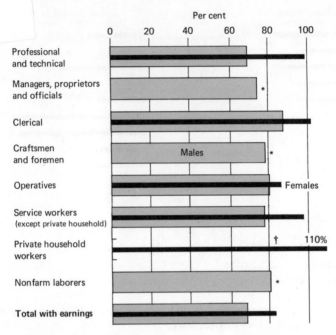

CHART 5. Median earnings of year-round full-time workers in 1970, blacks as percent of whites, by sex

an especially sharp increase in demand in those occupations which attract mainly women—clerical workers, teachers, and nurses. Hence, opportunities for moving up into better-paying jobs were probably greater for black women than for black men. In addition, black women have, on the average, higher levels of educational attainment than black men—55% of the black women in the labor force in 1971 had at least a high school education compared with 45% of the black men. Consequently, black women were better able to take advantage of the greater availability of higher-paying jobs.

Another reason why black women have made greater gains than black men in reducing the lag between their earnings and those of their white counterparts is that wages and salaries of white women have risen proportionately less than the earnings of white men during the past decade. Sex discrimination may have restrained gains in earnings of white women.

The gap between earnings of blacks and whites for all full-time workers, both men and women, is greater than within individual occupational groups since there are proportionately far more blacks than whites in the lower-paid occupational groups and proportionately fewer in the higher paid ones.

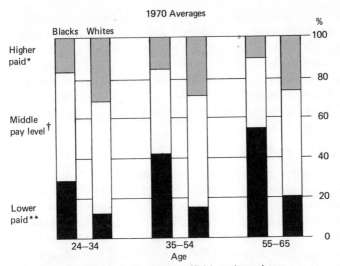

CHART 6. Distribution of employment by occupational levels for selected age groups
Source: Bureau of Labor Statistics

To what can the earnings differentials between whites and blacks within each occupational group be attributed? A combination of factors probably contribute to this reality:

- There is a broad range of jobs within each occupational group with an equally broad range of wage levels, and blacks and other minority groups tend to be somewhat more heavily concentrated in the lower tiers of the occupational scale within each broad category.

- Particularly in the better-paying jobs, blacks tend to be younger than whites. Consequently, on the average they earn less than whites in specific job classifications, reflecting less experience and seniority. Also, at entrance levels, blacks often are less qualified owing to inferior educational opportunities at segregated schools.

- A disproportionately large number of blacks live in the South where earnings are significantly lower than in the rest of the country.

- Discrimination, while declining, doubtlessly still exists and operates as an earnings depressant, e.g., opportunities for promotions and advancement may still be more limited for blacks than for whites.

The disproportionality in occupational distribution between whites and blacks, it should be noted, is considerably less pronounced among younger workers than among older ones, particularly at the middle- and lower-pay levels. In 1970 the proportion of persons aged 24 through 34 who were in occupations at the middle-pay level was 55% for both blacks and whites, while 35% of the blacks between the ages of 55 and 65 were in the middle-range occupations compared with 52% of the whites. Conversely, some 29% of the blacks in the 24–34 age group were in lower paid jobs compared with 13% for whites. But for those aged 55 through 65, fully 55% of the blacks were in the lower-level occupations as against only 21% of the whites (Chart 6).

BLACK BUSINESSES

Blacks are particularly underrepresented as entrepreneurs. According to a recent study of the U.S. Bureau of the Census,[6] in 1969 blacks owned 163,000 firms, or only 2.2% of the total 7.5 million firms in the United States. An even more dramatic indicator of the relative paucity of black-owned businesses is their share of all minority-owned firms. While blacks accounted for about three-fourths of the minority population,[7] they possessed only one-half of all minority-owned businesses.

The share of business activity accounted for by minority firms is especially tiny. Gross receipts of black-owned businesses represented only 0.3% of gross receipts of all firms, and other minorities had 0.4%.

Minority-owned businesses are far more likely than the rest of the business population to be small, one-person or family-run operations. Over three-fourths of the black-owned and two-thirds of other minority-owned firms had no paid employees; in 1969 they had average gross receipts of $7,000 and $8,000, respectively. For firms with one or more paid employees, those owned by blacks averaged four employees and gross receipts of $95,000; similarly, those owned by other minority groups also averaged four employees and gross receipts of $102,000. A mere 2% of the firms owned by blacks, as well as by other minorities, had gross receipts of $200,000 or more in 1969.

Minority-owned businesses are overwhelmingly sole proprietorships, constituting 91% of black-owned firms and 84% of other minority-owned firms. Conversely, the corporate form of business, which accounts for some 19% of U.S.

---

[6]U.S. Bureau of the Census, *Minority-Owned Businesses: 1969.* The study embraces all private industries with the exception of agriculture, railroad transportation, offices of physicians and dentists, legal services, and nonprofit organizations. Most of the data have not been compiled for earlier years so no information on the time trends is available. However, the Bureau of the Census plans to prepare a similar set of tabulations for 1972, scheduled for 1974 publication. It would be interesting to see whether, in the three-year period from 1969 to 1972, blacks and other minority groups have made significant gains as owners of business enterprises.

[7]"Minority population" as used in this context includes blacks, Spanish-speaking groups (of Mexican American, Puerto Rican, Cuban, and Latin American ancestry) plus Orientals and American Indians.

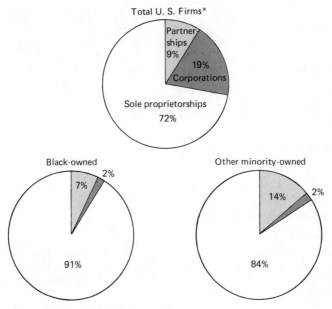

Total U. S. Firms*

Partnerships 9%

19% Corporations

Sole proprietorships 72%

Black-owned

2%

7%

91%

Other minority-owned

14%   2%

84%

*Data for 1967. See footnote in Table 2.
Note: Note to Table 2 also applies to data in this chart.

CHART 7. Distribution of firms by legal form of organization, 1969

Source: Bureau of the Census

business firms, is relatively rare among minority-owned firms; only 2% are corporations (Chart 7).

In view of the rarity of the corporate form, which is designed to enlist comparatively large investments through the participation of many persons, it is not surprising that black-owned firms are substantially underrepresented in industries which tend to require relatively large amounts of capital and/or relatively high levels of managerial skill. These industries are manufacturing, wholesale trade, finance, insurance, and real estate. (Table 2).

The kinds of business where black ownership is relatively large are selected services (dominated by beauty shops, barber shops, laundry and dry cleaning plants, building maintenance services, and auto repair services and garages), retail trade (nearly three-fifths of the firms are eating and drinking places or food stores), and transportation and other public utilities (four-fifths of the firms in this group are in taxicab service or trucking and warehousing).

The geographic distribution of minority-owned firms, as would be expected, conforms rather closely with the geographic scatter of the minority populations. Hence, the black-owned firms are heavily concentrated in the South, while the majority of other minority businesses are located in the West (including Hawaii and

Industry Division	All Firms*		Black-Owned Firms		Other Minority-Owned Firms	
	Number (000's)	Percent of Total	Number (000's)	Percent of Total	Number (000's)	Percent of Total
All Industries, Total ...	**7,489**	**100.0**	**163**	**99.9**	**159**	**99.9**
Contract construction	856	11.4	16	9.8	14	8.8
Manufactures	401	5.4	3	1.8	5	3:1
Transportation and other public utilities	359	4.8	17	10.4	7	4.4
Wholesale trade	434	5.8	1	.6	4	2.5
Retail trade	2,046	27.3	45	27.6	52	32.7
Finance, insurance and real estate	1,223	16.3	8	4.9	14	8.8
Selected services	1,803	24.1	56	34.4	45	28.3
Other industries and not classified	367	4.9	17	10.4	18	11.3

TABLE 2. Number of firms in 1969

*From the Internal Revenue Service, "Statistics of Income, 1967," latest year for which complete data are available. The Bureau of the Census study notes that the 1969 data for all firms are expected to show approximately the same relationship between minority-owned firms and total firms as is shown by using 1969 data for the former and 1967 data for the latter.
Note: These data exclude the following businesses: agriculture, railroad transportation, offices of physicians and dentists, legal services, and nonprofit organizations.
Source: Bureau of the Census

	Number of Firms	Gross Receipts (Millions)	Percent of Total	
			Number of Firms	Gross Receipts
Black-Owned Firms				
Northeast	24,392	$ 675.1	15.1	15.4
North Central	36,635	1,188.3	22.6	27.0
South	83,262	2,054.5	51.4	46.8
West	17,761	476.1	10.9	10.8
United States [a]	162,050	4,394.0	100.0	100.0
Other Minority-Owned Firms				
Northeast	18,891	$ 614.2	11.9	10.0
North Central	12,330	418.4	7.7	6.8
South	41,873	1,491.0	26.4	24.3
West	85,374	3,606.2	53.9	58.8
United States [b]	158,468	6,129.3	99.9	99.9

TABLE 3. Regional distribution of minority-owned firms in 1969

[a]Excludes 1,023 firms, with gross receipts of $80.3 million, not specified by region.
[b]Excludes 417 firms, with gross receipts of $35.3 million, not specified by region.
Note: Note to Table 2 also applies to this table.
Source: Bureau of the Census

Alaska) where the bulk of Mexican-Americans, Japanese, Chinese, Filipinos, and Hawaiians reside (Table 3).

EDUCATIONAL ATTAINMENT

The gradual shrinkage of the wide gap in educational attainment that has traditionally existed between whites and blacks has contributed toward the economic gains of blacks. In 1959 the median years of school completed by persons in the civilian labor force 18 years and over was 8.7 years for blacks and 12.1 for whites. By 1971 the figure of 11.9 years for blacks was only a half-year less than the 12.5 years for whites. While the number of school years completed by white workers has been virtually the same for men and women since the late 1950's, black women have been averaging one more year of schooling than black men.

The relative change between 1959 and 1971 in the proportion of persons in the labor force 18 years old and over that had not completed high school was virtually identical for blacks and whites. For blacks it fell from 73% in 1959 to 50% in 1971; for whites it dropped from 47% to 31%. However, the relative gain in the percentage of blacks in the labor force who are college graduates was much larger than for whites. For blacks it rose from 4% in 1959 to 7% in 1971, and for whites it rose from 10% to 14%. The share of the black labor force that had at least graduated from high school but had not graduated from college grew from 20% in 1959 to 42% in 1971, a relatively greater increase than for whites, which expanded from 42% to 55% over that 12-year interval.

While younger persons in the workforce are on the average better educated than older members among both blacks and whites, the educational gap between younger and older workers is considerably more pronounced for blacks. Moreover, among young adults, the educational differential between whites and blacks seems to be disappearing.

In 1971, for persons between the ages of 20 and 34, including those who were not in the labor force as well as those who were, the median years of school completed was 12.3 years for blacks, closely approaching the 12.7 years for whites. For persons 35 years old and over, blacks averaged 9.1 years of schooling compared with 11.3 years for whites.

While there is concrete statistical evidence that impressive strides have been made toward closing the educational gap between blacks and whites in terms of quantity, particularly among young adults, changes in quality are more difficult to ascertain. However, it is probable that the quality lag has also begun to shorten. This assumption is based on the large-scale shifts of the black population from the rural South to the metropolitan North and West where standards of education are higher; the greater proportion of blacks being educated in desegregated institutions at all levels—elementary, secondary, and universities and colleges; and efforts to improve instruction in ghetto schools.

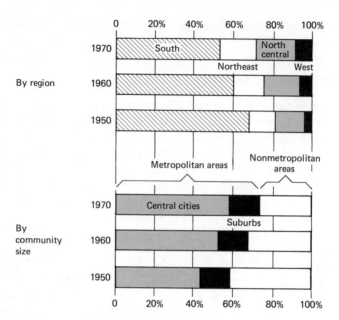

CHART 8. Geographic distribution of black population
Source: Bureau of the Census

BLACK MIGRATION

Another trend of recent decades which probably has had a salutary effect on the income of blacks is their large-scale exodus from the South, together with their passage from rural areas to central cities; i.e., the migration from lower-earnings areas to those of higher earnings. While part of the farm-to-city migration of blacks was intraregional, most of it was from the rural South to the urban North and West.

As a result of these geographic shifts, the proportion of the black population living in the South dropped from over three-fourths in 1940 to two-thirds in 1950, and then to slightly over one-half in 1970; the proportion living in central cities climbed from 44% in 1950 to 58% in 1970, while those residing outside metropolitan areas declined during the past two decades from 41% to 26% (Chart 8). The chief impetus for these shifts has been the shrinkage of employment opportunities in rural places, particularly in the South, as agriculture has become increasingly mechanized since the 1930's. Many submarginal farms have been withdrawn from cultivation and the land allocated to nonfarm uses, while industrial expansion has taken place in the metropolitan areas.

The migration pattern of the whites in recent decades has differed markedly from that of the blacks. While larger numbers of whites have also left rural areas for reasons similar to the blacks, the dominant trend for the whites has been away from metropolitan centers to suburban communities. By 1970 only 28% of the whites lived in central cities compared with 35% in 1950; the proportion living in suburban rings of metropolitan areas rose from 28% in 1950 to 40% in 1970.

As family needs and preferences are not uniform, so the impetus for the flight of whites from inner cities to the suburbs is not traceable to a single cause. Undoubtedly, some white families were motivated, at least in part, by the heavy influx of blacks. Others may find suburban residence more gratifying than urban for any number of reasons: greater safety in the streets, less noise, cleaner air, better schools, more play area for children, more spacious accommodations in a suburban house than a city apartment, and the appeal of home ownership and the building up of equity in a house.

It should be noted that many blacks, primarily those in the middle class, have also fled the city for surburbia in the past two decades. However, this trend has been minimal compared to the rather massive exodus of blacks from farms and other rural areas to the city.

REDUCING THE GAP

The ineluctable conclusion that emerges from a comparison of the economic status of blacks and whites is the vastness of the chasm that has historically existed between the two. However, available evidence unequivocally demonstrates that there have been significant advances in reducing that breach, particularly in the past five or six years.

The gains have not been uniform for all blacks, of course. The younger generation of black workers, those under 35 years old, have benefited more than older workers from the improvement of the economic climate for minorities during the 1960's. This is only to be expected. Expanding educational opportunities, together with expanding opportunities for better-paying, higher-prestige jobs, apply mainly to the young, rather than to middle-aged or older persons who, for the most part, are unable to avail themselves of these additional options for upward mobility.

Also, the black-white lag in earnings has been diminishing faster for women than for men. While there has been a substantial reduction in the number of black families below the poverty threshold, some 29% of black families were still below the low income level in 1970 as against 8% of the white families. Despite the South's having made proportionately greater gains than the rest of the country in reducing the black-white income discrepancy during recent years, the black-white ratio of median family income is still lowest in the South.

Women and Business:
Agenda for the Seventies
Business implications of equal rights
for women

General Electric Company

One of the most significant social events in America today is the movement for equality in women's rights. Analysis of current and prospective trends suggests that this is indeed a major social force, *not* a fad or an aberration. To understand the true significance of this movement we must look beyond the extremism and flamboyant demonstrations sometimes associated with "Women's Lib" to the basic forces and issues that provide its dynamism.

There is a curious dichotomy about the development and impact of the women's rights movement. Viewed in one light, it can be seen as the logical, but delayed, fulfillment of some traditional American ideals—equality, freedom, individual worth and dignity, justice. Viewed another way, it represents a radical social revolution of historic proportions, that will have a growing impact on every institution from the family to the Federal government.

While the women's rights movement is broadly based and has considerable momentum, there is considerable divergence in women's attitudes toward some of the issues involved. Quite obviously, for instance, the aims and aspirations of the white middle-class housewife differ from those of the black mother on welfare; not every woman wants to be "liberated" (according to some definitions). Again, the "moderates" in the movement concentrate their efforts on bringing about changes (such as the elimination of sex discrimination in employment) with which many men would agree; but "radical feminists" espouse much more sweeping changes (such as the elimination of *all* sex role differences) with which few women would agree. Such divergences do not, however, detract from the scope and seriousness of this new (or, more accurately, renewed) social movement.

THE HISTORICAL PERSPECTIVE

The principle of equality, embodied in the American Revolution and the Constitution, was not generally defined in terms of sexual equality, either socially or politically. In fact, the Industrial Revolution tended to emphasize rather than eliminate traditional occupational differences between men and women, and to take men out

Business Environment Studies, General Electric Company, 1972. Reprinted with permission.

Women's Views on Women's Rights

It is often argued that "most women don't want Women's Lib." Depending on what exactly is meant by this statement there may be some truth to it; but it hides some very important facts.

A recent Louis Harris poll revealed that there is a very close division on the question of support for "efforts to strengthen and change women's status in society"—42 percent are in favor, 43 percent opposed. *What is perhaps most surprising, at this relatively early stage of the movement, is that there should be such a close division, rather than a clear negative majority, on so sweeping a question.*

Most opposition is expressed about some protest tactics; but there is strong support for specific principles such as speaking up to right wrongs. Pressing most strongly for change are the young, the best educated and black women.

An earlier Gallup Poll found that nearly two-thirds of women felt that they get "as good a break as men;" but only 53 percent of college-educated women agreed with this statement. Significantly, disagreement with this statement was based mainly on matters of employment policy (wage discrimination; poorer jobs)—and most women in the survey either had a job (32 percent) or wished they had one (27 percent).

A general conclusion that might be drawn from this survey is that, *while there is not widespread discontent among women with their family and social position, there is a strong desire to work outside the home,* coupled with a belief that women do have talents which should, but do not usually, meet with equal opportunity to be realized.

---

of the home into factories, leaving women behind in the home. And pragmatism won out over principle in the political arena, it being considered impractical to extend suffrage to women at that time.

Not until 1848 was the Suffragette Movement born; and not until 1919 was the woman's suffrage amendment to the Constitution passed.

The turning point in the economic arena came in World War I which drew more than one-fifth of all American women into the labor force. Women served in practically all occupations, including the munitions factories. Not only did massive numbers of women perform what had previously been traditionally considered male jobs; they performed these tasks deftly. Recognition of this performance led several countries, in postwar years, to give, or to widen, female suffrage.

World War II, as World War I, brought with it greater employment of women in the labor force. The U.S. Department of Labor wrote the equal pay principle into defense contracts. This helped to lure "Rosie the Riveter"—wife and mother—into the work force. This dramatic increase in female participation in the labor force helped to set the stage for the emergence of [the] women's rights movement as a social force. Just as after World War I, with peace came the desire for a "return to normalcy." However, the pendulum had swung too far during the war: women had proven they could do the work. Thus the climate was created for the development and current flowering of the women's rights movement.

Having gained momentum in two World Wars, the women's rights movement has developed, first slowly, then more rapidly, as social forces created a climate that became steadily more propitious for the full flowering of the movement:

> • *Rising levels of education* have caused many women to feel growing dissatisfaction with the traditional boundaries of a woman's life, and at the same time has made men more supportive of the basic issues of the women's movement.
>
> • The *changing character of work* and the economy has led to a large increase in jobs in the services sectors which are less physically demanding and more open to women.
>
> • There has been a growing emphasis on the concepts of *equality and social justice* in our hierarchy of values.
>
> • *Changes in the size of families and in the family life-cycle* have given more women more years without children to care for; and labor-saving devices have eased the burden of traditional housekeeping tasks.
>
> • The *civil rights movement* generated a climate of opinion which helped to set the stage for the women's rights movement (see box, however). It also set the legal precedents and established the techniques of confrontation (sit-ins, boycotts, disruptions, law-suits).
>
> • The *consumerism movement* has provided an issue and a platform on which women can take a leadership role in society and politics.

On balance, therefore, it seems clear that there are many societal forces—the drives for equality and individualism, technology, education, consumerism, and economic trends—which are likely to be supportive of the basic thrust and demands of the drive for women's rights. This drive should gather momentum and impact rather than fade away as a short-lived fad. Its significance for business, as for other institutions is predictably great, even in the short-run, and even more sweeping as its longer-term implications unfold.

Women's Rights and Minority Rights

Comparisons between the women's rights movement and the minority rights movement are complex, subject to numerous caveats, and have to be handled with care and sensitivity. Yet from such a comparison it is possible to get some insight into the attitudinal problems raised by the drive for women's rights, and to assess the manner in which these two movements might interact with one another.

It is perhaps as well to begin by pointing out some obvious *differences* between women's situation in society and that of racial minorities. In the first place, of course, women are not a minority: they are a majority. In the second place, women are not, as a group, as socially and economically disadvantaged as are minorities. There is an order of magnitude difference, as has been pointed out, between "being black and oppressed and being a woman and suppressed."

Having noted these caveats, it is possible to go on and note some *similarities* in the two situations, starting with a comment on the matter of attitudes—male, toward female; white, toward black. In a 1969 article in *Mademoiselle,* authoress Ellen Willis wrote:

"Just as blacks live in a world defined by whites, women live in a world defined by males . . . To be female or black is to be peculiar; whiteness and maleness are the norm . . . Racial and sexual stereotypes also resemble each other. Women, like blacks, are said to be childish, incapable of abstract reasoning, innately submissive, biologically suited for menial tasks, emotional, close to nature." (Emphasis added)

The extent of male-female attitudinal problems should not be underestimated. What they lack in active outbreaks of animosity (as compared with the hatred that constantly simmers in interracial relationships), they may make up in depth of cultural rooting. It has been pointed out that, while the U.S.A. has had a 300-year history of slavery and discrimination against minorities, there have been many millennia of cultural evolution leading up to today's pattern of male-female relationships. So, *while slavery is scarcely to be compared with "male domination," there are points of similarity in the attitudinal problems confronting these two movements.*

The parallel between the women's movement and minorities is a close one in other respects. Both movements are manifestations of the trend to greater individualism and pluralism. On the one hand, they view themselves as groups—not just accumulations of persons, but political entities, united by a sense of some shared grievances. On the other hand, they stress their worth as individuals and demand to be treated for their abilities, not for their sex or racial role. It seems to many observers that the main thrust of the women's movement is to get "in": it is not separatist. Rather, it wants women to have the jobs, responsibilities, pay packets, and eventually, the feeling of self-respect that men have.

In assessing the impact of the established minority movement on the developing women's movement, we must bear in mind that *the minority movement has the potential both for accelerating the women's movement and for impeding it.* The social groundwork for protest was laid by the minority groups, and public discussion and business awareness of equal opportunity was initiated by them. Then, too, minority groups have tried and tested many of the weapons of social protest—sit-ins, boycotts, demonstrations, class-action lawsuits—that women's groups might use; and the framework has been established for vigorous government enforcement of anti-discrimination laws, on the grounds of sex as well as of race.

But there are conflicts. The public may have a limited attention span for the hearing of grievances. Already blacks and women's groups are competing for that attention. Employers may find themselves in an awkward position in the middle, needing to be a kind of arbiter between the demands of blacks and women. If there are just so many jobs to go around, who should get the available jobs? who should get promotion?

Further, from the point of view of the women's movement, black males are sometimes regarded as part of the problem rather than as allies. The subordinate role of black women, and the tendency toward male machismo, in black and Spanish-American groups are matters of increasing concern to advocates of women's rights.

CHANGES WITHIN THE NEXT DECADE

While specific predictions must be hedged with all the usual caveats, it is possible to predict that, during the Seventies, the beginnings of a redefinition of sex roles will appear in American society, and—of greater immediate impact—major changes in the employment field as the result of women's drive for equality.

On the broad, societal level, there is likely to be a marked trend toward a greater sharing of responsibilities for the home and family. The extent and nature of such a shift toward a better balanced family life-style between partners will, of course, depend on the individuals involved. As many experts point out, however, there is a rapidly growing national and international trend which seeks to free *both* women *and* men from their traditional roles. Men will be "liberated" along with women, many contend, in critical ways which will benefit all of society. First of all, men and women will be able to share the pressures and excitement of the working world. Men will no longer be the only ones forced by social norms and mores into the role of family provider. Other options will be open to them.

By the same token, other options will be open to women. Most experts agree that a more equal sharing of the responsibilities of the home will produce a more stable "two-parent" environment for children. In general, a consequence of this breaking down of traditional male/female roles will probably be a less "uptight" society, with more people playing the roles their talents best suit them for, rather than those roles which they must now accept based on their sex.

On the political front, there will be a renewed, self-conscious activism by women, comparable to the surge that brought them the right to vote fifty years ago. This time, however, a major characteristic of the drive will be its focus on increasing the representation and influence of women in political institutions, rather than merely a diffused "register and vote" effort. This sharper focus is already the basic aim of the Women's National Political Caucus, a multi-partisan organization, formed in the summer of 1971: its emphasis will be on winning political power for women. As Rep. Shirley Chisholm (D., N.Y.) said, "*No one gives away political power. It must be taken, and we will take it.*'' While the caucus will support men ''who declare themselves ready to fight for the needs and rights of women and all under-represented groups,'' there is every reason to anticipate an increase in ''women power'' in the political arena, in at least two specific ways:

- the election and appointment of more women to positions of responsibility at every level of government.

- the emergence of women as a separate, identifiable constituency whose interests must be specifically considered by political parties and candidates.

Reflecting the many facets of attitudes, opinions and politics, legislative changes will occur. Attempts to change/liberalize laws governing women's legal, marital and employment rights will most likely produce concrete results within the next ten years. These results will presumably reveal themselves in the areas of abortion laws; in the establishment of child development centers; in public accommodation bills; in an Equal Rights Amendment to the Constitution; and in increased powers being given to OFCC, EEOC, and the Consumer Protection Boards.

A recent study (in the *Yale Law Journal*) analysed some of the practical legal consequences of passage of the Equal Rights Amendment. The study predicts some ''wrenching changes'' in social thinking and mores, but points out that this is what the concept of equal rights is all about. Among predictions offered by this study are the following:

- The automatic invalidation of virtually all labor laws ''protective'' of women (e.g., regarding hours of work, lifting of weights);

- Availability of alimony to either spouse;

- Modification of child-custody laws that specify a preference for the mother;

- Drafting of women into the armed services;

- A wife might retain her maiden name rather than automatically assuming her husband's name.

The study concluded with a recommendation for a two-year delay between ratification of the amendment and its effective date, to allow for the passage of needed changes in federal and state laws, and so to ease the transition.

The next decade is likely to bring sweeping changes in the field of employment. In response to Title VII of the Civil Rights Act of 1964, and to social justice in general, an opening up of more jobs and training programs for women can be expected, leading to a better balance of women/men throughout all job and skill levels. Commenting on the initial steps leading to this better balance, Elizabeth Duncan Koontz, Director of the Women's Bureau, U.S. Department of Labor, notes: *''Tokenism is the way it gets started.''* Tokenism carries with it special problems; but, as more people are exposed to women holding positions that had previously been considered "male jobs," we can expect to see a lessening of attitudinal problems—both on the part of the "rare woman" in business, and on the part of her peers, male as well as female.

Hand in hand with the opening up of jobs to women will go a review and reclassification of jobs to ensure equal pay for equal work. As an issue, the principle of equal pay probably commands the widest support—from men and women; from those who work and those who stay home—so it is to be expected that the broadest gains would occur in this area.

Throughout this period, changing family and life-style patterns will generally support, and be supported by, changing work patterns. Set in motion by laws and social awareness, tokenism followed by greater increases of women in all job areas will bring with it certain adaptations in work schedules. Presumably, these adaptations will manifest themselves in a greater utilization of part-time work. This will occur not only among operatives, maintenance staffs and the like, but at the technical, professional, and managerial levels as well. Approaching part-time work with a slightly different idea, an organization entitled Newtime, Inc., offers to bring business and women together through creative scheduling on the basis of a five-hour day, five-day week. People in general are seeking shorter work hours or even shorter work weeks. This will certainly add to the understanding, and maybe to the acceptance, of such requests by women.

Within the next decade, child care centers will probably grow in number and in importance. Some industries, some communities, and some government-run day care centers have already been in existence for several years. It seems likely that these centers will continue, as they have done in the past, only with increased influence, to serve as models for the establishment of new day care facilities.

A further area of change is likely to occur in the business world—in the sphere of advertising practices. Certainly, many observers anticipate pressure from women's groups against Madison Avenue practices that are deemed to treat women as "sex objects," or that address women on the level of an elementary school education.

In many of these areas of change, the potential for disruption and even violence will never be far below the surface (as the President's Task Force on Women's Rights and Responsibilities acknowledged). The tactics of boycotts, sit-ins and confrontations—in addition to lawsuits and government pressure—may well be employed against what are viewed as "recalcitrant" organizations. In tense situations the possibility of sporadic violence cannot be discounted, even though it remains the exception to the general pattern.

In conclusion, it is important in forecasting possible developments, to restate the need to make and maintain a clear distinction between the issues of specific equality (such as in pay, promotion, education, etc.) and the issue of sex role redefinition. Progress is certain to come much faster in the former areas, if for no other reason than that the principles underlying them seem to so many to be quite unexceptionable and resistance to them will be predictably less.

WOMEN IN THE LABOR FORCE: PAST, PRESENT AND FUTURE

We have noted how two World Wars brought large numbers of women into the labor force to meet the nation's manpower needs. In the post-World War II period education, technology and economic growth have all combined to bring about, on a continuing basis, a much higher rate of participation in the labor force by women.

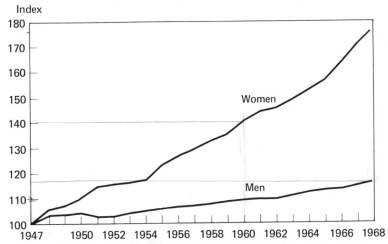

Relative Growth of the Labor Force, by Sex, 1947–68*(Index 1947=100.)
Source: U.S. Dept. of Labor, Bureau of Labor Statistics.

The fact is that the number of women in the work force has increased dramatically, as shown by the (accompanying) graph representing the relative growth of the labor force by sex, between 1947 and 1968.

In this twenty one year period the number of women in the civilian labor force increased by 75 percent (from 16.7 to 29.2 million), while the number of men rose only 16 percent (from 42.7 to 49.5 million). Consequently, in 1968 women were 37 percent of the total civilian labor force compared with only 28 percent in 1947.

By 1970, over 31 million women were working, representing better than 38 percent of the total civilian work force. On this basis, 50 percent of all women between the ages of 18 and 64 had chosen—or were forced by circumstances—to work.

One striking fact to emerge from this overall statistic is that, contrary to the popular image of the young single girl as the typical female employee, married women accounted for nearly three-fifths of all women workers.

Another significant fact is that education is a major factor in the composition of the female labor force. More and more jobs require better educated workers, and there seems to be a definite correlation between the education of women and their participation in the labor force. In 1970, for instance, of the women who had done some post-graduate study, 71 percent were in the labor force, compared with only 31 percent of the women with eight years of schooling.

A third significant fact is that mature women now represent a major proportion of the female work force. By 1968, women aged 45 and over made up 39 percent of all women workers, compared with 38 percent for those 25–44 years old and 23 percent for the under 25 age group.

A major implication of these facts is that, compared with the past, there is likely to be greater stability in women's work and career patterns.

However, despite this dramatic increase in participation in the labor force, women are typically employed in the lower-paid, lower-skilled categories of operatives, services and clerical workers. They are correspondingly underrepresented in, for example, managerial, professional and technical ranks.

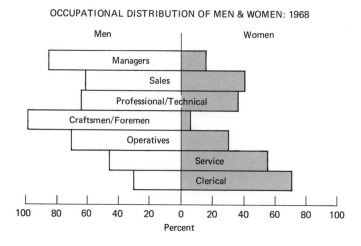

OCCUPATIONAL DISTRIBUTION OF MEN & WOMEN: 1968

Each bar of the second graph represents 100 percent of employment in a given occupation, divided by sex. At the lower end of the skills spectrum, the chart reveals that 73 percent of all clerical workers are women, and only 27 percent are men. Women are correspondingly underrepresented in the occupations nearer the top of the pyramid—accounting for example, for only 15 percent of the managers. Even what is shown here is an overstatement because many of the sales positions occupied by women are retail store clerks, and many of their professional and technical positions are in elementary school teaching and in nursing. The general conclusion to be drawn here is that, as skills, status and presumably income go up, so women's representation goes down.

This distortion in women's participation in the labor force has, in fact, been accentuated during the past decade. At the same time that women have increased their overall share of the labor market, they have been increasing even more their share of the lower skills (the very ones that are projected for lower demand in the future), and losing opportunities in the higher skills (which are expected to be in high demand in the 70's).

In some jobs male and female labor has been used interchangeably; but, by and large, the demand for labor has been "sex specific." Women workers have clustered in jobs which have acquired sex labels; and these sex labels have persisted through time, showing little tendency to change until very recently.

For the future, women will be a growing factor in the labor force. In the next decade, approximately 6.3 million women will be added to the labor force, accounting for 42 percent of the overall increase. By 1980, therefore, some 37 million women will be employed.

A Temple University study projects that 4.9 million, or over three-fourths of this increase, will result from increases in the female population, and 1.3 million, or nearly one-fourth, from increases in participation rates.

Other points brought out by this study include the facts that:

- *2.5 million of the increase in female participation will occur in the 25–34 age group*; 1.1 million in the 10–24 age group; and 1.0 million in the 55–65 age group. (The remaining 1.7 million increase is divided among the 14–19, 35–54, and over 65 groups).

- *The non-white female work force will increase at a somewhat faster rate than the white female work force*—25 percent increase vs. 20 percent. (By 1980, the totals will be approximately 5 million and 32 million, respectively).

- *Women's labor force participation rate will increase by 3.8 percent* in the period 1970–80, compared with a virtually static (0.3 percent increase) situation for men.

It is possible that the participation rate can be increased even more dramatically than projected, if business and other employers work to make it attractive to more women, and if they aggressively recruit women into their work forces. In fact, the *actual* labor force participation rate for women in 1969 already exceeded earlier Labor Department projections. If this actual rate is applied to the 1980 female population statistics, the projected female labor force for that year would increase by 7.2 million over 1970—or an increase of nearly one million over current 1980 projections of women workers.

Given the possible labor force participation rates, it is important here to review the employment outlook for the 1970's. Creating a framework for the improved utilization of women, we find that jobs in the skilled trades, for instance—which exist in almost every community—are expected to rise from about 10.0 million workers to nearly 12.2 million, or more than one-fifth, between 1968 and 1980. Noting specific examples, we find:

> *Appliance Servicemen.* An increase in demand by 1980 of one-third over the number employed in 1968 is projected. This means that 275,000 workers by 1980 will be required as a result of growing population, rising levels of disposable income, and increased numbers and new types of appliances.

Business Machine Servicemen. Here the demand is expected to almost double the number required in 1968: 225,000 workers will be required. Business machine servicemen do much of their work in the offices where the machines are used, and the physical demands of the job are light.

These are but two examples of expanding employment opportunities in the services sector, involving relatively light physical work and skills for which women can readily be trained.

In reviewing the outlook for women workers, the Women's Bureau noted:

> Shortages of skilled workers in selected professional and technical, clerical and service occupations provide excellent opportunities for qualified women workers. Legislation enacted during the past decade barring discrimination in employment on the basis of sex should open up new opportunities for women to train for and enter more diversified jobs, and to advance to jobs of higher skill level.

Women and Work: Myths and Facts

Over time several reasons have been advanced to explain women's general failure to advance into more responsible, better paid jobs, despite the fact that they constitute 38 percent of the labor force. *On closer examination many of these explanations turn out to be more myth than fact.*

"Women are intellectually unsuited for professional work"
   Studies show that two-thirds as many females as males among 11th grade students tested have engineering aptitude. Women's lack of professional and technical training does not follow from a deficit in potential ability, but rather from education, counselling and general socialization processes that direct women away from such careers.

"Women are physically unsuited for many jobs"
   Specific aptitudes, including finger dexterity and hand-eye coordination, required for a number of crafts, are found as frequently among female as male students. As to weight lifting ability, men on the average are stronger than women, but clearly there is some overlapping, with some women being stronger than some men. (The Equal Employment Opportunity Commission is taking an increasingly critical look at any claim of sex as a "bona fide occupational qualification.")

"Women are emotionally unsuited for executive work"
   Even professional opinion is divided on this point, but doctors point out that men as well as women have physical/emotional problems which interfere with their work. They assert that it is not the case that all women have difficulty performing work during menstrual periods or menopause.

FOCUS ON THE ISSUES

Broadly conceived, the issues involved in the women's rights movement can be divided into two categories:

a) Family and social issues

As opposed to immediate business-related demands and issues, there is a range of broader societal issues which relate to less well defined questions of family life and social role structure. These are areas which are characterized at present by debates rather than demands, and by being more fluid, having less currency, and attaining less public support and understanding than the business-related demands.

Perhaps the main thrust of the women's movement can best be characterized as a movement toward diminution of sex/role differences. As discussed earlier,

---

And studies by Dr. Estelle Ramey of Georgetown Medical School have proved repeatedly that women stand up to stress, on average, better than men do.

"Women don't have to support families"
   Most women *do*, in fact, work to support themselves or others. 19 percent of working women are widowed, separated or divorced; 22 percent are single; and 25 percent have husbands with annual incomes below $7,000.

"Women have a higher rate of absenteeism"
   Two major studies show there is a very little over-all difference between men and women in this regard. In one study, the annual time lost due to illness or injury was 5.6 days for women, 5.3 days for men; in the other, it was 5.3 days for women, 5.4 days for men.

"Women aren't seriously attached to their jobs"
   Over-all *turnover* rates are indeed higher for women because they are disproportionately represented in lower occupations, where turnover is highest for both sexes. When compared with men in similar occupations, however, women's turnover rates are only marginally different. In terms of *occupational mobility,* men change jobs more frequently than women (10 percent vs. 7 percent). Women's *work life expectancy* is, on the average, only 25 years compared with 43 years for men. However, between 1900 and 1960 it more than tripled (from 6.3 years to 20.1 years), and it is still increasing rapidly.

   Clearly, there is evidence that tends to overthrow or seriously modify many of these preconceptions. One must conclude, therefore, that the real reasons for the failure of qualified women to advance equal footing with men are to be sought in cultural biases and structural discrimination in employment.

many—if not most—of the probable changes in the next decade in the social and political fields will raise issues of sharp and prolonged debate. Although progress in this area must come mainly as the result of changing attitudes and education, there will be specific efforts made by women's groups, for instance, to give women equal property-owning rights in states where such discrimination still exists.

For purposes of this study, however, attention should focus on the twin issues of day-care/child development centers and abortion law repeal. From a business point of view, these proposals can be considered as means toward reducing absenteeism and turnover, so managers should seek to understand some of the issues involved.

i) Day care/child development centers As one approach to promoting greater equality of opportunity to choose working careers, women's groups, as well as advocates of welfare reform, are proposing the establishment of more day care/child development centers. During World War II many companies set up day care centers, but these were dismantled soon after V-J Day. Within the past few years new corporate attention has been focused on these centers; and, according to Urban Research Corp., about a dozen companies operate their own day-care facilities, while many others contribute to community centers.

Day care would help the welfare recipients who could become self-supporting, the increasingly large numbers of women who are moving into blue and white collar jobs, and the large number of professional women. "Motherless homes"— where the father is divorced, separated, or widowed—also would be affected favorably by the establishment of day care centers. The centers might even serve as an inducement to attract male workers—who, under Title VII of the Civil Rights Act of 1964, would have equal use of the facilities—to join a particular company.

There are, however, many problems of finance, legislation, and organization associated with the establishment of day care centers. Many day care licensing regulations were adopted from other codes rather than developed on a basis of careful evaluation of the special nature of day care programs. Many states, therefore, now find themselves applying a licensing code that is inappropriate, antiquated, and unnecessarily difficult to administer.

What is even more distressing is that many states have discovered that, where licensing regulations do provide for adequate facilities, they do not necessarily provide quality programs for children. Quality cannot be measured in narrow definitions of square footage or space available, and the type and amount of equipment acquired.

The Federal government is now entering the day care field, with plans for annual outlays of $750 million. Other Congressional proposals call for expenditures of up to $10 billion a year. So far no serious proposal has been advanced for implementing the demand of some women's groups for universal day care—which would entail a program costing some $30 billion annually.

i) **Abortion law repeal** The second major element under the family and social issues category is the debate over repeal (or amendment) of laws governing abortion. The question of whether the goal here should be "reform" or "repeal" is itself symptomatic of a division of opinion within the women's movement. There is general agreement among women that there should be an expansion of the conditions under which abortion is legal, but there is a stronger opinion held by some that women should have "control over their own bodies," and so should be able to get an abortion for *any* reason. They reason that only repeal will give women this full option, and that reform would still keep a measure of the decision in the hands of "the male medical establishment."

From the point of view of employment, observers point to a direct and obvious link between the availability of abortions and job continuity. Reform legislation has been passed in New York, Hawaii, Colorado and other states, and is an indication of changing social attitudes on this highly controversial subject. However, there is a growing body of evidence that the legislative changes have not as yet resulted in a substantial alteration of actual conditions facing women in need of abortion.

b) Business-related issues

Business-related issues primarily concern:

i) **Equal pay for equal work** Here there are clearly two branches of concern and discrimination. One is the use of different pay scales for men and women for *identical* work. A growing number of laws bear on this point, generally barring large companies from differentiating in wages paid to men and women in the same location for equal work. Exceptions are permitted only for bona fide seniority or merit systems, and do not alter the basic principle.

The second involves different pay scales for work which contains only *marginal differences* in actual work, e.g., when under 10 percent of the total work time is required for divergent tasks. In these cases, while pay differences are tied to differences in job classification, questions are now being raised, by government, women's groups, and the courts, as to the legitimacy of what had previously been regarded as differences in job classification. The courts are developing a concept of "substantially equal" job classifications for which equal pay is required.

In short, the objection here is that women are frequently doing the same jobs as men, but are not getting the same money. Gross statistics are generally supportive of this claim. For instance, in 1970, the median earnings of women in the professional and technical field were only 67 percent of their male counterparts. Women sales workers fared even worse: they earned only 43 percent of salesmen's salaries.

Over-all the pay gap between men and women has been widening. Whereas in 1955 women earned nearly 64 percent of men's salaries, by 1970 this ratio had fallen to 59 percent. While the median earnings of full-time male workers in 1970 was $8,966, women had a median wage of only $5,323.

However, these are gross statistics, subject to much debate and attack; and as Elizabeth Waldman of the Bureau of Labor Statistics wrote in the June, 1970, issue of the *Monthly Labor Review:*

> Comparisons of women's earnings with those of men are subject to innumerable qualifications . . . This is not to overlook job discrimination, some of which exists today. But the overwhelming majority of statistical evidence available does not permit a valid comparison of men's and women's earnings that would reveal the extent of discrimination.

However, there is prima facie evidence of discrimination when the President's Task Force report can quote the U.S. Department of Commerce statistics to show that *"women with some college education, both white and Negro, earn less than Negro men with eight years of education."*

ii) Equality of opportunity Part of the explanation for the differential in median income between men and women undoubtedly lies in the fact (already mentioned) of women's overrepresentation in the lower paying jobs with little advancement potential. However, such an explanation can give little satisfaction, for in effect it seems merely to substitute discrimination in hiring and promotion practices for discrimination in pay as the cause of this differential.

To what extent does denial of equal opportunity exist? Any objective rereading of history, or of our present employment picture, must reach the conclusion that, nationwide, our employment systems are not designed to ensure the full utilization of all our human resources; and that women are among those whose talents are not fully utilized, and who find institutional and attitudinal barriers to their advancement. The reasons for this particular form of discrimination are many and complex, including simple neglect, well-intentioned protective laws (e.g., re overtime, weight-lifting), "male chauvinism" and women's own attitudes and aspirations.

In whatever proportions these (and other) elements may have been compounded in the past to create this problem of inequality, all are destined for future re-examination and change under the combined pressure of changing social attitudes, economic conditions and governmental policies.

It should be emphasized that, in pressing for this equality of opportunity, women's groups and their supporters are *not* saying that *all* women must, or want to, work (though 59 percent do work or want to). Rather, they are asserting that those women who make the choice to work should have an equal chance with men for employment and promotion. Their aim is to establish the principle that, inherently, virtually all occupations, at all levels, should be open to women. Though the language may be different, their attack on "sexual stereotypes" in employment has the same thrust as the EEOC's critical examination of "bona fide occupational qualifications." There should be little hesitancy about predicting the need for progressive, and fairly rapid, elimination of all institutional barriers to women's advancement in whatever career they choose.

IMPLICATIONS FOR BUSINESS

This study's assessment of the basic issues and demands of this movement has brought out the striking fact that many of them are business-related. For instance, in the August 26, 1970 celebration of the 50th anniversary of women's right to vote, the key demands were for (a) equal pay for equal work; (b) day care centers, and (c) abortion reform. Of these, the first (equal pay) is clearly business-related; and the demands for day care centers and abortion reform are both largely adopted as means to the end of promoting equality of opportunity to work.

So the key issues that give this movement much of its dynamism are also the ones that pose a challenge to business—and lead to the involvement of government. Clearly, then, business *cannot* escape involvement in the issues. The only choice is between merely reacting to demands after they develop, and more constructively seeking to maximize the opportunities that the movement opens up.

Business response to this movement in the Seventies should primarily be dictated by a recognition of the basic equity of many of the proposed actions and of the real opportunities that are presented. As in the case of minority relations, the moral and legal rightness of helping employees develop their fullest potential (and so their productive contribution to the enterprise) can scarcely be argued. Both the interest of the individual (man or woman, white or nonwhite) and the interest of the enterprise are best served by a policy of developing and utilizing *all* available human resources to the fullest.

The advent of the women's rights movement also happens to coincide with the onset of a decade of projected tight labor markets in some age groups. Labor shortages are likely to be most marked in the 35–54 age brackets and in the managerial, professional, technical and skilled trades categories. And it is in these sectors that women present the largest potential manpower reserve by virtue of their numbers, increasing labor force participation rates, and aptitudes.

There is, clearly, a tremendous competitive edge to be won by those companies which are farsighted and imaginative enough to structure jobs, work schedules and benefit programs to meet women's needs and aspirations; to recruit aggressively at all levels; and to open to promotion opportunities on the basis of individual ability. Besides gaining needed additional skills and talent, such action can also do much to enhance a company's image and sales in consumer goods markets, and to win women's support on business issues in the political arena.

Against these opportunities there is a range of business risks that companies should be alert to, including consumer boycotts, strikes and disruptions, individual and class-action suits, and government action through compliance reviews and enforcement procedures. The prudent assumption to make in business planning is that the Federal government will be as vigorous in its enforcement of laws against sex discrimination as it has been on matters of racial discrimination. The legal framework for enforcing equal rights for women is already largely in place, and the enforcement of equal employment opportunities for minorities has already set the needed precedents and procedures. From a government point of view, the two aspects of enforcement can be, and are being, readily joined together.

The first and most important need is to recognize that the women's rights movement and the trend to a greater participation by women in the labor force are indeed long-range trends, not temporary aberrations. Business planning should, therefore, recognize these facts and respond accordingly.

The principal elements of an adequate business response will be a rethinking of, and adjustments to, the overall personnel planning and development system, and affirmative action programs of sufficient intensity and duration to realize the needed degree of change. In this regard General Electric is fortunate in having already developed a "systems approach" to the problems of equal employment opportunity.* Originally designed as a comprehensive approach to dealing with racial discrimination and minority problems, it is transferrable, in its major principles, to an attack on sex discrimination in employment. Illustrative of the elements to be included in such an approach are the following:

a) The possibilities for reorganization of work

There are two principal lines of investigation in this area. One is the restructuring of jobs and the reclassification of job categories to maximize the potential employment openings for women. The second is a reconsideration of the manner in which part-time work is viewed, and an examination of the options that are open to the Company for rescheduling work to make increasing use of part-time resources.

b) The possibility of revisions in pay and benefits programs

Beyond the need for ensuring "equal pay for equal work" (which ties in with the need for job reclassification) are other areas for examination, including the provision or support of day care centers, and adjustment of other benefits programs in the light of possible increases in part-time work.

c) The possibility of restructuring the supply of women workers

(to improve the quality of the work force and increase the upward mobility of women):

• **External** On the recruiting front, a great deal can be done by building up corporate relationships with women's colleges, working with vocational schools on designing programs for women, and otherwise seeking new avenues of approach to increase and restructure the supply side of the labor force equation as it relates to women.

• **Internal** Within the Company, serious attempts must be made to increase women's participation in apprenticeship programs and management/professional devel-

---

*"General Electric's Commitment to Progress in Equal Opportunity and Minority Relations" (ERC-49, 8/70).

opment programs to ensure a more equitable representation of women in the higher skilled trades areas and to enhance upward mobility into professional and management ranks.

What Does "Equal Employment Opportunity" Really Mean?

William H. Brown III*

As you know, recent amendments to federal law make discrimination in employment illegal, and assign responsibility for its identification and elimination to the federal agency of which I am Chairman. I want to discuss with you implications of this legislation for your operations.

THE ISSUE

First, I want to tell you about a magazine article I read recently about a County Executive of one of our larger counties.

The article told of the executive's warning to his department heads to "alert all staff" against the possibility of "some ultraliberal organization" prodding job applicants into taking advantage of the new federal law. The warning came in a memorandum which said that the county might have problems if a departmental head *said the wrong thing* and the applicant subsequently filed a charge of discrimination.

"Frankly," the memorandum stated, "I expect the county will have a charge filed against it, in any event, by some ultraliberal organization attempting to create an issue." Well, we at EEOC have news for that county executive: No one has to "create" an issue of discrimination. Discrimination exists today in both public and private employment, in all types of jobs, at all levels, against every minority, and both sexes.

What I want to discuss with you today is the dimension of that discrimination, the way in which it has been defined by the courts, and the amendments to Title VII which give EEOC increased powers to eliminate it.

Reprinted from *Proceedings, 1972 International Conference on Public Personnel Administration,* courtesy of the International Personnel Management Association.

*Chairman, Equal Employment Opportunity Commission, Washington D.C.

MEANING OF "MERIT" EMPLOYMENT

I am particularly glad to have an opportunity to discuss the legal requirements to eliminate discrimination with a group such as yours. You represent official state and local government agencies charged with the responsibility for the administration of state and local government merit systems. These systems have been designed to establish the principle of merit employment—the principle that the selection and promotion of employees must be based, not upon some extraneous factor, but upon their ability to do the job.

Title VII of the 1964 Civil Rights Act, the law which we enforce, requires basically the same thing. It requires that the particular extraneous factors of race, sex, or ethnic origin must not be a factor in any employment system; it establishes instead a "merit" employment principle of ability to perform the job for which the individual is being considered, recruited, selected, or promoted.

As you may know, the jurisdiction and coverage of EEOC to enforce Title VII has recently been expanded by amendments which became effective on March 24th of this year. Whenever a new law is passed there is some delay in understanding its full impact until cases work their way through the courts. While the applicability of Title VII prohibiting discrimination in employment is new to your agencies, the basic principles of Title VII are not. A body of precedent has been established by the courts which will, I believe, offer sufficient guidance to you in considering the implications of the new law.

The new law reinforces the principle of merit employment—employment based upon the ability to do the job. However, to be completely frank, I also think that a careful examination of the way in which the state and city personnel systems of this country have been run in recent years will suggest that full compliance with the law will require some new thinking on your part. It will require a new and careful look at the way in which you do business; it will require careful understanding of just what discrimination is and how it exists in your operations, and it may require new types of employment action to eliminate discrimination. It may, in short, require a whole new understanding of the full dimensions and scope of the term "merit" employment.

Let me explain. I view the term "merit employment" the same as the term "job relatedness." This is the standard imposed by the United States Supreme Court for determining whether employment practices comply with Title VII. Just because some state and local agencies say they are operating on the basis of the merit system doesn't mean they are in compliance with Title VII. Indeed, there is a substantial possibility that many of them are in violation, or at a minimum, in serious need of re-examination, because the mechanisms that they use to evaluate "merit," albeit in good faith, are not in fact, job related. They are not, in fact, adequate predictors of job performance.

DEFINITION OF DISCRIMINATION

This standard of "job relatedness" has developed over the last several years as we have become more sophisticated in our understanding of what discrimination in employment really is. I find that there is much misunderstanding about this term, both in terms of the law, our history, and our society. Over the last seven years, we and the courts have gone through several stages in our understanding of how discrimination works.

Stage I: Evil intent

The first stage is fairly simple to understand. It assumed that discrimination was essentially a human problem—an evil state of mind on the part of some individual. It was evidenced by signs such as "No Irish Need Apply"; or the advertisements in many newspapers dividing job opportunities into those for "white" and those for "colored." The investigation of this kind of discrimination focused on proving the intent of the employer and whether he "meant" to exclude someone for an unlawful reason. The remedy focused on educating the person and establishing brotherhoodly activities designed to eliminate this type of evil state of mind.

Stage II: Unequal treatment

The second stage focused not on the intent or the state of mind, but on the actions of the person accused of discrimination. The standard applied was one of "unequal treatment." Was a black person treated differently than a white person; an Anglo treated differently than a Chicano, or a man treated differently than a woman? The investigation focused primarily on what happened to a specific identifiable individual or limited group of individuals, and attempted to determine whether they had been treated differently than someone of another racial, ethnic, or sexual group. If illegal or unequal treatment was identified, the remedy was fairly simple: Find the people who had been treated unequally and treat them in an equal fashion.

Stage III: Unequal effect

Recently, a third stage of the definition of discrimination has been developed in legal decisions. The most important decision was the case of *Griggs* v. *Duke Power,* in which the Supreme Court considered two hiring standards applied equally and uniformly by the Duke Power Company—a requirement that a job applicant pass a written test and a requirement that a job applicant have a high-school diploma. Requirements similar to those exist in most merit systems.

The Supreme Court determined that these requirements were applied equally to all applicants regardless of race. Therefore, there would have been no violation of the law if the definition of discrimination were limited to "unequal treatment." Further there was no "evil intent" involved, as the Supreme Court found that the company was even engaging in various community activities to improve job opportunities for minorities.

With such a record, how could the Duke Power Company possibly be in violation of the law? It can be and it was, because the Supreme Court has made it perfectly clear that employment practices, even those which are neutral on their face and equally applied to people of all races, might still be illegal if their impact is to exclude people of one group more than those of another. Specifically, speaking for an unanimous court, Chief Justice Warren Berger said:

> "If an employment practice which operates to exclude Negroes cannot be shown to be related to job performance, the practice is prohibited."

What does this mean? It means that in examining employment practices we must go through a two-part analysis. Part one: Does the employment practice operate to exclude Negroes or women or Chicanos or another protected group? This can usually be discovered by a simple examination of the statistical make-up of your work force. The second step in the analysis is to determine what particular practices have operated in such a fashion as to exclude minorities and women, and to determine whether those practices are job-related. In this examination, the court made it clear that the burden of proof is not upon the minority group individual who believes that the practice which has excluded him is not job related, but the burden is on the employer utilizing the practice to prove its job relatedness.

While the Supreme Court decision focused on two specific employment practices—the use of certain tests and requiring a high-school diploma—the language used by Chief Justice Berger has much broader application than these two practices. Clearly his language requires a complete reevaluation of all our employment practices. I should like to outline for you some of the court cases interpreting Title VII in the private sector and those dealing with public employment under the provisions of earlier federal laws, so that you may anticipate the types of practices that may be illegal and begin to eliminate them with nondiscriminatory remedial practices.

The most important thing to remember is that discrimination need not be a matter of malicious intent. Not only the courts but the Congress have made it clear that general business rules and procedures may in themselves constitute systemic barriers to minorities and women.

The same indictment must be made of the operation of many aspects of the civil service system. Indeed, the report of the Senate Labor Committee on the recent amendments clearly observed that:

> Civil service selection and promotion techniques and requirements are replete with artificial requirements that place a premium on "paper" credentials.

This report also points out that similar requirements in the private sector had been held illegal in cases such as *Griggs,* and called upon the United States Civil Service Commission to:

Undertake a thorough reexamination of its entire testing and qualification program to ensure that the standards enunciated in the Griggs case are fully met.

I think you should undertake a similar "reexamination."

DISCRIMINATION IN STATE AND LOCAL GOVERNMENT

Measured against the standards established by *Griggs* what, then, are some of the particular troublesome areas of state and local government to which such examination should be devoted?

1. Recruitment

The courts have recognized that recruitment systems are often discriminatory. Specifically, if you have an all-white or male work force, and there is a heavy element of word-of-mouth recruitment in which job applicants learn about vacancies from existing employees, this may perpetuate the all-white or male character of the work force. This is clearly illegal under Title VII. A recent survey showed that your major recruitment sources are your job-announcement, local employment services, and a heavy dose of referrals from present employees. If any or all of these systems produce a segregated recruitment pool, they must be changed or improved. The remedy is to institute new recruitment systems which will have the result of obtaining an integrated recruitment pool.

2. Hiring standards and criteria

Any hiring standard such as educational level, amount of experience, requirement that an applicant not have an arrest record, or requirement that an applicant not have a garnishment against him, which may operate statistically to exclude more blacks than whites, or such as a height requirement which may exclude more women or Chicanos than Anglos, are illegal unless you can establish, by a clear-cut validation study, that the requirements you are utilizing are specifically related to the job performance for the specific jobs for which the individuals are being selected.

Incidentally, the survey showed that 28 per cent of you use residence as a requirement for unskilled jobs. Unless you can prove people with a certain residence do the job better, this may be illegal in a geographic area that is predominantly of one race. The survey showed 66 per cent of you disqualify applicants if they have arrest or conviction records. The courts have already said that to use arrest records this way is probably illegal unless you can prove specific job relatedness. It is probably also illegal, at least, for certain types of convictions. The survey also showed 22 per cent require a high-school diploma for unskilled jobs, and 94 per cent require it for the entry-level office worker.

3. Written tests

It is the position of our agency that if you are utilizing a written test as a pre-employment selection device, which 88 per cent of your agencies are, and the failure rate for blacks, Chicanos, or women is higher than the failure rate for whites, Anglos, or men then you must sustain the burden of proof of establishing a clear preponderance of statistical evidence that the test can actually predict adequate performance of the actual job for which the individual is being tested. If it is not accomplishing this, then its use must cease.

The demand for validated employment tests does not mean an end to *merit* employment principles but, rather, the opposite. It means return to true merit. It means that you must be able to prove that you are in fact measuring "merit" in terms of the ability to perform the job. That is the only merit which we should be measuring anyway.

4. Rule of three selection system

Another method commonly used in personnel systems to help appointing officials select qualified candidates for vacant positions, is the Rule-of-Three or the Rule-of-Five, which requires officials to select from the top three or the top five in the list of candidates. Some methods require the selection of the highest ranking candidate. Of 300 state and local government personnel systems in one sample, only 43 per cent permitted an appointing official to select any qualified applicant.

I think the courts will deal very critically with these selection systems requiring selection from a list of the top three or top five, for the same reason that mandating a high-school diploma is unlawful. If you find that a system utilizing the "Rule of Three" operates in such a way that Negroes are, in fact, qualified for the jobs but not appearing on the final selection lists, then the system is operating to exclude Negroes. I think you will be required by the courts to prove the job necessity of this selection system. This will be very difficult. Remember that the others on the list of those qualified are, by definition, qualified even if they are not included in the top three. I think you will find the courts looking with some substantial lack of sympathy upon any system which permits exclusion of qualified blacks.

5. Promotion systems

There are significant deficiencies between seniority systems utilized in private industry and promotion systems used in public employment. There are sufficient basic similarities, however, that the principles developed with respect to the former are applicable to the latter. For example, courts have required the elimination of seniority systems in private industry in which departmental or job seniority had operated to freeze blacks into jobs to which they were discriminatorily assigned at the time of their initial hire. These were replaced with plantwide or other broader-based seniority systems, which avoid continuing to penalize blacks because of prior discrimination.

Similarly, rigid civil-service job classification systems which freeze categories of employees into certain lines or job series may be discriminatory since they limit rights to move from one series to another. Where the failure to be assigned to that series in the first place was discriminatory, the failure to permit their promotion out of that series or their transfer into another series will simply perpetuate the discrimination and is therefore illegal.

REMEDIES

If discrimination is found to exist, what will you be required to do? The answer is to eliminate it, all of it, to make certain it won't return, and develop a remedy for those who have been victims. Prior to the passage of Title VII, the courts had already begun to do a thorough reexamination of state and local government standards and required remedial action. For example, in a case involving the Mississippi Highway Patrol, the court enjoined the use of a test "not proved to be significantly related to successful job performance."

The patrol was ordered not to introduce new standards more stringent than those applicable prior to the case; it was ordered to affirmatively recruit blacks by advertising in black media, visiting black schools, and other actions; and it was, of course, required to maintain records on applicants by race in order to determine compliance with the court order.

In another case involving the Alabama Highway Patrol, a court ordered that 50 per cent of those hired be black until such time as 25 per cent of the patrol were black; and that no training be implemented unless 25 per cent of those in the training course were black. The court required aggregating existing registers and waiting lists, if necessary, to reach this remedial goal, and further ordered affirmative recruitment efforts including "regular recruitment visits to predominantly Negro schools." Similar decisions requiring numerical remedies have been required by the courts in dealing with the Minneapolis Fire Department and a number of other government employers.

Recent newspaper stories regarding reactions to statements by the President have led some public commentators to ask whether there has been or will be a change in the policy of the federal government or the EEOC in requiring this type of remedy for employment discrimination. I should like to reassure this group that regardless of what interpretation may have been placed upon certain developments by the press, there is no change in the policy of the federal government or the Equal Employment Opportunity Commission concerning appropriate remedies for the elimination of discrimination in employment. These remedies are based upon the statutory duty of the Equal Employment Opportunity Commission to identify and eliminate discrimination in employment. We are not concerned with "quotas" or "preferential treatment" in the abstract where there is no discrimination. What does concern us at EEOC and throughout the federal government is the legal obligation to eliminate all discrimination. Sometimes the action taken to eliminate discrimination may be voluntary if an employer—such as the merit systems for which you work—conducts a comprehensive self-audit and determines that certain action is necessary to bring its operations into compliance with the law.

For example, the state of Pennsylvania recently conducted an extensive survey and examination of its employment practices. It concluded that certain substantial remedial steps were necessary and subsequently developed an excellent remedial program. More often, such action is necessary in the context of an enforcement or compliance procedure before an administrative agency such as EEOC. In either case the standard of remedy must be consistent with those required by the courts.

The Supreme Court has given us a great deal of guidance regarding a standard of remedy, and has made clear the distinction between preferential treatment, as some might call it, and remedial treatment which is necessary to eliminate discrimination. In the case of *Swann* v. *Charlotte-Mecklenberg Board of Education, 402 U.S. 1*, the court spoke directly to the issue in pointing out that if all things were equal, certain remedial practices might not be necessary or appropriate. All things, however, are not equal where segregation or discrimination have existed. The remedy for such discrimination may be:

> . . . awkward, inconvenient, and even bizarre in some situations and may impose burdens on some; but all awkwardness and inconvenience cannot be avoided in the interim period when remedial adjustments are being made to eliminate the . . . (discrimination or segregation).

Among the cases which the Supreme Court discussed was the case of *United States* v. *The Montgomery Board of Education,* 395 U.S. 225, in which the District Court had set a remedy requiring a specific racial ratio in faculty assignments and the Court of Appeals had changed this part of the remedy. The Supreme Court reversed the Court of Appeals decision and reinstituted the numerical remedy. It specifically permitted the use of a mathematical ratio as a starting point in the process of shaping a remedy. The Supreme Court pointed out "awareness of the racial composition of the whole school system is likely to be a useful starting point in shaping a remedy to correct past" discriminatory practices. Careful reading of the Supreme Court decision makes it clear that where discrimination exists it must be entirely eliminated and the remedy adopted must be appropriate to such elimination.

The use of what, I believe, may appropriately be called "numerical remedies" was clearly endorsed by the Supreme Court in this case. Such terms as "quotas" and "preferential treatment" and "discrimination in reverse" have had many meanings to many different people and have unfortunate connotations. The important thing to this agency and the Federal Courts is that, where discrimination exists, it must be eliminated, and where such elimination requires a numerical remedy, it is part of the policy of our agency to obtain the remedy that has been approved by the Supreme Court. Much public controversy has developed in this area because newspaper reporters and others may not be aware of current legal definitions of discrimination established by the courts and followed by the EEOC in its case-processing activity. Thus, much of the action including the requirement of a "numerical remedy" necessary to eliminate discrimination in employment appears harsh to those who do not understand the law, and the fact that discrimination is defined as more than just plain evil-intent or unequal treatment. But even if they do not understand the legal definition of discrimination, they certainly can understand the words of the Supreme Court that "all things are not equal" where discrimination exists.

PROCEDURE UNDER NEW LAW

In closing I should like to outline very briefly the procedural context in which we will be applying the principles I have outlined above:

> 1. *Charge Filed with EEOC.* The case begins when an aggrieved party files a charge with us or the initiation of a charge by one of our Commissioners where the possible existence of discrimination has been brought to (his/her) attention.
>
> 2. *Investigation.* Extensive investigation of the facts is conducted in order to determine exactly what happened and how your employment systems operate.
>
> 3. *Deferral.* In a situation where there is a state agency administering an enforceable fair employment practices law, our investigation is delayed for at least 60 days to permit deferral of the case to a state or local antidiscrimination agency administering legislation comparable in scope to Title VII.

Our records indicate that there are presently 33 state fair employment practices commissions to which deferral is appropriate.

A number of the agencies represented here have asked us whether we will be deferring to agencies administering state grievance procedures or other employee appeal procedures which include a nondiscrimination component. The statute does not permit such deferral. It makes it clear that a state law or city ordinance must prohibit the practices prohibited by Title VII and establish an agency specifically for the purpose of providing remedies for such practices and it clearly does not contemplate deferring for investigation to those agencies, which, in fact are the agencies against which the charge might be filed. This does not prohibit your agency from taking vigorous action to assure that its practices and those of other state agencies are in compliance with the law, but it does prohibit us from deferring to you for investigation charges against yourself or against other agencies.

> 4. *Finding and Conciliation.* If discrimination is found you will be notified of that fact and provided with an opportunity to eliminate the discrimination through informal methods of conciliation.
>
> 5. *Enforcement.* If conciliation fails, the statute provides two enforcement mechanisms—one governmental and one private. The EEOC can refer the case to the United States Attorney General who may bring

a suit in Federal District Court. If the U.S. Attorney General does not bring such a suit, the individual who filed the charge with us in the first place may bring one on his own, and if the experience in the private sector is any guide, will do so in many cases.

In concluding, let me urge you to start immediately on the work of extending the principle of merit employment to individuals of all races, ethnic origins, and sex. Let me urge you to conduct the first step in the examination of your practices proposed by the Griggs case, that is, determining whether there is a statistical disparity in your work force. Let me suggest that if our experience with state and local governments today is a guide, you will not need an elaborate computer but simply a glance around the room to determine that violations exist. Let me suggest finally that as you reexamine the operation of your employment systems in order to eliminate this statistical disparity, you do so with an imaginative and creative hand to extend the principle of merit employment to its fullest possible extent, which was not limited to rigid rules and tests but was instead designed to assure that the taxpayer gets his money's worth every time a government employee is recruited, hired, or promoted.

Merit principles were not implemented to assure the rigid following of procedures which no longer serve their purpose. They were not implemented to require the utilization of "phony credentials" nor were they implemented to protect the jobs of those of us who design, administer, and interpret written tests. Everytime a black, Chicano, or a woman is excluded from recruitment, hiring, or promotion by the rigid operation of the system that does not in fact measure merit or job relatedness, the taxpayer is gypped and the principles of merit employment sabotaged.

I look forward to joining with you in a great common effort to extend the concept of merit employment and to assure that all government jobs are filled with people who really can do their job regardless of race, religion, sex, color, or national origin. Gentlemen and ladies, you have my best wishes for success in this great common endeavor and my promise that, if you do not succeed voluntarily, we will use the full powers of the law recently passed by Congress to encourage your compliance with whatever steps are necessary to obtain it.

How "Equal Opportunity" Turned Into Employment Quotas
Some strange things have been happening, in government and industry, in the name of "nondiscrimination."

Daniel Seligman

Soon after it came into office, the Nixon administration proposed that critics "watch what we do instead of listening to what we say." By this eminently reasonable standard, the administration today might be judged to favor quotas in employment. The President has repeatedly assailed them; in fact, the elimination of quotas was identified in a major campaign statement as one of ten great goals for the nation in his second term. Yet during his years in office, and with some powerful encouragement from the executive branch of the U.S. Government, quotas have taken hold in several areas of American life. The controversies about them have centered on their appearance in the construction industry and on university campuses. Oddly enough, very little attention has been paid to employment quotas in large corporations.

The omission is very odd indeed, for it is in corporate employment that quotas are having their major impact on the American labor force and on relations between the races and sexes. Nowadays there are scarcely any companies among, say, the FORTUNE 500, that are not under pressure from the government to hire and promote more women and minority-group members; and many of these companies have responded to the pressure by installing what are, in effect, quota systems.

In most of the controversy over quotas, there is no real disagreement about ultimate objectives. Most educated Americans today would agree that several minorities, and women, suffer from discrimination in employment, that the discrimination is destructive and irrational, and that working to end it is a proper activity for government. Unfortunately, it is not clear what government should do—and all too clear that wise policies do not flow naturally from good intentions.

In discussions of this issue, people who don't define their terms can dither on for quite a while without getting anywhere. Let us begin, accordingly, with some definitions and distinctions. Among companies that have no intention of discriminating against women or minorities, four different postures may be discerned:

Reprinted from the March, 1973 issue of *Fortune* magazine by special permission. © 1973, Time, Inc.

1. Passive nondiscrimination involves a willingness, in all decisions about hiring, promotion, and pay, to treat the races and sexes alike. However, this posture may involve a failure to recognize that past discrimination leaves many prospective employees unaware of present opportunities.

2. Pure affirmative action involves a concerted effort to expand the pool of applicants so that no one is excluded because of past or present discrimination. At the point of decision, however, the company hires (or promotes) whoever seems most qualified, without regard to race or sex.

3. Affirmative action with preferential hiring. In this posture, the company not only ensures that it has a larger labor pool to draw from but systematically favors women and minority groups in the actual decisions about hiring. This might be thought of as a "soft" quota system, i.e., instead of establishing targets that absolutely must be met, the top officers of the company beef up employment of women and minority-group members to some unspecified extent by indicating that they want those groups given a break.

4. Hard quotas. No two ways about it—specific numbers or proportions of minority-group members must be hired.

Much of the current confusion about quotas—and the controversy about whether the government is imposing them—derives from a failure to differentiate among several of these postures. The officials who are administering the principal federal programs tend, of course, to bristle at any suggestion that they are imposing quotas; they have been bristling with special vigor ever since the President's campaign statements on the subject. Their formulations tend to be somewhat self-serving, however. The officials turn out, when pressed, to be denying that the government is pushing employers into posture No. 4. The real issue is No. 3, preferential hiring, which many government agencies are indeed promoting. Meanwhile, the President and a few other administration officials concerned with equal-employment opportunity sound as though the objective of the program is to promote pure affirmative action—posture No. 2.

THE CONCILIATORS HAVE MUSCLES

The U.S. government's efforts to end discrimination in employment are carried out through two major programs. One was set in motion by Title VII of the Civil Rights Act of 1964, which forbids discrimination based on race, color, religion, sex, or national origin. The act established an Equal Employment Opportunity Commission, which now has two main functions. The first is enforcement: the commission may sue in a U.S. district court, on its own behalf or for other claimants, when it believes that discrimination has taken place. The EEOC has had the power to sue only since March, 1972—previously it was limited to conciliation efforts—and has filed only about twenty-five suits in that time. Chairman William H. Brown III believes that when the commission gets warmed up it might be filing an average of five suits a week.

In practice, Brown suspects, not many of these are apt to be litigated; the right to go into court is useful to the EEOC mainly for the muscle it provides in conciliation efforts. If the EEOC did get into court, it would have to prove outright discrimination; in principle, that is, an employer might comply with Title VII simply by practicing passive nondiscrimination—posture No. 1. However, the conciliation agreements extracted from those accused of discrimination typically call for more than that. Most of the agreements negotiated thus far involve preferential hiring.

The commission's other main function is information gathering. Every enterprise with 100 or more employees must file annually with the EEOC a form detailing the number of women and members of four different minority groups employed in each of nine different job categories, from laborers to "managers and officials." The minority groups are Negroes; Americans of Mexican, Puerto Rican, Cuban, or Spanish origin; Orientals; and American Indians (who in Alaska are deemed to include Eskimos and Aleuts). With some 260,000 forms a year to process, the EEOC is having some difficulty in staying on top of the data it is collecting. "Obviously, we can't look critically at all the reports," Brown concedes. Eventually, however, he hopes to develop some computerized procedures for finding patterns of discrimination, i.e., procedures somewhat analogous to those employed by the Internal Revenue Service in deciding which tax returns to audit.

Meanwhile, the EEOC is getting a fair amount of help from people who believe they are being discriminated against. When any complaint is received at the commission, even one with no visible substance to it, an EEOC staff member pulls the file on the company in question and looks for patterns of discrimination. In fiscal 1972 more than 30,000 charges were filed.

SPECIAL RULES FOR CONTRACTORS

The other major federal program is based on the special obligations incurred by government contractors. This program may be traced all the way back to 1941, when President Franklin D. Roosevelt issued an executive order outlawing racial discrimination by defense contractors. Every President since Roosevelt has issued one or more orders extending the reach of the ban. It applies now to subcontractors as well as primes, to civilian as well as military purchases, and to services as well as goods. It affects every division and every subsidiary of any company with a contract worth $10,000 or more. It covers women as well as racial, religious, and ethnic minorities. And it has entailed increasingly expansive definitions of "nondiscrimination." Right now, about a quarter of a million companies, employing about a third of the U.S. labor force, are covered by the executive orders.

At the time President Nixon took office, most government contractors were operating under Executive Order 11246, which had been issued by President

Johnson in September, 1965. The order as later amended by Johnson, required "affirmative action" by employers—but did not specify what this meant in practice. The Office of Federal Contract Compliance had never developed guidelines for determining whether contractors were in compliance. It was left to the Nixon administration to make the program operational.

The administration's first major decision about the program was to make it, in the marvelous label applied by the Labor Department, "result-oriented." Affirmative action could have been defined so that it required companies to incorporate certain procedures into their personnel policies—but did not require that any particular results follow from the procedures. The difficulty with this approach was that companies determined to discriminate might simply go through the motions while continuing to exclude women and minority-group members. "It just would have been too easy for them to make patsies of us," said Laurence Silberman, who was solicitor of the Labor Department at the time, and who participated in the formulation of the program. An alternative approach, which was the one essentially adopted, would require each company to set goals and timetables for hiring specified numbers of women and minority-group members; would allow the government to review the goals to ensure that they were sufficiently ambitious; and, if they were not met, would require the company to prove that it had at least made a "good-faith effort" to meet them.

This approach was certainly calculated to produce results. The difficulty was that it also seemed likely to produce *reverse* discrimination by companies fearful of losing their contracts. The administration recognized this problem from the beginning, and agonized over it quite a lot. "No program has given me greater problems of conscience than this one," said Silberman recently, just before leaving the Labor Department to go into private law practice in the capital. In the end, however, the administration always came back to the view that a program that didn't achieve results would be a charade—and that the only way to ensure results was to require goals and timetables.

The rules of the new game were first set forth in January, 1970, in the Labor Department's Order No. 4, signed by then-Secretary George P. Shultz. At the time, it seems clear, businessmen did not pay a great deal of attention to Order No. 4. It is perhaps worth noting that the momentous changes signaled by the order had never been debated in Congress, not even during the great outpouring of civil-rights legislation in the 1960's. Anyone looking for examples of the growing autonomy of the executive branch of the federal government could do worse than focus on this quite unheralded administrative regulation.

TRYING TO BE REASONABLE

Specifically, Order No. 4 requires that every contractor have a written affirmative-action program for every one of his establishments. Every program must include a detailed report on the company's utilization of each of the four basic minorities in each of its own job categories. (A "Revised Order No. 4," issued by Secretary of Labor J. D. Hodgson in December, 1971, called for reports on women, too.)

Whenever there are job categories with fewer women or minority-group members "than would reasonably be expected by their availability," the contractor must establish goals for increasing their utilization.

Well, how does one determine the appropriate utilization rates? The order makes a great show of being helpful in this regard, listing eight criteria that contractors should consider in trying to answer the question. The first is "the minority population of the labor area surrounding the facility"; others include "the availability of minorities having requisite skills in an area in which the contractor can reasonably recruit," and "the degree of training which the contractor is reasonably able to undertake as a means of making all job classes available to minorities." The criteria certainly give contractors a lot to think about, but they do not, in the end, make clear what would be a reasonable utilization rate for, say, black mechanics. A contractor focusing on this matter might find himself utterly confused about the number of blacks in town who were already trained as mechanics, the number who were "trainable," the amount he was expected to spend on training, the distance he was expected to travel to recruit, etc.

In practice, contractors are encouraged to assume that they are underutilizing women and minorities and, accordingly, they have goals and timetables just about everywhere. For example, International Business Machines Corp., which has long been a model employer so far as fair-employment practices are concerned, has goals and timetables today at every one of its 400-odd establishments in the U.S.

Because the criteria are so vague, the goal-setting procedure often becomes an exercise in collective bargaining, with the outcome dependent on the respective will and resourcefulness of the company's top executives and the government's compliance officers. The government is ordinarily represented in these matters by whichever of its departments is contracting for the company's services; the OFCC does some, but not much, coordinating. On the whole, the enforcement varies considerably in both fairness and effectiveness from one company to another. Furthermore, some companies deal with several different departments; Union Carbide, for example, is monitored by the Atomic Energy Commission and the Departments of Defense, Transportation, Labor, Interior, and Agriculture.

The compliance officers themselves are career civil servants, and they seem to come in all varieties. Two quite different criticisms of them are often heard. One is that they are apt to be knee-jerk liberals, persuaded in advance that the big corporation is guilty. The other is that they have often lazily adopted the position that anything the company proposes is fine with them. Herbert Hill, the labor specialist of the National Association for the Advancement of Colored People, is prepared to regale anyone who wants to listen with tales of compliance officers who have been co-opted by corporate personnel departments. One senior official of the Labor Department who has been in a good position to observe the contract-compliance program was asked recently what he thought of these two criticisms. "They're both true," he answered, adding, after a moment's reflection, that the compliance officers also included many thoughtful and conscientious public servants.

WHAT'S HAPPENED TO MERIT?

There is no doubt that, between them, the EEOC and the contract-compliance program have transformed the way big business in the U.S. hires people. Even allowing for those co-opted compliance officers, the government has gone a long way toward wiping out old-fashioned discrimination in the corporate universe. But it is increasingly evident that, in doing so, the government programs have undermined some other old-fashioned notions about hiring on the basis of merit.

The undermining process can be discerned in the campaigns, waged successfully by EEOC and OFCC, against certain kinds of employment standards. Employers who demand certain skills, education levels, or test-score results are presumed to be discriminating if their standards have the effect of excluding women or minority-group members. To counter this presumption, the employer must demonstrate conclusively that the skills are in fact needed for the job. If test-score results are involved, he must also demonstrate that the tests reliably predict the skills in question and, finally, that "alternative suitable . . . procedures are unavailable for his use." One argument the employer *cannot* make is that he had no discriminatory intent in establishing the requirements. Under Title VII, as administered by the FEOC, the intent is irrelevant: it is only the effect that matters—which represents a major alteration in the law of discrimination.

The altered concept became the law of the land in March, 1971, when the U.S. Supreme Court upheld the EEOC's view, and overruled a court of appeals, in *Griggs* v. *Duke Power.* The company had required applicants for certain jobs to

---

A.T.&T. Gets the Message

The American Telephone & Telegraph Co., which had been spending a lot of time with the equal-employment opportunity forces of the U.S. government, made a remarkable settlement with them in January. Back in 1970, A.T.&T. had a request for rate increases pending before the Federal Communications Commission. The Equal Employment Opportunity Commission asked the FCC to deny the request on the ground that the company pursued discriminatory hiring and promotion practices and was, in fact, "the largest oppressor of women workers in the U.S." The petition clearly reflected an effort by the EEOC, which then had no enforcement powers, to use the muscle that comes naturally with the FCC's power over rates.

The FCC inquired, naturally, what discrimination had to do with rates. The EEOC responded that if the company did not discriminate against women, its costs would be lower: discrimination resulted in high turnover rates, the commission argued, and these saddled the company with heavy training costs. Early in 1971 the FCC began hearings on discrimination in the company.

Meanwhile, as a leading federal contractor, A.T.&T. was negotiating

have a high-school diploma and also to score at certain levels in aptitude tests. There was no contention that Duke Power intended these standards to have a discriminatory effect, and it was agreed that they were applied impartially to blacks and whites alike. It was also agreed that the standards resulted in very few blacks being hired. The company argued that it wanted to use the standards to improve the over-all quality of its labor force; but it could not demonstrate that the standards had a direct relationship to the jobs being performed. In ruling that the standards had to be dropped, Chief Justice Warren E. Burger, who wrote the Court's opinion, upheld the EEOC's contention that Title VII "has placed on the employer the burden of showing that any given requirement must have a manifest relationship to the employment in question."

Anyone pondering the particulars of the Duke Power case would have to feel sympathy for the black workers involved. Growing up in a society that had denied them a decent education, they were unfit for many skilled jobs. When they applied to do some relatively unskilled work that they could perform, they were excluded by educational standards—which, the facts suggest, really were extraneous to the company's needs. Unfortunately, the logic of the Duke Power decision suggests that some perfectly reasonable standards are now in trouble, too. Companies that have high standards and want to defend them will immediately perceive that the ground rules, which not only place the burden of proof on the employer but require coping with some formidable-looking validation procedures, are not inviting. Many will obviously conclude that it is simpler to abolish their standards than to try justifying them.

The new law presents special management problems to the numerous companies that have traditionally hired overqualified people at entry-level jobs, expecting

with the General Services Administration on goals and timetables for greater utilization of women and minorities. In September, 1972, GSA and the company reached an agreement under which 50,000 women and 6,600 minority-group members were to get better jobs over a fifteen-month period. The agreement was immediately questioned by two other agencies, the Office of Federal Contract Compliance and the EEOC, both of which undertook to renegotiate it.

The terms accepted by those agencies in January called for lump-sum payments of some $15 million to 13,000 women and 2,000 male minority-group members, who had been discriminated against in the past. It also called for immediate raises, aggregating $23 million, for some 36,000 workers who had been discriminated against. Finally, it roughly doubled the company's "ultimate goals" for hiring male operators and clerical workers and females employed in craft jobs. Ordinarily, goals are supposed to be set in detailed "utilization analyses" at each of the company's establishments (A.T.&T. has about 700). But in this case no one was pretending that the goals had any scientific basis.

them to compete for the better jobs. Dr. Lloyd Cooke, who monitors Union Carbide's equal-employment-opportunity program, suggested recently that most big companies like his own could no longer assume there were a lot of highly qualified people searching out their own paths to the top. "Now we must develop upward mobility models that include training along the way."

In addition to all their problems with tests and formal standards, federal contractors often face a new kind of pressure on the informal standards they may have in mind when they hire and promote people. Revised Order No. 4 specifies: "Neither minority nor female employees should be required to possess higher qualifications than those of the lowest-qualified incumbent." The logic of this rule is inexorable, and it too implies lower standards. In any organization that has a number of people working at different levels of skill and competence—a corporate engineering staff, say, or a university economics department—whoever does the hiring would ordinarily be trying to raise the average level of performance, i.e., to bring in more people at the high end of the range. If the organization must take on applicants who are at the low end or face charges of discrimination, it can only end up lowering the average.

Professor Sidney Hook, the philosopher, has assailed the possibilities of this "fantastic" requirement in universities. "It opens the door," he has written, "to hiring persons who cannot meet *current standards of qualification* because, forsooth, a poorly qualified incumbent was hired by some fluke or perhaps ages ago when the department was struggling for recognition."

WHAT CONGRESS HAS PROSCRIBED

For reasons that are certainly understandable, neither the EEOC nor the OFCC has ever said in writing that it believed the law to require some hiring of less-qualified people. To do so would apparently conflict with some of President Nixon's animadversions against quotas. In addition, it would seem to go against the plain language of the laws in question. It is, after all, logically impossible to discriminate in favor of blacks without discriminating against some whites; thus anyone espousing preferential hiring of blacks would be bucking Section 703(a) of Title VII, in which it is deemed unlawful for an employer "to . . . classify his employees in any way which would deprive or tend to deprive any individual of employment opportunities . . . because of such individual's race, color, religion, sex, or national origin." In *Griggs,* Chief Justice Burger reaffirmed the intent of the law in plain terms: "Discriminatory preference for any group, minority or majority, is precisely and only what Congress has proscribed."

In pushing preferences for women and minorities, the government's lawyers and compliance officers repeatedly offer the assurance that "you never have to hire an unqualified person." Since unqualified persons are by definition unable to do the job, the assurance is perhaps less meaningful than it sounds. The real question is whether employers should have to hire women or minority-group members who are less qualified than other available workers.

The answer one gets in conversation with EEOC officials is clear enough. If hiring someone who is less qualified will help an employer to utilize women or minorities at proper levels, then he should do so. Chairman Brown was asked recently what an employer should do if he was presumed to be underutilizing women and there were two applicants for a job: a fairly well qualified woman and a man who was somewhat better qualified. "If it's just a question of 'somewhat better,' you should probably hire the woman," he replied.

THE LAWYER'S PREDICAMENT

How can the lawyers who run the federal programs justify preferences that seem to violate the intent of the basic statutes? Not all the lawyers would respond in the same way, but most of them would point to some court decisions at the appellate level that call for preferential hiring and even hard quotas. They would also note that the Supreme Court has declined to review these decisions. In one important case, for example, the Alabama state troopers were ordered by a federal judge to hire one black trooper for every white man hired until the overall ratio was up to 25 percent black. Most of the lawyers would also agree with this formulation by William J. Kilberg, the Labor Department's associate solicitor for labor relations and civil rights: "In situations where there has been a finding of discrimination, and where no other remedy is available, temporary preferential hiring is legal and appropriate."

Kilberg himself believes strongly that preferences should be limited to these special circumstances—in which it is indeed hard to argue against them. But other government lawyers view them as natural and desirable in a wide range of circumstances. They argue, for example, that it is unnecessary to require a finding of discrimination; they contend that companies underutilizing women or minority-group members are, *per se,* guilty of discrimination and that it is appropriate, in reviewing their goals and timetables, to push for some preference. Furthermore, the EEOC tends to the view that any past discrimination justifies preferences, i.e., it often fails to consider whether other remedies are available.

Last fall H.E.W.'s Office of Civil Rights made a major, but only partially successful, effort to clarify the ground rules of the contract-compliance program. J. Stanley Pottinger, who has headed the office for most of the past three years (he recently moved over to the Justice Department), put together a volume spelling out some guidelines. At the same time, somewhat confusingly, he issued a covering statement that went beyond anything in the volume. It said, "Nothing in the affirmative-action concept requires a university to employ or promote any faculty member who is less qualified than other applicants competing for that position." That statement was, and indeed still is, the only formal declaration ever issued by any contract-compliance official ruling out a requirement for hiring less-qualified job applicants.

Many contractors who read the statement took it for granted that the same rule would apply to corporate employment. Unfortunately, anyone talking about this matter to officials of the Labor Department soon discovers that they regard university hiring problems as somewhat special. There is a view that faculties have a unique need for "excellence," but that in the business world, and especially at the blue-collar level, most jobs are such that employers suffer no real hardship when "less-qualified" people are hired.

A MESSAGE TO JACK ANDERSON

Meanwhile, corporate executives tend to take it for granted that, in practice, reverse discrimination is what affirmative action is all about. Whoever it is at International Telephone & Telegraph Corp. that leaks internal memorandums to columnist Jack Anderson recently sent along one on this subject. In the passage that Anderson published, Senior Vice President John Hanway was proposing to another executive that thirty-four rather high-ranking jobs "lend themselves readily to being filled by affirmative-action candidates," i.e., they should be filled by women or minority-group members.

Companies' public declarations about affirmative action do not ordinarily propose so blatantly to prefer these groups, but the dynamics of the program more or less guarantee that there will be preferences. Revised Order No. 4 says, "Supervisors should be made to understand that their work performance is being evaluated on the basis of their equal employment opportunity efforts and results, as well as other criteria."

Supervisors are indeed getting the message. At I.B.M., for example, *every manager* is told that his annual performance evaluation—on which the prospects for promotions, raises, and bonuses critically depend—includes a report on his success in meeting affirmative-action goals. A memo last July 5, from Chairman C. Peter McColough to all Xerox managers in the U.S. (it was later published by the company), warned that "a key element in each manager's overall performance appraisal will be his progress in this important area. No manager should expect a satisfactory appraisal if he meets other objectives, but fails here." At Xerox, furthermore, the goals are very ambitious these days. Something like 40 percent of all net additions to the corporate payroll last year were minority-group members.

In principle, of course, a line manager who is not meeting his targets is allowed to argue that he has made a "good-faith effort" to do so. But the burden of proof will be on the manager, who knows perfectly well that the only surefire way to prove good faith is to meet the targets. If he succeeds, no questions will be asked about reverse discrimination; if he fails, he will automatically stir up questions about the adequacy of his efforts and perhaps about his racial tolerance too (not to mention his bonus). Obviously, then, a manager whose goals call for hiring six black salesmen during the year, and who has hired only one by Labor Day, is feeling a lot of pressure to discriminate against white applicants in the fall. "In this company," said the president of one billion-dollar enterprise recently, "a black has a better chance of being hired than a white, frankly. When he's hired, he has a better chance of being promoted. That's the only way it can be."

SOME KIND WORDS FOR ABILITY

The future of the "quotas issue" is hard to predict, for several reasons. One is the continuing blurriness of the Nixon administration's intentions. For a while, last summer, these appeared to have been clarified. In August, Philip Hoffman, president of the American Jewish Committee, sent identical letters to Nixon and McGovern expressing concern about the spread of quota systems in American education and employment. Both candidates replied with letters assailing quotas. The President wrote to Hoffman: "I share your support of affirmative efforts to ensure that all Americans have an equal chance to compete for employment opportunities, and to do so on the basis of individual ability ... With respect to these affirmative-action programs, ... numerical goals ... must not be allowed to be applied in such a fashion as to, in fact, result in the imposition of quotas."

This declaration was followed by a number of newspaper articles suggesting that the administration was preparing to gut the affirmative-action program. The articles were wrong, however. Before the reply to Hoffman had been drafted, a number of administration officials—they included White House special consultant (on minorities) Leonard Garment, Silberman, and Pottinger—met to discuss the program and to consider whether the time had come to change it. Specifically, they considered whether to drop the requirement for goals and timetables. And they decided, as they had in earlier reviews, to resolve their doubts in favor of standing pat.

It seems clear that the Nixon letter to Hoffman temporarily shook up some members of the equal-opportunity bureaucracy, but it doesn't seem to have led to any major changes in the way the federal program is implemented. Many executives, including some who are vigorous supporters of the program, confess to being baffled by the contrast between the President's words and the bureaucracy's actions. General Electric's man in charge of equal-employment-opportunity programs, whose name happens to be Jim Nixon, remarked recently that he kept reading in the papers that "the other Nixon" was cutting back on affirmative action, but "around here, all we see is a continuing tightening of the noose."

Perhaps the simplest explanation of that contrast between words and actions lies in the very nature of the program. It is logically possible to have goals and timetables that don't involve preferential hiring—and that happy arrangement is what the Administration keeps saying we have now. But there are built-in pressures that keep leading back to preference: the implicit presumption that employers are "underutilizing" women and minority-group members; the further presumption that this underutilization is essentially the result of discrimination; the extraordinary requirement, quite alien to our usual notions about due process, that unmet goals call for the employer to demonstrate good faith (i.e., instead of calling for the government to prove bad faith). It seems reasonable to speculate that at some point the administration will abandon goals and timetables, conceding that they lead in practice to preferential hiring and even quotas. Indeed, some of the program's senior officials regard the present format as temporary. Pottinger, who has spent a lot of time in recent years arguing that goals don't mean quotas, nevertheless says, "I sure hope they're not permanent."

In any case, one would have to be skeptical of the long-term future of any program with so many anomalies built into it. For a democratic society to systematically discriminate against "the majority" seems quite without precedent. To do so in the name of nondiscrimination seems mind-boggling. For humane and liberal-minded members of the society to espouse racial discrimination at all seems most remarkable.

THE CRUELTIES OF REVERSE DISCRIMINATION

One immediate threat to the program may be discerned, meanwhile, in a number of suits against corporations and universities, alleging some form of reverse discrimination. H.E.W. now has an "ombudsman" working full-time on such complaints. It seems likely that companies engaged in preferential hiring will be hit by more such suits as the realities of their programs sink in on employees and job applicants.

But even aside from all the large litigious possibilities, there are surely going to be serious problems about morale in these companies. It is very difficult for a large corporation to discriminate in favor of any group without, to some extent, stigmatizing all members of the group who work for it. G.E.'s Nixon, who is himself black, says that talk about hiring less-qualified minority-group members makes him uneasy—that "it puts the 'less-qualified' stamp on the minorities you do hire." In companies where reverse discrimination is the rule, there will be a nagging question about the real capabilities of any black man who gets a good job or promotion. The question will occur to the white applicants who didn't get the job; it will occur to customers who deal with the black man; and, of course, it will occur to the black himself. Perhaps the cruelest aspect of reverse discrimination is that it ultimately denies minority-group members who have made it on their own the satisfaction of knowing that.

In short, businessmen who are opting for preferential hiring, or who are being pushed to it by government pressure, may be deluding themselves if they think they're taking the easy way. It seems safe to say that at some point, even if the government does not abandon its pressures for preference, more businessmen will begin resisting them. It should go without saying that the resistance will be easier, and will come with better grace, if those businessmen have otherwise made clear their opposition to any form of discrimination.

SELECTED READINGS

Boyle, B. M., "Equal Opportunity for Women is Smart Business," *Harvard Business Review*, (May–June, 1973).

"Changes in the Labor Force Status of Women," *Monthly Labor Review,* August, 1973.

"The Chicanos Campaign for a Better Deal," *Business Week,* May 29, 1971.

Cross, T. L., *Black Capitalism.* (New York: Atheneum Publishers, 1969).

Domm, D. R., and J. E. Stafford, "Assimilating Blacks into the Organization," *California Management Review,* Fall, 1972.

Fletcher, A., "What Happened to the Philadelphia Plan?", *Business and Society Review/Innovation,* Spring, 1973.

Gelb, B. D., and B. M. Enis, "Affirmative Action in Housing and Beyond," *California Management Review,* Winter, 1973.

Ginsberg, E., and A. M. Yohalem, eds., *Woman's Challenge to Management.* (New York: Praeger, 1974.)

Holsendolph, E., "Black Executives in a Nearly All White World," *Fortune,* September, 1972.

Kreps, J., *Sex in the Marketplace: American Women At Work.* (Baltimore: Johns Hopkins Press, 1971).

Pati, C. C., and P. E. Fahey, "Affirmative Action Program: Its Realities and Challenges," *Labor Law Journal,* June, 1973.

Purcell, T. V., and G. F. Cavanaugh, *Blacks in the Industrial World.* (New York: The Free Press, 1972).

"White Males Complain They Are Now Victims of Job Discrimination," *Wall Street Journal,* February 28, 1974.

Cases

CALVIN COOLIDGE CHAIR CO.

Article 16 of the collective bargaining agreement provides as follows:

ARTICLE 16. PROMOTION AND BIDDING

When a vacancy occurs in an existing job classification or when a new job classification is created, the Employer will promptly post a notice of such vacancy on each bulletin board for a period of not less than five (5) days.

A notice of vacancy will state that interested employees shall have ten (10) working days after the first day of posting within which to bid for the vacancy by filing a written bid with the Personnel Office.

If two or more employees shall bid for the vacancy, seniority shall govern between employees whose ability to perform the job is relatively equal.

If, in the opinion of management, employees who bid for the vacancy lack sufficient qualifications, the employer may hire qualified persons from the outside.

On May 14 the Employer posted the following notice on each employee bulletin board:

NOTICE OF JOB VACANCY

Forklift Operator, Shipping & Receiving Dept.

Rate—$3.90 per hour

Qualifications—Prior experience preferred, not required.

Closing date—May 28.

E. Dubinsky,
Personnel Manager

On May 29, Personnel Manager Dubinsky called for the bids for the forklift operator's vacancy. To his surprise there were only three bidders. From a brief study of their job bids and a look at their personnel files, Dubinsky put together these brief profiles:

John C. Bach—age 19.

Present job: mail clerk.
Present rate of pay: $2.15.
Education: High school graduate.
Family: Unmarried.
Physical: Height—5'6"; weight—145.
Attendance: Excellent.
Prior experience with forklift: None.
Seniority: 10 months.

Gloria C. Vivaldi—age 28.

Present job: Packer.
Present rate of pay: $2.33.
Education: High school graduate and AA degree in business from King Tut Community College.
Family: Married; no children.
Physical: Height—5'6"; weight—120.
Attendance: Good.
Prior experience with forklift: None.
Seniority: 8 years, 3 months.

Mario Delmonico—age 63.

Present job: Janitor.
Present rate of pay: $2.28.
Education: 8th grade.
Family: Married; grown children.
Physical: Height—5'11"; weight—225.
Attendance: Average.
Prior experience with forklift: 6 weeks' experience approximately 10 years ago when employed by another firm.
Seniority: 29 months.

Dubinsky reviewed these profiles with a sense of disappointment. He regarded Delmonico as the best qualified because of his prior experience and because he seemed psychologically best suited to getting along with the tough, all-male crew that works on the shipping and receiving dock. On the other hand, Dubinsky had doubts about Delmonico's age. (Dubinsky knew, but neither the Union nor employees knew, that the Employer was contemplating implementation of a mandatory retirement policy for employees upon reaching age 65.)

Dubinsky had different kinds of reservations about John Bach, who had effeminate mannerisms and about whom employees circulated nasty little rumors. Although Bach's overall employment record was quite satisfactory, Dubinsky wondered whether the young man's personality was unsuited to operating heavy equipment and to the social environment of the shipping and receiving dock. In Bach's favor were his youth and his good record for attendance and punctuality.

Dubinsky regarded Gloria Vivaldi's bid as something of a joke—but not entirely. She had a reputation as a practical joker. She was attractive and well liked by her co-workers and supervisors. In her present job classification, she was required occasionally to lift heavy boxes which she did with apparent ease. She had talked about running for the presidency of the Union, and a number of female employees seemed eager to support her candidacy. In recent weeks it was suspected, but not proven, that she and friends had pasted little stickers around the plant which said: "OFF the MCP's." *

If her bid were rejected, would she file a grievance under the contract? Would she go to the Equal Employment Opportunity Commission? Or what else?

The following day, after a long discussion of the matter with Mrs. Nickelmoose, Dubinsky notified each of the three bidders that, in the opinion of management, he or she lacked "sufficient qualifications" to

---

*Male chauvinist pigs.

perform the forklift operator's job and that management intended to advertise the job outside the plant. Simultaneously he sent the following notice to the Modigliani office of the U.S. Employment Service:

> The Calvin Coolidge Chair Co. has an opening for an experienced forklift operator. $3.90 per hour. Contact E. Dubinsky, Personnel Mgr.

The next afternoon Dubinsky interviewed and hired an applicant referred by the U.S. Employment Service, E. V. Debs. Debs, a white male, age 34, had had five years' experience as a forklift operator.

Through the plant's grapevine, Bach and Vivaldi heard about Debs's employment. Each of them, without the knowledge of the other, called the chairman of the Union's grievance committee and demanded that the Union file a grievance on his or her behalf.

CORBIN PHILATELICS

Stan Corbin had been a philatelist since he was six years old, becoming interested in postage stamps when his teacher brought some into school to use in a history lesson. Corbin collected right up through his college years at Notre Dame, where he majored in marketing and business administration.

While at Notre Dame—during 1963 to 1967—he earned his spending money by operating a small stamp approval business. Approvals are stamps sold through the mail with the customer receiving them, selecting those wanted, and returning the rest to the dealer along with payment for those kept. It's a risky business and hundreds of would-be stamp dealers go in and go out in short time. Corbin bought collections, broke them up, either mounted the stamps on sheets or placed them in glassine envelopes, and sent them out to his customers. He had about 130 customers while in college and grossed over $1500 a month while spending about four hours a day plus about 15 hours on weekends on his hobby–business. After deducting losses for nonreturns, fortunately only 0.5% of sales, Corbin figured he netted about $300 per month. By the time he left college, he had accumulated a nice-size inventory for a small dealer with a retail value of about $13,000.

Corbin was in Air Force ROTC at Notre Dame and was called to active duty in September of 1967. He sold his inventory to a Chicago dealer for $6,400. On his release from the service in 1970, Corbin took a job as a sales trainee with a large oil company, but he secretly wished to get back into the stamp business. He restarted his approval business and slowly gained some 175 customers. His method of operation was still like that of his college days, buying old collections, breaking them down and sending the stamps out to his customers. He operated out of a basement room in his home, spending most of his spare time on the business. Corbin grossed about $3,000 per month on stamps on which he figured he netted about $500.

In 1971, Corbin decided that the time had come to either go full-time into stamps or forget the whole thing. He found himself having little spare time for his family, and the business was just getting to be too much for him to handle on a part-time basis. One weekend, he spent considerable time analyzing his alternatives and the possible way he might operate a full-time stamp business.

He thought that traditional stamp merchandising was archaic. Typically the dealers were small, one person or so did all the functions, there was little specialization, and in general the business was very disorganized. He thought that most dealers rarely thought about the costs of serving customers or of handling particular items. The key to success, he reasoned, was not necessarily in buying collections and breaking them down completely—that consumed inordinate amounts of labor— but in getting the inventory turned over fast. Also, the costs involved in selling penny stamps were generally the same as selling more expensive ones. Finally, there were so many countries issuing so many stamps these days that to be a new-issue dealer—stocking worldwide stamps —was virtually suicidal.

Corbin decided that if he went into business, the following principles would guide him: First, the minimum price for a stamp or set of stamps would be 75¢. Groups of singles could be combined, but nothing under a unit price of 75¢ would be sold. Second, in breaking down collections, only complete sets or better singles would be extracted. The remainder of the collection could be assembled into packets and wholesaled. Thirdly, the business must be operated in such a way that nonstamp collectors could be rapidly trained to break down collections, price the stamps, put them into inventory, and handle customer mailings. Corbin felt that a professional philatelist should be needed only for specialized collections and evaluation of very rare material.

He started to think about systems. He thought that he would spend the bulk of his time buying and appraising collections and lots. This was not an easy process, as he had to peruse auction catalogues, go to some of the larger sales, visit sellers' homes, and appraise material sent to him. If Corbin were to go into stamp dealing in a big way, purchasing would consume most of his time.

He would then need someone with some philatelic knowledge to administer the office and handle the breakdown of more expensive material. In the office, two separate procedures would be needed. One would be the breakdown of collections and inventory-replenishing process. People would have to be trained to take a collection, get out the complete sets or valuable singles, catalogue them according to the standard American catalogue, price the material (usually at 50 percent of catalogue value), grade the stamps, package the stamps in glassine envelopes, and place them into inventory.

The other system involved customer service. Corbin thought that each customer could have a card on file. When the customer was sent his stamps, the amount of material sent would be noted on the card. Attached to the card would also be a listing of the material sent in terms of country, catalogue number, value, etc. When the stamps were returned, the amount of purchases would be tallied and recorded. The returned merchandise would be checked against the inventory sheet as well. Also on the card would be noted the customer's specialties and particular wants, and an employee could then assemble another selection to send, prepare a new inventory sheet, and return the card to the file. Some cards would have a maximum selection value noted, and this could periodically be upgraded if necessary.

Stamps not purchased would be returned to inventory by the person handling the breakdown of lots and collections. Periodically, Corbin thought that he or his manager would scan the cards, deleting customers whose purchases consistently ran below 25 percent of the selection sent.

Corbin thought about the kinds of people who could best fill the proposed positions. No particular skills would be required except for the manager and bookkeepers. He was convinced that he could reasonably train people in less than a week to break down collections; order fillers could be trained in about the same time provided the inventory was broken into special categories by country and location (such as British Commonwealth, Western Europe, Asia, etc.). Corbin thought that any reasonably intelligent person could handle the jobs. He decided that a high school diploma would be sufficient educational background, but just to be safe, he would administer one of the intelligence tests—the Wonderlic Personnel Test—that he knew his present employer was using. Finally, since stamps had high value in small size, he knew he must be assured of complete honesty in his employees. He decided to check credit, arrest, and previous employment records.

Corbin's decision was probably made before he even started to think about the particulars of opening the stamp business. Late Sunday night, he announced to his wife that he was quitting his job at the oil company and going into business for himself. She was a bit frightened, but she knew Stan's love for stamps; she reluctantly agreed to the change.

After buying some old library-card cabinets and some used office furniture, and renting an office in downtown Chicago, Corbin started.

Sales		$643,600
Cost of Goods Sold		385,000
Gross Profit		258,600
Expenses:		
Salaries	143,000	
Rent	12,000	
Supplies	16,000	
Postage	4,700	
Depreciation	1,500	
Losses from Accounts	11,400	
Utilities	4,800	
Advertising	9,000	
Insurance	3,000	
Total Expenses		205,400
Net Profit		53,200

He hired a friend from the Evanston Stamp Club to be his manager; at first, the manager performed many of the routine tasks of breaking down collections and sending out selections. Corbin initially did the bookkeeping as well as the buying, and his wife sometimes came in to help sending out selections. He hired his first two employees about three months later, and they took to his systems quite well.

By 1974, the business was a success. Corbin had 6,200 active accounts and was grossing about $57,000 a month. The company had 17 active employees besides the manager and himself. "Things were really looking good," he thought. The 1973 income statement showed a net profit of over $53,000.

Corbin thought that, despite the hard work and long hours, the money he was making in this business was a lot better than the $24,000 he would be making at the oil company. Besides, he was enjoying this work. He also now had an inventory valued at over $500,000.

After the initial few months, Corbin left the hiring to his manager, Fred Towne. One day in April, Towne interviewed a young black woman, Joan Clark, for a job in the selection processing system. Ms. Clark responded to an advertisement in the *Chicago Bugle.* Corbin Philatelics employed no blacks, but most of the employees were women. Ms. Clark wasn't a high school graduate, but seemed extremely alert and capable. While her scores on the tests were not too high, Towne was reasonably impressed. On checking her credit and employment references, however, Towne learned that she was once detained by police on alleged shoplifting charges. She was released, however, when the shoplifter turned out to be someone else. Ms. Clark was one of six black women detained and released before the shoplifter was identified. Although Towne realized that the arrest was improper, he decided not to take chances and rejected Ms. Clark's application. There was just too much valuable merchandise around to take risks, he reasoned. Besides, she wasn't a high school graduate and her tests scores weren't very high anyway. He informed Ms. Clark that she didn't meet the qualifications for the job.

About a month later, Stan Corbin was sitting in his office working on auction bid sheets when a young woman knocked at his door. "Mr. Corbin?" she asked. "My name is Susan Wright and I'm from the Equal Employment Opportunity Commission."

C. *Business and the Physical Environment*

A decade ago, pollution and ecology were two terms rarely found in the lexicon of business. Today environmental survival and pollution abatement are major topics of the times and receive prominent exposure in the literature of business and economics. If any one issue provides the sustenance for social responsibility proponents, that issue must be the effect of business operations and practices on the physical environment. Probably more words have been written on this subject than on most others of a business and social problems context. We reflect this wealth of material, along with the diversity of viewpoints, in this section of the book.

Before proceding much further, we might define, more precisely than we have heretofore, two terms the student will meet often, particularly in a discussion of the physical environment—*externalities* and *external costs.* Externalities are the side effects of a process or transaction that neither positively nor negatively directly affect the primary participants in that process or transaction, but do affect others who are not party to the transaction. With pollution, the wastes dumped into a river or the smoke spewed into the air are externalities; they are ancillary to the production process and affect (through disease, uncleanliness, and even death) individuals not primary to the production or transaction process. The *costs* imposed by such practices are not paid for by the firm or included in the transaction price. Hence, they are called *external costs.*

External costs are borne by others than the primary participants in the transaction; the primary participants or producers pass the costs of externalities onto others. For examples, the costs of treating a disease contracted by a swimmer in a polluted river are borne by the swimmer, not by the firm which polluted the river; the costs of cleaning a building abutting a factory are met by the building owners, not by the factory owners whose smokestack let the dirty exhaust escape. The essence of the pollution problem, from an economic point of view, lies in the assigning of external costs. If the costs are assigned "correctly," then the price system would include the full costs of production, and the firm (or whatever economic unit one is considering for analysis), in seeking to minimize that cost, might lessen its pollution. Should society so desire, costs could be assigned in the form of taxes which could then be converted to public pollution control efforts.

Although a relatively large part of this nation's pollution (air, water, noise, and land) is attributable to nonbusiness sources—public institutions, individuals as consumers, schools, hospitals, and government agencies (a recent episode involved a citation to the San Francisco branch of the U.S. Mint for polluting the air while destroying (burning) old, worn currency)—a disproportionately high share of the criticism falls on business and industry. Perhaps the scenes of factory complexes replete with belching smokestacks (those scenes so proudly reproduced on earlier stock certificates of some corporations) are too firmly fixed in the public mind. So are the foul-smelling waterways that pass by waste-producing plants.

One should not get the idea from the previous paragraph that business firms are not guilty of polluting and that only symbolism accounts for their being criticized. They are often quite guilty, and the waste pipes, smokestacks, and solid-waste disposal of industrial plants are not figments of the imagination, but serious sources of pollution. We are simply saying that critics in many cases have failed to maintain reasonable perspectives or acquire adequate knowledge. One of your authors, for example, vividly recalls lecturing a group of nonbusiness majors on pollution and business; while the students consistently berated business firms for polluting, not one knew where the sewage treatment plant of his home town was located (many did not even know whether their towns had plants), or where the plant in their college town was located (even though it is less than 1000 yards from the University's major dormitory complex). None of the students had any idea of the complexity of pollution control or of the extent of industry's clean-up efforts.

A discussion of pollution problems, relative to business, is not as easy as some would have us believe; nor are the solutions as glib. Business firms come in all sizes; they range from the smaller, perhaps marginal firm to the giant with considerable monopolistic power. Plants also come in many age brackets; new plants may be efficient and less costly to operate; older plants may be more prone to closure from minor changes in costs or markets. Machinery may differ among plants and, of course, the competence of managers and the availability of capital are nowhere near standard across firms. New plants, old plants, large plants, and small plants also may all have their profitability affected by events well beyond the control of many managers: a cancelled government contract, a sudden oil embargo, a tight money market, or a million-dollar lawsuit for an automobile accident 3500 miles away.

In essence, the abilities of firms to absorb the costs of pollution and still remain in business vary greatly and depend on a wide range of events. Even when the proper technical capabilities exist, other factors can clearly constrain the effective implementation of pollution-control efforts. One error often made by critics of industry is their assumption of identical or similar cost, market, and other environmental conditions for each and every firm. But just as one person may have a different lifestyle from another, so may one business firm be quite different from even its closest competitor.

The issue is far from clear-cut as to what the proper stance of business should be in the environmental cleansing effort. Some business leaders take the traditional approach, arguing that firms should do nothing unless forced to by government. Despite lip service given to voluntary efforts, the traditional approach may be more operative than business would care to admit. Rhetoric aside, the fact remains that a good deal of pollution abatement on the part of firms comes after a law is passed and the government inspector has made his rounds. The traditional approach echoes the theme that *the business of business is business* and that the firm has just as much right to use a stream, for example, as do fishermen and bathers. (This argument, by the way, raises an interesting point put forth by many economists, and one worth pondering: who creates greater externalities, the firm depriving swimmers of their beach, or the swimmers depriving the firm of its cesspool?)

Others call for voluntary efforts by business to clean up the environment. In essence, the business firm is asked to voluntarily absorb the external costs of its pollution. This, of course, is the social responsibility approach to which we have been exposed.

Between these two extremes fall a large number of proposals for industry–government–public cooperation. Included in this range are various combinations of taxation, subsidies, shared facilities, and the like.

As we mentioned earlier, the pollution problem is not one that can easily be resolved. Values, comparative costs, equity and efficiency, economic dislocations, and convenience all play their roles in this issue. It is not simply an issue of business be damned or business be praised. At stake are jobs, livelihoods, and ethical dilemmas.

One example can point out how a seemingly insignificant environmental decision can have monumental impacts. Vermont and Oregon now have laws prohibiting the use of nonreturnable beverage containers. Several other states, including Massachusetts, are considering similar legislation. The consumer, under this legislation, pays up to ten cents extra as a deposit on the bottle. In essence, the regulation is designed to force consumers to reduce externalities (litter) associated with their drinking, by adding a cost to their pleasure. It is quite possible that consumers may be more than willing to absorb the cost (thus in effect raising the price on nonreturnable bottles and defeating the whole purpose of the exercise), and still toss the containers on the roadsides (and note that the payment for the containers under many of these laws goes not to the state highway departments, but to the bottling companies). Irrespective of these possibilities, one must still consider the short-run effects of a widespread adoption of this type of law. First, can and glass companies could experience lower sales and either be forced to close plants or seek new products or markets; the result could be some increase in unemployment far from the state where the law was passed. Bottlers might be forced to add delivery trucks and thus increase costs because the system is now geared to one-way delivery and each truck would probably deliver less if the drivers had to load and carry empties. Packaging machinery and vending equipment would have to be reengineered, the former from light bottles and cans to heavier bottles and from screw tops to crown tops, and the latter to handle returned bottles. Stores would have to convert valuable warehouse space to holding unprofitable empty bottles. All of these conditions could increase costs, perhaps create unemployment, and possibly force some firms out of business. On the other hand, the cost of a bottle could be spread over many users, although cleaning and handling costs may negate those savings. Incidentally, some critics of this law note that glass is extremely cheap, uses no precious natural resource, and, when disposed of properly, makes excellent land fill.

In the long run, in theory at least, capital and labor should be sufficiently mobile to move into new undertakings. Glass workers might even become beer-truck drivers and can manufacturers might even manufacture soda truck bodies. In fact, however, the reallocations of labor and capital are not affected so smoothly; quite serious dislocations could result. Jobs might be at stake, livelihoods destroyed, or perhaps even welfare problems exacerbated. And because the new proceeds from the deposit do not go to the state, there is no guarantee that the cleanup of remaining litter would be any better than before.

We mention this one issue not because we accept litter or are especially enamored of the glass, can, or bottling industries, but simply to alert students to the fact that pollution problems need maximum study; many apparently attractive solutions have too many ramifications for one to rush headlong into them.

THE READINGS

The paper by Arthur Elkins centers on the two concepts of economic growth and environmental pollution. Many critics see these concepts as mutually intertwined; pollution comes with growth. The author attempts to define the concepts, relate the economic system to the problems of environmental enhancement, and discuss some of the strategies, processes, and problems for balancing high standards of living with high-quality living. Finally, Elkins relates the concepts to some American societal values and political processes and problems.

We include next a short compilation of the legislative history and the authority of the Environmental Protection Agency in relation to air, water, solid waste, and noise pollution. Students are encouraged to check out the laws and powers of agencies in their own states, counties, and municipalities.

A tale of woe is provided by Richard Haverka in "The 'Ironic Castings' Story: Cleanliness is Next to Bankruptcy." The article is a case study of how a company sank progressively into deeper problems as systems failed because of poor design, standards became increasingly rigorous, and enforcement became more severe.

Finally, Dale McConkey's article (from *Business Horizons*) details the problems of small business in responding to the environmental cleanup effort. McConkey suggests some managerial strategies for the small businessman, to cope with environmental issues that arise in the face of the inadequate resources that small businesses typically possess.

Pollution Control
and Economic Growth:
Strategies, Processes,
and Problems
in Striking the Balance*

Arthur Elkins[†]

It should be ample testimony to the fact that society undergoes changing whims, to note that an issue forming an important and relatively exciting part of the 1960 Kennedy–Nixon presidential race became the qualified issue in the 1972 campaign, even though the same underlying problems were present. Many in our society doubt the system's capacity for change, its ability to absorb new ideas and issues. But note the change in focus on the dominant issue of the 1960 election, that of economic growth.

In 1960, with the United States easing its way out of a recession, suffering unprecedented balance-of-payments problems, and an unemployment rate hovering about the seven-percent mark, the key issue was getting the growth curve moving upward again. Somehow, we had to adjust our goals and the means to increase the historic three-to-four-percent annual rate of growth, and keep pace with or surpass other countries, notably the Soviet Union.

Twelve years later, in 1972, with the country emerging from another recession, with the unemployment rate again around six to seven percent (and up to 12 to 15 percent in some areas of the country), and the balance of payments problems still persisting, economic growth was still an issue, but was often qualified by statements on controlling the *composition* of that growth.

Now, words relatively insignificant in 1960—environment and pollution— equally dominate discussion; and in some quarters, at least, the economic growth we craved for in the 1960s is the antithesis of the ecological survival goal we now seek in the 1970's.

*This paper (now slightly revised) was originally prepared for the Faculty Colloquium on Comparative, International, and Global Survival Studies at the University of Massachusetts in August, 1972. The Colloquium was conducted as part of Grant #16069231 from the U.S. Office of Education.

†The author would like to thank Dean George B. Simmons, Florida International University, for reading and commenting on an earlier draft of this paper. His critique was most helpful; obviously, any remaining errors of commission or omission are the author's alone.

It is the purpose of this paper to discuss these two concepts, economic growth and environmental pollution, define them, relate the economic or productive system to the problems of environmental enhancement, discuss some of the strategies, processes, and problems for striking the balance of the "good" life to the "quality" life, and finally to relate these concepts to some of our societal values and political problems.

ECONOMIC GROWTH AND GNP: WHAT THEY ARE AND WHAT THEY AREN'T

With the term "economic growth," we simply mean the "increase in national product, measured in constant dollars."[1] A more significant measure might be the increase in national product *per capita,* since that levels out the increases in population.

Both of these figures do not mean economic progress *per se,* nor do they measure a general increase in economic welfare. As Denison points out, the "measures take no account of the increasing leisure hours of the working population, of changes in the distribution of income, or of the uses to which the national product is devoted."[2] The product can come in many forms; guns count, as does butter, pollution control equipment is counted, as well as automobiles.

Many commentators have leveled criticism at the idolization of GNP or absolute economic growth. Caroline Bird points out some of the deficiencies. First, GNP does not measure quality of goods and services. If a consumer has to pay three times to get his automobile repaired correctly, all three payments count in GNP (but the time lost by the consumer does not). In essence, according to Bird, "GNP actually fattens on inefficiency." Secondly, GNP leaves out "all the good things that money cannot buy." A beautiful view, fishing on clean water, breathing fresh air, etc., are not included. Finally, she cites the view of many that the concept of GNP is amoral. "A war increases defense spending and with it, the GNP, but it would be hard to find anyone in this country who seriously believes we are better off for it."[3]

What determines economic growth or the rate of that growth? Basically, in any society—free or not—the rate of growth results from the total of individual and/or collective decisions on employment mobility, resource mobility, knowledge accumulation and transfer—in short, technological change, investment or capital formation, and optimum employment of labor and materials.[4]

---

[1]Edward F. Denison, *The Sources of Economic Growth in the United States* (New York: Committee for Economic Development, 1962), p. 3.

[2]*Ibid.*

[3]Caroline Bird, "The GNP—A Beast to be Bridled?" *Think,* XXXVI (May–June, 1970), p. 5.

[4]Denison, *op. cit.,* p. 11. See also, Neil H. Jacoby, "The Environmental Crisis," *The Center Magazine,* III (November–December 1970), pp. 37–48. Reprinted in *Issues in Business and Society,* ed. George A. Steiner (New York: Random House, Inc., 1972), p. 189.

In a "free" society, these decisions are largely individual and corporate—or private. In a less "free" society, these decisions are largely public or centrally made. In both cases, growth is probably not maximized. Not everyone shifts to the highest paying jobs, nor do consumers devote their entire incomes to research and investment. And even that investment that is made may not be maximizing.[5] Several writers, for example, have criticized the American steel industry for building new capacity based on older technologies, when the Basic Oxygen Process, a clearly more efficient method of producing steel, was well developed.[6]

Suffice it to say at this juncture that any society can, through a change in values or a collective decision (basically a government decision), change its rate of growth or its form of growth. But in the free market society, these decisions rely less on government fiat and the change is more of an evolutionary process than a revolutionary one.

POLLUTION

The word "pollution" or the term "environmental protection" leads us to a multitude of definitions, and the problem of limiting the frame of reference for this paper. One can find the term environment covering such problems as conservation, land use, population dispersion, population limitation, as well as the polluting ancillary side-effects of human activity. Thus resource conservation may become part of the multitude of issues, and environmentalists will concern themselves with the preservation of supplies of oil, gas, timber, etc.

For our purposes, however, resource conservation essentially is concerned with the input side of productive activity and will not be covered herein. What will be covered here are the ancillary side-effects of producing and using products or resources; and hence our concern is with the throughput and output side of the productive system.

This limiting of our frame of reference is not meant to belittle the importance of conservation—it *is* important. But resource shortages, as a constraint to economic and human activity, are more easily encompassed by the market system and reflect themselves directly in prices. The ancillary side-effects of producing and consuming are what the economist calls "externalities." Traditionally, the costs of these externalities have been shoved off onto others, and the problems of returning them to the producers (and their consumers) are quite difficult. But basic input-resource shortages, as constraints to economic activity, are more easily taken in by the price mechanism; that is, scarcity imposes a direct increase in costs, absorbed by the system when resources are purchased, and paid for the price transaction. These increases in costs are, of course, passed on directly to the final consumer.

---

[5]Denison, *op. cit.*

[6]See Walter Adams and Joel B. Dirlam, "Big Steel, Invention, and Innovations," *The Quarterly Journal of Economics,* LXXX (May, 1966), pp. 167–190.

Most of the ancillary effects, or external costs, affect resources that economists have traditionally called "free goods." The costs of using these resources are not easily transferred to their users, nor have they historically been transferred or absorbed in the cost of the user's product.

Thus, our definition of pollution or our concern with environmental protection centers chiefly on those effects which are now passed on freely.

COSTS OF POLLUTION: WHAT WILL IT TAKE TO CLEAN UP?

Estimates of the cost of pollution control vary and, with each passing month, the estimates from all sources tend to increase. The Harvard Center for Population Studies estimated that the United States must spend $13.5 billion annually to clean up the pollution now existing ($5.1 billion for capital investment and $8.4 billion for operating costs). Of this, they estimate that $4.1 billion will have to be spent for air pollution, $4.7 billion for water, and $4.7 billion for solid waste disposal.[7]

Another estimate by the Federal Water Pollution Control Administration comes to a cost of $26 to $29 billion over a five-year period for streams and lakes alone.[8] Finally, a third estimate comes from the President's Council on Environmental Quality, which calculated the cost to be $105.2 billion for the 1970–75 period, and recently increased the projected outlay to $287 billion for the decade until 1980.[9]

While these costs, at first glance, look astronomical, one must view them in the perspective of the size of the economy and the savings in damage that a cleanup will result in. "The new total of $287 billion represents only 2.2 percent of the $13.2 *trillion* Gross National Product estimated for the 1971-to-1980 period."[10] Even more significant, however, is the fact that aggregate savings from damage now done by pollution will probably more than offset the cleanup bill. For example, measured damage from air pollution alone was calculated in 1970 at an annual rate of over $2 billion, with several effects yet to be costed out.[11]

DETERMINANTS OF POLLUTION

Historically, the supply of amenities—air, water, and open space—has been so great relative to the demands on them, that no price could be set for their use.

---

[7]George A. Steiner, *Business and Society,* (New York: Random House, Inc., 1971), p. 171.

[8]*Ibid.*

[9]"Ecological Outlays Rising to $287 Billion In 10 Years Through 1980, U.S. Panel Says," *Wall Street Journal,* August 8, 1972, p. 3.

[10]*Ibid.*

[11]Council on Environmental Quality, *Environmental Quality: The First Report of the Council on Environmental Quality* (Washington: U.S. Government Printing Office, 1970), p. 72.

Hence, the economist's term "free goods." No one would deem it necessary to charge for air or water because enough was available in consistently good quality to satisfy all needs. Why, all of a sudden, do we concern ourselves with these free resources? Certain growth patterns have taken place that now impinge on that vast supply, reduce its bulk relatively, and make people willing to pay or impose a cost to preserve it and obtain some for their own use.

Technology

While technology increases our capability to handle pollution control, it also is the source of that same pollution. Quite obviously, the power plant, the steel mill, the plastics factory, and the spreading industrial complexes are the most visible signs of technology's impact on the environment. And one can cite the myriad products which today are more polluting than the ones they replace—detergents replacing soap and plastics replacing glass being two of the most notable examples.[12] But consider, also, technology in the change of social organization or in the change of distribution systems. For example, the major change in distribution has been the mass merchandising technique, starting with the supermarket of the 1930's and leading up to the multi-line discount stores of today. Key emphases of mass merchandising are on packaging and point-of-purchase visibility. These merchandising techniques mean that plastic packages, paper bags, cardboard, and other byproducts have been added to the system through "technological changes" wrought in marketing. While output per man hour in retailing has increased, so have the social costs of waste disposal.

Increasing affluence

The increase in disposable income also allows families to purchase more goods. While that statement is not too profound, consider the mix of goods that are bought. Increased disposable income can compound pollution merely by encouraging families to buy increasing numbers of goods that pollute or products that require disposal. For example, automobile sales were over 10 million in 1972, with a total of over 105 million vehicles on the road. Harking back to only 1930, the automobile and truck population was only 26 million.[13] The purchase of labor-saving devices, washing machines, dishwashers, electric sewing machines—all products of the affluent society—adds enormously to the demand for electric power. In essence, increasing affluence adds demands for more complex labor-saving devices, which, in turn, directly or indirectly create pollution.

---

[12]See Barry Commoner, *The Closing Circle* (New Yorker: Alfred A. Knopf, 1971), Chapter 9.

[13]D. Philip Locklin, *Economics of Transportation* (7th ed., Homewood: Richard D. Irwin, 1972).

Population

Free goods can remain free only so long as the supply is capable of fulfilling the demand in overabundance. What has happened to most of our free goods is that demand is now outstripping the supply. This imbalance relates to numbers of people and is particularly visible in most of our urban areas. The cities are simply no longer capable of supplying air, water, and recreational facilities to the greater numbers of people and their demands. This is not to imply that the cities' air and water were ever pristine pure; far from it. But levels of pollution in past years were either much smaller than they are now, or fewer people put fewer demands on the resources available, or people didn't care as much and hence put less value on the media carrying the pollution.

Relating pollution to population carries possibilities beyond the mere control of pollution and/or population density. The total population may grow to some limit and still cause little environmental impact, but let that population *congregate* —and supply it with sufficient affluence and product—and the environmental problems surface very rapidly. Air becomes polluted, garbage mounts up, and waste multiplies.

In this sense, then, a 10-percent increment in population in New York City is much more environmentally disastrous than that same number of people spread out over, say, 1000 smaller towns. Perhaps, then, part of the solution to pollution implies population dispersion (as well as a decrease in the rate of population growth) and methods to encourage such dispersion. More on this in later sections.[14]

ISOLATING THE CULPRIT

To what extent is each of these factors—population, affluence, and technological change—responsible for today's level of pollution? Barry Commoner attempted to measure the effect of the three factors, utilizing the following formula, and applying it to several products and product categories:

$$\frac{\text{Pollution}}{\text{emitted}} = (\text{Population}) \times \left(\begin{array}{l}\text{Economic good}\\ \text{per capita}\end{array}\right) \times \left(\begin{array}{l}\text{Pollutant output per unit}\\ \text{of economic good produced}\end{array}\right).$$

Commoner defines the *economic good per capita* as affluence, and *pollution output put unit of economic good produced* he views as attributable to technical change. He found for the relevant products and categories that the *increase in population* accounted for from 12 to 20 percent of the various increases in total pollutant output since 1946, whereas the *affluence factor* accounted for from one to five percent. "The technology factor—that is, the increased output of pollutants per unit of production resulting from the introduction of new productive technologies since 1946—accounts for about 95 percent of the total output of pollutants,

---

[14]For a discussion of the urban and population problem, see Jacoby, *op. cit.*

except in the case of passenger travel, where it accounts for about 40 percent of the total."[15]

Commoner's formula seems lacking, however, in several respects. Economic good per capita is, of course, related to technological change and also to population. It cannot be labeled as simply affluence. Increasing pollutant output per unit of economic good produced can just as easily result from constant technology as from an increasing "introduction of new productive technologies." Old-fashioned plants pushed beyond scale, old-style equipment, and less control can all contribute to an increased pollutant output *per unit of good produced* as total production is increased. Nevertheless, Commoner's reasoning on the determinants of pollution goes to the root causes: population, affluence, and technological change.

It is easy to see why economic growth becomes the whipping boy of some environmentalists. Its roots and those of pollution are quite similar: increasing productivity, population growth, and technological change. Does that mean that the two are mutually inclusive? Let us examine briefly a school of thought that does hold that view.

THE ZERO GROWTH APPROACH

Zero economic growth has been offered as a solution to the pollution problem. Since it is growing production and growing consumption that lie at the base of society's ills, this school of thought would have society stop growth and fix some balance between man, production, and nature.

Kenneth Boulding seems clearly in this camp. Describing the growth-oriented economy as a "Cowboy Economy," Boulding then compares that to what he calls the "Spaceman Economy."

> In the spaceman economy, what we are primarily concerned with is stock maintenance, and any technological change which results in the maintenance of a given total stock with a lessened throughput (that is, less production and consumption) is clearly a gain. This idea that both production and consumption are bad things rather than good things is very strange to economists. . . .[16]

Jacoby points out three faults in the Zero Growth argument. First, Zero Growth does not consider the *pattern* of growth. Were current patterns of production and consumption merely maintained, we would simply stabilize at current levels of pollution. Second, since growth is a function of investment and technology as well as of population, this would imply *stopping all three.* Population growth is extremely difficult to stop in a short period of time, saving rates show little inclination to decline, and a paralysis in technological change is virtually inconceivable so long as man remains a thinking animal.

---

[15]Commoner, *op. cit.,* pp. 175–177.
[16]From Kenneth E. Boulding, "The Economics of The Coming Spaceship Earth" reprinted in Sheldon W. Stahl, "Social Cost—The Due Bill for Progress," *Monthly Review, Federal Reserve Bank of Kansas City,* (April, 1972), p. 16.

Finally, Jacoby argues that Zero Economic Growth is undesirable. "A rising GNP will enable the nation to easily bear the costs of eliminating pollution." What is needed is a *redirection of the growth* that will inevitably take place.[17]

In addition, Edwin Dale points out that the American labor force for the next twenty years is already born. "It is hard . . . to imagine a deliberate policy to keep a large portion of it unemployed." The only way to reduce growth of output might be to cut hours of work, but even then, Dale forsees a growth rate of 2 percent rather than 4 percent. He simply writes off the hope for zero growth.[18]

Our next step is to investigate methods of curbing pollution within the context of economic growth. Few economists would argue that we could shut off growth even if we wanted to, but many do offer programs for making pollution control compatible with economic growth. After a brief digression to cover the concepts of costs involved, we move into some of those methods.

THE COSTS OF PRODUCTION

Before moving into methods for curbing pollution, perhaps we should investigate briefly the area of costs, since it is in this area, most economists believe, that our most powerful weapons for curbing industrial pollution lie.

Production of goods and services involves several types of costs. Most of our economic thinking considers only the private internal costs of producing: What does it cost a company to make a particular product and get it out on the market? This means that our calculations include as costs labor, materials, marketing costs, interest on borrowed money, etc. In pure economic theory, costs also include a return to capital invested and a return to entrepreneurship. Most analyses of production costs do not include anything the company does not have to pay for, or the costs that the company, through its actions, imposes upon its neighbors.

But another type of cost—external costs—are now beginning to show up in the calculus; and it is through working on these that most economists seem to find the means of controlling pollution. Externalities are those hazards or inconveniences inflicted upon another person or community of persons for which the originating party does not pay. Smoke, soot, dirt, water pollutants, etc., are viewed as reducing the well-being of the other person or persons, yet the original producer is not required to pay compensation for this reduction of well-being or pay to *prevent* the polluting output in the first place. As long, however, as the inflicted party had no demand on the resources polluted or had so much of the resources

---

[17]Jacoby, *op. cit.,* pp. 189–190.

[18]Edwin L. Dale, Jr. "The Economics of Pollution," *The MBA,* (January, 1971), pp. 9–10.

he couldn't be bothered in caring about them, external costs were nothing to be considered.

The concept of omitting external costs from the total cost, then, rested on two assumptions: that there was an absence of objective criteria for evaluating social dangers; and that externalities were of little import in the overall determination of costs. Hence, the fascination with the concept of "free goods."[19]

With the increase in awareness by many elements of society, it is now clearly evident that total (social) costs of production involve both the previously contained internal costs and the now relatively important external costs. Can external costs, however, be allocated by the market mechanism inherent in the free enterprise system? The answer is no, unless the external costs are imposed upon the polluter.

Wenders cites the following hypothetical paper-producing problem to illustrate the weakness of the market mechanism relative to external costs.

Suppose there are two methods available for the production of paper at the rate of 100,000 tons per year. Method A has no external costs (i.e., there is no pollution resulting from its production) and thus has private costs equal to (total) social costs. Method B, even though having less private costs to the firm, has very high external costs in the form of pollution, so its (total) social costs are much higher.

Hypothetical Costs for Producing 100,000 tons of Paper Annually

	Private costs	External costs	Total costs
Method A	$20,000,000	0	$20,000,000
Method B	$10,000,000	$50,000,000	$60,000,000

Obviously, the rational cost-minimizing firm will choose method B, and it would have little choice if it is in competition with other paper mills facing the same situation. Barring some legal compulsion, there is nothing in the market system to compel or even induce the producer to choose any system whose costs are over the minimum internal costs of production.[20]

Another example relates to consumers. In 1970, General Motors Corporation tried to sell a pollution-reduction kit for $26. During the first month only a relative handful of kits were sold in a market with several hundred thousand buyers. This lack of interest takes little explanation; "an automobile owner would not install the

---

[19]Stahl, *op. cit.,* p. 14.

[20]John T. Wenders, "An Economist's Approach to Pollution Control," *Arizona Review,* XIX (November, 1970), pp. 1–5.

device, because other people would reap the benefits of the cleaner air made possible by the expenditure."[21]

In sum, the market is incapable of handling or assigning external costs without the intervention of the governing power. "When large external costs or benefits are involved, there is conflict between the decision that serves the self-interest of the individual and that which serves the collective welfare of society."[22] The market mechanism is capable only of enforcing private economic efficiency.[23]

A DIGRESSION: SHOULD WE CHANGE THE SYSTEM?

One might be tempted to ask, given the inability of the market system to independently internalize or allocate external costs, whether the system itself ought to be changed. There are many variations on this theme, of course, ranging from complete socialism to private ownership with *complete* state regulation. Let us briefly examine two variations.

First, socialization of industry and business. This ultimate step would transform the multitude of free market decisions now being made privately to a central planning apparatus and state ownership. But there is nothing automatic in this step toward the solution of pollution problems. The Soviet Union, the world's most notable example of a centralized industrial society, would have seen no need to sign an environmental treaty with the United States if it were not suffering similar environmental problems. In fact, pollution problems in the Soviet Union are now being seen as quite immense. And as Jacoby points out, "Managers of socialist enterprises are judged by the central planners on the efficiency of their operations, and are under as much pressure to minimize internal costs and throw as much external cost as possible on the public as are the managers of private firms in market economies who seek to maximize stockholder profits."[24]

Moreover, he adds, a state combination of political and economic function dilutes one of the checks on economic processes present in the market system.[25] Under our present system, separation of the social–political functions from the

---

[21]Jacoby, *op. cit.,* p. 192.

[22]*Ibid.*

[23]"Economic efficiency requires that rates of return should be equalized among different uses, but the market mechanism is only capable of equalizing the *private* rates of return, thus the total of social rates of return will differ whenever external costs are present." Wenders, *op. cit.,* p. 3.

[24]Jacoby, *op. cit.,* p. 189.

[25]*Ibid.*

economic is an advantage, since the sociopolitical system can intercede with the economic to correct social imbalances. For example, antitrust laws have as much a political and social rationale as an economic one. Without the check of the political system, the economic system's dysfunctional qualities could not be mitigated easily.

A second approach stresses what are called "misplaced priorities." The proponents here would argue that private spending encourages multitudes of polluting products and hence results in a lack of resources available for public necessities such as schools, hospitals, public transportation, etc. The solution would be to tax away larger proportions of disposable income, dampen consumption, and devote more of the nation's product to public need. This concept is quite similar to that of John Kenneth Galbraith's approach in one of his earlier works, *The Affluent Society*.[26] But while Galbraith's approach was aimed at solving pressing social needs, others have decried "a pursuit of consumer gadgetry with all its senseless by-products of waste and pollution."[27]

At an initial glance, this seems like an attractive proposition. But looking deeper, one finds that almost one-third of our total product is now publicly generated, and the prospect for increasing this proportion would run into formidable opposition.

Practical politics is not alone, however, in mitigating against the misplaced priorities approach. Edwin Dale points out another obvious flaw in the argument. Simply shifting spending from private to public needs does not reduce total spending, and there is no immutable law which states that publicly initiated projects use less resources or generate less external costs than does private spending. Public employees consume, just as do private employees; schools require steel, lumber, tile, brick, and carpeting just as private homes and offices do; public employees (presumably government spending will add to the army of these) spend their paychecks just as private employees do; and even a sewerage treatment plant requires steel and electricity. In short, the same criticisms leveled at private spending can be leveled at public spending; nothing is inherent in the system of public spending that will guarantee us any less pollution than we have now.[28]

BUSINESS VOLUNTARISM

Many commentators have suggested that business firms might voluntarily absorb the costs of pollution control. Voluntary absorption falls under the rubric of the

---

[26]John Kenneth Galbraith, *The Affluent Society*, (Boston: Houghton-Mifflin Co.).

[27]Dale, *op. cit.*, p. 12.

[28]*Ibid.*

social responsibility approach,[29] a doctrine that has become a favorite topic of business meetings, courses in business schools, and interestingly enough has provided something of a confluence of evolving business ideology and the social idealism of the young. In essence, business is being asked to act not like the rational economic man shown in our previous examples, but like something akin to an eleemosynary institution voluntarily absorbing the added costs.

The doctrine of social responsibility includes pollution control under the umbrella of a whole host of social issues that proponents insist the corporation should be involved with: urban renewal, minority employment, better government, consumerism, and the like. Under the doctrine, management becomes an arbiter of sorts, parceling out corporate resources to competing claims on the corporation. The stockholders, who might demand maximum profits, are considered only one of the claimants. The community upon whom the corporation heaps external costs becomes another.

Jacoby abruptly dismisses the expectation that social responsibility will result in corporations absorbing the external costs voluntarily. The competitive market puts each firm under pressure to minimize costs, and few firms—particularly if they lack some degree of monopoly power, where the increased costs can simply be passed on—will voluntarily put themselves at a cost disadvantage relative to other firms.[30]

Milton Friedman rejects social responsibility on philosophical grounds as well. He terms it a "fundamentally subversive doctrine." "There is only one social responsibility of business—to use its resources and engage in activities designed to increase its profits so long as it stays within the rules of the game . . ."[31]

Paul Heyne voices a similar objection on the grounds that the businessmen are "placed in positions where they must make decisions that they are not competent to make." He goes on to say:

> A decision against stream or air pollution must be a collective decision, because it requires simultaneous action on the part of many people. It is therefore properly a political decision. It is up to the legislature or some other appropriate body to determine the public interest and establish the appropriate sanctions.

---

[29]Many sources provide some background to the social responsibility doctrine. One of the earliest, and still one of the best, is Richard Eells, *The Meaning of Modern Business* (New York: Columbia University Press, 1960). See also, *Social Responsibilities of Business Corporations* (New York: Committee for Economic Development, 1971).

[30]Jacoby, *op. cit.*, pp. 192–3.

[31]Milton Friedman, *Capitalism and Freedom* (Chicago: University of Chicago Press, 1962), pp. 133–6.

> When we cast this burden upon the businessman's conscience, we are being just neither to the public nor to the businessman.[32]

What is being said here on several grounds is that the rules of the game must be changed. One cannot expect—indeed *should not* expect—businessmen to voluntarily do things if the evaluation of their performance is to be based on profit. Nor is voluntarism fair; there will always be those businessmen who will reject social responsibility, leaving those who voluntarily undertake it at a severe disadvantage. We simply have here a case of idealism smacking into practical reality.

Now that we have established the problem in terms of the market's inability to assign external costs; seen, however, that another system might not necessarily be any better; found faults with alternative systems; and pointed out reasons why any expectation of business voluntarism is impractical, let us examine the possibility of changing the rules of the game.

Basically, the issue centers on the relation of the political system to the economic system. The problem resolves itself down to the necessity for government intervention in the productive system to restore the equity between pollution producers and those affected, indirectly using as tools of enforcement the price mechanism and self-interest.

Of course, ample precedent exists for government's role here; all sorts of social problems, ranging from child labor, social security, and labor legislation, on the one hand, to antitrust on the other, have been handled through government intervention into the economic system. Indeed, one school of thought suggests that businessmen welcome this sort of intervention, since it relieves them of decision-making and establishes firm, consistent, and in many cases, self-serving standards.[33]

Before proceeding, however, let us remind ourselves of the basic problem of economic growth versus environmental pollution. None of the mechanisms to be described in the next few pages are designed to slow growth *per se*. What might result from some of the methods described below is a change in the composition of the national product and/or some redistribution of income. The systems are designed to charge polluting firms (or consumers) the full (or at least partial) costs of their actions.

CARROT APPROACHES

The carrot approach involves basically the paying of part or all of the costs of pollution by the public. Its mechanisms are tax credits or, in some cases, subsidies

---

[32]Paul T. Heyne, *Private Keepers of the Public Interest,* (New York: McGraw-Hill Book Co., 1968), p. 92–4.

[33]See, for example, George T. Stigler, "The Theory of Economic Regulation," *The Bell Journal of Economics and Management Science,* II (Spring, 1971), pp. 3–21.

granted to the polluter in an effort to impel him to clean up. Businessmen, naturally, favor this approach. In a 1966 survey by the National Industrial Conference Board, the vast majority of the 441 companies surveyed seemed to prefer these types of incentives over programs involving penalties.[34]

At present, most of these programs involve the states rather than the Federal government. The federal government does offer some tax advantages, most notably the allowing of accelerated depreciation of pollution-abatement equipment. Seven states also allow such accelerated depreciation.

Exemption from the property tax on pollution-control facilities is allowed in 24 states, but some states disallow the exemption if the facility produces a marketable by-product. Twelve states exempt such equipment from sales and use taxes, while six states allow a direct income-tax credit. New York allows the option of "taking either the usual one-percent tax credit allowed for new equipment of any kind, or deducting the entire cost of the pollution control equipment from taxable income."[35]

Some basic problems are involved with the incentive approach. First, opponents argue that society's concerns with pollution stem from a basic inequity in the system, with society on the short end. Why pay polluters—even a part of the costs—for the loss of a right (to freely pollute) when that right is inequitably held.[36]

Secondly, with external costs absorbed by the public, the wealthier, who may pollute relatively more, pay proportionately less of the cost. From this point of view, the distribution of the external costs continues to be inequitable and the sources of pollution don't pay their full share.[37]

A third criticism goes right to the heart of the matter, the incentive. Without some concurrent regulation, polluters have no incentive to use pollution control unless the subsidy or tax credit were 100 percent or more. Why should a firm add costs voluntarily even if the government ends up paying 90 percent?[38] Furthermore, tax credits or exemptions have no effect on the marginal firm, since it probably pays no tax anyway; marginal firms many times are the foremost pollut-

---

[34]National Industrial Conference Board, "Pollution Abatement in Industry: Policies and Practices," Reprinted in *Issues in Business and Society,* ed. William T. Greenwood (Boston: Houghton-Mifflin Co., 1970), pp. 475–81.

[35]*Pollution Control: Perspectives on the Government Role,* (New York: Tax Foundation, Inc., 1971), pp. 21–22.

[36]Jacoby, *op. cit.,* p. 194.

[37]*Ibid.*

[38]Wenders, *op. cit.,* p. 3.

ers.[39] To some extent, this argument repeats the social responsibility problem all over again, and some would argue that, since the firm must be regulated anyway, then the total cost ought to be placed where it belongs, on the polluter and his product.

Another disadvantage of tax incentives is that they create preferences for equipment rather than changes in the productive process. It may be that some simple reworking of production methods or research into changing the process may be more useful and efficient, but the tax-credit incentive pushes the firm toward a solution of pollution-control equipment rather than to the only partially recoverable costs of research or managerial effort involved in production-process redesign.[40]

Related to the preceding criticism is the argument that aid is given to polluters and that incentives may conceivably distort production patterns by rewarding the dirty producers, but giving no rewards to the clean ones.[41]

Finally, our history of paying people *not* to do things has not been all that successful. Farm subsidies, for example, have a notorious history of favoritism, overpayment, and bureaucratic inefficiency; many would argue that the benefits do not seem appropriate to the costs.[42]

It is too easy, however, to write off the tax incentive and subsidy approach, however. Despite the arguments to the contrary, a certain amount of equity rights are acquired by the polluting firm if only because society, by doing nothing in the past, has allowed a firm to lock itself into a mode of business operation. To that extent, and to the extent that other methods of control may create problems of unemployment and community readjustment, some temporary subsidy or tax incentive (or some relaxation of other regulation methods and standards) to allow the firm to unlock itself, might well be in order.[43]

STICK APPROACHES

The most equitable approaches and the methods calculated to yield the most efficient allocation of resources may be those forcing the *internalization of external costs* or the absorbing by the firm (or polluting consumers) of the total cost of production (or consumption).

---

[39]Tax Foundation, *op. cit.,* p. 32.

[40]*Ibid.*

[41]*Ibid.,* pp. 32–3.

[42]Wenders, *op. cit.*

[43]Jacoby, *op. cit.,* p. 194.

Many methods have been proposed to force such internalization: taxation, regulation, amenity rights, and product taxes, to name a few.

Direct regulation

Direct regulation of polluters involves government action in setting the standards of environmental quality and prescribing the mechanisms to achieve the reduction in pollution. All polluters would then be required, under some penalty, to reach the prescribed level of pollution abatement.

But straight regulation has some serious disadvantages. It may not allow polluters to choose a least-cost method of pollution abatement. Standards and procedures set at some central level may not be flexible enough to allow producers to make a choice of equipment, process change, or product change.[44]

In addition, there may be situations where the cost of the prescribed abatement procedures may be so high for an individual producer that he would be driven out of business, whereas the cost of collectively handling the wastes of several similar-size polluters may inflict relatively less of a burden. Thus, one could conceive of a situation where the minimum costs for installation of pollution-control equipment would drive an individual mill out of business, whereas a *public processing plant* to handle wastes generated by several such smaller mills would be economically financed through a less onerous taxing scheme. Direct regulation, with no thought to flexible programming, would thus drive out those mills whose scale of operation was too small to support the installation of relatively expensive equipment.

Operationally, our history of regulation is even bleaker than the history of subsidies. Regulatory commissions come under all sorts of political pressures, and hence become the vehicle for disastrous compromise. Indeed, many commentators have noted that regulatory commissions go through a life cycle, with the last stage of that cycle being one where the commissions become captives of the regulated.[45]

Scarce resource rights:

One novel solution, possibly less popular because it grants a "right" to pollute, views air, water, and land as scarce resources whose use for waste disposal may be paid for by effluent producers.

> Generally, the mechanism would operate as follows: First, a technical survey would determine approximately how much waste matter the air and water in a given region could accommodate without deleterious effects. Certificates entitling the holder to utilize the purifying capacities of the river for a specified

---

[44]Wenders, *op. cit.,* p. 4.

[45]For example, Marver H. Bernstein, *Regulating Business by Independent Commission* (Princeton: Princeton University Press, 1955).

number of units of waste material would be issued and sold, up to a total fully utilizing the natural resource. Only holders of certificates would be entitled to discharge waste; all others would be required to process wastes to render them harmless, meeting standards to be established by the certificate-issuing board before releasing them.[46]

Several unique points ought to be recognized in this proposal before it is unceremoniously brushed off. First, the rights themselves would be marketable, and hence, the cost of the rights should be pushed very close to the costs of installing in-plant pollution control equipment.

Second, maximum efficiency in the use of the natural resource would result, but since the certificates would be scarce (and become scarcer as time goes on), there is an incentive to develop more efficient in-plant pollution-control measures.

Finally, groups that want a cleaner environment and would want standards higher than the minimums calculated would be able to take some direct action, where their attempts at political action are too slow or unsuccessful. They could buy up blocks of certificates and thus withhold further effluent while concurrently forcing further and speedier development of pollution-control equipment, as the available resources for dumping are taken off the market and become scarcer.[47]

Amenity rights

An interesting approach to internalizing the external costs involves the guarantee of amenity rights to abutting property owners. Jacoby proposes a constitutional amendment to guarantee those rights. Owners of abutting property would then be entitled to sue for redress in the event of noise, soot, and water damage. In theory, at least, producers of pollution would internalize the costs of paying the legal bills and damages, or by installing the control devices necessary to save the costs of litigation and legal liabilities.[48]

On the other hand, this proposal puts forth a costly and time-consuming process for the plaintiff as well as the defendant and, given the state of under-capacity in today's judicial processes, other mechanisms of internalizing the costs might be preferable.

The pollution tax

A final method of pollution abatement that we might discuss is the pollution tax. Under this scheme, the polluter would pay a tax on his pollution output. The tax

---

[46]Tax Foundation, Inc., *op. cit.,* pp. 36–7.

[47]*Ibid.*

[48]Jacoby, *op. cit.*

would be so calculated as to force the polluter to pay the total costs (internal as well as external) of production.[49]

Presumably the effluent of an industrial establishment would be metered (just as water is now metered) and the tax per unit calculated from comparing the total outflow with the costs of reducing the pollution by the desired percentage.

Now the firm would be confronted with several alternatives. It could cease polluting, with a key advantage to the firm under the tax scheme being that it would be free to choose whatever method might accomplish that goal most efficiently.[50] Or the firm could continue to pollute, but would have the costs of the tax added to its total costs of producing. Both of these alternative courses of action internalize the total costs of production.

Critics might argue, however, that the second alternative still leaves the firm polluting, and undeniably this may be true. But several points of rebuttal may be made. Most important, it is the aggregate level of pollution that must be reduced, not that of each individual firm. Some firms may find it relatively cheap and easy to avoid the tax and may have a scale of operation big enough to sustain the costs of a pollution-control system efficiently. Other firms may have a degree of monopoly power in the marketplace and be able to pass on the increases in costs. Other firms, however, may be too small to need a system and these would prefer to pay the tax. So long as the *total industry pollution output* was reduced, the problem of the single firm polluting should not be troublesome. And as a further safeguard, the tax could be adjusted to make the number of firms willing to install pollution-control equipment sufficient to decrease the level of pollution to its desired state. One would have to argue for zero pollution to complain about a single firm's impact, and to my knowledge, few proponents of environmental quality support that view.

The tax system also sets the stage for community or concerned action. Communities could build regional systems—at least for water pollution and solid waste disposal. Firms that are too small to support internal pollution-control systems or systems that require large capacities to be economically viable, could be included in pollution-abatement programs through the use of the tax system. This would mean that a community could build a treatment plant; the polluters would pay the costs; marginal firms would pay only their share; large firms could process part of their effluent internally and be taxed on the other part while filtering it through the community system; and a genuine community or regional solution would decrease the pollution to a level desired.[51]

---

[49]Wenders, *op. cit.*

[50]*Ibid.,* p. 4.

[51]Allen Kneese and Blair Bower, *Managing Water Quality: Economics, Technology, and Institutions* (Baltimore: John Hopkins Press: 1968) cited in Stephen W. Campbell, *A Survey of Industrial Water Pollution in the Pulp and Paper Industry of the United States,* unpublished thesis, University of Massachusetts, 1972.

A tax system has some added quality even if only from the point of view of efficiency of enforcement. Somehow, the United States has had a history of success with its various taxes that it hasn't had with other forms of regulation. Taxes seem to be paid with a lesser amount of litigation. Finally, the mechanism for collection already exists and has shown some degree of efficiency.

THE POLLUTING CONSUMER

Up to now, we have dealt principally with the polluting producer and have covered schemes designed to assign or internalize the costs generated by the production processes. But many products generate costs during and after *consumption,* the primary examples being exhausts from automobiles during use, and the disposal of packages and solids after use. Quite obviously, if the producer must internalize his costs, a complete system should require the consumer to do so also.

Most of the methods described for the producer can easily be applied to the consumer, where the act of consuming can be individually and easily isolated. Thus, taxing polluting exhausts, or adding a tax to products requiring solid waste disposal have been proposed. With automobiles, the United States has adopted the regulatory approach; simply requiring each vehicle produced to come equipped with emission-control equipment. But the obvious fault with this system is already apparent; some consumers have simply disconnected the systems; others do not maintain them.

For solid waste, a unique proposal is to add the cost of disposal to the unit when sold, with a refund granted upon proper disposal. Thus a sum (say $35 for an automobile, one cent for a beer bottle) would be added to the purchase price (somewhat like the way an excise tax is added), and when the consumer brought the used product to a disposal station, he would receive a credit. While this would not resolve and apportion the costs of solid-waste disposal, the tax would still provide the incentive for proper disposal. Since solid-waste disposal is a generally accepted municipal or regional function, assuring its use and discouraging litter and abandonment may be all that is necessary in the regulation of consumer habits.

With air pollution, the tax system seems useful. Controllers could meter the air pollutants from consumer heating systems, car exhausts, etc., and set the tax appropriately. Some consumers would then be induced to install the necessary equipment or maintain that already installed at peak efficiency.

EFFECTS OF INTERNALIZING TOTAL COSTS

Whichever method is adopted of forcing producers (and consumers) to internalize the external costs of production, there will be an effect on the relative price structure of various products. Products which are polluting in production or in end-use would now become *relatively* more expensive than those which do not pollute. Electric power would be charged at its full cost; so would automobiles, paper, and the myriad of other products used. Thus, the search for cleaner alternative ways to produce and consume would also be enhanced; for example, hydroelectric plants might become more useful (less costly) than steam generating or atomic plants.[52]

Another result of forcing the internalization would be the development of uses for presently polluting by-products. Conceivably, methods would be introduced for allowing recovery of valuable materials that now go up in smoke or down the drain. Some critics might ask why this is not being done now, if the recovery is a profitable operation. But most firms rank projects on a rate-of-return basis. If a productive project is ranked against a recovery project and the latter yields a lower rate of return, management effort will be devoted to the former and the effluent will continue to flow. But if the firm is forced to absorb the costs anyway (that is, undertake the project previously rejected), then what was previously an unsatisfactory project on a ranking basis becomes relatively attractive.

Finally, the internalization of total costs could have an effect on the distribution of income. Costs now incurred for health, property maintenance, recreation, and travel would be reduced. This reduction would aid low-income people. People who buy or use discretionary products would now find their costs increased. In effect, the subsidies now granted to those who consume more would be eliminated; automobiles would cost more, as would other polluting products; the means of producing and consuming polluting products would cost more. This would mean that resources now flowing freely to the affluent, with the tacit subsidy granted by society at large, would be paid for by the consumer with some benefits concurrently flowing to the less affluent.[53]

A PROBLEM IN ABSORBING INTERNAL COSTS

Before one gets too caught up with plans for internalizing the external costs of production and consumption, he ought to be aware that there are problems in installing the system as well. While it is easy to armchair formulate a system for internalizing costs, it is much less easy to implement it. One author comments:

> Setting these prices on a comprehensive scale just once, not to mention changing them as conditions alter, would be an operational nightmare. Aside from the complexities of the administrative task, there would be widespread inducements to fraud, which probably would not be completely resisted. Furthermore, much pollution is the result of joint activities of industry and others, which raises questions of joint costs and their allocation.[54]

---

[52]Wenders, *op. cit.,* p. 4.

[53]Jacoby, *op. cit.,* p. 194.

[54]Steiner, *Business and Soceity, op. cit.,* p. 175.

THE QUESTION OF STANDARDS

Most observers agree that any standards set must be national in origin and in scope.[55] Allowing states and political subdivisions to devise and enforce standards might mean a repeat of the dangerous game played in the 1950's with industrial development. Some states would develop low standards or no costs in an effort to achieve more industrial development, just as they granted tax holidays and free plants to induce firms to move. On the other hand, the setting of standards on the national level does not preclude their being set at some minimally acceptable national level with the states and political subdivisions free to develop more stringent ones. Nor does it mean that there will not be any differential in costs among various areas of the country.

Suppose national standards are set for pollution control and we taxed so much per unit of effluent, with the total tax to equal or exceed the costs of cleanup necessary to reach the standards. It would seem that less congested places and more rural areas would have *no* costs (or lower total costs) than places such as New York City or Los Angeles. This would mean—at least up to the situation where a high minimum fixed cost is necessary regardless of the effluent flow—that the tax per unit would be lower for the firm in rural, less populated, less industrialized areas, than it would be for the one in the urban concentrated area.

Theoretically, then, a natural inducement is created. Firms and people should be induced to move to a less polluted area (even when the standards are similar) to avoid paying the higher tax. This will reduce the level of pollution, and hence the tax, in the urban areas and increase both in the rural areas. Theoretically, at some point, equilibrium will be reached.

The level of pollution need not be allowed to exceed standards in any of these areas. The tax can be varied according to the increasing and decreasing costs of abatement to standards, and the total tax bill will guide the firm in appropriately making the decision to install control equipment. But population and industrial dispersion should lessen the demand for public amenities in cities and be beneficial in bringing the actual level of pollution to the desired standards.

How high should standards be set? Generally speaking, the higher the standards, the higher the cost. "The optimum level of pollution is [reached] when any further reduction of pollution is not worth the cost." But how do we measure some of these costs and benefits? What is the value of a natural vista unaffected by smoke and soot? These are decisions we have just begun to contemplate and these are areas where environmental specialists can make their greatest contributions. The question becomes one of trade-off, and only society can make these decisions through the political process.[56]

---

[55]Wenders, *op. cit.,* p. 5.

[56]*Ibid.*

But critics should recognize some of the side-effects of higher than necessary standards. We have already noted the fact that internalization of costs will raise the prices of "dirty" products relative to those of "clean" products. Clearly some products will cost less—chiefly services such as recreation, health, etc. Some will cost more. But nobody has yet pointed out the effect that these increased product costs (inflation) will have on international trade and our already adverse balance of payments.[57] Obviously, the effect will be substantial and will entail large amounts of planning and indeed compromise.

OTHER NECESSARY PROGRAMS

The transfer of costs to identifiable polluting parties is an equitable solution, but a program consisting of only that step is clearly inadequate. Much pollution results from the little polluters, individuals and small businesses, as well as from governmental units (and one must appreciate that government accounts for almost one-third of Gross National Product), and other public institutions such as hospitals, universities, etc. It has generally been accepted that society will provide services where the cost would be intolerable for the individual citizen, where some widespread public need is demonstrated over a large portion of the population, where the scope of the action is too great for one person or small group of persons to handle the problem individually, where the solution of one problem would lead to others unless that solution was handled centrally, or where the public health and safety were at stake due to an unattended need. So governments have often provided, for example, solid-waste disposal, sewerage, and water supplies.

However, government does not always do a total or efficient job, and that which it does do, ofttimes has harmful side effects. Thus, a town may have a sewerage system, but the effluent may also flow untreated into the nearest stream.

While it is not within the bounds of this paper to analyze public needs, most observers agree that sewerage treatment, waterway management, rapid transit, and other public systems are clearly inadequate. Some call for massive programs shared by all levels of society to remedy the deficiencies, in addition to the control and taxes where individual polluters can be isolated and controlled.[58] Whether society is prepared or amenable to making the sacrifices, however, is another question.

POLITICAL AND VALUE PROBLEMS IN POLLUTION CONTROL

Technical and allocational problems are not the only constraints on strategies for improving the environment. Our very political heritage and governmental structure also offer problems and mitigate against fast and revolutionary change. Against that background, the change accruing over the past ten years has been phenomenally rapid and profound.

---

[57]Steiner, *op. cit.,* p. 174.

[58]Jacoby, *op. cit.,* pp. 195–6.

The Tennessee Valley Authority to the contrary notwithstanding, in general, public control and ownership is anathema to most Americans. While increasing erosion of this anathema is evident, the fact remains that it is present, and any control over private affairs must be applied gradually in small increments.

Another problem, however, is even more profound. Our political and governmental division of powers is not geared to tackling a problem such as pollution. The Federal system creates boundaries where natural boundaries don't necessarily exist, and pollution does not follow political boundaries. Pollution problems often call for regional compacts and districts, whose formation is often accompanied by calls for local autonomy and compromise.

Additionally, any environmental planning and control must take place within the context of planning for other needs. One of the key constraints on environmental control, for example, has always been the concept of "environmental unemployment," most typically associated with the smaller marginal firm or the older mill town. With increasing unemployment from decreases in defense expenditures, for example, it is fairly difficult to add unemployment resulting from environmental control.

A final constraint concerns the organization of various governmental bodies. Typically, governments are organized around defined constituencies; farmers, veterans, labor, business, etc. But environment is a much broader concern cross-cutting many of the traditional government agencies.[59] So far, governments have not been prone to handle well the pervasive and boundary-spanning problems such as pollution control.

With these problems in mind, let us now look at some of the additional pressures present at various levels of government.

Local

Some of the most effective work on environmental protection should probably take place at the local level. Pressure can probably be most easily applied on local officials and the results are most visible and easily measured against grassroots desires and values. But local pollution-control measures and participation have definite limits. First, resources are probably most limited at the local level; the tax base in most local communities is already severely strained. Second, as already mentioned, pollution does not stop at political boundaries. But the key constraint to local action is the fact that the pressure that can be brought to bear by citizens' groups can be just as effectively counterbalanced by industrialists, particularly when jobs are at stake. This leads to the possibility that local communities will engage in competition to assure minimal pollution standards rather than maximal ones.

---

[59]See Lynton K. Caldwell. "Environmental Quality as an Administrative Problem," *The Annals of the American Academy of Political and Social Science,* CD (March, 1972) pp. 108–15.

State and regional levels

Here the citizen is less a part of the "system" and compromise more a part of the process. But where air travels and rivers flow through political boundaries, efforts must be either state- or region-wide.

Clearly, centralizing decision-making to a higher level—state and regional—must have a rationale and criteria for application. For examples, several local areas must use the same medium, standards by necessity have to be identical or compatible among local units, and communities must be incapable of mustering the technical skill or resources necessary to adequately handle the problem.

Increasingly, these criteria have been recognized as regional compacts and multi-community or multi-state consortiums have come into being. But the trade-off between local autonomy and centralized control is always present.[60]

National level

Clearly, it is at the national level that most effective action *can* take place. The federal government possesses the resources and the power to effectively set and enforce standards to get the job done. But there are several constraints on action at the Federal level, just as there are at the local and state levels. National standards must allow variance to account for local needs and values and by their very nature may be diluted because of the necessary consideration given to varying needs.

Highly organized pressure groups have more visibility at the national level in comparison to the grassroots action by common citizens. Only recently have public-oriented citizens' groups started to effectively organize; and there is a serious question as to whether they will represent substantial numbers of people or just determined small groups. In any event, at the present, paid lobbyists, industrial representatives, and commercial groups may be more active at the Federal level.[61]

Finally, the federal government is not monolithic in nature. Often, the action by one office is negated or offset by an opposite action of another. The celebrated case of the Surgeon General's warning against smoking, concurrently with the Agriculture Department's campaign to increase smoking in Thailand is illustrative of the problem.

International level

While no government body exists on the international level, the effect of the environment movement upon international relations can be seen in the recent international conference on the environment held under United Nations auspices

---

[60]See "U.S. Steel Forced Into Vast Antipollution Program," *New York Times,* (August 27, 1972), p. F–3 for a demonstration of local and regional "power" versus a major corporation.

[61]See R. Joseph Monsen and Mark W. Cannon, *The Makers of Public Policy,* (New York: McGraw-Hill Book Co., 1965).

in Stockholm, and the treaty on the environment signed by the United States and the Soviet Union.

But, given the present state of international relations and the nonexistence of international government, the question of effective pollution control imposed by some international organization or even by treaty seems remote. Controls may indirectly as well as directly affect many other kinds of activity; and while industrially advanced nations may be able to absorb the costs of pollution control, many of the less developed nations, already at a disadvantage relative to the more advanced countries, are not willing to have the control imposed upon them while they are attempting to develop and industrialize.

While international relations remains a game of competing nationalism, it seems that little beyond the conference stage can be expected at that level.

It seems, then, that any political action must be predicated upon several relatively strong traditions and certain political realities. First, time-honored values do not change overnight. Such institutions as private property, economic freedom, etc., must be considered as relatively inflexible constraints in the control process.

Second, we must consider pollution abatement a relatively long-term project. Education becomes the primary vehicle for sustaining the commitment to concern with the environment.

In addition, anyone who proposes to work in the pollution field must realize that, whereas standards of environmental purity are technically objective, they are politically subjective. Thus, compromise, almost by definition, is built into the process.

Finally, in the United States, at least, pollution control must work within a Federal system, with its various levels of power, and its emphasis on as much local autonomy as possible. In addition, it must work within a governmental organization structure which is constituent-oriented rather than problem-oriented.

A ROLE FOR CONSUMER GROUPS

The necessity to organize politically for environmental action seems to mean slow and diluted results, so long as the organizers rely solely on persuasion and less on economic clout. If it is cheaper for a business firm to fight pollution control because of the political weakness of opposing forces, then the odds are that the firm will do so. When, however, protesting groups can couple political clout with economic clout, the chances for short-run success become better.

One set of groups that seems to have promise in this respect are the various consumer groups. Right now, they are concerned with product quality, advertising truth, unit pricing, fair labeling, and similar issues. And to a certain extent, raising the prices of products through full costing might seem the antithesis of their present action.

But consumer groups could concern themselves with whether the product in question has absorbed the full costs of production. They could detail which products are "dirty" and which are "clean" in the production sense, and which products add to a consumers' tax bill by requiring special waste disposal. To my knowledge, no consumer group has yet calculated the savings on tax dollars to be gained by returning to returnable bottles, biodegradeable detergents, or other products requiring less processing.

In sum, then, consumer groups, which are developing some degree of power to reward or punish producers and seem to be gaining some degree of credence, could make another major contribution, by shifting some of their concern to the environment crisis.

SUMMARY AND CONCLUSIONS

In this paper, we have discussed the concepts of economic growth and its basic determinants, defined pollution and its basic sources, and indicated the magnitude of the costs. We have investigated what might be called grand schemes such as zero growth, a change in the system of production, and a change in the priorities of society. We have discussed the concept of production costs, and catalogued the various approaches within the free market system designed to allocate and perhaps internalize external costs and curb pollution. Finally, we pointed out some of the political and value problems involved in any pollution-abatement program and then set out a mild challenge to consumer groups.

If anything is made clear by this paper, it is that the problems are easy to talk about and write about and the solutions can glibly flow, but the ramifications are indeed immense. Instituting that grand strategy may not be impossible, but it is a great deal harder than it looks at first glance.

The Challenge of the Environment:
A primer on EPA's statutory authority

AIR

The alarming deterioration of the quality of the air we breathe has forced us to take a hard new look at air pollution, its causes, its results, and the means we have at our disposal for stopping it. While it is difficult to measure with any precision the costs Americans are paying for polluted air, we know the dollar total is enormous. Our most careful estimate is that about $6 billion each year is lost because of pollution-rated sickness and premature death. If we add an estimated $10 billion in property losses each year, we come up with a total of $16 billion a year for polluted air—a pollution bill of about $80 per American per year.

Excerpt from "The Challenge of the Environment: A Primer on EPA's Statutory Authority," U.S. Environmental Protection Agency, December, 1972.

EPA estimates that it will cost $15 billion spread over the next five years to control air pollution from existing sources. Simply letting pollution continue will be far more expensive than spending what it takes to curb it.

Statistics do not tell the entire story. The abatement of air pollution[1] in many cases will force industry to reduce obsolescence and inefficiency in its operations. For in many industries, the older and less efficient plant is also the biggest polluter. Forced to clean-up, many plants will be compelled to be more efficient. Moreover, the recaptured byproducts of industrial activity may provide usable, marketable products. Taking all of these factors into account, it makes good practical sense to end air pollution in America.

Legislative background

The Federal government's concern with air pollution officially began with the Air Pollution Act of 1955, authorizing the first Federally-funded air pollution research. Passage of the Motor Vehicle Pollution Control Act of 1965 expanded Federal activity to include setting emission[2] standards for automobiles.

Current Federal activity in air pollution abatement and research stems from the Air Quality Act of 1967 and the Clean Air Act of 1970. This undertaking is perhaps EPA's most controversial and comprehensive program and is certainly the most sweeping Federal pollution control scheme. The Clean Air Act set up a new system of national air quality standards and called for a roll-back of auto pollution levels.

Research

Specifically, the Clean Air Act, as amended, directs EPA to conduct research on the causes, effects, extent and ways to control air pollution. The agency is charged with the duty of providing technical and financial assistance to State and local air pollution control agencies and special investigations by EPA may be instituted at the request of State governments. Federal interagency cooperation is encouraged and EPA's own research is directed into specific areas, including health problems, fuel combustion, aircraft emissions, cost-benefit studies, and control technology.

Ambient air quality

The 1970 Act was the first law to call for national, uniform air quality standards based on geographic regions. Ambient air quality[3] is regulated by two sets of

---

[1] *Pollution Abatement*—ending pollution. Distinguished from pollution control (which may only reduce pollution) and penalties (which principally punish violations).

[2] *Emissions*—what is discharged into the air by a pollution source. Distinguished from "effluents" which are discharged into water.

[3] *Ambient Air Quality*—the average atmospheric purity as distinguished from discharge measurements taken at the source of pollution. The general amount of pollution present in a broad area.

standards, both determined by EPA. Primary standards concern the minimum level of air quality that is necessary to keep people from becoming ill. These levels are based on the proven harmful effects of individual pollutants. Secondary standards are aimed at the promotion of public welfare, and the prevention of damage to animals, plant life and property generally. EPA has now set primary and secondary national standards for six pollutants: sulfur oxide, particulate matter, carbon monoxide, hydrocarbons, photochemicals, and nitrogen oxide. Standards for these pollutants establish the maximum amount of each pollutant that will be permitted in the atmosphere consistent with public health and welfare.

Interstate regions

Since pollution does not follow State boundaries, the Administrator was given expanded power to establish interstate air quality regions;[4] each State however, retains authority for implementing national standards within its portion of an interstate region.

Implementation plans

State governments within each air quality region determine how national air pollution objectives are to be reached, subject to a three-year deadline for primary standards and a more flexible timetable for secondary standards. The States have submitted implementation plans showing in detail how and when they will achieve these standards within their own territory.

Federal standards apply to a list of identified pollutants that constitute the chief health problems associated with air pollution. The States have the broad responsibility of deciding which activities to regulate or prohibit in order to achieve the national standard. The Administrator will then review the individual implementation plan under prescribed criteria set out in the act itself: whether it expeditiously meets primary standards within the three-year timetable; whether it includes appropriate emission limitations, schedules, and timetables for compliance; whether it provides for sufficient monitoring capabilities; whether it provides for review of new sources of pollution; whether it is sufficient from the point of view of intergovernmental cooperation within the air quality region; and whether it provides for sufficient personnel, money, review, and inspection. The Administrator must substitute a plan of his own if the State fails to submit one, or if the State fails to revise its plan to meet the objections he has raised.

Although States are required to meet the national primary standards by 1975, the Clean Air Act provides for waiver of that deadline for up to an additional two years if compliance is technologically impossible and reasonable alternatives are inadequate.

---

[4]*Air Quality Control Regions*—the law requires the country to be divided into geographical units, reflecting common air pollution problems, for purposes of reaching national standards.

WATER

Three out of every four people in the United States get their drinking water from public supply systems. In 1969, a Federal study found half of these systems substandard. Health specialists are increasingly concerned about neutralizing toxic substances and viruses when natural water purification fails. We are finally realizing that there are limits to natural purification—that our nation's waters cannot indefinitely absorb an endless avalanche of waste.

Legislative background

Federal water legislation dates back to the nineteenth century, when Congress enacted the River and Harbor Act of 1886, recodified in the Rivers and Harbors Act of 1899. It is only within the last seven years, however, that major water pollution legislation has been passed.

Recognizing the threat that dirty water posed to the public health and welfare, Congress enacted the Federal Water Pollution Control Act (FWPCA), in order to "enhance the quality and value of our water resources and to establish a national policy for the prevention, control and abatement of water pollution." FWPCA and its several amendments set out the basic legal authority for Federal regulation of water quality.

The original Act was passed in 1948. Its amendments broadened the Federal government's authority in water pollution control. The Water Pollution Control Act Amendments of 1956 strengthened enforcement provisions by providing for an abatement suit at the request of a State pollution control agency; where health was being endangered, the Federal government no longer had to receive the consent of all States involved. The Federal role was further expanded under the Water Quality Act of 1965. That act provided for the setting of water quality standards which are State and Federally enforceable; it became the basis for interstate water quality standards. The Clean Water Restoration Act of 1966 imposed a $100 per day fine on a polluter who failed to submit a required report. The Water Quality Improvement Act of 1970, again expanded Federal authority, and established a State certification procedure to prevent degradation of water below applicable standards.

Despite the improvements achieved by each amendment to the original Act, the result of this sporadic legislation was a hodgepodge of law. Eleven reorganizations and restructurings of Federal agency responsibility compounded the difficulty of effectively implementing the law. To solve these problems, the 1972 amendments to the FWPCA restructured the authority for water pollution control and consolidated authority in the Administrator of the Environmental Protection Agency.

Goals and policy

The objective of the Act is to restore and maintain the chemical, physical, and biological integrity of the nation's waters. In order to achieve this objective, the Act sets two goals. The first national goal is the elimination of the discharge of all pollutants into the navigable waters of the United States by 1985. The second national goal is an interim level of water quality that provides for the protection of fish, shellfish, and wildlife and recreation by July 1, 1983. In this framework, Congress gave the Administrator the legal tools necessary to make inroads into the problems of water pollution control, while continuing to recognize the primary rights and responsibilities of the States to prevent, reduce, and eliminate pollution.

SOLID WASTE

America's high level of technological developments combined with our standard of living has produced a staggering accumulation of waste and refuse. Our appetite for resources promises to continue to swell, but our methods of dealing with the waste products of our way of life remain rather primitive. This nation generates 360 million tons of solid waste each year—garbage, trash and other solid materials, exclusive of sewage and dissolved material. That 360 million tons may double within ten years. In 1970, each American consumed 578 pounds of packaging material alone. While the levels of solid waste continue to grow, the most common method of disposing of the by-products of America's consumption is the same as it was a century ago: open dumping.

We have historically operated on the assumption that the earth, water and air around us will absorb all of our waste products indefinitely. We now are beginning to realize that the earth, the oceans, and the atmosphere are finite, and that nature's capacity to assimilate more waste is coming to an end.

Legislative background

In 1965, Congress enacted the Solid Waste Disposal Act, the first Federal legislation to attempt to deal with the effects of solid waste disposal on the environment. Up to that time, only five States had made any kind of organized effort to address the problem. The Federal program under the 1965 Act was largely a system of grants which stressed State and local responsibility.

By 1970, the more far-reaching implications of disposing of used resources and waste products were widely recognized. Congress amended the 1965 Act with the Resource Recovery Act of 1970, which officially recognized the potential economic benefits of recovering a portion of the "trash" we were casually discarding. That legislation also directed new grant programs to urban areas, where solid waste problems were getting out of hand.

Nature of federal role

Although the primary responsibility for the management of solid waste materials clearly resides with State and local officials, Federal activity was directed by Congress into several areas:

(1) construction, demonstration, and application of waste management and resource recovery systems for the preservation of air, water, and land resources;

(2) technical and financial assistance to agencies in planning and developing resource recovery and waste disposal programs;

(3) national research and development programs to develop and test methods of dealing with collection, separation, recovery, recycling, and safe disposal of non-recoverable waste;

(4) guidelines for the collection, transportation, separation, and recovery and disposal of solid waste;

(5) training grants in occupations involving design, operation, and maintenance of solid waste disposal systems.

NOISE

Our experts define noise as "unwanted sound." The national recognition of noise as a pollutant is relatively recent, probably because it is generally confined to a specific geographic locality and temporal period, and because its deleterious effects are less patent than those of other forms of pollutants. Each of us has noticed such "garden-variety" pollutants as waste in rivers, or auto emissions in the air. We may shrink back from a river because of its peculiar color or odor, or be offended by noxious fumes from the antique buses that still service many cities, but noise, being less tangible and enduring, tends to be less sensually and aesthetically offensive.

Legislative background

The Airport and Airway Development Act of 1970 and the Federal Aid Highway Act identify noise as one factor among others to be considered in the planning, development, and construction of airports and highways. EPA is required to evaluate environmental factors involved in such projects and to report its findings to the Secretary of Transportation. He, in turn, must take them into consideration before making a final decision on the feasibility of a given project.

The Noise Pollution and Abatement Act of 1970, directed that substantial research be undertaken to study a wide range of problems concerning the harmful effects of noise. In 1971, EPA set up its own Office of Noise Abatement and Control to study the effect of noise on public health and welfare.

With enactment of the Noise Control Act of 1972 came the first major piece of Congressional legislation in this area. The stated purpose of the Act is to establish a vehicle for the effective coordination of Federal research and activities in noise control, to authorize the establishment of Federal noise emission standards for products distributed in interstate commerce, and to provide information to the public respecting the noise emission and noise reduction characteristics of such products.

In addition, the Act amends the Federal Aviation Act of 1958 to provide for interdepartmental action between FAA and EPA in the prescription of standards and regulations relating to the control and abatement of aircraft noise and sonic boom. It further provides for similar cooperation between the Department of Transportation and EPA in the promulgation of standards and regulations relating to the noise emission of interstate railroad and motor carriers.

Noise emission standards

Under the Noise Control Act, the Administrator is given the authority to prescribe regulations for products designated as major noise sources, where noise emission standards are feasible and where the product falls into one of the following categories: construction equipment, transportation equipment, any motor or engine, electrical or electronic equipment. Each regulation must include a noise emission standard which sets the limits on emissions from a given product, and which, based on published criteria, is a requisite for the protection of the public health and welfare. Factors for consideration are the magnitude and conditions for use, the degree of noise reduction achievable through the application of the best available technology, and the cost of compliance. The Administrator is also authorized to devise regulations for other noise sources where standards are feasible and when it is determined that the source poses a threat to the public health and welfare. The Administrator must give labeling instructions for designated products, which will put the prospective user on notice of either the product's exceptionally high noise emission level or its effectiveness in reducing noise.

Enforcement

Under the Noise Control Act, the Administrator may issue an order, after notice and a hearing, specifying such relief as he deems necessary to protect the public health and welfare, and may request judicial action to restrain violations of the Act. There are criminal penalties for the following willful and knowing acts: the distribution in commerce of any new product not conforming to the emission standards specified or the designated labeling requirements; the noncompliance with an order of the Administrator; or the failure to maintain certain records, make certain reports and tests, or provide certain information. Private citizens also can bring civil actions for violations of the Act.

The 'Ironic Castings' Story: Cleanliness is Next to Bankruptcy

Richard Haverka

"Ironic Castings" is a pseudonym for the foundry division of a major manufacturing corporation. Our writer, who is intimately familiar with the foundry's story, was allowed access to normally private information, with the promise that neither the foundry, its parent company, nor its suppliers would be named. But Ironic's problems with pollution control contain broad lessons: Company management and engineers should carefully monitor their consultants' work; a supplier with proven competence in one field is not necessarily competent in another; pollution-control standards are indeed forever-tightening, but the "moving target" of changing standards can be hit squarely if designers agree to provide more than the minimum controls called for by current laws.

In 1965 management men at a midwestern foundry, referred to hereafter as Ironic Castings, read the fine print of air-pollution standards then proposed for the county in which the foundry was located, decided that the young Turk responsible for drafting the standards meant business, and elected to clean up the plant before the county did it for them.

Eight years, six million dollars and several attempts later, Ironic Castings is further behind in its cleanup program than when it started. Court action is pending and the plant's resident pollution control engineer refers to the whole mess as "an open-ended race" between tightening standards and tighter pollution controls.

The decision to start the cleanup wasn't difficult to make. While Ironic had never been cited for air-pollution violations, smoke from its stacks had long served to guide pilots making VFR approaches to a nearby air field, and downwind newspapers had used its smoke as editorial grist for years.

Management asked for bids on systems for air-pollution control, and the treatment of any wastewater that might be produced by them. Several proposals were received. Only one firm entered a bid to handle the total problem. For controlling particulates there were wet scrubbers which, because of space limitations at the foundry, had to be uniquely designed, proprietary systems. For treatment of the scrubber water prior to its release into a small but navigable river alongside the plant, the design firm proposed the geometric enlargement of a system used almost solely for cleaning swimming pool water—a diatomaceous earth filter.

The design firm, on the basis of its pilot tests, projected that the elaborate filtration system would yield water containing less than five milligrams of suspended solids per liter. The firm got the contract despite internal memos from lower-echelon engineering personnel arguing that the pilot project set up by the bidder to prove the system was handling only 100 gallons per minute while the foundry would be flushing out 4,000 gallons per minute. And there were unknown scaleup problems because no similar large system had ever been built.

Moreover, no attempt was made in the pilot project to test the diatomaceous earth filter with the type of particulate-laden water that would be representative of the foundry's waste. Rather, according to one critic at the time, "the pilot project was by comparison being operated with tap water with handfuls of dirt thrown in."

Management countered these arguments by pointing out that the supplier had served the firm's manufacturing division unerringly for 25 years. This record should be worth something. And this was the only total package offered. Accepting separate air and water systems would double the number of consultants and design teams to keep track of.

The system went into operation in the summer of 1967. The wet scrubbers, one for each of the four cupolas, worked acceptably by the relatively low standards of the day, reducing particulate emissions by more than 80%. But the filter system, which went on line shortly thereafter was, in the words of one witness, "instant catastrophe."

The eventual analysis, long in coming, was that the particulates gleaned by the scrubbers would form a seal over the diatomaceous earth, rendering it useless minutes after going into operation. As obvious as this explanation should have been, it wasn't universally accepted until a decision was made to scrap the water treatment portion of the system in late 1969.

In the intervening two years the vendor was given complete freedom to do what it could to breathe some life into the system. Making allowances for the precision of hindsight, one observer now opines that "using diatomaceous earth to filter foundry waste is like trying to dig the basement of an office building with a shovel . . . not a spade, a shovel. You cannot use it to collect gross solids."

The supplier was handicapped in that it was unable to deviate from that one filtering agent. Unable to tackle the cause of the problem, it seized on noncauses —toying with them in all but infinite variety. Various piping patterns were tried and a number of other metals were used to replace the pumping system, which was originally stainless steel. Nothing worked.

By late 1969, the young Turk in the county air pollution office hadn't even cocked an eyebrow at the facility, primarily because the wet scrubbers were reducing atmospheric emissions to within standards. Unfortunately, since the filtration system wasn't functioning, enough particulates were being discharged into the river to interfere with navigation. The state's water conservation agency then ordered Ironic to defray Army Corps of Engineers costs of keeping the channel open until a new system was working. That expense: $85,000 a year.

The $1.3 million diatomaceous earth system was ripped out. An Ironic management source commented on the vendor: "They tried in good faith and failed miserably. It was a case of trying to fix something that was inherently wrong. They're not in the [water treatment] business any more. I think they found the track too fast."

The water agency gave Ironic until Nov. 15, 1971 to have a new system in operation. Plant engineers designed their own conventional filtration system and management subcontracted for its installation. One drawback: the system took up more land than was initially available for that purpose. Total cost of the new package: $1.9 million.

Three months before the new system went on stream the young Turk finally struck. The county approved new air-pollution control standards which rendered Ironic's wet scrubbers, the good half of that two-part system, inadequate.

For better than half a year Ironic received a number of what-do-you-plan-to-do-about-this letters from the young Turk, prompting a series of meetings. Ironic representatives explained their problems and county engineers pressed for a commitment to their resolution.

Unsatisfied, the county took Ironic to court in mid-1972 in an effort to force development of a suitable corrective program and establishment of an acceptable timetable for its implementation.

With the qualified endorsement of the county, Ironic is proceeding to make the charge doors of its batch-loaded cupolas smaller, and to install vibrating charge systems to replace bucket charging. The company likes this idea because it feels it will get a better melt job and better charge distribution. Almost as an afterthought, it's explained this way at Ironic: "with a better spread of the charge over the bed, we will drastically reduce the induced air going through the open door. If we do that we think our collectors will just about clear the hurdle so far as particulates go."

The first pair of cupolas was scheduled to be revamped by December, 1972, and the second pair is slated to be in operation by mid-summer, 1973. Cost for the four cupolas: $1.3 million.

The young Turk holds out little hope for Ironic's latest project. "We have great reservations on this approach. . . . I think we're going to have to let them try it, but we've been saying all along that eventually they are going to have to do something more fundamental in terms of changing the design of the scrubbers they've got."

He then added, distantly, "The records will show that back when [Ironic] was putting those collectors in, even though we didn't have jurisdiction over them yet, we held talks on the plans and we told [Ironic's men] that the equipment they had in mind wasn't going to work."

Will Ironic get off the hook? For the moment the company is buying time, at a cost of $1.3 million, by altering the charge doors. Meanwhile the county will keep after it, pressing in court-ordered conferences for the establishment of "commitments of what Ironic's going to do and when. We want something that we can translate into a final order of the court, or into a consent judgment or, if we can't get everything done that we want, into an interlocutory order that will get us some of the things we want."

Over at Ironic the charge-door program is proceeding on a crash basis but there's a hint of resignation that this isn't the final solution. It's possible, says the plant's pollution-control expert, that the situation could go on indefinitely.

This feeling of hopelessness may explain why Ironic elected to carry out a stop-gap measure that few believe will be adequate. After all, if nothing else, its company does get a better product out of it. If it weren't for that, Ironic's return from attempting to curb pollution since 1965 would be nil.

Will Ecology Kill Small Business?
Managers must control pollution effectively

Dale D. McConkey

Ecological concerns have created pressing problems for the managers of small business. Already coping with immediate emergencies, including the capital requirements for day-to-day operation, they are now faced with complying with governmental regulations designed to preserve our environment. The author describes a number of cases in which companies must quickly solve waste disposal problems or cease operations. They are at a disadvantage, compared to large businesses, for they are less influential, less flexible, and do not have the budgets that would permit them to enjoy the advantages of long-range planning or internal expertise. A number of suggestions are made that will allow the small company to survive. These include waste utilization, government assistance, gradual phase-ins, and prompt adjudication.

Small business does not need the ecological and environmental problem; it has enough already. Especially, it does not need the urgency associated with these issues.

Traditionally, small business has been plagued by several wants; chief among them has been the capital required for the day-to-day operations of the present and

From *Business Horizons,* April, 1972. Reprinted by permission.

for growth in the future. In this respect, the average small company probably exists on a hand-to-mouth basis, maintaining its inventory at the lowest possible levels and turning it over as rapidly as possible. The disadvantages of short-term borrowing and high interest rates must be coped with, and planning, as frequently as not, is for the immediate present rather than for the future.

The small company is also forced to compete with large companies in the area in its attempts to attract or retain its managers and employees. It is not easy to attract the best employees when one is unable to match the higher wage and salary rates, fringe benefits, and better physical working conditions usually provided by the larger employer. Many times the small employer must satisfy himself with the workers and managers who are left after the better ones have been skimmed off. Lower productivity, less quality, and disproportionate training costs frequently result.

The smaller employer is at a similar disadvantage when he attempts to compete in the marketplace. Unless he is fortunate enough to be producing a highly unique product or be located in an insulated marketing area, he is at a serious disadvantage. He cannot afford costly distribution channels or extensive advertising and promotion. To retain his accounts and compete against his bigger brother, he is often forced to provide services that are completely out of line with the profit generated, for example, more frequent deliveries of smaller quantities.

In the production area, outdated plant and equipment are not unusual in the small company, which has never been able to operate with generous capital appropriations and outstanding preventive maintenance programs. Small production runs and higher unit costs compound other production problems. All of these exert an impact at the output end of the company's production lines.

Organization and management pose additional problems. The management group of the typical small company does not usually include the needed, but expensive, services and expertise of the staff specialist—a top-drawer financial manager, the personnel and employee relations specialist, research and development personnel, and engineering and maintenance personnel, who could make sizable contributions to higher output and lower costs.

It is almost a truism in the small company that each manager wears at least two hats, devoting most of his time to his primary job and what time is left to one or more of the staff specialties. It is not surprising when management gets its priorities confused. A president who must spend an inordinate amount of time acting as a treasurer to secure needed financing is not likely to have enough time to guide and direct the over-all affairs of the organization. Significant research breakthroughs are not likely to flow from a company in which the manager responsible for the research effort must devote most of his working time to meeting daily production requirements.

AND NOW—ECOLOGY

For many years the over-all objectives of the small business involved, primarily, profits, sales, return on investment, product mix, and earnings mix. Except for marketing and sources of supply, external matters seldom arose. But now the issues created by the new emphasis on ecology and environment must be added to the traditional problems. Unfortunately, this has happened before small business has learned, or been able, to live with its own problems. Thus, the combination of the old and new problems, plus the urgency with which solutions for the new ones are being sought, poses a formidable challenge to the small business. How well it succeeds in meeting this challenge will significantly affect its management and employees, its owners, whole communities, and the economy itself.

The writer recently conducted a survey among the presidents of fifty small companies with annual sales ranging from $3 million to $25 million. Participants were asked to list the ten most pressing problems which they would face within the next ten years and rank these problems on the basis of how critical they would be to the company's future. Over 80 percent of these presidents ranked "ecology" in the upper portion of the list, and of this 80 percent, a significant 56 percent ranked the time and costs of coping with ecology as either number one, two, or three. Naturally, the responses to ecology were closely related to the type of business and the degree to which the company's process contributed to pollution.

In many instances, the cost of ecology facilities and the management time and effort projected as required in dealing with ecology outranked problems of production, marketing, and securing capital. One president cited his current predicament. He had been devoting all of his time to attempts to secure refinancing for his company just to keep it going; suddenly, he had to drop completely this number one priority and concentrate instead for a full two weeks on a pollution charge which threatened to close his plant.

Examples of the problem

An upstate New York food-processing company with annual sales of about $15 million has been disposing of its product waste for over twenty years by channeling it into the municipal sewer system. This practice caused no particular problem until the number of residential dwellings began to multiply. Now the combination of the residential sewage and the company's product waste has taxed the present system to the point where new facilities must be financed and constructed. The town, supported by state health officials, has ordered the company to build and maintain its own primary treatment plant or to cease operations that produce the waste. The initial capital cost and on-going expense of the treatment plant are imposing a hardship on this none too profitable company.

Originally, a small Middle Western steel foundry-fabricating company built its plant and facilities in the rural area not far from a residential community. The area's population expansion has now surrounded the foundry, and the noise and fumes have become a matter of high priority among the foundry's neighbors. The cost of insulating the old plant with noise-deadening materials and revamping the work process to suppress smoke and fumes will probably be prohibitive as will be the cost of relocating the plant.

Several small companies operating cattle and hog feed lot operations in the grain producing areas of the United States are also facing pollution problems. In the past, feed lots were not located near populated areas, and the waste and odors caused few problems. However, population expansion has now created pressures to either close or move many of these lots, which are charged with both stream and air pollution. Prevailing winds can carry animal and waste odors as far as two miles, and streams can carry waste pollution for several miles. Feed lot operators, already operating on a relatively small margin, face a problem of considerable magnitude, which is aggravated by the almost weekly passage of rules and regulations.

Concern for ecology has had a pronounced impact on another small company in the agricultural industry. The main business of this company was to operate pea viner stations, where peas are separated from the pods, vines, and foreign matter. Naturally, peas are grown in farm areas which also contain creeks and rivers harboring fish dear to the hearts of conservationists and sportsmen. Both the juices from the vines and pods and the waste water resulting from the process of washing and blanching contain elements that are injurious to fish life. The outcry over dead fish in the area of the viner stations culminated in an injunction against the company, which forced it to cease operations until extensive corrective action could be taken. Such delays, even when short-lived, are costly when perishable products are involved.

The president of a Wisconsin company which each year sells $8 million worth of items converted from forest products has had his priorities changed dramatically. Since founding the company, he has grown accustomed to having as his number one priority the initial capitalizing of the company. At present, his primary priority and problem is to find some way to cope with the wastes and water pollution which usually accompany the pulp and paper-related industry.

Even those who seek to promote enjoyment of our outdoor heritage have caused problems. The number of camping and tenting grounds has increased dramatically. A small company that franchises campgrounds sees the consumer demand and has the wherewithal to finance ground clearing, swimming pools, and utilities. The cardinal problem, both to the franchisor and his franchisees, is the ecological one. How does the campground operator properly handle the garbage and human waste resulting from a high concentration of population within a confined area?

Two small home construction companies in Pennsylvania have ceased business recently. Up until last year, these companies had prospered by building modest second or vacation homes in housing development style. The first few caused no problem; however, the increasing number plus soil conditions in the area have caused health officials to severely restrict new home construction. The cost of meeting the new regulations priced these construction companies out of the market for second homes.

As an Ohio businessman discovered, even those engaged in waste-disposal businesses are not immune from repercussions of ecological concerns. This businessman had been operating a sanitary landfill and refuse dump where residents for miles around disposed of their garbage and junk by paying a modest fee. Even though the dump was located in the country, was burned over several times each week, and then covered by bulldozing, it was closed by state health officials until the businessman complied with certain standards. The cost of the heavier equipment and new procedures required for compliance rendered the operation uneconomical, and the business was closed permanently.

On Nov. 5, the U.S. Army Corps of Engineers started an inspection and clean-up campaign in the New England area. Most of the companies affected are small ones which pared their operating costs by pouring wastes into local streams. The Federal Refuse Act Permit Program required the filing, by July 1, 1971, of applications for permits to continue this dumping. So far, the federal agency has begun on-site investigations of 58 waste discharge operations in order to gain evidence of violations, and an additional 130 cases have been brought to the attention of the agency. Violators are given fifteen days to state their intentions with respect to corrective action. Out of the 1,400 applications for permits, 1,304 are still being reviewed by the Environmental Protection Agency, which jointly administers the program along with the Corps of Engineers. Employers paid $210,000 in fees to file the 1,400 applications.

Disadvantages of smallness

Compared to large business, the small business has less community and political influence, less money to spend on public and community relations, a weaker voice in industry and labor, less availability to lines of credit, and less ability to control its own destiny generally.

The manufacturing process of a very large company, the dominant employer in a small Midwest city, dumps residue on the homes, lawns, automobiles, and the outdoors in general for miles around the plant. As if this were not objectionable enough, the process is accompanied by a highly obnoxious odor comparable to a mixture of rotten eggs and chlorine. The company's attempt to lessen the nuisance and damage by increasing the height of its smokestacks has not succeeded. Thousands of people, numerous businesses, and the economy of the area within a twenty-mile radius are closely tied to the operation of this company; therefore, unofficial complaints are nonexistent and official complaints few. Would a small company enjoy the same immunity?

Often both the short- and long-term flexibility of the large company when coping with ecological problems are denied the smaller company. The cost of making ecological improvements aside, the larger company is usually better able to afford the delays, interruptions, and even complete cessation of business which retooling, installation of pollution control devices, or court orders may entail. The loss of production and sales for only a few days is often critical to a small company. Unlike the larger company, which may have several geographically dispersed plants producing the same product, the small company cannot switch production to another plant when one of ecology's policemen knocks on its door.

Concentration on short-range planning precludes the small operator from capitalizing on the advantages of long-range planning. The manager of the large company usually has the funds to construct the basics of his business, step by step, for several years ahead, and can plan the most effective and least costly ways and means of coping with ecological issues. Unlike the typical small businessman, he has the staff to help him minimize the impact of the problem. The problem often arises without warning in the small company, and little time is available to meet it effectively.

Last, the small company cannot usually afford even the most rudimentary services that would permit it to deal with the day-to-day activities for promoting ecological objectives. In large businesses, these services are provided by smoke control experts, sanitation engineers, and the research personnel for long-range projects, such as devising methods of converting present wastes into salable by-products.

Possible solutions

One can well argue, as many have, that the small company which fails to generate sufficient profit to operate according to normally accepted standards—including ecological and environmental requirements—is a marginal operator at best and should be allowed to go by the boards. Indeed, it is probable that many small companies will succumb to this built-in condition of a competitive market economy. Unfortunately, such failures affect the countless employees and communities that depend upon the small company for their very existence. In addition, the real health in the long run of a economy comprised primarily of a concentration of larger companies is highly suspect.

Before suggesting possible methods of helping the small company meet the ecology issue, it is in order to establish certain prerequisites which these companies must meet if they are to receive help from external sources. First, for the economic benefit of all, the company should be basically sound, one in which the problem is truly caused by the ecology issue and not one whose ability to survive was already in question. There will always be a limit to the number of dollars available for assistance; therefore, funds must be channeled to deserving companies where they will exert the greater impact.

Second, any assistance granted should not be in the form of a handout; it should be based on the demonstrated performance and ability of the recipient to meet realistically established environmental standards and valid, periodic checks of progress at various points in the assistance schedule. Third, where dollar assistance is involved, major emphasis should be devoted to payback schemes such as long-term, low interest-bearing loans. Top emphasis must be placed on providing the small company with an opportunity, not an absolute right, to stay in business.

Several avenues of exploration can be suggested if the mortality rate of small companies is to be lessened as a result of a continuing emphasis on the ecology issue. Clearly, a major and continuing effort is called for on the part of the public, government, labor organizations, employees, and the management of small business.

Utilizing wastes

In certain instances, it is possible to turn a present disadvantage into a future advantage by converting wastes into desirable by-products, which may be added to the product line or which will at least defray the cost of the conversion. Examples of success in this regard include the processor who now sells as cattle feed the tons of residue remaining from the pressing of apples used to make cider and vinegar; previously the residue was dumped. Formerly, the oil industry burned off several gases resulting from the refining process or let them pass into the atmosphere; now they are collected and sold.

Wood chips and particles left over from lumber mills are now collected, packaged, and sold as flower and garden mulching agents, landscaping supplies, and for weed control; still others are used for making hardboard and other composition materials for the building trades. Animal waste solids are now collected, sterilized, and sold as organic fertilizer, a demand which the ecology drive helped create.

Unfortunately for the small company, many of these ways of utilizing wastes are discovered only after years of research and experimentation. This long-range payback and the sizable expenditures in research time and money remove much of the promise of this alternative for the small company.

Government assistance

Care must be exercised here to ensure that companies that are inherently inefficient are not protected and allowed to stay in business only for principle's sake. Assistance could take several forms: accelerated investment credits or other forms of tax relief for ecological improvements; guaranteed long-term, low-interest financing through banks; relocation allowances; technical assistance to alleviate or eliminate the ecological problem; research for determining new or improved uses for wastes; and partial subsidies during the short run if the long-term future of the company is judged to be sound.

The value of the Civilian Conservation Corps was debated during its existence in the 1930's, but it did make substantial contributions to the nation's outdoors. Thousands of parks, flood and erosion control projects, and the outdoors in general were protected and beautified by CCC workers. Comparable projects, hopefully made more efficient through past experience, should be considered as one way of helping small employers construct ecology facilities. Concurrently, such projects would provide worthwhile employment for the scores of unemployed, persons living in depressed areas, and the minority groups which are worthy of assistance. In many instances, no increase in costs would result; earned wages would be substituted for relief, welfare, and unemployment payments.

Community action

Many towns and cities, especially those heavily dependent upon one or two small companies, are going to be forced to determine just how much they want to retain the small company and then devise every possible way to assist it. To be effective, this will require concerned action on the part of all members of the community—the company, unions, municipal governments, banks and other money institutions, and the local citizenry.

A two-pronged thrust is called for: first, to find more and better ways to increase the company's productivity so that it can better afford the new facilities which will be required, and, second, to find more and better methods of assisting the company in financing the new facilities. Positive understanding and constructive action aimed toward the mutual benefit of all parties are absolute requirements for the success of this community action.

Switching products

In certain instances, it may be possible for the small company to switch to new or changed products by either eliminating the waste which causes the problem or manufacturing products which generate a higher return, thus permitting the company to afford the increased costs of waste control. Each small company will be required to complete an exhaustive analysis of its primary objectives, especially the objective that is revealed when it decides what kind of business it can afford to be in.

Potential advantages to the small business from this alternative are limited considerably by the inability to afford the rather large product development staff and costs that accompany this type of endeavor. Retooling and adding new equipment involved in switching from one product line to another also involve considerable costs.

Better facilities

A more advanced ecological technology will provide some answers. The Warner Company of Philadelphia, for example, is experimenting with a new method of eliminating the ecological problem of garbage and other forms of refuse; the refuse is dumped and covered with asphalt, which prevents contamination from filtering into the water and ground. The Western Company in Fort Worth has devoted considerable research effort to develop methods of pumping refuse deep into underground collection areas where it will no longer act as a pollutant.

A specially organized division of a large company in Pittsburgh is addressing itself to find better and cheaper ways for other companies to treat their waste prior to discharging it. Other organizations are attacking similar issues, and it is certain that better, less expensive answers will be found. Whether the speed of these technological advances will keep pace with the accelerating ecological problems is debatable.

Company combinations

Several companies situated in a limited geographical area might explore the possibility of combining efforts when attacking the ecology problem. Certainly it is less expensive for four or five companies to construct and maintain one common treatment or dumping facility than it would be for each one to construct and operate its own. Also, the pooled resources of several companies should make it easier to secure longer-term financing on more favorable terms.

There is ample precedent for such combinations. They have been used successfully by small operators in the form of purchasing cooperatives, labor relations councils, area development associations, and in management education groups. Its potential should be explored fully where ecology is concerned.

Mergers

The small company, which is often defined as being one with annual sales of $25 million or less, represents an attractive acquisition candidate for many larger companies. Among other reasons, the cost of acquiring the small company is commensurately less and the company is easier to assimilate. While this alternative may be repugnant to many small company owners, it may represent one of the more practical solutions to furthering his company as a viable entity.

This is particularly true of those small companies which would constitute a synergistic fit when absorbed by the larger one, and when the larger company could provide the long-term financing and initial low return on investment contemplated by the new pollution control facilities. Many times the small business must realize an immediate return on all capital just to stay in business tomorrow. While management of a small company might prefer to run an independent company, its preference may have to be relegated to the alternative of remaining independent or becoming a smaller fish in a bigger pond.

"Mini" consulting

As noted previously, the average small company cannot afford to retain on its internal staff the costly expertise of the sanitary engineer, pollution control experts, and others whose efforts are designed to combat the problems of ecology. Nor can it defray the usually high costs of securing these needed services from the outside through paid consultants.

One method of filling this need is through government services such as those provided for many years by the Extension Division of the U.S. Department of Agriculture. This division provides the nation's farmers with expert advice and on-the-spot guidance in such matters as disease and erosion control, irrigation, types and sources of planting media, animal raising, cultivating practices, and other services. The only cost to the farmer are the taxes which he pays. More recently, the Department of Agriculture has started paying up to half of the cost of agricultural practices that aid the farmer but also help to promote valid ecological objectives.

A second type of consulting assistance could be carried on by the numerous business extension divisions of state and city universities. An excellent example is the Management Institute of the University of Wisconsin's Extension Division, which annually conducts hundreds of seminars and in-company training sessions; many are directed toward the problems being faced by the countless small companies in Wisconsin. The sessions, led by experienced members of the university staff and practicing businessmen from the outside, cover every aspect of the manager's job. The cost to participants in these sessions is only a fraction of the cost to the company if the experts who conducted these sessions were on the company's payroll or were retained as consultants to the company. In light of the large number of tax-supported schools in each state, this alternative has the potential for making a sizable contribution.

Gradual phase-in

The various governmental organizations and agencies responsible for pollution prevention and enforcement can lessen the immediate impact of their programs by giving the small company more time to correct its ecological problems. Such a respite would be especially permissible in those instances in which the pollution is confined to the local area and would cause no lasting harm if permitted to continue for a time.

Indeed, it would appear that the suddenness with which the ecology issue appeared on the industrial scene will cause irreparable damage to all companies —especially the smaller ones—if correction is attempted with the same speed. Problems which developed and existed over the years are not going to be solved wisely overnight. A gradual phase-in based on an order of priorities would be in order. Pollutants causing the most serious damage would be scheduled for immediate correction; those causing less damage would be given additional time.

Prompt adjudication

The small company operator must be provided promptly with a decision when he encounters an ecology problem or is charged with an offense. Enmeshing him in red tape for several months will lessen his already poor chances for survival. The federal Environmental Protection Agency and other federal, state, and local agencies must take cognizance of his situation with respect to action.

A recent article in the *Wall Street Journal* reported on the magnitude this problem may assume. Six months ago the federal government issued a requirement that any industry must obtain a federal permit to discharge waste into a navigable waterway or face court action. Since this requirement has been on the books,

20,000 permits have been applied for—but fewer than 10 permits have been issued. The small company can ill-afford such bureaucratic delays, nor can it afford the sizable costs that accompany these government measures. The same article estimates that industry's cost for preparing the permit applications could reach $40 million or more.

The permits previously mentioned covered only industrial discharges into navigable waterways. More recently, the Senate passed a water-cleanup bill that would extend the permit program to cover industrial discharges into municipal systems and municipal discharges into navigable waterways.

Another problem that may plague the small employer is the question of which agency or agencies has jurisdiction over a particular pollution issue. So far, major debates have arisen between agencies and groups within the federal government, particularly between the Environmental Protection Agency and the Corps of Engineers over jurisdiction on inland waterways.

Small business management must take the lead in coping with the ecology issue; after all, the Lord helps him who helps himself. A manager who fails to do so is likely to find his company going down the drain along with the wastes responsible for causing his trouble in the first place.

He must examine his total operation and arrive at methods of making it more efficient and productive. He must find better ways of dealing with pollution by eliminating the causes where possible and then arriving at the most efficient approach and facilities for treating the pollutants that cannot be eliminated. He must do a better job of working with his community to demonstrate his worth and contribution as a corporate citizen. He must make his voice heard before governments and governmental agencies at all levels. Above all, he must resolve to himself that he will do everything possible to support valid ecological considerations in the day-to-day management of his company, including the realization that he has no right to continue to pollute just because his company is small and may not be able to afford the costs of pollution control. Clearly, the necessity for all of this action on the part of a small company adds up to a problem it does not need but one it must resolve successfully if it is to stay in business.

SELECTED READINGS

Alexander, T., "The Big Blowup Over Nuclear Blowdowns," *Fortune,* May, 1973.

Bowerman, F. R., "Managing Solid Waste Disposal," *California Management Review,* Spring, 1972.

Clean Air and Water News, Commerce Clearing House, N.Y. (Weekly).

Commoner, B., *The Closing Circle.* (New York: Alfred Knopf, 1971.)

The Conference Board, *Corporate Organization For Pollution Control.* (New York: The Conference Board, Inc., 1970.)

DeNevers, N., "Enforcing the Clean Air Act of 1970," *Scientific American,* June, 1973, pp. 14–21.

Edmunds, S., and John Letey, *Environmental Administration.* (New York: McGraw-Hill Book Company, 1973.) Note particularly Section 1 and Chapters 12, 16, 17, 18, 22 and 23.

Environment Reporter, Bureau of National Affairs, Inc. A Weekly Review of Pollution Control and Related Environmental Management Problems.

Fir, R. W., "Facing Up To Pollution Controls," *Harvard Business Review,* March–April, 1974.

Goldstein, J., *How to Manage Your Company Ecologically.* (New York: Rodale Press, 1971.)

Lessing, L., "The Salt Of The Earth Joins The War On Pollution," *Fortune,* July, 1973.

Ross, S. S., "By and Large, The Environmental Cleanup is Progressing Quite Nicely, Thank You," *MBA,* February, 1973.

"Technology Isn't The Villain—After All," *Business Week,* February 3, 1973.

"Water Cleanup Becomes A Booming Industry," *Business Week,* April 7, 1973.

Case

R. B. BRISTOL, INC.*

On July 28, 1972, R. B. Bristol, Inc., an Uxbridge, Massachusetts textile manufacturing firm, filed with the Department of Public Health a request for variance from the "Regulations for the Control of Air Pollution in the Central Massachusetts Air Pollution Control District." Specifically, the request was for variance from Regulation 5.1.2. which prohibited the firm from burning fuel oil with a sulfur content in excess of 1 percent. R. B. Bristol, Inc., was requesting permission to burn 2.2-percent sulfur-content fuel oil. The firm subsequently submitted testimony on its behalf at a public hearing conducted on August 15, 1972. After a review of the evidence, the Department of Public Health at its meeting of February 22, 1973, voted to deny the requested variance.

COMPANY BACKGROUND

R. B. Bristol, Inc., founded in 1813, is a manufacturer of fine woolen fabrics and materials. The firm's textile products include a wide variety of finished and unfinished apparel fabrics, both woven and knitted, for

---

*While this case was based on a true corporate situation, names, dates, places, and selected facts and figures have been changed in order to maintain anonymity of the firm actually involved. © Copyright 1974 Dennis Callaghan and Arthur Elkins.

men's, women's, and children's wear. A smaller portion of their output includes unwoven textured and spun yarns. All of their products are of the highest grade and are used by some of the most exclusive garment designers and manufacturers in the U.S. Additionally, Bristol holds a contract from the U.S. Government to supply fine woolen materials for selected military apparel and equipment.

Bristol's main office and four of its plants are located in the town of Uxbridge, Massachusetts. Uxbridge is a relatively small town with a population of 8,300. Bristol serves as the largest industrial operation and dominant employer in the town, employing 823 from a work force of approximately 3,000. Three other smaller textile mills are also in operation in Uxbridge. Bristol's fifth plant is located ten miles away in Worcester, a city with a population in excess of 180,000.

There are 23 stockholders of R. B. Bristol, Inc., and all are individuals or trusts domiciled in Worcester County. The majority of the stock is held by individual stockholders who live in Uxbridge and are active full time in the management of the business. The President and Chairman of the Board is R. H. Bristol, a fourth generation direct descendant of the founder, R. B. Bristol. The First Vice President is the sister of R. H., Mary Lou Bristol Adams. The Second Vice President is a cousin of R. H., Baker C. Bristol.

For many years, R. B. Bristol, Inc., has been a healthy company operating in the black as a national leader in its field. The firm has continually invested substantial amounts in the modernization and updating of plant and equipment in Uxbridge and Worcester. This had aided in keeping the company healthy, profitable, and competitive. In 1970 through 1972, the total expenditures averaged 1.8 times the company's net profit after taxes. The Company anticipated further major capital-expenditure projects in Uxbridge and Worcester which are expected to continue at least at the 1970–1972 levels for the foreseeable future. The expenditures will finance replacement, expansion, and modernization of the textile manufacturing equipment, and the company's share of the Town of Uxbridge's contribution to expansion of the local joint town sewage-treatment plant. Capital expenditures for plant, machinery, and equipment for the 10-year period ending December 31, 1972 totaled $14,500,000. Substantially all of this was for facilities directly related to production and manufacturing operations, for stream improvement, and for research and development facilities. (See Exhibit I for financial data.)

Since 1961 the firm has had a profit-sharing plan which distributes a percentage of net profit (before income taxes) to all employees relative to their individual base earnings. Distribution is made to a deferred fund or partly in cash, as elected by the employee. Further, since 1953, the firm has had a funded pension plan. Pension liability for all employees is now fully funded.

R. B. Bristol, Inc., for many years has been actively contributing to local charitable and community service organizations. (See Exhibit II for total annual expenditures which flow into the local community.) Most recently, the firm has contributed properties for use as recreational areas, including Granite Lake to the Town of Linwood, Bolton Lake to the Massachusetts Department of Natural Resources, and land in the Woodbury Park area of Uxbridge to the Town for playground purposes. In process now is a contribution of property to the Town of Uxbridge for sanitary landfill purposes. It is anticipated that company policy will include further contributions providing the firm is economically able to do so.

Owners and management of the firm encourage employees to actively participate in community affairs. Areas in which employees have and are serving in responsible capacities are:

Uxbridge Town Government and School Committee
Uxbridge Community Chest
Worcester Medical Center
Central Massachusetts Health Planning Council
Uxbridge Community Recreation Association (YMCA)
Worcester County Natural Resources Council, Inc.
Association of Business and Commerce, South Central Massachusetts
Salvation Army
Goodwill Industries
Worcester Boys' Club
Boy Scouts, Campfire, Girl Scouts
Uxbridge Rotary and Lions service clubs
Local churches

In addition to contributions of time, personnel, funds, and properties to the local community, Bristol management believes that it has consistently maintained a keen awareness of the general environment in which it operates. Among the areas in which Bristol owners and managers claim the firm has been far ahead of others in forecasting and meeting social demands are fair-labor practices, union recognition, equal employment opportunity, and, most recently, pollution control.

EXHIBIT I

R. B. BRISTOL, INC.
CONSOLIDATED INCOME ACCOUNTS
Years Ended January 31,

	1971		1972	
Net Sales		$32,930,016		$27,407,093
Cost of sales	$24,409,104		$21,102,420	
Selling and other expense	3,264,640	27,673,744	2,475,729	24,078,149
Operating Profit		$ 5,256,272		$ 3,828,944
Interest expense	$ 474,729		$ 571,104	
Income taxes	2,401,054	2,875,783	1,693,365	2,264,469
Net Income		$ 2,380,489		$ 1,564,475
Previously retained earnings	$588,297		$402,214	
Less: Distribution				
Credit	−72,000	516,297	−265,000	137,214
		1,949,538		901,360
Retained Earnings		$ 4,330,027		$ 2,465,835
Earnings per common share		$1.35		$0.98
Average number of common shares		1,762,151		1,600,000

EXHIBIT (continued)

R. B. BRISTOL, INC.
CONSOLIDATED BALANCE SHEET
January 31, 1972

Assets

Cash	$ 837,803	
Receivables, net	3,650,680	
Inventories	5,227,930	
Prepayments	183,152	
Total Current Assets		$ 9,899,565
Property, etc., net	$6,283,798	
Other assets	517,577	6,801,375
Total Assets		$16,700,940
Net Current Assets		$ 4,631,310
Depreciation		3,397,432

Liabilities

Notes payable	$ 787,375	
Accounts, etc., payable	4,279,998	
Income taxes	200,882	
Total Current Liabilities		$ 5,268,255
Long-term debt	$2,483,115	
Common stock ($1)	1,840,000	
Capital surplus	2,779,543	
Retained earnings	4,330,027	11,432,685
		$16,700,940

EXHIBIT II

Total Annual Expenditures from R. B. Bristol, Inc., which flow into the local
community:

Property taxes to Uxbridge (20% of total tax revenue comes from Bristol) and Worcester . . . . $	393,000
Added payments to Uxbridge and Worcester for sewer and water services	57,000
Payroll including profit-sharing distribution, and payments to pensioners.	8,454,000
Payments to local suppliers and contractors	2,576,000
Charitable contributions, principally to local charitable and community service organizations	63,000
Total to local community	*$11,543,000*
Income and machinery taxes to *Commonwealth of Massachusetts* . . . . $	*264,000*

INVESTMENT IN POLLUTION CONTROL

The operations involved in textile manufacture were (and are) inherently "dirty." The first two stages of operation include fiber preparation,
yarn spinning, and weaving, knitting, and/or braiding of yarns into gray
or unfinished fabric. These processes result in a great deal of solid
waste. The final stage of finishing the fabric requires bleaching, dyeing,
printing, waterproofing, coating, and/or other treatments. In this stage
the waste is primarily in liquid form, consisting of heavy concentrations
of raw chemicals diluted in water or other liquid agents. Traditionally,
Bristol, like other textile firms, dumped all of the liquid and a substantial
portion of the solid waste into a nearby river. On occasion, Bristol
would add additional bleaching agents to the waste emitted in order to
remove the color from what often became unsightly slicks around the
discharge port.

In 1958, Bristol undertook a voluntary program to substantially reduce the effluents emitted by its plants into the Blackstone River, along
which the four Uxbridge plants are located. In years past, the firm had
concentrated on minimizing solid discharges, but in 1958 it began to
concentrate on liquid wastes. Adapting existing technology to its requirements, Bristol installed a $250,000 treatment plant which far sur-
passed the effectiveness (and cost) of any others employed by firms of
comparable size in the textile industry. The equipment and treatment

processes were far more sophisticated than would have been needed to meet the Federal Water Pollution Control Act of 1948, as amended in 1956, had Bristol been dumping *four times* its volume of effluent. (Bristol had been complying with Federal and State standards prior to installation of the treatment plant.) Since 1958, the firm has spent over $1,250,000, in combating the effluent problem (including funds spent at the Worcester plant). Continuing operation of the waste-treatment plant costs in excess of $120,000 per year. Its efforts have been recognized through awards presented by the Sierra Club (1969) and the Audubon Society (1970). The Blackstone River leaving the Bristol mill sites in Uxbridge far surpasses the standards established by the Massachusetts Department of Water Pollution Control. By 1971, fish had begun to return to the river, after an absence of over 100 years. The firm has, throughout recent years, kept well ahead of Federal and State regulations regarding water-pollution control.

Although Bristol's primary voluntary interest in pollution control centered on stream pollution, the firm has, in past years given some voluntary attention to air-pollution abatement. Owners and management have become actively concerned on those few occasions when area residents have complained of "heavy" concentrations of malodorous smoke in the air. Recognizing that on these occasions the wind was out of the north, the explanation normally given was that industrial emissions from Worcester were being blown southward over Uxbridge and that the Bristol plants on the north side of town were, if anything, adding just slightly to the problem. In any case, Bristol management was concerned and in 1968 offered to install pollution-abatement equipment at its main steam-boiler facility as soon as the "appropriate technology" was available. Since that time management has kept abreast of recent developments in air-pollution control equipment with the intention of installing such equipment when proven effective for the kind of abatement needed in their plants.

Bristol's main air polluter is its steam generating plant which is located centrally to the four mills in Uxbridge. Steam is an essential element for the company, being used in heating, drying operations and pressure-operated equipment. Additionally, Bristol uses excess steam for the generation of electricity in its steam turbines. The firm produces only a small portion of electricity in this manner, purchasing the bulk of its requirements from the Massachusetts Electric Company. On occasion, however, the firm has produced enough electricity so that it was able to sell back to the utility company a portion of its output.

In order to produce the necessary steam, Bristol uses fuel-oil fired boilers, a most efficient means of steam generation. With recent technological innovations and proper operating procedures, Bristol has managed to operate the plant at 80 percent efficiency which is about as good as possible. Excess heat and smoke is exhausted through two 110-foot stacks. The stack emission is nearly invisible except when the "tubes are blown" for about 1½ minutes per day. On a Bailey Meter Smoke Density Recorder installed by the firm, normal emissions are at a level below 1 on the Ringleman chart of 0 to 5, except when "blowing tubes." During these short periods a dense pitch-black smoke is emitted, which normally dissipates within minutes. On certain days, when a temperature inversion occurs, the blown smoke has lingered for hours. A few complaints have been registered by area residents during these periods, but mention of the influence of the weather has relieved the tensions. After two particularly bad days of smoke retention, the firm ran small commercial advertisements in the local newspaper explaining the temporary effect of the weather on dissipation and also mentioning that Bristol was not emitting any more smoke than usual.

BRISTOL'S AIR POLLUTION AND THE LAW

The Federal Clean Air Act of 1963 had little impact on the operators of the Bristol mills. Being limited to interstate air pollution, the law had little applicability to Bristol except when winds were out of the north creating the possibility that emissions could be blown seven miles south into Rhode Island. Although the possibility existed, the Act was never applied in legal suit or used as an order of compliance in any cases involving Uxbridge area firms.

The 1967 Air Quality Act (actually an amendment to the 1963 Act) did, and still is, having an indirect effect on Bristol operations. This law set the ground rules for Federal–State standard-setting for air quality-control regions. A direct result of this law was the division of Massachusetts into eight air-pollution control districts. The Massachusetts regulations, administered by the Department of Public Health, established a number of limitations and requirements for each of the districts. Regulations were established for the Central Massachusetts Air Pollution Control District in 1970 and included the Uxbridge area in the jurisdiction.

The new State regulations of 1970 were drafted by the Division of Environmental Health of the Department of Public Health and were approved by the National Air Pollution Control Agency.* The rules and

---

*In July, 1970, shortly before the effective date of the State regulations, the Environmental Protection Agency was established according to reorganization plans initiated at the White House. Henceforth, the EPA would have jurisdiction over coordination and approval of state-drafted regulations.

regulations for the Central Massachusetts District were such that many firms in the district would have to make significant adjustments in operations in order to comply with them. R. B. Bristol, Inc., was among those firms affected.

The most significant portions of the regulations included first, the establishment of an acceptable level of particulate emissions. For a fossil fuel plant the size of Bristol's, the limit was set at 0.12 pounds per million BTU output. Secondly, any facility burning residual fuel would be required to use fuel oil with a sulfur content of one percent or less by weight. Most plants, including Bristol's, had been burning 2.2-percent sulfur content fuel. These new regulations included a one-year "grace period" such that affected firms would be required to be in compliance by November 1971.

IMPACT OF THE REGULATIONS

By October, 1971, the Bristol steam generating plant was operating on one-percent sulfur content #6 fuel. The immediate impact of the use of one-percent fuel was an increase in cost of 2¢ per gallon. Also, the one-percent fuel was 2 percent less efficient than the 2.2-percent sulfur fuel used previously. The 2.2-percent oil gave an average of 110 pounds of steam per gallon, while the one-percent oil gave only 107 pounds of steam per gallon. This efficiency differential resulted in the use of approximately 300 gallons more per day at the preexisting annual usage of 5,800,000 gallons. This loss of efficiency plus the substantial difference in cost per gallon means an added cost to the company of $116,000 per year.

Fuel oil is the third largest cost item to Bristol. Raw materials are first, payroll second, fuel oil third, and electricity fourth. In this fourth largest cost item, electricity, Bristol also felt the effects of the pollution regulations. Massachusetts Electric Company was also within the governance of the regulations and it, too, found increased costs through losses in efficiency and higher costs per gallon when it switched to the lower sulfur-content fuel. These costs were passed on, at least in part, through increasing electric power prices. Between 1969 and 1972, the power costs incurred by Bristol increased $120,000 per year, at least a portion of which was a direct result of the State regulations. (Reference Exhibit III for Increases in Major Elements of Expense, 1969–1972.)

Technical problems were also incurred as a result of the use of the lower sulfur-content fuel. Bristol, like most other #6 fuel-oil users, had purchased relatively low-cost Arabian oil prior to the State Regulations. Arabian oil, a high sulfur-content, asphalt-based fuel, had presented few technical difficulties in transfer from storage tanks through a preheating injection system, into the burners of the steam generating system. In

EXHIBIT III

Increases in Major Elements of Expense

	1969	1972	4-year percent increase
Freight	$248,542	$ 283,024	14%
Avg. straight-time hourly rate	2.60	3.50	35%
Fringe benefits	987,190	1,198,625	21%*
Electricity	462,761	582,333	26%
Fuel oil	312,199	625,586	100%
Local real estate taxes	224,342	348,693	55%

*A further increase in Blue Cross–Blue Shield is expected to substantially increase this figure for future periods.

order to supply a low sulfur-content fuel, however, refiners and suppliers often distribute Venezuelan oil, which is a lower-viscosity, higher-pour oil and has a naturally lower sulfur content. The Venezuelan oil is paraffin-based; this results in the possibility of separation of the paraffin during preheating. If the paraffin were to separate, it could solidify and "gum up" the injectors, resulting in a shutdown of all operations for a lack of steam. In order to prepare for this possibility, Bristol contracted with Roger Dentley, Inc., a large reliable engineering firm, to study the problem. The engineers recommended changes to existing Bristol equipment in the amount of $48,570, not including engineering contingencies or the overhead and profit for the engineering firm. As of May, 1973, Bristol had not made the recommended changes, but it had not experienced any particular difficulties with the paraffin-based fuel.

Bristol continued the use of one-percent sulfur-content fuel until June, 1972. At that time, a temporary four-month variance went into effect, allowing all plants in the Central Massachusetts Pollution Control District to return to the use of 2.2-percent fuel. This decision had been made earlier in the year by the Division of Environmental Health upon the urging of many firms in the District. It was felt that the threat of sulfur-dioxide pollution would be reduced during the warmer months because of the likelihood of fewer severe temperature inversions and greater dissipation of all gaseous emissions. Nearly all firms in the District, including Bristol, returned to the use of 2.2-percent fuel oil. During the summer of 1972, the Massachusetts Department of Public Health conducted periodic tests for sulfur-dioxide concentrations in the district and found that all were below the Federal and State primary and secondary standards.

Aware of the impending lapse of the four-month variance, Bristol management and the firm's attorney prepared an application for a 1-year variance from the State regulations so that it could continue to burn the 2.2-percent fuel. Application for variance was the accepted procedure provided for in the regulations themselves. Associated with the request for variance was the requirement to submit formal written testimony on behalf of the firm. Bristol submitted its application on July 28, and presented its formal testimony at a scheduled public hearing before a Hearing Examination Board of the Department of Public Health on August 15, 1972.

THE HEARING AND TESTIMONY

The hearing was held in an open chamber room in the County Office Building in Worcester. In attendance were three Department of Public Health officers serving as the Examination Board, a number of Bristol management people including R. H. and Baker C. Bristol, Bristol's attorney, Weston Miles, a number of witnesses testifying in behalf of the firm, and two "regulars" at pollution-control hearings who attended in order to testify against award of the variance. There were no unattached spectators.

Weston Miles opened the testimony on behalf of R. B. Bristol, Inc. In his prepared presentation he emphasized the "unfavorable economic conditions" affecting the firm and the "relatively stagnant Uxbridge economy." He mentioned the recent erosion of Bristol's competitive advantage by disproportionate increases in taxes, wages, and benefits, raw materials costs, and particularly fuel costs, noting the 100-percent increase in the prior three years. He further mentioned Bristol's contributions to the local community and the possibility that future contributions may be affected by these increasing costs in manufacturing.

On the matter of proving economic hardship, which is normally a means by which a firm can earn a variance award, Miles said, "In our opinion it should not be just the marginal companies who are helped by variances. The healthy companies are the ones who provide steady jobs without layoffs, provide support to the communities, and are able to keep their pollution-control equipment operating effectively. They should be regarded as assets to the community and State with all reasonable cooperation given to them to keep them healthy."

The attorney continued the detailed testimony mentioning most of the facts favorable to the firm's position covered earlier in this case. He mentioned the Department of Health report indicating that the sulfur-dioxide concentrations in the County were well below the Federal and

State primary and secondary standards during the past two months when 2.2-percent fuel was burned. He also related the technical problems and associated expenses involved in handling the 1-percent fuel.

At the conclusion of his first round of verbal testimony, the attorney turned the floor over to State Representative William Ryan. In a brief statement, the Representative emphasized the importance of Bristol to the economic life of Uxbridge, noting the value of Bristol's equipment, payroll, taxes, and contributions to community activities. He urged that the variance be granted since the one-percent sulfur-content fuel requirement did appear to be having an adverse financial effect on the firm's well-being.

The next witness was Mayor Daniel Lanham of Woonsocket, Rhode Island. Woonsocket is a city of 50,000 located seven miles downriver from Uxbridge. The Mayor, in a very brief statement, noted the company's well-recognized efforts in the area of water pollution. As on other occasions, the Mayor publicly praised the work of Bristol management in bringing the Blackstone, "one step closer to its natural state."

Following the Mayor was Lewis L. Robertson, Deputy Commissioner of the Department of Community Affairs. Mr. Robertson reiterated many of the arguments presented by Attorney Miles. In each of his references to the town in which the Bristol plants are located, however, he mentioned the Town of Oxford, a small town eight miles west of Uxbridge. His closing remarks included, "The community looks to Bristol for employment, tax payments, and civic leadership. To weaken this connection by reducing the competitive advantage of Bristol through a variance denial would inevitably harm the community of Oxford both economically and socially . . . For this reason, and because of the excellent ambient air quality existing in the southern portion of Worcester County, the Department of Community Affairs recommends favorable action on this request."

Alan C. Blake, Executive Director of the Worcester County Development Commission spoke next. He noted Bristol's increasing employment levels, which were particularly profound in light of a decline in the number of residents employed by textile manufacturers in the county from 3170 (1970) to 2828 (1972). He further pointed to the "economic as well as physical aspects of the 'quality of life' in Worcester County." Mr. Blake additionally stated that "economic hardship would see a multiplier effect on the town of Uxbridge." He closed with, "The Commission respectfully submits that the possible decrease in air pollution is not worth, at this time, the economic hardship and the serious consequences that may be presented by failure to grant the variance."

Next, John J. McKie, Chairman of the Uxbridge Board of Selectmen, spoke on behalf of the firm. He pointed to the philanthropy of the Bristol family, stating that the family, "has been in effect, one of the outstanding pillars of strength to the community for years long past." He further mentioned that Philip Bristol, former President of the firm, was for many years Chairman of the Southern Worcester County Stream Pollution Committee. "His efforts resulted in the construction of the Blackstone Interceptor Sewer in conjunction with local towns. This project was, in a sense, a pioneering effort in the field of pollution control."

Ralph L. Wilanski, Executive Director of the Central Massachusetts Natural Resources Council, Vice President of the Massachusetts Association of Conservation Commissions, and presently a member of the Governor's Committee on the Environment, served as the last witness for Bristol. "We are concerned that the overall State standards take into consideration regional differences and that we do not lose sight of the fact that the achievement of environmental quality is interdependent upon sustaining a healthy economic climate for Worcester County . . . Therefore, we respectfully request that the Public Health Council grant this variance with consideration for overall investment planning to achieve a better environment."

In closing the testimony on Bristol's behalf, Attorney Miles pointed to two alternatives to the use of one-percent fuel on a continuous basis. His first suggestion to the Hearing Board was the use of "fuel switching." "At Bristol we have the capability for immediate fuel switching. The engineer on duty has authority to carry out this procedure. We have one tank which could be filled with one-percent sulfur #6 oil for use during an air-pollution episode. Some minor piping installation will be necessary before this can be used, but if our variance is dependent upon having the ability to fuel-switch, we will set up the system in this manner. The tank capacity is 20,000 gallons, a one-day supply. We could easily switch over to the lower sulfur oil on five minutes' notice. Our fuel oil suppliers have assured us that they could keep this tank filled with one-percent sulfur oil, if necessary, for extended pollution episodes."

As a second alternative, Miles mentioned the future possibility of using "stack scrubbers," which would require a major investment on the part of the firm in order to adapt and improve existing technology to meet the needs of the textile industry. As a compromise, Miles indicated that Bristol would prefer to invest the differential fuel cost of $116,000 per year in the research and development of such a system rather than "pouring funds into the use of one-percent sulfur-content fuel which has highly questionable results."

Miles formally closed the testimony on behalf of R. B. Bristol, Inc., with, "We respectfully, but urgently request that this petition of a variance to permit us to burn 2.2-percent sulfur oil be granted at the earliest possible moment, for one year from the date of allowance of this request."

Speaking against the request for variance were the two "regulars" of pollution-control hearings. The first was a representative of the Audubon Society and the second a representative of the Tuberculosis Association.* Both had attended many hearings on issues similar to Bristol's, delivering much the same testimony at each of them. Without referring to specific details surrounding the Bristol case, each delivered long and impressive presentations on the perils of air pollution in the Commonwealth. Citing specific cases of the results of uncontrolled air pollution, each speaker effectively portrayed the need for strongest application of pollution-control laws in the maintenance of public health. Both speakers mentioned the effectiveness of the enforcement of existing regulations in stabilizing the pollution levels in the State. Although appearing not to listen attentively, each member of the Board was well aware of the positions taken by the "regulars" in opposition to the variance request.

At the conclusion of testimony the Chairman of the Hearing Board, as per standard procedure, indicated that the proceedings of the hearing would be brought before the Board of the Department of Public Health at a future meeting. There a decision would be made as to disposition of the variance request. The Board meeting was to be public, but no preannounced date could be set for consideration of the case.

THE DECISION

Although no Bristol representative attended the Department of Public Health Board meeting, Bristol obtained word of the decision shortly after the February 22, 1973 meeting at which the case was considered. Late in March, 1973, the firm received the only official response to its application from the Department of Public Health. The entire text of the body of the letter follows:

> The Department of Public Health, in response to your letter of July 28, 1972 for a variance in the application of Regulation 5.1.2. of the "Regulations for the Control of Air Pollution in the Central Massachusetts Air Pollution Control District" to permit the use of 2.2-percent

*In 1970 the wife of a financial officer at Bristol had been asked by the Tuberculosis Association to serve in the post of representative at air-pollution hearings. As a member of the Association, she considered, but declined the offer.

sulfur-content residual fuel oil at your plants in Uxbridge, Massachusetts, conducted a public hearing on August 15, 1972.

After review of the evidence, the Department, at its meeting of February 22, 1973, voted to deny the variance.

Signed,

The Commissioner of the
Department of Public Health

OTHER DEVELOPMENTS

During the months between the hearing and the decision, Bristol management had met with representatives of Smith Electric, a large manufacturing firm in Worcester, with the hope of developing an acceptable alternative to the use of one-percent sulfur fuel. Together the two firms hired Dr. James N. Voelexen, Associate Director of the Atmospheric Sciences Research Center in Boston. Dr. Voelexen outlined a plan which he stated would be the most sophisticated in the U.S. It involved the installation of sensors in the Worcester area and as far away as 30 miles, to measure pollution levels of both the background and stack plume. There would also be a meteorological tower in Worcester to collect local data on wind direction and velocity, temperature, etc., from ground level to 1000 feet above ground level. All of the information collected would be transmitted by telephone lines to a real-time computer in Worcester. The computer would continuously work with a model to predict the air-pollution levels 24 hours in advance. As soon as high levels were predicted, participating firms would be notified and would switch to low-sulfur oil.

On April 15, 1973, Smith Electric applied for variance, based on "economic hardship and public good," as did Bristol. In testimony Smith Electric outlined its fuel-switching proposal. In July, 1973, Smith received denial of its application.

In April 1973, Bristol was asked, "off the record," if it would install sulfur-dioxide monitoring devices at its own expense if it were allowed to return to 2.2-percent fuel for the coming summer months. If it would not agree, the State indicated that it was not likely that the EPA would approve the State's request for a temporary variance for the Central Massachusetts District for the June-through-September period. Also mentioned was the fact that only a few of the larger firms in different sections of the District had been asked to install such equipment, although all firms would reap the benefits. Bristol and four other firms in the District agreed; the temporary variance was granted.

In the summer of 1973, Bristol management learned that the (U.S.) Energy Policy Office had proposed a federal regulation which, if it became effective, might prohibit Bristol from burning low sulfur-content fuel for a period of 12 months from its effective date.* The proposed regulation was introduced in light of an expected heating-oil crisis in the winter of 1973–74. Although the regulation had not been acted upon by late August, Bristol's attorney had suggested that the firm alert their fuel suppliers to the need for high, rather than low, sulfur fuel for the winter. There was no assurance that the regulation would become effective in the near future.

---

*EPO REG 2 (Proposed) "Priorities for Use of Certain Low Sulfur Petroleum Product," *Federal Register,* Vol. 38, No. 167, Wednesday, Aug. 29, 1973, Regulation pursuant to Section 203(a)(3) of the *Economic Stabilization Act of 1970* as amended.

D. Business And The Energy Crisis

Enough has been written about the energy crisis to fill volumes. Apart from Watergate, the energy crisis is the topic of the 1970's. While the most severe deprivations occurred after the Arab oil boycott of October, 1973, the energy problem involves much more basic political, environmental, economic, and social factors. In fact, many believe the Arab action to be a blessing in disguise; it provided the impetus for the United States and other industrialized societies to take stock and attempt to solve the basic problems of energy use and supply. With the relaxation of the boycott, however, there is fear that concerns about energy will subside and the nation will resort to its traditional voracious and wasteful use of energy.

The basic problem seems to be that energy provision and use is a complex web, in which shortages in one sector set off repercussions throughout the entire system. In the short run, at least, the supply is relatively finite, given the configurations of use and supply channels of distribution. In the past few years, demands have been pressing the ability of domestic sources to supply energy in the forms in which it is being used. The breakdown in the delicate chain can start quite simply. One example will serve to illustrate. For years, the Federal Power Commission had been regulating prices on natural gas. When, in 1954, gas was plentiful and alternative sources of energy were cheap, the low price was no problem. But by 1970, the price of natural gas was less than one-third that of refined petroleum. As a result, utilities used gas to generate electricity because it was so cheap, but the low price also took the incentive out of exploration for new sources. The inevitable happened in 1971. Gas deliveries were cut and utilities started converting to oil. Oil refineries were hard pressed to supply heating oil and therefore curtailed the refining of gasoline. And so the problem broadened.

Compounding the energy crisis is the balance-of-payments deficit. Foreign sources of energy in 1974 met about fifteen percent of United States needs; by

1985, given pre-boycott conditions, they were expected to supply thirty percent of U.S. needs. This would have meant an outflow of $30 billion in 1985 at 1973 prices; with the increase of oil prices following the boycott, $70 to $80 billion in outflow might be a reasonable figure to expect.

Yet basic sources of energy within the United States seem to be plentiful. It has been estimated that the United States possesses, in known and proven reserves, a 65-year supply of oil, a 50-year supply of natural gas, a 300-year supply of coal, a 35-year supply of uranium, and a 35-year supply of recoverable shale oil. While these figures are, of course, calculated at present rates of consumption, they do not account for new resource discoveries or technology (breeder reactors and nuclear fusion, coal gasification and liquefaction, geothermal and solar energy, and conservation measures) that will reduce reliance on traditional fuels and methods.

But the problem persists, in the short run, of providing fuel and energy from existing sources and channels. Technology is a longer-run source of relief, since the capital equipment required to supply energy does not appear overnight. One estimate is that capital costs by 1985 will be well over $500 billion. Moreover, it takes several years to find and tap a new oil field and over ten years to build a nuclear power plant.

THE ENERGY CRISIS AND BUSINESS FIRMS

Basically, we can isolate three relationships of the energy crisis and business firms. First, some firms are in the energy provision business. Their problem is essentially a production and marketing one; they must provide energy sources while at the same time dealing with the increasing constraints imposed by political and environmental protection forces. Secondly, all firms are energy users to some extent, and face the problems of switching sources, converting to other fuels, or conserving energy. In the face of mounting costs across the board and environmental constraints, as well as competition in markets for their products, these firms face some difficult decision-making. Finally, many firms produce energy-consuming devices such as automobiles, air conditioners, toasters, and electric toothbrushes. These firms are under increasing pressure to build energy efficiency into their products.

THE ENERGY PROVISION PROCESS

The energy-provision process is a quite complicated chain of events and interrelationships. Even without political and governmental regulation or environmental constraints, the provision of energy is a costly, complex system. The figure below illustrates some of these interconnections in very simple form.

All energy starts as a basic material—usually extracted from the earth—such as coal, oil, uranium, gas, or solar light. About half (at present forms of use) is ready for immediate consumption—principally coal and gas. But other forms of basic energy—oil, uranium, increasingly large volumes of coal—require some refining before being usable. From basic extraction and refining, energy moves to consumption and to conversion—to electricity—which is also consumed. Great efficiency

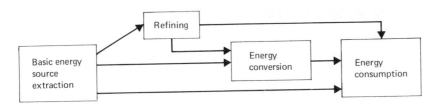

is lost in the conversion process as well as in the consumption process—about two-thirds in electricity generation and 30 percent in gas heating.

The various problems all along the chain are immense. Basic production is expensive, is subject to high risk of failure, and is environmentally hazardous. Coal mines underground are often dangerous and dirty places to work; strip mining is more efficient, but environmentally destructive. Oil reserves are found increasingly offshore; aside from being expensive to tap and long-run propositions in terms of the exploration-to-production cycle, the chance of environmental damage to beaches and marine life is always present. Refineries take three to five years to build, must operate near capacity to be efficient, and pose a variety of environmental hazards. Conversion units (power plants) are increasingly difficult to site. Nuclear plants are involved in the controversy over radiation leakage and safeguards against catastrophe; it takes as much as 10 to 15 years to plan a nuclear plant, get it approved, and build it. Both steam-generating and nuclear plants use large volumes of water, which, when returned to its source, often is warmed enough to cause thermal pollution. Coal, the most abundant energy source, is a prime polluter, and cleansing methods to eliminate stack gases are still not well developed. Finally, increased capital costs for utilities pose problems in building any generating capacity.

Between the links in the chain are pipelines, ships, and other methods of transportation. Pipelines can no longer be built routinely. The Alaskan pipeline from the North Slope, whose reserves, at the 1972 consumption rate, were estimated to be capable of supplying 40 percent of total U.S. oil demand for 25 years, was delayed in process because of its potential for environmental spoilage. Tankers of increasing size also pose increasing risks from ruptures and oil spills. Dangerous nuclear wastes must be transported and disposed of safely.

Energy provision has its competitive aspects too. Gas and electricity fight fiercely for the home heating market and both compete against oil. With increased technology in the coal industry, that energy source might return as a viable heating fuel. Nuclear plants compete with coal- and oil-fired power plants. While many of the major oil companies have vast coal reserves and are in the nuclear fuel business as well, the energy industry is still highly populated. Business Week aptly summed up the competition in a quote from Walter Meade, an energy economist at the University of California: "The energy business is like a big tent that covers everyone in the business. When they all step into that tent, I think they're going to kill each other.

BUSINESS AS ENERGY CONSUMER

Manufacturing consumes about 27.5 percent of the energy used in the United States, and transportation another 24.4 percent. This consumption is exclusive of energy being used as feedstocks for manufacturing processes (in plastics, for example). Energy shortages, then, pose several hard decisions for fuel-consuming firms. First, regularly used fuels may no longer be in ready supply, nor may they still be the cheapest, so managers are faced with evaluating alternative fuels. Second, conservation and efficiency become the order of the day. Certain inefficient uses of energy will be eliminated or changed simply because the increased price no longer keeps them tolerable. For examples, office buildings might be redesigned, no longer being sealed compartments but structures using more natural heat and cooling; and freight could be shipped by rail instead of trucks.

In many ways, the price system (or market) should spur conservation simply by raising prices; in other ways, regulation might be necessary. For example, using scrap in many industries consumes much less energy than processing newly mined ore. Yet recycling may not be undertaken despite the higher fuel costs, particularly if the industry has sufficient market power to pass on increased costs to its customers. Some regulation may then be required to *force* recycling.

In any event, the era of cheap, abundant energy seems to be over, and energy is becoming a more important parameter in managerial decision. It would seem, however, that, barring unforeseen complications or some nonefficacious government regulation, businessmen and managers might be able to react chiefly to market forces in their decisions, although the decision-making will be increasingly difficult.

BUSINESS AS A PRODUCER OF ENERGY-CONSUMING DEVICES

Like business, the consumer is faced with some difficult energy-conservation choices. Gasoline prices have nearly doubled in less than six months, and electric rates are up by thirty to fifty percent in some parts of the country; as a result, many consumers are becoming energy-conscious. This means that energy-consuming products will increasingly be examined for their energy-use efficiency as well as for other attributes. Air conditioners, housing (through the use of better insulation), automobiles, washers, dryers, and the whole host of consumer products using electricity or other forms of energy, can be made more efficient. For example, according to the Environmental Protection Agency, reducing the average car's weight from 3500 pounds to 2500 pounds would save an estimated 2.1 million barrels of crude oil a day, or one-seventh of the daily usage in the United States at 1970 rates.

In addition, business might find whole new groups of energy-conscious customers to serve. Solar-heated houses are already being built, and it is quite possible that solar energy could find more consumer uses. Some people have suggested windmill power and geothermal power, opening up whole hosts of exciting possibilities. Finally, firms selling energy or energy-using products might find related markets to tap. One of your authors has met with a group of fuel-oil dealers who were concerned about not getting enough oil to expand their businesses. In a brainstorming session, all sorts of new approaches to service and products (not necessarily related to energy) were suggested.

Thus energy producers, energy users, and producers of energy-consuming products all face challenges as a result of the energy crisis. Technology may provide many of the long-run solutions, but in the short run, at least, managers will face not only technical problems, but social, political, economic, and environmental ones as well.

THE READINGS

In our first article, Paul H. Frankel argues that oil will still be the major energy source for several years to come; it will be the cheapest and most easily accessible resource. With the geographic concentration of oil reserves in the Middle East, however, prices should rise and alternative sources of supply will be developed. Frankel feels that the resource reserves will be found adequate and that our technological potential frees us from concern. "Not only can we safely assume that we shall further develop our faculties for locating and making available more and still more fossil fuels and for improving the efficiency of using their locked-in potential, but, in addition, the advent of nuclear energy has fundamentally changed the whole aspect of the problem . . . The simple fact that we now know how to bring forth energy as we go along . . . makes it admissible for us to use up fossil fuels without having to worry that our grandchildren will freeze and starve to death."

Stephen B. Shepard's "How Much Energy Does the U.S. Need?" (from *Business Week*) discusses the various studies conducted to project energy needs until the year 2000, along with predicting the effects of various substitutions. The price mechanism seems to emerge in most of the models as the primary effective way to cut the growth of energy use—from the 1973 rate of about 4.8 percent a year to a necessary 2-percent growth rate—without necessarily altering standards of living or lifestyles.

Much has been written on the need for alternate energy sources as the industrialized societies face the longer-run problems of energy supply. Philip W. Quigg, in our third selection, examines the possibilities of alternate sources along with their prospects and environmental impacts.

Finally, we include a recent survey from the *Conference Board Record* on "The Energy Crisis and the Manufacturer." Managers are found to be facing a variety of problems in all areas—marketing, purchasing, production, logistics, planning—because of the energy crisis. And they are taking such measures as price increases, conservation, substitution, altering production processes, rationing, and in some cases, closing down.

Prospects of the Evolution of the World Petroleum Industry

Paul H. Frankel*

I

In the decades of world-wide rapid growth of the economy which followed World War II oil and natural gas were far out in front. Their volume has not only grown in line with that of the economies, but their coverage has increased by their having replaced coal as the backbone of energy supplies. Furthermore, their availability at comparatively low cost has in itself been a spur to allround growth.

This spectacular role, of being the foremost exponent of the growth phenomenon, has brought hitherto undreamt of opportunities and with it profitability to the industry, but has left it, for the very same reason, exposed to the concomitant risks and perils. The oil industry[†] in all its phases, including that of the end-use of its products, is a prime target for the criticism now being levelled against the impact that modern industry is making upon the fabric of life as we have known it. On a different level, the prodigious use of finite resources, consisting of subsoil reserves, has raised once again the spectre of their exhaustion in a foreseeable future.

Reprinted from the *Middle East Information Series,* vol.XXIII, May, 1973. Published by the American Academic Association for Peace in the Middle East. Reprinted by permission of the author.

*Dr. Frankel is a London-based international oil expert. The above is a paper delivered at the International Symposium on Petroleum Economy held at the Université Laval, Quebec, on March 12–13, 1973.

[†]Where the terms "oil" or "oil industry" are used in this paper they generally also cover natural gas and its industry. Not only are the two quite often produced together ("associated" natural gas) but their properties, in the eye of the user, overlap to a great extent. "Economics of a liquid" has become known as one of the characteristic features of oil, and in fact natural gas is a "liquid," only one with pressure as a third dimension. This creates certain specific problems at the storage and transport stage (for overseas transportation, the gas has to be transformed into a liquid). Generally speaking, natural gas transport is several times more costly than that of oil, hence its location is more critical. On the other hand, the environmental handicap of oil, to which reference will be made, is not shared by natural gas.

However much one favors supporting a trend towards establishing safeguards against excesses of the industrial impact upon the environment, the moment will come, sooner rather than later, when the pendulum will swing back. This will be the case when it becomes evident that the standard of living to which the inhabitants of the developed countries have become accustomed, and to which those of the developing countries fervently aspire, cannot be maintained or for that matter achieved, without a positive attitude towards industrial operations. Unless the world is prepared to adopt a pre-industrial kind of pastoral, mode of life—that of the Good Old Days which look so good only in retrospect—it has to put up with the fact that late-20th century living involves certain changes from earlier ways of life. We cannot do with less industry. What is needed is more of it, but of the right kind.

This simple truth—that one cannot have it both ways—will in the first instance be brought home to people as soon as the inhibitions now imposed upon the energy industries result in the actual failures of services which one has come to take for granted. Heatless schools in the U.S. Middle West in the winter of 1972/73 and, still more telling, inoperative air conditioning plants at the height of the summer heat, a thing soon to come, and perhaps also some local industrial recessions, will concentrate peoples' minds. When the feet are cold (or worse, when the stomach is empty) the nose gets anaesthetized.

Whereas we are perhaps justified in considering the anti-industrial spirit, now propagated by the more extreme of the environmentalists, as a phenomenon which will be of but marginal and passing importance for the energy industries, the problem of the availability, of the location and of the control of fossil fuel reserves is of fundamental and enduring relevance.

II

In respect of the amount of known or "proved" reserves of fossil fuels there is a need for more discriminating definitions that are usually applied. Coal reserves are always reported to be very substantial and to amount to many times those of oil known to exist. This is partly, though not exclusively, due to the fact that it is comparatively easy (and therefore not costly) to locate the incidence of coal in the subsoil, whereas it is difficult (and therefore costly) to do the same for liquid and gaseous hydrocarbons. From that point onwards, however, the positions are reversed. Great effort in capital investment and manpower is required to bring coal to the surface where deepmining is involved, whereas, at least in the earlier periods of a field, oil comes up to the surface under its own gas pressure.

Thus the term "reserves" covers entirely different circumstances in the two cases. Coal reserves are known to be ample but their potential is in many cases difficult (or impossible) to realize, whereas in view of the high cost of locating actual oil reserves it does not make sense actually to "prove" much more oil than can be industrially used within a timespan of industrial calculations. But once it is proved it is within our reach. Hence the simple fact that, in spite of huge coal reserves, it is hard to get more coal. Hence too, the perennial phenomenon of the world getting along nicely with a visible oil reserve cover of but a few decades, yet being shaken now and again in its confidence in the future, resulting in the kind of panic we are now witnessing.

The current concern about the limits of natural resources has the same root as the preoccupation with industry impinging on its environment. The exponential growth which we have witnessed and which some of us see continuing does make it sound possible that—false alarms in the past notwithstanding—this time (or the next) the wolf might really come and we shall in fact run out of oil.

Yet fundamentally, there is no reason to be particularly concerned about the world-wide prospects of our exhausting the irreplaceable resources of fossil fuels, which were accumulated over millions of years and which are now being exploited more and more extensively in the course of barely two centuries. We are justified in maintaining a somewhat serene attitude in the circumstances because of the knowledge of our technological potential. Not only can we safely assume that we shall further develop our faculties for locating and making available more and still more fossil fuels and for improving the efficiency of using their locked-in potential, but in addition, the advent of nuclear energy has fundamentally changed the whole aspect of the problem. In fact we revert happily to the pre-coal era when we used wood and waterpower, i.e., *renewable* sources of energy. The simple fact that we now know how to bring forth energy as we go along,* instead of merely carving up what we have not created, makes it admissible for us to use up fossil fuels without having to worry that our grandchildren will freeze and starve to death. This leads to the conviction, on the one hand, that there are now virtually no limits to technological achievements—neither in the realm of chemistry nor (*vide* the moon landings) in that of engineering, and on the other hand, that the constraints there are belong to the sphere of economics—and of politics, for that matter.

One should perhaps add that our belief in the limitless scope of technology has to be qualified by a time element. The time it still takes to develop and to perfect some processes once they are scientifically established is, more often than not, a constraint which is felt acutely. The prospect of a brilliant future is not always enough to light up a dismal present.

III

There is, however, yet another constraint, that of comparative cost.

The cost picture is complicated by the fact that oil in general has a lower cost than do, in most instances, virtually all alternative sources of energy, be it coal (outside the U.S.), additional hydroelectric power, tar sands or oil shales. This

---

*In this context we can ignore the need for uranium as a starting point in view of the expectation of fast breeder reactors and eventually of the fusion route to be developed.

factor, added to the amenity of transporting, storing and using a liquid or gaseous rather than a solid material, has caused the spectacular ascendency of oil and natural gas to which I referred at the beginning. All this would not have been possible had there not taken place at the very time when coal, wage-determined as its costs are to a great extent, became progressively dearer, the discovery and rapid development of large (and comparatively low-cost) oil reserves in Venezuela and, much more massively, in the Middle East.

It would be a worthwhile exercise to trace the way things might have gone in the second half of this century had there been no Middle East oil. It is almost certain that (perhaps for a while not in the U.S. but there too eventually) oil would have remained what it had been earlier on: a fuel for road transport and a provider of specialized services such as lubrication and road building. Coal as the provider of basic energy and as the raw material of a chemical industry would have been maintained and probably further developed and some alternatives might have been found for industrial power and electricity generation. One can safely assume that energy would have been more costly to the user and it is more than likely that the overall growth—especially in the Eastern Hemisphere, which we witnessed in the 'fifties and 'sixties—would not have been quite so spectacular, had the economy not been fired by a comparatively cheap fuel which was readily available and developed and pushed by the oil companies, those most formidable entrepreneur-marketers of our time.

There is one facet of this saga which does not seem to have been generally realized. The "new" oil from the Middle East (and later from North and West Africa) involved only a small fraction of the actual cost which was known to be associated with finding and developing oil in North America, hitherto the fountain-head of oil and whose prices had traditionally determined world market prices. The low-cost oil was eased into its world market gradually. Priced at first as though it had come from higher-cost sources, it developed, in due course, a competitive dynamic of its own—hence the progressive erosion of prices in the late 'fifties and throughout the 'sixties. Yet the starting point of profit margins was so high that it provided first for the oil companies alone, then for a while for them jointly with the producer country governments ("50/50 Profit Sharing"), a substantial economic rent* which lately, however, has come overwhelmingly into the hands of the oil producing countries themselves.

Before going more deeply into the present and the likely future oil scene, one element of the cost/price structure for oil should be given the attention it deserves. This is the fact that at the outset plentifully available oil enjoyed a position in which it could be—and actually was—sold at prices which bore no relationship whatsoever to its own low cost. The present policy of OPEC (the Organization of Petroleum Exporting Countries) would not have been possible had it not been able

---

*Payment to owners of a productive resource which in the long run is in excess of the minimum payment necessary to keep the resource in current use.

to adopt and adapt a system prefabricated by the international oil companies. All this may be galling to the buyers of oil, yet to some extent it was preferable to some of the alternatives. Had low-cost oil been yet cheaper than it was (as it could have been) it would have replaced other sources of energy still more thoroughly and more rapidly than it did, and our dependence on it (and the atrophy of alternatives) would have become more crushing than it is anyhow. Also, the margins thus earned have become available for reinvestment by the oil companies and by the producer countries, thus facilitating the development of the oil industry in all its phases and making possible the rapid economic progress witnessed in countries such as Venezuela, Iran and a few others. It would have been quite different had energy had to be made available the hard way as it were, by massive physical exertions (such as must be involved in developing more coal and transforming it to a liquid or gas and in developing tar sands and oil shales), soaking up means of investment which would then not have been available for the other uses just mentioned. Obviously this is a thought to be borne in mind should we have to plan for massive development of sources of energy other than oil at a time when the latter is technically available at minimal *physical* cost.

IV

Having surveyed, briefly, the role which the oil industry as a purveyor of energy plays in our world, we have to look more intently at the structural problems within the industry itself.

The first main feature of the present (and of the medium-term future) is the extreme concentration of the resource in terms of geography. 35% of the world's 1972 crude oil production, or rather 55% of it outside the U.S. and the U.S.S.R., originated in the Middle East and almost all of this came from the Persian Gulf alone.[†] The percentages for proved reserves are still higher, i.e. 54% and 65% respectively. What is yet more significant (and to some extent results from the comparison of the share in production and in proved reserves) is that whereas most other areas produce at or near their optimum capacity, it is mainly to the Persian Gulf that we have to look for readily available growth, a most relevant feature at a time of rising demand. Even these figures do not give a full picture of the degree of concentration, since 34% of the Persian Gulf production and 42% of its proved reserves are located in one single country: Saudi Arabia.

Such locational concentration is not without precedent. Sugar, copper and tin come to mind as falling into this category at one time or another, and, more poignantly, rubber, whose South East Asian origin created a major stumbling block for the Allied war effort after the takeover of that region by the Japanese. The fact is that virtually all such bottlenecks have been bypassed in due course by technological developments which, more often than not, were dictated by political and military exigencies. Rubber provides a most illuminating example. Germany,

---

[†]Excluding N. Africa.

locked inside Europe and afraid of being cut off from overseas raw materials, devoted thought, time and money to developing synthetic rubber (and for that matter motor fuels by way of coal hydrogenation); the maritime powers happily relied on the freely available and cheaper real stuff brought in from overseas. It is a piquant aside to history that it was the U.S. which really benefited from the German synthetic rubber spadework to which it had access, when it found itself, after all, cut off from Malaya.

What happened later was only a repeat of earlier experience. The synthetic material for which "Ersatz" had to be found for non-economic reasons developed after its baptism of fire, technical and economic features which made it an equal or more-than-equal competitor of the natural one.

It is tempting to expect that politically motivated interruptions (or the danger thereof) to the supply of a locally confined commodity, especially when such danger is accompanied by what the buyer considers to be extortionate price levels, will, in the case of oil too, lead to substitution—by oil looked for and developed elsewhere and by "synthetic" hydrocarbons. There is no doubt that tendencies of that nature will be strong and it may well be that by the end of the century the position will be quite different from what it is now. Yet the very magnitude of the task—determined by the exceedingly great volume of energy requirements and the extent of the capital investments required—does put the process of a shift away from the now prevalent supply sources and from the existing supply channels into a category for which there are no relevant precedents.

V

Our understanding of the present state of the oil industry and its future prospects will be enhanced by a brief review of the developments which have resulted in the setup of the late 1960s, just before the turn of the tide.

We have already talked of the wide range between low-cost and higher-cost crude oils and of the fact that the former were "eased" into the markets. The reasons why that process was slow and remained within certain bounds were three-fold.

Firstly, there was the sheer, physical magnitude of the process and of the capital investment involved, not only in the production phase but in that of transport and refining, which inevitably hampered the rapid substitution of high-cost by lower-cost energy.

Secondly, problems of national security and considerations of domestic politics in the countries where higher-cost energy was being produced (and which were also massive users of energy) caused most of these countries to prefer to safeguard their indigenous supply (and suppliers) to the availability of cheaper foreign oil. In this respect, West European coal and U.S. oil were birds of a feather. To survive, both had to be protected and/or subsidized, a task that became the more onerous (and at times more perilous politically) as the bigger the gap was between the two cost levels.

Thirdly, and most significantly, the low-cost oil was found and developed by a small number of large oil companies whose interests were global and included, in most cases, a vital stake in the U.S. market—which could have been upset by massive imports. There were two further elements of substantial general importance. Large-scale enterprises with a highly diversified business tend to be conscious of the fact that "orderly progress" is what is best for them. Any violent upswing in one instance is likely to involve downward pressure in another or, as the saying goes, "what you gain on the swings you lose on the round-abouts."

There was yet another motive that made most of the companies belonging to the charmed circle go easy in their maximizing the amount of low-cost oil in the supply pattern—although there was *some* divergence of interest and opinion among the few companies involved. The economic rent they derived from being the only ones who had such oil was to be reduced by this oil becoming a price-determinant, rather than being price-determined by a whole range of higher-cost supplies.

It was from the mid-'fifties onwards that the position changed, because then enough low-cost oil was available for its suppliers to compete with each other in earnest and on the new level—hence the continuous price erosion (only briefly interrupted by the political supply crises) which prevailed right up to the events of 1970. Yet it is the wide gap between the various cost levels which oil companies themselves enjoyed and managed to preserve for some considerable time, which provided the pattern of margins which the oil exporting countries have now come to consider as being their own by right.

This chain of events has resulted in a very unusual relationship between cost and price being established in the first instance and being consolidated thereafter. There is apparently no precedent for a situation in which a commodity in ample supply is being sold at twelve to thirty times its actual cost of production, and where more than eighty percent of the difference is accounted for by a kind of export tax.

To go back to first principles: the price of a commodity cannot, over a period, fall below its "cost" (i.e. below what it takes to make it available) nor can it rise for any length of time above its "replacement value" (i.e., the price of alternative means of fulfilling the respective demand). However, *where* the actual price is positioned between floor and ceiling depends on the degree of competition—or the absence thereof—among the operators.

In our case—based on the assumption generally held for a long time of ample supply of low-cost oil—the floor would be (or could have been) exceedingly low —much lower than the "market prices" were even up to 1970, but the ceiling is undoubtedly very high, indeed higher than was the price in 1970 or even as it is now, in 1973. Not only is coal, in many parts of the world, more expensive than oil, even with its heavy tax/profits load, but the simple fact is that demand for energy has far outpaced the availability of coal. Hydroelectric power has, in most instances, reached its economic (and environmental) limits and nuclear energy, however promising for a most distant future, is now as little a market factor as are tar sands or shale oil.

Hence, the alternative sources of energy—until far into the 'eighties—are not only, one and all, more costly than oil prices are now, there just are not enough of them to provide a credible and thus market-relevant alternative to oil supplies.

To gauge where, in fact, the oil prices are likely to stay (or move) within these extremes which are so widely apart, we have to try to sketch into the picture the forces at work now and in the years to come.

VI

It is perfectly justifiable to attribute a great deal of what is now happening in the field of international energy supplies to political elements, such as the trend towards establishing and exercising sovereign power in oil exporting countries, yet the degree to which such tendencies can make themselves felt effectively is really a matter of the relationship of supply and demand. If demand for energy had not risen as it did and/or if further oil reserves at the Middle East level of magnitude and cost had been found, no political operation *per se* would have provided the leverage and therefore the power which the OPEC countries now have.

Their strength, and the consumers' current weakness, stem from the fact that we have—rightly or wrongly—entered into one of the periods of "agonizing reappraisal" of the balance of future reserves and of estimated demand. This is not the time and place to restate the available figures—one can confidently state, however, that the known and expected reserves of oil in the world, especially in the Middle East, are sufficient to meet demand even if the higher range of estimates will prove to have been correct. But there is less certainty as to how the several decision-makers involved will act and react in the circumstances.

From the experience of the last few years one might have to draw the conclusion that although there is not likely to be a *physical shortage,* due to the lack of the reserve potential, the high concentration of the main reserves might result in a state of mind leading to the *absence of a surplus.*

Since the position of actual quotation between the possible floor and the ceiling of prices just mentioned depends on the state of competition, it is necessary to envisage the kind of competitive field which can be expected.

Traditionally, both producer countries and oil companies tended to be interested in as high an output in as short a time as possible—the companies being constrained in this respect only by their knowledge that any violent move of theirs might rock the boat in which they have all been sitting.

The erstwhile attitudes—trying to optimize returns by increasing the volume of output—were perfectly rational as long as (a) most of the oil exporting countries were in dire need of more cash *now;* (b) the reserves, in several instances, looked like being bottomless pits and (c) the companies making a great deal of money upstream were interested in going for additional output whilst the going was good.

(The current curtailment of their concessionary rights justifies such policies retro-spectively.)

None of these terms of reference appears to be applicable now:

a) Some countries, especially Saudi Arabia and most of the skeikhdoms, have more money coming to them than they can possibly use or perhaps could even prudently invest.

b) Increased demand for their oil and in some cases, such as Kuwait, second thoughts on the true magnitude of reserves, have generated a greater con-sciousness of the time limit attached to the exploitation even of the largest reserves. The memory of once flourishing gold-rush towns, now deserted shells, must be haunting the oil-country rulers.

c) The oil companies, seeing their freedom of action in oil-producing countries progressively curtailed, are more likely to look for profitability per barrel which they handle than for aggressive expansion of their crude oil output.

In these fundamentally changed circumstances, the particular experience of the success of Libya, which in 1970 gained power *and* money, not by increasing but by curtailing output, has left its mark. Added to the considerations just men-tioned, this feature seems to assure that, in the years to come, restrictive or conser-vationist tendencies will outweigh the straight competitive ones.

VII

What is the guidance we can derive from this analysis for a preview of the prospects of the oil industry?

If we take this term in its narrower sense, i.e. comprising the oil companies only, their status is undoubtedly being reduced, although their role is by no means played out yet.

What has changed for them in the first instance is that their function as *international* operators—looking for oil where they could, refining it where this was most economic and selling it where they might—has been severely affected by the rising tide of sovereignties. The companies represent the concept of global optimization, as it were, a concept which is not necessarily acceptable to individual nations—much of the world's economic infrastructure would be different if the world was one unit but it is not, and thus each country (oil producing and importing) has its own kind of national optimization. Global and national (or regional) optimi-zations are not always mutually compatible and the more each country pursues its own brand of national policies the less effective organizations designed to span the world become.

Such weakening of supra-national networks is particularly critical since—as they are bound to do—the incentives and the means for world-wide long-term investment are attenuated. Oil, being the biggest item in international trade, both in respect of volume and of value, can develop more readily in a climate which favors unhampered interchange of capital and of people. It inevitably suffers when there are a large number of smaller units of sovereign decision-making separated from each other by a whole series of barriers which keep on being adjusted as to their height—and at short notice too.

The supply role of the internationally operating companies is the one of which one first takes note, but it is their function of investment planning which is the one which really matters. Their high degree of geographical diversification, as well as their integrated activities—right through from exploration via transport and refining to the end-user marketing of products—make it possible for them to take risks consistently and to play long odds, simply because they can survive failure at any one point. Also, they can invest in exploration because they know that the oil they (might) find has a home downstream. Conversely, they can invest downstream because they are assured of regular supplies of crude oil on adequate terms.

If activities are boxed into small compartments without the benefit of the 'law of averages,' one of the mainsprings of development might break. It is easy to harass those who have made the investment, but to make people invest is another matter altogether.

If the wide-ranging system of international oil companies were to be consistently and massively affected by acts of sovereign governments of producing and importing countries alike to such an extent as to inhibit the flow of capital for the investment needed to provide the supplies of tomorrow, an alternative *modus operandi* would have to be set up if real shortages of oil are to be avoided.

VIII

Looking beyond the international oil company setup, which is the result of certain economic and political circumstances prevailing in the early days of our century, it is only rational to assume that the vastly changed general climate demands—and will probably create—an energy supply structure quite different from the one to which we have become accustomed.

It is quite inevitable now to talk of energy rather than of oil: in the developing stage of the oil industry, when it grew much more quickly than energy demand as a whole and, especially during the period after World War II, when its cost and price were (at least outside the U.S.) well below that of alternatives, it was oil that determined the direction and the pace of events. For the reasons which emerged from the analysis presented here, these circumstances have ceased to apply with their erstwhile force, or can be expected to cease to do so within the foreseeable future. Consequently, oil can now be seen only in conjunction with the whole range of sources of energy.

The determinants of a new setup likely to meet the changed requirements, as they can now be seen, are:

1. The possibly reduced share of oil in the total energy pattern will require a substantial and rather rapid flow of capital into alternatives, all of them highly investment orientated.

2. The rising tide of sovereignties in the world will make it increasingly difficult for international industrial groups to provide, on their own, the ways and means of development which will be required.

These two elements as such, and still more so the two of them together, appear to make it necessary that the basic investment decisions must now be taken—or at least backed—by authorities who are able to see them through in all circumstances or, as the case may be, who can shield an entrepreneur against a change of circumstances due to governmental policies. In a world of sovereignties, in other words, only a sovereign government can provide the basis of long-term investment.

In respect of the first of the above determinants, the capital requirements of nuclear energy and the long lead-time of its projects have, from the outset, made it inevitable that the state take the initiative and provide the money—and it is not likely that this position will change in the course of this century.

For similar reasons, the investment in alternative sources of energy—all of them requiring capital of a high order which, in turn, is expected to make their output high-priced in comparison with today's and even tomorrow's inflated oil prices—will be undertaken only if a situation is guaranteed by the governments: they will have to provide or protect an adequate return of the investment. This, incidentally, is likely to become manifest when the U.S. begins to develop and to display its long-term energy policies.

In respect of oil in particular, the current uncertainty as to the security of tenure of investment which is subject to the policies (and changes of policies) of other sovereign governments has made it virtually impossible for industrial enterprises to go forward without some kind of backing or guarantee by their own government. This state of affairs is somewhat obscured by the fact that the main part of the current operations in virtually all oil exporting countries still relates to investments whose basic stratum dates from earlier periods of greater overall security of tenure and of terms made by well-balanced firms, which in most cases, have seen their money coming back many times over. Furthermore, the additional investments they have to make as they go along are not particularly high in most cases, and are well justified if this helps to conserve the privileged position which they still enjoy on the strength of their original concessionary status.

The position is entirely different when it comes to making altogether new investments. Whereas, less than ten years ago, freelance operators (most of them Americans) swarmed into prospective areas to take their share in the bonanzas to come, there are hardly any such Merchant Adventurers left now. It is just not possible to face the risk of dry holes *and* the risk of being dispossessed—and the second risk gets all the greater the more successful one has been in surmounting the first.

It has become obvious that an approach from scratch is now possible only with state finance and guarantee. Hence, the only ready operators to take up new exploration ventures in OPEC territory are, in 1973, the Japanese, the Brazilians and (at some distance) the Germans, all of them strongly government backed.

The position is obviously different in politically 'safe' areas such as the North Sea, although even there the change of direction decided upon in early 1973 by the Norwegian authorities, and which appears to affect some interested parties retrospectively, must have had a chilling effect on would-be explorers everywhere. Even within the home country, the non-technological and extra-economic risks have gone up. In a recent public debate in New York a question asked about the political risks involved in oil imports from foreign lands received this response: true, these supplies are far from being secure but they are somewhat safer than are those from Alaska where, through environmentally related political pressure, oil found within the confines of the U.S. is inaccessible to those who need it.

The lesson to be learned from this survey of the problem is that even if one's preference lies in the direction of private enterprise and freedom of international trade, the general framework of our current positions renders it necessary for sovereign authorities to cope with situations set by other such sovereign authorities. The form this adaptation may take will depend on a whole series of local, national and regional conditions, but there remains, in all cases, the need for a clear understanding of the 'objective situation' and for the formulation of policies which are designed to meet these conditions rather than for futile endeavors to paper over the cracks in the traditional edifice.

IX

By way of conclusion it might be appropriate to consider in what way the several forces described will lead to a new balance or imbalance of power and, as a result, to a price level for oil.

The concentration of the only reserves which can provide the upward flexibility to match the curve of demand for their oil, especially taking account of the rapidly rising U.S. import requirements, puts an unprecedented degree of power into the hands of those under whose sovereignty these reserves happen to fall.

On the other hand, it is the dependence on their oil supplies (which the U.S. is now to share with Western Europe and Japan), which makes it likely that the weight of political influence wielded, especially by Washington, will be sufficient to avoid a degree of alienation of the main producing countries liable to provoke such a drastic step as that of complete withholding of supplies.

It is, however, quite likely that there will be no very strong resistance against a further scaling up of the monetary benefits which the OPEC countries derive from their oil exports. Hence it would not be surprising to see a further increase in the tax-paid cost of oil over the rest of this decade. Whereas most of the industrialized countries are likely to be able to take such increases in their stride (since they are bound to recoup some of it as suppliers of goods and services to the OPEC countries and, in a different way, as recipients of the monies which these countries will place and invest in the rest of the world) it is the oil-importing countries in the developing stage—some of them with very low GNP per capita—which will be hardest hit, and it would be strange indeed if means could not be found to channel towards them a slice of the unprecedented accretion of wealth now enjoyed by a very limited number of countries, some of them exceedingly small.

Inevitably, the price increases for what is still low-cost oil, and the potential political pressures to which oil importing countries now feel exposed, will lead to an ever increasing interest in developing alternative sources of supply. This will be a slow process and will hardly influence the going price for oil for some time to come; but, eventually, its results should be far-reaching and long-lasting.

The role of the existing internationally relevant oil companies is changing, but it will not be extinguished overnight—their sheer operational position is, for the time being, unchallengeable. Yet their character would be fundamentally affected over a period if, as was envisaged in this paper, they were no longer able (or willing) to take on the world-wide exploration function. Bereft of it (or perhaps spared its risks and perils) they will, in fact, become providers of well defined services, whereas the main decision-making will take place elsewhere. Where it will take place, and who will have the responsibilities, and thus the power, is one of the questions to which there does not yet seem to be a clear-cut answer.

How Much Energy
Does the
U.S. Need?

Stephen B. Shepard

In the five months that it was in effect, the Arab oil embargo did what no amount of environmental rhetoric could have done: It dramatically spotlighted the need for energy conservation. As a result, most specialists now agree that U.S. energy problems must be solved not only by boosting supply, but also by curbing the explosive growth of demand. "Long-term conservation is absolutely essential to achieve the goals of Project Independence," says John C. Sawhill, head of the Federal Energy Office.

But long-term conservation implies more than a laxly enforced 55-mph speed limit or a switch to year-round daylight savings time. It means a sharp cut in the 4.8% energy use growth rate the U.S. reached last year. For if that sizzling rate were to continue, U.S. energy consumption would double in 15 years, foreclosing any chance for energy self-sufficiency. What, then, is a reasonable level of energy growth? And, more important, would a sharply reduced energy growth rate choke economic growth?

A CONSENSUS

In recent weeks, many answers have been suggested. Russell E. Train, head of the Environmental Protection Agency, has called for a 2% average energy growth rate for the rest of the century, and Russell Peterson, chairman of the President's Council on Environmental Quality, thinks 1.8% is feasible. At the FEO, Sawhill says 3% can be achieved as early as 1980, while the agency's planners are working with a 2% rate in the Project Independence blueprint that will go to the White House next November. And the Ford Foundation's Energy Policy Project claims that the U.S. can achieve an average rate of 1.7% a year from 1975 to 2000.

In short, a consensus is forming somewhere around 2% a year, and if that can be achieved, the savings would be vast indeed. By the same arithmetic that governs compound interest, the difference between 2% and the current 4.8% adds up to 128-quadrillion Btus a year by 2000—more energy than the U.S. now uses and a 50% saving over the next 25 years. C. Howard Hardesty, Jr., of Continental Oil Co., puts it more dramatically. A saving of only 10%, he says, is equivalent to 200,000 new oil wells, or 2,930 new coal mines, or 211 additional nuclear plants.

All the proposals currently making the rounds emphasize energy-saving technology—what Ford calls a "technical fix scenario." In this view, the U.S. is an energy glutton, wasting billions of Btus on overweight cars, underinsulated homes, and inefficient manufacturing processes. By designing products and processes to use energy more efficiently, the reasoning runs, the U.S. can save energy with little adverse economic impact. At the same time, the nation would also have to shift to more mass transit, greater use of railroads to haul freight, and more material recycling.

The Ford study claims that such technological changes would produce a 1.7% growth rate "without reducing the standard of living or significantly changing lifestyles." Though this assertion has drawn criticism in some quarters, it is now backed by an econometric model designed by Data Resources, Inc., a consulting firm under contract to Ford.

RADICAL DEPARTURE

The DRI projections, prepared by economists Dale Jorgenson and Edward Hudson, are rather startling. They show only a tiny shortfall in gross national product by 2000 even if the energy growth rate is cut from 3.4% a year, the U.S. average since 1950, to 1.7%. Moreover inflation increases only 0.2 percentage points a year, even though energy prices are drastically higher. And total employment actually increases slightly, even though energy growth has slowed. Says Hudson: "Energy can be saved with little loss in GNP and without more unemployment."

The Jorgenson-Hudson conclusions represent a radical departure from previous thinking about energy demand. Energy has long been deemed the *sine qua non* of industrial society: Cut the use of energy and industrial growth will grind to a halt. Indeed, the amount of energy used to produce one dollar of GNP is about the same now as it was in 1955, reinforcing the notion that the U.S. needs a certain energy input to achieve a desired GNP output.

Jorgenson, who is a professor of economics at Harvard, rejects this approach, which he calls "engineering thinking." Instead, he and other econometricians see energy as a commodity subject to the laws of supply and demand, which, of course, means a sensitivity to price. "We cannot consider the need for energy independent of price," says Hendrik S. Houthakker, a Harvard economist who served on the Council of Economic Advisers during President Nixon's first term.

As obvious as this may seem, many energy projections made by energy companies and their banks still ignore the impact of rising energy prices on demand. As a result, they show energy demand rising much as it did when energy prices were lower. Such studies, Jorgenson and Houthakker believe, all overstate future energy consumption.

To the econometricians, energy growth soared in the U.S. over the last 20 years not because of need but because real energy prices declined to bargain-basement levels. Between 1951 and 1971, for instance, real electricity prices dropped 43%, refined petroleum prices fell 17%, and coal prices dipped 15%. These declines stimulated energy consumption by encouraging users to substitute energy for labor and material, which were rising faster in price.

REVERSE GEAR

Now that energy prices are rising faster than labor, capital, and material prices, the econometricians say substitution will reverse, slowing energy growth. Thus, a homeowner will invest in better insulation (substituting capital for energy), a manufacturer might switch from plastic to wood (substituting material for energy), or a company might use hand assembly rather than automation (substituting labor for energy and capital).

"Our view is that the U.S. economy has a lot of flexibility to substitute for energy with a small cost in GNP," says Jorgenson. In short, he believes, total output will not change much, though the way it is generated will shift to more of the energy-saving technology favored by the Ford team.

To forecast how energy demand will vary as prices rise, economists need a model that accurately quantifies the scope for substitution. Conventional input-output analysis does not help much because it uses a fixed relationship between inputs and outputs—what economists call fixed coefficients. No substitution is possible in these models, and a decline in energy is simply reflected as a decline in output—precisely the sort of "engineering thinking" that Jorgenson rejects. The DRI model, by contrast, avoids fixed coefficients, simulating instead the response of producers and consumers to rising prices in nine key industries.

Because widespread substitution is possible in the DRI model, energy demand growth declines sharply as prices rise. This is reflected in the high price elasticities projected by the model, ranging from -0.58 for coal to -0.62 for electricity. Thus, a 10% rise in coal prices spurs a 5.8% decline in coal use from what it might otherwise reach. Similarly, a 10% rise in electricity rates slows future kilowatt consumption 6.2%. The use of coal and electricity will still grow a lot, but at a slower rate than if lower prices had prevailed.

ESSENTIAL POINT

The response to price in the DRI model is great enough to drive energy growth down to 2.9% a year. If the nation wants to go further, say to the 1.7% rate favored by the Ford team, some government action is necessary. For example, Washington might spur railroad use by increasing subsidies, or it might encourage recycling of scrap by lowering the depletion allowance on virgin material. But the essential Jorgenson-Hudson point remains: Even a 1.7% rate would not cripple output or employment.

The two economists also claim that if the U.S. wanted to reach all the way to zero energy growth by 2000, it could do so by imposing a 15% energy sales tax that would artificially boost energy prices still further. And by pumping the tax revenue—$131-billion by 2000—into health care, education, and other low-energy industries, the DRI model predicts, GNP growth and employment would hardly suffer.

Obviously, the accuracy of the DRI projections depends on the validity of the model, and some economists criticize the DRI approach. They do not dispute the idea that demand depends on price, but they question the wisdom of using only nine industrial sectors to draw macroeconomic projections. And they say that substitutions that occurred when real energy prices decline may not be reversed now that prices are rising. Says one critic: "Jorgenson has ground out a lot of projections from a limited data base. His method will give you numbers, but I'm not sure how useful they are."

PRICE MECHANISM

If the DRI model is reasonably accurate, its findings carry profound implications. First, price is a much more effective way to curb energy demand than previously thought. Jorgenson's conclusion: Energy prices should be allowed to rise if conservation is to be effective. But the government is already under great public pressure to control energy prices or even roll them back. "It's politically difficult to talk about price as a regulatory mechanism to control demand," says Sawhill.

Second, work-force participation rates may increase if labor is substituted for energy as the model predicts. The result is lower productivity—more man-hours for slightly less output. That is normally bad news for the economy. But because the number of people in the work force will grow sharply by 2000, increasing the utilization of labor compared with other resources may be a social blessing.

Third, notes Hans Landsberg of Resources for the Future, if energy prices stay high, the U.S. lifestyle might begin resembling that of Western Europe: small cars, greater use of railroads, and patterns might change. According to a new study by the Council on Environmental Quality, planned high-density housing takes 44% less energy than unplanned urban sprawl.

Finally, the shift to service industries might accelerate. The CEQ's Russell W. Peterson looks for growth in what he calls "resource-lean jobs." But not all services use little energy, and Landsberg cautions that the so-called service economy is no panacea. "How many people can work in services," he asks, "without letting the store go to hell?"

Many questions still remain, and the DRI model needs careful scrutiny by economists. But for now, a consensus seems to be emerging that rising energy prices will save much more energy than once thought. To a nation long accustomed to the notion that more is better, the new conservation economics may require some wrenching changes. The rewards, however, are substantial. If energy growth is cut by half or more, the nation will achieve a cleaner environment, cut billions from its foreign oil bill, and conserve precious energy resources. Says Jack Gibbons, a conservation specialist at the FEO: "History will show that the oil embargo was a gift from the Arabs."

Alternative Energy Sources
Part I

Philip W. Quigg

The vast verbiage devoted to the energy crisis has dwelt largely on its immediate impact and on measures to cope with it. Less attention has been given to alternative sources of energy, because they cannot help us in our present predicament. Nor, in fact, can coal, oil, and gas in the very short term, for it will be some time before substantially larger quantities of those traditional fuels can be produced. The easy assumption that an abrupt switch to coal would save the situation has now been seen as an illusion; the coal industry can hardly meet its present commitments.

Nevertheless, it is indisputable that coal will recapture its former importance; no other source can make a major contribution to the energy supply over the next two decades. Coal now provides only 17.2 percent of U.S. energy—considerably less than that of Europe, substantially more than that of Japan. The environmental

Reprinted by permission from World Environment Newsletter (February 9 and 23, 1974), appearing as a regular feature in *Saturday Review/World.* © Philip W. Quigg.

consequences of increased reliance on coal will be profound, even if ways of purifying it are perfected.

The ready availability of coal in the United States must not be allowed to delay the search for alternative sources that are less detrimental to the environment. It is significant that Japan, which has no oil and limited coal, is planning to spend a far higher proportion of its GNP on research and development of non-fossil fuels than is the United States or Europe.

In examining the following analysis of so-called esoteric energy sources, one is struck by how long they have been around. Some, like coal gasification, geothermal, wind, and tides, have been in use for decades or centuries, while the theoretical potential of others has been known for at least a generation. With the sudden doubling and tripling in the costs of energy, every one of them appears to be economically competitive, if the technology can be developed or perfected.

For twenty-five years, cheap fuel and the promise of limitless nuclear energy have deterred any concentrated research into alternatives to oil and gas or the more efficient use of coal. In retrospect, our lack of foresight seems astounding. Yet more remarkable is the fact that even now in the United States, research into solar and geothermal energy, not to mention more remote technologies, is not being adequately funded. Of the projected $11 billion that the administration proposes to spend over the next five years on energy research and development, 96 percent is to be devoted to nuclear power (more than half) and fossil fuels, plus conservation. Even the $11 billion total is less than "the minimum viable effort" recommended by expert panels appointed by the administration.

The paucity of fundamental research and, even more, of pilot projects to test the feasibility of alternative energy sources enhances the difficulty of forecasting when and to what extent "new" sources will become significant. Billions of dollars have been spent so that we may learn how difficult it is to produce nuclear energy by means that are clean and safe. Having hardly begun to examine other alternatives to fossil fuels, we cannot know what technological pitfalls lie ahead.

But much more is involved than discovering new technologies. Most close observers of the energy problem agree with Chauncey Starr, who wears many energy hats, that "the most pressing energy need is for a coherent and long-range program to plan and manage our national and international energy systems. It takes ten to twenty years for a significant alteration in the trends of these huge systems. Waiting until the situation becomes intolerable must now be recognized as intentionally planned neglect—a societal irresponsibility difficult to condone."

Although there is enormous variation among estimates of how much energy may be derived from non-fossil fuels by the end of the century, a measure of consensus prevails on the following points: (1) none will be a significant factor for at least a decade, and (2) even by the end of the century, no new source of energy will have replaced fossil fuels. Most students of the energy problem (though not, apparently, governments) also agree that all potential sources should receive public financing—whether or not they have reached the pilot stage.

It can be argued, too, that the United States has special responsibilities to develop alternative sources. As consumer of 35 percent of the world's energy, as the largest producer of oil, and as the country with the largest reserves of coal, the United States not only is unusually blessed but also is in no small part responsible for the global energy shortage and soaring prices. What most countries of the world need is not merely the opportunity to buy fuels at now-inflated prices but also indigenous sources of energy. Some of the misnamed esoteric energy sources, notably the sun, are more promising prospects in the developing world of the tropic zone than in the industrialized nations. But it is the latter that must develop the technologies.

Concentration in this two-part series on new supplies of power neglects the importance of reducing the growth in demand through conservation and more efficient power generation. A leading example of the latter is the combined gas-steam turbine systems, in which propulsion technology developed by the aircraft industry is being applied to stationary power plants. The expectation is that present conversion efficiencies can be increased from a high of about 40 percent to 58 percent or even more in coal-fired systems that are virtually free of sulfur. Greater efficiency in power generation, mining and smelting, transportation, construction, and manufacturing, combined with a revised sense of values, may be the most promising alternative of all.

COAL GASIFICATION

The gaslight era was illuminated by coal. Since then research into ways to increase the heating value and lower the cost of coal gas has been occasionally energetic, more often fitful. Most of the research has been conducted in Western Europe, which had ample coal but no oil or natural gas until the recent discoveries in the North Sea. When pipeline technology made it possible to bring natural gas from the American Southwest to the East Coast, U.S. research on coal gasification withered. Now at least four different processes are being investigated.

To the layman, they all seem basically similar. The variants have to do with the size of the coal and how it is fed into the reactor, whether air or oxygen is used in combustion, whether the operation occurs under pressure, and whether the raw gas is methanated (by combining carbon monoxide and hydrogen). Some choices depend on whether the objective is to produce a gas high in BTUs, suitable as a substitute for natural gas and economically transportable by pipeline over long distances, or whether the aim is a so-called producer of gas of relatively low heating value but adequate for on-site electric generation. Each plant must be tailored to the characteristics of the coal used, which may vary enormously.

For humanitarian, environmental, and economic reasons (a rare and happy combination), the most desirable possibility is that coal can be gasified right in the underground seams—an idea first explored in the Soviet Union in the early Thirties. Following World War II, in situ gasification attracted worldwide interest, but experiments thus far have had very limited success. The process has proved difficult to control and has produced a gas of low quality. But experiments go on. In a new variant, which the AEC's Lawrence Livermore Laboratory is now testing, explosives are detonated at the bottom of a seam, making the bed permeable. Then the coal is ignited from the top, a mixture of steam and oxygen is pumped down the shaft, and gas is recovered from the bottom of the hole.

Environmental impact

Successful underground gasification is a goal ardently to be wished for. It will reduce the need for strip-mining, avoid the hazards of deep mining, minimize pollution, and reduce costs. Other methods of gasification do not have all those advantages but will reduce air pollution from the direct burning of high-sulfur coal. (See also "Coal Liquefaction.")

Prospects

The first commercial conversion plants are not expected until 1980, but with increased funding that schedule may be shortened, at least for producer gas. The newer processes have not reached even the pilot stage, and much engineering work is required.

COAL LIQUEFACTION

The technology for obtaining oil from coal has not proceeded much beyond the achievements of the Germans during World War II, when price was no object. The two processes they developed then still appear to be the most promising. Both remain complicated and expensive, and both require gasification as the first step. The more efficient of the two requires extremely high temperatures and pressures, which make reduction in costs difficult.

A distinction needs to be made, however, between coal oil that can be refined into synthetic substitutes for various natural petroleum products, such as gasoline, and that which can be made into a low-sulfur fuel for industry and utilities. The former involves more expensive and complex processes, but a modified form of coal liquefaction, designed primarily to remove pollutants before or during combustion rather than afterward, may prove more practical and economical than expensive stack-gas scrubbers.

Under one system—*solvent refining*—coal at high temperature and under pressure is converted into a molten mass in a solvent containing a small amount of hydrogen. The undissolved sulfur is then filtered off, and the solvent is distilled away. The refined coal can be fed in its molten state directly into a furnace, or it can be allowed to cool into a shiny solid for transportation elsewhere. The by-products removed in the process offset some of the costs, and the refined coal is both low in impurities and exceptionally high in heating quality.

Another system is called *fluid-bed burning,* because the combustion process gives the appearance of a bubbling boil. Finely ground coal is sprayed into a chamber and mixed with chips of limestone, which react with oxides of sulfur to form calcium sulfate. This can then be extracted, separated, and the limestone recycled.

Environmental impact

The most detrimental aspects of coal conversion, whether to gas or oil, lie in the vast quantities of coal—much of it strip-mined—that will be needed. To produce 100,000 barrels of synthetic oil requires 35,000 tons of coal per day—more than twice the output of the largest mines now being worked. Similarly, there will be an astronomical demand for water, which may have to be brought from long distances. Whatever the price to the environment, it simply is not known whether sufficient water will be available for coal gasification and liquefaction on a significant, hence economical, scale. (A liquefaction plant may cost half a billion dollars.)

Moreover, liquefaction produces nitrogen oxides, which can be removed only at high cost and with the consumption of large amounts of hydrogen.

Prospects

Obtaining oil from coal is technically more difficult and more expensive than coal gasification; hence its commercial production is probably more remote. The great attraction of liquefied coal is that it could be fed directly into existing pipelines and ultimately could alleviate the petroleum shortage. The U.S. Department of the Interior has one liquefaction plant in operation and another under construction. The navy has successfully tested a destroyer powered by oil produced from coal and hopes to start converting other ships within a few years. But unless there is a crash program, refined synthetics from coal oil are not likely to be widely available commercially until the next decade.

MHD

For the past ten years, studies have been conducted on the possibility of converting coal directly into electricity—an effort somewhat comparable to the alchemist's dream of turning lead into gold. MHD, or magnetohydrodynamics, involves burning coal or other fuels at high temperatures (4000° to 5000°F.) to produce a very hot ionized gas. The charged gas is passed through a strong magnetic field, and electrons are drawn off to form electric current. That is the theory; the problems have proved formidable and do not appear close to solution. Not the least of these is the formation of high concentrations of nitric oxide. MHD is still in the stage of fundamental research, although the Soviet Union is said to have two pilot plants in operation, and it appears to be further advanced with the technology than other nations are. Some scientists believe that other processes for achieving high thermodynamic efficiencies may completely overtake MHD, thereby making it redundant. Thermonuclear fusion would have the same effect.

OIL FROM SHALE AND TAR SANDS

In many countries shale oil was produced commercially before petroleum was discovered. In the intervening years, new processes for extracting oil from shale have continued to be tested, often in large pilot plants, but the estimated costs then seemed excessive. When the Department of the Interior offered leases on three tracts in 1968, no serious bidders could be found. But starting last month, six new tracts are being leased in Colorado, Utah, and Wyoming, which are thought to have 1.8 billion barrels of oil recoverable from shale. Each tract is 5000 acres in size but geologically different.

Oil shale is widely available, though its quality varies. The best yields thirty-five gallons or more per ton of shale. In the United States the oil potentially available in shale is believed to be forty times greater than proved oil reserves, including Alaska. Federal lands alone are believed capable of yielding 600 billion barrels of shale oil.

Vast quantities of oil or tar sand also exist; the largest and richest known are in Alberta. The Athabasca deposits are thought to contain 80 billion barrels of oil recoverable by methods now in use—and potentially much more. A sudsidiary of the Sun Oil Company has been operating there since 1967 at a loss of several million dollars a year. A large U.S.-controlled consortium, Syncrude, which hopes to be producing by 1978, is already spending $2 million a month on start-up costs.

Economics and technology

After oil sand has been mined, it is treated with a mixture of steam and hot water so that the oil can be extracted. Syncrude expects capital costs of $1 billion just to produce enough oil for a 100,000-barrel-a-day refinery.

Development of oil shale is likely to be more rapid, partly because scientists consider its chemical properties more promising. Even with high-grade shale, it takes 1.4 tons to produce a barrel of oil and leaves 1.2 tons of waste. The sheer volume of the raw material required virtually dictates that the oil be extracted where the shale is found. The shale may be mined first and then processed, or it may be liquefied *in situ*. The latter is accomplished by breaking up the shale to ensure permeability, then igniting the shale at the bottom of a hole drilled into the formation. At a temperature of 900°F, the hot gases created distill the hydrocarbons from the shale, and the oil is then drawn off into a second hole.

A variant of that method, now being tested, is to dig a cavern under the shale and set off an explosion. The fragmented shale collapses into the cavern and is thus made permeable in one stroke. It has not gone unnoticed that this process might be achieved even more simply and economically with nuclear explosives.

Environmental impact

It will be evident that obtaining oil from shale will impose heavy environmental costs in disruption of the land and in visual, air, and water pollution. A study by the Environmental Impact Assessment Project, sponsored by the Ford Foundation, asserts that in Colorado shale waste and water made saline in the mine operation will be dumped into the Colorado River. It also warns that toxic by-products released will include mercury, cadmium, lead, and fluorine.

Not only is the waste material enormous, but also by volume it will be considerably larger than the original shale, having been altered from finely stratified rock to rubble. A plant producing 50,000 barrels of oil daily will have to dispose of more than a ton of shale waste every second. The open firing of the shale will obviously cause air pollution; how much is a matter of dispute. Finally the process will require huge amounts of water; and in Colorado, where the highest grade of shale is found, water is already in short supply. Several environmental organizations are protesting the mining of oil shale, charging the Interior Department's final impact statement is inadequate.

Similarly, extracting oil from sand will require large amounts of water and leave vast quantities of waste. However, the Athabasca field is in a remote area several hundred miles north of Edmonton. Since the ground is spongy and sticky, alternative land uses are limited and sufficient water is available. Thus, the environmental impact should not be particularly adverse.

Prospects

The cost of producing shale oil commercially is believed to be in the neighborhood of five dollars per barrel, which would make it already competitive. But both the risks and the initial capital investment are high. Production in the United States is expected to start in 1978, and the Interior Department calculates that by 1985 approximately 1 million barrels per day may be produced. That is approximately 10 percent of the anticipated increase in demand for oil between now and then.

The Athabasca oil sands are now producing about 50,000 barrels a day. That figure may quadruple by 1980 and reach 1 million barrels by 1990—equivalent to the daily amount that Canada exports to the United States today.

WASTE

The great attraction of using waste as an energy resource is that it is there; no exploration is required to find it. On the contrary, means must be found to get rid of it. The burning of municipal waste to generate electricity and to provide steam for home heating has been practiced in Europe for many years. Now at least twenty U.S. cities and several industrial plants are doing, or planning to do, likewise.

In Milan, Italy, streetcars and subways will soon run on electricity from generators fueled by waste. A Philadelphia company intends to convert 90 percent of that city's waste into a marketable fuel that will be sold either in a finely shredded form or as briquettes. General Motors is planning to burn 55,000 tons of refuse a year from its own plants in the Pontiac, Michigan, area to furnish much of the energy needed by its truck and coach division. Nashville, Tennessee, will soon be burning its solid waste to provide air conditioning as well as heating.

The technology for separating waste into its component parts (organic matter, glass, metals) is available and advancing rapidly. After it has been shredded and separated by air blowers and vibrating screens, the combustible material (about 80 percent) is normally mixed with coal or oil so that it will burn more efficiently. In the much-publicized St. Louis experiment, waste makes up only 10 percent of the fuel. In a few instances boilers are fired entirely by shredded refuse; the most notable example is a generating plant on the outskirts of Paris.

Gasification and liquefaction

In more sophisticated systems, the refuse may be converted to gas or oil in much the same way that is being tried with coal. Hydrogenation converts the carbon content of the trash to oil, using high temperatures and pressures. A ton of dry waste produces about two barrels of oil (before subtraction of the fuel used in the process).

A slightly less efficient method is pyrolysis, a distillation process that produces both oil and a low-energy gas. Though it, too, requires high temperatures, the process takes place at atmospheric pressure—a considerable economy. Both of those methods are still in the experimental stage, but encouraging progress is being made. The Coors Brewery, outside of Denver, which has the largest brewing plant in the world, is experimenting with a gasification project fueled entirely by municipal trash and garbage. If early successes continue, all of Denver's municipal waste will be used to provide all of the brewery's fuel requirements.

The principal drawbacks to using refuse as a fuel are that its BTU output is low; it may cause corrosion in boilers; the variations in the content of the material from season to season and from place to place complicate efforts to achieve uniform combustion; and because neither the supply of refuse nor the demand for energy is constant, garbage may accumulate at times when demand for power is low and be insufficient at times of peak load. Also, since refuse can be used efficiently only in large generating plants, the costs of collection over a wide area may be high. In most cases, however, those costs are borne by the municipality and do not add to the costs of the fuel.

Fermentation

Many of these drawbacks do not apply to anaerobic decomposition, a method of accelerating decay of organic matter to produce the odorless, colorless gas, methane. Small plants can be highly efficient. There are more than 2500 bio-gas installations in India alone, and throughout East Asia many are just large enough to provide for the needs of a family or farm. The notion of "an anaerobic digestor in every home" is not entirely fanciful. Since there is an upper limit to the size of a digestor (the fermentation vessel), an installation to serve a city would require many digestors. But a farm family could meet all its energy requirements with a single unit, and urban dwellers might reduce their external needs by half.

Unlike methods that use waste for combustion, fermentation needs moisture and benefits from a combination of solid waste and sewerage; their chemical properties complement one another, and sewerage can provide the water that is needed. Thus waste from animal feedlots, dairies, canneries, and other agricultural processing; municipal trash and garbage; sewerage; and much more are grist for the fermentation mill. Each pound of organic matter can produce about ten cubic feet of methane, and the residue at the end of the four-to-seven-day process can be used as a clean, rich fertilizer, either sprayed onto fields in liquid form or dried for easier distribution. It may also be recycled as an animal feed.

Methane is inescapably produced in sewerage plants. In many places in Europe and Asia, the gas is captured and piped to homes and factories. In the United States it has generally been considered a nuisance; certainly no effort has been made to maximize its production. Elsewhere, too, fermentation has been used to reduce the bulk of waste or to produce nutrients rather than gas.

Environmental impact

The use of solid waste for power generation offers immense environmental benefits. It reduces the misuse of land for dumping refuse and lessens water and soil pollution. It also encourages the recycling of the glass and metals that must be removed.

To be sure, refuse is by no means a "clean" fuel when it is burned, and what goes into the garbage will affect what comes out as air pollutants. But as plants are converted to accept refuse, or new ones constructed, pollution controls can be built in.

Flywheels

Many means of storing energy are being explored. One of the most intriguing is flywheels. By virtue of stronger, lighter materials and more advanced design, engineers foresee giant flywheels operating in a partial vacuum at 3500 revolutions per minute and charged with 10,000 to 20,000 kilowatt-hours of energy for use in peak periods of demand for electricity. Smaller units with about 30 kilowatt-hours of stored energy would drive a small car for 200 miles at 60 miles an hour, and they could be recharged in five minutes. In terms of a barrel of crude oil, such a flywheel system would be five times more efficient than the internal-combustion engine and would be totally free of pollution in operation. Unused, the flywheel would keep its "charge" for at least six months.

Above all, perhaps, flywheels offer a means of storing the intermittent energy of sun, wind, and tides.

Processes for producing gas and oil from waste are cleaner and in turn produce fuels that are low in pollutants. Fermentation takes place in a closed system, and in terms of the process and the product (methane), it deserves the highest environmental marks of all conversion systems in commercial use.

Prospects

Most estimates of the potential of waste as a fuel are still highly theoretical, partly because we do not know how much waste we can practically collect. One U.S. estimate (by the Bureau of Mines) is 15 percent, though the smaller countries of Europe should easily exceed that figure. The least efficient process is burning of solid waste for direct generation of electricity or space heating and cooling. That is unlikely to exceed 1 or 2 percent of energy consumption anytime in the future. The greatest potential is for the production of methane, because fermentation uses all forms of waste, wet and dry, and because it requires minimal fuel in the process of conversion. Here the constraints are largely structural and institutional and, therefore, most difficult to forecast. Nevertheless, the mounting problems of waste disposal and the need to recycle metals, in combination with the energy shortage, should provide strong incentives to increase the use of waste as an energy source.

FLOWER POWER AND ALGAE

The farming of vegetable matter especially for burning (after sun drying and shredding) is most frequently proposed as a waste supplement to ensure a constant supply of fuel. Sunflowers and sugarcane are among the plants being tested, but the amount of farmland and water required to make a significant contribution to the fuel supply is staggering. Artificially stimulating algae growth may be more practical but the problems of harvesting and drying would be substantial. Others have suggested tree farms for fueling an on-site generator. One calculation has it that a tree plantation of 400 square miles could produce about 400 megawatts of electricity.

Although these fuels would be low in sulfur and their ashes could be returned to the soil, their use is otherwise unappealing. It would seem more logical to find ways to collect and utilize the lumbering and agricultural wastes that already exist. In terms of efficiency and land use, flower power (promoted as a form of solar energy) rates poorly and seems unlikely to come into commercial use.

Part II

THE NUCLEAR OPTION

The fission reactor

Of all non-conventional sources of energy, nuclear fission has received far and away the most development support. When the U.S. Atomic Energy Commission was founded in 1946, it expected that nuclear reactors generating electricity would become, without undue difficulty, our most important source of energy. It was anticipated that by about this time conventional fission reactors of the light-water or gas-cooled type would provide energy almost equal to that of the fossil fuels. The fission reactor's unique "clean air" characteristics appeared to make it a most desirable option. Nuclear fuels are a compact source of energy, and their use involves lower mining and transportation costs than coal requires: Water pollution, land disruption, and human injuries associated with mining are correspondingly reduced.

The rate at which nuclear power has entered into the production of electricity has been greatly disappointing to its supporters. In the United States there are some three dozen operating reactors, supplying about 5 percent of the nation's electrical capacity. Initial delays were largely related to the problem of establishing reliability and safety for commercial operation. More recently, fears have mounted concerning the environmental impact of large-scale use of nuclear fission. The optimistic period for fission technology ended around 1970.

Unforeseen natural disasters and human actions ranging from carelessness to deliberate sabotage are of critical concern. Of all sources of energy, nuclear fission is potentially the most hazardous to human health and to the environment.

The breeder

A further disadvantage of the conventional fission reactors in commercial operation today is that they utilize less than 1 percent of the energy in naturally occurring uranium. These reactors consume the fissionable uranium isotope U-235 (0.71 percent of natural uranium) and convert only small amounts of the dominant uranium isotope U-238 into fissionable plutonium. While experts differ as to the quantities of uranium that are economically recoverable, reliance on conventional fission reactors for a significant portion of our electrical energy demand would require the use of expensive, low-grade uranium ores. As a consequence, great emphasis has been placed on the development of the "breeder" reactor, which produces more fissionable material than it consumes and theoretically utilizes between 50 and 80 percent of the uranium.

However, breeders pack more energy into less space than the ordinary reactors do, making the possibility of a meltdown more frightening. Their radioactive wastes are much richer in highly toxic plutonium, the stuff of which weapons are made.

In the United States, the AEC is predicting that by the year 2000 there will be 900 nuclear power plants in operation, and the Federal Power Commission is renewing the prediction of three decades ago: that nuclear plants will meet 50 percent of the nation's energy needs within twenty to thirty years. Japan and some European countries foresee even greater dependence on nuclear fission, but some are meeting stubborn resistance from significant sectors of the public.

Fusion

The possibility of obtaining power from a controlled thermonuclear reaction has steadily receded in time. Some believe that the process will never be perfected; others forecast that significant power from fusion is possible by the end of the century.

The fusion process involves the interaction of very light atomic nuclei, such as hydrogen, to create highly energetic new nuclei, particles, and radiation. Over-simplified, the problem is how to contain the reaction at astronomically high temperatures and pressures. The fusion processes being explored include the magnetic containment of the fusion plasma (ionized gas) and laser-induced fusion. In the first process, the plasma is surrounded by a neutronmoderating blanket and contained by very large super-conducting magnets. The other process uses a giant laser pulse to impinge on a deuterium-tritium pellet.

The advantages of nuclear fusion are now legendary: for all practical purposes, an inexhaustible source of clean energy with minimal environmental impact, primarily thermal pollution. But control of the fusion process involves many scientific phenomena that are not yet adequately understood, and research has not yet reached the stage of engineering feasibility. Controlled nuclear fusion is conceptually attractive but has a highly uncertain outcome.

GEOTHERMAL

At least eighty nations have geological conditions indicating that the earth's heat is within potential reach as a source of energy. Today, usable geothermal energy is being produced only in the United States, the Soviet Union, Italy, Iceland, Japan, New Zealand, and Mexico. For the most part these developments are not recent but go back many decades—in the case of Italy, to 1904. The total electric power produced amounts to about 1100 megawatts, or the equivalent of a single large fossil-fueled power plant. Geothermal power is now being tapped in Kenya and Ethiopia, and serious exploration is proceeding in Turkey, Chile, El Salvador, Nicaragua, and Taiwan. It is in lands having a history—however ancient—of earthquakes and volcanoes that heat from the earth's molten interior can be expected to be within man's technological grasp.

Geothermal energy need not be converted to electricity to be useful. As in Reykjavik, Iceland, hot springs may be used for home and industrial heating, or they may be applied to desalinization and mineral separation. While some geothermal reservoirs have very hot water with temperatures as high as 550°F, others, such as those underlying Hungary and parts of the Soviet Union, are of relatively low temperatures (around 200°F) suitable for space heating and residential hot water.

The limited energy that has so far been tapped from the earth's interior has come entirely from sites of natural outcroppings of steam or hot water. These occur in only a few places in the world; the most notable example in the United States is the Geysers, ninety miles north of San Francisco, where efforts are being made to increase output from 237 to 1000 megawatts.

Any widespread use of geothermal energy requires exploratory drilling deep into the earth to reach either steam, hot water (also brine), superheated rock, or possibly magma (molten rock and gases).

The economics and technology

Geothermal steam is cooler than that normally used in power generation. This means lower efficiency and a higher capital investment per watt of output.

A Hydrogen Energy Regime

A chemical fuel having attractive qualities for replacing oil and gas is hydrogen, which is non-polluting and virtually inexhaustible. Moreover, it is an ideal form in which to store and transport other forms of energy, especially from such intermittent sources as the sun, wind, and tides. The proponents of hydrogen have used the term "the hydrogen economy" to describe a regime in which it would be the predominant fuel. As a gas, it would be delivered by pipeline to homes or plants for use directly by burning or by conversion to electricity in on-site fuel cells. Hydrogen would be burned in engines, as gasoline and other petroleum products are. It is a clean and efficient fuel for internal-combustion engines and appears to have good promise for aircraft propulsion. The range of aircraft would be increased two to three times for the same weight of fuel. Liquid hydrogen does have the disadvantage that it must be kept at very low temperatures.

Hydrogen is not a "natural" fuel, but it can be synthesized readily from conventional fuels or it can be produced simply by splitting molecules of water—including ocean water—into hydrogen and oxygen. This electrolysis process requires an input of electrical energy derived from new or old energy sources. Hydrogen may also be produced by biological processes and photosynthesis. Any organic matter would serve, including waste. Of all these processes, electrolysis now seems the most practical for large-scale use.

Environmental Impact

Hydrogen is a clean, non-polluting fuel. It is, however, a hazardous material that must be handled with all due precautions. We have had extensive experience with pipelining hydrogen over short distances, using

Hot water at high temperatures may be converted into steam for direct power generation. This is being done successfully, though with low efficiency, in New Zealand and at the relatively new plant at Cerro Prietto, Mexico. At lower temperatures the water must be used to heat a liquid that has a lower boiling point, such as Freon or isobutane, which in turn drives the turbines. One such plant using this so-called binary system is in operation in the Soviet Union, and another is planned.

The geothermal fluid may in fact turn out to be brine—with up to 30 percent solids (salt, silica, carbonates)—and highly corrosive. In this case a binary system is essential in order to keep the brine isolated. Enough hot brine is believed to be under the Imperial Valley in California to produce 20,000 megawatts for a century.

The most widespread and possibly the richest source of geothermal energy is probably dry hot rock, which can be used to heat water fed from the surface. To permit the water to pass over multiple surfaces of the rock and absorb its heat, water is initially pumped down the bore hole under high pressure, thus hydraulically fracturing the rock. The heated water then rises by natural convection through

---

pipeline materials and pressures similar to those for natural gas. Liquid hydrogen is regularly shipped in railroad tank cars and truck trailers. Handled with proper practices and in equipment designed to ensure its safety, hydrogen could be used without undue risk.

The transmission of energy via hydrogen in underground pipelines avoids the visual pollution, loss of energy, and misuse of land characteristic of the transmission of electricity via high-voltage power lines. Electrolysis facilities can be placed in the optimum locations either for utilizing fuel sources or for dispersing polluting by-products of the power production.

Among the most important advantages of hydrogen is that it adds to the feasibility of other energy sources, which may be limitless but variable (sun, wind, etc.) and can be converted to hydrogen at peak periods.

Prospects

A hydrogen-energy regime is already technically feasible. The cost of hydrogen produced from electricity must always be higher than the cost of the electricity. But its storage advantages and the lower transmission and distribution costs, compared with electricity, make it attractive. It should already be possible to sell hydrogen energy to the average customer at a price lower than he now pays for electricity and lower than he soon will pay for natural gas.

Perhaps the principal obstacle to be overcome is public fear of the hazards of hydrogen, sometimes described as the "Hindenberg syndrome." In part because of this concern, some have suggested "the methanol economy" could be a transition route from an oil to a hydrogen economy. Methanol, a synthetic compound of hydrogen, has the advantages of being safer, possibly cheaper, and more easily adaptable to the automobile.

a parallel bore hole, and after its heat has been tapped, it is returned by gravity to the underground rock in a continuous cycle.

So far this is theory, but it has been successfully tested to the extent that hydrofracturing (developed by the oil industry for reviving tired wells) can be achieved in granite and other crystalline rock formations at relatively modest pressures; and the cracks will not cause the water to leak away, as some feared. Thus the technology appears promising and will receive a full-scale test soon.

Scientists are now assessing a two-by-five-square-mile area near Marysville, Montana, where hot rock lies only a mile below the surface at a temperature of at least 932°F (500°C). It is estimated that for a period of thirty years, this relatively small source could provide nearly 10 percent of all the electricity now used in the United States. Experiments on removing this dry-rock heat will begin next summer, when an exploratory hole will have been completed.

Environmental impact

Geothermal energy is not so free of environmental consequences as some of its proponents suggest; its impact will vary widely with the quality of the steam and/or water that emerges and will be dependent on whether subterranean pressures prevent returning them to earth. If so, the problems of disposal may be formidable, though having adequate water for cooling is an asset, and relatively pure water may find agricultural and other uses. In the case of hot dry rock, substantial quantities of surface water will be required. In other respects, hot rock seems the most environmentally satisfactory source of geothermal energy. The fear that hydrofracturing, especially in earthquake-prone areas, may cause dangerous geological instabilities has been somewhat lessened.

In populated areas noise and odor pollution may be serious, though not insurmountable. Steam escaping under high pressure is ear-splitting, and the frequent presence of hydrogen sulfide, unless extracted, will fill the neighborhood with the odor of rotten eggs.

As with other forms of on-site power generation, which will be increasingly common, the electricity must be carried to where it is needed. This means an expansion of transmission lines with their attendant problems of land use, visual pollution, and energy loss.

Prospects

There is no question that geothermal energy offers a gigantic potential. For example, the Russians estimate that their geothermal potential is probably equal to their reserves of petroleum, coal, and lignite combined. Moreover, unlike many other so-called esoteric sources, the basic technology is at hand. The uncertainties lie largely in economics and geography. Little is known about costs of exploration and extraction. If geothermal energy is to be competitive in the near term, it will be only in those areas where the earth's heat is closed to the surface. In the United States, that means in the West, where the energy shortage is less severe.

Development in the United States has been excruciatingly and inexcusably slow. The R&D budget for this fiscal year is a paltry $11 million—and scheduled to rise to $40 million next year. Only this year are the first leases being issued for exploratory drilling on federal land—where most of the best prospects exist. Nevertheless, a study by the National Science Foundation estimates that by 1985 the United States will generate 132,000 megawatts of electricity from geothermal energy and that by the end of the century the output will reach 395,000 megawatts —or more than the total generating capacity of the United States today. From a different perspective, the Joint Atomic Energy Committee estimates that by the year 2000, geothermal will provide less than 5 percent of U.S. energy requirements.

SOLAR

The limitless potential of solar energy today captures some of the excitement generated by thermonuclear energy two decades ago, when its promise seemed imminent. The new interest in solar radiation is deserved, but again high expectations may be disappointed; years of neglect of this primordial source will not be overcome quickly.

By now every literate person has read something about solar energy; therefore we will encapsulate this section even further than others.

The possibilities

• *To supplement conventional methods of heating and cooling homes and commercial buildings* through the use of large panels that "collect" the sun's radiation and store it by transferring the heat to water, rocks, or (more recently) special salts. The technology is available, but each system and its components must be custom-designed. The usual objective in the north temperate zone is that solar energy should meet half the space-conditioning requirements of a given structure.

• In addition to heating, *to install solar cells that will convert the sun's heat directly into electricity* for household light and appliances. Excess power might be stored in conventional batteries, in flywheels, or chemically as hydrogen for use at peak periods of demand on public utilities. One experimental house combining space heating and photovoltaic conversion exists at the University of Delaware. Though the findings are not yet published, it is hoped that solar energy will provide 80 percent of the building's heating and electric needs at an added capital cost of 10 percent. With a fifteen-year amortization and abundant fuel savings, such a system would be highly competitive.

• *To capture the sun's thermal energy in a solar furnace by concentrating large amounts of solar radiation.* With parabolic mirrors or plastic lenses, automatically steered, the sun's rays would be focused on a large boiler, probably mounted on a tower. The heat would be converted to electricity initially by a steam turbine generator, with possibly more sophisticated methods to follow.

• *To generate massive quantities of electricity from solar heat captured in hundreds of miles of pipe containing a liquid with a low boiling point.* The pipe, laid out in deserts or raised above grazing land, would be coated with a material designed to allow solar radiation to penetrate but not to escape. In theory, the amount of electricity that could be generated is limited only by the high capital costs and amount of land that could be devoted to the purpose. Such a project would be practical only in areas of maximum sunshine. Much further research is required.

• *To put into synchronous orbit one or more giant satellites with solar cells spread out over several miles, which would transmit electric energy by microwave to earth stations.* Placed in pairs, so that one was always outside the earth's shadow, such satellite stations could provide an uninterrupted supply of energy. The financial and energy costs of placing the satellites in orbit would, however, be astronomical.

Of these possibilities, only space heating and cooling and small-scale conversion to electrical energy are in any sense imminent. Since the basic technology is available, the key question is how far and how rapidly mass production can reduce costs.

Environmental impact

Although solar energy may be the most non-polluting of all sources, it of course has environmental implications.

Solar ranching clearly has important consequences for land use. Hundreds of miles of heat-absorbing pipe extending over vast areas of desert may be viewed either as a productive use of waste land or as an insult to the natural environment and especially to its fauna. The same would be true of the huge antenna required to receive microwaves from space and convert them into electricity.

Extensive use of solar energy may cause one other form of pollution not often mentioned: visual pollution. The incorporation of solar collectors into structures of attractive and varied design will be a severe challenge to architects. Because these solar panels must be oversized in relation to the structure, because they must all face south (in the Northern Hemisphere) and at approximately the same angle, the appearance and orientation of houses may leave much to be desired.

In any case, the environmentally adverse aspects of solar energy are minor compared with its assets as a potentially unlimited source of clean energy that is available everywhere.

Prospects

It is possible that solar heating units will be commercially available in five years. Much testing remains to be done to determine which systems and their components are most reliable and economical. How rapidly solar heating is thereafter adopted will depend on many factors involving attitudes and incentives. The most important motivation will be the shortage of fuel oil and electricity as it is felt by the individual consumer at the end of the decade.

More ambitious schemes for converting solar radiation to electricity are fairly distant. Thus the use of the sun as an energy source will evolve slowly, in part because there are no economies of scale.

In the United States, the Joint Atomic Energy Committee anticipates that solar energy will constitute about 6 percent of the supply by the year 2000. Taking a longer look, a Solar Energy Panel formed by the National Science Foundation and NASA estimated that by the year 2020 solar energy "could" provide as much as 35 percent of the nation's space heating and cooling and 20 percent of its electricity.

Perhaps the brightest prospect for solar energy is in the developing world. If photovoltaic cells can be mass-produced at reasonable cost, there is the possibility that the most remote area can have enough electricity.

WIND

Windmills were first used to generate electricity in Denmark more than eighty years ago, and it is in that country that the most successful large wind turbine is found. Yet its output is only 200 kilowatts. The most ambitious experiments have been in the United States, the Soviet Union, Germany, and India; most were undertaken many years ago, and their lack of success did little to encourage further research and development.

Today, however, there is not only fresh motivation, but also new, lighter materials, improved understanding of aerodynamics, and more efficient means of storage. Whereas the most celebrated U.S. experiment (in the Forties in Vermont) used a two-bladed propeller 175 feet in diameter and weighing sixteen tons, today's experiments use lightweight propellers with a diameter of six to twenty-five feet and advanced aerodynamic design.

Since the energy available in a twenty-mile-an-hour wind is eight times that at ten miles an hour, there is obviously a premium on placing turbines where the wind is strong as well as steady. One suggestion is to put floating windmills off the Atlantic coast. Twenty to fifty thousand would provide the base load for a good part of the East Coast; when the wind fails, conventional power plants would meet power needs. Another plan is to place windmills atop existing transmission towers. One student calculates that there is enough wind over the western plains to supply half the electric-power requirements of the United States.

Almost the only objection that can be raised to wind power on environmental grounds is that it will cause visual pollution. Technologically advanced wind generators scattered by the tens of thousands over several states would lack the appeal of windmills of old.

A new age of sail?

One of the most fascinating possibilities is that square-rigged cargo ships, entirely automated and capable of speeds of twelve to sixteen knots or more, can be made as reliable as, and more economical than, freighters fueled by oil. As with windmills, the technology relies on new light materials and on advanced aerodynamic design. According to plans developed by German engineers, sails would be set, trimmed, and furled by push button from the bridge. The ships would have auxiliary power and would not be suitable for all runs. But in the heavily trafficked North Atlantic, for example, the wind is said to be reliable 85 percent of the time.

TIDES

Despite millennial interest in the power of tides, there are only two places on earth where it is being harnessed to generate electricity—one in the Soviet Union, which generates 400 kilowatts, and one in northern France, which generates 240,000 kilowatts. Though much more could be done to capture tidal energy, the opportunities will always be limited geographically: There are not many places where the difference in elevation between high and low tide—the head—is sufficient to make electricity generation practical.

Tidal installations of the future will almost certainly have special holding basins, pumped storage, flywheels, or hydrogen conversion to provide constant power from intermittent tides. The most likely site is Canada's Bay of Fundy, where the fifty-foot head is the highest in the world.

The required dams across bays or estuaries obviously will have an impact on the marine environment, which must be studied in each case.

OCEAN CURRENTS

The unimaginable energy in ocean currents may be tapped using "underwater windmills." The Florida Current, only one component of the Gulf Stream, is said to carry fifty times the flow of all the freshwater rivers of the world. Near the surface it moves at speeds that sometimes exceed 5.5 miles per hour. If the total flow between Miami and Bimini could be harnessed, it would amount to about 25,000 megawatts.

So far, an experimental turbine has not even been designed, and some doubt that the low RPMs could generate electricity economically. But the attractions are obvious: Usable currents are moderately widespread in the world; they are relatively constant; the energy would be pollution-free; and the environmental impact on the marine or coastal environment would be minimal.

THERMAL GRADIENTS

These same qualities apply to thermal gradients, a term that describes the fact that surface waters in the ocean may be as much as 45°F warmer than the water at 1000 feet or more. This difference can be a source of energy.

The warm water would flow through a heat exchanger, causing another fluid —probably ammonia—to boil. The vapor would drive a turbine to produce electricity, which might be carried to shore by cable or used *in situ* to extract hydrogen from seawater. Cold water from lower depths would then be used to cool the vapor back into a liquid, and the cycle would start over.

The potential of thermal gradients has been known for at least half a century. In 1929 a Frenchman produced 22 kilowatts of useful power, using a thermal gradient of less than 20°F. Until quite recently, almost all research in the field was conducted by France.

Although efficiency is low, many claim that the system can easily be made competitive. An added bonus is the fact that nutrients from deep-sea water can be used to great advantage in the cultivation of shellfish. From an environmental viewpoint, thermal gradients appear to be most desirable.

Its wide adoption may be slowed by the fact that extremes of water temperature are not found where energy demand is greatest. The principal potential is in tropical or sub-tropical waters. In the long run thermal gradients could become an important source of energy for many developing nations.

The Energy Crisis and the Manufacturer

James K. Brown

Since the onset of the energy crisis the sales of a Midwest manufacturer of truck and car equipment have increased. So have the sales of a maker of energy-related machinery. Another firm in the same field has gained business from entrenched competitors—and believes, furthermore, that the prospect of crisis-related layoffs will help the firm's position in its upcoming labor negotiations.

But reports of such blessings in disguise are few and far between among most manufacturers, at least according to a recent Conference Board survey of the

From *The Conference Board Record,* June, 1974. Reprinted by special permission of The Conference Board.

sector. Of 242 firms representing 32 industries,[1] over 80% describe the effects of the crisis as "severe or worrisome" in terms of both the cost and the availability of raw materials; and almost half of them have had considerable difficulty in controlling production costs and meeting consumer delivery schedules.

Selected Effects of the Energy Crisis

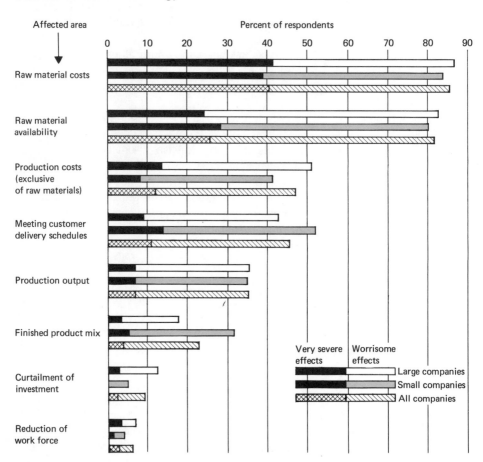

[1]The participants in this survey included: 157 members of the Board's Survey of Business Opinion and Experience panel comprised of manufacturing companies ranging in size from annual sales of about $50 million to the largest firms in the country ("large companies" in this article); and 85 manufacturing members of the Board's Managing the Moderate-Sized Company survey panel, made up of companies with, a couple of exceptions aside, sales considerably less than those of the smallest firms on the first panel ("small companies" in the text).

Among small firms there has been a greater incidence of "severe" problems than among large firms in three areas—in cost and availability of materials and in meeting schedules. In general, however, neither size of company nor type of industry affected the pattern of response—negative effects of the shortfalls have been uniform and pervasive. Furthermore, while very few firms report layoffs or curtailment of investment, the ranking of problem areas (see chart) accords roughly with the typical sequence of the production process—which suggests that the areas in which the impact of the crisis has been relatively light may become troublesome if the shortages persist.

Only 16 firms describe their problems as minor or nonexistent in the eight areas specified by the survey. However a number of companies report severe problems outside of these eight categories. Shortages of fuel, construction and maintenance materials, purchased equipment and hardware were cited by seven firms. Seven others have experienced marketing problems—reduced customer demand (in the case of automobile makers), cancelled orders, reduced mobility of salesmen and increased sale call expense. Others tell of difficulties in planning, forecasting and budgeting, of increased transportation costs, supplier delays, problems for commuting workers and curtailment of new product development.

A number of firms qualify their responses by noting that for them the impact of the energy crisis varies from negligible to very severe, depending upon which operating unit is in question; and some observe that shortages of particular forms of energy have been experienced only in certain geographic areas. For one or another of these reasons others surveyed find it difficult to describe the overall impact of the crisis.

What forms of energy have caused significant problems for these manufacturers? Fuel oil and natural gas are cited by over half the companies. Gasoline and petrochemical feed stocks have been especially troublesome for between 40 and 50% of the firms. Electric power comes fifth, cited by 38.1%, and coal stands at the bottom, with only 16.1% designating it as a significant problem.

To the question of whether it has been high cost or lack of availability at the root of the problem, the predominant answer is "both"—for all forms of energy except electric power for which high cost has been by far the most common experience.

COMBATIVE MEASURES

By far the most common reaction among manufacturers to problems caused by the energy crisis has been to raise prices to cover cost increases—more than three-fourths of the companies queried have done so.

Speaking to the gravity of the cost/price spiral, a chemical company spokesman comments:

> The shortages are having a greater proportionate effect on prices than at any time I can recall. For example, we are now paying three times as much for fuel

oil as we were four years ago. The price of polypropylene resin has already jumped 32% in 1974. The rapidity of price changes associated with this energy crisis seems to be its most unique characteristic.

And an executive of a construction company observes:

> The principal impact of the energy crisis on our company has been in the production area with costs soaring as a result of fuel price increases. These increases since early 1973 have ranged up to almost 300% for fuel oil. 100% for natural gas. These dramatic increases have led us to convert three of our cement plants to petroleum coke as a replacement for either fuel oil or natural gas. However, this fuel is now in short supply, and conversion of other plants does not appear feasible.

More of the small companies surveyed have raised prices than large ones; however, a number of firms, both large and small, point out that on account of competition or price controls they have been able to offset cost increases only partially or only for certain products. It is not surprising, then, that some 73% of the companies have turned to energy conservation measures, sometimes incorporating them in a formal program with specific goals and monitoring of results. Such measures include curtailing office use of fuel and light or reducing use of company vehicles (or replacing old ones with small models).

Other steps taken, in order of incidence, include: using substitute raw materials, changing production processes or techniques, investing in energy-saving equipment, simplifying product lines, rationing customers and, in very few instances, closing production facilities. Some firms report special efforts to keep in close touch with their utilities and with the energy problems of their suppliers. Others have been able to develop their own energy sources, or have used substitutes—oil and coal

---

Confusion Still Prevails . . .

In this community in the Middle West where many employees live in countryside situations and drive to their place of employment, gasoline lines have been long, gasoline supplies replaced sex as the top priority subject of locker room conversation, and indignation at oil companies, gas pump jockeys, tank truck operators, and wandering Arabs, runs high. Nevertheless, the buses of our public transporation system still run empty, the parking lots at the local high schools are jammed, the ear-splitting whine of the snowmobile and the Yamaha is heard far into the night, and our rather carefully studied efforts to assist employees to set up car pools based upon carefully plotted and widely distributed residential zones has been received with a wave of apathy.

In our part of the Middle West the electric companies, several years ago, thoughtfully commenced collaboration with the manufacturers groups, talking about projected energy demands, sources of fuel, costs of

for natural gas, for example. Still others have initiated programs to reclaim and recycle materials.

ENDURANCE TEST AHEAD?

Over half the companies surveyed believe they will be severely and indefinitely hampered by energy shortfalls. Another 25% think the worst will be over within a year.[2] Smaller companies seem more optimistic in this respect than large ones.

A variety of comments and suggestions are offered along with these predictions. One firm sees the crisis disappearing with the lifting of wage and price restraints. Another says the situation will remain severe until that unknown time when new energy sources or processing capacities are on stream. A third believes conditions will improve in the next six to 12 months—and then worsen again until new refinery capacity is available "some years hence." And a fourth, more pessimistic still, is convinced that the era of low-cost energy is a thing of the past.

The spokesman for a manufacturer of office equipment and computers predicts "intolerable squeezes on the conventional resources" and capital investments of "huge amounts never before contemplated" to solve the long-range requirements of industry. But dramatic cost increases are, in his opinion, "not all bad," and he offers a relatively calm appraisal of the near future: "It merely requires a reordering of how we use our energy sources and in what quantities. For the next five years industry and the general public must reduce their consumption. All of us have become extraordinarily wasteful in our habits. We must and can learn to live with a lot less power. Since there is only a finite amount of energy available from known sources, these should be conserved in a more diligent manner. Technology eventually will find new and substitute sources, but in the meantime we can all live very normal lives if we use our heads."

---

fuel, lead time for generating stations and new sources for energy. The net result has been the orderly development of nuclear plants, including their activation, and we do not face a brownout.

However, as I view the situation nationwide—and we have a number of widely distributed plants—the country is not yet at the point where enough collective sanity has developed to bring about a collective cool-headed approach to the problem analysis. Intellectually, the approach to our energy adequacy challenge is still on the same level as the discussions of the Equal Rights amendment to the U.S. Constitution or permissive abortion laws. Until we can get the discussion moved away from the microphones and the television cameras and into conference rooms and laboratories, confusion is likely to prevail.

—A Wisconsin hardware manufacturer

---

[2]The survey participants made their responses in March.

Several companies hesitate to isolate their energy-related problems from others they have experienced in recent months. A communications and electronic equipment manufacturer, for instance, attributes its own hard times to a combination of inflationary pressures, raw materials shortfalls, and overloaded production facilities. Inflation is named the major problem, too, by a motor vehicle maker. A hardware company cites "impractical OSHA requirements and environmental laws" as more worrisome than the energy crisis. And a drug manufacturer finds that "shortages in many areas, particularly petrochemical feed stocks, have been exacerbated by domestic price ceilings which are too low relative to world prices."

The difficulty of singling out a problem center is perhaps best summed up by the executive of a chemical company:

> Many of the problems we are encountering in regard to raw material costs and availability are not due solely to the energy crisis. A more chronic situation has existed for a number of years. While connected with energy, it is due to a number of seemingly disparate but actually interlocking factors such as: controls of natural gas prices at the wellhead, environmental concerns and legislation, oil importation quotas and, recently, economic controls. The latter have led to severe anomalies in supply due to artificially high exports and the hoarding of materials.
>
> The other factors have occasioned the major oil companies to invest in refining capabilities overseas rather than in this country; thus, given an adequate supply of crude, there will still be shortages of petrochemicals synthesized from feed stocks. This problem has been with us for two to three years now and will persist for another two to five years. It's a complex situation which goes beyond the rubric, "The Energy Crisis."

One Prescription . . .

What the nation and the energy producing companies need is a floor— not a ceiling—price for crude oil that will cause a market level for energy equivalent to approximately $7.00 per barrel for crude oil.

We feel that very few economists, politicians, members of the Administration or citizens can comprehend the need for this price floor: Since the 1950s the price of oil and natural gas have determined, and thereby severely limited, the development of coal, shale oil and nuclear energy. Given this historical record there is too much reticence on the part of the energy companies to develop these forms of energy.

If by government edict or by law there were set a floor price of $7 to $8 a barrel for crude oil it would remove the doubts and fears of many companies, I believe, and they would proceed to develop these other forms of energy which are so sorely needed.

—A supplier of equipment to drillers and
producers of crude oil and natural gas

SELECTED READINGS

"Energy Crisis, Shortages Amid Plenty," *New York Times,* April, 1973 (a series of articles).

The Energy Problem and the Middle East. (New York: American Academic Association For Peace In The Middle East, 1973).

"Enough Energy—If Resources Are Allocated Right," *Business Week,* April 21, 1973.

Faltermayer, E. "The Energy Joyride Is Over," *Fortune,* January, 1972.

Freeman, S. D. *Energy: The New Era.* (New York: Walker and Company, 1974.)

Lessing, L. "Capturing Clean Gas: Oil From Coal," *Fortune,* November, 1973.

Netschert, B. C., "Energy vs. Environment, *"Harvard Business Review,* January–February, 1973.

Wilford, J. N., "The Long-Term Energy Crisis," *The New York Times,* April 19, 1973.

Case

ALLIED POWER AND LIGHT COMPANY*

Jim Bell, vice-president for operations at the Allied Power and Light Company, was facing his perennial problem again. The 1974 forecast for electric-power use in the 3000 square miles covered by Allied showed at least a fifteen-percent increase in demand. This would be the second year in a row that usage increased by 15 percent. Over the last three years, electric-power use in the area had jumped by over 13 million kilowatts.

Allied's six major power-generating stations—at their present peak output—could produce ninety percent of forecast demand and the situation promised to be tight. Over the past few years, Allied had little difficulty in purchasing power from the Northeast Power grid. Now, however, Bell knew that there would be little help in meeting the increased demand from that source. The Northeast grid was being severely strained and already was buying as much Canadian electricity as possible. Allied had also been told that the Mid-Atlantic grid could not help either. For short periods in the past, Allied had even purchased

---

*This case was researched by Joseph Thomas. Copyright 1974 Joseph Thomas, Dennis Callaghan and Arthur Elkins. All rights reserved.

power from TVA and the North Central grid, but these sources could not be considered reliable full-time suppliers.

Bell also knew that his maintenance schedule called for the shutdown for thirty days, in August, of the company's 3-million-kilowatt generating station at Dunston. August was generally a fairly predictable month, with power requirements rarely going above ninety-two percent of peak capacity. Barring an unexpected lengthy heat wave, Allied could probably get through the shutdown period. Potentially more serious was the projected September shutdown of the 2.26-million-kilowatt Mount Catherine plant. It would be three months before Catherine was on line again and, even though that plant's output would be doubled, Bell was banking on a mild autumn and a late winter. And of course, the company also planned on no delay in the delivery of the new generators, no unexpected damage or additional repairs to the present generators, and no accidents during start-up. Bell always remembered, with some hope that it wouldn't happen to Allied, Consolidated Edison's year-long loss of *Big Alice,* their enormous generator in the Catskills. Three months of repair work slowly drifted into a year of brownouts, customer irritation, and increases in costs. The *Big Alice* story was very useful in sobering the sometimes overly optimistic estimates of utility engineers. However, at both of the Allied stations, maintenance shutdowns were predicted to be routine. Even if everything went wrong, Allied could perhaps be able to buy replacement power from the grid, and customers wouldn't be inconvenienced to any great extent, provided the plans for the Southport facility were fulfilled.

The cornerstone of Allied's system was the Southport plant, now delivering just over 12 million kilowatts at peak. Careful planning by Bell's predecessor and top management resulted in completion of the installation at Southport of two huge turbines and four new generators, whose added capacity would permit Allied to face the future with equanimity—12 million additional kilowatts would become available, doubling the capacity of the plant. Allied could even sell power to the grid if it could simply get these new turbines rolling.

However, the new steam-generated plant at Southport was built to be oil-fired, and the additional oil wasn't readily available. Allied had been forced to renegotiate its contracts for oil deliveries when prices had risen drastically, and the old three-year level-price contracts seemed to be gone forever. Only annually renewable contracts were being written and these contained escalator clauses; and no contracts could be negotiated with new suppliers or for increased oil supplies. Bell even requested that the company look into the possibility of arranging for the purchase of tanker loads of oil from a broker, but either purchase price or tank-farm storage fees were found to be prohibitively high.

Now he was considering alternative fuels, all with immediate and long-range difficulties.

Bell's initial reaction was to consider converting his boilers from oil to gas. The cost of changing burner tips, atomizer plates, and distribution piping and valves was found to be minimal—little more than $25,-000. Should oil subsequently be more readily available, reconversion in short order was possible. The alteration of one storage tank was considered necessary because the gas company felt that a high-volume tank was required. Otherwise, fluctuations in line pressure because of changing firing rates could have serious effects on service to other customers. Cleaning, repair, and alteration of a tank and its piping would cost about $110,000.

Difficulty arose when Bell asked the gas company to quote him a cost forecast. While the gas at present prices was a real bargain, compared to the cost of oil, the gas company warned that the price differential probably would not continue. They stated that the oil companies were confident that controls on natural gas wellhead prices would soon be lifted and that natural gas prices would rise to the level of oil prices. If that did not occur, the gas company predicted that oil firms would curtail their gas production, since the low return makes natural gas insufficiently profitable.

With supply a problem, Bell asked one major supplier about the possibility of negotiating an option for the purchase of natural gas. He estimated an annual usage of 15 billion cubic feet, and in order to obtain the best possible leverage, offered to convert Mount Catherine to gas-firing; in the late spring of next year, either Mount Alpin or Dunston could be converted. The supplier's representative refused, explaining that he could not consider granting an option on such a quantity of gas at present prices. Some gas customers had to accept smaller supply allocations, so he could not accept new large orders even if customers were willing to pay premium prices. He referred to the problems being experienced by two Southern California utilities, each of which held purchase options on natural gas; now there was a hotly contested attempt by the larger utility to raid the smaller utility's allocation, on the grounds of the greater good for the greater number.

Bell looked into coal as an energy source. He found that coal could be used in any of three ways to fire his boilers. It could be powdered and blown in, pumped in as a slurry, or liquefied (or gasified) outside the boiler and then introduced as a synthetic oil. The latter procedure was technically the most sophisticated and the costs promised to be competitive with oil, provided the process could be carried out in large enough quantities. The startup costs appeared to be high and the waste disposal was a problem not yet solved, since much of the coal was not liquefied. The major problem, however, was that, while the process was theoretically sound, and limited pilot runs had been promising, the actual hardware was untried, the long-term effects on the firebox efficiency were unknown, and the operating techniques were neither complete nor proven.

Atomization (or introduction of powdered coal under pressure) had been demonstrated with apparent success several times. Special equipment, however, was required; crushers and mills were needed to powder the coal, special piping was required to bring the coal to the boiler front, and unique burners were needed. It appeared, too, that the boilers were altered significantly in their operating characteristics. They could, because of the high efficiency of the burners, easily be overfired. They were slow to adjust to changes in the firing rate, because of the very intense heat of the flame, which kept firebox temperatures very high. The cost of the new equipment amounted to about $50,000 per boiler; for Southport with seven boilers, this would mean a significant expenditure. Reconversion usually required reconstruction of the boiler and would cost on the order of $100,000 per boiler.

Slurry was more efficient. Again, crushers and mills powdered the coal and the powdered coal was then suspended in water. This suspension was agitated and injected into the boiler piping at very high pressure, using special booster pumps. The mixture was then forced through atomizing orifices and injected into the firebox as an aerosol, which burned with remarkable efficiency. It was a sophisticated and efficient system; after installation its cost of operation was very competitive with oil. It did require special pumps, mixing tanks, high-pressure lines, special burners, and special handling equipment, and reconversion was slow and expensive, since the entire boiler front had to be dismantled. Bell estimated that the cost for installation would be about $65,000 per boiler, and reconversion would be about the same price. It would not be necessary to reconstruct the firebox, however.

Coal was available and favorable contracts appeared negotiable. It would be possible to store the coal on land now owned by Allied and on land that could be leased. A land owner was already contacted and had no objection to storage of coal on his property; he tentatively agreed to a figure for rental of his land and granted the utility an option on the property, giving it first refusal of lease rights.

However, other problems were present with coal usage. The state environmental protection commission had to be consulted; a request was submitted to them for a waiver of certain provisions of the air-pollution standards. Allied emphasized that the request was purely preliminary.

Bell quickly found that coal was not an easy solution to his problem. The state environmental protection commission was by no means eager to grant a waiver. It was their contention that the conversion to coal was not necessary, and that the utility had not yet exhausted the possibility of purchasing additional fuel oil. They pointed out that the state public-utility regulations permitted the increased cost of fuel oil to be passed on to the consumer. They felt therefore that the higher cost of fuel oil was not germane to the request for a waiver.

Bell knew, however, that the state legislature was seriously consider-ing eliminating the fuel factor pass-on provision. Over the past year, electricity consumers had found that their bills had nearly doubled and that this increase was due solely to increased fuel costs. Some were refusing to pay the special fuel assessment. This movement was not a serious threat to Allied at the present time, and there was no expectation that a widespread consumer revolt was about to take place, but the sentiment had reached the legislature and some lawmakers were seri-ously considering repealing the authority granted to utilities to pass on the increased fuel cost.

Repeal of the fuel factor would mean that the utility would be forced to put particular emphasis on fuel costs in the future; the extra costs of conversion of boilers and their ancillaries and fuel storage would be ever more serious, and, of course, profits would be sharply reduced—all at a time when capital costs for utilities were extremely high.

Bell knew that the environmental protection commission was reason-ably amenable to permitting the burning of low sulfur-content coal. Low-sulfur coal was available in quantity from a number of mining firms in southern Illinois; the price was competitive with oil and the average sulfur content was low enough to permit its being burned with a minimal variance from the state's air-pollution standards. Unfortunately, a long-standing policy of the utility prohibited the purchase of strip-mined coal. The policy dated back nearly forty years when members of the then controlling board of directors, who also held interests in several Penn-sylvania anthracite mines, managed to enact a prohibition against the utility's purchasing anything but anthracite coal from deep mines.

While Bell thought such a policy was out of date, the present board, knowing the distaste with which many of the company's customers viewed the operations of strip mines (there were nine colleges with over 55,000 students in Allied's service area) refused to lift the prohibition. What started as a matter of self-interest for individuals became a matter of enlightened self-interest for the firm. Bell approached the chief exec-utive officer about the possibility of changing the policy on the purchase of coal, but was discouraged. The board of directors had no desire to give any appearance of supporting strip mining when so many of the utility's customers were ardent environmentalists.

Thus Bell couldn't supply his present customers' needs without additional fuel; he could purchase little additional oil, and natural gas supplies seemed unavailable at any price. Low-sulfur coal was available but the costs of conversion were high and the company's policy against purchase of nonanthracite coal seemed unlikely to be altered.

Present Capacities of Generating Stations

Jefferson	8,000,000 kw	
Southport	12,000,000 kw	(Presently being modified)
Mount Alpin	5,000,000 kw	
Hancock	4,000,000 kw	
Dunston	3,000,000 kw	(To be repaired in August)
Mount Catherine	2,260,000 kw	(To be modified, Sept.-Dec.)
Total	34,260,000 kw	
Present Demand	*38,062,125 kw*	
Shortage	*3,802,125 kw*	

Projected Capacities by January

Jefferson	8,000,000 kw
Southport	24,000,000 kw
Mount Alpin	5,000,000 kw
Hancock	4,000,000 kw
Dunston	3,000,000 kw
Mount Catherine	5,200,000 kw
Total	49,200,000 kw

Projected Demand

1974	38,062,125 kw
1975	43,771,444 kw
1976	50,337,161 kw

E. U.S. Investment Abroad: South Africa

A little over one percent of total United States overseas investment is in South Africa —about $1 billion. Yet that relatively small stake in another country has created an issue for some American managers as to the appropriateness of American investment in a society with policies distasteful to most Americans.

The problem raised by South African investment revolves about the official racial policy of the South African government: apartheid. Apartheid (literally, separation of the races) encompasses a broad spectrum of laws and regulations designed to prevent whites and blacks from integrating. Officially, the policy is said to encourage separate development of the races with eventual independence for the black-populated areas (bantustans). However, critics contend that the policy, which involves petty harassment as well as more serious racial restrictions and is resulting in quite uneven development of whites and blacks, is discrimination, pure and simple, and is designed to maintain white supremacy.

South Africa is a relatively large country situated at the lower tip of Africa. The country is one of the world's leading producers of diamonds and the world's largest exporter of gold, major sources of its wealth. South Africa sits on the crossroads for the major markets of Europe and Asia, and its geographic position is strategic. Even with the Suez Canal open, major ships, which cannot navigate the Canal, must round the Cape of Good Hope at the tip of Africa.

The total population of South Africa is 21.4 million, of which 3.8 million are white, 15 million black, and 2.6 million Asian or colored, the official South African term for people of mixed race. The white population is divided between Afrikaaners, or the descendants of the Dutch, German, and Huguenot settlers (the Boers) and English-speaking peoples.

South Africa has an interesting history. The Dutch East India Company settled the original colony in 1652 and administered the land until the British occupied the territory in 1795. Independent Boer republics, the Orange Free State and the Transvaal, were established in the 1850's, and a confederation of the Boer Republics and the British colonies was attempted in the 1870's. But the British and the

Boers had several irreconcilable differences, not the least among them the less liberal policy of the Boers toward the native population. In 1899, the Boer War broke out; it ended in 1902 with British occupation of the two Boer republics. In 1910, the various states (Orange Free State, Transvaal, and the former British colonies, Natal and the Cape of Good Hope) were merged into the Union of South Africa, until 1961 a self-governing dominion of the British Empire. In 1961, South Africa, under the administration of the Afrikaan Nationalist Party, withdrew from the British Commonwealth of Nations and declared itself a republic.

South Africa's geographical position isolates it from the ferment against racism and colonialism present in the rest of the African continent. Partially separating South Africa from newly independent African nations are Rhodesia and Mozambique,* both white-dominated areas, as well as the United Nations Trust Territory of Namibia, currently controlled by South Africa. South Africa is under fire from the vast majority of the nations of the world for her unwillingness to relinquish control of Namibia, formerly South West Africa. Although the original mandate granted South Africa by the League of Nations in 1919 has been rescinded by the United Nations, and a World Court opinion has ruled South Africa's continued domination over Namibia illegal, South Africa refuses to relinquish jurisdiction.

Today almost four hundred United States firms are involved in the South African economy (including many of the giants of American industry). One group of critics contends that this involvement bolsters an essentially racist regime and is demanding that U.S. firms pull out of South Africa as a means of weakening apartheid. Some corporations remain silent on the issue, hoping the clamor will dissipate. But others respond that their presence actually benefits the black population, a position supported by another group of critics, who, nevertheless, would like to see American firms take steps (beyond mere presence) to combat apartheid.

Like most matters, there is probably some substance to the positions of both sides. No doubt, industrial development strengthens the economic system of South Africa, nourishes self-sufficiency, and increases the state's ability to withstand external pressures. But with a limited white population, there is also no doubt that economic development means greater employment opportunities for blacks since fewer whites are available to fill jobs. This does not mean that, in the short run, blacks will necessarily move up to positions of social and economic power. Given South African values, however, without industrialization and commercial development, all jobs would be reserved for whites. In essence, the growing economy, with a limited white population, essentially forces the society to bend its racist posture when the economic growth rate is threatened by the lack of workers. Some evidence suggests that this is already occurring. To that extent, the presence of outside investment is an effective limitation to apartheid.

But the mere passive activity of *presence* is not sufficient to calm the protests of groups seeking to change South African policy. Critics contend that, in many cases, the personnel of foreign firms are as racist as the South Africans, and that

---

*As of this writing, Portugal has announced plans to grant Mozambique independence.

American corporations—if they stay—should be taking positive steps to speed change in the South African society. Limited evidence suggests that some firms are moving beyond mere presence and becoming actively involved.

An interesting case in this regard involved the Polaroid Corporation. Polaroid had no direct investment in South Africa; its products were distributed by a locally owned company. Polaroid's sales through its South African subsidiary were relatively modest: $1.5 million out of a total of $500 million worldwide. Nevertheless, Polaroid film and equipment was used for the identification photos in the passbooks carried by all nonwhites.

In the United States, Polaroid was considered a model company by social responsibility proponents. Its work force was 10 percent black and its organizational and personnel policies were based on affirmative action long before that process became fashionable. Quite early, an all-black Volunteer Committee was established to expedite the grievances of black employees against top management.

In October of 1970, a group called the Polaroid Workers' Revolutionary Movement, led by a Polaroid design photographer, staged a protest demanding that Polaroid completely sever its ties with South Africa. Edwin Land, inventor of the original Land Camera and President of Polaroid, first banned the direct sales of film and cameras designed for identification photos to the South African government. But rather than accede completely to the demands of the PWRM, Land dispatched an employee committee to South Africa to study the effects of apartheid and the role that Polaroid products played there. In late 1970, Land announced that Polaroid would continue to sell consumer film, cameras, and sunglasses to its South African affiliate, but would embark on a program to improve the lives of blacks living in South Africa. Polaroid encouraged its distributor to give equal pay for equal work and to promote blacks into supervisory positions. In addition, funds were granted to organizations to underwrite the education of South African blacks.

Obviously, Polaroid's action alone is not going to have major impact, but it does offer some evidence of response by American firms to the growing expressions of concern.

The Polaroid case also offers some interesting insights into the related protest tactics and their possible effects that are no less important to managerial decision-making than the South African situation itself. Polaroid's decisions cut short a threatened boycott of its products in the United States and a potential strike situation in its plants.

Boycotts and strike action may become increasingly utilized weapons of activists concerned about American corporate behavior overseas. The effects of such boycotts on corporate profits as well as reputations then become important variables in decision-making. There can be little doubt that managerial responses in terms of policy changes in another country are made as much to forestall domestic challenges as they are to mitigate conditions in the foreign country.

And South Africa is not the only issue. Domestic boycotts have also been threatened and attempted against Gulf Oil, because of drilling operations in Angola; against Pepsi Cola, because of its trade with the Soviet Union (emigration of Soviet

Jews being the issue), and against Standard Oil Company of California because of a letter sent by SOCAL Chairman, O.N. Miller, to shareholders and employees urging sympathy with the Arab cause in the Middle East (SOCAL has vast investments in Arab countries).

Thus, the manager must consider what effects and actions in the home market the firm might have to deal with as a result of activities in another country. How does the firm react to boycotts, strikes, and other pressures called against it in domestic markets and U.S. plants?

THE READINGS

The first article by Cotter, Denerstein, and McKeon is a detailed catalogue of proxy challenges being faced by U.S. corporations over South African investment. A discussion of the pros and cons of doing business in South Africa—from a "social" point of view—is also included.

The second article, "The Proper Role of U.S. Corporations in South Africa" by John Blashill (from *Fortune*) reports some of the activities being undertaken by subsidiaries of U.S. firms to upgrade the status of South African blacks. Blashill also cites the lagging of U.S. firms even in areas where South African law allows companies wide latitude in pay and job assignments irrespective of race.

The Proxy Contests Over Southern Africa

William R. Cotter,
Robert Denerstein, and
Nancy McKeon

This spring, thirteen of America's major corporations are facing or have faced proxy challenges over their operations in southern Africa. Although southern African issues are hardly business's top social responsibility problem, they rank high on the list of problems that most corporate executives least understand.

To date, the southern African protest movement in the U.S. has been mainly the handiwork of a small group of dedicated activists, operating mostly within the

Reprinted from the Spring, 1973 issue of *Business and Society Review/Innovation,* copyright © 1973 by Warren, Gorham and Lamont, Inc.

structure of the Protestant Church. Largely as a result of this movement—which has grown in strength over the past three years—the debates on the options open to U.S. firms are beginning to sharpen. The protesters have gathered strength and gained experience, and the business executives are taking a closer look at their southern African operations. While some observers predict that peak pressure on the corporations may be as much as five years away, the choices now confronting American business operating in that troubled part of the world are beginning to narrow to two options—either reform employment practices or get out.

South Africa, with its system of legalized white supremacy and its grand design for the ultimate separation of people along racial and ethnic lines is familiar to most Americans. It is not widely known that there are four other territories in the region known collectively as southern Africa.

Two of these—Angola and Mozambique—are Portuguese controlled, and are the last important vestiges of European colonialism in Africa; companies which operate here are being asked by opponents to disengage entirely. A third territory —Namibia (Southwest Africa)—is a former German territiory, now controlled by South Africa, and has been declared by the World Court to be the legal responsibility of the United Nations. Here, too, most activists advocate total withdrawal of American investment. The fourth, Rhodesia, unilaterally declared itself independent in 1965 and has been the subject of mandatory United Nations economic sanctions since 1966. American business dealings with Rhodesia are forbidden by law, except for importation of chrome and certain other products, allowed as the result of last year's Military Procurement Act.

THE PORTUGUESE TERRITORIES

Gulf Oil's $150 million investment in Angola constitutes the major portion of total U.S. investment there, and American investments in Mozambique have been estimated at $15 million. About 20 U.S. firms operate in these two Portuguese-controlled areas, primarily in extractive industries—mineral and oil exploration.

Many political analysts view the Portuguese territories of Angola and Mozambique as the key to fundamental change in southern Africa. They speculate that if these territories move to majority rule, a significant blow would be rendered to white southern African hegemony.

Politically, Angola and Mozambique are quite different from South Africa. Aside from their avowed policies of racial toleration (arguable in reality, critics contend) and current moves by Portugal to confer some form of multi-racial local government in Angola and Mozambique, they represent to many people the last important vestige of overt European colonialism in Africa. (The Portuguese consider these territories an integral part of Portugal itself.) African guerrilla groups have been fighting anticolonial wars in the Portuguese territories for the past 10 years, whereas there are no guerrilla forces operating inside South Africa. In addition, the percentage of whites in Angola and Mozambique is small (a combined average of 4.3 percent, compared with South Africa's 17.2 percent) and is composed of people who are colonial transplants, as opposed to the South African whites who consider the land their home.

Official U.S. policy toward the Portuguese territories supports self-determination for the people of Angola and Mozambique but rejects violence as a means to that end. The policy, as articulated by Secretary of State William P. Rogers, also states that because force is "in no one's interest, we imposed an embargo in 1961 against the shipment of arms for use in the Portuguese territories. We have maintained this embargo and will continue to do so."

Those who call for the withdrawal of U.S. business from the Portuguese territories contend that U.S. investment helps Portugal fight its colonial wars against the African nationalists, and that U.S. investment, though smaller than in South Africa, is much more critical. There can be no doubt that the oil and mineral wealth discovered in Angola and Mozambique during the past 15 years has immensely increased the value of the territories to Portugal, bolstering, as it has, its treasury. It is also likely that royalty and tax payments by American firms have contributed to Portugal's ability to finance its war effort, at least by making possible the release of other funds.

Because the issues in the Portuguese territories are seemingly so well defined, the Protestant Church project on southern Africa entertains no prospect of "constructive involvement"; the call for American withdrawal is plain and simple. Although the major American investor in Angola, Gulf Oil, has been a church target company in past years and has been praised by the churches for revealing the details of its operation there, the Gulf position firmly discounts withdrawal.

Gulf is not the target of a church-sponsored resolution this year, but another oil company, Exxon—which has applied for a license to prospect in Angola—is being asked to examine all the implications of setting up an Angolan operation. Some shareholders distinguish Exxon from Gulf, noting that Exxon has no preexisting stake in operations in Angola and that it is more difficult for a company to pull out than to avoid going in. The seemingly vague resolution filed with Exxon is viewed by some as part of a church tactic to keep the southern Africa issue alive. Withdrawal resolutions never have garnered much shareholder support, and the modified language of the Exxon proposal suggests an attempt on the part of the church group to gain allies among its fellow institutional investors (the ultimate church goal still being withdrawal). Many nonprofit institutional investors—particularly universities facing student protest—have noted that it is difficult for them to oppose resolutions demanding either information or thorough investigation.

NAMIBIA AND THE TSUMEB MINE

The U.S. government, which does not officially discourage or encourage investment in the Portuguese territories or South Africa, has taken a definite stand in the case of Namibia: it actively discourages new American investment. South Africa has ruled Namibia since 1920 under a League of Nations mandate. The United Nations, successor agency to the League, has now demanded, without success, that South Africa relinquish its control. Washington upholds the World Court decision (of June 1971) that declared South Africa's control over Namibia illegal, and has informed investors they will receive no government assistance in protecting investments made after 1966 against claims of a future lawful government in the territory. In addition, the U.S. Treasury Department is now considering denial of U.S. tax credits to American firms that pay South African taxes relating to their Namibian operations.

Accurate figures on the amount of U.S. trade and investment in Namibia are impossible to arrive at, because neither the United States nor South Africa separates the Namibia figures from South Africa as a whole. The U.S. investment amounts to about $50 million, mainly in the Tsumeb Mining Company. American Metal Climax and Newmont Mining own about 60 percent of the mine.

Although South Africa controls Namibia, the racial climate in Namibia differs from that of South Africa. Africans in Namibia are subject to similar discrimination and working conditions as in South Africa, but rigid apartheid legislation has not been introduced. According to 1970 figures, there were only 90,000 whites in Namibia's total population of 746,000.

Because of its legal status, Namibia often has been called the Achilles heel of South Africa. Strategically significant, Namibia links South Africa with Angola and helps provide a buffer against majority-ruled Africa to the north. Protesting groups generally call for the withdrawal of American firms as part of an overall strategy that they believe would hasten South Africa's downfall. One church group, an exception, has adopted a "realistic" stand, calling for Newmont to establish equal opportunities worldwide, with special reference to Namibia.

SOUTH AFRICA: THE GREAT DEBATE

Inevitably, all discussions of southern Africa circle back to South Africa. The Republic of South Africa always has commanded the lion's share of the American investment dollar in southern Africa. In fact, it accounts for about 25 percent of American investment in all of Africa, a continent of forty-one independent countries. According to Department of Commerce statistics, U.S. direct private investment in South Africa reached $964 million at the beginning of 1972, about one percent of all U.S. direct foreign investment. Half of U.S. business in South Africa is in manufacturing,

---

What Is Apartheid?

Apartheid is a system of legislation exerting control over nearly every aspect—political, social, religious, work, and sexual—of the lives of South Africa's 14 million blacks. The most all-pervasive of these restrictions are the "Pass Laws." These laws require every African over the age of 16 to carry, and produce to any policeman on demand, a book containing his photograph, his number, and the various stamps he needs in connection with residence, movement, and work—in other words, to explain satisfactorily why he is where he is. If asked, he must produce various other documents as well. Every year some 640,000 Africans are tried for the violation of these Pass Laws.

Other laws forbid official recognition of African trade unions, while tradition keeps most African workers unskilled and poorly paid. The South African Department of Statistics in late 1972 released figures showing that whites were paid 560 percent higher than blacks. Built into this system of control is the legal machinery necessary to stifle opposition, its most powerful weapon being the Suppression of Communism Act of 1950. This law gives the government power, without referring to the courts, to ban periodicals, meetings, organizations, and individuals (black or white) of its choice.

primarily of automobiles, drugs, cosmetics, and industrial equipment; other substantial U.S. investment is in petroleum, mining, and smelting.

Although it is difficult to catalogue all the American firms operating in southern Africa—because of the "invisibility" that sometimes masks ownership of multinational corporations, and because many U.S. firms work through foreign-owned distributorships—it is estimated that between 300 and 400 American companies operate there. Their average rate of return (earnings as a percent of book value) ranged between 17 and 23 percent from 1962 to 1970 (it dropped to a 10-year low of 12.4 percent in 1971). These rates of return are the source of many critics' most ardent charge: that American firms in South Africa make enormous profits because of low wages for oppressed blacks.

An examination of American companies' return rates in other parts of the world helps in weighing the validity of this charge. In 1971, worldwide return on American investment was 13.1 percent, while investment in the developing nations yielded 20.0 percent. In Africa, excluding South Africa, the rate of return was 22.1 percent, although if investment in oil-rich Libya is also excluded, the return on the relatively limited American investment was only 6.4 percent.

While it is true, as many American businessmen argue, that black workers in South Africa generally earn more than their counterparts elsewhere on the continent, it can also be argued—in line with United States Department of Commerce policy which considers South Africa a developed country—that the proper comparison is between South African wages and those in other industrialized economies. In South Africa, black workers spend their wages in an industrial setting with developed-world prices.

Under the Group Areas Act of 1956, the government has designated 81 scattered "black" spots on the map of South Africa—surrounded by "white" areas—as homelands or Bantustans for the black population. This land comprises 13 percent of the territory, in accordance with the Native Land Act of 1912, which prohibits Africans from owning land in 87 percent of the country. This 87 percent, belonging to the one-sixth of the population which is white, includes every seaport and gold mine, as well as 99 percent of industry and all advanced farming areas. The Separate Amenities Act of 1953 authorizes separate, racially segregated facilities in public places.

The South African Institute of Race Relations says that there are no accurate figures available for racial comparison in the areas of education and health, but the United Nations Unit on Apartheid has culled a few: The South African government annually spends $159.74 to educate each white child and $18.90 for each African child, amounting to a total of $333 million spent on white education and $20.3 million on African education. Whereas school attendance is compulsory for white children, it is not for Africans.

It is in South Africa where white power is most firmly entrenched, and where the government has voiced the staunchest pledges to defend the existing system. South African protest strategies fall basically into two camps: one calls for the withdrawal of American firms; the other argues that American business should reform employment practices in their South African operations ("constructive involvement").

Those advocating constructive involvement pin their hopes for cracking the apartheid system on the notion that American business, indirectly at least (and perhaps inadvertently), can be an important force for progressive change within South Africa. They note that South African law and custom allows U.S. businesses to upgrade the economic well-being of black employees—equal pay for equal work, wage increases, job-training programs, more rapid promotions, educational programs for children of employees, inclusion in company pension and life insurance plans, health and disability insurance programs, housing subsidies, medical care, transportation allowances, recognition of black bargaining units, and other such measures. No American firm (or any other company, for that matter) has yet approached the limit of what is permissible under South African law.

They further argue that even if disengagement were the better course in theory, it is so unlikely to happen that one might as well take what one can get and hope it will have impact. Withdrawal will not damage the South African economy, so the argument goes, since other firms would simply take over U.S. interests. Further, even if South Africa's economy were to be hurt, this would reduce, rather than increase, the power of blacks to pressure for change. They believe that meaningful, evolutionary change is possible in South Africa and that enlightened employment practices can help bring about desired progress—although there is no clear agreement by this group of advocates on what constitutes "progress."

The case for withdrawal of American business sees U.S. involvement as strengthening white supremacy and white control. Proponents of withdrawal claim that business seeks to operate without offending the South African government and is really committed to maintenance of the status quo. Tim Smith, executive secretary of the Interfaith Committee on Social Responsibility in Investment (the Protestant Church group), contends that business commitment to social progress in South Africa is highly questionable, since the entire argument for constructive involvement developed only after critics began campaigning for withdrawal. "The case for constructive engagement always has the ring of rationalization rather than the true force of argument—especially when businessmen make the case," Smith charges.

Smith further argues that U.S. investments in certain sectors strengthen the South African government where it most needs help. "The South African government is involved in a frantic search for oil, aided by U.S. companies such as Mobil and Caltex. This search is motivated by political and economic reality: South Africa is not self-sufficient in oil."

Thus the opposition to constructive involvement points to two major obstacles to the position: (1) Even if American firms paid equal pay for equal work and made other improvements, they would still be supporting apartheid because of the direct and indirect support of the white minority government; and (2) Employee benefit improvement would not affect the majority of nonwhites and could not crack the apartheid system that so limits and circumscribes the fundamental human rights of nonwhites.

Because violent revolution seems unlikely at this point, and because many observers think that this is the only way for blacks to change the apartheid system, there are those who feel that all policies should be based on moral objections to the oppressiveness of that society, and not on the likely result within South Africa. The argument here says, "We may not be able to change South Africa, but we certainly need not participate in its society."

Neither the constructive involvement nor the withdrawal camp has advanced a clear scenario of precisely how either course would bring about change in the current status of black South Africans. Those who demand withdrawal suggest that it might serve as a giant impetus to black organizing and be a morale booster within the black South African community. Ironically, advocates of constructive involvement also argue that their course of action can have important repercussions for strengthening black organizations and morale.

Official U.S. government policy toward South Africa condemns apartheid and prohibits military sales, but neither encourages nor discourages investment (although the Commerce Department does actively promote whatever trade and distribution of American goods will better the U.S. balance of payments position). According to Assistant Deputy Secretary of Commerce Harold B. Scott, the department's policy is to tell potential investors of the problems of operating in South Africa, to point out investment possibilities in neighboring black countries and, if the investor is still committed to establishing himself in South Africa, to encourage him to implement "enlightened" or "progressive" labor practices.

THE PROTEST MOVEMENT

Although indignation over South Africa has a long history in the United States, especially in the black community, protests against corporate involvement did not capture public attention until the late 1960s. The American Committee on Africa, headed by a Methodist minister, Reverend George Houser, had consistently called for American business withdrawal, and it was this group that carried most of the protest burden in the early part of the decade. They were rebutted by many who saw themselves as liberals but who also had economic interests in South Africa. David Rockefeller, chairman of the Chase Manhattan Bank, was one of the first to advance the constructive involvement argument. In 1967, Rockefeller remarked that, over a period of time, the "bank can exert a constructive influence on racial conditions in South Africa."

Toward the end of the 1960s, students began to pressure universities to divest themselves of stocks of companies operating in southern Africa. In March 1969, Princeton University's faculty requested that the university sell its $127 million of holdings in firms operating in South Africa. Princeton's trustees refused, and their decision was protested by 75 students who occupied an administration building.

Universities struggled with questions pertaining to southern Africa and other socially related investments, and were forced to cope with what are not traditional proxy questions. Three years after the student protest, Princeton abstained on disclosure resolutions against Gulf Oil, General Motors, and American Metal Climax; the university wrote to the management of each company, explaining that its committee on social responsibility had recommended the abstention but urged the companies to disclose pertinent information voluntarily.

Harvard University also abstained on the 1972 resolution calling for Gulf's disclosure, arguing that Gulf already had disclosed much of the information sought. Prior to the filing of the resolution, student protesters at Harvard had demanded that the university divest itself of Gulf stock because of the company's role in Angola. The university responded by sending Stephen Farber, assistant to Harvard President Derek Bok, to see Gulf's installation for himself. The report issued by Farber appears to reconfirm Harvard's decision not to sell its $17,500,000 worth of Gulf shares. Talks with "social responsibility" committee representatives at other colleges have indicated that benchmark schools, such as Harvard, are watched carefully by other institutions.

The first major sign of the American black community's dissatisfaction with American business over southern African issues came in 1970. A group of black workers at Polaroid Corp. demanded that the company end all sales to South Africa and contribute prior South African profits to African liberation groups. (Ironically, Polaroid has a relatively minimal South African presence. The company sells its products there through an independent distributor and derives only one-half of one percent of its total revenues from such operations.) Polaroid sent a team of workers, black and white, to South Africa to examine the situation firsthand. As a result, the company publicly announced its abhorrence of apartheid, agreed to upgrade the black employees of its South African distributor, and made arrangements to help pay educational expenses of about 500 black students. Additionally—and most significantly, according to critics like Tim Smith—Polaroid refused to sell to the South African government its ID-2 system, which, it said, was used to classify people by race.

Critics of Polaroid contend that the company had an easy choice to make because its involvement is so small. Others contend that the Polaroid Experiment, as the company's action has become known, was more public relations than substance.

Other protest efforts—mainly small scale, local, and generally lacking in a coherent strategy or follow-through—have been staged by such groups as the Madison Area Southern Africa Committee, the New York-based Committee for a Free Mozambique, and the Denver Committee on Southern Africa. The Gulf Boycott Coalition, based in Dayton, Ohio, is an exception. It succeeded in getting that city to cancel its gasoline contract with Gulf for city vehicles, even though Gulf was the low bidder for the $56,000 contract. But Gulf has yet to suffer great financial loss from the coalition-organized boycott, and southern Africa, as an issue, has yet to work its way into the league of table grapes and iceberg lettuce.

In the past two years, the most visible demonstrations against southern Africa have been black, sometimes involving thousands of demonstrators (the May 1972 Washington demonstration in support of African liberation drew some 12,000 supporters). This contrasts with the 100 or so that predominantly white organizations can usually muster for protest.

Although attention shifted to the Washington demonstration for a day last May, there was no immediate follow-up. (A similar rally and march are planned for this spring.) The students who occupied President Bok's office, to protest Harvard's Gulf Oil holdings, did not follow up with any strong protest following publication of the Farber report. There has been sporadic talk about boycotting South African goods or Angolan coffee, but no effective follow-through. Some longshoremen have refused to unload Rhodesian chrome ore on occasion, but the ships go elsewhere, are unloaded, and the protest subsides.

The most systematic pressure on American corporations has been at the shareholder level. Board chairmen, chief executive officers, and other business leaders have, during the past two years—usually in response to proxy challenges—visited South Africa, examined their operations there, and, in some cases, instituted changes in employment practices. General Motors, for example, recently finalized plans to establish a sports center for black employees, and said it had raised the wages of some of its black hourly workers.

To date, however, no U.S. corporation has withdrawn from South Africa on the grounds that its continuing presence there supports apartheid. And only Polaroid has publicly condemned apartheid. To be sure, statements by other companies indicate some recognition that operating in South Africa presents an American firm with special problems. E. M. "Pete" Estes, executive vice president of General Motors, last year told a group of institutional investors: "My comments today will focus specifically on South Africa, a country where human equality does not exist as we know it in the U.S. . . . It should be emphasized that General Motors is deeply concerned about the complex moral issues which exist in relation to the mandatory classifications of races, but that our approach is to help build a climate within which the desired social changes can be implemented. . . ."

The problem the shareholder activists have is that, even while they are the most likely force for affecting corporate policies vis-à-vis South Africa, they have no real grass roots support. And such support does not appear to be forthcoming.

Several major questions remain with regard to the future of the South African protest movements. How strenuously and through what channels will the American black community increase its involvement in the issue? Can a movement with minimal grass roots support be kept alive if its base doesn't grow? To what extent will organized labor play a role in future South African protest? How effective will corporate actions such as upgrading black employment (presuming it can be verified) and company publicity be in quelling opposition? Will student groups federate around this issue as they did on Vietnam, or is the campus not a likely place for increased protest? Will U.S. government policy toward South Africa change and take the lead away from protests which so far have been directed largely at the private sector? Will America be able to confront the issue of racism in another country when it has not yet resolved the issue at home?

With little press coverage, little organized political activity, and perhaps a shrinking from international involvement, it is easy to be doubtful about any major revision in America's posture toward South Africa. But the limited protest which began in earnest a mere three or four years ago has grown continually, and has accomplished more than would have been suspected at the outset. Many point to this fact as evidence that pressure on U.S. corporations won't let up.

The Proper Role of U.S. Corporations in South Africa

John Blashill

The Republic of South Africa has always been regarded by foreign investors as a gold mine, one of those rare and refreshing places where profits are great and problems small. Capital is not threatened by political instability or nationalization. Labor is cheap, the market booming, the currency hard and convertible. Such are the market's attractions that 292 American corporations have established subsidiaries or affiliates there. Their combined direct investment is close to $900 million, and their returns on that investment have been romping home at something like 19 percent a year, after taxes.

And yet South Africa is also the home of apartheid, where 4,000,000 whites rule some 15,000,000 "Bantu" (blacks), 2,000,000 "coloreds" (mulattoes), and 600,000 "Asiatics" (mostly Indians). The intense moral fervor aroused in its critics by apartheid has made South Africa an international pariah. The United Nations has passed more than thirty-five resolutions aimed at South Africa, including an arms embargo. South African trade unions have been forced to withdraw from the International Labor Organization. South African athletes have been banned from the Olympics. It has become a highly attackable place, one that stirs up explosive emotions. In the U.S. those emotions are beginning to explode at stockholders' meetings—and even in the boardrooms—of corporations doing business in South Africa.

Many of these companies are now being forced to face the question that Polaroid Corp., under pressure from some of its black employees in the U.S., asked itself in a series of advertisements a year and a half ago: "Is it right or wrong to do business in South Africa?" It was a fairly uncomplicated question for Polaroid, since the company sells its products through a local distributor and has none of its own money invested in the country. The answer Polaroid came up with cost the company itself little or nothing, and proved to be a triumph of good public relations. Polaroid decided to continue its South African sales on condition that its distributor "improve dramatically the salaries and other benefits" of its nonwhite employees (which has been done).

The issue of American corporate involvement in South Africa has been taken up by civil-rights leaders, labor unions, churches, stockholder groups, the Ford Foundation, the State Department, and Congress, with varying bias and varying answers. Some, including Representative Charles Diggs, a black Congressman from Detroit, have decided that American corporations can stay—if they mend their ways. A number of critics, however, are demanding that they get out. "American firms in South Africa are partners in apartheid," asserts George M. Houser, executive director of the American Committee on Africa, a privately funded organization in New York that promotes freedom for Africans. Representatives of six Protestant denominations returned from a three-week tour this winter to report that "most of us believe that American corporations should totally disengage from South Africa."

The issue profoundly affects the lives of all of South Africa's nonwhites, as well as many of its white citizens. But those who cry "Abandon ship" have not consulted the passengers. Many of South Africa's blacks, on whose behalf the issue is supposedly being fought, want U.S. business to stay. "I feel if the Americans withdraw it will lower the general standard of living here, and the Africans will be the first to suffer," says Lucy Mvubelo, general secretary of the National Union of Clothing Workers and one of the nation's few African labor leaders. Aside from whatever moral cleansing might be gained by refusing to dine with the devil, it would serve no useful purpose at all for American corporations to get out. Indeed, the closing of U.S. subsidiaries would throw at least 100,000 Africans out of work immediately, and could eventually cost the jobs of 150,000 more. "Foreign investment can help us," says Julius Moikangoa, a white-collar worker in Johannesburg, "by working for us from within." That is the crux of the South African challenge for U.S. corporations.

FACING AN OBVIOUS TRUTH

The withdrawal of American investment would not bring down the apartheid system. More likely, the system would be worsened, for an enforced U.S. retreat would almost certainly cause a violent reaction among South Africa's whites. In fact, American withdrawal might be the only thing that could save apartheid in the long run.

For perhaps the first time, most South African whites are becoming aware that there is something wrong with their elaborate structure of apartheid laws. Not only does it not work justly, it just doesn't work. The society is beginning to move—slowly, perhaps, but fundamentally. Some of South Africa's leading industrialists have long opposed restrictive labor practices, under which the whites get all the best jobs and the blacks only the worst. "It is just a plain, obvious truth," says Harry Oppenheimer, chairman of the giant Anglo American Corp., "that a country that refuses to allow something like 80 percent of its labor force to do the best work of which they are capable cannot hope to progress as it should or hold its place in the world."

The ferment is beginning to permeate South Africa's political life. Apartheid was invented by another generation, and reflects the views of the old Boer pioneer, who could claim as much land as he could cover on horseback in a day. The system was, in many ways, the legal application of the Boer's ancient tactic of self-defense: when attacked, he "went into *laager,*" barricading himself inside a circle of covered wagons. Stringent apartheid laws are still very much on the books, but such tactics don't fit an industrialized society, and South Africa's younger voters—those now forty or below—do not live in fear of the Africans to the extent that their elders did. They are increasingly concerned with torments that are more universal: taxation, traffic jams, inflation, and keeping up payments on the house. And since these younger voters will be in the majority by the next election, their attitudes are an important fact of life in South African politics today.

The climate is ripe for change. What strikes an observer forcibly, however, is that few American subsidiaries in South Africa seem to know it—or want it. With some notable exceptions, they are behind the times, even for South Africa. They should not be compelled to leave the country, but for their own good they should reform their ways. "We should be in the forefront of the social changes that are happening here," says Bill Marshall Smith, fifty-nine, a South African who is managing director of Caltex, which is jointly owned by Texaco and Standard of California. "It just makes bloody business sense," declares Peter Loveday, forty-two, another progressive South African. He is managing director of Standard Telephones & Cables (S.A.) Ltd., the principal I.T.T. subsidiary in the country.

But most executives who run U.S. subsidiaries in South Africa like the system as it is. In 1969 a market-research organization conducted a poll of 106 American and Canadian businessmen living in the country. More than three-quarters of them approved of apartheid as "an approach that is, under the circumstances at least, an attempt to develop a solution." Only 20 percent opposed it. Less than one in ten felt it was "altogether incorrect." In 1970, Jim Hatos, the managing director of the International Harvester subsidiary, told a visitor from New York's Council for Christian Social Action: "I am sympathetic to what the South African Government is trying to do. I don't want hundreds of Africans running around in front of my house."

The truly extraordinary thing about that statement was its frankness. A good many of Hatos' colleagues might agree with the views he expressed, but they would no longer dare say so in public. Most of them, in fact, have become afraid of saying anything about anything. "We are justifiably proud of our record, but it would serve no useful purpose to talk about it," said the manager of a factory where African workers with ten years of service earn less than 50 cents an hour. "My home office doesn't want to give any publicity to the fact that we have a South African operation," pleaded another man, whose company has one of the world's best-known trademarks.

The nervousness among these executives bears its own message. American companies are finding their records in South Africa suddenly very embarrassing, for the very good reason that they don't live by the same rules they practice at home. "American firms aren't really any better than the Boer firms," says Dabulamanzi Tantsi, a lawyer in Johannesburg's sprawling African township of Soweto.

There are exceptions—including Caltex, I.T.T., General Motors, Ford, Mobil, Gillette, and, most notably, I.B.M. These companies and a few others pay their nonwhite workers considerably more than the usual wage rates. For example, even though its union keeps the top ranks of jobs for whites only, I.T.T.'s nonwhite workers—mostly colored and Asian—get an average of $135 a month. Loveday raised their wages 19 percent last year and plans to keep moving toward what he calls "wage parity."

DOUBLE NAUGHT IS STILL NAUGHT

Could Americans alone, by paying top wages, have any meaningful effect on the living standards of South Africa's nonwhite population, particularly the blacks? An African teacher in Soweto supplies an answer: "I, personally, would derive no immediate benefit if the Americans decided to pay fair wages. Not many of us would. But this would spread. It would have to. If Factory A increases wages, Factory B will be forced to increase wages too, and before you know it, everybody's wages go up, even mine."

All companies in South Africa do give occasional raises to their African employees, and the management of most firms can pull out seemingly impressive figures on how much they have raised the salaries of their Africans over a term of years. But the figures are apt to be flawed. "You double naught and it's still naught," explains Fred van Wyk, director of the South African Institute of Race Relations, a private foundation that has been fighting against apartheid for years. Besides, white wages have gone up more than those of the Africans. Because they have replaced white workers with black, moreover, some companies actually find themselves spending less on their payrolls than they did ten years ago.

Another claim often made by American companies is that "we pay the rate for the job, regardless of race." In the U.S. that would mean equal pay for equal work. In South African jargon, however, the statement has a special meaning. "There is no such thing as equal pay for equal work," says F. P. Sauls, national secretary of the colored National Union of Motor Assembly and Rubber Workers

Union of South Africa. Most companies that say they pay "the rate for the job" operate under union agreements in which all jobs are categorized and assigned minimum rates. But the rates are pegged artificially low, and invariably all whites are paid considerably more than the minimum.

Moreover, blacks and coloreds are often employed at jobs for which they are not "rated." A colored shop foreman, for example, will be rated as a group leader (sometimes called a "team leader" or "charge hand") and paid 50 cents to $1 an hour less than if he were a white doing the same job. In the electrical industry there is a union rule forbidding black electricians to be called electricians or to work from blueprints. They can, however, be called electrical assistants and are allowed to work from pictures, even if the pictures happen to be photographs of blueprints. But their pay is less than half that of white electricians.

Only at the middle grades of the factory pay scales do blacks and whites work at the same wages. The blacks start at the bottom and can rise no higher than the middle. The whites start no lower than the middle and can go to the top. It's a pyramid, all black at the base, all white at the top, with a few zebra stripes in a thin line at the center. Or, as Ford's industrial-relations manager Fred H. Ferreira explains it, "There is an upward movement of the whites as they make way for the progression of nonwhites."

SCRAPING THE LABOR BARREL

Ferreira's comment is an accurate summary of the pattern in South Africa. Black workers are being allowed to rise, but in most cases only to fill jobs vacated by upward-moving whites. It's a process of massive readjustment, all of it motivated by the same fundamental cause. South Africa, whose economy was largely based on mining and farming until World War II, is rapidly transforming itself into an industrial power, and the accompanying demand for labor has far outstripped the traditional labor supply. One survey showed 6 percent of all "white" jobs to be vacant because there was no one to fill them. Unless these jobs can be filled, the Federated Chamber of Industries (South Africa's equivalent of the National Association of Manufacturers) has warned, the projected growth of the economy will be curtailed by 20 percent.

But filled by whom? Not, certainly, by whites, for there are no more left to employ. The white unemployment rate is officially calculated at less than 0.2 percent—a total of some 3,000 workers, including assorted drunks and misfits, who are unemployed only because they are absolutely unemployable, An additional 50,000 whites, perhaps, would be classified as unemployables in any other country, even though they hold jobs. "You can imagine," says Ian Hetherington, the British-born managing director of the Norton Co. plant near Johannesburg, "how deep into the barrel we've scraped."

Faced with the prospect of empty assembly lines, industry has had no choice but to turn to African workers. "If I had to depend on white labor to run my plant, I'd have to close down tomorrow," says a typical American manager. Another tells this story: "When we came here at government request ten years ago, we were told that we could hire only white workers. Well, we couldn't get them. Five years ago a government labor inspector came around and found the place full of non-whites. So we told him, either we employ them or you don't get your equipment. And that was the end of it."

Given their choice, many employers would rather hire blacks than whites. The whites, pampered and protected by tradition, tend to be unreliable and shoddy workers. They often wander from job to job, quitting on the slightest pretext. Sometimes they refuse to work at all unless management provides them with African "assistants," who do everything for them—brew their tea, hand them their tools, and even fill in for them when they play hooky. In one American heavy-equipment plant, where welding jobs are reserved for members of the white union, the managing director reports that the welders seldom come to work more than two days a week, and go fishing—without pay—the other three. When they're absent, the welding is done by their supposedly untrained African assistants—who work twice as fast at one-third the pay. "I get six times the production per dollar out of my Bantu," the manager says.

I.T.T.'s Peter Loveday calls this indefensible exploitation. "In practically every situation where you've got whites and nonwhites doing the same job," he says, "you're dealing with the cream of the coloreds and blacks, and the dregs of the whites." Yet the blacks cannot afford to be prima donnas, for there is a vast pool of unemployed African labor. Once an African lands a job, he does his best to keep it. If he quits or gets fired, he runs the very serious risk of being shipped back to his "homeland," or reservation. In most American subsidiaries the only employees with twenty years' service are Africans.

Under the circumstances, industry in South Africa might be expected to make better use of black and colored workers. Yet there are some important barriers. Some white unions enforce closed-shop rules on the skilled jobs and forbid their members to train nonwhites; this is the case at I.T.T., among others. White artisans usually refuse to accept nonwhite apprentices. There is an unwritten rule against putting blacks in charge of whites. In most industrial areas management must obtain government permission to increase the number of African workers.

But as the manager of a major American industrial plant puts it, "If you're smart enough to recognize an impediment, you're smart enough to find a way around it." Unions can be cajoled, artisans can be trained elsewhere, and permission to hire more Africans usually can be obtained: 72 percent of all such applications have been approved, according to Prime Minister Balthazar Vorster. The trouble is that most American companies don't appear to try to overcome the impediments.

LOOKING AFTER THE GARBAGE DRIVERS

Among the abused and misunderstood bars to the advancement of African workers are South Africa's so-called "job-reservation laws," which reserve for whites a variety of jobs in specified industries and areas. Job reservation is cited by countless

American managers as the principal reason why they cannot promote their blacks. But so far only twenty-seven specific job-reservation "determinations" have been issued by the government, and they affect only 2,080 individual workers. Most of the determinations are either riddled with exemptions or apply to only a handful of jobs. Determination No. 9, for example, concerns only the twelve white garbage drivers in the town of Springs, near Johannesburg. With all the exemptions taken into account, it appears that the only American company subject to a specific determination under the job-reservation laws is Chrysler.

One of management's responsibilities is to know the laws that affect its operations, but in too many cases in South Africa the top men in U.S. subsidiaries seem not to bother. "They believe the myths," says a senior American diplomat with long service in South Africa. "They think everything is illegal, and they don't care." Ignorance of the law is especially prevalent in subsidiaries headed by Americans. South Africa may be just another step in their corporate careers, and their stay is likely to be a short one. Their success is measured in the short-run terms of this year's profits, and many of them are simply not interested in anything else. They come and they go, and what happens after they leave South Africa does not concern them. "They're semiskilled barbarians," concludes the American diplomat. "They have little minds." Adds Loveday of I.T.T.: "It's bad management."

In the past, of course, South Africa has not been regarded as a corporate problem area, and so it has been assigned a fairly low rung in the overseas promotion ladders of many American corporations. Too many of the managers sent to South Africa are like the man who runs an American subsidiary's factory in the state of Natal, southeast of Johannesburg. Accountable only to his home office in New York, he likes to get his picture in the paper from time to time with African community leaders because "it's good for P.R." He directs a work force of more than 400, of whom 150 are nonwhite. His starting wage for Africans is $13.17 a week, which is far below the poverty datum line for the area.

There is one rather bold innovation in his factory. He employs both white women and African men on his assembly line. This could be an explosive combination, he says, "except I let those Bantu know that the first sign of trouble, they're out." The white women earn 3 cents to 6 cents an hour more than the black men —even though the blacks have proved more productive and more reliable. The managing director doesn't know how much it would cost him to pay equal wages, because he has no intention of doing so. "If New York orders me to pay the rate for the job, I'll pay it," he says. "But if I don't have to , I won't. I'm here to make profits. If the Bantus don't like it, they can work somewheres else."

This manager would like to convert his assembly line to only black workers, thereby reducing his total payroll somewhat. But he says he cannot do so because "it would be against the law. I have to maintain a quota of white workers." In point of fact, there is no specific law setting race quotas on his industry in Natal. He could fire all his white workers tomorrow, if he wanted to.

GETTING AWAY WITH HERESY

Even some companies that are serious about change in South Africa have made only token gestures, such as not having separate water coolers and not putting signs on restroom doors to indicate whether the facilities are for whites, coloreds, or Africans. But other actions are more substantive, such as putting the desks of black stenographers next to those of white ones.

Now and again there are calculated frontal attacks against the underlying structure of the apartheid system. A heavy-equipment manufacturer in the Capetown area has installed an interracial cafeteria for its white and colored workers; that is plainly illegal. The manager of a plant near Johannesburg says that "whenever we can safely employ a black to do a job, we'll discriminate against a white to do it." He has installed a black supervisor over a partly white assembly line; this, although not strictly illegal, is at least heretical. He has also hired black security officers who have the authority, though they rarely use it, to search the persons of white workers coming off shift—and this is not only heretical in South Africa, but absolutely unthinkable.

The miraculous thing is that the managers who have ventured into heresy have [gotten] away with it. Their white workers have not complained, because great pains have been taken to prepare the ground. Where blacks have been put in sensitive positions, they have been chosen with care and know their jobs.

Of the companies willing to talk about what they're doing, the two most impressive are Gillette and I.B.M. Like the majority of progressive U.S. subsidiaries, both are managed by South Africans. Gillette's wage scales are not as good as I.B.M.'s—"We still have some warts," concedes Denis Sanan, forty, managing director of Gillette. But his company is moving aggressively to wipe out its warts. Says Sanan: "We can't wait for opportunities to appear for the blacks. We have to create areas of opportunity."

A colored chemist is chief of Gillette's research and development department, two black quality-control inspectors work on its production lines, and there are nine black salesmen and a black field supervisor on the sales staff. The chemist, Sanan reports, is so capable that he is being sought out by white department heads for advice on production problems. The quality-control inspectors enjoy "excellent relations" with the whites whose work they inspect. The black salesmen "are my most effective sales force, at least in the amount of territory they can cover. They average twenty-seven calls a day, versus eleven a day for white salesmen." As for the field supervisor: "He's tops. He could eventually become this company's general sales manager."

BLACK AND WHITE AT THE COMPUTER BANK

I.B.M. is unbelievable—in the sense that Africans outside the company cannot believe what it manages to do for its workers. The company's starting wages for

Africans are above $200 a month, which is by far the highest minimum rate in the country, and more than the maximum in most companies. I.B.M. still has few black workers, but is aggressively seeking more. Once it hires a talented individual it keeps moving him up, regardless of race. Frank Molobi, for example, is a twenty-four-year-old black. He joined the company five years ago as a junior clerk and is now a trainee programmer—a title that means he has completed his programming courses but has less than a year's experience.

I.B.M. is entirely open about its color-blind corporate policies. In its show windows on Johannesburg's Rissik Street, a computer bank is in constant operation, and the operators are both black and white. The mixture is more than a window display; it is a symbol of deep-seated company philosophy. "What the companies here should ask themselves is whether they have a basic philosophy of human dignity that they apply," says Morris Cowley, forty-six, I.B.M.'s managing director for South Africa.

Among other companies that do apply such a philosophy are Caltex and Mobil. Their subsidiaries are both based in Capetown, and both are headed by enlightened South Africans. "We give equal pay and equal conditions and are proud of it," says Caltex' Bill Marshall Smith, a squirish and sometimes eloquent man who grew up in the interior of Natal and learned Zulu along with English. "We try to stay about ten yards ahead of the troops," says Mobil's William de la Harpe Beck, forty-nine, a former rugby player from the Orange Free State who is fluent in Sotho. "If you get much further ahead than that," he adds, "you start running into fire."

Both Marshall Smith and Beck have turned to Africans and Capetown's large colored population to find the skilled workers they need. Mobil uses colored computer operators and key punchers, for example, and Beck says that approximately one-fifth of his 750 nonwhite workers are employed at skilled jobs, earning salaries comparable to whites. For laborers, Mobil's starting wage, including a Christmas bonus that amounts to an extra month's pay each year, is $123 a month; the total is well above the poverty line and almost unrivaled in South Africa.

Caltex starts lower—$112 a month—but the wages it pays go up rapidly. Most of the company's 700 nonwhites are doing skilled or semiskilled work, and "we're looking for areas to employ more nonwhites." One remarkable accomplishment —remarkable for South Africa, at least—is that Caltex now has Africans driving its oil tanker trucks in the Johannesburg area. Their starting wage, as trainees, is $207 a month, and they can eventually earn $500 once they have been on the job long enough (none earn that much as yet). Most remarkable of all, these drivers make deliveries to Afrikaner gas-station operators in Johannesburg. This means they must cross traditional color bars. "They're more than drivers," says Marshall Smith. "They have to discuss how much the client wants, make out the bills, and collect his money. It was touchy, at first. The whites didn't like it. They'd never had to explain to a black man why they couldn't pay until next time. It was losing face before an inferior, as they saw it. But they got over it."

CHAPS WHO ARE GIVEN AUTHORITY

The biggest American companies in South Africa are the three major auto makers, each of which has a plant measurable in the hundreds of acres—Ford and General Motors in the Indian Ocean city of Port Elizabeth, Chrysler near Pretoria in the north. Among them, they employ nearly 13,000 workers, and account for nearly 40 percent of all new-car sales in the country. All three companies are now beginning to give more attention to the welfare of their nonwhite workers.

Ford, with a labor force totaling 5,576, is the largest American employer in South Africa. Its lowest rate is 53 cents an hour, which is a livable wage. Ford has more colored workers than blacks and offers them opportunities for advancement that are considerably above average. Twelve colored employees are now ranked as group leaders, according to Sauls, the national secretary of the colored auto workers' union, "and these chaps are really given authority."

Until recently, Ford's medical plan made a sharp distinction between white and nonwhite employees: the families of white workers were covered after three months' employment, the families of nonwhites only after ten years. Last January all employees, regardless of race, were given coverage for their families after three months. Ford still has no coloreds or blacks in the top two of its eleven labor grades, and Sauls does not credit the company's claim that it gives equal pay for equal work. "A colored with fifteen years' experience gets the same pay as a white starting out," he says.

General Motors, which is smaller than Ford in South Africa, has roughly 5,000 workers (70 percent of them nonwhite), and treats them well. Its wage scales and fringe benefits are approximately the same as Ford's. Even more important, says van Wyk of the South African Institute of Race Relations, "General Motors is very aware." One sign of G.M.'s awareness is the practically constant flow of company officers from Detroit to inspect the plant in Port Elizabeth. One such visitor was Chairman of the Board Richard C. Gerstenberg, who flew to South Africa in April "to assure myself that General Motors is doing everything it can to hasten the day of equality there."

Much has happened at G.M. in the past six months alone. The number of workers enrolled in in-plant technical programs has been doubled. G.M.'s African workers, forbidden by law from belonging to registered unions, were encouraged to form a "Works Committee," which can take up grievances with management. The company also announced it would pay full tuition for any employee who wished to continue his education after hours.

Potentially more important in the long run is a program, similar to one started by Gillette, to help black children go to school. (In South Africa, education is free and compulsory only for whites; for blacks, with their low incomes, going to school can be a prohibitively expensive proposition.) Under its program, G.M. will pay tuition and the cost of books for the children of its African workers; that amounts to $7.53 a year for each child, which could take care of about one-third of the total cost in the lower grades. Since January, when G.M.'s education subsidy was announced, 475 black children have started to school with company support. In addition, G.M. has provided 125 scholarships of $33.25 a year for high-school students; small as it is, the sum is enough to take care of a large part of their total costs.

As with Ford, there are still areas where G.M. falls short in the view of its nonwhite workers. Sauls, the union secretary, complains that "the communication between employer and employee is not very good," and criticizes the technical training courses as having no visible results. "They train the chaps," says Sauls, "but once they graduate they don't give them the jobs. It's a dead end." G.M., however, insists that this is being changed. Several colored group leaders, it says, have been trained to become foremen; the first of them will be installed—title, salary, and all —in his new post by the end of the year. Because of pressures from the white union, however, those new foremen will be given supervision only over nonwhite workers.

In the past, Chrysler has lagged behind both Ford and G.M. in its treatment of nonwhite workers, but that is now changing. Since 1968 the average wage paid African workers by Chrysler has nearly tripled. This occurred even though the company has moved its main plant from Capetown, a high-wage area, to a location near Pretoria, where the going rates are lower. The new plant is not far from an African township, which provides a considerable pool of potential labor. About 1,000 of the plant's 2,038 workers are black, and another 111 are coloreds. Under a job-reservation determination issued in 1970, Chrysler is required to keep 30 percent of the assembly-line jobs at this new plant for whites, but it has undertaken an active training program to upgrade the skills—and pay—of its African employees.

SOOT IN THE CAFETERIA

Not all American companies involved with the auto industry get high marks for their treatment of nonwhites. Firestone, for example, recently built a new factory near an African homeland in a location that has been designated as a "border area"; the designation means that the normal minimum-pay scales do not apply there. This factory—at Brits, a town near Pretoria—has 140 workers, almost all African (there are twenty whites). Firestone put some of the blacks through a five-month training course to equip them for better jobs, but it has not been paying them as skilled labor. The going rate for skilled blacks in Brits industries is 45 cents an hour.

At the main Firestone plant in Port Elizabeth, where there are almost 1,400 workers (380 whites, 450 coloreds, and 525 blacks), minimum rates do apply, and the average wage of nonwhites is higher than at Brits. But the company's wages at Port Elizabeth are low for the area. For example, Firestone starts its colored workers at 40 cents an hour, or considerably less than Ford or General Motors, its two largest competitors for labor. The result, according to Sauls, is that Firestone has to take "the dregs, the people Ford and G.M. don't want." Firestone recently installed a cafeteria for its colored workers, but Sauls says: "It is so bad that our people won't eat there. The tables are covered with soot. The food is covered with soot."

And what of Polaroid, the company that started all the fuss? Having no direct subsidiary in South Africa, Polaroid has no employees of its own there. Since the "Polaroid experiment" began, however, the company has persuaded Frank & Hirsch, the local (but independent) distributing company for its products, to give black employees wage increases of 22 percent. Frank & Hirsch now pays its 151 Africans an average of $121 a month; the increases cost the distributor $39,500 a year in additional wages. Polaroid itself has provided grants totaling $75,000 to promote education of Africans. That may not be a great deal, but it is considerably more than most American companies have done.

"STOP HIDING BEHIND THE LAWS"

All together, there are probably not more than twenty-five subsidiaries of American corporations that can be considered to be reacting responsibly to the growing pressures for change. In addition to those already mentioned, they include companies such as Norton Co., PepsiCo, Coca-Cola, and General Electric.*The others— and there are more than 250 of them—either oppose change or are dragging their feet. The O'okiep Copper Co., for example, 57.5 percent owned by Newmont Mining Corp., still maintains a feudalistic labor system that has long been standard in South African mines. O'okiep has 2,000 black workers. It recruits them from poverty-ridden tribal areas, signs them to one-year contracts at wages averaging about $40 a month (plus bed and board in the company compound), then ships them back home when their year is up.

Even in the manufacturing industries, American employers as a whole are falling short—and not just in their pay scales. "They have no communication with their Africans." say Dudley Horner, of the South African Institute of Race Relations. "It's just hire and fire. How can you run a plant if you don't even talk to your workers?"

What most American subsidiaries need is thorough, fundamental, and genuine reform. The first thing they must do, says Morris Cowley of I.B.M., is to "stop hiding behind the laws." They should pay a living wage, which means roughly $50 a month above the local poverty datum line, even to common laborers. They should train Africans for skilled and responsible jobs, then put them into those jobs and

---

*Time Inc., the publisher of Fortune, maintains a business office for Time magazine in Johannesburg with six employees, including an African messenger-chauffeur who is paid $144 a month. In addition, Keartland Press of Johannesburg prints 55,000 copies of Time each week on a contract basis. About half of Keartland Press's 407 workers are Africans. The minimum wage for these black workers is $79.80 a month, their average wage is $159.60 a month.

pay them for performing them. They should encourage their Africans to form a Works Committee that can serve both as a union and a channel of communication with management. Whenever possible, they should put blacks and whites at the same job in the same room. Finally, they should prepare the ground for putting black supervisors in charge of whites.

Daring as some of these measures may seem, they have all been put into effect in today's South Africa by one or more companies. Such changes have to be made quietly of course, and with discretion. "Any employer who goes whole hog, publicly, can expect retribution from the government," concedes Robert Kraft, assistant general secretary and economist of the Trade Union Council of South Africa. On the other hand, there is a widespread belief that the government would like to see a general liberalization of labor practices, though it cannot afford to admit it openly because of pressures from rigid Afrikaners. "Vorster is happy to see the laws bent and broken," says Loveday, "but he cannot openly condone it." The strongest position for an enterprising employer, according to Kraft, is to "present the public and government with a *fait accompli,* a situation that has been working for a year or two. There's nothing anyone can do about it then."

Many of the actions open to employers are subject to no pressures at all. Any manager can insist that his African workers be treated with the same basic human dignity as his whites. He can give financial support to such worthwhile South African institutions as the National Development and Management Foundation, which has recently started a series of courses designed to train Africans for management positions. He can also, and at a minimal cost, follow the lead of Gillette and G.M. and subsidize the education of African children. Along with higher wages, what most African workers want most is education for their children.

DIRECTION FROM THE TOP

Only top management in U.S. headquarters can take the steps necessary to improve the lot of their nonwhite employees in South Africa. "The direction for change must come from the boardrooms back home," says Bill Marshall Smith of Caltex. "And let's face it, we could all be moving faster." Too often, however, home-office decisions must be made on the basis of faulty or misleading information from the field. An auto-company executive, resident in South Africa, explains the danger: "Corporate decisions are made from tiny slips of paper with maybe just the figures written on them. The slips are the distillations of reports from the field. But no subsidiary tells its home office the truth. We all lie as much as we think we can get away with. We even lie about figures, so you can imagine how much we lie about everything else. If anybody back there really knows what we're doing, it's certainly not our fault."

Top managements that want to protect the future of their companies in a changing South Africa will face a difficult, and perhaps painful, task. One important step would be to quit judging local managers solely by the size of their current profit margins. Instead, they should be encouraged to act in the longer-term interest of the company, with power to increase wages and improve the benefits of African workers. In most cases, the profits from South African operations are so substantial that the increased labor costs would not be overly burdensome—especially since productivity would be likely to improve.

The challenge U.S. corporations face in South Africa was capsulized last year by a fast-growing black group called South African Students Organization. Its manifesto declared: "The white man must be made aware that one is either part of the solution or part of the problem." The words are hardly original, but the implicit challenge to U.S. business is all too real.

SELECTED READINGS

"A Black and White Issue Faces Polaroid," *Business Week,* November 14, 1970.

"Churches Lose Bid On G.E. Disclosure," *New York Times,* April 26, 1973.

"Churches Mount First Joint Campaign Against U.S. Firms in Southern Africa," *Wall Street Journal,* February 15, 1972.

South Africa, A National Profile, Ernst and Ernst International Business Series, May, 1971.

"Polaroid To Continue South African Program To Aid Black Workers," *Wall Street Journal,* December 31, 1971.

Vicker, R., "Some U. S. Firms Ignore Urgings to Leave, Instead Seek to upgrade Status of Blacks," *Wall Street Journal,* September 22, 1971.

Case

CRAMPTON OIL CORPORATION INVESTS IN NAMIBIA

Crampton Oil Corporation, although doing $325 million in annual sales, is small by industry standards. The company's operations are principally confined to domestic drilling, exploration, and refining. The company refines about three-quarters of its own crude, selling the products to independent heating-oil distributors and small, privately-owned chains of gasoline stations. Although the company is located in Oklahoma, its principal outlets for heating oil are in the Northeast and for gasoline in the states of Ohio, Indiana, Illinois, and Kentucky. The remainder of its crude is delivered by pipeline and tanker to a refinery in New Jersey belonging to another small firm.

Crampton's first overseas venture is in Namibia (South West Africa) where it is currently drilling exploratory wells. Crampton won the concession to drill at a recent auction conducted by the government of the Republic of South Africa.

South Africa administers Namibia under a League of Nations mandate. That mandate, however, has been voided by the United Nations. Despite a World Court opinion that South African jurisdiction over Namibia is illegal, the Pretoria government refuses to relinquish control. Apartheid, or racial segregation, is practiced in Namibia, although the legislation applies only to South Africa proper. Worldwide calls for self-determination for the inhabitants of Namibia have been issued; indeed, South Africa is on numerous boycott and trade embargo lists.

Investment by United States corporations, however, is increasing despite the fact that the United States Government discourages it. In fact, the Treasury Department is considering disallowing the credits paid for foreign taxes relative to operations in Namibia.

Crampton management views the prospect of an oil strike in Namibia as high despite the fact that three dry holes have been sunk so far. Geological tests in the area were very encouraging. Crampton's relationship with the government of South Africa are described as formal, but cordial and good. Crampton bid in on the South African auction to assure the company of continuing supplies of crude. The company's domestic fields may last for 10 years of economical production, and Crampton is not equipped to tackle offshore drilling, where most of the new finds are being made; nor could the company always be assured of buying crude on the open market, although surpluses of relatively cheap crude are quite common.

Several shareholders, principally church groups, view Crampton's new investment in Namibia with displeasure. George Crampton, Chairman of the Board, and Walter Gunn, President, were both of the opinion that the Namibia operation was essential for the company's viability. They thought that Crampton Oil, being a small company, should be immune from the swirl of protests engulfing General Motors, Polaroid, Gulf Oil, and other business giants, since Crampton's impact would be minor, and smaller companies, fighting for their lives, must be allowed concessions that larger firms could be called to task for. Although Crampton and Gunn both grew up in the rough-and-tumble of the early oil business, they were thought to be model contemporary businessmen. Crampton Oil hired without regard to race or religion and was a strong supporter of local and regional civic and social activities.

Three church groups holding 2000 shares of Crampton stock (one-tenth of one percent of the total shares outstanding) have announced that they are combining forces to raise the issue of Namibia investments for discussion at the annual meeting. They also announced that, if Crampton management would not agree to put the issue on the meeting's agenda, they would petition the Securities and Exchange Commission. Crampton Oil Corporation is incorporated in the State of Delaware, under whose laws a company can dispense with its annual meeting for proxy matters if shareholders so indicate. George Crampton and Walter Gunn, along with their families, own six percent of the shares outstanding.

Crampton and Gunn called in Jim Jenkins, a corporate staff public-relations officer, to discuss the strategy and substance of responding to the church groups. The two men lectured Jenkins for over an hour on the importance of the Namibia operation, on the role Crampton could play in developing Namibia's economy, and on their opinions of the groups seeking to raise the issue. Then they gave Jenkins the assignment of devising the corporate strategy and drafting the corporate response. It was also suggested that Jenkins handle the annual meeting if and when the Namibia question came up.

Jenkins, who is a member of one of the church denominations involved in the issue, hadn't really thought about the issue before. He returned to his office and slumped into his chair. "I've got some hard thinking to do," he mused to himself.

F. *U.S. Business Abroad: The Ugly American*

United States culture, politics, technology, and society do not encompass the total environment faced by many firms. Most of the giant American corporations and indeed, many smaller and medium size firms, have some exposure to other countries and cultures, whether through the purchasing of materials and products made abroad, the exporting of products, or the establishment of offices and plants in other countries.

We have already encountered one of the issues faced by companies with international operations—apartheid in South Africa—and we should like to explore some of the other issues here. At this point, we might note that expanding numbers of young executives are being offered challenging overseas assignments. We might also note that American business firms are being increasingly prodded to explore opportunities for trade in foreign lands. Thus, the probability that a young graduate will someday be stationed overseas is increasing. That the executive posted overseas should be attuned to some of the problems and differences he will meet overseas needs hardly to be mentioned.

STAFFING

Probably the most important consideration that an American firm must consider in establishing plants and offices in another country is the extent to which citizens of the host country will be employed in top or sensitive management positions. This is not an easy question to resolve. In some cases, qualified personnel are not available. In others, the relationship of all the firm's branch offices to the home office is governed by a control policy that requires that someone familiar with corporate organization and planning be in charge at the satellite locations. Still other firms are concerned with the security of proprietary secrets or processes, and are not yet ready to entrust these matters to foreign nationals. Yet, many times, the American firm (and, to an increasing extent, the Japanese firm operating abroad) finds itself the target of nationalist emotions when all of the top management positions are staffed by Americans. Some firms, in response to pressure for staffing with local managers, initially appoint American managers while simultaneously engaging local personnel. Gradually, if all goes according to plan, the Americans phase out and the local managers phase in.

CULTURAL INVOLVEMENT

Then there is the question of how deeply an American based firm becomes involved in the culture of the host country. Does the firm passively react to another culture, conform to it, or attempt to change it? Here the American firm is sometimes in a quandary. The power of an American firm or group of firms, resulting from sheer size alone, may have a cultural impact in another country despite as passive a posture as possible. In Canada, for example, there is deep resentment of the Americanization of Canadian culture that results chiefly through American ownership of a large segment of Canadian industry and media. Although there may be no conscious effort on the part of American firms to dominate or impose American culture, sheer size has its own impact. Most Canadian cars are of American design and make, most of the movies are American, and many of the familiar products in United States supermarkets line the shelves of Canadian supermarkets as well. Indeed, many Canadian unions are part of U.S.-based organizations.

Conversely, some American firms do attempt to dominate the culture of the country in which they locate. Managers often insist on conducting business in English. Firms introduce U.S. production and marketing methods that may seriously undermine family, tribal, or cultural traditions that have long governed and provided the weft of the social fabric in another country. And many American managers have an innate conviction that only the American way is the correct way. These types of managerial postures can have serious repercussions, and can result in a not too pleasant relationship between a firm and its host country.

MULTINATIONALS

Sometimes firms declare themselves multinational, with offices all around the world, managers drawn from many cultures, and business conducted in several languages. These firms ostensibly declare allegiance to no particular culture or society. Obviously there are advantages to multinational status, not the least of which are the traditional business-decision parameters: ready access to markets and sources of raw materials, lower taxes, ability to find pools of able and cheap labor, the securing of acceptance, and worldwide financing, to name a few.

A multinational corporation, however, does not shed its national affiliation simply because it declares itself a worldwide firm. There is no international government to which a corporation can declare its allegiance, and multinationals are still considered firms of the countries in which they were founded or in which they maintain their largest installations or head offices. Multinationals run the risk of criticism in their countries of origin if they use the designation to rationalize decisions made to the advantage of another country and the disadvantage of the country of origin. Many of the oil companies claim they are multinational corporations even though their parent operations are in the United States and they are identified chiefly as U.S. firms. When the Arab oil embargo was declared, the major oil companies obeyed an order from the Saudi Arabian government to cease deliveries of Arab oil to U.S. military installations. Although many of the companies claimed they were able to divert non-Arab oil to U.S. military needs, nevertheless they were sharply criticized for their acquiescence to Arab demands. On the other hand, the oil companies were caught in a squeeze because they did have substantial stakes in the oil-producing countries and were bound to obey the laws of those countries, also.

In another case, the Argentinian subsidiary of General Motors Corporation was solicited to sell several thousand vehicles to Cuba, currently on the U.S. government's total embargo list. United States government policy calls for foreign subsidiaries of U.S. firms to be governed by the embargo listing. Argentina, however, was prepared to order that the sale go through. The question of national allegiance for the multinational firm was thus crucial. In the end, the United States raised little complaint and the sale went through; relations between the U.S. and Cuba have shown signs of improvement and many authorities cite an improved climate of international relations as the reason for the mild U.S. government reaction. If, however, the United States government had objected and the Argentinian government had insisted, the key problem facing U.S.-based multinationals would have been brought into sharp focus. Similar predicaments face the firms operating in South Africa. Military supplies are on the embargo list for South Africa. What would happen if the South African government ordered military equipment from Ford or General Motors plants in that country?

AMERICAN FIRMS AND FOREIGN POLITICS

A related question concerns the involvement of American firms in the politics of the host country. In some degree, the call for American firms to involve themselves in a change of South African apartheid policies is the converse of the posture firms typically are being urged to adopt. Most observers are urging U.S. firms to keep out of local political and governmental controversies or elections, but for others perhaps the *issue* is most important, not the process.

In the most celebrated case of involvement, the International Telephone and Telegraph Corporation came under heavy fire, both in this country and in Chile, when columnist Jack Anderson released documents purporting to show that ITT sought to prevent the inauguration of President Salvadore Allende Gossens of Chile in 1970, and then tried to influence the United States government to bring pressure on Chile to prevent expropriation of ITT property in that country. Of course, American business and U.S. foreign policy have come a long way since the U.S. Marine Corps constituted business's private army and the protection of U.S. business assets was a primary mission of U.S. foreign policy. Every once in a while, however, a manager or his firm does become overly zealous in trying to maintain some concession or status in another country and an embrassing and potentially explosive situation quickly develops.

NEW DANGERS IN INTERNATIONAL BUSINESS

Businesses operating abroad have always faced the dangers of being caught in international wars, or internecine expropriation and nationalization, and changes in governments. They have also faced situations where they were labeled "Yankee imperialists" by political groups seeking change. But recently they have faced terrorist threats to executives and installations; and bombings and arson have been directed at American-owned firms all over the world. Some executives have been kidnapped. Esso paid over $11 million to gain the release of one of its executives kidnapped by guerillas in Argentina. With different outlooks toward political violence, and with American-based firms forming convenient targets, such occurrences might be increasingly common in future years.

DAY-TO-DAY RELATIONSHIPS

The involvement of American firms in the culture and politics of other countries is usually less sensational, however, than the episodes we have recounted. Thousands, of American executives and managers are sustaining productive and rewarding relationships in other lands.

It is the less sensational problems and cultural adjustments that are most pervasive, however, and indeed these loom important in the successful conduct of business. Language, customs, eating etiquette, punctuality, dress, entertainment, male and female status, and the rest of the day-to-day things that managers must be aware of when they are assigned to another country, are the primary lessons in an overseas manager's education.

Since many of the less developed countries may seek out American investment and know-how, living in those countries may involve whole new learning experiences for American managers used to dealing with, say, European cultures. Without a knowledge of the customs and cultures of the less-developed countries, what might be considered an unimportant and irrelevant indiscretion by an American manager could become the cause of a substantial loss of business and strained relationships.

Thus, we broaden the scope of the manager's environment. It may be trite to say that the world is getting smaller, but for the manager involved in overseas operations, certainly a broadening of his environmental perspective is very much in order.

THE READINGS

Our first article, from *Business Week,* focuses on the multinational corporation and the new tensions arising between the multinationals and their host countries around the world. "Designed to operate easily and profitably across national boundaries, [the multinational] is running up against the economic and political aspirations of increasingly assertive national states. Indeed, there is some question whether the multinational company can survive in its present form."

From the *Management Review,* we include the article "Business Customs from Malaya to Murmansk" by H. K. Arning. Arning covers the seemingly innocuous but, in reality, significant differences in customs between nations. Personal manners, privacy, meals, pride and status, truth, terms of payment, and gifts are among the areas covered in this interesting survey.

Finally, Richard D. Hays, in the "The Executive Abroad," discusses the "behavioral problems and difficulties of an individual moving from one cultural environment to another . . ." He covers problems associated with culture shock, self-reference tendencies, and national stereotyping which "represent the root of a substantial portion of behavioral difficulties associated with international business."

New Era for the Multinationals

Business Week

The multinational company, probably the most successful secular international organization in history, is moving into the most critical state of its evolution. Designed to operate easily and profitably across national boundaries, it is running up against the economic and political aspirations of increasingly assertive national states. Indeed, there is some question whether the multinational company can survive in its present form.

For one thing, the number of socialistically tinged governments is on the rise. None of these administrations looks with much favor on the untrammeled existence of powerful entities committed to profits through the free employment of capital and labor.

"From being welcomed, the multinationals have moved to a stage where they are reluctantly tolerated," suggests John Dunning, professor of economics at Britain's Reading University and a specialist in multinational matters. "It is somewhere between uneasy alliance and open hostility."

Flareups between multinationals and their host governments are increasing in both number and severity. The most dramatic confrontation, of course, involves the world's major oil companies and the Middle East kingdoms. In addition, Jamaica has hit Reynolds Metals Co., Kaiser Aluminum & Chemical Corp., and several more of the biggest aluminum companies with a $200-million levy on bauxite exports from the tiny Caribbean country. And F. Hoffmann-La Roche & Co., the big Swiss drug company, is battling bitterly with the British Parliament over the transfer of enormous profits out of Britain.

The list grows longer every day. What is more, a number of convenient mechanisms that smoothed the way for multinational operations—from customs unions to monetary cooperation—are breaking down. And just to make life more difficult, economic growth is slowing throughout the world.

THE QUESTION OF SOVEREIGNTY

All this is not to say that the giant worldwide companies lack the resources to operate profitably under difficult circumstances. Their 1973 profits were handsome indeed, and many of them are forecasting good years ahead. Indeed, the multinationals may do a lot better than smaller companies limited to national markets. But in the long run, they will have to substantially alter their way of doing business if they wish to hold onto their positions.

The driving force behind this pressure for change is the delicate issue of sovereignty, both national and commercial: Does the parent company or the host government have final control over the actions of the multinational subsidiary? Which decides whether technology should be imported or withheld? Which decides whether capital flows freely from one subsidiary to another? Which decides whether an unprofitable plant closes or stays open?

The questions are critical because multinational subsidiaries are often major factors in key sectors of the economy. In France, for example, Westinghouse Electric leads the way in nuclear reactor orders. International Telephone & Telegraph subsidiaries have the largest share of the telephone equipment market. IBM and Honeywell-Bull dominate in computers.

In a time of economic slowdown, such dominance has the potential for conflict. The multinational companies, controlled by managers with a worldwide view, will act at variance with the policies of a government struggling to fend off inflation, maintain employment, and support a weakening currency. An example cropped up last month when Chrysler Corp., the U.S. auto maker, tried to lay off workers at a French plant and ran into the establishment. Chrysler reconsidered.

Some multinationals must change their ways faster than others. The greatest pressure is being exerted upon those corporations in the highly visible and politically sensitive area of natural resources.

The days are fading fast when a multinational group can retain equity control of a major project. In the future, the companies will provide indispensable services —technology, managerial skills, or marketing networks—to nationally controlled entities in return for a share of the product. Charles W. Robinson, president of Marcona Corp., has a grisly image for the future of relations between companies and countries: "The only thing that counts is whether you are worth more alive than dead. If you are worth more dead, you'll be dead."

The companies that will be able to retain the most control for the longest time will be those with an advanced technology in great demand. International Business Machine Corp.'s computer skills, for example, give it tremendous leverage in its effort to retain 100% of its multinational operations.

Says IBM Vice-Chairman Gilbert E. Jones: "It is economically unfeasible to build components in every country. We split the manufacture so that the whole European market for, say, printers will be supplied out of one plant." But even so independent a company as IBM must sometimes bend its planning to suit national interests. For example, it will probably bow to pressure from the Spanish government and build a plant in Spain to maintain access to that booming market.

Ford Motor Co.'s problem in the developing world is slightly different. Although Asia is a growing market, few nations can support an automotive manufacturing facility. In order to mollify national desires to participate in industrial development, Ford is using rationalization—which it calls "complementation"—to assign manufacture of specific auto components to various Asian countries. The assembly itself is centralized in still another nation. The ultimate problem is that no country wants to be a cog in a larger wheel, and each eventually presses for a more broadly based industry.

LOCAL PARTICIPATION

Furthermore, there is growing pressure from individual governments to allow more local involvement in the operations of multinational subsidiaries. The more thoughtful corporations have moved nationals into top managerial spots wherever possible —IBM boasts that it could fly the bulk of its U.S. nationals working abroad back home in one 747. But this will not be enough. Larger involvement will translate as more domestic equity, leading to control or, as is the case in Germany, a larger say for workers in management.

Major local participation cannot help but crimp the style of the multinationals. "For example," says a foreign affairs analyst of a major U.S. auto company, "we cannot take a loss in one country for the benefit of the total corporation. It makes it tough to operate." Local partners from the private sector often want to see the profits returned to them rather than plowed back or shifted out of the country. Government local partners, on the other hand, might want the profits reinvested, and they would take umbrage at a multinational that pulled out large dividends because it believed the local currency was about to be devalued.

WHERE IT'S AT

Yet no matter how fast or how fundamentally the rules change, the multinationals have to remain in the game. For some it is a matter of retaining access to raw materials in an increasingly resource-short world. One Tokyo banker expects Japanese overseas investment to climb from $10-billion to $40-billion by 1980.

For other multinationals, particularly U.S. companies, abroad is where the growth is. And foreign sales have often proved more profitable than the domestic variety. B. F. Goodrich Co., the Akron tiremaker, is a case in point. Right now, foreign business accounts for 28% of its $1.7-billion in sales and 33% of its profits. Goodrich Chairman O. Pendleton Thomas is pushing expansion in the parts of the world that have the least restriction on foreign investments, such as Brazil. Thomas realizes that Goodrich will have to relinquish his goal of 100% ownership in most places. But this judgment is that "the demand for tires will grow faster out of the U.S. than in it."

Thomas' judgment is echoed by U.S. corporate managers in other industries. Says J. Paul Lyet, chief executive officer of Sperry Rand Corp.: "Thirty-five percent of something is a lot better than 100% of nothing."

The multinationals are hardly likely to become objects of pity. Their size and international breadth give them alternatives that national companies lack. They can outbid most competitors in the scramble for high-priced raw materials. What is more, they have the flexibility to extricate themselves from ticklish situations. Sperry Rand's Lyet tells how his company faced the politically inflammable prospect of closing down an unprofitable operation in Italy. Instead, it switched the production of a higher-profit product to the Italian factory and kept it going.

Perhaps the greatest irony for the multinationals, most of whom naturally espouse free trade, is that they may lose some of their muscle in the western and developing world but become a major force in the détente developing between East and West. C. Fred Bergsten, a senior fellow at Brookings Institution, argues that only the multinationals have the clout and flexibility to deal with state economies. "And ironically," he says, "the multinationals probably will find that it's safer to operate in Communist countries than some others."

Business Customs from Malaya to Murmansk

H. K. Arning

The cultural differences between nations have developed on the basis of religious, political, and economical traditions. Some of them may appear unimportant to the foreigner—but ignorance about them can be dangerous to the success of business operations abroad. It is worthwhile, therefore, to look at some of the areas in which international marketers may experience difficulties that can be embarrassing or costly—and that in some cases can cost the company further business.

Reprinted by permission of the publisher, from *Management Review,* October, 1964. © 1964 by the American Management Association, Inc.

PERSONAL MANNERS

Business outside North America follows rather conservative rules, and the personal appearance, including dressing habits, are more formal than in Canada or the United States. To arrive at a business appointment without coat and tie indicates lack of respect in any country, but particularly in Asia the question of respect is more important than in many other parts of the world. One can always take off his coat if everybody else does, but as a rule it is advisable to keep on the formal side. Physical attitudes can also be important: For example, it is considered rude in Southeast Asia, particularly in Thailand and Laos, to display the sole of the foot or to sit with the legs crossed. In the same area it may be considered offensive to place your hands on your hips; many Chinese will regard it as signifying that you are angry.

Physical contact should be avoided throughout the Middle and Far East. Handshaking is commonly accepted in most of the Asian countries, but particularly in India and Thailand the initiative in this respect should be left to the national hosts, who often regard any physical contact with strangers—even handshaking—as distasteful. In Moslem countries, avoid linking arms or putting your arm around the shoulders of your wife; it may be unlawful, and would in most cases cause some embarrassment, since such physical contact is regarded as a private matter that should be confined to private quarters.

There is a sharp contrast between the attitude toward physical contact in large parts of the Middle and Far East on the one hand, and Latin America on the other. Again, it is undoubtedly helpful to let the host take the lead. Foreign visitors to Latin American countries have often attempted to avoid the repeated embracings, but such attempts are as a rule misunderstood by the local nationals, who interpret them as a sign of reserved attitude—which in turn breeds distrust. The same applies to a certain extent in respect of the distance between the faces. Asians will as a rule prefer a substantial distance compared to North American standards, while Latin Americans tend to be more comfortable with a distance of just a few inches. Thus, a businessman from North America may easily appear to be crowding in Asia, and give the impression of running away from his host in Latin America—neither of which is conducive to a relaxed business climate.

NO TRESPASSING

The European concept of privacy may sometimes appear unreasonably exaggerated to North Americans. Europeans consider it distasteful to talk about their family in the office or the plant, and it is not usual to meet colleagues on a social basis after business hours; family, evenings, and weekends are private matters that most Europeans prefer to keep separate from business. People may live for twenty years in the same house without ever inviting their neighbors over for a cup of coffee or a drink; they are courteous and friendly to each other, but they preserve their privacy. Such attitudes may possibly explain why the American-style cocktail party has not gained very wide popularity in Europe.

First names are seldom used outside the Western hemisphere, possibly because of the differentiation of the word "you" which occurs in many languages. The polite form of "you" expresses respect, while the familiar form is more intimate and is employed only within the family or between very close friends. For business purposes the respectful form is used almost without exception, and to combine it with first names would be comparable to saying Mr. Bob or Mr. Jim in English. The resentment against use of first names is particularly evident among North Europeans, who often will feel embarrassed when business acquaintances infringe on what they consider strictly private.

DINNER AT EIGHT

In most countries it is not customary to invite non-relatives to dinner at home; business acquaintances are entertained in clubs or restaurants. To receive an invitation to a private home is a great honor, and it should be kept in mind that an Indian, for example, never extends such invitations for the purpose of furthering business aims; that would be a violation of sacred hospitality rules. The codes in this respect vary with geographical areas and, generally speaking, only Australasia and the Scandinavian countries come fairly close to North American practices. A detail worth remembering overseas, especially in Scandinavia and the Netherlands, is the custom that the visitor brings some flowers or a box of confectionery to the hostess when he is invited to dinner. The cost or size of the gift is not important; it is the courtesy that matters.

All over the world it is usually appreciated when foreigners follow local eating customs. Often, the local food can be very worthwhile, and to experiment with chopsticks, for example, can be highly entertaining—particularly for the host. It is a practical exercise in applied good will, and if you give it an honest try and prove that you cannot manage, your host will not be offended if you ask for knife and fork. It may be useful to remember that Chinese dinners usually consist of eight courses, and that the guest is supposed to remain hungry throughout the seven first ones. The eighth course is usually fried rice or noodles, and at that stage it is customary for the guest to help himself to a modest quantity, thus indicating that he has had enough; otherwise the host will order still further dishes. In Chinese homes it is common practice that the guest will respectfully decline to be the first to help himself from any course, no matter how much the host insists. In Scandinavia it is proper etiquette to shake hands with the hostess thanking her for the meal when the dinner is over. It is much appreciated when foreign visitors are aware of this courtesy.

The Asian attitudes to consumption of alcohol range from partial prohibition in India to various degrees of liberal drinking in Chinese and Japanese company. Contrary to common belief, the local brews are not very potent, and although the principle of temperance is highly recommended, it may be wise to follow the hosts even into simulating a slight degree of intoxication. Complete abstinence from drinking is often regretted, but it is also respected.

In this context, it should be noted that in an Asian society where a rigid code of formality has been deeply ingrained from childhood, the relaxing effects of alcohol may perhaps be more appreciated than in Western societies; for business purposes there may be special reasons to keep that in mind.

In Mediterranean countries and in Latin America, it is rare indeed to see intoxicated people in public. The nationals of these countries are proud of their wines and they enjoy them frequently, but in modest quantities. Scandinavians are said to be heavy drinkers, but that reputation is hardly justified, at least not in business circles.

PRIDE AND STATUS

In countries that recently have obtained political independence, the government and its policies are a matter of considerable pride. Most people will be delighted for an opportunity to explain political and also religious questions to foreigners, but it is advisable to avoid unfavorable comparisons with other systems or religions. There is little satisfaction and still less business to be derived from hurting the host's pride or from questioning his religious convictions.

Some North American businessmen tend to judge business acquaintances abroad on the basis of their status symbols. Many times such judgments are made subconsciously or automatically, and it may be useful to keep in mind that the yardsticks abroad are different. The top floor is not necessarily the executive suite; in Japanese department stores, the top floor is reserved for bargain counters. The location and size of the office or the carpeting of the floor may be subject to practical, legal, or climatic considerations. In fact, in a number of countries the nationals will flatly deny that they have any system of material status symbols at all. There may be many reasons for that, among which could be mentioned that differences in caste or class may make such symbols distasteful; sometimes the language or diction will express status, sometimes the name or title will indicate proud tradition or great wealth. Family, relatives, connections, and friendships are in most cases by far the most important status symbols and, actually, materialistic symbols would often be completely out of place.

BUSINESS MANNERS

Through the centuries, it has been a custom in most countries that the eldest son follow the line of his father in career fields such as civil service, the armed forces, and certain professions. The introduction of communism brought an abrupt end to such bourgeois traditions in Eastern Europe. Presently, however, there are indications that the former aristocracy in the communist countries quietly continue their old traditions: the medical families still raise doctors, and the offspring of the merchant clans join the state trading monopolies. This does not in any way imply a change in the communist doctrine, but it is noteworthy that some of the old and proud traditions are carried forward, notably the sense of honor and integrity that prevailed in business circles in Russia, Poland, Hungary, and Czechoslovakia before the communist upheaval. At that time, the East European countries were in many respects similar to the conservative Western Europe, and some of the old cultural attitudes are still recognizable. Due to the nature of the political system, however, the businessmen have not been exposed to the modifying influence of frequent contact with foreigners, and consequently, they often appear rigidly formal, which is evident in their dress, speech, and observance of traditional business rituals—as well as in their meticulous fulfillment of contract obligations.

BEHIND THE IRON CURTAIN

Westerners sometimes find it difficult to appreciate that import and export agencies in the East European countries are part of the enormous communist civil service, and considerable time is required before a decision can be made on a Western business proposal. Plans and suggestions have to be approved by a seemingly endless number of committees, and in some cases it has happened that several years have elapsed before a final word is forthcoming.

Russian negotiators often have formal training in both bargaining and chess playing, which may explain why every move they make is so carefully planned. They never seem to get tired, and their negotiating skills may often test the Westerner's professional and human endurance. When agreement on one point apparently has been reached, they may start the next day by going through all the same motions again, pinning down every little detail. As purchasing agents they are shopping all over the world for the most advantageous deals, and they are fully aware that the centralization of the communist purchasing functions put them in a favorable bargaining position: The orders are not numerous, but they are sizable.

Late deliveries are a nuisance in most countries, but they may be more than that for East Europeans: A delay of just a few days may upset their quota system, and thus deprive them of their bonus. Western suppliers who are unable to meet the rigid communist system of quotas and deadlines will be unlikely to receive new or additional orders.

LITTLE WHITE LIES

It may not be pleasant to learn that truth is a relative matter, which actually is the case in a number of countries both in the Far East and in Latin America. Form may be more important, and it is obvious that that may complicate regular business transactions. If the foreign visitor is pressing hard to obtain an agreement, he may find that his host will sign the deal just to be pleasant, and without any intention of keeping to the contract. Similarly, and particularly in the Far East, it may be considered rude to say straightforwardly that the Westerner's product or service is unsuited for the Oriental customer's purpose, and the sale may be kept hanging in the air simply because the buyer does not want to be unpleasant.

When a trader in the Middle East asks a price that is twenty times higher than what he actually expects to obtain, we have a situation where the buyer obviously will be pleased when he has managed to haggle the price down to size. Both seller and buyer have made a good deal, and both are satisfied. Pleasantries are considered important, and the time required is immaterial.

Both in Latin America and in the Orient it is customary to spend considerable time talking around the business on hand, sometimes about completely irrelevant matters. One of the reasons for this habit is a traditional distrust of foreigners, which they try to overcome by developing a first stage of friendship before they come down to business. It should be noted in this context that friendships in many parts of the world are considered obligations to a much greater extent than is customary in North America, and that such obligations may imply substantial help over and beyond what may be agreed on in the contract. (This is one of the reasons why business with relatives and close family friends has priority over any other business in most parts of the world.)

FROM HERE TO ETERNITY

In Japan, it is not unusual to have long periods of silence in the middle of negotiations. Although it may be nerve-racking, it usually pays off handsomely if the Westerner can restrain himself enough to outwait the silence of his hosts. It may take thirty minutes, perhaps more, but in the meantime his silence is negotiating for him, usually better than he could do orally. Sometimes Oriental businessmen take advantage of the fact that time has become almost an obsession in Western countries. A Japanese once said that Westerners have a most convenient weakness: If they are kept waiting long enough they will agree to almost anything. Consequently, negotiators visiting Japan will often be asked how long they have planned to stay. Once that is known, they will be pleasantly entertained, while negotiations are kept inconclusive until a couple of hours before they are scheduled to leave, when the real business starts. Another aspect of time is the common lack of punctuality for business appointments in the East. The Westerner will learn that an hour or two is just an insignificant slice of eternity.

In fact, the question of punctuality is considered liberally in most parts of the world except in Northern Europe, where it is customary to arrive before the scheduled time. To be late for a business appointment in Northern Europe is often regarded as so disrespectful that it may hamper subsequent business relations.

CASH AND CREDIT

The terms of payment in many countries follow rules that are different from what is commonplace in North America. In Japan, it is not unusual to regard ninety-day or six-month promissory notes as cash payment. Good customers of Chinese business houses have an almost unlimited credit. A Chinese does not want to ask a rich man for money, and consequently the renowned Chinese tailors in Hong Kong may wait for years before they issue a bill to Westerners living in the Crown

Colony. On the other hand, a Chinese is highly reluctant to grant credit to strangers, even if he knows that the customer has an important position in a large business corporation and carries fully satisfactory credit credentials. There are old and deeply ingrained traditions which form the reasons for this apparently contradictory attitude.

For exporters it may be useful to remember that interest rates in Asia often range from 8 to 12 per cent per year for bank loans—in Latin America, from 1 to 2 per cent per month. A liberal extension of credit may therefore be a strong sales argument in both areas. In Europe, the cost of capital is comparable to North American levels.

In most of the Orient, entertainment bills should be checked before they are paid. It is not at all unusual to overcharge foreigners, and if one only starts to add up the items, the bill will frequently be taken away for correction. In a number of Asian countries, the price for smaller services should be agreed on in advance, as the negotiating right is forfeited when the service has been performed. It may be rather embarrassing, for instance, when taxi drivers in the Middle East at the end of the trip start arguing at the top of their voices and with arms raised over the head, claiming a fare that is many times higher than what you are used to or might have agreed on before you hired the taxi.

BRIBES OR GIFTS?

Bribery is a relative matter, depending on the country and the circumstances. In Asia, the practice of giving gifts follows local rules which are too complicated to be discussed here. It should be noted, however, that in a number of countries civil servants are notoriously underpaid, and it is more or less understood that they perform certain services against a reasonable reward, provided receipts are not required. Such services may consist of such things as speeding up the handling of applications, arranging meetings with higher officials, cutting red tape, or extending the validity of visas and import licenses. It is highly advisable, however, to ask reliable advice, preferably from your consular service, before doing anything that might be construed as compromising the integrity of a civil servant abroad. What may be common practice in one country may be severely penalized in another.

ADVERTISING ABROAD

A substantial amount of literature about international advertising is available in North America, but as almost all of it is intended for West European or Latin American markets, it may be useful to mention a few points that should be taken into consideration when advertising is prepared for communist countries and for the Far East.

Marketing of Western consumer products in the Soviet Union may not be so remote any longer, and it may be worthwhile to note that since consumer articles have been in short supply for a long time in Eastern Europe, there has been no need to advertise whatever was available. However, advertising has been resorted to in order to dispose of slow-moving or substandard articles, and that has to a certain extent brought advertising into disrepute. The situation would make marketing difficult for Western businessmen who are accustomed to rely heavily on advertising, and it would appear to be advisable to put stress on quality and guarantees if an advertising campaign is to be launched.

Another difference between Western and communist advertising is in the use of female models: East Europeans regard as distasteful the use of models to attract attention for commercial purposes. An enterprising Russian garment manufacturer was recently criticized in Pravda because he used models in advertisements for bathing suits. The display of naked skin was, in Pravda's opinion, a sign of degeneracy.

Some elaborate advertising campaigns that have been launched in Asia have turned out to be complete failures because the marketers did not research and explore beyond the conventional data, particularly regarding the religions and superstitions of the countries concerned. Asia is composed of so many countries, religions, languages, and cultures that only wide diversification of the advertisements and a careful selection of media will render satisfactory returns.

There may even be a diversity of languages within the boundaries of the same country: the Commercial Manager of Air India, Mr. S. K. Kooka, has suggested that advertisers may use the Tamil language in South India, Hindu in North India, and Gujerati around Bombay. Also, it is almost impossible to translate directly from an alphabetic language into the characters and symbols of Chinese and Japanese, and still retain the same message.

The choice of illustrations is largely influenced by religious factors, for pictures of birds or animals or animal products may have specific religious connotations. Even pictures of people have to be selected to fit the cultural environment of the local market.

LUCKY COLORS

Colors have to be used with utmost care. To the Chinese, red is a lucky color; the Thai would prefer yellow for the same reason. The combination of purple and green is acceptable in several Asian countries, supposedly from the time when the leaders of the Shinto religion wore those colors. On the unfortunate side, the combination of black, white, and blue is suggestive of a funeral to the Chinese. Throughout the Far East there is a substantial amount of what Westerners usually call superstition connected with almost any color or combination of colors. For business purposes, superstition has to be respected; one cannot ignore it.

There are many pitfalls in international business that are caused by cultural differences, and to be trapped in one of them may have undesirable and sometimes costly consequences. Among foreign businessmen there is a small but increasing awareness of the existence of such differences, and over the long run the most extreme of them may be modified so that the gap is lessened. It is important, however, that visitors do not openly attempt to speed up any such development or to change the cultural habits of the local nationals. Such attempts will understandably be resented, and the repercussions on business will hardly make them worthwhile. Even when people are imitating knowingly, they like to feel that they have developed something themselves, and to tear down their illusions in that respect does not serve any useful purpose—at least not as far as the cultural differences that affect international business are concerned.

The Executive Abroad
Minimizing behavioral problems

Richard D. Hays

The range of problems faced by a firm broadens greatly as its interests and activities become more international in scope. The details and execution of technical business functions—such as marketing, accounting, and finance—all change dramatically as the international perspective replaces the national one. However, the area which probably holds more changes than any of these, and yet about which less is known, is the behavioral performance of individuals as they cross cultural and national boundaries.

As products and outputs are moved from one national market to another, changes must be made. As marketing, accounting, and financial systems are broadened to include multinational facets, fairly major changes and revisions must also be made. However, these changes tend to be along complex but nonetheless fairly determinable and predictable lines. The behavioral issue lacks this certainty. It is impossible to predict the behavior of individuals, with the accompanying vicissitudes and indeterminant states, when they are introduced into a new and different cultural environment. There is substantial evidence to indicate that many of the failures of international business ventures (as well as many suboptimal performances) can be attributed to the behavioral problems associated with transnational personnel rather than to technical difficulties.

Although the behavioral problems and difficulties of an individual moving from one cultural environment to another are complex, three particularly important areas of behavioral difficulty have been isolated for consideration here. The problems associated with culture shock, self-reference tendencies, and national stereotyping do not constitute the totality of behavioral problems, but they certainly represent the root of a substantial portion of the behavioral difficulties associated with

From *Business Horizons,* June, 1972. Reprinted by permission.

international business. A familiarity with the nature of these three problem areas is vital to businessmen associated with the cross-cultural transfer of personnel.

CULTURAL SHOCK

Each individual is a product of his own culture and background—probably much more so than he would suspect or admit. Each adult has learned, through a long series of experiences in his specific cultural environment, to behave in specified ways and to expect particular kinds of behavior from those around him. The child-rearing process is largely an attempt to inculcate within the child the "proper" set of behaviors and expectations, so that child may become a well-integrated member of the society in which he lives. Most of the rules relating to behavior standards are culture-bound, in the sense that they are uniquely generated and taught to help the individual get along in that particular culture.

This system of appropriate behavior and expectations is extensive and ranges from such simple acts as the accepted way to deal with merchants or to obtain directions for travel to such a complex problem as the way to obtain employment or effect a political change. Each individual learns how to carry out these actions in his own cultural environment extremely well and has generated, over the years, a firm set of expectations as to how those around him will respond to his own behavior.

A confrontation, however, results when he faces individuals from another culture who operate under different behavioral assumptions and expectations. When he tries to carry out the simplest actions (which always worked in his home environment), the response from the new cultural environment may be totally unexpected and unintelligible to him. As pressures continue to mount because of this divergence from the sets of assumptions and behaviors that he has grown to know and understand, it becomes clear that the assumptions which he has used to guide his behavior in the past are no longer applicable. The people which surround him in this new setting think and act according to rules which he does not understand, and the inappropriateness of his own set of assumptions and internal rules is all too evident.

Unfortunately, however, the individual usually has not had sufficient training in the new culture to learn the subtleties of expected behavior which govern the actions of the local residents. Since his own frame of reference has been shown to be inadequate and since he has not had time to develop a new set of behavioral reference points, he is left with a void in the set of assumptions upon which he can base his behavior and expectations. Quite predictably, this void may cause a high level of anxiety disorientation, more familiarly termed "culture shock."

A universal experience

The severity of culture shock will differ among individuals, but some generalized statements about typical responses can be made. First, it should be noted that culture shock is a universal phenomenon which is precipitated when individuals are confronted with environments that are substantially different from those in which they were reared. Culture shock can affect the casual American tourist to England, the experienced multinational businessman in Thailand, or the foreign diplomat in Argentina. It often can be noted even when a family moves from one section of the United States to another.

One could expect the more severe cases to develop when the new environment was substantially different from the previous one, or in cases in which the individual concerned had not had much previous exposure to new and varied cultures. Therefore, we could expect that moving from Philadelphia to Phoenix would induce less shock than moving from St. Louis to Saigon. Similarly, it would be less severe for an individual who had spent his life traveling and exposing himself to different cultures and varying assumptions governing behavior than for an individual who had been exposed to only one environment.

Usually, the initial encounter with a new cultural environment evokes curiosity and amazement. However, as the newness of the experience begins to wear off, between one and three weeks from the first exposure, the negative impact of culture shock begins to set in. The weeks following the initial enchantment can be weeks filled with agony for the victim of severe shock. This period can be characterized by a strong rejection of the "way things are done here" and a wish that "these people would do things the right way—like we did back home."

During this period, the typical victim will grope for reference points which he may use to more adequately assess his own behavior and to provide him with more valid expectations regarding the behavior of those around him. He will find some type of accommodation to his problems. For some, the solution is escape from the difficulties of operating in this new environment. They may retreat to the security and familiarity of known environments; in fact, many of the failures of U.S. executives abroad can be directly traced to their wives, who decide that they can no longer take the foreign environment and must return to the United States. Or they may retreat to a local "colony," a transplant of the home culture with behavior patterns and expectations that are understood and shared.[1]

Another and usually more desirable resolution of the stresses of culture shock lies in the adaptation to the realities of the new culture. An individual can begin to learn the more subtle behavioral guidelines and therefore become less uncertain of his own actions and more knowledgeable in his expectations of the behavior of others. (The extreme form of this avenue of adjustment is "going Native," a phenomenon feared by multinational personnel officers but not a common occurrence.)

---

[1]For a more complete examination of the importance of wives' decisions see R. D. Hays, "Ascribed Behavioral Determinants of Success-Failure Among American Expatriate Executives," *MSU Business Topics* (Spring, 1971).

For an excellent insight into the details of the latter type of adjustment, see Anne D. Eggleston, "The Bored Wives of Tatapoto," *Worldwide P & I Planning* (January-February, 1960), pp. 61–68.

This learning process and the accompanying improved effectiveness in the new environment tends to lessen the stresses of culture shock. If an individual can remain immersed in a culture long enough to allow this process of adjustment and learning to continue to a mature stage, he can reduce his problem to a minor personal anxiety.

Minimizing shock

Since culture shock is a phenomenon expected from nearly all individuals, how can its negative effects be prevented or at least minimized? The Peace Corps and several multinational firms have found that if the individual who is contemplating a foreign assignment understands the universality of the problem and the details of its nature, he is more capable of coping with it once it occurs. If an individual understands, once the effects of culture shock set in, that he is not unique but is undergoing an experience that has been endured by thousands before him, he is going to be more capable of finding a more positive method for resolving his difficulties.

Therefore, many organizations have prepared their new international personnel with an orientation to the general nature of the phenomenon of culture shock so that these individuals may be better able to deal with it. A second device which seems to help is the provision of an environment which is as helpful as possible during the time the individual may be in a high stress condition. Although international assignments are often made on an emergency basis, many firms, whenever possible, provide periods of orientation and adjustment to their international employees which can help accelerate learning regarding the new cultural environment and consequently diminish the disorientation.

For example, if an executive is allowed time to help his wife get the family household operating, the severity of culture shock could be expected to be somewhat less for both. The shock is often greater for the wife than for the husband. While many things change in the husband's world, he does have the fairly familiar environment of his work to provide some mental reference points which are common between his new and old environments. For the wife, however, few possibilities for behavior common to a former life exist, because the entire mode of household management is vastly different in most cultures.

Other measures used to a lesser extent include psychological testing for individuals who may be highly prone to severe culture shock and screening these individuals out of an international assignment possibility. However, these types of approaches have not been highly predictable in their results, and consequently are not in widespread use.

SELF-REFERENCE TENDENCIES

A second problem that is a behavioral stumbling block in international business is closely related to the culture shock problem. However, the difficulty, rather than adjustment to a new culture, is the tendency to use oneself as a behavioral reference point. This problem is related more to effectiveness of behavior and influence in a new cultural environment.

Whether one's purpose in moving to a foreign environment is to achieve a business, political, or personal goal, the success of the venture will depend on effectiveness in relating to other individuals in the environment. In trying to achieve effectiveness in interpersonal relationships, one has to make certain assumptions about the behavior of others. Whether one is trying to make a decision about how to market a product abroad, or how to best set up a new production facility, these assumptions are crucial to the success of the venture.

However, one problem that seriously inhibits the effectiveness of many individuals in a foreign culture is a strong tendency to rely almost totally on themselves as reference points in making behavioral assumptions and judgments. This tendency is very natural. In situations where behavioral decisions must be made, the easiest assumption to make is that "others will behave as I would behave in this situation." If one is talking about individuals of one's own culture, this assumption can be quite valid and can produce effective behavior, but, in the international sphere, it can result in highly unsatisfactory situations.

One author has listed three examples in which Americans use themselves as reference points to make behavioral judgments in foreign environments, often with poor results.[2] The first concerns lateness for appointments. American standards for promptness and the obligations incurred by making an appointment sometimes differ dramatically from those used by foreigners. If an American executive has no real understanding of the nature of foreign thinking regarding lateness for appointments, he may find his actions severely at odds with those of members of the local culture.

A second example of use of the self-reference model relates to postponement in getting down to business. In the United States, only preliminary social amenities are exchanged prior to dealing with the business at hand. However, in a foreign culture one often experiences long delays (as judged by American standards) as seemingly endless social amenities and unnecessary niceties are exchanged. This system can be frustrating to an American using his own experience as a reference point without a real understanding of the reasoning behind this postponement.

The third example concerns the immensely varying commitments which are incurred in various cultures by virtue of a promise. In the Orient, an individual's promise that a certain act will be completed by a certain date does not necessarily mean that the act will be carried out as agreed. Judging by American standards, this is a breach of promise and onerous action, but an understanding of the Oriental rationale for this type of behavior can reduce the probability of an erroneous judgment regarding a colleague's promise.

---

[2]James A. Lee, "Cultural Analysis in Overseas Operations," *Harvard Business Review* (March-April, 1966), pp. 106–114.

Many other examples could be cited. But in each case, the foreigner's behavior, as seen by the foreigner himself, is eminently reasonable and logical. However, this same behavior, as seen through eyes using American bases for judgment, seems foolish or inefficient. These two differing interpretations arise because of the differing reference points of the observer. In cross-cultural situations, the use of one's self as a reference point in making decisions about the behavior of others may cause dysfunctional results. Self-reference tendencies can become a problem either because no better reference system is available or because the person involved forgets how strong this tendency is and how often it is used.

The first source of problems mentioned above can be overcome only by sufficient exposure to the new environment. Other improvements can be effected simply by understanding the nature of the problem itself. Information concerning the strong tendency to use one's self as a reference point can help an individual become more sensitive to decisions made in this manner.

Finally, and probably more important, a conscious effort to identify the specific kinds of cultural and behavioral reference points used in relating to the behavior of others can be extremely useful in preventing erroneous judgments. A specific and organized process of identifying the precise kinds of assumptions that one makes can be extremely fruitful in producing more effective outcomes for multinational personnel. Also helpful is an attempt to identify the different behavioral assumptions which might be appropriate in the culture in which one is working.

NATIONAL STEREOTYPING

A third behavioral stumbling block in international business relates to the phenomenon of national stereotyping. As individuals try to organize their thoughts about other groups of people, certain mental short cuts are taken. One of these short cuts is a grouping and labeling phenomenon commonly called stereotyping.

A stereotype is a mental picture used to identify and think about certain groups of people and usually contains a label, which is the title given to the group of people, and a mental list of traits that are associated with members of this group. The world is complex, and no one has the mental facility to file away each individual piece of information received during his lifetime regarding experiences and encounters. Therefore, we tend to group experiences and data and file them away in a more organized and easily accessible manner. These simplified data can now be called forth from memory as needed.

However, not all stored data are exact representations of reality, and the process of simplifying and classifying is a mental exercise involving bias and slanted views—even for the most objective individual. In the case of national stereotyping, this process is important to the business manager going abroad. He should understand not only the types of national stereotypes which he himself uses in thinking about other people, but the kinds of trait associations which mention of his own nationality brings forth in the minds of the members of the local population. Here the "truth" about a particular national group is much less important than the local beliefs incorporated into the local stereotypes of that national group.

For example, an American business executive traveling in a country where the label "American" is regarded negatively by the local population will probably act differently than he would in a country where Americans are looked upon favorably. He would find his reception and the general view of his activities much cooler in the first country and would probably respond by behaving in a more reserved and retiring manner. Obviously, all Americans will not act in ways that are congruent with the list of traits which others may assign to an American. However, everyone finds it useful to use these broad generalizations as a method of improving the organization and certainty of the expectations which we may have about the behavior of others.

In a study involving national stereotypes, U.S. college students were asked to list the characteristics they associated with certain national and ethnic labels. This experiment was first conducted in 1932 and again in 1950. The results are listed in the table on page 392.

For example, students in 1932 thought Italians were artistic, impulsive, passionate, quick-tempered, and musical. These were strong definers of Italians in the typical American national stereotype. By 1950, however, a much lower percentage of Americans assigned these traits to Italians. Two things had happened during that eighteen-year period. First, the mix of traits in the American stereotype of Italians had changed; in 1950, "impulsive" had slipped to fourth place. Second, in 1950 none of the traits were assigned to Italians in as high a frequency as in 1932. The stereotype of Italians in the mind of Americans had weakened and grown less definite.

Americans in 1950 seemed to have a much more diverse and open mental picture of the traits assignable to other nationalities. One might conclude from these data that Americans were becoming somewhat more sophisticated in their view of foreigners, and were using a more subtle and open structure in categorizing others (other less complimentary explanations are also possible). But, regardless of the explanation of this particular phenomenon, the knowledge that national stereotypes are often strong determinants of one's behavior toward others, and that national stereotypes can change over time, are important pieces of information for the multinational businessmen.

As more and more firms become multinational in their operations, the problems involving the transfer of individuals from one culture to another grow more intense and important. Three specific behavioral stumbling blocks in international business are culture shock, self-reference tendencies, and national stereotyping. Each has its unique details, but each is rooted in the mental reference system that we use to guide our own behavior and expectations concerning the behavior of those around us.

Stereotypes held by Americans concerning national and ethnic traits*

	1932 (N=100)	1950 (N=333)		1932 (N=100)	1950 (N=333)
Americans			*Germans*		
Industrious	48	30	Scientific-minded	78	62
Intelligent	47	32	Industrious	65	50
Materialistic	33	37	Stolid	44	10
Ambitious	33	21	Intelligent	32	32
Progressive	27	5	Methodical	31	20
English			*Japanese*		
Sportsmanlike	53	21	Intelligent	45	11
Intelligent	46	29	Industrious	43	12
Conventional	34	25	Progressive	24	2
Tradition-loving	31	42	Shrewd	22	13
Conservative	30	22	Sly	20	21
Negroes			*Chinese*		
Superstitious	84	41	Superstitious	34	18
Lazy	75	31	Sly	29	4
Happy-go-lucky	38	17	Conservative	29	14
Ignorant	38	24	Tradition loving	26	26
Musical	26	33	Loyal to family	22	35
Jews			*Irish*		
Shrewd	79	47	Pugnacious	45	24
Mercenary	49	28	Quick-tempered	39	35
Industrious	48	29	Witty	38	16
Grasping	34	17	Honest	32	11
Intelligent	29	37	Very religious	29	30
Italians			*Turks*		
Artistic	53	28	Cruel	47	12
Impulsive	44	19	Very religious	26	6
Passionate	37	25	Treacherous	21	3
Quick-tempered	35	15	Sensual	20	4
Musical	32	22	Ignorant	15	7

*Source: G. M. Gilbert, "Stereotype Persistence and Change among College Students," *Journal of Abnormal and Social Psychology,* LXVI (1951), pp. 245–54.

Action to minimize the negative effects of these stumbling blocks can take place on two fronts. First, awareness of the existence and nature of the problems of culture shock, self-reference tendencies, and national stereotyping can provide increased sensitivity and understanding of the difficulties of cross-cultural operations. Second, specific actions may be taken toward ameliorating the effects of each of these. These might be selective screening of potential international executives, provision of a supportive environment that will enable the transnational manager to better accommodate the problems of behavioral adjustment, and specific training and monitoring activities. The importance of understanding and dealing with these behavioral adjustments can be expected to increase dramatically as the degree of involvement of American business in multinational affairs increases.

SELECTED READINGS

Bates, T. H., "Management and the Multinational Business Environment," *California Management Review,* Spring, 1973.

Davis, S. M., *Comparative Management.* (Englewood Cliffs: Prentice-Hall, Inc., 1971.)

Hesseling, P., "Studies in Cross Cultural Organization," *Columbia Journal of Business,* Winter, 1973.

Lee, J. A., "Cultural Analysis in Overseas Operations, *Harvard Business Review,* March–April, 1966.

Thiagaran, K. M., "Cross-Cultural Training for Overseas Management," *Management International Review,* 1971.

Vernon, R., *Manager in the International Economy,* 2nd ed. (Englewood Cliffs: Prentice-Hall, Inc., 1971.)

Yousef, S. M., "Integration of Local Nationals into the Hierarchy of American Overseas Subsidiaries: An Exploratory Study," *Academy of Management Journal,* March, 1973.

Case

FILTCO, BELGIUM*

In July, 1972, John Hartley, President of Filtco Corporation, headquartered in New York City, was contemplating whether to allow the Managing Director of Filtco, Belgium, to assume control of the sales and marketing functions of the Belgian operation.

---

*Case prepared by Thomas M. McAuley. All rights reserved.

BACKGROUND OF WILLIAM PATTERSON

In 1961, William Patterson, Export Manager of Filtco Corporation, had developed a $2,000,000 export business. Export sales included various types of precisely engineered filter products used in industrial plants and in products they produced. Ninety percent of Filtco export sales were made to companies in Germany, France, Switzerland, Italy, the Netherlands, Belgium, and the Scandinavian countries. Primary growth had been in the European Common Market countries. Overseas sales of Filtco products were handled by Patterson, a salesman in Brussels, and agents in Italy, Germany, Sweden, and Switzerland. Since the number of customers was relatively small, this sales staff could manage the job satisfactorily. Shipments of products were made from three U.S. manufacturing plants.

Patterson had started his career with Filtco in 1945, after serving five years in the U.S. Army. He had gone to college for two years prior to entering the Service, but he decided not to continue his formal education after leaving the Army. He joined Filtco as a sales trainee and rapidly gained a reputation as an outstanding salesman. When Filtco decided to enter the export market in 1955, Patterson was chosen because of his superior sales skill, his thorough study of sales prospects, and his sensitivity to customer needs and personalities. In addition, he was a bachelor. Since his export sales job required considerable travel (often 50 percent of his time outside the U.S.A.), this was a critical factor in the decision to select him. (Patterson could not speak or write any foreign language.)

PLANNING THE FUTURE

In 1961, Patterson, Hartley, and Robert Bailey (Manufacturing Vice-President) met to review the objectives of the corporation, with special emphasis on what the strategy should be concerning its export business. In this review, consideration was given to long-range domestic plans, opportunities in the U.S.A. and abroad, threats to the domestic and foreign business, and a long, hard look at the future. The products made by Filtco were growing in domestic sales at the rate of 12 percent annually, and export sales growth exceeded 20 percent. Hartley and Bailey knew that additional plant and equipment would be required to achieve long-range sales forecasts. Patterson believed strongly that a European manufacturing operation would be necessary to accommodate the future health of Filtco's export market, which he had so carefully developed.

Filtco Corporation had accumulated an excellent patent estate on its processes and products, and patents had either been issued or applied for in all the countries to which the company exported products. In spite of this, Hartley was reluctant to establish a foreign operation that in any way would jeopardize the know-how which had been achieved. There had been two instances where foreign-born technical employees had left the company and had allegedly divulged certain critical technical information regarding its manufacturing operations. This had caused embarrassing problems, though it had not hurt Filtco's business. Patterson agreed that this could be a problem, but he strongly believed that either a foreign manufacturing facility must be built or the export business would decline rapidly and eventually cease.

Patterson pointed out several compelling factors favoring a foreign operation:

1. Boat shipments to Europe took up to three months in some cases. Furthermore, the incidence of dock strikes had caused late deliveries at an increasing rate.

2. Problems in quality or the use of Filtco products on its customers' machines were becoming more difficult to solve. Salesmen and agents were not equipped to handle technical problems adequately.

3. Freight costs and tariffs were becoming prohibitively high when consideration was given to competitive products available in foreign countries. Though U.S. manufacturing costs were relatively low, freight and tariff costs amounted to over 20 percent of sales.

4. Because of the potential and real growth in the market for Filtco's products, several European companies were starting to make competitive products. At this time, they were not of good quality, but Patterson did not underrate the ability of these companies to develop improved products.

5. Raw materials represented over 50 percent of the cost of Filtco products, and these materials were available in Europe at costs lower than those in the U.S.A.

6. The concept of the "Ugly American" was strong in Europe. Although Filtco had excellent relations with its customers, Patterson had been told several times by many of them that they would prefer their own domestic sources rather than U.S. products. He further related that, even with customers who appeared to understand English well, there was language confusion and often distrust.

This "side of the coin" was strong, but Hartley saw difficulties. There would be high investment to get an operation going, large training costs, language barriers, and lack of familiarity with the culture and laws of a foreign country. There would be difficulty in selecting a good manager. There were nascent, competitive technologies which might make Filtco's equipment obsolete. The narrow product base and the possibility that major customers would integrate backwards and make their own product bothered Hartley. He was also cognizant of the possibility of shrinking U.S. demand, which might idle some of the company's domestic capacity. He wanted to make sure that all avenues were considered before a decision was reached.

BAILEY'S CONCERN

Robert Bailey was a long-time Filtco employee, having spent over twenty years working his way up in the manufacturing organization to his present job as Vice-President and Manager of Manufacturing. He recognized the problems he would face in starting a manufacturing operation in Europe. He had an adequate engineering staff, and machine builders had service personnel they could send to overseas locations to assist Filtco's men. Bailey was concerned about the language barrier and the difference in culture of any continental European country compared to the U.S.A. He knew he would be the one responsible for getting the operation started, and he was very uncertain as to how quickly foreigners could assimilate the complexity of company operations. He also felt that the three U.S.A. plants were all that he could comfortably control.

THE DECISION

Hartley reviewed the pros and cons and concluded that a site search should be undertaken. It was decided that a plant should be located as geographically central as possible to potential markets, that it would start as a small operation in a rented building, and that preferably it should be located in a small community. A further requirement was that a nearby site should be available on which to locate another company-owned plant should growth occur as anticipated. Hartley also concluded that the operation should be managed by a national and that no Americans should be in plant management after the initial engineering and installation work. The national manager would report to Bailey. Patterson would maintain supervision over sales and marketing.

FILTCO, BELGIUM

A site was eventually selected in the quiet little town of Brusk, Belgium. The 40,000-square-foot building on the site would be adequate as a starting point. Hartley, Patterson, and Bailey had made several trips to Belgium. They talked at length with local government officials, bankers, and national officials exploring the source of employees, local and national laws and practices, and the attitude of the Belgians regarding a foreign-based manufacturer entering their country. Hartley knew that Filtco could succeed in Brusk only if it contributed as much to the community as (or more than) the community contributed to the company. The decision to locate in Brusk was made quickly, however; there was a genuine feeling of mutual trust.

JON VODER

Bailey's knowledge of Belgium and its languages was nil, and now he faced the responsibility of finding a manager for Filtco, Belgium. After many interviews (during which he happily discovered that many Belgians spoke English well), he selected a 26-year-old engineering graduate, Jon Voder, who had some experience in a field related to Filtco products. Bailey immediately recognized that Voder was bright. His relative youth and limited industrial experience bothered Bailey somewhat, and Voder's stiff and formal demeanor disturbed him. Voder had excellent references, however, among which was high acclaim by the local mayor (who had considerable power and prestige in this little town). Bailey considered Voder the best prospect of any of those he interviewed.

Voder immediately got to work, and he assisted in negotiating a renewable three-year lease on the property which had been selected. He spent two months in the U.S.A., familiarizing himself with Filtco equipment, processes, products, cost systems, work assignments, financial reports, quality control, etc. He became acquainted with company personnel, with whom he and his staff would later have contacts. He became "the manager" immediately; it was his operation in Belgium even before anything was physically in existence. Baily was often upset by Voder's self-confidence, his almost arrogant manner at times, and his reluctance to be informal. In a shirt-sleeve conference, Voder always wore a jacket. Bailey cringed at this.

OPERATIONS

Engineers were sent from the U.S.A., and servicemen from U.S. machinery builders assisted in the installation of equipment. Voder hired a few supervisors and workmen who became familiar with operations through vestibule training and on-the-job experience in helping the machine erectors. Luckily, most of the men Voder hired could understand some English, certainly enough to grasp what was going on. The Americans did not understand the Belgian languages, and because of their limited time there, they made no attempt to learn. This disturbed Voder, but the other personnel did not appear to mind. Machinery and equipment were in place and ready to go less than a year after the decision was made to establish a plant in Belgium. The job had gone smoothly, although Bailey and Patterson continued to have difficulty in understanding Voder. Patterson commented to Bailey many times that he was glad that Voder was Bailey's responsibility and not his.

Startup problems were normal, no greater than those experienced in America. Voder established reliable sources of raw materials, selected excellent associates and workmen, and dedicated himself to make Filtco, Belgium, an asset to the community. For all his rigidity, he was a good manager. He knew the Belgian people and what was acceptable and unacceptable in the community. Though he was highly ambitious, he knew that he must establish this little plant and make it successful. It was evident early that he wanted to manage the plant with as little interference as possible, and very often he eloquently expressed this point of view to Bailey and Patterson.

In 1963, it was decided to build a larger plant in Belgium. Voder's staff developed the plans and hired the contractors. A review of the plans by Hartley and Bailey revealed that Voder had planned a huge office for himself and a large hall "for me to give talks to employees." Voder defended his desire for these forcefully, much to the chagrin of Hartley and Bailey. He finally agreed to a sliding partition in the middle of his office to make half of it available as a conference room. "You Americans just do not understand us," was Voder's lament. Aside from the two "luxuries," the plans were accepted and a beautiful plant was built. Filtco, Belgium, continued to grow, and Voder continually pressured Hartley and Bailey for additional plant and equipment. Over the next several years production expanded tenfold.

GROWTH

Contributing significantly to the growth of the Filtco, Belgium, operation were the efforts of Patterson. He had built a sales force of ten men on the continent, with his Brussels salesman now being Sales Manager. He hired two Belgians as Product Managers, reporting directly to him. Though these two men were housed in the Filtco, Belgium, office building, Voder made sure that they were given the smallest offices and that they were not involved with his operations or invited to attend any of his meetings. Both of the Product Managers, as well as the Sales Manager, told Patterson they would resign if they had to report to Voder. Patterson tried to get these men together, but Voder remained aloof. At the same time, however, Patterson recognized that Voder's men had done an outstanding job in assisting customers. Despite more competitive conditions in Europe and the necessity to lower prices, profitability of Filtco, Belgium, was excellent, having a higher rate than the U.S. operation.

The manufacturing operation of Filtco, Belgium, was fully mature by 1972, and Bailey felt strongly that he no longer could add anything to the activity. He suggested to Hartley that Voder was capable and that it was no longer necessary for Bailey to be involved. Hartley agreed and made plans to have Voder report directly to him in the future.

When Hartley announced this to Voder in a late-morning meeting, Voder was dismayed, not because he was no longer reporting to Bailey, but because he had anticipated that Hartley was also going to give him responsibility for sales and marketing. "It is five minutes to twelve," said Voder toward the scheduled close of the meeting.

Hartley was very upset by the apparent arrogance of Voder's remark. Voder had the nerve to tell him that the time had arrived for him to come to the decision to consolidate the sales and marketing functions with manufacturing! Hartley was not aware that such a comment was considered perfectly acceptable in Belgium as a means of ensuring that a decision is made prior to the scheduled termination of a meeting. He simply interpreted it as another evidence of Voder's rigidity.

Patterson was a sensitive man. He was still relatively young, only 52. His entire career was in selling and he had done an outstanding job. Where was his future? He felt very strongly that Filtco, Belgium, was his creation. He prided himself on the organization he had built in Europe. His subordinates were intensely loyal to him. Relationships with customers were never better. His Brussels Sales Manager was extremely competent, and his Marketing Manager (previously one of the Product Managers) was doing a splendid job. Both of these men spoke French, German, and Dutch fluently, and knew the cultures of every country in which Filtco, Belgium, sold products.

Hartley was also proud of Filtco, Belgium. He was thankful for his decision to initiate this operation. He was elated over the respect that the company had in the Brusk community and indeed in the country of Belgium. He had often smarted under Voder's demands but could not deny that Voder had done a very fine job. Perhaps he did not really understand the Europeans.

G. *Business and Government*

The commonly held needs and values of a society's members are reinforced by all sorts of social mechanisms and conventions, not the least of which is government. When new needs or new values coalesce into some form of unity (or older values become more widely held), that unity is expressed very often through some action by the government of the society in terms of legislation. This is not meant to imply that government always responds with knee-jerk reaction. The transformation of social values to law is a slow and evolutionary process subject to cultural lags, competing values, and political power.

Relative to business, if the social body comes to view a business practice with enough alarm, then that alarm may be manifested in some action by government. Put another way, when the social costs of a business practice become onerous, legislation may be enacted to force business firms to absorb those costs. All sorts of laws and regulations come to mind in this regard—child-labor laws, pollution-control laws, equal-opportunity acts, occupational safety and health acts, noise requirements, zoning and billboard restrictions, and hazardous-substance regulations, for examples. Thus, business–government relationships—both legislative and enforcement—are increasingly crucial elements in the managerial decision process.

Business relationships with government can be classified for our purposes in four fairly distinct categories: the seller–customer relationship, government as the keeper of competition, government as the regulator of price and entry, and government as the promoter of citizen well-being.

GOVERNMENT AS THE CUSTOMER

We do not intend to cover this seller–buyer relationship in great depth; the topic more properly falls under marketing. With the increasing governmental share of the national product, however, governments at all levels become valued, but fickle, customers; this relationship raises some serious ethical and social power issues. One has to do with firms hiring high-level military officers and governmental officials in sales or administrative posts. This practice is widespread, particularly among defense-related firms, leading some to question the potential for conflict of interest and cooperative processes. Many commentators, viewing noncompetitive bidding practice as well as staffing crossovers in the defense business, argue that, for all intents and purposes, the industries involved are close to being nationalized. Some have suggested that the arrangement be formalized.

Another issue concerns the power of government to force firms to comply with side regulations in order to obtain or retain government contracts. For example, all government contractors must now abide by affirmative action regulations promulgated by executive order. Firms with government contracts are now required to set guidelines or goals on minority or female hiring and file written reports on compliance. Side regulations pose few operational problems for the new bidder or the bidder with a small portion of his business in government contracts; the firm can simply opt out of the bidding process or adjust its practices to conform to government requirements. But, for the contractor locked into a long-term government contractual relationship, or one with a substantial part of its business geared to government work, the value of the relationship may be decreased markedly with side conditions imposed.

One shouldn't look on the previous paragraph as a criticism of affirmative action; we are not passing judgment on that issue. We are more concerned with pointing out the power of government to impose side conditions on contracts. The power of government looms as the crucial issue, not the substance of the requirement. If the substantive issue involved contributions to the political party in power, loyalty oaths, or the nonuse of imported materials, the question of power might be more easily focused on.

GOVERNMENT, THE KEEPER OF COMPETITION

The federal government (as well as the states) has antitrust legislation on the books whose objectives are to maintain competition, preclude economic conspiracy, forestall monopoly, and prevent unfair competitive practices. While it is impossible here to cover very much of this exciting field, we should like to highlight some of the more important points and examine some of the issues.

Antitrust is an old doctrine, much older than the 1890 Sherman Act, the first federal antitrust law. The roots of antitrust go far back into common law, where practices such as monopoly and restraint of trade were held illegal. The Sherman Act was enacted because of the growth of the trusts and the activity of the so-called "robber barons." The states were unable or unwilling to control that growth.

It should be noted, however, that both the enactment and enforcement of antitrust laws are just as much politically inspired as they are necessitated by economic conditions. The Sherman Act was enacted in a period of populist unrest, along with a number of other laws to control business. The enforcement or nonenforcement of antitrust laws is related to political expediency, political power of the party controlling the White House, international relations, and other political processes; sometimes these factors have a greater effect on antitrust action than do economic criteria.

At a minimum, managers ought to know the rudiments of antitrust and be aware that the field is a complex one necessitating competent legal counsel. The Sherman Act generally covers monopolization and conspiracy to fix prices, allocation of markets, and restriction of competition. For monopolization, the "rule of reason" prevails; the question to be decided by the courts is: "Were the actions of the firm reasonable business practices, or was the intent of the firm clearly to create or sustain monopoly?" With a conspiracy (involving more than one party) the *per se* doctrine generally is applied. Price fixing, market allocation, and similar anticompetitive practices are *per se* illegal; no defense based on the reasonableness of the results of the conspiracy is allowed. Thus, in the celebrated 1959 electrical manufacturers' price-fixing case, once the managers admitted meeting to fix prices, the case was closed. Some companies attempted to mollify shareholders by stating, in their annual reports, that no customers were harmed by the actions of the managers. These statements may have been good public relations, but they were bad law. Such pleas are inadmissible for the court.

The Clayton Act covers chiefly price discrimination, tying contracts, and mergers, "where the effect . . . may be substantially to lessen competition or tend to create a monopoly . . ." Unlike the Sherman Act, the cases under the Clayton Act need not require the establishment of intent, or proof of predatory practices. The Act's key words are "may be" and a potential merger, for example, may be disallowed if the government is able to establish its case that the merger would tend to diminish competition.

Antitrust is also covered in Section 5 of the Federal Trade Commission Act, which declares unlawful "unfair methods of competition in commerce, and unfair or deceptive acts or practices in commerce . . ." While the two major statutes in antitrust remain the Sherman and Clayton Acts, the Federal Trade Commission does have concurrent jurisdiction with the Justice Department in enforcing the Clayton Act.

For the manager, the key questions concern his behavior and the possible penalties for running afoul of the laws. Civil penalties concern the firm as an entity and are aimed at restoring conditions to those that obtained prior to the case at hand, or preventing new conditions from occurring. A merger may be disallowed, a cease-and-desist order or an injunction issued, or a divestiture may be ordered. Criminal penalties—or punishment for wrongdoings—can directly affect the manager. The Sherman Act provides for penalties of up to $50,000 in fines per offense and/or up to a year in jail per offense. Monetary sentences are most common, but the 90-day jail sentences meted out in 1959 dispelled any notion that penalties of incarceration were *not* being applied. Even more important to the manager than penalties, however, may be the effect that a conviction has on his reputation and his chances for advancement.

Antitrust is a complex and confusing area. Many businessmen complain that they don't know what is expected of them. Others cite the contention that the administration in power or the social or economic tenor of the times have more to do with the enforcement of antitrust than the economic issues involved in any one particular case. At least one economist has commented that, in merger cases, antitrust is grossly unfair. While the large firms are generally immune from prosecution under the Sherman Act, the merger of two smaller firms would tend to reduce competition under the Clayton Act and hence be subject to challenge. Finally, some writers have complained about the lack of expertise of the courts in adjudicating economic cases. Judges have little training or expertise in economics, and they get little assistance in the area. As an administrative agency, the Federal Trade Commission is supposed to apply this expertise, but the fact remains that major antitrust cases end up in the courts.

GOVERNMENT AS A REGULATOR OF PRICE AND ENTRY

Many firms are vested with what is called the public interest—their services are indispensable, and if they were left to operate freely, they could cause harm to the public welfare. Hence, the business practices and the scope of operations of these firms comes under government scrutiny.

Here we deal with such natural monopolies as electric power, telephone services, and water provision. These natural monopolies are regulated because it is inconvenient to have several sets of utility lines or pipes serving a community, because the services are deemed essential to the public welfare, and primarily because the industry incurs large capital costs in relation to the market; in essence, the size of the market relative to the technology *requires* a monopoly. No electric company, for example, adds 10 kilowatt-hours of capacity to service a new home; the company would add millions of kilowatt-hours at one time, because power plants of that size are the minimum necessary to yield economically optimum output.

Thus utilities are generally regulated in terms of price. Their prices are set to allow all costs to be recovered, along with a reasonable return on investment; the price is supposedly set below a monopoly rate of return. The public, in theory at least, is guaranteed prices below those of an unregulated monopolistic seller, while the utility is guaranteed sufficient income to pay all operating costs and sustain its capital base.

Questions are continually raised about the efficiency and effectiveness of regulation in protecting the public. Calculating costs and valuing the rate base continue to consume the time of economists and accountants, and recent controversies over the fuel-factor charge (in some states, utilities are allowed to adjust electric rates based on the cost of fuel, without going to the utility regulatory commission) have stirred legislative study of utility pricing.

Government also regulates the prices and/or entry of many professions, trades, and industries beyond those classified as natural monopolies. Liquor stores, funeral parlors, airlines, taxicabs, doctors, lawyers, plumbers, electricians, truckers, are all examples. Indirectly, some local communities, through the use of zoning regulation, limit the entry of many types of firms even though areas for commercial and industrial use exist. Many communities, for example, bar the operation of fast-food operations. Entry regulations are usually rationalized in terms of guaranteeing expertise, or because of some moral or ethical positions of the community. In the case of liquor stores, for example, limiting consumption of alcoholic beverages both in total and to specified age groups are primary objectives.

The question raised by many economists is whether all of this regulation is really in the public interest. Some commentators have opined that businesses might prefer to be regulated. Regulation can limit competition and free the industries regulated of the uncertainties of market mechanisms. Others perceive that regulatory commissions go through a life cycle, the last phase of that cycle being virtual captivity by the very industry they were supposed to regulate. The practice of limiting entry is also subject to question. Does limiting the number of liquor stores benefit the public or the fortunate few liquor-store licensees? Does the passage of requirements for funerals benefit the public or the funeral directors? Does the regulation of passenger fares benefit the public or the airlines?

PROMOTION OF CITIZEN WELL-BEING

Finally, government regulates all businesses in many social areas related to the well-being of the citizenry. In some cases, the regulation is strictly convenience-related, such as when the business firm may act as a tax collector for government (withholding Social Security and income taxes, collecting sales taxes, etc.). In others, the laws simply extend government's role as a protector of the public welfare into the workplace, where much of the public's time is spent. OSHA, child-labor laws, and equal-opportunity acts are illustrative here. In still other instances, government may act to force business to be more open to the public; unit-pricing regulations, for example. Under the social well-being category, we can also include our pollution laws, plant-beautification regulations, flammable-product restrictions, and many others.

The essence of many of these laws (although this is not articulated when the law is passed) is that government is taking action to mitigate effects on the public and force business to absorb social costs. Those side-effects for which business typically does not pay (lung damage, foul odors, polluted water, unsafe or unsanitary conditions) are now forced back on the firm in terms of real rather than external costs.

Obviously, the area of business–government relations is a huge one, and we can sample but a few of the relationships in this book. But the student is encouraged to think critically in this area. One might consider, for example, just what government really is. Most people refer to government as some monolithic body when in fact it is a multisided institution in which one hand often moves in different directions from the other. It is not unusual to find the Pentagon awarding a contract to a firm which is under investigation by the Internal Revenue Service or the object of an antitrust case by the Justice Department or the Federal Trade Commission. Nor is it unusual for a state or a municipality to be at loggerheads with the Federal government over pollution or desegregation. Thus, the locus of power within our governmental system is a key consideration.

Students are also encouraged to think critically about regulation: Is a particular regulation good for society? Or is it good for business? Or perhaps it might only be good for *government,* where often regulatory agencies refuse to depart the scene even when no longer relevant.

Government is a powerful social tool, and its wise use accomplishes many valued social ends, but like any institution, its virtues usually are accompanied by problems.

THE READINGS

The first article, by Carl Kaysen, explores the discrepancies between business ideology on government on the one hand and the real business relationships with government on the other. Buttressing his argument with several examples, Kaysen concludes ". . . that the business community gets the style of government policies it wants, even if this is not at all the style it commends in abstract discussion of appropriate relations between government and business."

The *Business Week* selection provides us with insight into some of the controversy surrounding antitrust proposals for change in the laws, new tactics of the Justice Department and the Federal Trade Commission, the concerns of businessmen and economists, and a consideration of the structural efficacy of U.S. industry.

Finally, we focus on an industry regulated only by the states. "Toothless Tigers" (a *Wall Street Journal* article) covers the regulation of insurance companies by state commissions. While some commissions are strong, others are relatively ineffective. Problems raised by the article include conflict of interest, inadequate regulatory staffs and insufficient resources to do an effective regulatory job. In this article, the captivity of the regulators by the regulated is only too evident. What is not so evident is whether Federal regulation, called for by many, would be any better. The article does not explore a third possibility advanced by some executives —*deregulation.*

Business and Government: Do Good Fences Make Good Neighbors?

Carl Kaysen

Relations between business and government have been high on the agenda of concern of the American business community at least since October 30, 1929. The intensity of that concern has fluctuated with the level and character of government activity. Currently, as our symposium itself indicates, the level of concern is high, raised by novel elements in the character of government activity. Not that government spending, government deficits, and changes in taxes have lost their capacity for arousing interest, but the additional elements of wage-price guidelines, and government targets for private business transactions in foreign markets represent both objects and modes of government activity in the economic sphere that have aroused intense new concerns in the business community. Other speakers will discuss these questions in specific detail; my purpose is to put them into a broader perspective.

There is wide agreement in our individualist society on the effectiveness of market institutions as the chief means of organizing and controlling economic activities. Accordingly, there is a presumption against nonmarket means in general, and against government activity in particular. Indeed, the conventional phrase for such activity is never milder than "intervention," and often enough it becomes "interference." A synthetic view of business discussion of government intervention in economic life suggests that three kinds of limiting criteria are usually applied to such activity: limitations on its appropriate sphere or objectives, limitations on the appropriate means or policy instruments, and limitations on its total extent. This same synthetic view would summarize these three sets of constraints in the following way.

In terms of scope, this view would admit some enlargement of Adam Smith's three categories of appropriate functions for the state: defense, the administration of justice, and the maintenance of such public works and institutions which, "though they may be in the highest degree advantageous to a great society, are, however, of such a nature that the profit could never repay the expense to any individual or small number of individuals, and which it therefore cannot be expected that any individual or small number of individuals should erect or maintain," or, in the terminology of modern welfare economics, those activities for which

Reprinted with permission from "Business and Government: Do Good Fences Make Good Neighbors?", by Carl Kaysen, *American Bankers Association Symposium on Business and Government Relations,* (1966), pp. 24–36.

external effects are significant. Smith further divided this category into two: those public works required for facilitating commerce, such as roads, bridges, canals, lighthouses, and the like; and those involving education, whether of the young or the whole population.

Perhaps the first modern enlargement would be one of emphasis, interpreting the administration of justice to give a greater role to lawmaking, law-interpreting, and law-enforcing institutions in providing the framework of legal rules within which private transactions in an enterprise economy can take place. The second enlargement would recognize several further categories of public works and institutions, including those relating to the public health, the advance of basic scientific knowledge, the conservation of irreplaceable natural resources, such as forests, or wild seashores—although this last may be less agreed upon than the others. In this category, there would also be a shift in emphasis from Smith's original insistence on the desirability of getting the bulk of the support for education from fees to a greater willingness to believe that education financed by tax-revenue or private foundations can be well conducted.

In addition, at least three wholly new categories would be added to Smith's original three. The first is the provision of relief or welfare for those unable to earn a minimum standard, and not otherwise provided for. The second involves the prevention of artificial or contrived monopoly and the regulation of technically inevitable or natural monopoly. It is now generally recognized that simple laissez faire does not guarantee the maintenance of competition, the central regulator of a market economy. Some policy to prevent the restriction of competition by those who would otherwise be forced to compete and suffer competitors is a necessary task of government. It is also widely—if not unanimously—recognized that in those industries in which the efficient scale of operation in relation to the size of the market makes monopoly or near-monopoly inevitable, regulation that prevents the monopolist from charging what the traffic will bear and from discriminating among his customers is necessary and desirable. In Adam Smith's day, the state appeared to be the source of all monopoly, and thus it is not surprising that he neglected this category of regulatory activities. The third additional category is the provision of a monetary mechanism and the regulation of the supply of money. Here again, new understanding since Adam Smith wrote has led to new views of appropriate policy.

Dare I add a fourth category: the regulation of aggregate demand at a level not so low as to permit unnecessary umemployment, and not so high as to promote inflation? This would clearly be recognized as an appropriate responsibility of government by the consistent, unprejudiced neoclassical economist, intent on getting the most efficient performance possible from the market economy. I am not yet sure, however, that the consensus in the business community recognizes this is as equally appropriate with the preceding three additions to Adam Smith's original list. My skepticism in this regard may be unwarranted, but it seems to me, in spite of the widespread enthusiasm for the results of the 1964 tax cut, that understanding of the requirements and possibilities of an active fiscal policy as the necessary prerequisite of honest acceptance may be lacking.

In respect to the mode of operation of whatever government economic policies are deemed appropriate, our ideal business view would be cast in terms of the polarity between "rules" and "authority," between a government of laws and a government of men. Government of law, embodied in well-defined rules, predictable in their scope and impact, is the desirable ideal. Conversely, the existence of wide areas of discretion for the decisions of governmental authority, bounded only by agreed-upon goals, which the authority can seek through any action appropriate to particular circumstances is undesirable. In terms of the political machinery of the American Government, this tends to translate into a preference for legislation and the Congress over discretion and the executive. If legislation cannot be self-defining and self-enforcing—as, regrettably, it so often fails to be—the "independent" commission is preferred to the department of the executive branch. Government is viewed essentially as a rule-maker and umpire for the actors on the economic scene, rather than as one of the actors, save perhaps in the sphere of defense. Since the executive is organized, however effectively, for action, this explains the logic of a preference against it. Further, the impersonality of rules helps to insure the equity and honesty of their application. By contrast, discretionary authority lends itself to favoritism and corruption on the one hand, and unfair "pressure" and politically selective application on the other. A further element in the choice of the suitable mode of government action is localism—a preference wherever possible for state over Federal, and local over state action.

Limitations on mode and limitations on scope need not fit neatly together. Not every objective of government policy seen as appropriate on this view can obviously be attained most efficiently—or even at all—by the use of what are considered appropriate policy instruments. An effective defense procurement policy, for example, might require a large degree of discretionary executive authority in both choosing sources of supply, and negotiating and renegotiating the terms of the contract, quite at variance with the notion of impersonal, universal, and uniformly applicable rules. The making of monetary policy provides another example of the need for a wide degree of discretion, as well as a question as to just where in the apparatus of government this discretion should be lodged, especially in relation to discretion in other areas of economic policy.

In general, the idealized business view that I have been sketching is directed to prescribing limits on government activity. Accordingly it emphasizes restrictions on appropriate modes at the expense of efficient performance of appropriate functions. This general orientation expresses itself in the third kind of limitation, resting on a quite different rationale: a limit on the absolute size of government activity. Less is more, and any increase in the total level of governmental activity is, *ipso facto,* bad. This proposition is frequently expressed in terms that go more than halfway in the range from a Lockean distrust of the element of coercion that appears to be inescapably bound up with government activity, to the Birchean belief that each dollar of government expenditures is one foot's progress down the road to socialism.

It is tempting to enter into a discussion of the correctness or incorrectness of the set of judgments embodied in this somewhat sketchy synthesis of what I have called the business consensus on business-government relations. The representative neoclassical economist might recognize several more categories of external effects warranting government action than those listed above, particularly in the area of urban development and industrial location. A more speculative economic observer might see a trend toward an increase in the extent and importance of external effects, deriving from increased population, income, and urbanization, and a corresponding growth in the demand for and necessity of government action. The equally representative political scientist might question the assumption that the democracy of the marketplace is less coercive, or more respectful of individual freedom than the democracy of the ward committee, the ballot box, and the legislature. Some quite unrepresentative scholars describing themselves as social critics or social philosophers might indeed question the basic individualist premises that underlie the argument for the virtues of a market economy with a minimum of government interference. But I wish to avoid this temptation and, instead, to look briefly into the sources of the views on the correct relations of business and government that I have described, and then to comment on the extent to which the business community itself chooses to support policies conducive to business-government relations of the sort they view as desirable.

One important element in explanation of the business view on these matters is that, historically, it has been substantially the American view. It is not merely a coincidence that the first edition of the *Wealth of Nations* was published in 1776. The American Revolution was, in great part, a revolt against the impact on the colonies of the mercantilist policies of the mother country. Though the Constitution did not enact Herbert Spencer's *Social Statics,* Lockean traditions of the value of private property and the dangers of government power were built deeply into the foundations of American ideas of the good society. These same traditional sources bear with equal weight on the choice of preferred modes of government action: executive discretion in the hands of the monarch spelled tyranny; a government of laws, freedom.

A century later, when much of the basic legislative foundation for the relation between business and the Federal Government was enacted, the climate of popular attitudes toward business did much to reinforce the effects of these earlier experiences, although operating in quite a different fashion. This was the period of Populist revolt, of farmer and Western agitation against Eastern moneylenders and monopolists. Popular hostility toward big business expressed itself in a variety of ways, including, most importantly for our purposes, the embodiment in the Interstate Commerce Commission and Sherman Acts of a particular conception of the proper relations between business and government. Government was to be the enforcer of rules of socially desirable conduct on a business community which was not naturally self-regulating. As such, the agencies which carried out the regulatory task and the business enterprises subject to their scrutiny stood at arm's length, viewing each other with some suspicion and even hostility. Basically, this attitude still remains, and, indeed, is considered the appropriate stance for regulator and regulated. To be sure, in the case of the I.C.C., long and familiar association has dulled somewhat the keen edge of this relation, and a similar process of growing intimacy between any regulatory agency with a fixed clientele and its clients, has occurred with similar results elsewhere. Nonetheless, in a broad sense, the hostile attitudes toward business, especially big business, which expressed themselves in the original legislation made a permanent imprint. Nor have the Populist sentiments themselves vanished, even though the social and economic settings which engendered them have. There is still a broad popular suspicion of Big Business, and the admiration with which the general public views its achievements is mixed with some fear of its powers. To be sure, this anxious regard is now shared by Big Labor and Big Government, but that does not diminish its import for our view of business-government relations. The ideological preference for the impersonality of formal rules over the intimacy of discretionary authority in business-government relations is reinforced by the attitude of hostility between the two parties.

This attitude is sometimes given fairly open expression in the administration of the antitrust laws. Businessmen often view prosecutions under these laws as simply attempts at punishment of success, or of inevitable business conduct; while, on their side, many of the officials of the antitrust agencies are sustained in their efforts by a crusading spirit of anti-big-business zeal. In this they reflect a widely popular note, which goes far to explain the continued vitality of the antitrust laws, three-quarters of a century after their original enactment. Indeed, it is noteworthy that in spite of a constantly high level of business grumbles about their capricious enforcement and their antieconomic effects, and the absence of any clientele who are their direct beneficiaries, these major pieces of regulatory legislation have suffered little significant legislative amendment and have, on the contrary, grown harsher in their standards and broader in their reach through the process of administrative application and judicial interpretation. In my own judgment, this reflects the depth in the public mind of the sentiments and attitudes they embody, rather than a widespread and passionate attachment to the normative significance of the equilibrium of perfect competition.

Beyond these traditional explanations, there is an important current element in the antagonistic relations between business and government: the struggle for power and prestige in a politically competitive and pluralistic society. In our highly industrialized and democratic society, big business is obviously a minority group, and it naturally views a government responsive to popular demands for welfare, economic security, and income distribution as at least potentially hostile. Further, in addition to actual and potential conflicts over these and other specific policy issues, there is a general struggle over the symbols of leadership and legitimate power. Business leaders and politicians are competitors in the race for generalized social leadership, and one side's gain is the other's loss. Certainly, competition in this respect was one of the more important facets of the dramatic clash over the price of steel between the Chief Executive of the United States and the chief executive of the United States Steel Corporation three years ago. This point may also be related to the importance of localism in business views about government, the preference for leaving responsibilities to the smallest governmental units with the least geographic scope, since they are obviously easier opponents in every way.

Although the same basic potential for political conflict exists in Europe, even the most superficial comparison between the United States and the industrial market economies of Western Europe—England, France, Germany, Italy, the Netherlands, et cetera—emphasizes the special character of American views on the proper relations of business and government. In none of these countries does the view prevail that somewhat hostile, arm's-length, formally prescribed relations should be the norm. Instead, every one shows, in one way or another, the acceptance of informal contacts and more or less direct—though not legally prescribed or circumscribed—negotiations between the executive authorities of government and business executives and business associations. To be sure, the difference between parliamentary and congressional government accounts for some of this difference, since the executive in the United States is simply less free to engage in such negotiation. But the difference lies deeper. The kind of relation between government planners and business groups on which the French planning process depends is hard to conceive in the United States, outside the circumstances of a war economy. Even then, it would depend on specific statutory authority to a much greater extent. Or to take a quite different kind of example, in the United Kingdom a Monopolies Commission proceeding can end in a recommendation to a Minister to discuss privately and informally with the executives of the companies investigated ways of improving the practices that were subject to complaint. We can hardly conceive of a similar outcome of an antitrust case here. Whether the different place of business and businessmen in European history and the high prestige of government and natural popular acceptance of broad government authority that results from continuity with a monarchical and aristocratic past is sufficient to account for the striking difference is not clear.

To these causes, I would add the existence of a purely ideological element in the hostility of American business to government. In legitimizing its own place in the social world, business has found it ideologically and emotionally useful to cast government in a negative role: to project onto it the responsibility, through misguided policies, for what goes wrong in the economy in particular and society in general, and to find in the politician a kind of antihero, whose vices underline the virtues of the businessman. Businessmen, or anyhow successful businessmen, are energetic, practical, inventive, responsible, subject to the discipline of the balance sheet and the test of the marketplace. Government, by contrast, is run by a mixture of politicians, seen more or less explicitly as corrupt and engaged either in pandering to the prejudices of the voters or deceiving them; and bureaucrats, who appear in the alternate images of routine time servers or impractical academic theorists—professors in disguise—who have never met a payroll. Since government can spend where it has not earned, it can never achieve that responsible conduct of its affairs that is enforced on business by the discipline of the marketplace. This of course is caricature, but caricature is the essential stuff of ideology, and—as I have amply documented elsewhere—it is what the public pronouncements of the business community and its agencies for public information do, in fact, say about government.

The ideological element in business hostility to government is important precisely because it does not yield the explanation on pragmatic grounds. While the struggle for power and prestige may be viewed as rational, the rejection of the strategy embodied in the old axiom, if you can't lick them, join them, is not. This ideological element is precisely what is absent in European business attitudes, and, by the same token, its absence is consistent with the much greater European tendency to follow the axiom.

Such are the precepts. Are they indeed followed in practice? On the whole, they are not. While I have not the space to demonstrate this in any comprehensive enumeration, I trust the few salient examples presented here will give this assertion sufficient weight to make the proposition interesting, if not indubitably convincing.

First, let us look at the antitrust laws, which often serve as useful symbols of just the kind of ring-holding function that government should perform. In general, business commentators on antitrust policy tend to argue for "rule of reason" doctrines, and against "per se" rules of liability. Yet it is just per se rules that provide the closest approximation to the automatic, uniformly enforced, impersonal rule, while the rule of reason allows for a wide variety of interpretation, in which prosecutors can select different cases as exemplifying illegal conduct, and different courts can come to different conclusions, and the predictability of the law's application declines. The recent amendment of the Bank Merger Act—which had your support, and that of the business community in general—exemplifies this point in concrete terms. The new act provides a wide latitude for decision to the Comptroller of the Currency and the Board of Governors of the Federal Reserve System in approving bank mergers. They may evaluate "banking factors" in relation to "competitive effects," and, even if a merger has a prospective negative effect on competition, may approve it if advantages in terms of banking factors outweigh competitive disadvantages. The situation before the enactment of this legislation had—through judicial interpretation of Section 7 of the Clayton Act and the earlier version of the Bank Merger Act—settled down to a quite predictable per se rule, and it could then be confidently said that any bank merger involving banks which in aggregate controlled as much as 25 per cent of the local market would be outlawed. From the point of view of banks which wish to grow by merger, the reasons for preferring the new to the old situation are clear; from the point of view of an ideal theory of business-government relations, the reason for the opposite position is equally clear.

Recent relations between the American Telephone and Telegraph Company and the Federal Communications Commission provide another example of a preference for authority over rules. The Commission has the power to regulate the interstate rates of the company. For some time now, this has been done by informal discussion between the company and the Commission. Recently, the Commission proposed a formal rate-making proceeding, with hearings, a written record, and an opinion of the Commission. The company reacted strongly and negatively; private negotiation had worked satisfactorily in the past, why not continue it? Again, the company's reasons for its position are not too hard to find. The formal proceeding would produce a record which some of the more aggressive state regulatory agencies—for instance those of California and New York—might find useful in their own proceedings, especially in the difficult matter of separating that part of the property of the company and its constituent operating subsidiaries used in interstate from that used in intrastate business. Further, the very formality of the proceedings might induce the Commission to deal more sternly with the company than it had heretofore in its informal proceedings. The company had a good basis for rising above principle; nonetheless, the fact that they did so is worth noting.

The case of wage-price guidelines, which are the center of much of the current controversy on our topic subject, is more complex and less dramatic. In general, individual business firms have accepted, sometimes rather reluctantly, what we might call government reminders on price guidelines. The business community as a whole, however, has reacted strongly and negatively to them, on the grounds that they represent a classic case of the "wrong" kind of government action, the kind that is described as "interference" with the functioning of the market. This view has, of course, been shared by the trade unions, but that is the subject of another paper, for some future conference. Today, it is doubtful that the guidelines alone could be depended on to achieve price stability in the face of already low levels of unemployment and continuing high aggregate demand. Some further restraints on aggregate demand also appear desirable. But this has not been the case over the four years since the wage-price guidelines were first articulated in the 1962 Economic Report. Criticism of them, however, was no less intense then than now, but no alternatives more in keeping with standards of appropriate government policy were advanced for moving toward high employment and maintaining price stability. I would speculate, however, that if the business community had been offered a choice between the guidelines, and vigorous enough antitrust policy in the relevent markets—including both movements against collusive pricing and structural reorganization in highly concentrated industries—to reinforce the competitive constraints on the wage-price interaction, it would have chosen the guidelines. This, of course, is only a speculation, and the difficulty of specifying how hard an antitrust policy of structural reorganization would have been needed to achieve the desired results makes the hypothetical choice involved less than perfectly precise. Further, the argument is complicated by the possible conflict in values between the business community and successive administrations on the relative importance of low unemployment and price stability. Since it was difficult for business to express opposition to lowering unemployment explicitly, attack on the guidelines offered a less direct approach, though, fortunately, not a particularly effective one.

Business reception of government policies directed toward eliminating or reducing the balance of payments deficit provides a final and sharper example of the divergence between precept and practice. Here again government has resorted to a set of measures that contradict the canons of proper policy. From the interest equalization tax to the targets for foreign transactions of individual firms, arrived at by private informal discussion between high officials of the government and the executives of the firms involved, enforced by public and private exhortation, and without the warrant of legislative authority, the whole process displays every characteristic of policy making that the business view condemns. Here there is a clear alternative, however; and the banking and business leaders, both by what they have said and what they have not said, have made it plain that they reject it and prefer the apparatus of informal controls. The alternative, of course, is to rely on the price system, either by devaluing the dollar or allowing it to float against the continental currencies. Devaluation would require agreement from the surplus countries, who might be reluctant to permit it; but a floating exchange is open to the United States as a unilateral choice. There are, to be sure, strong arguments to be made against both these choices of policy, but not such overwhelming ones as to rule them out of consideration. Yet no business critic of foreign investment guideposts and other informal controls on international capital movement has, to my knowledge, put the alternative forward. Indeed, it is my impression that, on the contrary, the strong attachment of the banking community to the present international monetary system has been one of the moving forces that has led the government to the kinds of policies it has chosen.

These examples suggest that the business community gets the style of government policies it wants, even if this is not at all the style it commends in abstract discussion of appropriate relations between government and business. Of course, in every case, particular pragmatic reasons can be discerned which account for the espousal or acceptance of a policy line so much at variance with professed ideal standards. But then, what is the function of the ideal standard?

Treating this question as literal and not rhetorical, two quite different kinds of answers suggest themselves. We can see discussions of the proper role for government, or the proper mode of government activity as simply an instrument in the political power struggle, a way of advancing the group interests of business against other group interests. The particular arguments used can be interpreted as a method of securing a more favorable bargaining situation for business interests, simply by attacking a variety of kinds and modes of government activities which historically have been used more on behalf of other interest groups than on behalf of business. Crudely put, government activity in the economic sphere has been in the direction of changing the *status quo,* whether in the distribution of income or the distribution of power. Business has resisted the change, and business arguments on the proper role of government have formed part of the instruments of resistance.

The difficulty of this explanation is its failure to account for the rejection of the alternative strategy—the espousal of close informal cooperation between business and government so that the ends and instruments of government policy are shaped more closely to business desires. The continental examples illustrate the feasibility of this alternative—if such an illustration is needed. In the United States, moreover, where no respectable or popular socialist party or movement exists, the obstacles to it would be even less than in Europe. It seems to me that, objectively viewed, this line is more likely to be successful than the line which has in fact been pursued.

Alternatively, we can recognize that business pronouncements on the role of government form part of a more general business ideology. The primary functions of ideology are not rational and instrumental; rather, they are responsive to demands for the affirmation of group worth and group solidarity, and for the justification—in sociologically rather than logically relevant terms—of group status in a larger world. From this perspective, we should not expect to find a particularly high correlation between what is said ideologically and what is actually done in a particular context, even though the ideology is cast in the form of prescriptions for right action. Thus the divergence requires no particular explanation. But, though ideologies are not blueprints for social action, they can and do influence it by the values they emphasize and the attitudes they embody. Business ideology has helped to nourish and reinforce a degree of hostility between government and business and deny legitimacy to some kinds of government policy in ways that were certainly not inevitable and need not correspond with a "rational" view of business interests.

As a proponent of reasoned discussion of public policy, including a reasoned evaluation of the gains and costs of alternative possible uses of the power of the state, I suppose I must deplore the large ideological element in business views on these matters. In this spirit, it is tempting to argue that business should either get what it says it wants—which I have argued it would frequently be most unwilling to accept—or change its tune, and confess to wanting what it gets. The second alternative would allow more open and focussed discussion of the genuine issues, in terms of the balance among competing values and competing power claims, as subjects for negotiation in terms of more or less, rather than ideological dispute in terms of all or nothing. This in turn might permit greater social harmony in matters of economic policy, which can be viewed as a valuable goal in itself.

But there is a contrary view. Hostility and conflict have their values, especially in a complicated, diverse, and pluralistic society. Ideology and counter-ideology generate the steam of emotional commitment which is important to the politics of democracy, and too much social harmony may be the inhibitor of social and political innovation. Merely rational discussion of problems that are viewed as technical may be insufficiently energetic to throw up as wide a set of alternatives and stimulate as searching an examination of them as do the more passionate debates produced when ideological commitments are involved. From this perspective, the views of the business community on the proper relations of government and business should not be evaluated merely in terms of the accuracy of their descriptions of the current state of those relations, or the sophistication of their underlying economic models, or the consistency and cogency of the political philosophy they embody, but accepted as the expression of a significant and persistent body of sentiment, which must be respected in the shaping of policy.

This is my own view. Perhaps I come to it more easily because I think that the business views I have here described have for some time been minority views in our society and will continue to remain so, and I appreciate the role of forceful expression of minority views in the shaping of social policy. Were these ideological views on proper spheres and modes of government action to replace the *ad hoc* pragmatism, largely free of a priori commitments, looking to problems and the best means to solve them, which I now believe is the majority view, though largely an unarticulated one, perhaps I would be stimulated to move from the stance of sociological explanation to that of ideological combat.

Is John Sherman's Antitrust Obsolete?

Business Week

The head of the major U.S. corporation spoke feelingly: "I would be very glad if we knew exactly where we stand, if we could be free from danger, trouble, and criticism." His plea could have been made yesterday, by executives at IBM, Xerox, GTE, General Motors, AT&T, Exxon, Standard Brands, Chrysler, or dozens of other large companies that have recently stood in the dock, accused of violating the nation's antitrust laws.

It was, in fact, said back in 1912 by Elbert H. Gary, chairman of U.S. Steel Corp. He was giving a Congressional committee his views on the need for updating the country's first antitrust law, the Sherman Act, to which Ohio Senator John Sherman gave his name in 1890. Echoing the sentiments of many executives, Gary complained bitterly of the restraints imposed by the antitrust law on his company's ability to compete in world markets. Business had grown too big and complex, Gary maintained, to be shoehorned into laws drawn from Adam Smith's economic model of many small companies competing in local markets.

Two years later Congress gave Gary an unwelcome answer to his plea. It passed an even more restrictive antitrust measure, the Clayton Act, and set up the Federal Trade Commission to police business practices and methods of competition even more closely.

Today business faces much the same danger, trouble, and criticism that disturbed Gary, and is raising much the same complaints against antitrust. The International Telephone & Telegraph Corp. scandal and corporate participation in Watergate has stirred up deep public distrust of national institutions, including business. In response, as in Gary's day, the antitrust wind is rising, blown up currently by the oil crisis and fanned by consumerists, such as Ralph Nader, who argue that antitrust weapons have been used like peashooters against dinosaurs. Business almost certainly faces even tougher antitrust enforcement and possibly even a new antitrust law aimed at breaking up the corporate giants in the country's basic industries.

This prospect points up the underlying question businessmen ask about antitrust: Are laws framed more than three-quarters of a century ago appropriate legal weapons in a market system grown increasingly large, complex, and multinational? In raising this basic issue, businessmen can point to a far-reaching, intricate web of laws and rules that has made the government the regulator, watchdog, and even partner of business. Wage and price controls, health and safety regulations, and disclosure laws, are all a far cry from the economy of Sherman's or Gary's day.

Businessmen complain of the unsettling vagueness of the antitrust laws, which permits antitrusters to attack many long-standing business practices in their effort to root out restraints of trade and monopoly. The FTC, for example, is now suing Kellogg, General Foods, General Mills, and Quaker Oats, alleging that such procedures as having route men arrange their breakfast cereals on supermarket shelves are anticompetitive. The Justice Dept. has a similar suit against tire makers Goodyear and Firestone.

Executives of International Business Machines Corp., caught by both government and private antitrust suits attacking pricing and promotion policies, privately declare that they are baffled over what they can legally do. Bertram C. Dedman, vice-president and general counsel for INA Corp., echoes a widely held view: "We never really know precisely what antitrust means. It's frequently strictly a matter of opinion."

Enormous economic stakes are involved in antitrust enforcement. Such current cases as those against IBM, Xerox Corp., and other giants involve billions of dollars' worth of capital investment and stockholder interests. Executives fear that such suits give broad power to courts not schooled in business, economics, or industrial technology. This power was dramatically illustrated last fall when U.S. District Judge A. Sherman Christensen announced a $352-million judgment against IBM and then confessed error, sending IBM's stock into wild gyrations.

Many businessmen wonder whether their companies are often targets of antitrust prosecution simply because they are big and successful. Philadelphia lawyer Edward D. Slevin sums up this attitude: "If the free market is pushed to its fullest extent, somebody wins. But the Justice Dept. seems to say: 'Now that you've won, you've cornered the market. We're going to break you up and start over.' "

All this, say many executives, makes it increasingly difficult for American business to compete internationally. Douglas Grymes, president of Koppers Co., argues that "big corporations are the only ones that can compete with big corporations in world markets." He says that the antitrust laws seem to equate bigness itself with monopoly and thus hinder American corporations from reaching the size necessary for world competition.

TOUGHER ENFORCEMENT LIKELY

Despite all these deeply felt concerns, the antitrust laws are likely to become even tougher and more restrictive. Starting with the Sherman Act, antitrust has been a product more of politics than of economics. Today's rising populist sentiment has led to demands for tighter antitrust enforcement. Only a decade ago historian Richard Hofstadter wrote, "The antitrust movement is one of the faded passions of American reform." Today it is the darling of reform. As James T. Halverson, director of the FTC's Bureau of Competition, sums up: "The political atmosphere is very favorable to antitrust right now."

The many signs of stepped-up antitrust activity in the last one or two years make an impressively lengthy list. They include:

New investigations

Last week three federal agencies—Justice, the FTC, and the SEC—as well as some congressmen, revealed that they are turning to a little-used section of the Clayton Act to investigate the complex of interlocking directorships among major oil companies.

New legislation

The industrial reorganization bill that Senator Philip A. Hart (D-Mich.) introduced in Congress last year would provide a new legal basis for breaking up leading companies in the nation's most basic industries: autos, iron and steel, nonferrous metals, chemicals and drugs, electrical machinery and equipment, electronic computing and communications equipment, and energy. It is given no immediate chance to pass, but its ideas could find their way into future legislation. Another bill introduced by Senator John V. Tunney (D-Calif.), already approved by the Senate and taking a back seat to impeachment considerations in the House, would increase the current maximum criminal antitrust fine from $50,000 to $500,000 for corporations and $100,000 for executives. It would also require the Justice Dept. to explain publicly its reasons for accepting a consent decree instead of preparing a case and actually going to trial.

Bigger enforcement budgets

The Administration is seeking large increases, by usually puny antitrust standards, in the fiscal 1975 budgets of both the Justice Dept. and the FTC for their antitrust departments. If Congress approves, Justice's Antitrust Div. will pick up 83 additional staff slots, more than half lawyers and economists. At the last big increase, fiscal 1970, the division got only 20. The FTC is due for an additional $3-million, or a 20% increase in its present antitrust budget.

Growing muscle at FTC

After a long hibernation, the FTC is stepping out as a feisty agency with a new esprit, a highly professional staff, and a taste for going after bigness. It filed the monopoly

---

How Justice and the FTC Compete

The antitrust laws exist to preserve the values of competition, so it may be entirely logical that two agencies compete to administer them. On paper, the Antitrust Div. of the Justice Dept. and the Federal Trade Commission are different kinds of agencies. Justice is the law enforcement branch of the Executive Branch, the FTC is an independent regulatory commission. But in their antitrust responsibilities they are quite similar.

The Antitrust Div., headed by Thomas E. Kauper, is responsible for enforcing the Sherman and Clayton Acts. It has the exclusive power to bring criminal prosecutions. It also tries to enjoin anticompetitive mergers and a variety of collusive practices. The FTC's power springs from the Federal Trade Commission Act of 1914. Over the years, the courts have interpreted Section 5 of that Act to include all offenses proscribed by the other antitrust laws, giving the FTC equal civil jurisdiction with Justice. In fact, it has a broader civil authority, since it is required to proceed against "unfair methods of competition" and, as added by the Wheeler-Lea Act of 1938, against "unfair or deceptive acts or practices in commerce." These phrases permit the FTC to go after business conduct that is not necessarily collusive. The FTC, for example, has premised the cases against four big cereal makers on a variety of practices that it charges are unfair methods of competition, allegations that are not open to the Justice Dept. to make.

Resources

The Antitrust Div. has an annual budget of some $14-million, the FTC $15-million for antitrust purposes. Both together represent tiny sums contrasted with the resources private business is able to draw on. International Business Machines Corp., for example, reimbursed Control Data

suits against Xerox Corp. and the four biggest cereal makers. It has a special unit with an extra $1-million appropriation to litigate its case to break up the eight leading oil companies. And it got important new powers from Congress last year, including the right to demand otherwise unavailable product-line sales and profit figures from companies without first clearing with the Office of Management & Budget.

Reorganizing justice

If the Justice Dept.'s monopoly case against IBM, filed more than five years ago, is successful, it would give new spirit to the Antitrust Div., which at least until recently has been demoralized by the successive shocks of ITT and Watergate.

Corp. $15 million in legal fees and expenses in settling the private suit CDC filed against IBM.

Occasionally the agencies take potshots at each other. The FTC last year finally got the power, formerly reserved to the Justice Dept., to go into court on its own to enforce its own decrees. The FTC complained that Justice sat on requests for action. Justice countered that the requests were poorly framed.

But the agencies usually work reasonably well together. Now, when good politics dictates making headlines as tough antitrusters, the brass at each shop says the rivalry between the two to bring and win significant cases serves as a spur to both. The rivalry, says Justice's Kauper, is a "friendly" one. "Each has kept the other at it," he says. The FTC's Halverson concurs, citing "good practical results" from the existence of two agencies.

Neither agency launches an investigation without first clearing it with the other. The first agency to propose a particular investigation gets it, provided there is no conflict with the other's on-going work. Disagreements are settled at weekly liaison meetings. When a conflict cannot be settled at meetings, the assistant attorney general and the chairman of the FTC, Lewis A. Engman, deal with it.

The home for a particular kind of case is partly a matter of historical accident and partly the predilection of staff lawyers. Price discrimination cases under the Robinson-Patman Act are traditionally prosecuted by the FTC, which also generally probes problems in food and textile industries. Justice almost always gets steel cases. While Justice must proceed on a case-by-case basis, the FTC has the power also to issue rules with the force of law, in effect to promulgate codes of commercial conduct. Until recently, Justice alone had specific authority to try to block an unconsummated merger. But the FTC just gained similar powers in the law authorizing the Alaska pipeline.

Even so, the division reorganized and beefed up its economics staff last fall to enable it to undertake investigations and prosecutions with a sharper eye to the economic impact of its actions.

More and tougher antitrust enforcement is foreshadowed by more subtle changes in mood and belief as well as by these specific developments. One such change is a growing recognition that the government itself creates monopoly power. Several weeks ago Columbia Law School called together many of the nation's leading industrial economists and antitrust lawyers for a conference on industrial concentration. The participants examined what business concentration means both for the economy and for antitrust policy. About the only thing generally agreed on was that governmental attempts to regulate an industry often result in preserving the monopoly power of those being regulated. In line with this belief, insiders say that the Antitrust Div. will step up its policy of intervening in other government proceedings to shape regulatory policy consistent with antitrust principles. Last January, for example, the division formally intervened in FCC proceedings in an attempt to deny renewal of the broadcasting license of Cowles Communications, Inc., in Des Moines, and those of Pulitzer Publishing Co. and Newhouse Broadcasting Corp. in St. Louis. All these companies also own newspapers.

Another change has been the dramatic multiplication of private antitrust suits —those brought by one company against another. These include the 40-odd private business suits against IBM, ITT's suit to split up General Telephone & Electronics Corp., and the large class actions against plumbing and wallboard manufacturers. In fiscal 1973 the government filed 45 antitrust suits. By comparison, businessmen and other private parties filed 1,152, making the business community itself a significant factor in antitrust enforcement.

All this is leading to an antitrust Congress. Victor H. Kramer, director of Washington's Institute for Public Interest Representation and a leading antitrust lawyer, expects that "more supporters of an effective antimonopoly program are going to be elected to the 94th Congress than to any previous Congress in many years."

THE ALTERNATIVES

But as antitrust action steps up, so do the conflicts over the direction antitrust policy should take. The populists contend that antitrust enforcement in the past has been spineless. Businessmen complain that current policy paralyzes corporations because they are uncertain what practices are lawful and that they are being punished for being successfully competitive. Who is right?

The conflicts lead many businessmen to push for an updating of the antitrust laws. Richard L. Kattel, president of Atlanta's Citizens & Southern National Bank, which has been sparring with the Justice Dept. over the bank's expansion plans, feels that the antitrust laws "need complete revamping."

Major revamping, though, will not come because there is no general agreement on what form it should take. Most of the Columbia conference participants believe that the economic evidence for a change in policy is scanty and inconclusive. Suggestions ranged from doing nothing to pushing the tough Hart bill through Congress.

In approaching antitrust policy, there are alternatives:

1. Abolish the laws altogether.

A very few economists, such as Yale Brozen of the University of Chicago, talk as though antitrust laws are largely unnecessary. But as Robert L. Werner, executive vice-president and general counsel of RCA Corp., told a Conference Board antitrust seminar earlier this month: "There should be little disagreement by industry over the basic validity of the doctrine of antitrust. Certainly no businessman would seriously suggest that we scuttle that doctrine and return to a pre-Shermanite jungle." The courts have ruled that such practices as fixing prices, dividing markets, boycotting, some mergers, and predatory pricing designed to destroy competitors unlawfully impose restraints on the market.

The High Court's Tougher Stance

Although there have been hundreds of antitrust decisions, the following Supreme Court cases would be on any list as landmarks on the road to tougher antitrust:

Standard Oil Co. of N.J. v. U.S. (1911)
Only "unreasonable" restraints of trade are prohibited. To be guilty of monopolization, a company must have "purpose or intent" to exercise monopoly power.

American Column & Lumber Co. v. U.S. (1921)
Control of competition through a trade association that distributes current price and inventory information and company-by-company forecasts is unlawful.

Maple Flooring Manufacturers Assn. v. U.S. (1925)
Mere dissemination of cost and past price and inventory statistics through a trade association is not unlawful.

U.S. v. Trenton Potteries Co. (1927)
Price-fixing is inherently unreasonable, and any such agreement is a per se violation of the Sherman Act.

Interstate Circuit, Inc., v. U.S. (1939)
Consciously parallel behavior, where each competitor knew, even without direct communication with the others, how to act in order to control the market, is unlawful.

U.S. v. Socony Vacuum Oil Co. (1940)
Program by a group of oil companies to purchase surplus gasoline on spot

2. Clarify the laws by specifying precisely what business practices are unlawful.

If various practices can be identified and prohibited through case-by-case litigation, why not draft a detailed code of conduct?

But the very difficulty of identifying such practices when business conditions are constantly changing led to the broad wording of the Sherman Act originally. No one has ever produced an all-inclusive list of anticompetitive conduct. No one can possibly delineate all the circumstances that amount to price fixing and other illegal practices. If publication of future prices by members of a trade association is unlawful, as the Supreme Court held in 1921, is dissemination of past inventory figures and prices equally unlawful? (No, said the Court in 1925. For other such cases, see box.) Moreover, as Thomas M. Scanlon, chairman of the American Bar Assn.'s 8,500-member antitrust section points out: "There's uncertainty in any kind of litigation. Laws intended to bring more certainty often bring less."

---

market from independent refiners in order to stabilize price violates the Sherman Act.

Fashion Originators Guild v. FTC (1941)
Group boycotts are per se unlawful.

U.S. v. Aluminum Co. (1945)
It is not a defense to a charge of monopolization that the company was not morally derelict or predatory in its abuse of monopoly power. Even though monopoly may have been "thrust upon" the company because of its superior foresight, actions designed to prevent competition from arising constitute unlawful monopolization.

International Salt Co. v. U.S. (1947)
Tying agreements are unlawful per se.

Theatre Enterprises v. Paramount Film Distributing Corp. (1954)
Parallel behavior in the absence of any collusive activity is not unlawful per se.

U.S. v. United Shoe Machinery Corp. (1954)
Business practices that "further the dominance of a particular firm" are unlawful where the company has monopoly power.

Du Pont-GM Case (1956)
The government may move to undo a merger not only immediately after stock is acquired but whenever the requisite lessening of competition is likely to occur, even if that is decades after the merger.

3. Replace antitrust laws with direct regulation.

U.S. Steel's Gary favored and Koppers' Grymes favors a business-government partnership with this approval. Its advocates agree with John Kenneth Galbraith that antitrust is a "charade," that it has not and cannot produce a competitive economy in the face of the technological imperatives of large corporations. University of Chicago's George J. Stigler concludes that antitrust has not been "a major force" on the economy to date. "The government has won most of its 1,800 cases," he points out, "and there has been no important secular decline in concentration." On the other hand, many economists and lawyers would argue that Stigler has drawn the wrong conclusion. As Almarin Phillips, professor of economics and law at the Wharton School of Finance & Commerce, puts it: "The success of antitrust can only be measured by the hundreds of mergers and price-fixing situations that never happened."

Brown Shoe Co. v. U.S. (1962)
For purposes of determining a merger's effects on competition, there may be broad markets "determined by the reasonable interchangeability" of products and also "well-defined submarkets," whose boundaries may be determined by examining industrial customs and practices.

U.S. v. Philadelphia National Bank (1963)
"A merger which produces a firm controlling an undue percentage share of the relevant market and results in a significant increase in the concentration of firms in that market is so inherently likely to lessen competition substantially that it must be enjoined in the absence of evidence clearly showing that the merger is not likely to have such anticompetitive effects."

El Paso Natural Gas Co. v. U.S. (1964)
A merger that eliminates substantial potential competition violates the Clayton Act.

U.S. v. Penn-Olin Chemical Co. (1964)
A joint venture by two competitors may violate the Clayton Act.

U.S. v. Pabst Brewing Co. (1966)
A merger with "substantial anticompetitive effect somewhere in the U.S." is unlawful..

U.S. v. Arnold, Schwinn & Co. (1967)
It is unlawful per se for a manufacturer to limit its wholesalers' rights to sell goods purchased from the manufacturer.

U.S. v. Topco Associates (1972)
All territorial allocations among distributors are unlawful, even if they might foster competition against others.

Moreover, in the view of an increasing number of observers, regulation that is designed to mitigate the effects of "natural" monopolies, such as telephone service, often winds up fostering them instead. Civil Aeronautics Board regulations, for example, have compelled higher airline rates than prevail on federally non-regulated intra-state flights. Wesley James Liebler, recently named director of policy planning at the FTC, says: "What the airline industry needs is a little competition. In the long run we should get rid of the CAB and let in some free competition." Liebler also wants to abolish fixed commission rates for stockbrokers.

Much of the energy of regulatory commissions seems to be devoted to anticompetitive ends. The Federal Communications Commission promulgated rules several years ago designed to stifle the growth of pay-cable television. Sports events, for example, may not be broadcast on pay-cable TV if similar events have been shown on commercial television any time during the previous five years.

Walter Adams, a Michigan State University economist, notes that regulatory commissions can exclude competitors through licensing power, maintain price supports by regulating rates, create concentration through merger surveillance, and harass the weak by supervising practices that the strong do not like. To combat this kind of government behavior, the Antitrust Div. itself has, for the past several years, been intervening or attempting to intervene in such agencies as the ICC, CAB, and SEC to force decisions that spur competition in industry.

In support of their position, reformers make a further point: Large corporations have the political muscle to force the government to support their anticompetitive goals. Adams charges that the government has established an industrywide cartel for the oil companies through publishing monthly estimates of demand; through establishing quotas for each state pursuant to the Interstate Oil Compact, which Congress approved at behest of the oil companies; and through "prorationing devices" that dictate how much each well can produce. It is illegal to ship excess production in interstate commerce. Tariffs and import quotas protect only the producers, Adams says.

What this all amounts to is maintenance of shared monopoly power with the active cooperation of government. Only when the power of large companies is reduced, argue the populists, will the government be able to guide a competitive economy rather than serve as a prop for large interests. This was one of the original arguments for the Sherman Act in the 1880s.

4. Move toward tougher enforcement.

Populist critics of antitrust, such as Nader and Senator Hart, agree with Galbraith that antitrust has been all too ineffectual, but they move in the opposite policy direction. Since they believe that government regulation usually entrenches the power of big firms and concentrated industries, they favor a get-tough antitrust approach. They argue for two related tactics: extending existing law through the courts to curtail many practices of large firms in concentrated industries and getting Congressional legislation such as the Hart bill to attack the structure of these industries.

The Hart bill would permit the prosecution of companies because of their size alone. The history of antitrust has largely been to define and prosecute practices that courts would rule were restraints of trade, such as price fixing by agreement among competitors. But with increasing fervor "structuralists" argue that size itself can be harmful.

HISTORICAL DEFICIENCIES

Before the Civil War, Americans felt uncomfortable with corporate bigness. The image of the yeoman farmer and the small, fiercely competitive businessman largely reflected economic reality. But the growth of railroads, with their "pools" carving up markets, changed all that. By 1871, Charles Francis Adams, grandson and great-grandson of presidents, was writing that corporations "have declared war, negotiated peace, reduced courts, legislatures, and sovereign states to an unqualified obedience to their will."

Populist politics, such as the formation of the Grange movement, picked up steam, but at the same time, in 1882, the first big trust, Standard Oil of Ohio, was born, followed by the Whiskey Trust, the Sugar Trust, the Lead Trust, and the Cotton Oil Trust. Senator Sherman warned that without federal action the country would confront "a trust for every production and a master to fix the price for every necessity of life." The upshot was his Sherman Act.

But federal prosecutions were limited, aimed mostly at fledgling labor unions, and the Sherman Act failed to curb bigness. Corporate mergers speeded up. U.S. Steel, Standard Oil (New Jersey), American Tobacco, American Can, International Harvester, and United Shoe Machinery were all put together at this time. As a result, antitrusters increased pressure for even tougher laws and an independent agency, which could develop industrial expertise, to enforce them.

These efforts came to fruition in 1914, with the passage of the Clayton and Federal Trade Commission Acts. The Clayton Act specifically banned anticompetitive mergers, while the FTC Act set up an agency to police "unfair competition" in the marketplace but not to regulate prices and output.

Like the Sherman Act, the Clayton Act proved ineffectual for many years, largely because of the way courts interpreted the law. As recently as 1948 the Court permitted U.S. Steel to acquire one of its own customers.

Partly in response to this decision, Congress passed the Celler-Kefauver Act in 1950, amending the Clayton Act to prohibit mergers through acquisition of assets or stock as well as those that would tend to foreclose competition in any market in the country. This effectively closed the door on many mergers. But the merger wave of the late 1960s comprised so-called conglomerate get-togethers of companies in different, often unrelated, industries. The case intended to settle this issue —ITT—never got to the Supreme Court because it was settled by a consent decree.

Mergers became the target of antitrusters because they mean the disappearance of independent competitors and lead to concentrations of industrial power. And, argue antitrusters, a few large companies may "share" monopoly power simply by dominating a given market. But unless collusion among competitors can be proved, there is no way under conventional enforcement to prosecute them.

CONFLICTING VIEWS

To remedy this supposed defect, Senator Hart's new law would create a presumption of monopoly power whenever:

- A company's average rate of return is greater than 15% of its net worth for each of five consecutive years.

- There has been no substantial price competition for three consecutive years among two or more corporations within an industry.

- Four or fewer companies account for half or more of an industry's sales in a single year.

Clearly, these criteria create a net that would sweep up hundreds of large corporations. Hart's staff estimates, for example, that a quarter to a third of all U.S. manufacturing concerns meet the third condition.

A company that met any of these criteria would not automatically have to divest. Its defense before the special agency and court the bill would create could be either that its position rests on legally acquired patents or that divesting would deprive it of "substantial economies." (At present economies are not a defense.)

Howard O'Leary, chief counsel to Hart's antitrust subcommittee, argues that without "some mandate" from Congress, the Justice Dept. would be unlikely to embark "on an antitrust crusade." The bill would provide that mandate.

Senator Hart asserts that statistics can be misleading. He cites concentration ratios which according to economists show competition in the oil industry. But, says Hart, "Look at the evidence of joint ventures, banking interlocks, vertical integration, joint ownership of facilities, joint production, absence of real price competition, and lockstep decision-making, and one must wonder."

Economist Walter Adams agrees. He points out that between 1956 and 1968, 20 major oil companies were involved in 226 mergers and thereby gained control over a variety of substitute fuels, such as coal and atomic energy. The oil companies also moved into allied businesses, such as fertilizers, plastics, and chemicals, through vertical integration. Adams believes that a new law is necessary to fragment the power of the companies in the oil and other industries.

The only businessmen to come forward so far in support of at least the thrust of what Senator Hart is trying to do, says O'Leary, are some in communications and data processing. Through a series of hearings the subcommittee hopes, says O'Leary, "to persuade politicians and to some extent the public that it is feasible to come up with more firms than now exist, that the market won't crash, and that jobs won't be lost."

Most other businessmen see little good in the Hart bill. Carl H. Madden, chief economist for the U.S. Chamber of Commerce, brands its basic thrust as "faulty."

He told Senate hearings last spring that the bill would thwart competition, not aid it, "by changing the legally permitted goal and cutting back the prizes."

Legal experts have many other objections. Richard Posner, of the University of Chicago Law School, feels that the Hart bill is symptomatic of "antitrust off on a tangent." Antitrust chief Thomas E. Kauper is not "satisfied with the economic evidence favoring broad deconcentration statutes." Kellogg Co. vice-president and corporate counsel J. Robert O'Brien says: "There is no reason whatever to assume that a 'concentrated' industry will necessarily be any less competitive than a fractionated industry. A course of antitrust enforcement that seeks to break up companies and restructure industries by looking at little more than concentration levels is misguided, to say the least."

Many have pointed out that among the defects in Hart's approach is the difficulty of measuring and the ease of manipulating rates of return. Further, even Ralph Nader, a supporter of the bill, says that deconcentrating an industry "is a 15-year job, at least."

OTHER TACTICS

Antitrusters are not holding their breath waiting for legislation. In a series of cases initiated during the past five years, they are using existing laws prohibiting monopolization and unfair methods of competition to check alleged anticompetitive conditions in concentrated industries.

The FTC's suit against Xerox and the Justice Dept.'s against IBM represent marked change from the past. The government has brought very few cases against single companies for alleged monopoly, partly because of limited prosecution budgets, partly because of political pressure from business, and partly because officials thought them unnecessary. These two recent suits single out a variety of practices—pricing policies, for example, and such things as announcing products embodying new technology far in advance of actual availability—that are alleged ways the two companies exercise monopoly power. The antitrust subcommittee's O'Leary says, "The IBM case is potentially very significant, if it is won and a remedy can be found. It is the first such case in 25 years."

The Justice Dept. also brought suit last August against Goodyear and Firestone, charging them with monopolizing the replacement tire market through a combination of practices, including acquisitions, periods of uneconomically low prices designed to drive out competitive products, service station tie-ins, and reciprocity deals. The two companies are charged with acting independently to maintain their dominant positions; they are not charged with collusion.

Perhaps the most innovative case is the FTC's suit against the four leading breakfast food makers, charging them with a variety of unfair methods of competition. The Commission is not claiming any conspiracy among the companies. It is trying to prove, instead, that a lengthy list of long-standing industry practices are anticompetitive and permit the companies, whose market shares have gone from 68% in 1940 to 90% today, to "share" monopoly power in their respective industries. If successful, this suit would strengthen the commission's ability to use its statute to go after many heavily concentrated industries.

The FTC's current prosecution against the eight major oil companies also attempts to break new ground. The key allegation is that the majors have been "pursuing a common course" in using control of crude oil and shipping facilities to stall the development of independent refineries. This includes eliminating retail competition by keeping prices low at the refinery and marketing end and high at the production end of the business. The FTC also charges the companies with such practices as using barter and exchange agreements to keep crude oil in their own hands and reluctance to sell to independent marketers. Unlike the cereal suits, the FTC charges that some of the oil practices are collusive.

When Companies Sue Each Other

Professor George J. Stigler of the University of Chicago, chairman of President Nixon's Task Force on Antitrust, finds the whole subject of antitrust "a dull field with few sensations." He makes an exception of the rise of the private antitrust case, which he calls "fascinating."

In recent years private companies have been suing each other furiously under the antitrust laws, far outpacing the government. In the past two fiscal years the government filed 108 antitrust suits against private business. But in the same period companies filed 2,451 suits against other companies. In fiscal 1960 there were only a paltry 228 private suits.

Dr. Irwin M. Stelzer, president of National Economic Research Associates, Inc., a large antitrust-oriented consulting firm, explains that private suits began to increase markedly following the electrical equipment price-fixing conspiracy cases in the early 1960s. State public utility commissions said, in effect, that if utilities had a remedy for overcharges as a result of antitrust violations but failed to bring suit to recover, the commission would not approve rate increases to cover the losses. The same principle applied to all corporations: Failure to pursue antitrust remedies could subject them to stockholder derivative suits. So, according to Stelzer, what had seemed to the big names in the antitrust bar as seamy litigation far beneath their notice, like chasing ambulances, suddenly became necessary and glamorous.

Maxwell Blecher, antitrust attorney in Los Angeles, sees the rise of private antitrust suits in the past 10 years as a transfer of power. "The government has failed to act and the private sector has filled the vacuum," he says. He attributes the change in part to different business attitudes. "Management is now result-oriented rather than concerned about being accepted at the club." He expects the number of private suits to continue to increase.

CAN WE COMPETE?

In the face of government attack, some businessmen wonder whether such antitrust action aimed at cutting down corporate size might not handicap U.S. companies in keeping pace with the growing number of multinational corporations around the world. Koppers Co.'s Grymes, who argues for permitting mergers, would prefer to see the government "adopt a whole new philosophy of life." He would like to see 26 steel companies, for example, merged into five or six. "Let them get together, produce together, sell together," he says. He concedes that to make up for the absence of competition, the government would have to levy an excess-profits tax or put limitations on investments. He vigorously opposes the Hart bill.

So does J. Fred Weston, a professor at the University of California at Los Angeles' Graduate School of Management, and for similar reasons. "The world market requires increasingly large firms," he argues. "If we hold on to the 18th

---

Anyone can sue.

Stigler strongly supports private use of the antitrust laws, a concept introduced into the Clayton Act in 1914. Anyone injured by a violation of the laws can sue as a "private attorney general." To sweeten the burden, courtroom success is rewarded with triple money damages plus attorneys' fees. "Anybody should be able to enforce the antitrust laws," says Stigler. "There is no way for bureaucrats to know what is happening. The only way the government finds out is through letters of complaint."

In 1966 the Supreme Court approved changes in the procedural rules governing class actions, making it easier for large classes of people or groups to pool common claims and seek relief through coordinated efforts of their attorneys. The number of private antitrust suits soared.

Businessmen began to see the specter of numerous nuisance suits. Victor H. Kramer of the Institute for Public Interest Representation agrees that there may be some but believes that "this is a fair price" for the meritorious suits. Thomas E. Kauper, Justice Dept. antitrust chief, says there is some basis for the businessman's concern, but he thinks that the courts will become increasingly experienced in using the class action rules to strike a fair balance. George R. Kucik, an antitrust attorney with Arent, Fox, Kintner, Plotkin & Kahn in Washington, suggests that consideration be given to changing the law with respect to the large class action sponsored by municipal or state governments in order to permit ordinary, not treble, damages. "If the pool is big enough to begin with," he says, "there is no need for the trebling." This idea is embodied in the Uniform State Antitrust Act, a new law being pushed by the National Conference of Commissioners on Uniform State Laws. It permits individuals and businesses to seek treble damages but holds governmental units to actual damages plus attorneys' fees.

Century idea of a nation of small shopkeepers and small farms, we will become a small nation." Unlike Grymes, Weston would not encourage mergers. Rather, he is against "fighting a rear-guard battle to prevent deconcentration based on invalid premises." Corporate size, he insists, should be judged in relation to the world market. "If there are firms of increasing size abroad and there are economies of scale, U.S. firms have to be able to compete."

Supporters of deconcentration policy do not quarrel with the premise that U.S. companies must be able to compete, but they do argue that existing levels of concentration in many industries are more than adequate. They believe that size alone is not a guarantee of economies of scale or of efficiencies. And they point to industrial studies indicating that economies of scale relate primarily to plant size but not necessarily to the numbers of plants that any one manufacturer controls.

Frederic M. Scherer, the FTC's incoming economics bureau chief, believes that economic studies show that many industries are more concentrated than efficiency requires. Nader argues that the best evidence is "clinical, not statistical." He says that studies of industries that have become less concentrated would show consumer gains without loss of efficiency. The arrival of a new supermarket chain in the Washington metropolitan area several years ago, he says, forced prices down, and he cites the aluminum industry after Aluminum Co. of America had to face competition. It was still able to compete.

Moreover, the fact that a company can be efficient does not mean that it will be. On the contrary, absence of competition may make the company fat and lazy —capable of efficiency but acting inefficiently because it is not spurred by the need to compete.

In the 1950 Congressional hearings on monopoly power, Benjamin Fairless, president of U.S. Steel, admitted that his company had less efficient production processes than its competitors, including much smaller foreign companies. Studies have demonstrated that American steel producers lagged woefully in innovation. Between 1940 and 1955, 13 major inventions came from abroad, yet American steel boasted the largest companies in the world.

The basic oxygen process, which Avery C. Adams, chairman and president of Jones & Laughlin Steel Corp., described in 1959 as "the only major technological breakthrough at the ingot level in the steel industry since before the turn of the century," was perfected by a tiny Austrian steel company in 1950. It was introduced into the U.S. in 1954 by McLouth Steel Corp., which then had less than 1% of American ingot capacity. Jones & Laughlin waited until 1957, and U.S. Steel and Bethlehem Steel Corp. waited until 1964 to adopt the process, resulting in lost profits to the steel industry, according to one study, of some $216-million after taxes by 1960 alone.

As for ability to compete abroad, there is practically no evidence that the Justice Dept. has impaired the competitive posture of U.S. companies in world markets. In the past few years the Justice, Commerce, and Treasury Depts., as well as Congressional committees, have practically pleaded for businessmen to come forward with examples of how Americans have been hurt, with minimal results. The Antitrust Div.'s recent release of business review letters from 1968 through 1972 indicates not a single turndown of joint export ventures.

David H. Baker, director of the Commerce Dept.'s Office of Export Development, made an intense search for examples of antitrust harm. A large food company wanted to enter a joint venture with another big U.S. outfit to bid on a plant an Eastern European government planned to build. The Justice Dept. indicated it might refuse to approve the deal, and the food company pulled out. A small U.S. company then bid for the contract on its own and won.

A NEW APPROACH

Some experts believe that the government cannot deal with business complaints adequately unless it develops a comprehensive approach to competition generally. Victor Kramer suggests the creation of an "office of antimonopoly affairs" within the Executive Office of the President. The function of this office, Kramer says, would be to implement a new executive order he would like to see promulgated, directing all federal agencies to act to promote a "free competitive enterprise system." It would require the federal departments and bureaus to prepare antitrust impact statements whenever they suggest action that would "significantly affect competition in the private sector."

Professor Neil H. Jacoby, of UCLA's Graduate School of Management, agrees with the general thrust of Kramer's suggestion. Jacoby, who believes that oligopoly is here to stay, proposes the creation of a Federal Competition Agency, either as an independent commission or within the White House. He would have it submit a "competition impact report" for "all proposed federal legislation."

Kramer concludes that his policy would have compelled the State Dept. to evaluate publicly the competitive impact of the voluntary steel import agreements with Japan and European nations. The Pentagon would have been called on to explain how the public benefits from the awarding of nonbid contracts. The Internal Revenue Service and the White House, he believes, would have to consider the competitive effects of proposed changes in tax laws.

This broadened approach to competition could come closer to resolving the conflicts between the tendency of companies to exert control over their markets and the public requirement that monopoly be held in check. Short of this, the evidence suggests that antitrust is the best we have.

The Toothless Tigers?
The states' regulation of insurance companies often viewed as farce

William Blundell and Priscilla Meyer*

A major scandal erupted, and the insurance company collapsed. Some of its assets were missing and a federal grand jury started a probe. By the time state insurance regulators took over the company, there wasn't enough money left in it to honor fully the contracts of policyholders.

The scenario in many ways fits Equity Funding Life Insurance Co., but the concern involved is actually Federal Old Line Insurance Co. which went belly-up in the state of Washington five years ago. The mess isn't cleaned up yet.

Almost 320 of the company's policyholders have since died, and their beneficiaries haven't gotten a nickel. "We've even had beneficiaries die in the interim," sighs Karl Herrmann, the state's insurance commissioner. (Equity Funding has at least paid death claims.) Living policyholders can't get the cash value out of their policies, either. (Nor can Equity Funding holders, at least for now.) "Most of them used the insurance as a method of saving," says Mr. Herrmann, "to put their children through school, for example. Now the children are in school, and the money isn't there."

The only essential difference between the Federal Old Line and Equity Funding cases is that the latter was a far larger company and collapsed amid national publicity over a particularly nervy fraud—the creation and sale to reinsurers of bogus insurance. All by itself, the Equity Funding case casts a glaring light on the weaknesses of state regulation of insurance companies. "It makes a tremendous case for federal regulation of insurers," says Robert Schultz, professor of finance at the University of Southern California and a consultant to many insurance companies.

113 CASUALTY CASUALTIES

But, as Federal Old Line suggests, there is more to the argument than that, for insurance company collapses aren't rare and unusual events. According to one tally, 113 casualty insurers collapsed from 1958 thru 1972—with little public notice.

From *The Wall Street Journal,* August 2, 1973. Reprinted with permission.

*Staff reporters of the *Wall Street Journal.*

Declared insolvencies of life insurers are far less frequent, and reliable numbers aren't available, but insurance regulators admit that many concerns have been in serious financial trouble. Most often, they are quietly bailed out by state regulators who negotiate behind the scenes to forcibly merge them or sell off their policies to well-financed larger companies; the policyholder seldom knows what a close call he has had until it's all over—or until, as in Federal Old Line, he is left holding the bag.

All of this belies the staid, gray image of safety and stability the insurance industry seeks to project. While most of the larger companies are solid enough, regulators concede that many smaller ones are not. Herbert Denenberg, the outspoken insurance commissioner of Pennsylvania, says flatly: "There has been improvement, but we still have too many weak companies. Informed buyers would avoid about 80% of the companies domiciled in the U.S."

Mr. Denenberg and others lay the blame on a whole complex of weaknesses that, in the view of many, make effective state regulation of insurance companies a farce. These flaws include state laws that allow insurers to set up companies on a relative shoestring and that leave policyholders unprotected when they fail; some regulatory personnel whose competence is in serious question, and who often are far too cozy with the companies they are supervising; enormous variation among the states' capacity to regulate, resulting in some states so weak they draw downpours of fly-by-night operators; and, finally, a creaky regulatory mechanism, devised decades ago, that has been unable to keep up with the growth of the industry or cope with such developments as the computer and the insurance holding company.

BURDEN ON REGULATORS

Life insurers now number more than 1,800, a fourfold increase since 1945, and they're writing about 10 times as much business as 28 years ago. The number of property-casualty companies, 2,700, apparently hasn't changed much over the same period, but these companies are writing about seven times as much insurance as in 1945. But the number of state insurance examiners, the men who perform the audits on insurance companies, has only about doubled. This places an immense burden on regulators, who keep falling behind in their insurance-company audits.

These state audits generally are supposed to be conducted every three or five years, depending on the state and the type of company. Some regulators think the audits are nearly useless in the current era of the giant company; it generally takes two years and more to audit a goliath like Allstate Insurance Cos. or Prudential Insurance Co. of America, and by the time the work is completed the picture the audit presents has all the freshness of the Dead Sea scrolls.

"What good is this?" asks James Steen, deputy director of the Illinois Department of Insurance. "It's a whole new company by the time you're finished." What's more, the data produced by the audit generally aren't compiled and available for another 20 to 29 months. Regulators and others generally wind up making most use of the annual statements prepared by the insurance companies themselves, statements that don't require certification by independent auditors.

Companies and some regulators also grouse about the waste involved in audits, particularly "zone audits." These occur when a state with the primary responsibility for auditing a company—usually the state in which it is formally domiciled—issues a zone call.

This is a notification to regulators in other geographic zones where the company may do business; representatives from states in these zones may then show up to help conduct the audit.

According to some regulators, they are more a hindrance than a help, since some of the zone representatives view a call as a chance for an expense-paid vacation. "We had one guy we just stuck in a corner, and we asked him to handle phone calls. He couldn't even do that," says one disgusted state insurance official. "Another time, we had a guy who absolutely refused to sign his name to the certification of the audit, which was all finished, because he still had three weeks left on the lease of the apartment he rented."

As for the companies, they don't like the disruption—and the expense. That's because they pay for their own audits, a procedure that many critics, including regulators themselves, believe reeks of conflict of interest.

The practice stems from the traditional view that insurance departments should generate money for the states instead of spending gobs of it; many are still regarded more as useful appendages to the treasury than as protectors of the public. According to the insurance industry committee of Ohio, the states collected $1.28 billion in 1970 in the form of insurance premium taxes and fees and spent only $58.8 million on their own regulatory operations.

State regulatory budgets are often kept low, and companies are charged more than the actual cost of audit, plus other fees, in order to cover the whole budget. Thus, in effect, the insurance departments often cost the states nothing at all to operate and states get to collect all the premium taxes besides.

COZY RELATIONSHIPS

The financial reliance of most departments on the companies they are supposed to be regulating is only part of the coziness. There is regular and routine movement of workers from insurance companies to regulators' jobs and vice versa. Commissioners often negotiate for and even announce new jobs in the industry while they are still in charge of regulating it.

And favors are exchanged. When Broward Williams, a former Florida commissioner, had trouble defending his position on insurance rates (a position favored by the industry) before state legislators, he requested and got the services of a top industry speechwriter to draft an address to the legislature. And when the National Association of Insurance Commissioners convenes, the regulators are engulfed by swarms of insurance executives, whose companies pick up the tabs for social events.

Similar cozy treatment extends down to insurance-department examiners, too, when they're auditing company books. All this makes some regulators distinctly uncomfortable. "How can you really be objective," asks Washington commissioner Hermann, "when you are wined and dined and paid by the people you are supposed to be regulating?"

The insurance watchdogs also complain about truck-sized holes in the regulatory net that allow insurers to evade effective scrutiny altogether. For example, they cite "farm mutuals," an unregulated type of insurer allowed, technically, to write only a few types of insurance in specific geographic areas. Frequently targets of the unscrupulous, some farm mutuals have been misused to write everything from auto insurance to costly commercial risks, then have collapsed at the drop of a claim form.

"PUPPET" INSURERS

Another regulatory gap is reinsurance—coverage written by one company and sold to another—which is barely regulated at all.

Though reinsurance is a necessary method for spreading large risks among many insurers and allowing the selling companies to raise cash to expand operations, it can be a vehicle for questionable deals and downright fraud, as in the Equity Funding debacle.

Reinsurance is also used in tax dodges such as "puppet" insurers. Many states levy stiffer premium taxes on companies that do business in their state, but aren't headquartered there, than on "domestic" insurers; to evade the stiffer tax, an out-of-state concern simply sets up a "puppet" subsidiary in the state as a separate company domiciled there.

Often the "puppet" consists of nothing but a sales force, and the insurance it writes is immediately sold to the parent or another of its subsidiaries. The proliferation of puppets in recent years has added immeasurably to the difficulties of regulation; state officials have the responsibility to audit all these extra companies but can't do it effectively because their books, records and officers are usually in another state, at the parent company.

THE COMPUTER

The regulatory machinery also isn't geared to cope with electronic data processing. Most insurers now have computers keeping their accounts, but the regulators are still oriented to physical records. Very few states have people on their payrolls who know anything about electronic data processing; real experts can make many times more money in private business than insurance departments can afford.

The result has been that examiners usually just take the company's computer printouts at face value because they have to. The peril of this is clear in light of what happened at Equity Funding, where the computer was programmed to produce deceptive or falsified printouts to gull auditors and examiners. Says Arizona Insurance Commissioner Millard Humphrey: "I'm scared to death by computers." He isn't alone.

The rise of the holding company also shows up glaring weaknesses in the regulatory system. Predatory parent companies can and do siphon millions out of the insurers they hold, legally or illegally, and effectively thumb their noses at the regulators. Some ploys include:

—The Bum Asset Swap. One of the most common ways of removing money from an insurance subsidiary, this involves a transfer of cash or gilt-edged assets from the insurer to the parent, who replaces it with something of dubious worth (often its own debentures).

—The Shell Game. In this, a holding company milks insurance subsidiaries for cash and other assets. The parent simply concentrates what assets are left in subsidiary A, when it's facing an audit, moves them to subsidiary B when that company is due for examination, and so on. Since insurance subsidiaries in different states usually are audited at separate times, the weaknesses never show up unless one or more of the companies finally goes under. Arizona's Mr. Humphrey recalls moving in to take over a troubled company and finding the same $8 million asset in two different subsidiaries. "They said it was just an accounting error," he says wryly.

—The Surplus Slurp. This is used to take cash out of insurance subsidiaries laden with money well in excess of their needs for reserves against insurance claims. The insurance subsidiary declares a hefty dividend to its shareholders—the parent. The biggest slurp on record—which was quite legal—was engineered in 1969 when Great American Insurance Cos. declared a whopping $174.5 million dividend to its happy parent, National General Corp. National General had gotten control of Great American shortly before.

Such dividends now are watched more closely by regulators, but parent companies have other ways of raising cash from insurance subsidiaries. One variation: acquire some real estate and immediately sell it to the subsidiary at a big markup, citing "improvements" to the property.

LAWS CALLED FULL OF HOLES

Locked into a fragmented and ill-coordinated system of regulation, enforcement officials concede they can't cope with the holding-company complex, especially since they have no power over the parent (only the separate insurance subsidiaries fall under state regulation.)

Says Mr. Humphrey: "I don't care what laws you have—there's little to prevent a holding company from taking money out of its insurance subs."

As for the laws, many regulators concede they are full of holes, too. "They have been written by and for the insurance industry and have been administered by and for the insurance industry," says Pennsylvania's Mr. Denenberg. In fact, few policyholders even realize state insurance departments exist; and negotiation over content of insurance regulations and such matters as auto-insurance rates are generally hashed out between the departments and insurers with the consumer a forgotten party.

And while depositors in banks and savings-and-loans, as well as brokerage-house clients have federally backed protection in case of failure, policyholders aren't nearly as well off. Forty-six states have special funds to cover policyholders of casualty companies that fail, but only nine protect holders of life-insurance contracts.

Heaped atop all these problems is the lack of quality regulatory workers. Some commissioners have strange backgrounds for the work; Cornelius Bateson, Oregon's former commissioner, was a chicken farmer, and Sherman Bernard of Louisiana lacks formal education and was a house mover. (A deputy says Mr. Bernard ran for office because he thought he was "getting robbed" on his own insurance.) No one accuses either of these men as being bad commissioners, though their backgrounds are unusual.

REVOLVING DOORS

Some commissioners, either elected or appointed, often aren't around long enough to make any difference. A new face in the governor's mansion or a cushy job in the industry or politics removes them; one industry man estimates that the average tenure in office of a commissioner is less than two years.

This means the regulatory burden is really carried by the salaried civil-service workers in the departments. Privately, many regulators say these ranks are riddled with incompetents embedded into place by civil-service provisions that all but forbid firing. Asked how his examiners compare with, say, junior accountants hired by the big accounting firms, one deputy commissioner snaps: "Miserably."

"We have two kinds of people," he says, "youngsters who don't know what they're doing yet and who will go to work in the industry just as soon as they learn, and older guys who have come here to retire and draw a paycheck at the same time."

The Equity Funding case illustrates a dearth of alertness at the departments. Equity Funding Life reported a near-doubling of insurance-in-force in 1970—astounding, as 1970 was an off year for insurance generally and a disastrous year for mutual-fund sales, which were tied to most of the company's insurance contracts. Apparently not one of the 41 states in which the company did business and filed reports seriously questioned these figures. Most of the "sales" turned out to be phony.

As grim as the regulatory picture looks now, it used to be worse. Regulatory staffs have been increased and laws stiffened over the past decade or so. A few states, notably New York, have reputations for fairly effective enforcement; New York had a computer expert on its payroll before the Equity Funding scandal and now is training examiners in data processing. Arkansas has gotten strong regulation since 1967, when new men stepped into its insurance commission and promptly put out of business more than half the companies domiciled in the state.

The Equity Funding case may bring more improvements, it's felt. Many states were rudely awakened to the potential for computer fraud and are making more use of outside consultants in their examinations. The National Association of Insurance Commissioners recently met and proposed a study toward modernization of the whole audit process.

Some states, including Arizona and Illinois, are cracking down hard on puppets, demanding that these companies' executives and books be physically moved to states with auditing responsibility. Illinois and New York have proposed scrapping the current three-to-five year examination system, New York favoring more flexible audits that zero in on potential problem areas, and Illinois suggesting that independent CPA firms conduct certified audits of insurers every year.

And some insurance departments are thinking about policyholder needs—by issuing insurance-buying guides, for example.

But as Mr. Denenberg notes, many problems are left unresolved, and "the climate now is right for fundamental change and reform."

Perhaps more fundamental than even the regulators suppose. Tides in the industry are quietly shifting toward federal regulation, which on the surface insurers have traditionally fought bitterly. As more insurers merge and grow into national companies, they need national marketing campaigns and standardized insurance policies. Here state-by-state nitpicking plays havoc, insurers say.

A number of insurance executives privately concede they'd welcome federal regulation, if only because it would free them of dealing state-by-state. And one man says so publicly. Ralph W. Leatherby, chairman of Leatherby Insurance Co. of New York, a subsidiary of Richmond Corp., says he "absolutely" favors federal regulation of insurance. The company currently writes workmen's compensation insurance in 28 states but has plans to expand into the other states within a year or so.

Mr Leatherby says he's annoyed by the petty corruption in a number of the departments. More importantly, he cites the cost of dealing with various state regulatory agencies. "It's widely said in the industry that it costs $1 million to get an insurance company licensed in all the states," he says. This represents local legal fees and lobbying costs as well as admission fees.

SELECTED READINGS

'The FTC Gets Tough," *Changing Times,* July, 1972.

Green, M. J., *The Closed Enterprise System,* Ralph Nader's Study Group Report On Antitrust Enforcement. (New York: Grossman Publishers, 1972.)

Liebhafsky, H. H., *American Business And Government*. (New York: John Wiley & Sons, 1971.)

Monsen, R. J., and M. W. Cannon, *The Makers Of Public Policy*. (New York: McGraw-Hill Book Co., 1965.)

Passell, P., and L. Ross, "The Cab Pilots the Planes," *New York Times Magazine*, August 12, 1973.

Select Committee On Small Business, House Of Representatives, *Congress And The Monopoly Problem*. (Washington: U.S. Government Printing Office, 1966.)

Stigler, G. J., "The Theory Of Economic Regulation," *Bell Journal Of Economics And Management Science*, Spring 1971.

Wilcox, C., *Public Policies Toward Business*, 4th Edition. (Homewood: Richard D. Irwin, 1972.)

Case

BERKELEY SAVINGS AND LOAN ASSOCIATION*

On September 1, 1971, the Berkeley Savings and Loan Association, in compliance with the New Jersey Savings and Loan Act of 1963, filed an application with the Commissioner of Banking of the State of New Jersey requesting permission to relocate its Chancellor Avenue, Newark, branch office to the Five Point Shopping Center in Union, New Jersey. Pursuant to the provisions of the Act, the New Jersey Department of Banking, which administers the law, held hearings on the relocation application and opposing arguments. On September 12, 1972, the hearing officer, Mr. Clifford F. Blaze, submitted a report to the Acting Commissioner of Banking, Mr. Richard F. Schaub, recommending approval of the application. Upon review of the case, however, Commissioner Schaub found that such a relocation would adversely affect the economic climate of Newark and therefore would not be in the public interest. Consequently the application was denied on January 24, 1973.

Since the case involves the issues of private versus public interests, business social responsibility, freedom of choice and movement in a free enterprise system, and the regulatory process and its attendant standards, it is fruitful to review the background and developments of the events leading to the commissioner's decision.

Company Background

Berkeley Savings and Loan Association is a mutual savings institution (that is, it serves the interests of depositors only) chartered and regulated

---

*Copyright © 1973 by Gordon K. C. Chen and Arthur Elkins.

by the State of New Jersey. The Association maintains its principal office at 421 Millburn Avenue, Township of Millburn, County of Essex, and operates two branch offices in Newark—one at 88 Lyons Avenue and another at 434 Chancellor Avenue, the one for which the Association has applied for relocation. Berkeley also has another branch office in East Hanover Township.

Berkeley's main office was originally located in Newark and had been relocated to Millburn only recently. All of Berkeley's facilities are currently located within the "first savings and loan district" of New Jersey, as defined by statute.

Berkeley was established in 1941 with assets of over $1 million and a reserve of a little over $61,000. The Association enjoyed a rapid growth and expansion during post-World-War-II years. By June 30, 1973, the end of the current fiscal year, its total assets amounted to more than $125 million, with reserves and deferred income totaling over $8.6 million. The bank offers a complete thrift and home financing service, having some 19,300 savings accounts and about 6300 mortgage accounts in 1971. The Association had 42 officers and employees in 1971. Berkeley's Chancellor Avenue Branch was opened for business in November, 1954. Because of the convenient location for its customers and the lack of competing institutions in the vicinity, the branch's deposits grew from a modest beginning of $400,000 in the first two months to $19.2 million in 1963.

Following the period of rapid growth, however, an increasing number of the branch's customers, starting in the early 1960's, were moving from the area into the suburbs of Essex and Union Counties. By 1971, 87 percent of its new savings customers came from the suburban communities.

Concurrently, a number of large thrift and banking institutions moved into the vicinity during the latter part of the 1960's. This combination of increased competition plus the out-migration of its older customers caused the branch, beginning in 1968, to experience a decline in deposits. In 1970, the branch suffered its highest annual savings loss of more than $2 million, while aggregate savings in New Jersey rose by $600 million in that year. Similar declines were felt in other types of thrift accounts, such as the Christmas Club.

Berkeley attributed the decline in business to a number of significant factors:

1. The suburban exodus of the residents.

2. The substantial increase in the number of competitive institutions.

3. The Newark riots in the summer of 1967.

4. The sharp increase in crimes of violence, particularly muggings.

5. The destruction of property for Route 178 displacing 1900 families and 7000 people.

6. The overcrowding of schools and the deterioration of the educational system.

7. The closing of most of the religious institutions, mostly of the Jewish faith as their members left the area.

8. The disappearance of most social and civic organizations.

9. Fear of safety.

10. Exodus of almost all of the Chancellor Avenue merchants.

11. Immigration of low income, financially burdened families into the Chancellor Avenue Area.[1]

THE APPLICATION

In view of the decline in business and the fear of further deterioration of its neighborhood (the condition of which was characterized as a "day-to-day state of siege"[2]) the management of Berkeley decided it was time to move the branch from the area. On September 1, 1971 Berkeley filed an application with the New Jersey Commissioner of Banking requesting permission to move the Chancellor Avenue office to a new site located in the Five Point Shopping Center, Union, New Jersey.

The 27-page application provided background information on Berkeley's history and operations, as well as analyses and reasoning for the proposed relocation. It also included attachments giving detailed facts and figures and exhibits in support of the application.

The proposed new branch site is located within the boundary of the so-called "second savings and loan district of New Jersey." Under the provisions of the New Jersey Savings and Loan Act (N.J.S.A. 17: 12B–26), three savings and loan districts were established. The first district consists of Bergen, Essex, Hudson, Morris, Passaic, Sussex, and Warren Counties of northern New Jersey. The second district includes Hunterdon, Mercer, Middlesex, Monmouth, Somerset, and Union Counties in the central part of New Jersey. The third district consists of the remaining eight counties in the southern part of the state.

The New Jersey Savings and Loan Act requires that a state-chartered Savings and Loan Association may establish a *de novo* branch only in the *same* savings and loan district of its principal office, but makes no mention about the relocation of any branches.

In compliance with Section 17: 12B–27. 1 (2) of the New Jersey State Acts, which requires that: "If the proposed new location is in another

municipality, the state association shall comply with the notice requirements set forth in subsection 2 of section 26 of the Act," Berkeley
served notice of its application to other associations having offices
located in Union Township or within two miles of the proposed site. The
New Jersey Department of Banking also notified the New Jersey Savings
League, the New Jersey Bankers' Association, and the Savings Banks'
Association of New Jersey of the pending application. In September
1971, a notice of the application was published in the bulletins of the
aforementioned associations.

THE HEARINGS AND THE REACTIONS

Following the announcement and notifications of Berkeley's intention
to relocate its Chancellor Avenue branch, objections to the application
and requests for hearings began to pour into the office of the Department of Banking. Among the objectors were the Colonial Savings and
Loan Association, the First New Jersey Bank, the Investors Savings and
Loan Association, the Union Central National Bank, and the Stonewall
Savings and Loan Association of Linden. The Greater Newark Chamber
of Commerce also objected to the move and requested a hearing, but
subsequently withdrew the request.

Upon receipt of the requests, the Department held a series of hearings
conducted by hearing officer Mr. Clifford F. Blaze, on February 14,
March 6, March 17, and March 20, 1972. The Department, in accordance with its usual procedures, placed all relevant materials in evidence as exhibits. Included in the exhibits were the brochures prepared
by Berkeley in support of its application, and some feasibility studies
prepared by Berkeley's consultants. Some objectors also submitted
documents and exhibits as evidence. Several people testified on behalf
of the applicant and some on behalf of the objectors. Among those who
testified against the application was Mr. William Cohen, Liaison Officer
of the Office of Economic Development of the City of Newark, who
appeared as a representative of Deputy Mayor Frisina.

At the conclusion of the hearings, the parties involved filed written
summations and legal briefs in support of their respective positions. At
about the same time, the Department of Banking received a letter dated
June 5, 1972 from Mayor Kenneth A. Gibson of Newark. Gibson stated
in part that:

> I do not believe that the proposed move of Berkeley Savings and Loan
> Association Chancellor Avenue Office to Union is in the public interest of the
> citizens of Newark. I would, therefore, strongly recommend that your De-
> partment refuse to grant this application.[3]

THE HEARING OFFICER'S FINDINGS

Subsequent to the hearings and upon review of the arguments and legal briefs submitted by both sides, hearing officer Blaze prepared and submitted a 26-page report and recommendations to Acting Commissioner of Banking, Richard F. Schaub. The hearing officer recommended approval of the application.

Blaze based his conclusions and recommendations primarily on the statutory criteria provided in N.J.S.A. 17:12B–27(2), which reads:

> If the proposed new location is in another municipality than that in which the existing branch is located, the State Association shall comply with the notice requirement set forth in subsection 2 of section 26 of this act, and the Commissioner, before approving the application, shall determine (1) that the establishment and operation of such proposed branch office is in the public interest, (2) will be of benefit to the area served by such branch office, (3) that such branch office may be established without undue injury to any other association in the area in which it is proposed to locate such branch office, and (4) that the conditions in the area to be served afford a reasonable promise of successful operation.[4]

In interpreting these provisions, the hearing officer found that the applicant had satisfied each and every procedural requirement set forth in subsection 2 of N.J.S.A. 17:12B–26. The critical issue that the hearing officer addressed himself to with greater deliberation was the question of the relocation of a branch office across district lines, as was contemplated by the applicant. On this issue, the Hearing Officer noted that the major positions given in the objectors' arguments centered around the following points:

1. It was the intent of the Legislature, in enacting the legislation pertaining to the three savings and loan districts, to make the Savings and Loan Act consistent with the Banking Act, but that in the instance at bar, banks would not be allowed to relocate branch offices across district lines, so the savings and loan associations should also be prohibited.

2. The applicable rules of statutory construction require that the savings and loan districts set forth in Section 26 of the Act be "read into" the provisions of 27.1 of the Act.

3. The applicant is attempting to accomplish by indirection what it cannot do by direction, i.e. to establish a *de novo* branch in a "foreign" district.

4. If the statute is read and interpreted as it has been by the applicant, results inconsistent with the purpose of the Savings and Loan Act would be reached.

5. The Savings and Loan Act, read as a whole, sets forth a consistent pattern of regulation and control, the obvious intent of which is to keep financial institutions from exercising statewide or semistatewide influence.[5]

It was the Hearing Officer's finding, after a careful search for legislative evidence, "that the recent legislative history with respect to the provision in question does not give us a specific indication of the Legislature's intent with respect to district and/or county lines when considering branch-office relocations for savings and loan associations."[6]

In his view. "as the statute in question presently stands, there is absolutely no direct reference to any district limitations."[7] He flatly rejected "the notion that the Legislature of the State of New Jersey intended that each and every branch-office relocation of a savings and loan association must be constrained by district lines"[8] and concluded "that there is not, and should not be, any complete prohibition contained within the wording and/or intent of N.J.S.A. 17:12B–27.1 which would prohibit the relocation, in all instances, of a branch office from one district to another."[9]

Concerning the objectors' charge that the applicant attempted to accomplish (i.e. to establish a *de novo* branch in a "foreign" district) by indirection what it could not do by direction, the hearing officer found no legislative restrictions in recent cases involving the movement of certain New Jersey Banks and bank holding companies. The fact that there has been a general liberalization of New Jersey banking legislation since 1948 is indicative of the desire of the state to achieve and maintain some degree of competitive parity between the state-chartered and the federally-chartered financial institutions, according to the examiner. He cited some recent cases in which the federal savings and loan authorities gave permission to several savings and loan associations to establish *de novo* branches across district lines. "If my reasoning and conclusions are sustained," he argued, "substantial parity between state and federal associations will exist. If my reasoning and conclusions are rejected, state associations would be left in a severely debilitated competitive position."[10]

Turning to the question of whether the relocation offered a reasonable promise of successful operation for the applicant, one of the statutory criteria to be met before approval of an application, the hearing officer heard and examined testimony and presentations of expert witnesses on behalf of the applicant and the objectors. The testimony centered around the issues of trade areas and projected clientele and sales of the proposed branch. It was the hearing officer's opinion that the estimates and projections made by the experts, in terms of relative influence of competing financial institutions within and between the trade areas, the rate of penetration, and the potential dollar deposits of the new branch in the first few years, could not be credited with any great degree of precision and are likely subject to errors. However, even giving allowance to those errors and reducing the experts' estimates by a wide margin, he concurred with the applicant that the branch could operate on a profitable basis with average deposits of $6.5 million or less. Thus, he concluded that he had reason to believe that conditions in the area to be served offer a reasonable promise of successful operation.

In deliberating the possibility of the proposed branch causing "undue injury" to other associations in the area, the hearing officer found that there were no mutual thrift institutions located at or near the shopping center, or within the trade area. In fact, there are no savings and loan associations located within a half-mile of the extremes of the trade area. Therefore, it was difficult for him to conceive that the establishment of the branch would inflict undue injury to others, in a statutory sense.

On the issue of whether the proposed branch was in the public interest, Mr. Blaze found that, inasmuch as the Five Points Shopping Center and its surrounding trade areas lacked any mutual thrift institution to serve their large numbers of local residents, the establishment and operation of the branch office *was* in the public interest and would be of benefit to the area residents. Whether or not the relocation was in the public interest of the Newark area seemed to be an irrelevant question. Mr. Blaze found that the New Jersey Savings and Loan Law provided no reference or guideline other than the requirements that notice of the application be made to the associations located within two miles of the proposed site or within the community in which the relocated office is to be placed, and that the *proposed branch* be in the public interest. It was his interpretation that the Legislature has not delegated the judgment of the public interest beyond that which pertains to the proposed branch. For this reason he felt he was not in a position to discuss this matter in a statutory sense even though he might personally think it a pertinent or relevant consideration.

However, in order to provide background information on this issue for the commission to reach a final decision, he summarized the arguments from both sides. The opponents' arguments are generally represented by those submitted by Mr. Manahan, on behalf of Investors Savings and Loan Association.

1. That a savings and loan association is quasi-public and therefore apparently owes a duty (undefined) to the persons residing in the area it serves.

2. That the "public interest" considers the public and not an advantage or benefit to a financial institution.

3. That the applicant's two expert witnesses ignored the issue.

4. That the Lyons Avenue office of the applicant could be the "next to go."

5. That an unhealthy precedent would be established.

6. That the situation in the Chancellor Avenue branch's area is not as bad as represented by the applicant.

7. That the old site has a better potential for the applicant than the new site.

8. That the denial of the application would help solve the problems in Newark to which the applicant has referred.[11]

Countering the preceding arguments, Mr. Blaze observed that "the record demonstrates that, for social, demographic and physical reasons, the applicant's Chancellor Avenue office has experienced a decline in deposits and influence in the community in recent years. It might well be concluded that the residents of Newark left the Berkeley before the Berkeley decided to leave Chancellor Avenue. Furthermore, the record demonstrates that, after the removal, there will remain in the Chancellor Avenue area, offices of savings and loan associations and mutual savings banks which are more than adequately located and equipped to handle the savings needs of the residents therein.

"No unhealthy precedent will be established here. The decision must of necessity rest on the facts of the case. No consideration can be given to a *possible* relocation application of the Lyons Avenue branch. Finally, even if the Newark site had a better potential than the Union site, such a fact could not be used to deny the application. As Mr. Manahan stated in his brief . . . the 'advantage to any banking institution, be it an *applicant* or an established objector' is not dispositive of the public interest."[12]

THE COMMISSIONER'S DECISION AND ORDER

Having concluded his hearings and deliberations, Mr. Blaze submitted his report and recommendation to Acting Commissioner Richard F. Schaub for final decision. Upon careful review of the complete file of the case, including all records and reports of the hearings and comments, the Commissioner made an independent evaluation and arrived at the following findings and conclusions.

The Commissioner agreed with the hearing officer that the applicant had satisfied the procedural requirements set forth by statute. He also concurred with Mr. Blaze that the trade area, as delineated by the applicant, was reasonable. On the issues of a promise of successful operation, of the potential of causing undue injury to other financial institutions, and of the likelihood of benefiting the area to be served by the branch, the Commissioner was again in agreement with the hearing officer.

However, on the concept of the public interest, the Commissioner departed from the hearing examiner's findings and opinions. It was his opinion "that in the applicable statute, N.J.S.A. 17:12B–27.1 (2), a specific distinction is made between the Commissioner's determining first, 'that the establishment and operation of such proposed branch is in the public interest,' and second, 'will be of benefit to the area served by such branch.' " He asserted: "If the fact that a branch would benefit a particular area does not in itself guarantee a serving of the public interest, then I am obliged to examine other criteria in considering this latter issue."[13] He cited a 1959 New Jersey court ruling in which the concept of "public interest" was broadly interpreted to mean the legislative objectives of achieving "(1) a sound banking structure, (2) healthily competitive, and (3) fully adequate for the needs of the community."[14] He believed, therefore, that his decision should be based on his evaluation of the alternatives—to relocate the subject branch or to retain it at the present site—and to select that alternative that best meets the objectives of the public interest.

On the question of healthy competition, he noted that, although the relocation may tend to introduce more competition in the proposed location, it also, in the meantime, would diminish to a similar extent competition in the existing trade area. Considering the issue of providing adequate service for the needs of the community by weighing the relative merit of improving service outside a central city against that of decreasing service within it, the Commissioner was of the opinion that "the continued presence of the applicant's branch office at the Chancellor Avenue location would convey both an actual and symbolic measure of economic stability (in the city)."[15] Although he recognized the physical and economic deterioration over the years in central-city communities which lack the means to reverse the trend of decline, he nonetheless felt "it is an acknowledged role of government at all levels to attempt to arrest such trends."[16] Thus, in his judgment, ". . . the detriment to the public interest which would result from the closing of the Chancellor Avenue office more than outweighs the favorable aspects relating to its relocation at the proposed site and . . . the subject application should therefore be denied."[17] This decision, he believed, would also contribute to the soundness of the New Jersey banking structure, also meeting the objective of public interest.

Having denied the application, the Commissioner conceded that, while finding it in the public interest to maintain this facility, it was beyond his power "to require an association to remain within an area where its employees and customers face a real threat of physical harm."[18] And he warned that "officials of the City of Newark who deem it important to retain the Berkeley at its present site have a responsibility to ensure the safety of its customers and the residents of the neighborhood."[19] Finally, having decided to deny the application based on the criterion of public interest, the Commissioner found it unnecessary to address the question of relocation across district lines.

NOTES

1. Berkeley Savings and Loan Association, *Brochure,* p. 16, August 1971.

2. *New York Times,* p. c 39, January 1, 1973.

3. *Hearing Officer's Report and Recommendation,* p. 54, Division of Savings and Loan Associations, Department of Banking, State of New Jersey, September 12, 1972.

4. *Ibid,* p. 5

5. *Ibid,* p. 8

6. *Ibid,* p. 9

7. *Ibid,* p. 10

8. *Ibid,* p. 11

9. *Ibid,* p. 13

10. *Ibid,* p. 16

11. *Ibid,* p. 24

12. *Ibid,* p. 25

13. *Commissioner's Decision and Order,* p. 7, Department of Banking, State of New Jersey, January 24, 1973.

14. *Ibid,* p. 7

15. *Ibid,* p. 8

16. *Ibid,* p. 8

17. *Ibid,* p. 8

18. *Ibid,* p. 10

19. *Ibid,* p. 10

H. *Business and Activism*

It is probably safe to say that few firms would have responded to societal or environmental issues had not some activist groups raised those issues. Practically all of the substantive problems that form the basis for today's corporate concern with its environment were (and continue to be) brought into focus by activists. This external generation of corporate substantive issues is unusual, in that it means that the corporation and managers must deal not only with the issue, but with the strategies and tactics of the activists as well—groups beyond the control of management hierarchy, policy, and internal procedure. No longer is it sufficient to deal with issues internally, with quiet contemplation and staff studies, and make decisions on the substance of the issues only. The activists cannot be filed away to be forever forgotten; they reappear often with new ways of badgering managers and with new issues to raise. Thus it seems appropriate that we close this section on operational problems with a discussion of activism and the tactics of activists.

Activism is not a new phenomenon in the United States, despite what legions of vociferous students might suppose. Activism preceded the American Revolution, and the populists, muckrakers, and pamphleteers of the turn of the last century take no back seat to today's radicals. Neither does the generation of the 1930's. What might be new is the use of the *campus* as a base for activism. Unlike Europe, or perhaps Latin America, the United States has little tradition of student activism or politically charged campuses. But, to some extent in the 1930's and very definitely in the 1960's, student activism peaked and produced strong forces for social change, innovation, and experimentation. If any one group was responsible for bringing the Vietnam war to the forefront of the nation's conscience, that one group had to be the student population of the country.

Many commentators think that we are now living in an activist age, albeit some perceive it as a fading phenomenon. Few know why activism is so particularly pronounced at this time. The Vietnam war was certainly one catalyst, and the successes of the various activist groups during that conflict certainly made them heady for further confrontations. Today the issues of racism, sexism, and the environment certainly are important, and they form the core issues for activist group cohesion. Some have suggested that the affluence and security of today's youth allow them to be "involved" with comparatively little risk; this may be accurate, for a cooling off on the campuses seems to have accompanied the decline in job availability. But the military draft and the Vietnam war ended also, so the link between affluence and activism may be a weak one.

However we explain activism, today's activist finds a primary and convenient target in the corporation and in business in general. Surveys show less and less confidence in the corporation in terms of its role in society. Critics are not prepared to accept corporations only as providers of goods and services; indeed, they question the efficacy of corporations in those roles as well. The surveys also show more and more people prone to change. As the Watergate revelations continue to unfold and the testimony on the participation of some corporations in election contributions and political payoffs becomes better known, one may expect the numbers of change-prone individuals to increase. Business simply hasn't made a good showing in recent years and the confidence of many people in the business system is ebbing. For the manager, consequently, activism is surely not a trifling issue.

Like Heinz products, activists and their tactics come in many varieties. The most serious variety for the immediate short run are the terrorists, with their practices of violence, destruction of property, and physical abuse. From the celebrated "Fox" who dumped Lake Superior sludge sewage on the carpets at the corporate offices of United States Steel Corporation (to protest, obviously, U.S. Steel's dumping of waste into the lake), to the extremist groups who deposit bombs or ignite fires in corporate offices and banks (e.g., a recent incident involving $350,000 in damage to Gulf Oil Company headquarters in Pittsburgh); from the protestors who carry magnets into corporate computer centers (and thus destroy records stored on magnetic tapes), to those who dump sand in the lubricating cups of expensive machinery, these actions pose both danger and expense to the business organization. Managers must now fear for their own safety and that of others, as well as for the security of corporate records and assets.

Violent actions have given corporations the task of developing elaborate alarm systems, taking extra care in the handling of corporate records (in many cases, ensuring that *multiple copies of everything* exist), and adding security personnel. These actions, of course, have the side-effects of making corporate offices less inviting and more restrictive places to work, in some ways further negating an already sagging business image. Fortunately, activists who are prone to physical violence are few in number; generally they are criticized not only by leaders of "establishment" social institutions, but by nonviolent activists as well.

The corporation has long faced the traditional gadfly at annual shareholder meetings. Wilma Soss, Lewis Gilbert, and other lesser known but equally sharp-tongued shareholder activists have been more or less permanent fixtures at the annual meetings of many of the major United States corporations. And while they often provided comic relief to what was normally a rather dull affair (box lunches notwithstanding), they rarely had much impact or success in altering corporate policy; the proxy machinery, firmly in the hands of management, clearly stacks any vote in management's favor.

A newer activist is of much the same pattern—seeking to use the shareholder's meeting to effect change—but the issues are less oriented to traditional shareholder concerns. Instead of stressing dividends, sales, profits, executive compensation, and other similar dollars-and-cents issues, the newer activist is more concerned with raising public responsibility issues: pollution, auto safety, minority hiring, political connections, and the like. Ralph Nader groups, church organizations, and some colleges and universities are trying to use the corporate annual meeting to effect broad corporate and social change.

Campaign GM, a Nader-launched attempt to force General Motors Corporation to deal with social issues, included focus on minority employment, South Africa, auto safety, pollution, product warrantees, mass transit, and wide representation on the Board of Directors. Even though the three-year Campaign GM may be classified as a failure from the activists' point of view (fewer than 2% of the shares in General Motors ever voted with the activists), for the first time some of the large holders of shares did not automatically assign their proxies to management. A number of university endowment funds, as well as some pension, mutual, and trust funds, either withheld their votes or voted for some of the proposals submitted by the Nader-inspired campaign. This voting with corporate antagonists represented a complete change of philosophy for many of the funds or trusts. Typically they espoused no interference with management. If the fund managers did not care for the way a corporation was being run (and this dissatisfaction usually related only to profits), they might have sold out the fund's holdings in the firm, but rarely would they use their votes to take issue with management.

As we have seen, activists also attempt to influence the corporation through the marketplace. Consumer boycotts are quite commonplace; many of the issues covered in earlier sections of this book were raised through the use of the boycott. SaranWrap, grapes, lettuce, Farah slacks, and Gulf Oil products have all been faced with boycotts (which had varying degrees of success) in order to force changes in corporate policy. SaranWrap and Dowguard were boycotted to force Dow Chemical Company, their manufacturer, to cease producing Napalm, a jellied gasoline used in bombs and flamethrowers (this boycott accompanied picketlines set up around college placement offices to prevent Dow recruiters from interviewing prospective applicants). Grapes and lettuce (and some wines) are still being boycotted to force growers to recognize and bargain with Cesar Chavez's United Farm-Workers Union. Gulf Oil Corporation was hit with a boycott undertaken to force a change in the company's exploration intentions in the Portuguese Territory of Angola (Gulf was also a target on college campuses, as activists attempted to force university administrations to remove Gulf stock from endowment portfolios). On a limited scale, a group of University of Massachusetts professors tried to eliminate Honeywell as a contender for a new computer installation because of Honeywell's defense contracting. More recently, boycotts have been called against Japanese and Russian products to protest the whaling carried on by those two nations; according to the activists, some species of whales are in danger of becoming extinct.

Most companies have attempted to ride out boycotts. Others, of course, have varied product lines, or sell their products to several classes of customers, so that a consumer boycott becomes virtually impossible. But for the single-product firm (marketers of grapes, for example) or the firm whose product is readily identifiable (Farah), a successful boycott can be particularly debilitating. Although consumer boycotts generally are extremely difficult to start and sustain, recent successes should be testimony enough to alert the manager to their potential effects.

In early confrontations between managers and activists, either the activists were superb tacticians or the managers were not. College and university administrators were caught flatfooted by activists in the 1960's. Few could respond; those who did respond often later regretted their actions. Many demands were met with little consideration of their impact or ramifications. Corporations often acted with no better effectiveness. Many credit General Motors Corporation with "creating" Ralph Nader; without the Corporation's hiring of a detective to trail Nader, he might now be just one more of the great body of social critics who faded into oblivion.

Activists learned early the cardinal principle of budgeting that operating managers know only too well: Ask for the extraordinary and get the desired. Yet a manager's dealings with activists who use that tactic are quite different from his dealings with subordinates who use it. Subordinates can be fired; activists cannot. The manager trying to deal with activists who use the "budgeting" strategy is caught on the horns of a dilemma. If the manager refuses to meet the demands of the activist, he opens himself up to all sorts of verbal abuse. The term "reactionary" may be the kindest appellation he acquires; other more colorful ones have been hurled at corporate executives. The manager may find himself the subject of critical press comment. Indeed, his actions may further inflame the activists to further, perhaps violent, response.

On the other hand, if the manager accedes to the "demands" of activists (even to a few of them), he may only whet their appetites for more. Activists may interpret a manager's cooperation as a sign of weakness, and "bore in" for more victories.

Activist confrontations demand that the executive apply all the skill at his command, tempering any accommodation with discretion and toughness. Any accession should be based on the soundness of the issue, and its value to management, the corporation, or society, rather than on the tactics of the activists. If the manager must refuse accommodation, he should be prepared to support his decision with reason, not, as so often happens, with utterances that fuel the passions of his critics.

THE READINGS

The first article by Gene I. Maeroff (from *The Nation*) offers a catalogue of activist confrontations (particularly in annual meetings), along with some insight into the issues and tactics of activists. While some of these tactics are no longer widely displayed, the legacy of Saul Alinsky, best known for his confrontation with Eastman Kodak, is still very strong.

The second article from *Business Week* brings up to date the activities of the new shareholder activists and their effects on corporate policy and support.

Finally, Ralph Nader, the best-known corporate critic, is the subject of Richard Armstrong's *Fortune* article. Armstrong discusses Nader's philosophies, the work of the various Nader groups, and some of the effects that Nader's activities have had on business and the Washington bureaucracy. Ralph Nader emerges as a deeply dedicated, driving, and complex individual. Armstrong comments, "Nobody has been able to explain the deep personal anger that erupts when Nader begins to speak about corporations. He himself simply denies that he is antibusiness . . . But anger of some kind is unmistakably there."

Stinging the Corporations

Gene I. Maeroff

In his mind's eye Saul Alinsky has a picture of Yankee Stadium, filled with 80,000 screaming people who are waving not pennants but proxies. Down on the mound where Mel Stottlemyre usually toils, the chairman of, say, Standard Oil of New Jersey is standing on a platform. It is the company's annual meeting and he is speaking into a microphone. The 80,000 have just voted "Yes" on a proposal and the chairman is telling them that on behalf of 90 per cent of the shares he is voting "No" and that the 80,000 people have lost. "I'd just love to see that happen. I'd like to see him try to call 80,000 people out of order," says Alinsky.

Of course, nothing resembling that scene is likely to occur soon. But this spring the corporate annual meeting came under assault as never before, and those who have been involved in bulldozing open this new avenue of social protest believe that the big corporations face some changes. "There will be progress," Alinsky insists. "Once the corporations are pushed into the corner on straight power they will do the right things for the wrong reasons. You've got the stockholders on one hand and the rest of the country on the other. If the United States goes down, the big corporations go with it."

It was Alinsky who invented the idea of using the annual meeting as a forum at which to urge big business to become responsive to the issues of the day. He started the practice three years ago in Rochester, N.Y., when he forced Eastman Kodak to improve job opportunities for blacks. This spring young protesters across the nation copied and improvised upon Alinsky's methods. They transformed what

From *The Nation,* June 22, 1970. Reprinted by permission of *The Nation.*

had been quiet gatherings of the semi-retired into arenas of raucous discontent. The annual meeting may never be the same.

A partial list of the corporations that have been thus besieged reads like a page from the *Fortune* 500: United Aircraft, American Telephone & Telegraph, Commonwealth Edison of Chicago, General Electric, Honeywell, Boeing, Gulf Oil and, most recently, General Motors. There has been little coordination, however; for the most part dissidents in each city planned and acted independently.

Chances are that next year there will be more central planning. Alinsky himself will create a focal point for anti-corporate activities when he takes a leave of absence in the fall from the Industrial Areas Foundation and his other responsibilities in Chicago. He will concentrate on fitting together the machinery for an organization to be known as Proxies for People. The group will solicit proxies from anyone, anywhere, for any corporation. "We will put together a radical, diversified portfolio," he says, laughing. Since announcing Proxies for People, Alinsky has been besieged by letters from share owners who wish to give him their proxies and become involved in the movement. He tells each of them to hold off until the fall.

Thus far, the dissidents appearing at annual meetings have had little specific effect on the corporations. However, it is entirely realistic to measure their gains in attitudinal terms. Corporate directors have been forced to think about matters that until now they could ignore. Share owners are awakening to their potential strength. The public is beginning to take notice.

"This movement is never going to be successful in a 51 per cent manner," explains Ralph Nader, who concedes that the corporations retain the raw voting power. "The success should be measured in other ways. Until now corporate power in this country has been successfully used without challenge. A challenge such as Campaign GM forced a corporation such as General Motors to look out at its support structure—the banks, colleges and others who hold large blocks of its stock—for the first time. It required General Motors to surface and use its power."

The more the corporations are criticized for abusing their power and the longer they refuse to help solve the great social problems, the more likely they are to alienate the masses, i.e., the consumers. Intransigence, in other words, could affect profits. Nader considers what has happened until now a first stage in educating public and institutional share owners. When it is completed there will, he thinks, be a tremendous upsurge of awareness. He says people will realize that "no street in any American city is safe from General Motors." The second stage will then involve the development of a different public concept of the role of the corporations in American life.

"Things will change," says Nader. "The role of the individual share owner questioning the corporation in terms of social responsibility will increase. The corporations will bend a little. General Motors was very concerned about Campaign GM. It hit them to the core. GM has been able to be so powerful because it never had to use its power.

"An institutional share owner not voting its stock in behalf of GM represents a loss of confidence. This weakens the silent legitimacy. If GM turns out to be totally inflexible it will make militants of those who are not militants. GM knows this, but they don't know enough to head it off. The whole thing is a building process and it will continue well beyond the annual meeting."

One way that it will be sustained beyond the annual meeting is through the continued existence of Campaign GM and other such organizations. In a sense, they will themselves become corporate consciences. This already has happened in Minneapolis. The Honeywell Project was founded there in November 1968, and devoted its first four months to researching the corporation. It has now been through two annual meetings. Honeywell's management has even extended grudging recognition, meeting three times for discussions with the group's leaders. The Honeywell Project served as one of the models for the Gulf Action Project and the Anti-Aircraft Conspiracy founded to challenge Gulf Oil and United Aircraft at their annual meetings this year.

Heading the Honeywell Project is Marvin Davidov, a 38-year-old veteran of many major New Left skirmishes, who has been in nine prisons since his entry into the movement in 1961 as a Mississippi freedom rider. He views with satisfaction the successes of his organization, and thinks that within a year or two, fifty to 100 such organizations will be aimed at specific corporations. "We're trying to develop a power base from which to launch our demands. We want immediate cessation of Honeywell's weapons production. [The company, a major producer of anti-personnel bombs, is the leading defense contractor in Minnesota and ranks eighteenth nationally.] We want the company to develop serious reconversion plans, so that none of the 20,000 workers in weapons production loses his job. We want control of the corporate power to pass from the board to the employees and the representatives of the community. The major achievement of our demonstration at the annual meeting was to show that there is not really a share owner democracy. There is no such thing as people's capitalism. It is socialism for the rich."

It may be that the anti-corporate movement will have its most immediate effect on the composition of boards of directors, but not because the dissidents will marshal enough votes to compel the corporations to accept their nominees. Rather, the corporations will hope, by adding token directors who meet with the approval of the protesters, to ease the pressure. The best publicized instance of a dissident group trying to elect directors was the bid made by Campaign GM. The Security and Exchange Commission required General Motors to include on its printed proxy ballot Campaign GM's proposal that three directors be added to the twenty-four-member board. It also required the management to list Campaign GM's proposal that the company create a "committee of corporate responsibility." Backers of Campaign GM wanted the three new board positions to be filled by Dr. Rene J.

Dubos, an environmental scientist; Betty Furness, consumer adviser under President Johnson, and Rev. Channing E. Phillips, a black minister in Washington.

Less widely publicized was the attempt made in Cleveland to replace three AT&T directors. Nominated from the floor were U.S. Sen. Stephen M. Young (D., Ohio), a leading Congressional dove; Dr. Sidney M. Peck, a professor of sociology prominent in the national anti-war movement, and George Maranuk, a student activist at John Carroll University in Cleveland. AT&T Chairman H. I. Romnes became so flustered that he forgot to invite a motion to close nominations, and a company spokesman had to bring the oversight to his attention. Senator Young led the dissident nominees with 9,398 votes. The management slate had 370,600,000.

But a month after the annual meeting it was apparent that the gnat had stung the elephant. Bell Laboratories, a satellite of AT&T, let it be known that it was getting out of the missile business. Various reasons were given, but the 3,000 protesters who assembled outside the annual meeting that sunny April day in Cleveland must have figured in the decision, even though Romnes denied the connection. No AT&T official will soon forget the Oberlin College student-share owner who, after being recognized by the chair, shouted into a microphone: "You shouldn't need cops on horses outside this building to suppress legal demonstrations. If that's the kind of company this is then screw it."

That is not the sort of language share owners are accustomed to hearing at annual meetings. Nor are they used to the rigid security measures to which they were subjected this year at most of the meetings. The prospect that someone might explode a bomb had corporate officials in a dither. Corporate secretaries compared notes on security provisions and read anxiously of demonstrations at one another's meetings. Marv Davidov thinks it possible that the annual meeting as presently constituted may be coming to an end.

Corporate officials dislike having police barricades erected outside their meetings and hordes of Pinkertons patrolling inside. They find tight security necessary, but nevertheless offensive. Share owners at the United Aircraft meeting had to pass three checkpoints. At the AT&T meeting all boxes and packages were to be checked at the door. Evelyn Y. Davis, the perennial gadfly of annual meetings, insisted on carrying a valise into the meeting hall, but had to let it be searched. Once inside, she made it clear that her sympathies were not with the new breed of gadflies, whom she denounced as Communists and radicals.

Most corporate officials have been more circumspect. They have avoided name-calling, have ignored obscenities, and in many cases have tried to make it appear that the protesters were being given a fair hearing. "Let's not scoff at them," Louis B. Lundborg, BankAmerica Corp. chairman, told his share owners at the annual meeting in San Francisco. He went on to answer questions asked him by members of the peace movement who objected to the bank's operations in Vietnam.

In Chicago, Commonwealth Edison officials soliloquized on how the company has spent $53 million to fight air pollution. Their explanations were unsatisfactory to the delegation of proxy holders representing the Campaign Against Pollution.

AT&T in Cleveland let its annual meeting run five hours and seven minutes as Chairman Romnes accepted a wide array of questions on the war and social issues. E. D. Brockett, Gulf Oil chairman, devoted most of his annual report in Pittsburgh to rebutting criticisms. Gulf's president, B. R. Dorsey, gave almost his entire speech to the firm's efforts in the field of ecology.

Attention, though, does not assure results and some officials are even unwilling to give that. W. W. Keeler, Phillips Petroleum president, says: "Protest of that type hasn't any place at an annual meeting. I don't know of any operation we have that such protest would have relevancy for and, in my capacity, I wouldn't recognize such protesters even if they were bona fide share owners." There's the problem; the corporation sets the ground rules. Before its annual meeting, Honeywell said: "We are very much aware that there are people who will be at the meeting who disagree with the company's policies. They have the right to attend the meeting and express their opinions and we will respect that right." But as soon as things began getting out of his control, Chairman James H. Binger proclaimed to dissidents: "You've forfeited your right to speak." He adjourned the meeting sixteen minutes after it had begun.

Corporations have many other ways to quash protesters. Republic Steel, for instance, chooses to meet in such an out-of-the-way place as Flemington, N.J. Some companies use small meeting rooms, thereby limiting the audience. Also, corporate officials at the door determine how many persons may be admitted on a single proxy. Finally, the chairman or presiding officer decides whom to recognize and when to entertain a motion for adjournment. Certain legal questions are raised by these management tactics.

Some of the corporation weapons are more subtle. Nader complains that General Motors lobbied among its institutional share owners against the Campaign GM proposals. Universities that could reasonably have been expected to be sympathetic refused to support the Nader group. The Rockefeller Foundation—owner of 195,000 shares of GM—issued a statement praising Campaign GM, but ended the statement by explaining that it would not support the two proposals because it had a responsibility to consider management's position. "A hell of a lot of debate was going on in these institutions," says Nader. J. George Harrar, president of the Rockefeller Foundation, admitted: "I have not seen anything like this before. Like other stockholders, we do have to think about this. We just can't dismiss it and pretend it didn't happen."

One of the first schools to support Campaign GM was Antioch College, which several years ago adopted a progressive policy that its investment decisions should reflect social concerns. As an offshoot of the movement, students around the country have begun pressuring trustees to divest school endowment portfolios of stock in companies that they consider to be war-oriented. In Cleveland, Case Western Reserve students picketed at the prestigious Union Club to which some trustees belong. They also went to the homes and churches of trustees.

But no one dreams that the corporations will become good citizens by the time next year's annual meetings roll around. Progress will be slow and protesters without high frustration thresholds will grow impatient—and perhaps violent. The corporations are bracing themselves. Staughton Lynd says the corporations are "our inevitable enemy in the coming years." Already various anti-corporate groups have scheduled summer strategy sessions.

In some respects public awareness has already passed beyond the initial stage. Stewart Mott has criticized General Motors and identified himself with Campaign GM, and Stewart Mott is the beneficiary of trust funds holding a reported 700,000 shares of General Motors stock. Similarly, sixteen Congressmen have issued a statement hailing Campaign GM and calling it "enormously successful, regardless of the outcome." It is also noteworthy that the president of the Detroit police officers' association has asked that the 29,000 shares of GM stock in the city's pension fund be voted in support of Campaign GM. Corporate officials show their awareness of public opinion when the president of Dow Chemical spends one minute reporting on sales and earnings and an hour telling what Dow is doing to keep from being a polluter and to develop anti-pollution products.

Activists Step Up Their Annual Attacks

Business Week

In New York, First National City Corp. shareholders this week heard Chairman Walter B. Wriston defend the minority hiring record of the nation's second-largest bank holding company, its investments in South Africa, and the membership of its board of directors. In San Francisco, three dissident candidates for director challenged BankAmerica Corp. on the way the nation's biggest bank is meeting its corporate social responsibilities.

In short, it is annual meeting time once again, and for the fourth year in a row, activists are challenging corporate managements on a variety of points. And if the challengers are less shrill this year than in the past, they are stepping up their pace. Some 30 corporations, compared with 20 last year, face attack from activist shareholders.

BETTER ORGANIZED

The challengers, working through proxy proposals and questions from the floor, include representatives of major religious denominations, foundations, and such veteran groups as the Washington-based Project on Corporate Responsibility. Their questions this year mostly involve corporate investment in South Africa, minority

Reprinted from the March 31, 1973 issue of *Business Week* by special permission. © 1973 by McGraw-Hill, Inc.

hiring, broadening the membership of boards of directors, and disclosure of military contract business, political contributions, and lobbying activities.

Further, based on early evidence, this year's effort is more polished and better coordinated than in the past. Both the National Council of Churches and the Council on Economic Priorities have compiled summaries of corporate challenges, listing the companies and the issues involved as well as the group waging the proxy contest. The dissidents are getting more practiced at making a pitch to institutional investors, trying to win these big blocks of stock over to their side. Indeed, one group of 50 institutional investors last December formed its own research outfit, Investor Responsibility Research, Inc., to report on proxy issues.

But if the results at BankAmerica and Citicorp are any guide, this year's proxy proposals still will not muster much stockholder support. The management slate of directors at BankAmerica, for example, got virtually all the votes cast. Black community leader Carlton Goodlett, Carol Hancock of the National Organization of Women, and consumer attorney Neil Gendel each received less than 1%.

And at Citicorp, three proxy proposals opposed by management were soundly defeated. Former employee John Allen, who says he was fired for pushing minority hiring and promotion policies, introduced a proposal that asked Citicorp to report on the advisability of enlarging its board and of minimizing the "interlocking relationship" of board members. That got only 0.9% of the vote. His second proposal, which would have required Citicorp to issue periodic reports on minority hiring, got even fewer votes.

The American Baptist Board of Education & Publication, operating with a coalition of Protestant churches in a "Church Project on U.S. Investments in Southern Africa," also failed to draw much support from Citicorp shareholders. Its proposal, asking for a detailed report on Citicorp's involvement in the Republic of South Africa, also received only less than 1%.

WINNING ISN'T ALL

To challengers, though, winning isn't everything. Even though proxy proposals dealing with social responsibility draw only nominal support, the activists still consider them an effective tool to get their message across. Says Susan Gross of the Project on Corporate Responsibility: "Proxy proposals have an enormous educational value for shareholders and the public. They keep pressure on, and there has been a lot of reexamination by management because of them."

This view is reflected in the larger number of proxy proposals this spring. The South Africa issue is likely to come up during shareholder sessions at American Metal Climax, Caterpillar Tractor, Continental Oil, Eastman Kodak, Exxon, Ford, General Electric, Gulf, IBM, ITT, 3M, Newmont Mining, Phillips Petroleum, Texaco, and Xerox.

The Clergy & Laity Concerned (CALC), a New York-based nondenominational peace group, has submitted proxy proposals to both Exxon and GE, seeking reports on military contract work and asking for the creation of committees to convert defense production to "civilian-oriented production." Last week, CALC was joined in its effort at GE by the National Federation of Priests' Councils. The entry of the federation, which represents 131 priests' councils around the country, marks the first time that a broad-based unit of the U.S. Catholic church has participated in a corporate-responsibility proxy contest.

The primary target of CALC, which claims 53,000 members in 50 local chapters throughout the U.S., is Honeywell, Inc. Honeywell's proxy statement includes a CALC proposal asking the company to stop production of "antipersonnel weapons." CALC has been waging its campaign for a year, calling for consumer boycotts of Honeywell products and for student demonstrations against Honeywell recruiters. It now is asking city governments in Ann Arbor, Mich., Palo Alto, Calif., and Boston to boycott Honeywell products.

While a CALC proxy proposal to require Honeywell to report on its military business last year drew just 1% of the shareholder vote, CALC program director Trudi Young predicts a better showing this year. More than 20 CALC chapters will be represented at Honeywell's annual meeting in Minneapolis on Apr. 25, she says.

POLITICKING

The Project on Corporate Responsibility, which pioneered the proxy power movement in 1970 at General Motors, this year submitted two proposals apiece to GM, Eastman Kodak, ITT, and Union Oil, seeking information on political contributions and lobbying activities. But the resolutions will appear only in GM's proxy statement, since the Project did not hold stock in the other target companies when it submitted the resolutions. Project spokesmen say they plan to attend the annual meeting of each company and raise their points.

The Project did better with a proposal to allow individual shareholders to have their nominees for board of directors included in a company's proxy statement. It was submitted to IBM, Levi Strauss, and Xerox, and all three companies are including the proposal in their proxy statements. The Project's argument, says Susan Gross, is that now only candidates backed by management are listed on a proxy statement and nominations by shareholders at the annual meeting have little impact. By that time, virtually all of the votes for directors have already been cast for the management slate listed on the proxy statement.

CONSUMERISM

The Citizens Action Program (CAP) will challenge AT&T at its annual meeting in Chicago on Apr. 18. CAP wants a 50% rate cut for senior citizens from AT&T's Illinois Bell Telephone Co. And its leaders say that "at least 1,000 senior citizens" will be at the meeting. "Senior power is not empty rhetoric," says a CAP spokesman, "but a full-fledged reality."

A coalition group in Minneapolis, representing 11 community groups and claiming a membership of 150,000, wants to put a consumer advocate on the board of Northern States Power Co. The group's candidate is Mrs. Alpha Smaby, a 63-year-old grandmother and former Minnesota state representative. Working with the group is the Council for Corporate Review, which is negotiating with the Securities & Exchange Commission to get Mrs. Smaby's name on the ballot. Says Council director Mary Smith: "It will all be legal, and we just might win."

SOCIAL DUTY

The Field Foundation in New York has submitted three proposals to Pittston Co. One requests that Pittston make periodic reports on how it is compensating victims of a West Virginia flash flood early last year, caused by the collapse of a dam owned by Pittston's Buffalo Mining Co. A second proposal would create a public policy committee to work on mine safety and ecology measures. The third asks the company to report the proceedings of each annual meeting to all shareholders.

When representatives of the Field Foundation asked for a flood-victim accounting from Pittston at last year's meeting, it marked one of the first forays of a foundation into the social responsibility fray. And Field still is the only foundation challenging a company whose shares it holds.

While other institutional investors have not gone so far as the Field Foundation, there is a growing awareness that corporate social responsibility proposals can no longer be ignored. Last year, Harvard University President Derek Bok wrote some 100 universities, foundations, and other institutional investors, asking if they would be interested in setting up a research group to gather facts on corporate-responsibility proxy contests. The response led to the formation of Investor Responsibility Research, Inc. The 50 institutions that support IRRI include universities, foundations, banks, mutual funds, and insurance companies.

So far, the Washington-based group has issued reports on South African investment and equal employment opportunity for its subscriber list. When the proxy season is over, IRRI will launch a series on such topics as strip mining, nuclear power safety, and employment for women. The reports analyze the issues, without attempting to side with one group or another.

The Passion that Rules Ralph Nader

Richard Armstrong

On a recent visit to Marymount College in Arlington, Virginia, Ralph Nader arrived at the school gymnasium an hour late. But he then proceeded to pacify an overflowing crowd of restless students—and earn a lecture fee of $2,500—by denouncing America's big corporations in venomous language. Afterward one question from the audience brought a rousing and spontaneous burst of applause. When, the questioner asked, did he plan to run for President?

A slightly more measured assessment of the Nader phenomenon came from Bess Myerson, New York City's commissioner of consumer affairs, when she introduced him as star witness at a recent hearing on deceptive advertising. "Mr. Nader," she said, "is a remarkable man who, in the last six years, has done more as a private citizen for our country and its people than most public officials do in a lifetime."

The remarkable thing about this tribute is that it is literally true. In the seven years since he moved to Washington from Winsted, Connecticut—without funds and with a narrow base of expert knowledge in a single subject, automobile safety—Nader has created a flourishing nationwide movement, known as consumerism. He is chiefly responsible for the passage of at least six major laws, imposing new federal safety standards on automobiles, meat and poultry products, gas pipelines, coal mining, and radiation emissions from electronic devices. His investigations have led to a strenuous renovation at both the Federal Trade Commission and the Food and Drug Administration. And if the quality and convenience of American life do not seem dramatically improved after all that furious crusading, Nader can point to at least one quite tangible result. Last year, for the first time in nine years, traffic fatalities in the U.S. declined, to 55,300 from 56,400 in 1969. Unless the decline was a fluke (and officials at the Highway Traffic Safety Administration do not think it was), then for those 1,100 living Americans, whoever they may be, Nader can be said to have performed the ultimate public service.

MORE THAN TEN KREMLINS

And yet, despite all this, it is easy to conclude after a conversation with Nader that he is not primarily interested in protecting consumers. The passion that rules in him —and he is a passionate man—is aimed at smashing utterly the target of his hatred, which is corporate power. He thinks, and says quite bluntly, that a great many corporate executives belong in prison—for defrauding the consumer with shoddy merchandise, poisoning the food supply with chemical additives, and willfully manufacturing unsafe products that will maim or kill the buyer. In his words, the law should "pierce the corporate veil" so that individual executives could be jailed when their companies misbehaved. He emphasizes that he is talking not just about "fly-by-night hucksters" but the top management of "blue-chip business firms."

The lawyers who provide legal cover for all these criminal acts are, to Nader, nothing but "high-priced prostitutes." As for the advertising profession, Nader recently served up the following indictment: "Madison Avenue is engaged in an epidemic campaign of marketing fraud. It has done more to subvert and destroy the market system in this country than ten Kremlins ever dreamed of." With the certainty of the visionary, Nader would sweep away that shattered market system and replace it by various eccentric devices of his own, such as a government rating system for every consumer product.

If, on the one hand, Nader has advanced the cause of consumer protection by his skillful marshaling of facts in support of specific reforms, he has, on the other hand, made reform more difficult through his habit of coating his facts with invective and assigning the worst possible motives to almost everybody but himself. By some peculiar logic of his own, he has cast the consumer and the corporation as bitter enemies, and he seems to think that no reform is worth its salt unless business greets it with a maximum of suspicion, hostility, and fear.

Nader is a strange apparition in the well-tailored world of the Washington lawyer. His suits hang awkwardly off his lanky frame, all of them apparently gray and cut about a half size too large. His big brown eyes in their deep sockets have a permanent expression of hurt defiance, and before a crowd he blinks them nervously. The eyes, the bony face, and a small, set chin give him, at thirty-seven, the look of an underfed waif.

Nobody has been able to explain the deep personal anger that erupts when Nader begins to speak about corporations. He himself simply denies that he is anti-business. "People who make that charge are escalating the abstraction," he told an interviewer recently, his long hands clasped together, his brown eyes flashing. "They don't dare face the issues." But anger of some kind is unmistakably there. It seems to spring out of some profound alienation from the comfortable world he sees around him, and perhaps dates back to his early days in the conservative little town of Winsted, where he was something of an oddball, the son of a Lebanese immigrant, the boy who read the Congressional Record. He recalls proudly that his father, who kept a restaurant and assailed customers with his political views, "forecast the corporate take-over of the regulatory agencies back in the 1930's." Princeton and Harvard Law School trained Nader's brilliant mind, but their social graces never touched his inner core. There seems something of the desert in him still, the ghost of some harsh prophet from his ancestral Lebanon.

According to one old friend, Nader has always had a conspiratorial view of the world, and when General Motors put private detectives on his trail in 1965 just before the publication of *Unsafe at Any Speed* that view was strongly reinforced. "He thought somebody was following him around," says the friend, "and then, by gosh, somebody *was* following him around." Apparently, at the time, Nader was convinced that G.M. planned to have him bumped off. He still moves about Washington in great secrecy from one rendezvous to the next.

THE FIFTH BRANCH OF GOVERNMENT

In his role as scourge of the regulatory agencies, Nader is aggressive and ill-mannered as a matter of calculated policy. "Rattle off a few facts so they will know you can't be bluffed," he tells his teams of young investigators setting out to interview government officials. "Get on the offensive and stay there." Says Lowell Dodge, who runs Nader's Auto Safety Center: "If somebody is messing up Ralph wants to embarrass them."

But Nader can be an engaging fellow when he chooses. He takes care to maintain good relations with Washington journalists—parceling out news tips with an even hand—and many of them pay him the ultimate tribute of calling him the best reporter they know. To these men he seems to serve as a sort of ghost of conscience past, a reminder of investigations not pursued and stables left un-cleansed. Both reporters and professional politicians find him extremely useful. "Nader has become the fifth branch of government, if you count the press as fourth," says a Senate aide who has worked with Nader often in drafting legislation. "He knows all the newspaper deadlines and how to get in touch with anybody any time. By his own hard work he has developed a network of sources in every arm of government. And believe me, no Senator turns down those calls from Ralph. He will say he's got some stuff and it's good, and the Senator can take the credit. Any afternoon he's in town you still see him trudging along the corridors here with a stack of documents under his arm, keeping up his contacts."

What Nader gets out of the intercourse is power—not the trappings but the substance—more of it by now than most of the Senators and Congressmen on whom he calls. When an important bill is pending he is quite capable of playing rough, threatening to denounce a Representative to the press unless he goes along on a key amendment. "Does Ralph like power?" The Senate aide laughed at such a naive question. "Good gracious, yes. He loves it." Compared to other powerful men in Washington, Nader enjoys a rare freedom of action, flourishing as a sort of freebooter who is able to pick his targets at will, unconstrained by an electorate or any judgment but his own. "You will find sensitive people around town who are saying it's time to take a second look at this guy," says the Senate aide. "There are people who wonder whether he ought to be the final arbiter of safety in autos or in the food supply. Nader has something the companies don't have—credibility—especially with the press. There is a danger that people will be afraid to go up against him for that reason alone."

REGRETS TO DAVID SUSSKIND

By any measure, Nader's power is still growing. He remains absolute master of his own movement, but he is no longer alone. "When I think of all the lean years Ralph spend knocking on doors—" says Theodore Jacobs, who was Nader's classmate at both Princeton and Harvard Law School and now serves as a sort of chief of staff. Jacobs had just concluded a telephone call that, from his end, had consisted only of various expressions of regret. "That was Susskind. He's got a new show, he wants Ralph, and I had to turn him down. Ralph hates New York—all that traffic and pollution—and I can't get him up there unless it's imperative. I spend a lot of my time saying no. Among other problems, he's got two people on his tail right now who are writing full-length biographies. He has to husband his time. He's down for the *Today* show next Tuesday, but that's right here in town. If there is an important bill pending in committee and they need some input, he'll be there. He'll duck anything else for that."

Jacobs presides, loosely, over a modern suite of offices in downtown Washington housing the Center for the Study of Responsive Law. This is home base for the seven most senior of Nader's "raiders" and is one of the three organizations through which Nader now operates. The other two are located a few blocks away: the five-man Auto Safety Center and the Public Interest Research Group, staffed by twelve bright young graduates of top law schools, three of them women. In addition, there are the summertime student raiders, who this year will number about fifty, only one-quarter as many as last year. The program is being cut back, Jacobs explains, because the students are a mixed blessing, requiring a good deal of nursemaiding by the full-time staff. "But we still think it's useful for the regulatory agencies to see a fresh batch of faces wafting through."

One of the center's main functions is to handle a flood of crank calls. "No, I'm afraid Mr. Nader isn't here," says the young girl at the switchboard. "Can you tell me what it's about?" After a protracted conversation, she explains with a grin: "He said it was something so big he didn't dare put a word on paper. No name either, but still he wants to speak to Ralph." Nader drops by for a few minutes every day or so, and the other raiders emulate his casual example; by the switchboard, message boxes improvised out of brown paper are filled to overflowing with notices of calls never returned.

The Center for the Study of Responsive Law is tax-exempt, supported by well-known foundations, such as Field, Carnegie, and Stern, and by wealthy benefactors such as Midas muffler heir Gordon Sherman and Robert Townsend, author of *Up the Organization.* (Townsend gave $150,000.) On a budget of $300,000 a year, the center is able to pay its raiders a stipend of up to $15,000 each. "A far cry from five years ago," says one of the veteran raiders, Harrison Wellford, thirty-one, "when Ralph was being trailed by G.M. gumshoes and we would meet at night at the Crystal City hamburger joint on Connecticut Avenue to compare notes. We'd work our heads off and then get gunned down by someone from Covington & Burling [a large Washington law firm] who had been on an issue for a corporate client for ten years."

Consumers Union is the biggest single donor to the Auto Safety Center, which operates on a slender budget of $30,000 a year. The Public Interest Research Group, or PIRG as it is called, is Nader's own nonprofit law firm, and he pays all the bills out of his own pocket, including the stipends of $4,500 a year to the twelve young lawyers. It is an irony that must warm Nader's heart that the money comes out of the $270,000 he netted in the settlement of his lawsuit against G.M. for invasion of privacy. Since PIRG's budget is $170,000 a year, Nader is obviously going through his windfall at an unsustainable clip.

CONSCIOUSNESS III DOESN'T GIVE A DAMN

Nader calls his own organization "a big joke really, a drop in the bucket compared to the size of the problem." It is in his nature to conceive of the enemy as being enormous, pervasive, and exceedingly powerful. "How many public-interest lawyers would it take to oversee the Pentagon? A hundred? Multiply that by the number

---

Notches on Nader's Gun

The Automobile

An auto-safety enthusiast while at Princeton and Harvard Law School, Nader went to Washington in 1964 to work on his pet subject as an aide to Daniel Patrick Moynihan, then Assistant Secretary of Labor, who happened to be interested in a field far removed from his assigned duties. Bored with office routine, Nader quit the following year and wrote *Unsafe at Any Speed* in ten weeks. During the Senate hearings on auto safety, he came out a clear winner in a much-publicized confrontation with James Roche, president (now chairman) of General Motors. The publicity assured passage of the Motor Vehicle Safety Act of 1966, establishing a government agency to set mandatory vehicle-safety standards, of which there are now thirty-four.

Unsanitary Meat

For his second campaign, Nader found ready-made evidence in a study done by the Department of Agriculture of state-regulated packing plants, considered to be in intrastate commerce and so not covered by federal law. Many of the plants were filthy and rodent infested, but apparently nobody of any consequence had ever bothered to read the study's report. Nader did. The result was the Wholesome Meat Act of 1967, giving states the option of bringing their inspection programs up to federal standards or having them supplanted by federal inspection. In 1968 the provisions of the act were applied to poultry products.

Federal Trade Commission

A team of student raiders assigned by Nader to the FTC in 1968 found one official at the agency literally asleep on the job, others frequenting nearby saloons during working hours, and still others who seldom bothered to come to work at all. President Nixon commissioned a study of the FTC by an American Bar Association panel, which confirmed the

of departments and agencies. This country needs 50,000 full-time citizens, including 10,000 public-interest lawyers. And I could get that many applicants if I had the money." Last month Nader began a campaign to raise $750,000 from students in two states, Connecticut and Ohio, where the money would be used to set up Nader-like centers for investigating state and local government. Students in two other states, Oregon and Minnesota, have voted to donate $3 each from their college activities funds to finance similar organizations. Nader hopes that one plan or another will spread across the country.

To the young, Nader is a hero of great stature. Thousands of students in law, medicine, engineering, and every other field want to "conform their careers and their ideals," as he puts it, by going to work for him. They are the mass base of his movement, and he is able to pick and choose among them for his staff. (They say on campus that getting a job with Nader is "tougher than getting into Yale Law School.") And yet this appeal is in many ways hard to fathom. Nader has no use at all for the "counterculture," and he abhors drugs. "There's a conflict between living life on a level of feeling on the one hand and Ralph's product ethic on the

---

major findings of the Nader report: low morale, lack of planning, preoccupation with trivial cases and timidity in pursuing important ones. Outcome: new faces and new vigor at the FTC.

Food and Drug Administration
Student raiders studying the FDA in the summer of 1969 compiled evidence on two important regulatory blunders: approval of cyclamates and monosodium glutamate for unrestricted use in the food supply. Alerted by the raiders, the news media covered both stories with unrestrained enthusiasm until the FDA banned cyclamates from soft drinks and manufacturers voluntarily stopped putting monosodium glutamate in baby food. In December, President Nixon fired the three top officials at the FDA.

Other Doings
Legislation inspired by Nader: Natural Gas Pipeline Safety Act (1968), Radiation Control for Health and Safety Act (1968), Coal Mine Health and Safety Act (1969), Comprehensive Occupational Safety and Health Act (1970). Published reports: *The Chemical Feast* (on the FDA); *The Interstate Commerce Omission* (it recommends abolishing the ICC); *Vanishing Air* (a critical look at air-pollution-control laws and industry compliance); *What To Do With Your Bad Car* ("an action manual for lemon owners"); *One Life—One Physician* (on the medical profession). Reports in progress on: the Department of Agriculture, nursing homes, water pollution, Du Pont, First National City Bank of New York, the Washington law firm of Covington & Burling, land-use policies in California, supermarkets, and "brown lung" disease in the textile industry.

other," admits Lowell Dodge. "To produce, to have an impact—that's what Ralph admires. Consciousness III doesn't give a damn about the FTC. Ralph does." Dodge thinks Nader is growing ever stronger on campus as revolutionary ideas begin to fade. "There's more interest in change *within* the system, and Ralph is the most effective example of an agent for change."

Nader hectors students mercilessly about their public duties, about their "anemic imaginations," about their "thousands of hours on the beach or playing cards." And they seem to love it. "Suppose students would engage in one of history's greatest acts of sacrifice and go without Coke and tobacco and alcohol, on which they spend $250 each a year?" he asked a student audience at Town Hall in New York. "They could develop the most powerful lobby in the country. Write to us! We'll tell you how to do it." Hands dived for pens as he called out his address in Washington.

It is possible to question, nevertheless, whether this enthusiasm would survive a close association with Nader. Although most of the members of his full-time staff plan to stay in public-interest legal work, many of them talk with enthusiasm about the day when they will be leaving Nader. One reason, of course, is money. "On $4,500 a year, it's tough," says Christopher White, one of the young lawyers at the Public Interest Research Group. And then these young people are blither spirits than Nader and have a spontaneity and graciousness he lacks. Although they refrain from criticizing him directly, the picture that emerges is of a boss at least as dictatorial as any they would find in a private law firm. "The emphasis is on production," one of them says. "Ralph thinks that if a brief is 90 percent right, it's a waste of time to polish it." Nader tells them that a work week of 100 hours is "about right." He lectures them about smoking, refuses to ride in their Volkswagens, and never has time to waste socializing. Lowell Dodge got a call from Nader last Christmas Eve, but only because Nader had a question to ask about work in progress.

The warmth and empathy so important to the young are not to be found in any relationship with Nader. Robert Townsend's daughter Claire, a pretty blonde student at Princeton, says with unblushing candor that she became a raider last summer partly because "I had a terrible crush on Ralph. All the girls have crushes on Ralph." But Nader apparently never has crushes on them. He still lives monk-like in a rented room. His most pronounced concession to cravings of the flesh comes in appeasing a voracious although picky appetite. He is leery of most meats but often tops off a meal with two desserts. It is somehow typical of the man that when the soon-to-be-famous blonde detective tried to pick him up, back during his fight with G.M., she found him in a supermarket buying a package of cookies.

TRYING TO FIND FREE ENTERPRISE

What young people admire in Nader is a dark and uncompromising idealism, coupled with a system of New Left economics that he is able to shore up with all sorts of impressive-sounding facts. They think he has got the goods on "the system." And he is completely free of any humdrum sense of proportion. A conversation with Nader makes the consumer society sound as gory as a battlefield: motorists "skewered like shish kebab on non-collapsible steering wheels"; babies burned to death by flammable fabrics improperly labeled; a little girl decapitated because a glove-compartment door popped open in a low-speed collision; "thousands of people poisoned and killed every year through the irresponsible use of pesticides and chemicals."

The corporate criminals responsible for this slaughter always go unpunished. "If we were as lenient toward individual crime as we are toward big-business crime we would empty the prisons, dissolve the police forces, and subsidize the criminals." The regulatory agencies are "chatteled to business and indifferent to the public," and Congress is "an anachronism, although a good investment for corporations." As for the market economy, it is rapidly being destroyed by the same corporate executives who are always "extolling it at stockholder meetings."

"Where is the free-enterprise system?" Nader asks, a sly smile lighting up his face. "I'm trying to find it. Is it the oil oligopoly, protected by import quotas? The shared monopolies in consumer products? The securities market, that bastion of capitalism operating on fixed commissions and now provided with socialized insurance? They call me a radical for trying to restore power to the consumer, but businessmen are the true radicals in this country. They are taking us deeper and deeper into corporate socialism—corporate power using government power to protect it from competition."

DOWN TO ZERO PROFITS

Nader is not exactly the first social critic to be astonished at the functions—and malfunctions—of a market economy, and to render them in overtones of darkest evil. But sinister tales of this sort, while they go down well enough with college crowds, throw no light at all on the issues Nader claims to want to face. It is true enough that unless consumers themselves are concerned about product safety, corporations have no particular bias in its favor. This is due, however, not to corporate depravity but rather to the economics of the case: an extra margin of safety is an invisible benefit that usually increases costs. When products, automobiles for example, are too complicated for consumers to make independent judgments as to safety, government must usually set standards if there are to be any —and it is a measure not just of business power but also of consumer indifference that safety standards for autos came so late.

Government must also counter the ceaseless efforts of corporations to escape from the rigors of competition through the acquisition of monopoly power, through tariff protection, import quotas, and the like. Granted that government hasn't done a very good job of this. All the same, most corporate executives, obliged to immerse themselves daily in what feels very much like competition, would be surprised to learn from Nader how free of it they are supposed to have become.

Given Nader's own diagnosis, it might be thought that he has been spending his time battling restraints on trade, but this is far from the case. He has instead been devoting his considerable ingenuity to devising new schemes for regulating and "popularizing" business, by such means as a federal charter for all corporations, "which would be like a constitution for a country," publication of corporate tax returns, and the election of public members to corporate boards. He would require an attack on pollution "with maximum use of known technology and down to zero profits."

Nader denies any desire to take the country into socialism, and in this he is apparently sincere. One of his raiders, Mark Green, told the New York *Times* recently that when Nader thinks of socialism "he doesn't think of Lenin but of Paul Rand Dixon," former Chairman of the FTC and, in Nader's mind, the quintessential bureaucrat. Yet Nader seems never to have grasped that when he talks about operating on "zero profits" he is talking not about a market economy but about a confiscatory, state-imposed system that would inevitably bring in train a host of other controls

In his "consumer democracy" of the future, as he outlines it, everybody could order business around. Tightly controlled from above by the federal government, business would be policed at the local level by what would amount to consumer soviets. Nader thinks it will be easy to organize them, by handing out application forms in the parking lots of shopping centers. "Then collectively you can bargain with the owners of the center. You can say, 'Here are 18,000 families. We want a one-room office where we can have our staff within the center that will serve as a liaison between us and you. And we're going to develop certain conditions of our continuing patronage on a mass basis.' It might take the form of banning detergents with phosphates, improving service under a warranty, or holding down prices." Nader's product-rating system, including a telephone data bank for easy reference, would force manufacturers, he says, to abandon their present policy of "severe protective imitation" for one of "competition on price and quality." (Nobody has been able to explain just how such a system would make the millions of decisions the market makes now, many of them involving subjective judgments as to quality or value.)

While otherwise holding business in low esteem, Nader seems to have a blind faith in instant technology, insisting that if corporations are given tough enough deadlines, on antipollution devices or on proving the safety of food additives, they will somehow manage to comply. While it is true that some corporations plead ignorance as a convenient alibi for doing nothing about pollution, it is also true that feasible systems have not yet been developed to control a number of crucial pollutants, including sulphur dioxide. On the question of food additives, James Grant, deputy commissioner of the Food and Drug Administration, says, "Scientific advances solve problems but also raise new questions. We can prove that certain chemicals are unsafe, but we can never prove, once and for all, that *anything* in the food supply is safe. We frequently are obliged to make absolute decisions on the basis of partial knowledge. If I have one criticism to level at the consumer advocates, it's that they're unwilling to take scientific uncertainty into account."

DOES SEARS, ROEBUCK CHEAT?

Economics, clearly, is not Nader's strong suit. He seems to think of figures as weapons, to be tossed around for maximum effect. To cite one of his current favorite examples of business fraud, he says that the orange-juice industry is watering its product by 10 percent, and thus bilking the public out of $150 million a year. And he adds: "You may wish to compare that with what bank robbers took last year in their second most successful performance to date: $8 million." Nader says he arrived at the 10 percent figure on the basis of "insider information." He applied it to total sales of the citrus industry and, lo, another "statistic" on business fraud. Even if the industry were watering, which it strenuously denies, it does not follow that the public is being gypped out of $150 million. On a watering job of that scale, the price would reflect the water content, and if water were eliminated the price would have to go up.

Another of Nader's current favorite targets is Sears, Roebuck & Co. "Nobody thinks Sears, Roebuck cheats people. But they charge interest from the date the sales contract is signed rather than from the date of delivery—a few pennies, millions of times a year." But Sears no longer has ownership or use of the merchandise once the contract is signed, and could not, for example, apply any price increase that might subsequently be decided upon. The contract is perfectly open and aboveboard and should be considered in the context of the total transaction, price versus values received.

Nader quotes and endorses an estimate by Senator Philip Hart of Michigan that the whole gamut of business fraud and gouging, from shoddy merchandise to monopoly pricing, costs the consumer over $200 billion a year, "or 25 percent of all personal income." That utterly fantastic figure is also more than four times as large as all corporate profits in 1970. For a clipping of that magnitude to be possible, even theoretically, it would have to run as a sort of inflationary factor through the whole economy—wages as well as prices—and thus the argument becomes something of a wash, but a grossly misleading one all the same.

Like reformers before him, Nader is extremely reluctant to admit that any progress at all has been made in any area of consumer protection, even where he has helped write new legislation. "Very little progress, really," he sums it up. "It's a push-and-shove situation." He still refers to the nation's meat supply as "often diseased or putrescent, contaminated by rodent hairs and other assorted debris, its true condition disguised by chemical additives." This is the identical language he used three years ago to arouse Congress and propel passage of the Wholesale Meat Act. Since then the Department of Agriculture has declared 289 packing plants "potentially hazardous to human health," and has told state authorities to clean them up or shut them down. The department says "much remains to be done" to eliminate unsanitary conditions—but perhaps not as much as Nader seems to think. Similarly, despite the thirty-four automobile safety standards enforced by law and 701 recall campaigns, Nader says that "the changes are purely cosmetic."

SHOCK WAVES AT THE AGENCIES

The most impressive documents to come out of the Nader movement are the reports on the regulatory agencies. In most respects they are detailed and thoughtful, written with surprising skill by various groups of amateurs working under Nader's direction. And they have sent shock waves through Washington's bureaucracy. Since their publication, agency awareness of the public interest has greatly increased, and a certain distance has crept into the previously cozy relations between the regulators and the regulated. That distance, however, is still not nearly great enough to please Nader, who wants industry policed with eternal suspicion. "Sharpness" is one word he uses to describe the proper attitude. Jail terms for executives, he says, would be far more effective than the voluntary compliance on which the agencies now mostly rely. "Jail is a great stigma to a businessman, and even a short sentence is a real deterrent," explains James Turner, who wrote the FDA report. "You would get maximum compliance with a minimum of prosecutions."

That may well be so. But in the atmosphere of hostility that would result, regulation might actually be less effective than at present. The agencies can now make sweeping judgments—that a rate is "discriminatory" or a trade practice "deceptive"—on the basis of a simple hearing. "If criminal penalties were involved, our statutes would be interpreted in a much less flexible way," says Robert Pitofsky, the new head of FTC's Bureau of Consumer Protection. Most regulatory matters are exceedingly complex, and the agencies have trusted the industries concerned to furnish the data. If this system were replaced by a program of independent government research on countless topics, the sums expended could be huge enough to dent the federal budget. "It has to be a cooperative effort," argues Administrator Douglas Toms of the National Highway Traffic Safety Administration, which sets auto safety standards. "We're not going to get anywhere with an ugly, persistent confrontation, where the two sides try to outshout each other. We'd be pitting a tiny government agency against the worldwide auto industry."

At the FDA, a new leadership is attempting to stay on cordial terms with the $125-billion food industry while attacking the two key problems documented in great detail in the Nader report, *The Chemical Feast*. First, the FDA is undertaking a comprehensive review of the hundreds of chemicals added to the food supply as preservatives, colorings, or flavorings. "None of these chemicals, perhaps, has been put to the most rigorous testing that present-day science could muster," admits Deputy Commissioner Grant, one of the new men at the agency. Second, the FDA has also acted on mounting evidence that many prepared foods are deficient in nutritional values, and is now setting guidelines for their fortification with vitamins and minerals. "In many ways the FDA was a bar to progress," says Grant, "and we are attempting to turn that around."

CONFESSIONAL FOR SINNERS

Among the agencies Nader has investigated, the FTC comes closest to the tough, pro-consumer point of view that he is pushing for. Under its new leadership the FTC has filed a flurry of complaints on deceptive advertising, and in a number of these cases it has gone far beyond the traditional cease-and-desist order (known around the FTC as "go and sin no more"). To the dismay of the advertising profession, the FTC now seeks what it calls "affirmative disclosure"—that is, an admission in future advertising, for a specific period, that previous ads were deceptive. Howard Bell, president of the American Advertising Federation, says this amounts to "public flogging."

"Somebody is going to take us to court on affirmative disclosure, and they should," Pitofsky cheerfully admits. "It is a substantial expansion of FTC power." The FTC is also insisting that claims be based on evidence. "We're not after something that 'tastes better,'" Pitofsky says. "That's just puffery. But if you say it's twice as fast or 50 percent stronger, we will take that to mean faster or stronger than your competitor's product, and it better be so.

By swinging to "a fairly stiff enforcement of the law," as Pitofsky puts it, the FTC hopes to encourage self-regulation by industry. "Voluntary compliance comes when companies see that they are better off cleaning house themselves than letting government do it for them." And that is what seems to be happening. Warning of "the regulatory tidal wave which threatens to envelop us," the American Advertising Federation is trying to establish a National Advertising Review Board, which would set standards for ads, seek voluntary compliance with the standards, and refer ads it finds deceptive to the FTC for action.

In all this unaccustomed bustle, the agencies are, of course, just doing what they were supposed to be doing all along. To say only that, however, is to ignore the extraordinary difficulty of the regulatory function when there is no counterpressure to the steady, case-by-case intervention of skilled lawyers with specific and valuable corporate interests to protect. Congress, like the agencies, responds to the pressures applied—it's a case of "who's banging on the door," in Nader's words. Yet the pressures applied by individual corporations in individual cases can work to subvert the larger interests of the business community as a whole. "Intriguingly enough," says the FDA's Grant, "the overwhelming majority of the food industry believes that it is better off with a strong FDA, because all get balanced treatment." It is Nader's accomplishment, and no small one, that he has given the agencies the other constituency they need, the public. "Until we came along," says Nader, "the people at the agencies had forgotten what citizens looked like."

Nader will bend all of his lobbying skill this year to persuade Congress to pass a bill that would give the consumer permanent representation before regulatory bodies. The consumer agency to be established by the bill would, in fact, attempt to do just the sort of thing that Nader is doing now, but with the help of government funds and powers. A number of other consumer bills have broad support this year, including regulation of warranties and power for the FTC to seek preliminary injunctions against deceptive advertising. But Nader says, "I'd trade them all for the consumer agency."

THE PROBLEM OF MAINTAINING CLOUT

But can a movement like consumerism, powerful and yet amorphous, really be institutionalized? Certainly the passion and craft of a Nader cannot be. Nor would the director of a consumer agency enjoy Nader's complete freedom of action. A Senate aide who helped draft the bill predicts that the new office might "have its time in the sun, like the Peace Corps or OEO. Then it will carve out a rather cautious domain of its own and become part of the bureaucracy."

That being so, there will still be opportunities for Nader, always provided that he can stay in the sun himself. His support is volatile, a matter of vague tides of public opinion. "His problem is maintaining clout," says Douglas Toms, the Traffic Safety Administrator. "He has a strange kind of constituency, people with a burr under their saddle for one reason or another. He has to constantly find vehicles to keep him in the public eye." Financing will continue to be a problem. Nader himself is well aware of all these difficulties. He says that a basic error of reform movement is expecting to succeed. "You will never succeed. All you're trying to do is reduce problems to the level of tolerability."

Nader's answer to that question about the presidency is this: "I find that I am less and less interested in who is going to become President. A far more interesting question is, who's going to be the next president of General Motors?" Despite any such disclaimers, it is easy to imagine the movement going political and Nader running in some future year as, say, a candidate for the U.S. Senate from Connecticut. Nader might do well in politics, as a sort of latter-day Estes Kefauver. A recent Harris survey revealed that 69 percent of the people think "it's good to have critics like Nader to keep industry on its toes," while only 5 percent think he is "a troublemaker who is against the free enterprise system." This is the sort of public response that most politicians, including Presidents, yearn for in vain.

Judging Nader on the basis of the specific reforms he has brought about, it would be hard to disagree with this public verdict. There has been some cost, however, and this cannot be measured. He has visited his own suspicions and fears upon a whole society, and in the end his hyperbole may prove to be a dangerous weapon. But this year at least, the public apparently expects its crusaders to be twice as fast and 50 percent stronger.

SELECTED READINGS

"Activists Adopt New Tactics, Goals," *Industry Week,* April 20, 1973.

"The American Corporation Under Fire," *Newsweek,* May 24, 1971.

"Corporate Performance and Private Criticism—Campaign G.M. Rounds I and II." in G. A. Smith, C. R. Christensen, N. A. Berg and M. S. Salter, *Policy Formulation and Administration,* 6th Ed. (Homewood: Richard D. Irwin, 1972.)

"Industry Faces More Activist Demands," *Industry Week,* April 8, 1974.

Leone, R. C., "Public Interest Advocacy and the Regulatory Process," *Annals of the American Academy of Political and Social Science,* March, 1972.

"Nader vs. G.M.," *Time,* August 24, 1970.

"Radical Confrontation and its Challenge to Management," *Financial Executive,* December, 1970.

"Ralph Nader Becomes an Organization," *Business Week,* November 28, 1970.

Sanders, M. K., *Professional Radical: Conversations With Saul Alinsky.* (New York: Harper & Row, 1970.)

Cases

McDONALD'S, INC.*

McDonald's, the nationwide chain of hamburger restaurants, has a policy that the American flag will fly in front of each of the company's outlets. The policy was personally promulgated by Ray Kroc, Chairman of the Board.

On Monday, May 4, 1970, four students at Kent State University were killed by National Guardsmen. The Guard was ordered to Kent State after students, like students all around the country, struck and rioted in protest to the Vietnam war and the invasion of Cambodia. At Kent State, the students had burned the ROTC building a few nights earlier.

On Tuesday, May 5, students about the country were in a state of shock and confusion because of the Kent State killings. At the Carbondale campus of Southern Illinois University, students were asking that all flags be lowered to half mast in memory of the Kent State students. When they confronted the manager of the local McDonald's, he complied and lowered the flag.

A neighbor who witnessed the confrontation reported it to McDonald's Chairman, who in turn called the manager and ordered the flag

---

*The substance of this incident was reported in J. Anthony Lukas, "As American as a McDonald's Hamburger on the Fourth of July," *The New York Times Magazine,* July 4, 1971, p. 26.

hoisted to full mast. The manager complied with the chairman's directive.

A few hours later, the students returned, disturbed that the manager hadn't kept his word. They threatened in no uncertain terms to burn the shop down.

The manager, perplexed, called McDonald's headquarters for guidance. The manager's call was put through to the President of the corporation.

NEW ENGLAND RETAIL CREDIT CORPORATION*

On June 17, 1974, a small article appeared in the business section of the *Boston Chronicle* describing a computer order placed by New England Retail Credit Corporation (NERCC). The brief article quoted an announcement by John P. Daunt, president of NERCC, in which he stated that the firm, the largest credit-reporting agency in New England, had signed a 7.2-million-dollar contract with one of the country's largest computer manufacturers to install a computer system in their Waltham, Massachusetts, office. Included in the system will be input/output devices for NERCC's eight regional offices, three banks, and a local franchised credit agency.

The new system is scheduled to be in operation by January 1, 1976. By 1979 it is expected that the firm will have input/output devices in 90 percent of the banks in New England and will have franchise operations in nearly all of the more than two hundred local credit bureaus in the six state area. NERCC will then (for all practical purposes) become the custodian of *all of the credit information* on New England residents.

After reading the *Chronicle* story, Philip Kleinglass, a Boston attorney who had worked on several cases with the Boston chapter of the Civil Liberties Protective Society, became concerned about the effect that this new system would have on the privacy of the citizens living in the area. After much thought, he contacted James Kohanek, executive director of the Boston chapter of the CLPS, and asked that they meet to discuss the implications of such a system.

On June 22, 1974, Kleinglass and Kohanek met and discussed the issue over lunch. From their discussions it became apparent that the executive board of the CLPS should look into the issue further. Kleinglass agreed that he would contact Daunt to find out more about the system and then would make a report to the executive board.

---

*This case was prepared by Leslie D. Ball, copyright 1974.

When Kleinglass contacted Daunt about meeting with him, Daunt appeared to be delighted to talk about his proposed system. At that meeting Daunt explained the background of NERCC, why the system was needed, and how it would benefit the individuals living in the area. Kleinglass was shown the final report from Long and Retz Associates (Exhibit A), which was commissioned by NERCC to investigate the credit-reporting business in New England and NERCC's role in that business.

Daunt pointed out that the volume of their business was increasing at an average annual rate of 22 percent, but that was still approximately 4 to 5 percent less than the growth rate of credit volume in the New England area. While they were experiencing this growth, they were also experiencing increasing errors in their reports and an increase in the amount of response time required to fill a credit-report request. Because of these problems, NERCC's profitability was decreasing at an alarming rate. The Long and Retz report clearly shows that a continuation of NERCC operations employing current practices would lead to eventual bankruptcy.

"The system now being planned will accomplish many goals," said Daunt. He pointed out that it will offer improved service to a person applying for installment credit, reduced expenses for the credit grantor, and centralized credit information in New England.

The current functions of NERCC are to answer inquiries about credit, make credit reports, and attempt to collect uncollectable accounts. An *inquiry,* Daunt pointed out, results in only the information in their files being reported, while a *credit report* requires that NERCC update all information in its file and *then* make a report to the client. Daunt gave Kleinglass a sample credit report (Exhibit B). When the new system is installed, the cost of inquiries will be immediately reduced to $0.75 per inquiry from the current $1.50 charge; the cost of credit reports will be reduced to $2.00 from $3.00; and the number of collections done by the firm will be reduced substantially. Because of the reduced costs and the added accuracy of the computer system, it is expected that the local credit agencies will begin using NERCC's services more frequently through franchised operations.

Daunt also noted that the computer system was a modular system. Because of the modularity, the storage capacity for the system could be increased, as need be, to an almost infinite size. In addition, eventually it might be possible for the system to tie into planned systems in other areas of the country.

When Kleinglass asked Daunt to explain how the firm was going to ensure (1) that the system contained only accurate information, (2) that access to that information would be made only by authorized users and for authorized purposes, and (3) that an individual could correct erroneous information, Daunt explained that the rights of the individual would be amply protected and that the system was "error-proof." He further stated that the system complied with the Fair Credit Reporting Act of April, 1971. In addition, the data base will contain a credit history of the individual containing both positive and negative items of objective information, and will *not* contain any *subjective* information, as most traditional credit reporting agencies usually include.

Following this meeting, Kleinglass reported to the CLPS. He first distributed copies of a summary of the Fair Credit Reporting Act (Exhibit C) and remarked that, if complied with, this act would protect the rights of privacy of the individual. In his report he stated that the need for credit information was, indeed, required for the effective operation of business and industry in the country. However, the past history of NERCC with respect to errors in their files raised a number of questions about the possible effect on the privacy of the citizens of New England. It was suggested that the CLPS work with NERCC to ensure that they complied with the Fair Credit Reporting Act. One board member recommended that the CLPS supply a computer programmer to NERCC to work with their staff in the development of the computer system and its related computer programs. Finally, it was decided that Kleinglass should approach Daunt with the offer of the computer programmer.

During the next two weeks, Kleinglass attempted to contact Daunt on several occasions. Daunt did not respond to over a dozen telephone calls and two letters. Kohanek and another member of the board received similar results when they attempted to contact Daunt.

On July 26, 1974, the CLPS petitioned Judge Warren Perry of Boston's Federal District Court to issue an injunction against the further development of the computer system by NERCC. In their petition, they stated that the central ingredient in a credit-reporting system was that the information about the individual be complete and accurate. The CLPS petition argued that the history of NERCC's activities showed a lack of concern for maintaining any standards of completeness or accuracy. Furthermore, the CLPS continued, it appears that the proposed system does not comply with the intent of the Fair Credit Reporting Act. A number of questions were raised: What personal information will the NERCC system include in credit reports? How accurate is the information reported by them? How complete are the derogatory entries in the file? What procedures are available for handling items of information which involve disputes between businesses and the consumer? And what precautions have been taken to prevent unauthorized access to NERCC's files?

The petition also pointed out that the system would have the capability of continuously monitoring various consumers with the intent of notifying all creditors when the consumer became late in any of the accounts that he owed. The petition stated that this would cause creditors to demand more rapid payments and would force individual bankruptcy upon many individuals unnecessarily. Further abuses of the system could also be possible.

CLPS asked the court to enjoin the system development until such time as these issues were cleared up to the satisfaction of the court, and appoint a panel to inspect the development of the system when, and if, it were given the go-ahead. Judge Perry then gave NERCC 48 hours to respond.

EXHIBIT A

Long and Retz Associates, Inc.
Consultants to Business and Industry
1272 Avenue of the Americas
New York, New York 10012

January 15, 1974

John P. Daunt, President
New England Retail Credit Corporation
Waltham, Massachusetts 01789

Dear Mr. Daunt:

Enclosed is the final report of a study conducted by Long and Retz. As the study is quite lengthy, I have decided to summarize a few of the major points made in the report.

Our study involved a review of your current operating practices, trends in retail credit in New England, your position within the industry, and different operating practices that you might follow. The results presented in our report are for each year from your inception in 1945 through December 31, 1973, with the time from 1974 to 1990 estimated. These estimates were based on currently available statistics and an evaluation of current trends. We believe that these estimates have a high degree of accuracy.

It is quite obvious that your firm is not operating as effectively as it once did. Net income as a percentage of sales has continually been declining, with the largest declines in recent years. In addition, net income itself declined in 1972 for the first time in the company's operating history and continued declining in 1973.

There are two principal reasons for the decline. First, the volume of your business is growing so rapidly that your current manual operating procedures have become ineffective. This large increase has caused an increased percentage of errors in reporting and caused an increase in the amount of time that it takes to respond to an inquiry or to make a credit report. For the period through 1960, less than 5 percent of your records contained errors in some form or another. Yet, in a sample taken during 1973, 37.6 percent of the records were in error. In 1960 inquiries were processed in an average of 7 minutes and it now takes approximately 18 minutes. Credit reporting has seen a similar increase. A report in 24 hours was nearly always possible in 1960, but it seldom is now. Most often reports are turned out within 48 hours but some have been as long as 96 hours.

Secondly, NERCC is facing a tremendous cost squeeze. The cost of labor has pushed your costs up rapidly but income has been unable to expand. You cannot increase the costs of your service as you are competing with many local credit bureaus and a rapidly increasing number of banks that provide the same service.

After World War II, installment loans became part of virtually every American's liabilities. Increased home buying also produced many more home mortgages. Thus, the ratio of private debt to GNP has grown from 69.4 percent in 1945 to over 135 percent today (Table I). While this growth should continue, it is expected to only reach 145 percent by 1990. However, due to the large increases in the GNP, private debt will increase by almost three-fold from 1970 to 1990. Conditions within the New England area are parallel to those of the nation. The large increases in your early years of operation are a direct result of this increase in installment loans and home buying and NERCC should put itself in a position to profit from future growth in these two areas.

Since you started operations, NERCC has been the largest credit-reporting agency in New England. A summary of your business activity appears in Table II. While NERCC remains number one, your business activity as a percentage of the total New England business is declining (Table III). This is largely attributed to an increase in local credit bureaus and the increase in credit information supplied by banks.

After reviewing your firm and the credit-reporting practices in New England, we find only two avenues open to NERCC. In what we call "Option A," you could continue operations as they currently exist. This, however, will lead to smaller profits in 1974 and substantial losses beginning in 1975 (Table IV). Option A is the "Bankruptcy" option.

Option B provides an exciting approach to credit information reporting, as well as satisfying the needs of businesses and individuals in the area and making NERCC a profitable firm once again. From our discussions with banks and local credit bureaus, it has been determined that a need exists for a central depository of credit information and a quick procedure for accessing it. No organization now exists that can fill this need and NERCC is the only firm that has the potential.

Initially, a computer system will be put in your home office. All currently available data would be converted to machine readable form. Once that phase is completed, video display tubes will be put in your branch offices and a few selected banks and local credit bureaus. These tubes will allow the user to request information from the computer. They will then receive the most up-to-date credit information that NERCC has on the individual. By typing a special code, a complete credit report will be generated on the computer in your home office and then be sent to the requester. Additions and deletions to the information will be transmitted from the various remote locations via the terminals, verified by your staff, and then entered into the computer system.

While this computer system introduces more opportunity for control than the hazards of the old procedures, it also provides a number of other benefits. Among them are:

1. Credit information will be at the grantor's fingertips which, of course, will save him time and the time of the individual applying for credit.

2. Fewer loans will be granted to high-risk individuals as a result of more up-to-date information.

3. Charges for this service can be reduced substantially due to, first, a reduction in the number of employees required to handle requests by approximately one-half and, secondly, the increased effectiveness of the system.

4. As costs come down, more requests will come in and more local credit bureaus and banks will become more interested in becoming a part of the system.

In conjunction with the establishment of the computer system, we urge that NERCC substantially cut back the collection segment of the business. This segment of the business has become a haven for illegal activities in other firms. Therefore, NERCC's collection business is also looked upon by some as illegal. It is suggested that, as a courtesy to clients, collection accounts be telephoned twice and then, if not collected, labeled as a "difficult" account and turned over to an agency specializing in difficult account collection.

While the above is very brief, the complete report gives details of our study and the resulting suggestions. If there should be any questions, please feel free to contact me. As always, Long and Retz Associates, Inc. is ready and able to serve you.

Sincerely,

Robert T. Long
President

TABLE I   Ratio of Private Debt to GNP (in billions of dollars)

Year	Private debt	GNP	% of GNP
1945	147	212	69.4
1950	221	284	77.7
1955	372	398	93.5
1960	597	503	118.5
1965	883	681	129.4
1970	1299	974	133.2
1975(e)	1787	1286	138.8
1980(e)	2261	1607	140.4
1985(e)	2790	1946	143.1
1990(e)	3321	2391	144.9

TABLE II   Business Activity (Options A & B included)

Year	Inquiries	Credit reports	Collections Number	Collections Dollars
1950	38,146	11,441	156	$ 15,674
1955	78,443	22,373	469	52,646
1960	131,396	30,490	1276	171,592
1965	259,482	59,387	2819	421,937
1970	612,561	151,076	2746	549,114
1971	758,792	197,145	2611	548,792
1972	912,356	226,780	2697	593,345
1973	1,125,000	281,000	2500	527,000
Option A				
1974(e)	1,337,000	343,000	2425	511,675
1975(e)	1,601,000	397,000	2350	498,200
1976(e)	1,937,000	482,000	2300	507,400
1977(e)	2,216,000	573,000	2250	518,600
1980(e)	3,236,000	806,000	2000	600,000
1985(e)	6,841,000	1,732,000	2500	875,000
1990(e)	15,896,000	4,001,000	3000	1,200,000
Option B				
1974(e)	1,400,000	360,000	2450	513,000
1975(e)	3,225,000	795,000	2800	735,000
1976(e)	4,149,000	1,035,000	3200	780,000
1977(e)	5,456,000	1,362,000	3600	825,000
1980(e)	8,891,000	2,345,000	6200	1,112,000
1985(e)	17,675,000	4,880,000	12,300	2,775,000
1990(e)	46,900,000	11,375,000	18,550	4,995,000

TABLE III   NERCC's Business Activity As a Percent Of New England Activity (Options A & B included)

Year	Inquiries	Credit reports	Collections
1950	7.1	7.4	6.2
1955	12.9	12.6	13.7
1960	26.4	26.1	31.4
1965	30.7	31.2	37.8
1970	31.4	30.7	32.6
1971	30.3	30.8	30.2
1972	30.2	29.7	28.9
1973	29.7	30.2	26.4
Option A			
1974(e)	29.4	29.1	24.6
1975(e)	29.0	29.6	21.7
1980(e)	26.0	25.4	12.0
1985(e)	24.7	25.1	8.1
1990(e)	23.2	22.8	6.0
Option B			
1974(e)	29.5	29.2	24.1
1975(e)	57.0	56.8	23.1
1980(e)	74.1	73.7	35.7
1985(e)	74.6	74.2	39.2
1990(e)	71.8	72.3	36.3

TABLE IV   Income projections (000's Omitted)

Year	Inquiries	Reports	Collections	Total	Expenses	Net income
1950	57	33	5	95	71	24
1955	117	66	18	201	148	53
1960	196	91	57	344	263	81
1965	390	180	141	711	569	142
1970	918	450	183	1551	1344	207
1971	1137	600	182	1919	1707	212
1972	1368	775	191	2334	2148	186
1973	1687	840	176	2703	2562	141
Option A						
1974(e)	2005	1012	170	3187	3161	26
1975(e)	2402	1200	166	3768	3871	(103)
1976(e)	2905	1446	169	4520	4848	(328)
1977(e)	3324	1719	172	5215	6058	(843)
1980(e)	4848	2412	200	7460	8880	(1420)
1985(e)	10261	5196	291	15748	19958	(4210)
1990(e)	23844	12003	400	36247	43747	(7500)
Option B						
1974(e)	1250	720	171	2141	3850	(1709)
1975(e)	2419	1590	245	4254	4120	134
1976(e)	3086	2070	260	5416	5019	397
1977(e)	4101	2724	275	7100	6246	854
1980(e)	6668	4690	371	11729	8620	3109
1985(e)	13256	9760	925	23941	17165	6776
1990(e)	35200	27750	1665	59615	37430	22185

EXHIBIT B

New England Retail Credit Corporation
Credit Report

NAME _Sharpe, John J._   DATE _6/13/74_
ADDRESS _365 Maple Street_   AGE _40_
        Brandon, MA 01356   S.S.N. _15-056-0609_
WIFE _Martha_   DEPENDENTS _5_
TELEPHONE _413-762-9873_

PREVIOUS _63 Fredrick Street_
ADDRESS _Rumney, N. H. 02273_

EMPLOYER _Atlas Sand & Gravel Co._   POSITION _Foreman_
         Brandon, MA 01356   SALARY _$245/week (a/o 2/1/74)_
SINCE   _January 12, 1961_

MORTGAGE OR _Federal Savings Bank_   ORIGINAL _$21,500_
RENT FROM _Brandon, MA 01356_   CURRENT _$16,757 (a/o 2/1/74)_
PAYMENT   _$252 pit_

WIFE'S _Brandon Gift Shop_   POSITION _Clerk_
EMPLOYER _167 Main Street_   SALARY _$1.95/hr. (a/o 2/1/74)_
         Brandon, MA 01356

CHECKING _First National Bank_   AMOUNT _$35.89 (a/o 6/13/74)_
         Brandon, MA 01356
SAVINGS _Federal Savings Bank_   AMOUNT _$842.13 (a/o 6/13/74)_
        Brandon, MA 01356

IN FILE SINCE: _1966_   LAST CHECKED: _2/1/74_
INQUIRIES: _Sears 2/66; 7/69; 11/73; FSB 1/66; IRS 6/69; Davis Ford_
           _8/66; 10/68; 3/71; 2/74_

CREDITORS	OPEN	HIGH	BALANCE	TERMS	RATINGS
Fed. Sav. Bk	21500	21500	16757	360@185	R-1
Sears	156	482	266	36@21	R-2
BankAm.		652	114		R-2
B&B Fuel		382	214	12@62	R-1
Mobil		112	54		R-1
Exxon		23			R-1
Singer	457	457	186	24@21	R-2
Ford M.C.	2600	3150	2213	24@116	R-2

PUBLIC RECORDS: _Small Claims 2/69 Acme TV $385.00 Pd. 4/69_
                Speeding Ticket 8/71 Fined $25.00 9/71

REMARKS: _Consistent low bal. in checking and savings_
         Youngest child is a mongoloid
         Dentist refuses to report
         Family reported to be nudists.

EXHIBIT C

SUMMARY OF FAIR CREDIT REPORTING ACT*

Purpose

To insure that consumer reporting agencies exercise their grave responsibilities with fairness, impartiality, and a respect for the consumer's right to privacy.

Requirements

1. *Accuracy of Information*—reasonable procedures must be followed to insure maximum possible accuracy of the individual's information.

2. *Obsolete Information*—certain items of adverse information may not be included after they have reached specified "ages" (i.e., 7 years old for paid tax liens).

3. *Limited Uses of Information*—a report about an individual can only be used for the following purposes:

   a) in response to a court order;

   b) from written instruction of the individual;

   c) to determine the individual's eligibility for (i) credit or insurance, (ii) employment, including promotion, or (iii) a license or other benefit for which the law requires a consideration of the individual's financial status;

   d) to meet a legitimate business need for a business transaction involving the individual.

4. *Notices to Individuals*—whenever credit, insurance, or employment is denied, information is reported that might adversely affect his employment, or an investigation report (includes interviews with neighbors, friends, etc.) is prepared, he must be so notified in advance.

5. *Individual's Right of Access to Information*—the individual has the right to be informed of the nature and substance, the sources, and recipients of information about him whether or not adverse action has been taken.

6. *Individual's Right to Contest Information*—when a dispute arises concerning the accuracy or completeness of information, the agency must reinvestigate and record the current status. If this does not resolve the dispute, the individual has the right to file a brief statement explaining the dispute.

---

*Portions extracted from: *Records, Computers, and the Rights of Citizens,* Report of the Secretary's Advisory Committee on Automated Personal Data Systems, U.S. Department of Health, Education, and Welfare, July, 1973, p. 66–69.

PART III
MEASUREMENT

Social Accounting and Reporting

With all the writing on social responsibility or the role of the corporation in solving social problems (as well as all the criticism on the softness of the whole topic), it should not be surprising that, in time, some forms of measurement or accounting for corporate social activity would be attempted. There isn't much to show yet in the area; for a topic so liberally strewn about the literature, the techniques are surprisingly nonstandard, underdeveloped, and often unaccepted.

Yet the area of social audit or social accounting is becoming standard fare at corporate and business meetings; it has absorbed the time of some reputable scholars, and is finding increased interest among practitioners.

Managers have all sorts of reasons to undertake or advocate social audits. Some simply seek to forestall activist protests. If these managers can present some form of data, they hope they can at least fend off accusations and condemnations. Other executives want to know how much they are really spending. After all, corporations have been lending executive time, operative time, facilities, and equipment for years to all sorts of civic and charitable causes; few ever bothered to calculate the real costs of these contributions. Still other managers firmly believe in the social responsibility doctrine and want to develop social audits for planning, control and reward purposes. In some companies, official policy, publically announced at least, is that lower-level managers will be rewarded according to social performance as well as profit performance. Finally, in the ultimate, some managers would like to find that nebulous net benefit figure.

The problem, of course, is that there is little agreement on what to measure and how to do it. As the concept has evolved, there seems to be at least two schools of thought on the approach an audit should take; one advocates starting now to

find a measure of corporate net social benefit, the other centers on a more traditional determination of costs incurred. These two approaches are illustrated in our
readings by the Linowes article and the piece by Bauer and Fenn.

Linowes proposes that firms develop what he calls a "socio-economic operating statement" (SEOS). Briefly, the Linowes approach sets onto paper voluntary
expenditures made by the firm for public or employee welfare. Set off against the
expenditures would be what he calls "detriments," the costs of projects which
have been brought to management's attention, but which were not undertaken.
The bottom line of a SEOS statement would be "total socio-economic contribution
or deficit for the year."

Bauer and Fenn are much more cautious. They propose that firms must first
get on the learning curve by initially designing the audit for internal purposes only
and by first focusing on programs and not on social impact. In essence, Bauer and
Fenn advise companies to start by listing items resulting from an "explicit corporate
policy involving a meaningful level of resource commitment." Then management
can proceed to include costs as well as measures to determine the effectiveness
of programs. For programs with no adequate performance measures, Bauer and
Fenn recommend the "process audit," which is a description of origins, goals,
rationale, and actual operations of the programs.

Since the area of social audit is so new, there are a number of critiques of the
early attempts at measurement. This is especially true of the Linowes approach. We
should like therefore to offer a summary of the critiques after the readings.

After Linowes and Bauer and Fenn, we include a general approach and rationale for the field by George Steiner (from *The Conference Board Record*).

What *Is* a Corporate Social Audit?

Raymond A. Bauer and Dan H. Fenn, Jr.

Once the murky notion of the social responsibility of business began to take on
popular appeal and specific shape, it was inevitable that public pressure would
begin to build for some sort of business accountability in the social sphere. After
all, if society really believes that corporations should broaden their concept of their
own function to include social responsibility, articulate members of society are

going to demonstrate and implement that belief by demanding some kind of accounting of corporate performance in noneconomic areas.

This demand that corporations be socially accountable has been augmented
by a growing realization among businessmen that corporate social programs have
been haphazard in their growth, poorly aimed and weakly coordinated, and little
known or understood—even within a given corporation. Further, if specific programs are hazy and obscure, the notion of "total social impact" has proved almost
completely opaque, not just to businessmen, but to society as a whole. Thus it
should surprise no one that the pressure for and talk about a formal "social audit,"
in some way analogous to a financial audit, have increased measurably in recent
months, both within and outside companies.

The social audit is indeed a relatively new development; it has only a thin
history prior to the 1970's. It first appeared on the scene when the accepted
definition of "corporate social responsibility" was no longer being formulated
primarily by businessmen, but rather by social activists who had reason to capital-
ize on a general suspicion of all "establishment" institutions, including business.
What the term means is commensurately vague, and there is precious little agreement on how such an audit ought to be conducted.

In the pages that follow, we present a description and analysis of some of the
problems encountered by those who are attempting to perform social audits and
outline an approach that appears to us to be viable. We term this approach the
"first-step audit." It is designed to provide data that are immediately useful for
corporate executives; it is also designed to put the whole effort toward social
accounting on an upward learning curve by combining descriptive information with
quantitative measures in a meaningful way. Hopefully, the first-step audit will be
helpful to businessmen who are trying to resolve such questions as: "What activities
should I be auditing? What measures should I use? And what standards of performance should I use to calibrate my record?"

Some readers will say that what we are proposing is not an *audit* at all, but
rather a form of social *report*. So be it; but we cannot see that the question of
terminology has much significance at this point. The loose usage of the word
"audit" has characterized discussions of corporate social audits and is sanctioned
neither by dictionaries nor the accounting profession. An audit means the independent attestation of facts by some outside party, but it is clear to us that independent
attestation is a step that still lies far down the road. The first-step audit we shall
describe will prove, we believe, a useful way station.

For the purposes of this discussion, we shall take "social audit" to mean: *a
commitment to systematic assessment of and reporting on some meaningful,
definable domain of a company's activities that have social impact*. This definition is a fairly disciplined one, and one that will allow the activities now carried
on under the social-audit banner to be included in a more embracing form, with
independent attestation, at a later date.

SOURCES OF PRESSURE

As we have said, there are powerful forces loose in the land that are demanding some kind of social audit:

1. Executives generally desire to acquire both an individual and a corporate image of social responsibility, one that harmonizes with a public concern which they (and we) do not believe is going to subside.

2. Businessmen, like everyone else, are caught up in the changing mores and priorities of the society and are concerned today about matters which only a few years ago did not worry them. The level of this concern should not be underestimated. Pollution, the disadvantaged and minorities, clarity and directness in advertising—issues like these have moved rapidly onto (and higher and higher on) the agendas of corporate executives.

3. Another influence is commercial. A number of consultants, sensing the possibility of a new source of business and inherently curious about the whole complex area, are trying to develop ways of performing social audits.

4. Then there is the stimulus of the outside "auditors"—the Naders, the Council on Economic Priorities, the new mutual funds, the recently established journal called *Business and Society Review,* minority groups, ecologists, and so forth, all of whom have a stake in making public almost anything that a company may want to hide. Obviously, such stimuli encourage managements to present their cases in ways they think accurate and proper; but, perhaps even more important, managements want to know what is in store for their companies if they are attacked. This second motivation has obtained in some of the companies with which we are acquainted, where managements actually do not (or did not) know what or how well they were doing, although they may have had some suspicions.

5. Nonprofit organizations such as churches and educational institutions have spurred the idea of social auditing. Urged by their constituents to establish a "social portfolio," to sanitize their holding of paper from companies adjudged irresponsible, or to influence the policies of those in which they have investments, these organizations have been seeking (usually with painful unsuccess) to establish some way of determining if Company X is or is not socially responsible.

6. Investment houses which, for a variety of reasons, are establishing funds specializing in "clean" securities are also generating interest. These houses face the problem of identifying companies that both act responsibly and promise to be good long-term gainers. This is not a simple matter: it begs a gaggle of questions turning on what is "good social performance."

7. The social activists themselves have an obvious stake in some kind of measurements. If they expect to have significant impact on corporate behavior, they need some yardsticks to use in advising the general public of the social health of this or that company.

CONFUSION OF METHODS

It is precisely this broad spectrum of pressures for social auditing that causes much of the confusion. Everybody is talking about the social audit, but scarcely anyone agrees with anyone else as to exactly what it is, and no two organizations are doing it quite the same way. To illustrate:

- In one company, the chief executive assigned the task of designing a social audit procedure to his public affairs group. This group, naturally enough, was primarily interested in increasing the company's role in community affairs and consequently designed an audit that would demonstrate a close linkage between social programs and long-range profitability.

- Another CEO wanted to satisfy his own conscience that his company was, indeed, behaving responsibly. Inevitably, the issues and norms selected for the audit were those which were important to him personally, and the nature and precision of the data generated were determined by how much he needed to know to sleep at night.

- One president wanted to make sure that his corporation's social programs were producing the maximum benefit to society for the investment being made. He focused the auditing effort on making an inventory of what the company was doing and evaluating the usefulness of each program vis-à-vis others in which the company might engage. Hence his audit was designed to answer such questions as this: "Should we be working with the public schools in town instead of sponsoring low-income housing?"

- The relevant question for a church or an educational institution is this: "Which companies are doing well in ways that are of particular concern to our constituency?" If a constituency is upset about apartheid, or antipersonnel weapons, or pollution, the only questions the audit must answer—within the bounds of financial prudence—are whether or not any companies represented in the institution's portfolio are viewed by the constituency as socially responsible on this particular range of points; and, correspondingly, the audit will be designed to provide just the data that show whether the criteria are in fact being met.

- Consider the social activist who seeks to force corporations to halt activities that have (as he thinks) antisocial effects, and who also seeks to enlist them in the effort to improve the world around them. Here, again, the task is different, and the audit will be different. The activist will select the issues that strike him as being especially significant and collect enough data to convince himself and the general public, which is the ultimate source of his influence, that improper things are being done.

• The consulting firm interested in helping clients with the auditing problem obviously wants to develop a version of the social audit which is financially and professionally feasible and applicable for as wide a variety of clients as possible. Its nonindividualistic approach is bound to conflict and contrast with those of other auditors.

• The company that is seeking either a good image or protection against attack will select those areas for investigation that, in its judgment, will satisfy the public it is trying to impress (which may, incidentally, include its own employees). Since the audit data must be made public, the company will probably need to make investigations and disclosures that are very extensive—extensive enough to convince an audience that is growing ever more skeptical of corporate pronouncements. Its audit is bound to be company-specific, by virtue of the nature and depth of the data required.

In short, many purposes and programs are currently crowding and jostling under the umbrella of the social audit. Nevertheless, the full vision continues to be that, in the future, companies shall report their social performance with the same regularity and the same appearance of precision with which they now report their financial performance.

The question to be asked is whether the audit can ever be developed to a state that will satisfy that austere vision.

THE VISION VS. EXPERIENCE

In the past few months, we have investigated a number of organizations that are engaged in one or another kind of social auditing. We have talked with consulting firms and looked at their efforts. We have met with and, in some cases, worked with companies in many different industries that are taking bites at the apple. We have been associated with several of the social action groups. We have studied some of the investment houses. And we have now reached the point, we feel, where we can define five significant difficulties imbedded in this auditing process.

1. How do we decide what to audit?

As the social auditor enters the thicket of implementation, the first bramble bush he will meet is the question of what to audit. What are the areas of social responsibility, anyway? As we have surveyed current practice, we have found almost as many answers as there are auditors.

Pollution and the hiring and promotion of minorities (including women) receive a roughly consistent priority, but after that things are fairly wide open. Some auditors virtually ignore corporate giving and community programs; others include them. Quite a few stress consumerist issues of various kinds; others go heavy on munitions manufacturing, or investments in South Africa or Portugal. Still others focus on employee well-being—fringe benefits, promotion opportunities, safety, and so forth.

The choice is not easy to make. When he comes to decide whether to include a specific factor, the auditor inevitably realizes the full complexity of some of these issues. For many, Polaroid's involvement in South Africa was a simple matter, but the company did not find it so. Finally, after a strenuous internal debate, the company came to the conclusion that it would better satisfy its social responsibility in the long run, even in the eyes of the groups pressing for withdrawal, by remaining in that unhappy land than by leaving it.

Equally, some of the components of social responsibility are as vague as they are complex. For example, how does the auditor grapple with a subject like "quality of work?" This term can—and does—mean everything from the adequacy of fringe benefits to the degree of employee participation in corporate decisions. Executives in one company found to their surprise that employees felt it was socially irresponsible for management to demand of them as much time and effort as the corporate mission required. Clearly, quality of work is too imprecise a quantity to be taken for granted.

Defining the *relevant parts* of social responsibility creates further difficulties. For some, a social audit is adequate if it simply examines the community activities in which a corporation is engaged. For others, this is ducking the issue: the relevant point, they feel, is the impact a company is having on society because of the business it is in or the way in which it is conducting that business. An insurance company might ask itself, for example, what good it does to audit its investment in low-income housing and minority enterprises but ignore its red-lining policies in the ghettos? Similarly, one might argue that a change in the traditional hiring practices of a company is going to have a far greater beneficial effect on a community than all the gifts it makes to the Community Fund.

Finally, the definitions of corporate social responsibility are still evolving. If one takes the recent past as a basis for prediction, he would have to guess that expectations will rise, that standards of performance will be hoisted, that new and unforeseen issues will be introduced, and that some of today's causes will become less relevant. Thus, in 1973, good labor relations is no longer much of an issue; similarly, if pollution laws are strengthened and enforced, pollution control may not be worth auditing in the future. Social responsibility is a moving target, and this fact greatly complicates the choice of what to audit.

Roughly, the decision as to what to audit has to be determined in one of two ways. Either the top corporate executives, on the basis of their interests and their perceptions of the concerns of their constituents, must make the choices, or some kind of survey of the relevant constituencies must be conducted. A good case can be made for either approach; it is largely a question of what purpose a company has determined for the audit.

2. What are the measures?

Once a company has defined the areas it wants to audit, it must decide how to measure its performance.

One obvious way is by cost—what it spends in each area. But even if a company selects only a narrow definition of social responsibility and focuses just on the costs of its so-called social programs (for example, English-language programs or housing rehabilitation), how does it determine what the true costs of such activities are? How does it measure the executive time that goes into them? How does it assign overhead to them? How does it assess the opportunity costs involved?

Furthermore, cost by itself is an inadequate measure, since the main question the company will want to answer about each activity is, "Was it a success?" The difficulty in answering this question is that such corporate activities can ordinarily be measured only in terms of such intermediate effects as the number of people who have received a given type of service—say, the number of community residents whose apartments have been rehabilitated. Few social programs can satisfactorily document what the delivery of these services did for the people who received them.

In addition, these activities are extremely expensive to evaluate, and it is doubtful whether any company would find it feasible to make frequent evaluations of its total contributions.

A compounding difficulty here is that the answer to the question, even if one gets it, may be valueless. If a company ascertains the number of high school students who use the computer it has donated, what has it really learned? Probably, not very much.

3. What constitutes success?

Thus we come to the problem of defining what constitutes success—that is, of defining the appropriate norms against which a company should measure. Even if a company can make a sound selection of items to audit and can develop some satisfactory measure for its performance on these items, how will it know when it has done a job right? How good is good?

Government standards (if they exist) may fill part of the need here, but most of us would feel that such standards are minimums for performance, not norms for judging success. Furthermore, in many areas such as pollution and minority hiring, there is so much variation of factors from industry to industry in the problems with which companies are confronted that one probably needs separate performance norms for each. Sometimes this is possible; more often it is not; but even when it is, it is rarely adequate. One would not expect Con Ed's records for hiring and promoting Puerto Ricans to look like those of PG&E. Specialized norms mean tougher comparisons in measurement.

In an effort to cut through such problems, some people have suggested that the effectiveness of a company's program in meeting a social issue is the norm that should be used. We have already referred to the difficulty of evaluating social programs and the even greater difficulty of comparing the ones selected with others which could have been undertaken.

There is also another difficulty with this approach. The success of a program for training the hard-core unemployed, for example, can be measured in terms of numbers completing the course, being hired, and being retained in the job. But if an observer tries to go the next step and judge whether a particular company's hard-core training program solved or even significantly contributed to the solution of a social problem, the verdict may well be dismal, simply because any one company's contribution is unlikely to solve a problem unless it is a very large company in a very small community.

4. Where are the data?

Next we should mention the difficulty of collecting data in this area. It is expensive and time consuming for a large, complex company to collect adequate data about its social programs, much less determine which of its activities have a social impact and thus should be studied. Quite frequently, outside auditors have difficulty getting at the kind of information they need. Even inside auditors may run into real problems. For example, one company with only minimal manufacturing operations but extensive retailing ones decided to hire a group of students to check on what it assumed were the few locations where it could be polluting. It very quickly became apparent that the job was truly immense, because the company was disposing of solid wastes in literally hundreds of company locations. The group could only sample, not study, the company's pollution programs.

Another reason for this difficulty is stubborn internal resistance. Even if the CEO wants a social audit, he is likely to encounter foot dragging, if not outright opposition, within his own family. In conglomerates in particular, division managers resent what they perceive as an intrusion into "their" private files.

Also, managers do not seem to care much for morale surveys to see what the people they supervise think of the company and its record in social performance. Others disagree philosophically with the whole social-responsibility idea; some even say that if the boss wants to fool around with it at his level and work with the Boy's Club somewhere, okay—but he had better keep his liberal do-goodism out of operations. This kind of controversy has forced more than one CEO to back off and scale down his internal audit from what he had intended.

In one company, the headquarters staff started to audit the condition of the employees because they thought it would be the easiest way to cut their teeth before they began to audit other matters. Believing that equal employment was well accepted in the company, both as the law of the land and the right thing to do, they sent people to check records in one of the divisions.

The division head, however, flatly refused to let them look at the files; and when he finally did consent to open the drawers as a result of a topside order, he continued to be as uncooperative as possible within the terms of the directive he had received. At this point, the company began to reconsider the whole social-audit idea.

5. How accurate can we be?

Unfortunately, there has been an inordinate amount of loose talk about the social audit, much of it in responsible journals or in responsible places. For example, Thomas Oliphant, writing in *The Boston Globe,* said: "Almost all of this data exists right now on some corporate executive's desk. What is lacking is the decision to put it all together and release it to the public in a manner modeled roughly after financial accounting standards to ensure a maximum of information and a bare minimum of public relations."[1] To that statement, and the many similar ones being made today, we reply, "Nonsense."

But, unfortunately, it is worse than nonsense. The twin myths that such a thing as a social audit exists and that financial audits are hard and precise have misled some businessmen into trying to create a report on their social performance which has the same precision and accuracy they attribute to the balance sheet.

The fact is that we are not yet at the point where such an audit is possible, and we may never get there—indeed, we may never have to. The social audit, even when we have learned how to do one that is credible internally and externally, may look nothing like a financial audit at all. We are only on the edge of the thicket, and what we really need is not a man with *the* answer, but a number of men with the courage to try to frame *an* answer—to experiment, to learn about how to measure and report on social performance, and to pass what they learn along to the rest of us.

The Abt experiment: Only one of the companies we studied, Abt Associates, had completed anything that could meaningfully be called a social audit.

The Abt audit of its own activities is a public document included in the firm's annual report. It is an effort to represent, in purely dollar terms, the company's social assets and liabilities—in other words, its social impact. This represents a diligent and ingenious pioneering work, especially on the part of the president, Dr. Clark Abt, who spearheaded the effort. However, considering the novelty of this effort, it is no surprise that the firm's accountants did not give it their official sanction.

There are various reasons why we think that this format is *not* the one most likely to be adopted by large, complex companies:

> • It does not appear to respond to the currently perceived needs of the executives of such organizations nor to the realities of their situations, as we understand them. For example, the Abt audit is organized around

---

[1]The New Accounting: Profit, Loss and Society," May 1971.

the total social impact of the company rather than around an assessment of its social programs. While this approach has great conceptual attractiveness, it is not particularly well adapted to the needs which are expressed by the executives with whom we are familiar, whose concerns, objectives, and aspirations for an audit are far more limited than Dr. Abt's.

• Abt Associates is a relatively small consulting firm. The total social impact of a large complex company is not nearly so amenable to this kind of financial summary.

• The goal of the Abt audit, once again, is to render social performance in dollar terms in balance sheet form. Thus it does not disclose (it may even hide) the firm's performance in social programs in which its executives are interested. For example, a company could be spending large amounts of money inefficiently, on pollution control or hard-core training, on giving substantial sums to irrelevant charities. And, indeed, in the course of conducting his audit, Abt found out some unwelcome facts about his organization and changed policy accordingly. But the actual rendering of his findings into balance sheet form was, in our view, a superfluous technical exercise. Our sense is that few companies are interested in supporting this last step of technical virtuosity *if the information can meaningfully be presented in other ways.*

• Abt's audit is designed for external reporting. However, most executives are interested at this time in internal reporting for internal assessment. The prospect of external reporting exacerbates the already considerable anxiety of such executives.

• Finally, the Abt form of a social audit is so abstract and complicated that we find few, if any, executives (never mind laymen) who claim to understand it as an overall entity—nor do we feel we can explain it as a totality.

We do, however, encourage the reader to consult the Abt annual report to form an independent judgment. We may well be too sharply critical; and, indeed, we have a personal bias to which we must confess. We feel that the attempt to reduce social performance to dollar terms is perverse. While monetary measures are of great utility in many contexts, this utility is, finally, limited; we feel there is likely to be fatal error in employing the dollar measures as exhaustive representations of social phenomena.

Our judgment is not so negative with respect to proposals for auditing the dollar *costs* of social contributions, although we are respectful of both the difficulties and the tricky judgmental questions imbedded in such calculating. Mainly we are skeptical of the availability and possibility of rendering the social *consequences* —whether positive or negative—in dollar terms.

All in all, given the complexities and complications of doing a social audit, given the various forms which an audit might take, and given the varying uses to which it might be put, we judge it a mistake to specify at this time just what its final form should or will be. Instead, we believe that the task of management for the immediate future is to get on the learning curve.

This is best accomplished by tackling the auditing problem in a way that is sufficiently modest to be attainable, yet of sufficient scope to have both some utility and some value as a base for more ambitious versions of the social audit. The first steps toward a social audit also should be defined with an eye toward the organizational conflicts that a social audit can bring about.

HINTS FOR GETTING STARTED

Thus our first suggestion is that the audit be initially designed for internal purposes only—that is, for aiding in the decision making process and for helping officers assess the company's social performance, both with a view to its vulnerabilities and to changes that management may want to make in its activities. Such a course offers dual benefits.

For one thing, it relieves the anxieties of those corporate officers who fear the embarrassment of disclosure, enabling the company to make corrections with a certain amount of privacy if it chooses to do so. Equally, it allows officers to take what guidance they can from data and judgments that may be too imprecise to present to the public, and it bypasses their natural fears that their professional and financial future may be adversely affected.

We make this suggestion—that the first effort to a social audit be aimed at internal decision making—in full recognition that the audit is likely to be reported to the public sooner or later. We only propose that there be no initial *commitment* to publication of the first-round audit, so that this learning experience can be entered into with a minimum of anxiety and a minimum of demand for technical elegance.

We also suggest that a company first focus on its programs rather than on its social impact. There are three strong practical reasons for this recommendation. Two of them are those we just cited for aiming the audit at internal decision making: the magnitude of the task and executive anxiety. The task of considering, measuring, and evaluating all the impacts of a large, complex company on society boggles the mind; it also seems very threatening to anxious executives, since the results of such an analysis may strike at the very core of the business. A deodorant manufacturer might become a stench in its own nostrils.

The third reason is the sheer difficulty of defining the limits of social impact, which is surely a conceptual haymaker, as terms go.

Again we recognize the limitations and counterarguments to what we are proposing. For many industries, one could argue that a company's social activities are merely cosmetics that conceal the impact of its regular business activities. There is little reason for crediting a drug company, say, with an excellent domestic employment policy without investigating its promotion policies and labeling practices in other countries. This counterargument concludes that the auditor's concern must be global. Nonetheless, we advise early simplification for the sake of avoiding endless debates that might well take on the color of theological disputes.

We also recognize that when a company is examining its social programs, it may also want to look at its regular business activities as a separate, parallel effort, especially if either its internal or external constituencies are demanding such an examination or are likely to do so.

For example, one bank is looking at the impact of its lending policies, realizing that these are related to the social audit it is undertaking; but the bank is not at this stage considering the policy investigation as part of the audit. Similarly, even where public pressure encourages or forces a company to look at one or more of its regular business activities—for example, munitions manufacturing, construction in Vietnam, or doing business in South Africa—such examinations ought to be handled separately from the initial audit.

If companies accept these two suggestions—focusing only on internal use and social program evaluation—life will be much simpler, but still complicated enough to be interesting. The audit will have a "meaningful, definable domain," as our statement suggests it must, but the domain will still be virgin wilderness.

We must point out, however, that a compromise is available which some companies may prefer to adopt. A company may feel it imperative to define those constituencies to which its actions are most relevant—employees, customers, stockholders, "the community," and so on—and survey these constituencies to determine for which aspects of social performance they hold the company responsible and what their expectations are.

This procedure would establish a "definable domain" for social auditing in a quite different fashion from the path we have recommended; but it has one defensive advantage worth mentioning, namely, public attitudes. Its disadvantage may be that it probably does not provide as valuable a learning experience as our more orderly first step does for the company that plans to build toward a more complete audit. Hence, on balance, we believe that concentration on social programs as the "defined domain" is the preferable route.

Inventory + cost

Assuming a company decides to review its social programs first, its next step should be to compile an inventory of its explicitly social programs. For almost every company, this list will include the currently popular issues of pollution control, minority and female hiring, and promotion practices. Let us say that it will also include corporate giving. From there on, the nature of the list is likely to vary with the corporation in question, and it will not always be easy to decide what ought to be included and what ought to be excluded, or why.

A typical instance of such a difficulty is whether to include executive participation in community affairs when the executives contribute their own time. Our advice is to exclude any item from the list that is not the result of an explicit corporate policy involving a meaningful level of resource commitment. We also advise companies to exclude any item that causes substantial argument. (Of course, a company would do well to keep a list of rejected items, for future perspective.)

There will be other kinds of difficulty as well. In some instances, management may discover that there is no central source of information on everything the company is doing in the social area; hence compiling the list may take more effort than one would expect or accept.

Once the inventory has been reduced to those socially motivated activities to which the company has clearly made a commitment and which it accepts as "social programs," management can begin to assemble the costs and performance data associated with them, to get a picture of the extent of the company's commitment to each one and to social programs as a whole.

The first area is the matter of costs. Generally, there will be less difficulty in getting the direct costs of each activity than in ascertaining the true costs, which is quite a different matter, as we have already pointed out. These true costs should include allocated overhead and opportunity costs as well, wherever the resources might have been put to different use. A company's ability to get such true costs readily will depend on how the relevant items are represented in its accounting system, what system it is using to measure work, and the like. One should also realize that even if the basic data are available, special allocation conventions may be required.

Since considerable expense and effort are required, the auditors and management should make an explicit decision as to whether they deem it worthwhile to establish the true costs of social activities, whether they are willing to go with a rough estimate, or whether they will be content with knowing only the direct costs.

Our sense is that the public at large is not likely to be interested in the true costs of a company's social activities. Even though the true costs would represent a more accurate picture of the company's level of effort, they are likely to be perceived as padded figures.

However, for *management* decision making, true cost will be important. If it proves difficult to get true costs in the first audit attempt, and a decision is made to forgo this information, this circumstance should signal the need for establishing mechanisms for assessing true costs in the future. It is highly probable that there is no thoroughly satisfactory way to do this at present, although Professors Neil Churchill and John Shank are currently researching this problem at the Harvard Business School.

The second area of quantitative measurement is performance data. The place to start is still readily available statistical data that show the level of effort expended and measure the output. For example, how many hard-core unemployed have been trained, or apartments renovated, or children served in a day-care center? It is true, as we have pointed out, that pulling together such material may be difficult. It is also true that this kind of material does not necessarily show, in and of itself, the *effectiveness* of the programs.

Perhaps the assistance extended to minority businesses has in fact done more harm than good in that the funds generated ultimately are spent outside the inner city, or the failures have served to discourage people from starting ventures instead of encouraging them to do so. But we shall return to this difficult matter of norms and social benefits in a moment. Suffice to say at this point that there are some figures that can be obtained, and that they do constitute legitimate data for a social audit.

Here again, we would opt for a kind of "creaming" approach. Rather than spending inordinate amounts of time either in determining what figures should be collected or which should be included, we would urge that the most obvious and easily ascertainable be the ones that are reported. It is too early in the state of the art to try to squeeze out the last, ultimate figure or to fight through the finest kind of judgments as to what should be in or out.

Ethics of public reporting. These first two steps of an audit will give a picture of the extent and nature of the company's social programs and of the resources committed thereto. The display of just these two sets of information will be of help to many managements in assessing their social performance. These sets of information could also be the basis for reporting to the public, should management choose to do so.

It may be argued that reporting data such as these is very little different than what is being done for public relations purposes by many companies in their annual reports or in special publications. We grant this. But we see nothing wrong in a company's communicating the extent and nature of its social activities and the magnitude of effort behind those activities, provided the coverage is complete and the reporting honest.

Such an audit would at least reveal the extent of the company's concern. One of us recently conducted a study of the reaction of Bostonians to the efforts Boston business was making to help the community, and we were struck by the fact that success or failure, or even quantity of effort, is outweighed in people's minds by evidence that companies or individuals actually are concerned and are doing something about it. Businessmen are not expected to solve the problems of the city, nor are they expected to be successful in every venture they undertake. However, they are expected to take the problems seriously.

Thus an honest and straightforward public reporting of what a company is doing, accompanied by the figures that are available, seems to us to be perfectly appropriate if public reporting is the name of the game.

Questions of measures and norms

We know a fair number of companies that have taken one or both of these first two steps—inventorying activities and assessing costs. Some have done it as part of a social audit activity; others, for the more straightforward reason that management wanted to know what the company was doing. None found that this was a trivial effort, and a number found that the mere assemblage of information as to what the company was doing was already of value to management.

However, we doubt that managers who take the concept of a social audit seriously will want to stop at this point. They will want to make an assessment of how well they are doing in their various social activities. Since this seems to us to be an inevitable direction for the social audit, we would encourage this step—but with moderation, because assessing performance is beset with grave difficulties. Assessment in the first audit should be limited to only several of the most important activities.

Here we must distinguish between cases where true measures of performance are available and cases where they are not (we shall discuss the second of these possibilities when we describe the process audit).

Now a true performance measure is a measure of the ultimate result that an activity is intended to accomplish. We have already identified the two types of program areas for which performance measures are most likely to be available—pollution and employment. Some of these performance measures may be the fallout of the "easily available" data which are noted at the inventory stage, but such data are bound to be incomplete; a company is very likely to have data available on emissions into the air and water, for example, but it is not equally likely to know about its contribution to solid waste. Personnel records, too, will vary with respect to the availability of information about the employment of minorities.

Norms, also, are required, and once again the picture is cloudy and uneven. There are laws of various kinds by which to judge one's levels of emissions into air and water, but not for emissions of solid waste. Nor are there likely to be industrywide norms of performance unless the industry in question has been studied by the Council for Economic Priorities or some similar organization.

Some commentators suggest that one should judge pollution performance by what is technologically feasible, and this may work out in some cases; however, cost/benefit trade-offs are only too likely to crop up. Again, companies can get industry norms for the employment status of minorities from the Equal Employment Opportunities Commission, but these industrywide norms may have to be adjusted to the idiosyncracies of the communities in which a company's installations are located.

However, while it may be possible to get adequate performance measures and norms for some of a company's social programs, for others it will be difficult to the point of virtual impossibility. The results of a community development program, for example, perhaps will not be clear until sometime in the future, and a particular company's contributions to these developments will be hard to isolate even then. Again, management might be satisfied with judging a program for training the hard-core unemployed by the number of candidates who graduate from the program and secure employment, but management might also view these numbers as only intermediate measures of the long-term effects which it regards as crucial.

Wherever the auditing team and management feel that there are no adequate performance measures of a social program—and this is likely to be true of almost all service programs—we advocate a *process* audit, which we shall now describe. We have not yet seen such a process audit completed. What we propose takes as its model such innovative efforts of the accounting profession as the management audit.[2]

THE PROCESS AUDIT

The first step in a process audit should be an assessment of the circumstances under which each social program being audited came into being. (We consciously avoid saying "the reason" for the program, since in many instances the circumstance is likely to be less rational than the term "reason" implies.) While this search into origins may at first glance look like navel gazing, it is likely to be crucial for informed future decision making. A company that does not know how it gets into things is likely to get into things it does not want to do.

The second step is to explicate the goals of the program—that is, to produce a statement of what it is intended to accomplish.

The third is to spell out the rationale behind the activity. A company should specify what it proposes to do to attain the goals, and why it thinks this set of actions will achieve them.

The final step in the process audit is to describe what is actually being done as opposed to what the rationale says ought to be done. We assume that this description will include any relevant quantitative measures, such as numbers and types of persons served, and any available intermediate measures of performance, such as proportions of defaults on loans.

The goal of such a process audit is to assemble the information that will make it possible for a person to intelligently assess the program, to decide whether he agrees with its goals, to decide whether the rationale is appropriate to the goals, and to judge whether the actual implementation promises to attain those goals satisfactorily.

Process audits are most likely to be appropriate for service programs, which are notoriously hard to evaluate but around which considerable amounts of expertise develop. Thus appropriate norms for process audits are likely to be standards of best practice. Where it seems in order, then, a process audit might be conducted

---

[2]See Olin C. Snellgrave, "The Management: Organizational Guidance System," *Management Review,* March 1972, pp. 41–45.

in part by one or another expert in the area, especially since companies vary considerably in their relevant in-house capabilities.

Even where the purpose of the audit is just to clarify internal decision making, a company may want to bring in an outside expert to help define the relevant factors to assess and to make the final evaluation of a program. When such expertise is brought to bear, management can better judge whether it is satisfied with present activities, whether it wants one or another changed and improved, and whether it wants to shift its efforts among activities.

Once all the above information is assembled for management scrutiny, and possibly for presentation to the public (an option always open to management), we would regard the first round of a social audit to be completed. It seems likely that the public will be uninterested in the first step of the process audit we have proposed—namely, the circumstances under which the company undertook the activity (though there may be instances where this is relevant). However, the remaining steps develop information that would be helpful and acceptable to the public in its evaluation of the company's performance.

There are many ways in which an initial process will be incomplete and imperfect, compared with what a company might aspire to later. It may be bulky and cumbersome. The format will be unstandardized. Only a portion of the company's social impact will be assessed. And of that which is assessed, only the most important activities will be given any treatment beyond bare identification, description, and specification of costs. Furthermore, such technical problems as assessment of true costs and performance measurement will be handled in a fairly rough and ready manner.

But the show will be on the road. Management will be in a considerably better position to make decisions and take actions. It will also know whether it wants to report to the public at this stage; and if it does, it will have a respectable report from which to work. Furthermore:

- The foundations for future auditing will have been laid.

- The nucleus of an auditing team will have been trained.

- The controller will have had his first taste of the problem of assessing the true costs of social programs.

- Management will have a realistic basis for estimating what an audit costs and is worth.

- Hopefully, the fears of corporate executives will be surfaced and assuaged.

- To the extent that management thinks it desirable, it can build expanded ambitions into future audits.

- The very fact that management has undertaken an honest, systematic effort will be a plus.

The reader will note that we have said nothing about the relationship between responsibility and profitability. This is intentional. We have specifically excluded from our version of a first audit any attempt to assess the contribution of social activities to the profitability of a company. We believe that this exercise is possible only in the case of a minority of such activities, and that the attempt to complete this exercise, while having a certain appeal to technical virtuosity, is likely to divert attention from the more straightforward objectives we have proposed—namely, management information and public reporting.

The future needs

We close on the question of whether a company can carry out such an audit on itself. As the reader would expect, there is not a yes-or-no answer to this question. It is better to rephrase the question and ask whether the company can benefit from outside help. In fact, at present, there is not much outside help to turn to. Only a few consultants have had any experience in social auditing, and the experience of even those few is limited.

Our conclusion is that a certain amount of outside help can be useful both as a source of discipline and direction, and as a spur to keep the audit moving. Most companies have had trouble on these scores. Outsiders can also supply technical help on such matters as assembling true costs, preparing information for distribution to management and the public, and the process audit.

Eventually, we assume, if the social audit develops viably, the accounting profession will be centrally involved, both in setting up systems to gather data and in attesting to the truth of the data for the purpose of improving its credibility. This is already a matter of considerable interest in the accounting profession, but at this point everyone in the race is standing on the same starting line. The most important task now is to start running. Only in that way will we learn what the track is really like.

An Approach
to Socio-Economic
Accounting

David F. Linowes

"Social audits" will be required within the next decade for most business organizations, the author is convinced. Prepared by an internal interdisciplinary committee and audited by an external socio-economic audit committee, they will be demanded by consumer groups, special institutional investors, and an increasing number of regulatory governmental agencies. Before long business will be expected also to prepare Socio-Economic Operating Budgets to project what the company expects to do in the social area during the succeeding year:

"Business managers must have available a meaningful measure of their long-range social and economic commitments for all the world to see and evaluate, along with the short-range measurement of profit-making operational activities which have always been given broad visibility through the profit and loss statements. The Socio-Economic Operating Statement fills this need."

Business management today is functioning in a new environment and is being forced to assume a share of society's problems. This is no longer news. But it is now also becoming apparent that the challenge to the role of business has become so widespread that executives can no longer look to dollar-profit measurement alone as an adequate reflection of their effectiveness. With the expanding exposure of business to the various facets of society, the traditional measurement of profitability and growth reflected both in the profit-loss statement and balance sheet are no longer adequate.

Financial analysts have always been aware that those managements which neglect their machinery and equipment and do not make expenditures to train junior executives often show a higher earnings picture during the short term than is justified. In time, of course, this neglect of equipment and executive personnel training takes its toll in the operating effectiveness of the company, but for the present, the profits look better.

Those companies which undertake actions which may benefit society and incur costs for such activity are in effect being "penalized" on their profit and loss

From *The Conference Board Record,* November, 1972. Reprinted by special permission of The Conference Board.

statements for such activity. Costs of hiring and training hardcore unemployables, making executives available to assist ghetto entrepreneurs, and incurring extra costs for environmental improvements presently serve to hurt the record of progressive management because they are charged as expenses against its operations. Obviously, business managements may show better operating profit results by not incurring these extra costs and by ignoring the harm caused by dumping production waste into streams or polluting the atmosphere.

In our present system of business reporting, however, we do not measure— or report in any statement of a management's stewardship—the damage done to that stream or to the air we breathe. Nor do we, on the other hand, give proper reporting credit for the "good" that management does, either.

Admittedly, social programs are sometimes difficult to define. That does not mean we should not try to deal with them, for I am certain that society will no longer condone further avoiding of accountability. And I believe, clearly defined or not, we know a social action or nonaction when we see it. As Justice Potter Steward said of obscenity. "I can't define obscenity but I know it when I see it."

GIVING THAT GOES BEYOND THE LAW

Basically, the concept of what is included in a social action program is what a business has given to or held back from society. If this seems somewhat vague, the purpose is to permit management the widest latitude in the measurement of these activities and to encourage innovation. We must also make distinctions between the costs of actions voluntarily undertaken and those social programs required by law and/or contract, e.g., with the union or with local authorities, since these are arm's-length negotiated business deals and therefore a necessary cost of doing business. Thus a voluntary social action program *today* may be a necessary cost of doing business *tomorrow* by the passage of legislation or the decision of a court.

It may be years before we can invent and use social measurement with the confidence and relative precision with which we use economic and fiscal measurements in business and government, but we do have enough standards available now with which to begin. Indeed, considering the softness of much of the economic and fiscal data used (and often misused) today, I would think that the results of social measurements with all their present limitations can be just as effective as economic measurements.

What we might do at once, then, is to borrow from economics and apply the "system" of economic and fiscal measurement to social areas. It is this that I call Socio-Economic Measurement.

Dollars involving social costs incurred by business are usually determinable. However, the fact that a prepared statement of these costs may not be complete is not sufficient reason for us to delay further the preparation and use of such exhibits. Traditional financial statements have never themselves been able to reflect significant facets of business affairs fully—e.g., contingent assets such as the value of trained manpower, extent of provision for executive succession, potential profitability of new inventions and product development, or contingent liabilities which include potential adverse legal actions for faulty products.

MEASURING SOCIAL "DETRIMENTS" AND "IMPROVEMENTS"

There should be no reason to forbid us from developing a Socio-Economic Operating Statement (SEOS). It would be prepared periodically along with a business organization's profit and loss statement and balance sheet. The SEOS I visualize is a tabulation of those expenditures made voluntarily by a business aimed at the "improvement" of the welfare of the employees and public, safety of the product, and/or conditions of the environment. Such expenditures required by law or union contract would not be includable, inasmuch as these are mandatory and necessary costs of doing business.

An item is determined to be a "detriment" or negative charge for SEO Statement purposes when a responsible authority brings the need for social action to the attention of management, but management does not voluntarily take steps to satisfy such a need, even though it is of such a nature that a *reasonably prudent and socially aware business management* would have responded favorably. The fact that this determination is a subjective one should not discourage its implementation. In traditional business accounting, research and development items, work in process inventories, allowances for bad debts, depreciation charges, price-earnings ratios are also largely subjective determinations.

Several guidelines to help identify and classify socio-economic items can be offered:

> • If a socially beneficial action is required by law, but is ignored, the cost of such item is a "detriment" for the year. The same treatment is given an item if postponed, even with government approval. Similarly, if a socially beneficial action is required by law and is applied earlier than the law requires, it is an improvement. (In an inflationary period this might mean a saving of money for the company and could be categorized as a contingent asset.)

> • A pro-rata portion of salaries and related expenses of personnel who spent time in socially beneficial actions or with social organizations is included as an "improvement."

> • Cash and product contributions to social institutions are included as "improvements."

> • Cost of setting up facilities for the general good of employees or the public—without union or government requirement—is an includable "improvement."

• Neglecting to install safety devices which are available at a reasonable cost is a "detriment."

• The cost of voluntarily building a playground or nursery school for employees and/or neighbors is a plus on the exhibit. Operating costs of the facility in each succeeding year are also includable.

• Costs of relandscaping strip mining sites, or other environmental eyesores, if not otherwise required by law, are listed as improvements on the SEOS exhibit.

• Extra costs in designing and building unusually attractive business facilities for beauty, health and safety are includable "improvements."

The results of an SEO Statement produce an amount of "Total Socio-Economic Contribution or Deficit for the Year." It can be effectively used by comparing such statements for various companies in the same industry. Also, analyzing SEO Statements for a particular company over several years helps establish the general directions of the social involvement of a company's management.

THE SOCIAL AUDIT AS AN OPERATING STATEMENT

The various positive and negative social actions and inactions mentioned are classified on the SEOS exhibit into three groups: *Relations with People, Relations with Environment* and *Relations with Product.* The Socio-Economic Operating Statement that I recommend be instituted would then have the appearance of the chart below.

XXXX CORPORATION
Socio-Economic Operating Statement for the Year Ending December 31, 1971

I *Relations with People:*
    A. *Improvements:*

1. Training program for handicapped workers	$ 10,000	
2. Contribution to educational institution	4,000	
3. Extra turnover costs because of minority hiring program	5,000	
4. Cost of nursery school for children of employees, voluntarily set up	11,000	
Total Improvements		$ 30,000
B. *Less: Detriments*		
1. Postponed installing new safety devices on cutting machines (cost of the devices)		14,000
C. Net Improvements in People Actions for the Year		$ 16,000*

II *Relations with Environment:*
   A. *Improvements:*
     1. Cost of reclaiming and landscaping old
        dump on company property $ 70,000
     2. Cost of installing pollution control devices
        on Plant A smokestacks   4,000
     3. Cost of detoxifying waste from finishing
        process this year   9,000

   Total Improvements $ 83,000

   B. *Less: Detriments*
     1. Cost that would have been incurred to
        relandscape strip mining site used
        this year $ 80,000
     2 Estimated costs to have installed purification
        process to neutralize poisonous liquid being
        dumped into stream   100,000
                                        $180,000

   C. Net Deficit in Environment Actions for the
      Year   ($ 97,000)*

III *Relations with Product:*
   A. *Improvements:*
     1. Salary of V.P. while serving on government
        Product Safety Commission $ 25,000
     2. Cost of substituting lead-free paint for
        previously used poisonous lead paint   9,000

   Total Improvements $ 34,000

   B. *Less: Detriments*
     1. Safety device recommended by Safety Council
        but not added to product   22,000

   C. Net Improvements in Product Actions for the
      Year $ 12,000*

   Total Socio-Economic Deficit for the Year   ($ 69,000)

   Add: Net Cumulative Socio-Economic Improvements
     as at January 1, 1971 $249,000

Grand Total Net Socio-Economic Actions to December 31, 1971 $180,000

PREPARING THE SOCIO-ECONOMIC OPERATING STATEMENT

The SEOS exhibits themselves would be prepared by a small interdisciplinary team headed by an accountant. Other members of the team could include a seasoned business executive, sociologist, public health administrator, economist, or mem-

---

*The starred items are summed to obtain the Total Socio-Economic Deficit for the year 1971.

bers of other disciplines whose specific expertise might apply to a particular industry or circumstance. Although SEO Statements would be prepared internally by an interdisciplinary group, they should be audited by an outside independent interdisciplinary team headed by a CPA.

Though determination of items to be included in the SEOS is to be based upon subjective judgments, a standard dollar value applied to these improvements or "detriments" would be a combination of what businessmen traditionally classify as capital expenditures and expense expenditures. For example, the full cost of a permanent installation of a pollution control device is included in the SEO Statement in the year the cost is voluntarily incurred, as is the annual operating cost of a hardcore minority group training program. For convenience of reference, the totals could be expressed in Socio-Economic Management Dollars (SEM$) so as to identify all expenditures made voluntarily of a socially beneficial nature.

Specific cost items which would be entered on a SEO Statement as "improvements" or positive actions would include:

1. Cost of training program for handicapped workers.
2. Contribution to educational institutions.
3. Extra turnover costs because of minority hiring policy. (The adverse of this item, the cost of not setting up adequate orientation programs, would be included as detrimental nonactions.)
4. Cost of nursery school for children of employees, voluntarily set up.
5. Cost of reclaiming and landscaping old dump on company property.
6. Cost of installing pollution control devices on smokestacks ahead of legal requirements.
7. Cost of detoxifying waste from finishing process this year, ahead of legal requirement.
8. Salary of vice president while serving on government Product Safety Commission.
9. Cost of substituting lead-free paint for previously used poisonous lead paint.

Contrariwise, these specific costs would be entered on the SEOS as negative or detrimental nonactions:

1. Postponed installing new safety devices on cutting machines (cost of the devices).
2. Cost that would have been incurred to relandscape strip mining site used this year.
3. Estimated cost to have installed a purification process to neutralize polluting liquid being dumped into stream.
4. Cost of safety devices recommended by Safety Council but not added to product.

I would emphasize that some of these examples may no longer be includable on a current Socio-Economic Operating Statement, but they serve to illustrate.

Should Business Adopt the Social Audit?
A review of some of the considerations which must be in the mind of management

George A. Steiner

The notion that a business should make a "social audit" of its activities was first proposed almost 20 years ago.[1] For almost as long the idea lay dormant. Within the past year, however, there has been a surprising revival of interest in it, both in and outside the business community.

Fundamentally, a social audit refers to an evaluation of the social, as distinct from the economic, performance of a business. But even now, there is no consensus about whether a business should or should not make one. Nor is there unanimity, assuming it should, about what it is, how to go about doing it, or the problems involved in making it. Nevertheless, there are a number of specific considerations an individual company may take into account in connection with audits, even though no general standards now exist.

Most chief executives of businesses, especially the larger ones, are quite familiar with rising public expectations of their company's performance. The stockholder expects rapid growth and either higher dividends or stockmarket per share prices, or both. Workers expect higher wage rates and fringe benefits. Consumers expect better products, at cheaper prices, and better service. The community expects the corporation to clean up the environment, hire the jobless, rebuild our cities, and to solve other difficult problems which exist in society.

It is important to note that, except for a very few voices, these pressures are expected to be relieved by improving the social performance of business rather than by having the state take over the operation of individual businesses. The accelerating pressures for better social performance of business is driving managers

From *The Conference Board Record,* May, 1972. Reprinted by special permission of The Conference Board.

[1]Howard R. Bowen, *Society Responsibilities of the Businessman* (New York, Harper & Brothers, 1953).

to think more carefully about and to assume more social responsibilities. Concurrently, a growing number of individuals, groups, and institutions are appointing themselves as evaluators of the social performance of individual companies. To illustrate, the following organizations have or are now measuring the social performance of individual companies: The United Church of Christ, the Dreyfus Fund, the Council of Economic Priorities, Ralph Nader's organization, and the National Association of Concerned Business Students.

Management's interest in social audits reflects pressures such as these. There is every reason to anticipate that these pressures will intensify and broaden in the future.

Top managers are on the horns of a dilemma. If they are insensitive to growing demands that their companies improve their social performance, they will be criticized and demands will be made for the government to act. If they go too far in responding to these demands, they can jeopardize their economic performance, be subject to different types of censure and perhaps invite government regulations of a different sort.

We are in need today of creditable criteria for determining what responsibilities individual companies have and how far they should go in meeting them. In the meantime, the business social audit is one step a company may take to begin the process of sorting out for itself which social responsibilities it wishes to assume.

The words social audit, social accounting, or social accountabiltity imply an arithmetical or quantitatively measurable evaluation. Such precision does not and probably cannot exist with respect to measures of social performance. If corporations are to measure their social performance, we stand in great need of acceptable standards. But even with a major effort to develop such measures it is not likely that standards can be sufficiently formulated to approach in accuracy and acceptability the accountant's audit of economic performance. Both the words "social" and "audit" have other characteristics which may not be too suitable for describing what is in mind here.

I prefer a different, but somewhat more cumbersome shorthand, namely, "evaluation of corporate societal policies and actions," or, "evaluation of business responsibilities." Among other reasons, I feel this phraseology is a bit more positive, a little less accusatory, somewhat more tentative, and more descriptive of what is going on.

It is pertinent to ask the question: Should social audits be made of individual business performance? If one accepts the classical view that the only responsibility of a business is to maximize profit, the answer is clearly no. On the other hand, if one accepts the view that there are social responsibilities which individual businesses must perform, the answer is yes. The question then becomes: What type of social audit should be made?

If one accepts the view that business does have social responsibilities, one then must ask: Precisely what are the social responsibilities of an individual business, and how far should it go in pursuing them? Unfortunately, there is no consensus about an answer to these questions.[2]

THE QUESTION OF GOALS

Individuals and groups outside business have different objectives in making their social audits of individual companies. Generally, however, the end result sought is to make business more socially responsible as the individuals and groups who are measuring the performance see that responsibility. So far as an individual business is concerned, I see five major purposes of a social audit.

First, it is to identify those social responsibilities which a company thinks it ought to be discharging. In commenting on this point it is important to have in mind a definition of social responsibilities which a business may perform. Very succinctly, business social responsibilities can be classified in three different ways. Conceptually, social responsibilities generally refer to actions which a company takes partially with a view to helping society achieve objectives which it sets for itself. They also may be classified into internal and external activities. Internally, they may refer to such matters as due process, justice, and equity in hiring, promoting, or firing employees. Externally, they may concern a wide range of actions from improving consumer products to training and hiring hardcore unemployed. Finally, they may be considered in terms of profit. Some socially responsible actions may increase both short- and long-range profits. Others can reduce both.

If these definitions are accepted, socially responsible business actions include those which traditionally have been encompassed in a concept of business integrity, business morality, and good citizenship. But there is an added dimension. It is that socially responsible business actions include those which will help society achieve its goals. Today, a very significant goal which business is expected to help achieve is the improvement of the quality of life of more people. Unfortunately, there is no consensus about what, precisely, are the goals that society collectively wishes to achieve. There are only general concepts. The fact that there is no set of firm social goals does not, however, reduce the pressure upon business to help meet what different people and groups consider the goals to be. It makes the problem more difficult for business.

So, the range of possible activities which a social audit may encompass is rather wide. There can be included product quality-service combinations to meet consumer satisfactions, designs of new plants to meet employee and community esthetic needs, or rebuilding the ghettos. It is obvious that the spectrum of possible action is well beyond the range of even the giant corporations. Every company, if it gets to the point of making a social audit, will have to choose the activities it wishes to concentrate on.

---

[2]George A. Steiner, *Business and Society* (New York, Random House, 1971). See especially Chapter 9, "The Social Responsibilities of Business," and the extensive bibliography.

Second, once the areas of concern are chosen the company then needs to examine what it is doing and how satisfactory is the performance. To measure performance one needs standards. At the present time, however, there are few generally accepted standards. It is important that business get involved in the development of standards for if it does not, government and private groups will set them.

For some types of activities it is possible to measure performance against quantitative standards, e.g., minority employment, employment of women, meeting pollution standards, or improving worker productivity. Many activities cannot be measured quantitatively, such as quality of advertising, or meeting employee demands for job enrichment. Some standards for such activities, however, may be developed by surveys of opinion.

Third, once performance is measured against a standard the next question is: If there is a gap, how far should the company go in filling it? Here, of course, it is necessary to make cost/benefit calculations which often are more matters of judgment than quantitative conclusions. This is a new type of equation for business and will be of growing importance to it. Costs and benefits must be defined in terms well beyond traditional financial or broad economic measures to include, for example, such matters as impacts of *not* doing something (costs) versus advantages to the community in taking some action (benefits). There is no universal method to make a broad cost/benefit analysis.

Fourth, an audit may be designed to determine whether a company is vulnerable to potential criticism and attack. This purpose, of course, is a defensive one. In a large company activities may be taking place, unknown to top management, which may be the cause of severe criticism if the public is informed about them. For instance, a remote plant may be polluting the atmosphere contrary to the policy of the company and the laws of the local community.

Finally, a company may make an audit in order to inject into the thinking of managers at all levels a social point of view. The idea is to institutionalize social concerns into the job of each manager.

Overall, of course, the objective is to make an evaluation which will put a company into a position to examine its actions in light of changing social expectations and, thereby, to determine whether it is or is not responding appropriately. The measure of appropriateness can be determined by management, by government, by interests focused on the company, or by a combination of all.

WHAT SHOULD BE INCLUDED?

What should be included in a social audit, as noted above, depends upon what the company wishes to include. Choice may be made from among a wide range of activities. One list of major fields in which a corporation could pursue its social responsibilities includes: economic growth and efficiency, education, employment and training, civil rights and equal opportunity, urban renewal and development, pollution abatement, conservation and recreation, culture and the arts, medical care, and government—and it detailed 58 subgroupings in these areas.

The list from which a company might choose could also be developed in terms of internal versus external activities, or it might be centered on the major social problems which face society today. If the focus is on problems, the fields to be listed, in addition to those noted above, would include: poverty, prices, people congestion, privacy, space and beauty, transportation congestion, minority entre-preneurship, and research and development.

All this illustrates two points: There is no consensus about the spectrum of activities from which a company might choose, and the list is rather broad in scope.

So, too, the depth of analysis, and the form of presentation will, of course, vary for each situation. The range can be from a comparatively quick appraisal by one staff man of a limited array of activities to a rather comprehensive analysis in considerable depth made by a study team.

WHO SHOULD "SOCIAL AUDIT" . . . AND FOR WHOM?

Bowen suggested that an outside team should make the audit for a company in order to assure high objectivity. But he cautioned that the team should be capable and include persons conversant with business practices and problems, socially oriented, and technically capable in major areas related to the audit (e.g., management, economics, government, engineering, sociology, etc.).

The opposite, of course, is for a company to set up a team of its own members. Other approaches would be to give the job to a committee composed of members of the board of directors, or to hire an outside consultant to work with managers of the company. Another possibility would be for a group of companies operating in a common area to employ a team to study all the companies.

Each of these possibilities, of course, has its own set of strengths and weaknesses and they vary with each company's situation. Experience to date provides few guidelines for determining the preferred approaches.

Each company must in its own wisdom come to a decision about whether the report, or parts of it, should be made public. Generally speaking the public interest is best served when there is public reporting. There are, however, thorny problems for a company in making public a social audit at this time.

For a large company complete evaluation would be impossible and, as a result, someone could always find a basis for criticizing the company because the audit did not go far enough. Also, a basic purpose of an audit might be to determine whether the company was doing enough or was vulnerable for an infringement of a standard officially set or one existing only in the minds of self-appointed evaluation groups. To make the audit public could provide ammunition for outsider attack. Also, if a report were made public a small problem could be blown out of all proportion by a dissident group. If a report were made public, whose standards of performance measurement would be used? Those of: The auditors? The Chief Executive Officer? Majority stockholders? Ralph Nader? The SEC? A local housewife? A student?

A compromise might be to make public only a generalized statement of the findings of the audit. The "nitty-gritty" detail would not be in such a public report. This runs the risk that people might not find the report to be credible. The company might be liable to the charge that it was not being completely forthright and the public statement was self-serving.

Another approach might be to regard any social audit as proprietary matter but periodically, in the annual report, or at annual stockholder meetings or at other times and in other media, to publicize what it is doing. There is a trend in this direction.

Eventually, public pressure may lead to a periodic reporting requirement for social audits. David Rockefeller observed recently that: "Because of the growing pressure for greater corporate accountability I can foresee the day when, in addition to the annual financial statement, certified by independent accountants, corporations may be required to publish a 'social audit' similarly certified."[3] This day, I think, is some distance ahead but it seems to be the direction in which we may be headed. That there will be risks and opportunities both for corporations and for society in attempts to measure the social performance of business, however, seems obvious.

There are risks that the corporations may be unjustly criticized either for omissions or commissions. There are risks that society may be less well served if excessive expectations lead companies to do too much. On the other hand, there are opportunities for individual companies and society if acceptable criteria for guiding and limiting businesses social performance can be hammered out.

It just may be that by the social audit we may develop an acceptable method to institutionalize in business desirable and evolutionary reforms which will make business both stronger and more able to serve the social purpose. And it may be that this experience will stimulate thinking about, and methods to make, social audits of institutions aside from business, such as government, nonprofit corporations, and universities.

Notes on Critiques of Social Auditing

Any critique of the social audit must, of course, consider that the doctrine of social responsibility is itself a "muddy" concept. As one of our colleagues put it, "Trying to analyze social responsibility is like trying to cut smoke with a knife." There is little agreement on the logic of the concept, let alone on what should be included or whether the ingredients can be measured.

---

[3]David Rockefeller, address to the Advertising Council, reported in the *Los Angeles Times,* January 3, 1971.

These inadequacies show up most in the Linowes proposal. Linowes' approach has been included in several journals and popular magazines. In one, his model was subjected to critique by six practitioners and scholars and found wanting in several respects.* Much of the criticism involves the subjectiveness of Linowes' work and the fact that his approach measures inputs only. For example, one critic bemoaned the subtraction of the undone from the completed projects as depreciating the value of the completed projects. He also asked who was to specify the "detriments." Others criticized Linowes' reliance on costs. A costly program could be impeding progress, yet look quite good on SEOS. Conversely, many lower-cost, but quite beneficial, programs would not show up well. Another critic thought that managers who were able to build social benefit into productive systems intrinsically would not appear as good as managers who had to add expensive gadgets to accomplish the same social purposes; in essence, the efficient manager might be penalized. Finally, another critic attacked Linowes' ground rules; because SEOS excludes the accomplishments of legally required activities, once legislation is passed, expenditures for a program initiated prior to the law would cease being counted, yet the firm may have been way ahead of others and receive little recognition in later years. And since SEOS is limited to one year's activities, debt service on a previously made expenditure would not be counted. In sum, Linowes' approach would severely penalize efficient firms, would open up firms to all sorts of subjective judgments on detriments, and would not really measure benefits.

The cautious approach of Bauer and Fenn also relies heavily on the reporting of cost information, although they suggest that, where possible, reliable impact measures can provide valuable control information. Listing and assigning "appropriate" cost values to social activities (as they suggest for the initial stages of implementation) is probably most appropriate as an internal expense-control device. Indeed, this initial approach is a logical extension of the popular "management audit" and reflects a broadening of the more traditional controllership activities of the firm.

Perhaps the key criticism of much of social auditing is that, *for societal purposes,* the techniques do not measure rigorously the real costs and benefits of externalities. They simply provide a list of good and evil compiled by management. Reporting the cost of a pollution-control device tells nothing but the out-of-pocket cost of the device. Reporting on the probable costs of a project that was not undertaken simply measures out-of-pocket costs that were *not* incurred. Reporting these data, of course, may have a cathartic effect for the manager. They may even be good public relations. From a societal point of view, however, the data are not so useful in measuring real social impacts. The social audit may simply provide the public with a corporate self-adulation sheet.

What is more useful (from a societal point of view) is a measure of external costs and benefits, and these can be determined best by those affected. And if those

---

*Business and Society Review/Innovation, Winter 1972–1973

supposedly affected don't really suffer costs, then there are no external costs despite what managers may think. The same holds for social benefits. Perhaps, then, from a societal point of view, businessmen are not the ones to engage in social auditing; *society* is! And when society calculates those external costs and finds them unbearable, they might petition their government to pass legislation to force firms to absorb them. But that is nothing more than the traditional business–society relationship.

SELECTED READINGS

"The Annual Report Becomes a Confession," *Business Week,* April 21, 1973.

Bauer, R. A., and Fenn, D. H., Jr., *The Corporate Social Audit.* (New York: The Russell Sage Foundation, 1972.)

Colantoni, C. S., W. W. Cooper, and H. J. Deitzer, "Accounting and Social Responsibility," Research Report #8, School of Urban and Public Affairs, Joint Urban Sciences Information Institute, Carnegie-Mellon University.

Dierkes, M., and R. A. Bauer, eds., *Corporate Social Accounting.* (New York: Praeger, 1973.)

"The First Attempts at Corporate 'Social Audit,'" *Business Week,* September 23, 1972.

Linowes, D. F., "Let's Get On With The Social Audit: A Specific Proposal," *Business and Society Review,* Winter, 1972–73.

Ross, G. H. B., "Social Accounting: Measuring the Unmeasurable," *Canadian Chartered Accountant,* July, 1971.

Sethi, S. P., "Getting A Handle On The Social Audit," *Business And Society Review,* Winter, 1972–73.

Case

SPECIFIC MOTORS COMPANY*

Specific Motors Company (SMC) overhauls manufacturing equipment for resale. When the company started in 1938, Mr. George McClendon bought out the machines and equipment of depression-bankrupt manufacturers in the New York City area, and resold overhauled pieces to new and established businesses. In those days he relied upon inside information and the grapevine for tips on new businesses and for spreading the word about his wares. His father, with whom George had immigrated to New York from Ireland in 1906 when he was nine years

---

*This case was prepared by Robert Comerford. All rights reserved.

old, worked with him as the business grew until his death in 1948. In those first ten years, the company grew from six employees, all of whom were cousins and uncles, operating out of a shed behind their tenement, to a small but adequate brick factory in Westford, Pennsylvania, with thirty-seven employees. Presently, the company operates five plants in the greater Westford area.

There were many business failures during the war, and many successes. In New Jersey, northern New York and New England, many of the latter employed SMC machines. Early in the fifties, George added a sales force and began industrial advertising, both of which by 1959 had boosted sales significantly. In 1957 one of the salesmen, who had been in sales for a small plastic color manufacturer, convinced George that there was a whole industry developing in which the product was molded plastic parts, toys, and oddities. This mini-industry involved buying the appropriate machinery and going into business. SMC's strategy capitalized on the high turnover of these new businesses, the presence of many marginally operable machines floating through the market, and the high prices of new ones.

With the addition, in the late fifties, of the new line, and the formation of industrial marketing techniques, SMC grew and prospered. The strategy remained the same—in George's words, ". . . buy low, invest a little labor, and sell high, but not as high as new. But most importantly, service, advise, and befriend your customers." The main line had inadvertently become electric motors, and SMC's electric-motor group was its largest. Industrial electric motors can cost thousands of dollars new. Secondhand ones were easy to overhaul or repair for experienced people, but very difficult for the inexperienced.

By 1965, SMC had customers all over the country and several in Europe and Japan, but they were thinly spread. It had relatively few customers, but they were firmly entrenched. Suddenly, George retired in 1964, turning the business over to his State University-educated son, George, Jr.

The company had incorporated years before, but it was closely held. George, Jr., wanted to expand because present facilities were quite dilapidated and operating near capacity. SMC was not heavily laden with debt, but George simply did not want to assume more. Almost ten percent of SMC's customers were located in the Albany–Troy, New York, area; and young George had in mind purchase of a large plant just south of Albany. It was in much better shape than the several Westford facilities, and he was thinking about moving his family to the upper New York state area. He said, "The people are friendlier up there, and it's more concentrated industrially."

The obvious solution to funding needs was to go public. Financially the company was quite healthy even though he wished to take on no more debt. George knew that the way to manage going public was to begin leaking information about it long before actually doing it. He planned to start locally with clients and suppliers and brag discretely about sales and profits and growth for a year or two.

George was worried, however, about some bad publicity the company had received recently. Several editorials had appeared in a leading Westford newspaper complaining about the ugly appearance of one of the Westford plants. In fact, it, and the others, were unkempt structures, which George, Sr., had saved from demolition years before when he purchased them. The consensus was that, while the McClendon family had become wealthy "buying junk, repainting it, and selling it to strangers," they had never done anything to improve the appearance of their facilities. There were piles of old, rusty machinery of all sorts piled in parking lots at the various plants. Those which were of wooden construction had not been painted or maintained externally since they were purchased by McClendon. Most of them had been bought from bankrupt companies and no capital had been "wasted" on cleaning them up. And they were eyesores!

The worst site, and the object of the public's interest, was the huge State Street shop. It was purchased for "a song" from a machine and tool manufacturer which had relocated in South Carolina. SMC occupied about one-fourth of its 275,000 square feet, the rest of which was empty and deteriorating. The building paralleled State Street, which was heavily traveled. Its windows were nearly all broken, clapboards were falling off, and it had not been painted in years. Across the street was a small park and a new high school. Since construction of both, the city had tried to force SMC to demolish the unused portion of the structure and upgrade the appearance of the remainder.

The issue had since degenerated into an emotional, highly unprofessional state of affairs. The city attorneys claimed that George, Sr., had made a verbal agreement with certain city officials to take care of the problem when the school and park were in the planning stages. George, Jr., flatly refused to do anything, stating that the company would need the space for warehousing and he would "shape it up when the time comes." Further, he said that he had the right to do nothing to the building if he wished, and no one could force him into it against his will. George, Sr., quite senile by now, did not remember any such agreement.

The elder McClendon had never encountered this kind of hostility. He was greatly respected for involvement in many community activities, charitable organizations, and a general propensity to share his modest wealth and his company's while he actively managed it. Many people felt that young George had swindled his way into the company and stories proliferated about his wresting the company out of the old man's hands. None of this was true, but George, Jr.'s arrogance and aloofness and his "devil-may-care" activities while growing up all contributed to paint a hostile local image. Additionally, word had gotten around town that George was "tight" with donations and contributions to local organizations. In fact, the charitable activities of his father were continued by George, Jr., but with little fanfare. Further, young George directed the philanthropy of SMC more discriminately than had his father. That meant that some recipients were given less, and others more than they had received when George, Sr., ran the company. The bases for George, Sr.'s philanthropy had been mostly emotional. His son, who had majored in finance and marketing at State, saw philanthropy more as an investment. He felt that gifts by his company should be managed so as to maxmize his perception of a sort of political, if not directly financial, return. Unfortunately, young George had taken no political science courses!

George and SMC's accountant and treasurer were afraid that this (heretofore not more than bothersome) set of problems would seriously interfere with the stock offering, or at least, keep the price down. At one meeting between the two, George launched into a tirade about the whole mess. He yelled, "What right have the people in this town to interfere with my operations? Last year we gave away over ten thousand dollars to solve all of their problems and in return they do this to us!" The accountant, John Wettereid, self-taught, very calm, usually mild-natured, and above all, competent, recommended that they stop giving SMC's money away.

George responded, "Oh sure, they'll burn us to the ground!" He then asked John to go back to his office and start putting together a list of all the company's charitable contributions. He felt that if the case ever got to court, such information had better be on the top of his head.

John said that he did not have "all that stuff around," and that "getting it would be one heck of a job."

With deliberately underscored finality, George made a statement about the size of John's paycheck and told him to begin immediately on the list.

The next three days saw John shuffling around the small offices, grumbling about "college kids," trying to track down all "the stuff." He was trying to find cancelled checks and receipts for the last year. George, Sr., had never recorded any of his charitable activities, and so none was accounted for when young George took over. Many of the earlier contributions were in cash; some of the company's employees were often loaned to public and charitable organizations, with no record, to work for a few hours or days. Almost every year for the last ten, for example, three or four men were sent over to the Boys' Club to paint. In 1959, a new swimming pool (and hockey rink) was donated to the city at a cost of $30,000. A fund was established which contributed $2,000 a year to the upkeep of the latter facility. There were memorials, other loans of employees, scholarship funds, free equipment, and donated services given by the company to the community.

Four days after their meeting, John notified George that he had accumulated all of the items he could identify. A meeting was called between the two men, in which John grumbled that if he was going to be held responsible for this information, maybe he should start keeping more detailed records of it. He also made it clear that George would have to notify him of any gifts he made.

The list presented to George at this meeting was as follows:

SMC Contributions, Donations, and Gifts for last year

	$ or Description
United Fund	$5,000
Westford High School Booster Club	200
Westford Public Library	300
American Cancer Society	400
Civil Air Patrol	50
Easter Seal Society	200
Kennedy Memorial	500
Audubon Society	100
McClendon Scholarship	500
Two ten-horsepower motors to Westford Vocational H.S.	220
Westford Jaycees	100
Westford City Hospital	1,200
NAACP	300
Red Cross	500
Salvation Army	200
Sickle Cell Anemia Fund	100
Christian College	200
State University	1,500
St. Ponts Church	1,000
Urban League	50
United Negro College Fund	200
Brothers Academy	500
Westford Lion's Club	75
Total	$9,395

George looked at the list and said, "This looks like just the things where we've written a check and given it to them!" John replied that it was precisely that.

George, irritated, replied, "There have been a lot more contributions than that!" He went on to say, "What about painting the Boys' Club —that was four two-hundred-dollar-a-week electricians for six days. And the pool—I sent two guys from Maintenance over there to fix the rest rooms. They worked for five hours. Those guys get a hundred and twenty bucks a week! And every wildlife conservation meeting has one of our secretaries taking shorthand. The Pollution Control Board—I'm vice chairman of that. I gave those old lawnmowers we got with the first Westford plant to the Boy Scouts so that they could raise some money mowing lawns. And you, John, you set up the bookkeeping system for that food co-op. I want all that stuff figured out! Do I have to hold you by the hand to get something done, John?! "

John responded that he had asked for a list of contributions and that was what he got! George counted to ten and calmed down a bit.

Then he said, "Ok, go back to your office and figure out everything we've done that has contributed to this town, this state, this country, poor people, sick people, rich people, and anything or anyone else! And John, don't make me wait four days this time!

"Oh, one more thing, I got a call from the State Street plant just before you came in here today—they haven't received their profit report for last month yet. Will you get on that—This whole operation is all of a sudden coming down around my ears!"

With that, John left the office and went to his own without saying a word.